DICKENS STUDIES ANNUAL

Essays on Victorian Fiction

VOLUME
28

Edited by
Stanley Friedman, Edward Guiliano, and Michael Timko

AMS PRESS
NEW YORK

DICKENS STUDIES ANNUAL

ISSN 0084-9812

COPYRIGHT © 1999 by AMS Press, Inc.
Dickens Studies Annual: Essays on Victorian Fiction is published in cooperation with Queens College and the Graduate Center, CUNY.

International Standard Book Number
Series: 0-404-18520-7
Vol. 28: 0-404-18548-7

Dickens Studies Annual: Essays on Victorian Fiction welcomes essay- and monograph-length contributions on Dickens and other Victorian novelists and on the history of aesthetics of Victorian fiction. All manuscripts should be double-spaced and should follow the documentation format described in the most recent *MLA Style Manual*. The author's name should appear only on a cover-page, not elsewhere in the essay. An editorial decision can usually be reached more quickly if two copies of the article are submitted, since outside readers are asked to evaluate each submission. If a manuscript is accepted for publication, the author will be asked to provide a 100- to 200-word abstract and also a disk containing the final version of the essay. The preferred editions for citations from Dickens's works are the Clarendon and the Norton Critical when available, otherwise the Oxford Illustrated or the Penguin.

Please send submissions to The Editors, *Dickens Studies Annual,* Ph.D. Program in English, Graduate School and University Center, CUNY, 365 Fifth Avenue, New York, NY 10016-4309. Please send inquiries concerning subscriptions and/or the availability of earlier volumes to AMS Press, Inc., 56 East 13th Street, New York, NY 10003-4686.

Manufactured in the United States of America

All AMS books are printed on acid-free paper that meets the guidelines for performance and durability of the Committee on Production Guidelines for Book Longevity of the Council on Library Resources.

Contents

Preface

Once more, we offer thanks to those scholars who submit essays to us, and we again express our gratitude to all who generously serve as outside readers and thereby allow us to benefit from perspectives that at times differ from our own. Moreover, these readers' suggestions for revision frequently serve to strengthen the submissions that are accepted.

This volume includes, besides scholarly studies of texts by Dickens, Wilkie Collins, Gaskell, and Hardy, five helpful review essays. We express our appreciation to Professor William J. Palmer, for his fine study of New Historicist approaches to Dickens; to Professor Elisabeth G. Gitter, for her extensive survey of Dickens studies published in 1997; to Professor Alicia Carroll, for her consideration of recent work on George Eliot; to Professor Lillian Nayder, for her comprehensive review of Wilkie Collins; and to Professor Margaret D. Stetz, for her incisive examination of selected books that illuminate the "vital amount of change at the end of the last century." In addition, we thank Professor Richard J. Dunn, who, in collaboration with Ann M. Tandy, has provided an updating of his noteworthy *David Copperfield: An Annotated Bibliography* (New York: Garland, 1981), and we are very grateful to Professor Duane K. DeVries, the General Editor of The Dickens Bibliographies (now being published by AMS Press, Inc.), for helping to make this bibliographical supplement available to us and for assisting with its editing. (This bibliography includes its own index)

For various kinds of essential support, we express appreciation to the following administrators: President Frances Degen Horowitz, Provost William P. Kelly, Ph.D. Program in English Executive Officer Joan Richardson, and Linda Sherwin, Assistant Program Officer, Ph.D. Program in English, all of The Graduate School and University Center, CUNY; President Allen Lee Sessoms, Provost John A. Thorpe, Dean Raymond F. Erickson, Department of English Chair Nancy R. Comley, all of Queens College, CUNY; and President Matthew Schure of New York Institute of Technology.

We thank Gabriel Hornstein, President of AMS Press, for his encouragement and his belief in the importance of our enterprise, Jack Hopper, our editor at AMS Press, for his skill and cooperation, and Jody R. Rosen, our editorial assistant, for her alertness and reliability.

Beginning with this volume, we are providing brief abstracts of the articles presented. Professor John O. Jordan, Director of The Dickens Project at the University of California, Santa Cruz, has kindly offered to include on the Project's website these abstracts, as well as the tables of contents for prior volumes of *Dickens Studies Annual: Essays on Victorian Fiction.* The Dickens Project can be reached at http://humwww.ucsc.edu/dickens/index.html

We are grateful to New York Institute of Technology for assistance with electronic formatting.

Notes on Contributors

JIM BARLOON is a lecturer at the University of Kansas and has published articles on Thomas Hardy and Charles Dickens, as well as numerous book reviews. His dissertation, "Charting the Boundaries: Secrets in the Novels of Charles Dickens," examines the role of secrets, from various perspectives, in Dickens's fiction.

SUNDEEP BISLA has just completed a doctoral dissertation entitled "The Borderless World: The Fictions of Wilkie Collins and the Victorian Copyright Debates" at the University of Sydney, Australia. An essay on Morrison's *Beloved* is forthcoming in *Cultural Critique.*

ALICIA CARROLL is assistant professor of English at Auburn University. She has recently completed a book on George Eliot, and her other work on Eliot has appeared in *JEGP, Novel,* and *Nineteenth-Century Literature.*

RICHARD J. DUNN is professor of English at the University of Washington. He is the author of *Oliver Twist: Whole Heart and Soul,* has edited *Approaches to Teaching "David Copperfield,"* Norton Critical Editions of *Jane Eyre* and *Wuthering Heights,* and *David Copperfield: An Annotated Bibliography.*

LAWRENCE FRANK is Professor of English at the University of Oklahoma. He is the author of *Charles Dickens and the Romantic Self* (1984). Recently, he has published essays on the nineteenth-century sciences of geology, archaeology, and evolutionary biology and their relation to the detective fictions of Charles Dickens, Arthur Conan Doyle, and Edgar Allan Poe. He is completing a book-length study, "Reconstructions: Science and Detection in Poe, Dickens, and Doyle."

ROBERT GARNETT is associate professor of English at Gettysburg College. He is the author of *From Grimes to Brideshead: The Early Novels of Evelyn Waugh* (Bucknell University Press, 1990), and most recently a number of articles on Dickens. He is currently working on a longer study of desire and spirituality in Dickens.

ix

ELISABETH GITTER is professor of English at John Lay College, City University of New York. She has written on numerous Victorian subjects, and her work has been published in a variety of journals, including *Victorian Poetry, Dickens Quarterly, Dickens Studies Annual, PMLA, Studies in English Literature,* and *Victorian Literature and Culture.*

LILLIAN NAYDER is an associate professor of English at Bates College, where she teaches courses on the English novel and on Victorian fiction. Her essays have appeared in various journals, and her book, *Wilkie Collins,* was published in 1997. *"Victorian Collaborations,"* her work in progress, examines the fiction coauthored by Dickens and Collins.

WILLIAM J. PALMER is professor of English at Purdue University and the editor of *Modern Fiction Studies.* His most recent book is *Dickens and the New Historicism* (St. Martin's, 1998) and he has written three Victorian history/mystery novels: *The Detective and Mr. Dickens, The Highwayman and Mr. Dickens,* and *The Hoydens and Mr. Dickens.*

JEANETTE ROBERTS SHUMAKER is an associate professor of English at San Diego State University, Imperial Valley. She has published articles on Victorian fiction in *English Literature in Transition, College Literature, Continuum* and the *George Eliot-George Henry Lewes Newsletter.* Her other research interest is twentieth-century fiction by Irish women.

MARGARET D. STETZ is associate professor of English and Women's Studies at Georgetown University. Her recent projects include *The Yellow Book: A Centenary Exhibition* (1994) with Mark Samuels Lasner; an article on Ella Hepworth Dixon for the *DLB,* vol. 197; essays in forthcoming volumes on women and aestheticism and on Victorian humor, an Introduction to the reissued 1898 feminist novel *A Writer of Books* (Academy Chicago); essay reviews for *Nineteenth Century Studies* and *Victorian Studies;* and a monograph on "George Egerton" for the Eighteen Nineties Society.

ANN M. TANDY is a doctoral candidate in English at the University of Washington, where she received her M.A. She also holds a B.A. from the University of Wisconsin—Eau Claire. Her primary work is in nineteenth-century British literature.

The Black Hole of London:
Rescuing Oliver Twist

Jim Barloon

An interesting conjunction of secrets and place appears in Charles Dickens's Oliver Twist. *Like the world generally in Dickens, London—the "abiding city" of his fiction—becomes increasingly mystifying and difficult to compass. Despite this, Dickens proved an ardent, tireless explorer of the city, and his "discoveries" play an important role in his fiction and make a significant contribution to our understanding, on a mythical as well as a literal level, of the great modern metropolis. Oliver Twist flees to London to lose himself in its labyrinthine vastness only to be threatened with perdition of various kinds. The novel, indeed, can be read as a contest between two opposed societies—with Brownlow and the Maylies on one side and Fagin and Sikes on the other—for the body and soul of Oliver. Whereas Fagin and Monks, purveyors of secrets, attempt to corrupt Oliver and to keep his true identity secret, the "congenial" class tries to rescue Oliver so that he can claim his birthright and assume his proper station in life. London, the* terra incognita *through which Dickens guides us, serves not only as the backdrop to this struggle, but also as a formidable complicating factor for Oliver and those who rescue him.*

Just as the city is central to the development and identity of the novel,[1] especially in the nineteenth century, so London occupies a preeminent place in the novels of Charles Dickens; in both cases, it is sometimes difficult to separate the city from the modus operandi of the novel. These are not original

---

Dickens Studies Annual, Volume 28, Copyright © 1999 by AMS Press, Inc. All rights reserved.

1

observations, however. Indeed, existing critical work on the role of the city in Dickens is nearly as vast and labyrinthine as the city itself. And though it would be presumptuous to attempt to boil this work down to its quintessence, one can say with some confidence that virtually all critics who discuss the role of London in Dickens agree that the city serves a dramatic purpose, and not simply a scenic one. In ''The Creation of Consciousness and Dickens's Vision of the City,'' for example, Raymond Williams argues that the conjunction of Dickens and the novel form led to the creation of ''a new kind of novel'': ''The central case we have to make is that Dickens could write a new kind of novel—fiction uniquely capable of realizing a new kind of reality—just because he shared with the new urban popular culture certain decisive experiences and responses'' (106). George Gissing, many of whose novels were inspired by London life, suggests what our view of London, if not the city generally, owes to Dickens: ''London as a place of squalid mystery and terror, of the grimly grotesque, of labyrinthine obscurity and lurid fascination, is Dickens's own; he taught people a certain way of regarding the huge city, and to this day how common it is to see London with Dickens's eyes'' (53). In a very real sense, Dickens was an explorer of new territory, perhaps the first English novelist of genius to depict the lower and middle urban classes and their environment with both understanding and sympathy. To many such readers, Dickens's novels showed them their own city in a way that, to borrow a line from T. S. Eliot, enabled them to ''know the place for the first time.''[2]

If, as most critics agree, Dickens's portrayal of London ranks among his greatest achievements,[3] we should at least acknowledge the groundwork that such a feat required: namely, a thorough, first-hand knowledge of London. Dickens even claimed, in a 1867 interview with the Rev. G. D. Carrow, that he ''[knew] London better than any one other man of all its millions'' (qtd. in Burke 661). This knowledge was necessary not only for the sake of verisimilitude, but to accomplish the artistic and other objectives to which Dickens aspired. For example, in *Oliver Twist, Bleak House,* and *Our Mutual Friend,* among other novels, Dickens's strategy for reform included exposing unsavory localities in and around London that many of its inhabitants knew nothing about. An early example is Jacob's Island in *Oliver Twist:*

> Near to that part of the Thames on which the church at Rotherhithe abuts, where the buildings on the banks are dirtiest and the vessels on the river blackest with the dust of colliers and the smoke of close-built low-roofed houses, there exists the filthiest, the strangest, the most extraordinary of the many localities that are hidden in London, *wholly unknown, even by name, to the great mass of inhabitants.*   (442, emphasis mine)

However, when Sir Peter Laurie, a London alderman, ''told a public meeting that Jacob's Island 'ONLY existed' in the pages of *Oliver Twist,*'' Dickens ridiculed him in the preface to a new edition of the novel (qtd. in Johnson 2:715–16)—as if Dickens latterly assumed that everyone but an incorrigible alderman was familiar with Jacob's Island. Dickens's reaction also betrays some resentment that Laurie was not sufficiently transported by his artistic creation to suspend his disbelief—a resentment made righteous by Dickens's certainty that he was doing more than telling a story: he was telling the truth. Besides, Dickens had seen such places with his own eyes, and his account could be verified, or so he believed, by anyone who cared to investigate. Dickens, who could not resist immense tasks, took upon himself the herculean task of exploring and revealing "the mysteries of London" to his less "ubiquitous" readers.[4]

Dickens's interest in London extended well beyond its topography, however. Indeed, what Dickens found most interesting about London was the human landscape, the inhabitants of London. From the beginning of his career as a writer, Dickens understood that the city can play a decisive role in forming individual identity: just as the "magic lantern" of London can exhilarate or overwhelm the senses, so the city can have a corresponding effect upon identity. Dickens's love-hate relationship with London—he could perceive it, alternately, as a "magic lantern" as well as "a mouth that swallows up multitudes"—stems in part from the realization that the city can either reconstitute or annihilate individuality. Many go to the city to remake themselves, but many more go there only to suffer the sort of figurative death that Dickens was among the first novelists to delineate. As F. S. Schwarzbach has noted, "One can lose one's pursuers [in a crowd], but one runs the risk of losing one's selfhood as well" (50).

Among the chief attractions of a large city is its promise of transformation and renewal. Although one's identity can be lost, or simply reduced to insignificance, in the city, this danger is offset by the opportunity the city affords for improvising a new, perhaps more fulfilling, identity; so while one might become a "nemo," a no-one, one can also become a "some-one." Thus, Wopsle, an unappreciated parish clerk in the village where Pip grows up, can move to London and becomes Waldengarver, "celebrated Provincial Amateur of Roscian renown" (*GE* 242). The transformation does not succeed—we actually witness Wopsle's descent into something worse than insignificance—but that is the fault of Wopsle's haplessness as an actor. Dickens, a better actor, transformed himself from a neglected blacking-warehouse drudge into a celebrated author of world-wide renown. But Dickens's case is exceptional; Wopsle/Waldengarver's fate is by far the more common. Nevertheless, Dickens, perhaps because he never quite overcame the sense of hopelessness and abandonment he felt as a child living on his "own account" in London, devoted himself to telling "Nobody's Story," the story of those who "bear their share of the battle . . . have their part in the victory . . . fall . . . [and] leave no name but in the mass" ("Nobody's Story" 66). His efforts constituted an attempt to save them, and in the process himself, from oblivion.

Dickens recognized that the immensity and maziness of London rendered it an ideal hiding place. In addition to being the preferred place to hide *things,* London is also the place where one goes to hide oneself—that is, to become lost, literally and figuratively. When Oliver Twist determines to run away from Sowerberry's, he knows almost instinctively where to go: "it was just seventy miles from that spot to London. The name awakened a new train of ideas in the boy's mind. London—that great large place—nobody–not even Mr. Bumble—could ever find him there!" (97). (Later, Noah Claypole also flees Sowerberry's and travels to London to "lose [him]self among the narrowest streets [he] can find" [378].) An underlying danger, however, one which Oliver fails to recognize, is that he might become morally and spiritually lost as well; this danger becomes real when we observe Oliver being guided into London by Jack Dawkins, a.k.a. the Artful Dodger. The "crooked" streets they traverse lead to an analogous destination. Thus, the unique opportunities for concealment that London affords also make it an ideal place for those whose characters and activities cannot withstand exposure. Oliver is only one of many characters in Dickens who seek escape and anonymity in the "great large" city only to find themselves nameless prisoners to a corrupt and demoralizing underworld; escaping *within* London nearly always proves much easier than escaping *from* London. The price of secrecy is the diminution or loss of one's identity, while the price one must pay to recover it is self-disclosure.

Even a partial list of Dickens characters who use the city as a hiding place is considerable: Oliver Twist, Rudge, Nemo, Darnay, Magwitch, and John Harmon. Each (except Oliver, who does not know who he is) adopts a pseudonym, among other devices, to disguise his identity, and each faces the threat of surrendering his identity to the same obliterating entity that makes concealment possible. In Dickens, hiding not only entails hiding from others, but also involves an attempt to escape from one's self. The nature of the city, which offers so many opportunities for concealment, only compounds the difficulty of maintaining a hold upon one's genuine identity. In his discussion of *Bleak House,* Richard Maxwell notes that a "favorite theme" of the philosopher Georg Simmel is "the difficulty of asserting [one's] own personality within the dimensions of metropolitan life' " (169). While the "dimensions of metropolitan life" make it fairly easy for someone to hide, they also render it difficult *not* to disappear altogether. Therefore, for those who choose to take advantage of the cover that London's immensity provides, perhaps the most terrible danger they confront—among the many other, more notorious dangers within the city—is that of becoming a "nemo."

Well before Dostoevsky, Dickens had a fascination with the class of "underground men" who, like rats or grime, almost seem to be spontaneously generated by large industrial cities.[5] In "Shabby-Genteel People," one of the *Sketches by Boz,* Dickens observes, "There are certain descriptions of people who, oddly enough, appear to appertain exclusively to the metropolis. . . . they seem indigenous to the soil, and to belong as exclusively to London as its own smoke, or the dingy bricks and mortar" (262). Such characters belong to that vast group of urban phenomena—bureaucracies such as Chancery and the Circumlocution Office (in *Bleak House* and *Little Dorrit,* respectively) merely represent the culmination of this focus—that defy human understanding and heighten the sense of mystery and inscrutability that permeates the city like a "London particular."

Another reason for the increasing inscrutability of the city is its sheer mass; the man-made city has grown so large, has become so gargantuan, that no one can control or make sense of it. As Maxwell puts it, "Greatest among artifacts, the metropolis eludes the grasp of the human mind; to revise a traditional dictum, the maker no longer knows what he has made" (3). Aristotle anticipated this danger centuries ago in his *Politics* when setting forth the attributes of the Ideal State:

> experience shows that a very populous city can rarely, if ever, be well governed; since all cities which have a reputation for good government have a limit of population. We may argue on grounds of reason, and the same result will follow. For law is order, and good law is good order; but a very great multitude cannot be orderly: to introduce order into the unlimited is the work of a divine power—of such a power as holds together the universe.   (Bk. VII: Ch.3)

Whether or not Dickens would have claimed, as a more self-conscious artist might, that introducing "order into the unlimited" describes what artists (along with "divine powers") do, a case can be made that Dickens grew increasingly concerned with discovering, or imposing, some sort of order, some means of "holding together" the diffuse, variegated, and *expanding* city.[6] Like that "old artificer," Daedalus, we become bewildered and trapped by a labyrinth of our own devising.[7] No longer viewed as the cynosure of the Empire, London came to be seen in the mid- and late-nineteenth century as a "problem,"[8] one that even the most sanguine of reformers often despaired of ever "solving."

II

For Oliver Twist, however, London is not viewed as a problem, but rather a means of escape. Oliver flees Sowerberry's for London directly after defending the honor of his dead mother against Noah Claypole's insults, yet Oliver soon finds himself living among men who pose a much greater threat

to the truth and honor of his parentage. Fagin and Monks, who devote themselves to corrupting Oliver and suppressing the truth about his identity,
threaten Oliver, both figuratively and literally, with extinction. Were they to
succeed in their design, Oliver would embark upon a road that could very
well lead to the gallows—thus fulfilling the gentleman in the white waistcoat's
prediction that Oliver would be hanged some day (58). However, even if a
"fallen" Oliver were only to suffer the fate of the Artful Dodger or Charley
Bates, the conditions of Oliver's father's will—that the boy would receive
his share of his father's property "only on the stipulation that in his minority
he should never have stained his name with any public act of dishonour,
meanness, cowardice, or wrong" (458)—would effectively serve to disinherit
Oliver, to sever the bonds between Oliver and the respectable world. Thus,
to avoid becoming a "nemo," to claim his birthright and assume his "proper
station" in life, Oliver must remain virtuous in surroundings infected with
vice.

In a sense it is entirely appropriate that Oliver, upon entering London for
the first time, is taken directly to Fagin's den, the locus of secrets and secrecy
in "deepest, darkest" London. Oliver himself unknowingly embodies secrets
that the two opposed societies in the novel—what Northrop Frye refers to as
"the obstructing and the congenial society"[9]—struggle to control. The task
that Fagin and Monks take up, to ensure that Oliver's true identity be kept
secret, simply represents an extension of their ordinary operations: Fagin
deals in secrets. The early scene where Fagin takes out and fondles his cache
of precious contraband while a somnolent Oliver, a piece of "contraband"
himself, looks on could well serve as a paradigm for the view of the novel
towards inner London[10] ("inner London" refers not only to central London,
but functions as an image of the claustrophobic sense Oliver has of being
contained and constrained, of being swallowed up by an entity of overwhelming mass and complexity). Nowhere in Dickens does London more closely
resemble a "nest of Chinese boxes"[11] than in *Oliver Twist*—secret places,
houses, rooms, and objects, contained one within another, are disclosed at
virtually every turn. By endeavoring to make Oliver one of their own, Fagin
and Monks also attempt to defuse the potential danger that Oliver's secret
identity poses. One way to view the conflict in the novel, therefore, is as a
struggle between those who seek to hide or destroy secrets and those who
strive to "rescue" them; the city serves not only as the backdrop to this
struggle but also as a formidable complicating factor for Oliver and those
who rescue him.

Numerous critics have commented upon the polarized, even "Manichean,"
relationship between the various elements in *Oliver Twist*.[12] Good versus evil,
light versus dark, country versus city: the list of starkly contrasting values
and properties aligned against one another in the novel seems almost endless.

What is less often examined is the spatial, territorial relationship in *Oliver Twist* between the "obstructing and the congenial society." In a way that eerily prefigures the relationship between the Morlocks and Eloi in H. G. Wells's *The Time Machine* (1895), society in *Oliver Twist* consists of two antagonistic classes: one, represented by Fagin and Sikes, lives underground in the shadows and preys upon the second class, represented by Brownlow and the Maylies, who live in relative ease and brightness above ground. A Marxist critic such as Arnold Kettle, however, would reverse this equation, maintaining that the Brownlows and the Maylies, that is, the bourgeoisie, are the predators.[13] And just as the Eloi do not like to be reminded of the Morlocks or where they live, so the "congenial society" in *Oliver Twist* prefers not to admit, or simply has no conception of, the conditions that propagate the predatory class and places like Jacob's island.

Although the narrator remarks that "They must have powerful motives for a secret residence, or be reduced to a destitute condition indeed, who seek a refuge in Jacob's Island" (443), it seems that in London merely being destitute renders "a secret residence" necessary—as though the "better" classes will not tolerate even the appearance of the impoverished.[14] More bothersome than children, the disreputably destitute are not to be heard or seen. When Nancy, for example, walks "headlong" for more than an hour to the Hyde Park hotel where Rose Maylie is staying—we should also keep in mind that the difficulty and expense of travelling from one part of the city to another, especially before the railroad, acted as a further, virtually insuperable divide between the rich and the poor—the hotel employees, simple housemaids, appear insulted by Nancy's mere presence among them (ch. 39). The dregs, then, seek out hiding places not only because their delinquency requires it, but also because the "congenial" society all but demands it. Even an apparently harmless stray like Jo, the crossing-sweep in *Bleak House,* is compelled to find a secret residence because he is continually being "moved on" by the authorities. However, as Dickens takes pains to show, especially in *Bleak House,* the insularity that the privileged attempt to purchase—attempting, in effect, to quarantine the lower classes—not only does not succeed, but only exacerbates the problem by propagating the very conditions that prompt the middle and upper classes to seek refuge in the first place.

In *Oliver Twist*, which revolves around the efforts of the "congenial" society to rescue one of its own, the divide separating the two classes can only be crossed by the "obstructing" class: members of this class, which J. Hillis Miller refers to as the "hidden society," are able to move back and forth between their territory and that of the privileged, while the privileged, those who belong to the "open society," demonstrate little or no ability, and certainly no inclination, to cross into the *terra incognita* occupied by the hidden society. And while those who belong to the latter class can only venture out of their territory for short intervals (again like the Morlocks), Sikes and his gang do threaten the Maylies in their home, and Fagin and Monks demonstrate that they can find Oliver out, even far from the madding crowd of the city. On the other side, as Schwarzbach points out, "it requires the ceaseless efforts of an entire community of rich and powerful grown men to save one small boy" (65). Even then, Brownlow and the Maylies must rely upon an "insider," Nancy, to deliver Oliver from those who intend to destroy him; without such mediating, inside help. Oliver might never have been delivered from the bowels of London.

Like most "good murderous melodramas" (168), which is how Dickens characterizes his own novel, *Oliver Twist* resolves itself by rewarding virtue and punishing wickedness. In one way or another, the major antagonists to both Oliver and society—Fagin, Sikes, Monks, and, to a lesser extent, the Artful Dodger—are eliminated as threats. But the "hidden society" and, most importantly, the environment that sustains it, are left intact. Earlier in the novel the narrator likens Fagin to "some loathsome reptile, *engendered in the slime and darkness through which he moved*" (emphasis added 186). Eventually, Fagin is "taken" and will soon be despatched, but the "slime and darkness" that *engendered* him—which include Jacob's Island and the other "cribs," dens, lairs, warrens, and mews that harbor the hidden society—remain. Despite the immutably-Good Oliver, *Oliver Twist* argues, especially in its delineation of Nancy, that the environment exercises a considerable effect upon character and destiny. Thus, Dickens realized that as long as parts of London remain off-limits and unknown to the respectable classes, they will continue to serve as an inexhaustible breeding ground for the sort of "vermin" who pose the greatest threat to the social order. At one point in the novel, Fagin cautions Monks, " 'we never show lights to our neighbors' " (243). But Dickens illumined the dark and blighted heart of the city for all to see, changing, as a result, how many Londoners viewed their own world.

Towards the close of the novel, Brownlow adopts Oliver and they move "to within a mile of the parsonage house, where his dear friends [the Maylies] resided . . . and thus linked together a little society, whose condition approached as nearly to one of perfect happiness as can ever be known in this changing world" (476). Although some critics—Steven Marcus, for example—consider this a feeble conclusion, the logic of the novel dictates, or at least warrants, the move from the city to the country. The city itself, and not only Fagin and Monks, has acted as an antagonist to Oliver throughout, and though Oliver has withstood its dangers and temptations so far, London still threatens, still has its "slime and darkness." Also, because the city tends to disclocate and diffuse individuals—consider how many times Oliver becomes lost—only in the country is a secure "little society" possible; even Fagin's gang, a resilient "little society," is thoroughly demolished.

In his commitment to explore and explicate the city Dickens was not alone among nineteenth-century novelists; indeed, he was in very good company. Donald Fanger, in *Dostoevsky and Romantic Realism,* a study of Dostoevsky, Balzac, Dickens, and Gogol, contends that the "common theme" of these writers, "at its most general, is the great modern city—Paris, London, Petersburg—whose transformation was going on before their eyes, signaling the end of 'nature' and the 'natural life,' and the beginning of 'modernity' " (viii). Born at a time when London was undergoing momentous growth and transformation, Dickens made the most of the artistic opportunities this propitious conjunction afforded. Left to fend for himself—an anonymous, neglected boy—at the age of twelve in the great large city, Dickens eventually became a kind of master and conquering hero of the monstrous city that had threatened his younger self with annihilation. He explored the interminable streets and arcana of London and then reconstructed through the "magic lantern" of his imagination what he had discovered for those who preferred to travel vicariously. But Dickens was not only an explorer, he was also an interpreter, an expositor of the "Modern Babylon." Like so many great artists, Dickens not only illuminated much that his readers had missed, but also taught them *how* to see.

It is true that in his later years Dickens became increasingly disenchanted with London, while at the same time he grew more enamored with Paris (partly because he could enjoy in Paris an anonymity—much desired when travelling with a young, unmarried woman—that his phenomenal fame precluded when he was in London).[15] Still, London remained the eternal city of his imagination, as well as of his fiction. Even in the uncompleted *Edwin Drood,* a novel set predominantely in a small cathedral town, Dickens incorporated material from his travels into the dark heart of the city. As Philip Collins has pointed out, Princess Puffer's opium den and its habitués probably owe their existence to a visit Dickens made with his investigative brethren, the police: "[Dickens] remained, in adult life, a frequent visitor to this and other notorious districts of London, right up to the end of his life: a tour, under police protection, of the opium-dens of Shadwell inspired some notable characters of *Edwin Drood*" (213). Whether Dickens grew weary of London or not, he knew that *it* was inexhaustible, that as an artist he could draw upon it unendingly. The most indefatigable of men, Dickens, like Eliot, understood that to know a place well, one must not only travel far, but deeply:

> We shall not cease from exploration
> And the end of all our exploring
> Will be to arrive where we started
> And know the place for the first time.[16]

NOTES

1. Ian Watt, in *The Rise of the Novel,* is one of many critics who have linked the rise of the novel to the development of large, industrial cities.
2. T. S. Eliot, "Little Gidding," *Four Quartets,* I. 242.
3. Gissing asserted that "To depict London was one of the ends for which Dickens was born" (88).
4. In *Charles Dickens,* a memoir written by G. A. Sala, a friend of Dickens, Sala remarks that "Charles Dickens, when in town, was ubiquitous. He was to be met, by those who knew him, everywhere—and who did not know him?" (10–11).
5. See Donald Fanger's *Dostoevsky and Romantic Realism,* particularly his concluding chapter.
6. In *Victorian People and Ideas,* Richard Altick reports that the population of London doubled between 1801 and the middle of the century (44).
7. Others writing on this subject have also invoked the myth of Daedalus, J. Hills Miller in "The Darkness of *Oliver Twist*" refers to the "endless daedal prison" of the urban labyrinth (47).
8. In *The City of Dickens* Alexander Welsh writes, "In the nineteenth century the findings of science and statistics, of journalism and parliamentary reports, and the literature of the city in general, had one main tendency: the discovery of the city as a problem" (31).
9. See Northrop Frye's "Dickens and the Comedy of Humors," 73.
10. This scene evokes Marlowe's *The Jew of Malta* and Barabas's line, "Infinite riches in a little town" (I, i. 37).
11. This image is borrowed from Donald Olsen's *The Growth of Victorian London:* "London came to resemble a nest of Chinese boxes, each containing a smaller if distorted, version of itself" (82).
12. Graham Greene, in his essay "The Young Dickens," uses the term "Manichean" to describe the world depicted in *Oliver Twist.*
13. See Arnold Kettle's *"Oliver Twist"* from his *An Introduction to the English Novel.*
14. Schwarzbach also makes the point that in *Oliver Twist* poverty is treated as a crime (63).
15. Claire Tomalin in *The Invisible Woman* is one of many critics who noticed Dickens's fondness for Paris: "Dickens could be critical of French immorality, dirt and disobligingness, but as the years went by he found less to complain of and more of love" (136).
16. Eliot, "Little Gidding," II. 239–242.

WORKS CITED

Altick, Richard. *Victorian People and Ideas: A Companion for the Modern Reader of Victorian Literature.* New York: Norton, 1973.

Burke, Alan R. "The Strategy and Theme of Urban Observation in *Bleak House*." *Studies in English Literature* 9 (Autumn 1969): 659–76.

Collins, Philip. *Dickens and Crime*. New York: St. Martin's, 1962.

Dickens, Charles. *Great Expectations*. 1860–61. New York: Penguin, 1985.

———. "Nobody's Story." 1853. In *Christmas Stories*. Oxford: Oxford Illustrated Dickens, 1991. 61–66.

———. *Oliver Twist*. 1837–39. New York: Penguin, 1985.

———. *Sketches by Boz*. 1836–37. Oxford: Oxford UP, 1991.

Eliot, T. S. "Little Gidding." In *Four Quartets*. New York: Harcourt, Brace, 1943.

Fanger, Donald. *Dostoevsky and Romantic Realism: A Study of Dostoevsky in Relation to Balzac, Dickens, and Gogol*. Cambridge: Harvard UP, 1967.

Frye, Northrop. "Dickens and the Comedy of Humors." In *Charles Dickens*. Ed. Harold Bloom. New York: Chelsea House, 1987. 71–91.

Gissing, George. *Critical Studies of the Works of Charles Dickens*. New York: Haskell, 1965.

Greene, Graham. "The Young Dickens," 1951. In *Charles Dickens: A Critical Anthology*. Ed. Stephen Wall. Baltimore: Penguin, 1970. 359–63.

Johnson, Edgar. *Charles Dickens: His Tragedy and Triumph*. 2 vol. New York: Simon, 1952.

Kettle, Arnold. *"Oliver Twist." An Introduction to the English Novel*. Vol. 1. London: Hutchinson University Library, 1951. 115–29.

Marcus, Steven. *Dickens: from Pickwick to Dombey*. New York: Basic Books, 1965.

Maxwell, Richard. *The Mysteries of Paris and London*. Victorian Literature and Culture Ser. 12. Charlottesville: UP of Virginia, 1992.

Miller, J. Hillis. "The Dark World of *Oliver Twist*." In *Charles Dickens*. Ed. Harold Bloom. New York: Chelsea House, 1987. 29–69.

Olsen, Donald J. *The Growth of Victorian London*. London: Batsford, 1976.

Rose, Phyllis. *Parallel Lives: Five Victorian Marriages*. New York: Knopf, 1983.

Sala, George Augustus. *Charles Dickens*. London: Routledge, 1870.

Schwarzbach, F. S. *Dickens and the City*. London: The Athlone Press, 1979.

Tomalin, Claire. *The Invisible Woman: The Story of Nelly Ternan and Charles Dickens.* New York: Knopf, 1991.

Welsh, Alexander. *The City of Dickens.* Cambridge: Harvard UP, 1986.

Williams, Raymond. "The Creation of Consciousness and Dicken's Vision of the City." In *Charles Dickens.* Ed. Harold Bloom, New York: Chelsea House, 1987.

Natural Values and Unnatural Agents: *Little Dorrit* and the Mid-Victorian Crisis in Agency

Claudia Klaver

We can notice a convergence between Charles Dickens's participation in the mid-Victorian administrative reform movement and his novel Little Dorrit, *produced during the same time period. While Dickens fully supported the efforts of the Administrative Reform Association, his novel goes further than the Association in diagnosing the cause of England's governmental, social, moral, and economic instability, placing the ultimate blame for these instabilities on the speculative economic relations at the basis of the capitalist commercial system. For Dickens, the only antidote to the instabilities of such speculative relations was to locate a solid moral or economic ground that could, in turn, stabilize the moral and economic relations that had been disrupted by England's speculative social and economic system. Deploying a modified version of the separate spheres ideology, Dickens locates this ground in the feminine figure and the influence of the childlike and virginal Little Dorrit. However, when this ground, too, is destabilized in the course of the novel, Dickens's feminine "solution" to the problem of moral responsibilities and value is sorely compromised.*

I

In a letter to his friend W. C. Macready in 1855, Dickens echoes the rhetoric of his novel *Little Dorrit,* voicing his extreme frustration with government

Dickens Studies Annual, Volume 28, Copyright © 1999 by AMS Press, Inc. All rights reserved.

13

corruption and incompetency and with the general political apathy he identified as a key factor in the mid-century crisis of public governance and administration. Dickens writes:

> As to the suffrage, I have lost hope in the ballot. We appear to me to have
> proved the failure of representative institutions without an educated and ad-
> vanced people to support them. What with teaching people to "keep in their
> station," what with bringing up the soul and body of the land to be a good
> child . . . ; what with having no such thing as a middle class (for though we are
> perpetually bragging of it as our safety, it is nothing but a poor fringe on
> the mantle of the upper); what with flunkeyism, toadyism, letting the most
> contemptible lords come in for all manner of places . . . , I do reluctantly believe
> that the English people are habitually consenting parties to the miserable imbe-
> cility into which we have fallen, *and never will help themselves out of it.* Who
> is to do it, if anybody is, God knows. But at present we are on the down-hill
> road to being conquered, and the people WILL be content to bear it, sing "Rule
> Britannia," and WILL NOT be saved.[1]

The frustration and sense of urgency about the governance of the British
public sphere that Dickens voices in this passage was shared by a large
number of middle-class Victorians in the mid-1850s. Much of this frustration,
in turn, found expression in the Administrative Reform Association, the
largest organizational articulation of exasperation with the antiquated English
government. Through his active participation in the Administrative Reform
movement, Dickens addressed the political manifestations of the corruption
he saw as "eating away at the foundations" of British society. At the same
time that he was working in support of the Administrative Reform Association, however, Dickens was also developing a broader, more pervasive diagnosis and critique of the English public sphere. This critique, as suggested by
his letter to Macready, was directed not only at the British government and
its many dysfunctional institutions, but also at "the people" themselves.
However, while in his letter Dickens associates much of the fault of the people
with lack of education and advancement, in his novelistic diagnosis Dickens
identifies the source of Britain's problems as a fundamentally speculative
mindset that individual Britons had carried over from the economic sphere
to all of their other activities and relationships.

In this paper, I argue that Charles Dickens's novel *Little Dorrit* develops
a broad systemic critique of the problems generated by mid-Victorian capitalist economics and ideology. While contending that governmental, social,
moral, and economic instabilities were all inextricably linked, Dickens placed
the ultimate blame for these instabilities on the speculative economic relations
at the basis on the capitalist commercial system. Implicit in Dickens's novelistic critique was the judgment that the Administrative Reform Association's
diagnosis of, and proposed solutions to, governmental corruption did not

reach the source of the problem. Thus, while supporting the efforts of the Administrative Reform Association through his participation, speechmaking, and journalism, in his novel Dickens moved beyond those efforts in order to explore possible solutions to the more fundamental social, moral, political, and economic problems his critique has identified.

For Dickens, the key to any such solution was to locate a solid moral or economic ground that could, in turn, stabilize the moral and economic relations that had been disrupted by England's speculative social and economic system.[2] Deploying a modified version of the separate spheres ideology, Dickens locates this ground in the feminine figure and influence of the childlike and virginal Little Dorrit. Constructing her as the idealized carrier of moral values in the novel, Dickens posits Amy Dorrit as the touchstone against which the narrator, reader, and other characters can test the moral worth of persons, transactions, and relationships throughout the narrative.[3] Yet the very femininity that marks Amy as the novel's touchstone of moral value also places her character at risk from the darker side of that femininity—female sexuality. While through most of the novel Dickens seems to be able to protect Little Dorrit herself from the contamination of any such sexuality, perverse forms of that sexuality proliferate in other of the novel's female characters. As a result of such proliferation, Dickens's feminine "solution" to the problem of moral responsibilities and value is sorely compromised. The very feminine otherness that enables Little Dorrit to oppose the moral, social, political, and economic corruption that pervades the novel manifests itself in phobic form in the character Miss Wade, whom Dickens overdraws as fallen, angry, ungrateful, and perversely sexual—the abject female other who must be excluded from the resolution of the novel.

The character of Miss Wade, then, constitutes a striking trace of Dickens's failure to develop a viable alternative to the system he critiques. The ideal femininity on which Dickens's individualized moral solution depends can only be maintained through a massive gesture of scapegoating—a gesture so large that it is virtually an advertisement of the fantastical inadequacies of Dickens's novelistic remodelling of capitalist economic and social relations. However, at the same time that Dickens's novelistic project fails fairly dramatically in its revisionary critique, it also functions to expose similar failures within the proposals of the more directly politically engaged administrative and parliamentary reformers of the mid-1850s. Just as Dickens's solution to social and moral corruption was to identify and embrace a supposedly stable ground of value through the figure of Little Dorrit, so the administrative reformers' solutions involved idealizing the private sphere of competitive business as the natural and, therefore, stable basis for all social and political organization.

II

The Administrative Reform Association was only the most implicit and public manifestation of a larger reform movement or impulse that was directed at Parliament and the military, as well as the British civil service. In the mid-1850s, a large portion of the educated British public became intensely, if briefly, interested in all of the ways its government was doing business.[4] Through quarterly review and newspaper articles, the Administrative Reform Association, and other forms of "out of house" pressure, members of the public began to agitate for change within the "mechanism" of the British government.[5] In 1854–55, the "Northcote-Trevelyan Report" on the civil service was prepared for Parliament and published in blue book form. Focusing its criticisms of the civil service on appointment by patronage and on promotion based solely on seniority, the report called for major changes in the way the civil service recruited and managed its personnel. In particular, the report called for open competition in the service's recruitment for entry-level positions and promotions based on merit for employees moving between different departments of the service.[6]

Government and Parliamentary response to the issue of administrative reform remained cool and the recommendations of the report were defeated. The tragic bunglings and mis-administrations of the Crimean War, however, further catalyzed the interest and concern of the middle-class public.[7] The dramatic failures of "the system" during the Crimean conflict activated latent concern over the state's civil service, as well as its military departments, and this area of the public service became the focus for the new Administrative Reform Association.[8] While the Administrative Reform Association was organizationally distinct from the Parliamentary committee responsible for the Northcote-Trevelyan report, the Association did adopt many of the report's recommendations. In particular, the Association joined the writers of the report in agitating for open competition in recruitment as the key to reforming the country's civil service, even appealing to the newly reformed Indian civil service as the model for an effective, competitive recruitment process. When Gladstone's government responded with an Order of Council that the Association considered "a thrown bone," the Association's leaders organized two mass meetings in the Theatre Royal, Drury Lane, to rouse public opinion and to pressure Parliament. At the first of these, one of the letters which was read at the meeting's opening—letters pledging support *in absentia*—was by Charles Dickens, and at the second meeting, 27 June 1855, Dickens made his first appearance at a political meeting and delivered the main address.

While in his address Dickens certainly supports the resolutions of the Administrative Reform Association, he does so through a rhetoric that emphasizes the threats posed to all aspects of British national culture—not simply the nation's military and civil service—by the current state of affairs. Using the language of a "general mind" that includes "all classes of society," Dickens explains,

> with little adequate expression of the general mind, or apparent understanding of the general mind in Parliament—with machinery of Government and legislation going round and round, and people fallen from it and standing aloof, as if they had left it to do its last remaining function of destroying itself, when it had achieved the destruction of so much that was dear to them—I did believe, and do believe, that the only wholesome turn affairs so menacing could take was an awakening of the people . . . in all patriotism and loyalty to effect a great peaceful constitutional change in the administration of their own affairs.[9]

In this passage, Dickens sentimentalizes the deleterious effects of governmental incompetence, through a kind of personalization ("the destruction of so much that was dear to them") and inflation ("affairs so menacing") of the cost of the current system. Dickens's speech closes with a further heightening of this rhetoric, in which the sentimental veers into the Gothic:

> In this old country, with its seething hard-worked millions, its heavy taxes, its crowds of ignorant, its crowds of poor, its crowds of wicked, woe the day which the dangerous man will find for himself, because the head of the Queen's government failed in his duty of anticipating it by a brighter and better one.[10]

The unnatural state of the English public sphere, Dickens threatens, is on the brink of producing the kind of unnatural revolutionary agent associated with the Gothic terror of the French Revolution.

During these same late spring and summer months Dickens was beginning work on the novel that was to become *Little Dorrit*. In fact, the image of "the machinery of the government and Legislation going round and round . . . [with] people fallen from it" which Dickens describes in his Drury Lane speech seems the germ of that whirligig which was to be the (absent) center of *Little Dorrit*'s England—the Circumlocution Office.[11] But the crossovers between Dickens's activities in the Administrative Reform Association and the shape of his new novel went beyond the sharing of satirical rhetoric. For, just as the novel favorably opposes Daniel Doyce to the Circumlocution Office, and as the Drury Lane speech praises "private progress . . . in matters of business" over "public folly and failure,"[12] so the entire administrative reform program was advanced through the opposition between a public governmental sphere of activities and a private commercial sphere. In fact, in whatever generic context the problem of public administration was defined by the mid-Victorians, that definition involved an implicit or explicit contrast with the commercial business activities of a predominantly middle-class "private sector."[13]

At the center of the administrative reformers' critiques of the government, then, lay a fundamental sense that the problem with the public was that it was not the "private," and that the "private" was considered the natural sphere of human activity (thanks largely to political economy). Thus, for example, the writers of the Northcote-Trevelyan report oppose "the unambitious, and the indolent or incapable" as those who seek Civil Service employment to the "norm" of those engaged in "other professions":

> Admission into the Civil Service is indeed eagerly sought after, but it is for the unambitious, and the indolent or incapable [i.e., "unnatural"], that it is chiefly desired. Those whose abilities do not warrant an expectation that they will succeed in other professions, where they must encounter the *competition of their contemporaries* . . . , are placed in the Civil Service, where they may obtain an honourable livelihood with *little labour,* and with *no risk* (emphasis mine).[14]

The report goes on to describe the effects of public service on even the best of its recruits. Contrasting the "open professions" of the private sector with the civil service, the report develops an opposition between the private and professional "correctives" of competition and accountability with public establishments where

> the general rule is that all rise together. . . . The feeling of security which this state of things necessarily engenders tends to encourage indolence, and thereby to depress the character of the service [and] those who are admitted into it at an early age are thereby relieved from the *necessity of those struggles* which for the most part fall to the lot of such as enter upon the open professions . . . (emphasis mine).[15]

These passages make it clear that the writers of the Northcote-Trevelyan report conceived of the civil service as an unnaturally secure and protected sphere of activity, in contrast to the natural challenges of the private—competition, labour, and the "risk" of accountability for one's performance. Given this opposition between the private and an unreformed public sphere, the report's proposals for reform can be more suggestively contextualized; for its main resolutions of appointment by open competition and promotion (only) by merit are precisely ways of bringing the naturally "self-correcting" mechanisms of the private into the public sector. The assumption implicit in the report is that by making the qualifications of the civil service more like those of private industry, the reforms will also bring the level of efficiency and effectiveness in that service closer to the high levels achieved by private enterprise. This assumption, in turn, is based upon the supposition that both the proposed means and the desired ends are natural standards of human activity.

At the core of the Victorian conception of the private sector lay the individual—the individual naturalized by classical political economy and liberal political theory. For the Administrative Reformers, the individual was seen as the sole possessor of a certain amount of talent and accomplishment (i.e., "merit") to be measured by a competitive examination. Even more important-ly for Dickens and his fellow reformers, the individual was perceived as the most basic responsible unit; that is to say, "responsibility" and "accountabil-ity" were thought to be naturally based in the single human "agent." Thus the only way to make an organization accountable was to link the responsibil-ity for its decisions and actions to the individuals who comprised that organi-zation.

Ultimately, it was just this basis in the private individual that the public sphere was seen to require—in legislative matters as well as administrative. If the problem of the public was that it was removed from the natural intra- and inter-subjective relations of the private, then the solution was to re-ground public organization and activity in that private dynamic. In the best of socio-political situations, then, the public would only *appear* to be opposed to the private: on a closer look one would find that "the public" was just an aggregate of private individuals. This, at least, is the logic informing the writings of the Administrative Reform Association, the Northcote-Trevelyan report, and Dickens's satires on the English government in his Drury Lane speech, in *Little Dorrit,* and in several articles in *Household Words.*[16]

A concurrent reform movement, however, and one that overlapped with the Administrative Reform campaign, suggests that there was a problem even more fundamental than the public/private split. Focusing on Parliamentary, rather than administrative, governmental reform, spokespersons for this movement argued that there was a "natural Parliamentary logic" that in-volved the relationships between electors and delegates. According to these writers, that relationship had been corrupted. While the immediate source of that corruption was party and patronage, its ultimate cause was diagnosed as the moral failure of the individual electors.[17] Cyrus Redding, one of the more conservative spokesmen on this problem, writes that "In the choice of high-minded and well-qualified representatives there is a *fearful laxity among electors,* who, in too many cases, have not the smallest conceptions of an *imperious duty*" (emphasis mine).[18] One major historian of these mid-century reform movements, Olive Anderson, describes this aspect of the reformers' appeal as "a moralizing call to *individual duty.*" By resisting the aristocracy's "corrupt inducements" at parliamentary elections, individual—presumably middle-class—electors "could undermine the political influence of the aris-tocracy and restore the ancient vigour of the constitution" (emphasis mine).[19]

In contrast to the diagnosis offered by the Administrative Reform Move-ment, according to these accounts, the problem with the public was in large part a problem with the private individuals who composed the electorate or "voting public" of the nation. Government legislative and administrative functions had floundered not just because they were disconnected from a natural private sphere of competing, self-determining individuals; rather, they had also floundered because those individuals themselves had failed in their moral-political responsibilities. The private dynamic that was intended to ground the public system had itself proved unstable. According to Habermas's theorization of the bourgeois public sphere, the conjunction between the private and public (in the form of civil society and the state) was essential to the emergence of modern European forms of governmentality. In the place of Cyrus Redding's call of "duty," however, Habermas sees the link of the public to the private in terms of interest, especially the commercial interests of the bourgeoisie. Arguing that the eighteenth- and nineteenth-century public sphere was dependent upon the emergence of a liberal or "free" market, Habermas writes that

> only property owners were in a position to form a public that could legislatively protect the foundations of the existing property order; only they had private interests—each his own—which automatically converged into the common interest in the preservation of a civil society as a private sphere. Only from them, therefore, was an effective representation of the general interest to be expected, since it was not necessary for them in any way to leave their private existence behind to exercise their public role.[20]

The problem with private interest as the ground for the government public sphere was that this "interest" was itself a highly contested and unstable category. Thus, Redding's corrupt electors might argue that they were only serving their own interests—in this case economic interests—by selling their votes to the highest bidder.

Furthermore, by the mid-nineteenth century, many political reformers, including working-class reformers, rejected material, economic property as the only criterion for suffrage, arguing instead that the franchise should be based on an individual's possession of subjective properties. Such subjective properties, in turn, could replace or at least supplement interest as the stabilizing link between the private individual and the sphere of governmental legislation and administration. According to the parliamentary reformers discussed by Anderson, however, it was just such subjective moral properties that England's electors and "people" were seen to lack. This same concern with individual moral failures as the source of England's social and political problems pervades much of Dickens's letter to his friend Macready. When Dickens writes in his letter that "the English people are habitually consenting parties to the miserable imbecility into which we have fallen, and never will help themselves out of it," he extends his critique down from the aristocratic oligarchies that dominated Parliamentary and ministerial politics to the apparent apathy of the English people.[21] Dickens's focus on the problematic dynamic of individual responsibility and irresponsibility becomes most apparent, however, in his treatment of these issues through the form of the novel. In *Little Dorrit,* Dickens not only identifies individual moral failures as the source of virtually all of Britain's problems, he also analyses those failures in order to generate his own solution to the current crisis.

III

Individual responsibility was such a crucial issue for Dickens when he was working with the Administrative Reform Association and writing *Little Dorrit* that he originally conceived of a novel entitled "Nobody's Fault." Edgar Johnson writes that, as Dickens had first imagined the book, "its central character was to have been a man who brought about all the mischief in it, and then, at every fresh calamity, said, 'Well, it's a mercy, however, nobody was to blame you know.' "[22] In place of the one signally irresponsible character of "Nobody's Fault," *Little Dorrit*'s narrative confronts its readers with a plethora of irresponsible institutions and characters, in particular "Society, the Circumlocution Office, and Mr. Gowan [as] . . . three parts of one idea and design."[23] Most critics who discuss "Nobody's Fault" (the novelistic beginning that was displaced by *Little Dorrit*) see Dickens's abandonment of the scheme as signifying his growing sense that the "fault" for the mischiefs and calamities of the mid-Victorian social situation was not traceable to an individual. Johnson writes, for example, that "this notion did not emphasize clearly enough his desire to portray a vast impersonal system of inefficiency, venality, and wrong, baffling all endeavor to fasten responsibility anywhere."[24]

On a certain level, Johnson and those who agree with him are, of course, right: *Little Dorrit* is a novel in which fault is ascribed via broad cultural and class critique, rather than through the "fingering" of one individual. "The fault" is a moral one that permeates all levels and corners of English society as represented in the novel—from the residents of Bleeding Heart Yard to Merdle's diners, from the Marshalsea prisoners to the "Lords of the Circumlocution Office." Yet emphasis on the breadth of Dickens's social critique can also obscure the fact that the moral illness that permeates the novel's societies is diagnosed by the narrator as precisely the failure of individual responsibility. It is individual moral failures, that is, that result in the situation in which fault cannot be localized. While this diagnosis is virtually as all-pervasive in the novel as the illness itself, it receives its most explicit articulation in regard to the British public's response to the Barnacles and their jobbery:

> When it became known to the Britons on the shore of the yellow Tiber that their intelligent compatriot, Mr. Sparkler, was made one of the Lords of their

Circumlocution Office . . . Some laughed; . . . [some said] that the sole constitu-
tional purpose of all places within the gift of Decimus, was, that Decimus
should strengthen himself. A few bilious Britons there were who would not
subscribe to this article of faith; but their objection was purely theoretical. In
a practical point of view, they listlessly abandoned the matter, as being the
business of some other Britons unknown, somewhere, or nowhere. In like manner, at home, great numbers of Britons maintained, for as long as four-'and-
twenty consecutive hours, that those invisible and anonymous Britons 'ought
to take it up;' and that if they quietly acquiesced in it, they deserved it. But of
what class the remiss Britons were composed, and where the unlucky creatures
hid themselves . . . and how it constantly happened that they neglected their
interests . . . was not, either upon the shore of the yellow Tiber or the shore of
the black Thames, made apparent to men   (LD 644).

It is precisely such individual abnegations of responsibility, Dickens insists,
which allow and support the corrupt reign of the Barnacles and the Circumlocution Office. "Administrative Reform" in itself cannot cure the fundamental
problem of English society, because such reforms depend on the integrity
and engagement of the private individual—an integrity Dickens sees as sorely
absent. Instead, what is necessary as well is the willingness of the English
people—particularly the English middle classes—to become visible and individually responsible, rather than remaining "invisible and anonymous."
    While Dickens's novel attributes the illness of English government and
society to the failure of individual agents, it also goes further, probing beneath
the surface of such individual irresponsibilities to the conditions that create
them. In the course of the novel, Dickens reveals these conditions to be
economic; specifically, he accuses Britain's speculative economy of un-
dermining individual moral responsibility.[25] Ironically, then, in Dickens's
novel the naturalized "private" sphere of free trade and business celebrated
by the administrative reformers (and at some points by Dickens as well) is
ultimately characterized as generating the corruption that has undermined the
individual moral properties of the English people. The speculative mindset
that Dickens exposes as essential to successful participation in the Victorian
capitalist economy has seeped into the country's moral and social relationships as well, thus creating a profound moral and epistemological instability,
as well the financial instabilities that continually plague the novel's characters.
The most dramatic example of speculative economic investment in the novel,
of course, is the mania that surrounds the character of Merdle; but also of
importance are the many small instances of investment or debts attendant on
past investments. William Dorrit is in debtor's prison, for example, not because he participated in any grand bubble scheme, but simply because he
was one investor in a business enterprise that failed.
    From the beginning of the novel, in turn, Dickens explicitly associates such
economic failures with equivalent moral failures. While this is a commonly

noted trope in the Victorian novel, critics such as Barbara Weiss and Patrick Brantlinger who discuss this conjunction have not fully explored the specific ways in which Dickens has linked moral to economic failure in this novel.[26] Dickens does not loosely equate these kinds of failure, but repeatedly interrogates their relationship. For example, later in the novel, Arthur Clennam incurs a financial debt as he is infected and caught up in Pancks's speculation sickness—a sickness that the narrative explicitly describes as a moral infection. He does not, however, allow his inability to pay off his debt to become a failure of responsibility. By voluntarily giving himself up to the Marshalsea, he bears upon his person the obligations he cannot meet with his financial accounts. His momentary financial-moral lapse, in fact, becomes the opportunity for him to complete his moral education, for it is while imprisoned in the Marshalsea (in a chapter entitled ''The Pupil of the Marshalsea'') that Clennam learns both what Little Dorrit has meant to him, and what he has meant to Little Dorrit. And it is Little Dorrit, in turn, who serves as moral epitome in the novel—the responsible emblem and embodiment of that great Victorian virtue, ''Duty.''

Before examining Amy Dorrit's role both for Clennam's own development and for the novel as a whole, I want first to explore the other and much more prevalent side of the issue of the moral-financial model of responsibility. For if Little Dorrit and Arthur Clennam represent the fulfillment of individual responsibility, the majority of the remainder of the novel's characters represent its failure—its failure either in terms of money, or morality, or, quite often, both of these at once. In fact, virtually every unpaid financial debt seems attendant upon a similar moral irresponsibility (though the reverse is not always the case). Mrs. Clennam is one of the most complex examples of this doubled failure of duty, for she herself calculates moral balances on the model of a financial account:

> ''Reparation!'' said she. . . . ''I endure without murmuring, because it is appointed that I shall so make reparation for my sins. Reparation! Is there none in this room? . . .''
> Thus was she always *balancing her bargains* with the Majesty of heaven, posting up the *entries to her credit,* strictly keeping her set-off, *claiming her due* (emphasis mine).[27]

The problem with these accounts is that they are ''rigged.'' According to her accounts, Mrs. Clennam's ''credit'' column will always be longer than the ''debit'' column. In fact, she finds within her own records that she has accumulated so much moral credit to her account than that credit can even balance out a certain moral and financial debit—the suppression of a will and virtual robbery of the rightful heir. This is only possible, however, because of her willful misrecognition of what constitutes moral duty and responsibility. She has "reversed the order of Creation, and breathed her own breath into a clay image of her Creator" (LD 844); and though that image is nothing but her "own likeness . . . [her] own bad passions" (LD 844), it suffices to occupy the opposite column in her self-serving, self-balancing book of accounts. Mrs. Clennam ultimately serves as a dark and unnatural parody by the connection between moral and financial responsibility: pretending to use her accounting to avoid either type of failure, she in fact uses those false accounts as a screen under which she accrues debts on both the moral and financial sides.

The novel's most infamous example of the simultaneous failure of financial and moral duty is Mr. Merdle's bankruptcy. Like Mrs. Clennam, Merdle's moral failure is not simply attendant upon his financial irresponsibility, but is, at least in part, inherent in and inextricable from it. He is not just a "bankrupt," as are Dorrit and Clennam each in their turns; rather, his bankruptcy results from his being "the greatest Forger and the greatest Thief that had ever cheated the gallows" (LD 777). Through his financial bankruptcy and duplicitousness, in turn, Merdle's moral failure injures or ruins thousands of others. What makes the phenomenon of Merdle so central to the plot and concerns of the novel is, in fact, less his own duplicitous corruption than the susceptibility of Victorian society to such ruinous deception. The "phenomenon of Merdle" is, finally, more one of "Society" in general than of "Merdle" *per se*. Ferdinand Barnacle seems only the narrator's cynical spokesman when he laughs at Clennam's hope that "[Merdle] and his dupes may be a warning to people not to have so much done with them again":

> "My dear-Mr. Clennam . . . have you really such a verdant hope? The next man who has as large a capacity and as genuine a taste for swindling, will succeed as well. Pardon me, but I think you really have no idea how the human bees will swarm to the beating of any old tin kettle. . . . When they can be got to believe that the kettle is made of the precious metals, in that fact lies the whole power of men like our late lamented [i.e., Merdle]"   (LD 806).

Men like Merdle can only succeed in deceiving society, that is, because society is so willing to be deceived—only because the individuals who compose that society are so morally debased. Just as the administrative reformers ultimately perceive the government's failures as the failures of individuals, so, Ferdinand insinuates, "Merdle's" grand fraud is really the combined effect of many individuals defrauding themselves and, if possible, others.

Ferdinand's illustration, however, implies not simply that in such cases those who are deceived are almost as much at fault as those who deceive. The illustration also implies the moral and economic basis of the faulted susceptibility, for inherent in the analogy of an "old tin kettle" is an opposition between real, true, or natural value and false or artificial value. A pot, the metaphor suggests, whether made of tin or of precious metals, has a natural and irreducible value. That value can, perhaps, be marked by the assignment of a "price" or "cost" for exchange; but even if its price is mismarked or its cost is mistaken, the essential value remains unchanged. Given this definition of value, the only legitimate and fair exchange is one that recognizes the value of the object exchanged and acknowledges that value with a comparable or "true" price. Speculation, in contrast to fair exchange, depends on the asymmetry of investment and return—on the gap between price and "true value." In speculation, one thinks one is getting more for less and it is precisely the desire to get more for less—to get without giving—that binds investors to the deceptions of the Merdles.

The problem with speculation, then, it would seem, is that it is based on a type of financial relationship which, because it is dependent on the appearance, rather than the established fact of value, leaves the speculators highly vulnerable to deception and fraud. Yet the analogy of the "old tin kettle" and its natural value also suggests an even deeper problem with the speculation model of financial exchange. For, in an economy of natural values, any surplus on one side of the exchange must be balanced by a debit on the other side. Dickens, that is, seems to be rejecting the economic model in which value, marked by money, *can* materialize in the asymmetrical space of unequal exchange. In both the financial and moral economies of the novel, no such creation of value "ex nihilo" can occur, as is overwhelmingly evidenced by the bursting of the Merdle bubble. Merdle's empire was based not, as everyone had thought, on his genius at investing, but on his genius at deceiving. Likewise, his banquets were not the materialization of invisible profits, but rather "the plunder of innumerable homes" (LD 776). The real value involved in those feasts, that is, could not come from nowhere, and so came instead from the unwitting pockets of Merdle's victims. Any society or individual who approves of, allows, or participates in the financial relations of speculation, then, implicitly condones and enables robbery and exploitation: an old tin kettle is an old tin kettle, no matter how much it can be sold for; and if it is sold for more than it is worth, then someone else will not receive the full value for the kettle of precious metals he has to exchange.

This is as true of the moral relations and values of the novel as it is of its financial economy. In fact, it is precisely Society's irresponsible social relations which facilitate the immorality of its economic relations. Ferdinand's "old tin kettle" could as easily represent the figure of Merdle himself as his too-good-to-be-true financial schemes, for it is society's inflated valuation of Merdle and his "glorious" name which enables him to extend his economic credit. Thus, it is appropriate that it is on the eve of a dinner party at the home of the character whom the narrator designates "Society's" one representative of reality, "the great Physician," that Merdle chooses to deflate his name and person through an act of ignominious suicide. Likewise, "Merdle's complaint'' to which Physician has attended so fruitlessly turns out to have been social and financial imposition—''simply Forgery and Robbery.'' Such social trading on appearances—rather than realities—of individual worth is, in fact, the most common disease of the novel. Just as the Merdle-speculation sickness permeates English society from the Barnacles and new-monied Dorrits down to Cavelletto and the residents of Bleeding Heart Yard, so does the moral illness which confuses the appearances for the truth of individual value.

If Mr. Merdle is the novelistic representative of financial speculation and fraud, Mr. Henry Gowan is the spokesman for its counterpart in the moral realm of social relations. Gowan captures both the essences of this social duplicity and its connection with financial fraud when he tells Arthur Clennam of his lack of artistic talent:

> ''To be candid with you, tolerably, I am not a great imposter. Buy one of my pictures and I assure you in confidence, it will not be worth the money. Buy one of another man's . . . and the chances are the more you give him, the more he'll impose upon you. They all do it. . . . Give almost any man I know ten pounds, and he will impose on you to a corresponding extent . . . a thousand pounds—to a corresponding extent . . .''   (LD 358).

Gowan here figures the gap of ''imposition'' between social estimation and essential worth in terms of economic value. Like Ferdinand's discussion of the Merdle phenomenon, Gowan's estimation of social relations might be seen as a cynical ventriloquism of the novel's narrator. Actually, however, the narrator is careful to contextualize Gowan's opinion, distancing himself from Gowan's smug cynicism through an unusually explicit critique of Gowan's character. The narrator writes of Gowan:

> The worst class of sum worked in the every-day world is cyphered by the diseased arithmeticians who are always in the rule of Subtraction as to the merits and successes of others, and never in Addition as to their own.
> The habit, too, of seeking some sort of recompense in the discontented boast of being disappointed, is a habit fraught with degeneracy. A certain idle carelessness and recklessness of consistency soon comes of it. To bring deserving things down by setting undeserving things up is one of its perverted delights; and there is no playing fast and loose with the truth, in any game, without growing the worse for it.   (LD 540)

Here again, as in Ferdinand's kettle metaphor, the narrator asserts the presence of a true or natural value, even as he discusses the misrecognition of that value. Just as the kettle is granted an irreducible, unchangeable value—whether it be that of tin or of precious metals—so Dickens asserts that ''merit'' and ''truth'' in the moral realm exist independently of social acknowledgment or misrecognition. Henry Gowan may be able to trade socially on ''the discontented boast of being disappointed'' (LD 540), but that boast has no value in the sphere of moral truth. Or rather, the content of the boast has no positive value, while the act of boasting is a moral hazard. It breeds, in fact, precisely the "carelessness" and "recklessness" as to true value, and to one's own natural duties and responsibilities, that the narrator isolates as the fundamental problem of English upper- and middle-class society.[28]

To offset the speculative attitudes and pervasive moral irresponsibility of such characters, the novel offers us the image of Little Dorrit.[29] From the very outset of the novel, Little Dorrit has occupied a paradigmatic moral position. She is introduced, in a chapter devoted especially to her, as "the child of the Marshalsea" who takes upon herself all the moral and financial responsibilities of the family: she protects her father from the knowledge of his own degradation; she works to support him financially; she finds employment for her sister and brother; and she provides her father with constant emotional ministrations. Moreover, Little Dorrit does all these things via a mystified "inspiration" that the narrator explicitly compares to that of a poet or a priest. Throughout the novel, Little Dorrit's earnestness, honesty, and integrity form a pointed contrast to the vanity, duplicity, and pretentiousness of her sister and, through her sister, Little Dorrit's virtues contrast with those of the larger "Society" with which Fanny is so concerned.

Little Dorrit is not simply a model of moral worth, however; she is a touchstone by which others can judge such worth—an index who points beyond herself to that idealized moral worth. As a moral index, Little Dorrit is more than a representation or embodiment of all the qualities privileged by the narrative; she is also the standard of these qualities within the novel. Little Dorrit's most significant narrative role is relational—pointing both the reader and the fictional characters to all that is "good and true" within the world of the novel. For, while the novel is filled with willful misrecognitions of both moral and economic value, it is also riddled with the earnest, well-intended misreadings that seem inevitable in a society whose morality, as well as its economy, is based on speculation.

Exactly how hard it is to distinguish between the "natural" values of fair exchange and the "unnatural" values of speculation and fraud is rendered salient in Clennam's conversations with Pancks and Doyce about speculation and investment. What Clennam has presumed to be speculative enterprises—Merdle's bank and financial schemes—Pancks insists are sound *investments*. He has "gone into it," Pancks tells Clennam, he has "made the calculations . . . worked it. They're safe and genuine." Throughout the conversation, Clennam continues to refer to Merdle's schemes as speculations, and Pancks just as insistently corrects him with the word "investments."

The unstable boundary between investments and speculation is foregrounded again when Clennam asks Doyce how best to manage the company's capital while Doyce is away. Doyce explicitly states that he objects to speculation, and Clennam immediately agrees with this prejudice. Even though he has already invested the firm's assets in the Merdle ventures he had earlier identified as speculative, Clennam now believes that this investment meets Doyce's and his own criterion of "safe." The plot of the novel soon reveals, of course, what the readers have suspected all along: that these investments are anything but safe, thereby confirming Clennam's initial instincts. Less significant than the correctness of his original judgment, however, is the exposure of how unstable that judgment is. When confronted by Pancks's calculations, Clennam seems to have no ground from or principles by which to resist the lure of a large profit. Even Doyce himself recognizes that *some* profit is necessary, that the firm's assets must be invested, rather than remaining idle. The issue is how to discriminate between a legitimate and an illegitimate margin of profit; that is, between investment and speculation. The problem is that capitalist economics render this distinction virtually impossible to make—in fact, capitalism's successful functioning depends on the blurring of the distinction that Dickens (and most of his contemporaries) were trying to make.[30]

Pancks himself, a character whom Doyce as well as Clennam considers "a cautious fellow," tells Arthur that it is his duty—especially his duty to his partner, Doyce—to "be as rich as [he] honestly can" (LD 642). The pursuit of large profit margin, in other words, is the duty of a moral man in a capitalist society . . . even if that duty results in the occasional pursuit of false instead of true value. The instability of this economic situation, however, completely undermines the notion that a natural private sector can be opposed to an unnatural public sphere of government corruption. Individual financial and moral failures, it turns out, are not necessarily failures of individual will. Instead, they are sometimes failures of the capitalist system that undergirds private enterprises; or more precisely, they are the individual failures that the speculative economy of the capitalist system requires.[31] For Dickens, then, the private economic sector turns out to be as dangerously unnatural as the public sphere of government: in neither realm can the morality of the individual man (figured as his will or intentions) be perfectly aligned with his actions.

As a novel, rather than an economic or political tract, part of the project of *Little Dorrit* is to expose the deleterious effects that this failure of alignment has within the social and emotional, as well as the economic and governmental, domains of Victorian experience. Clennam's participation in the Merdle bubble may be the novel's most obvious instance of a well-intentioned misjudgment of value that has harmful effects, but Clennam also proves unable to judge the true nature of Little Dorrit's feelings for him during the majority of the narrative. This misjudgment results not only in his own pain, but also in the even more acute pain of Little Dorrit herself. The narrator repeatedly describes scenes in which Arthur's dwelling upon his own "old age," Little

Dorrit's youth, or their parent-child relationship function as a form of torture for the woman he addresses.[32] Clennam fails to recognize Little Dorrit's romantic feelings toward him, in part because he had earlier failed to acknowledge his own romantic feelings for Pet Meagles.[33] Though Clennam's self-deception about his feelings for Pet Meagles seems relatively harmless, and certainly understandable, Dickens marks his condemnation of even this degree of self-imposition by discussing it with the same indefinite personal pronouns—nobody and somebody—that he at other points uses to explicitly criticize individual and institutional apathy. The failure of Clennam's self-estimation, then, ultimately results in the same irresponsibility witnessed in Little Dorrit's father and English bureaucrats: all these men "impose upon" themselves concerning the person they are and the responsibilities that involves, and in each case, the result is a harmful abrogation of responsibility.

Conversely, only through Clennam's recognition of Little Dorrit's feelings for him is he able to see himself truly and, as a result, to rectify his earlier misjudgment and the harm it had caused. In other words, only when Clennam sees himself in relation to Amy Dorrit—or even through her eyes—can his moral intentions produce consistently positive results. Clennam himself, after his moment of self-recognition, realizes that Little Dorrit is his "vanishing point":

> Looking back upon his poor story, she was its vanishing point. Everything in its perspective led to her innocent figure. He had travelled thousands of miles toward it; previous unquiet hopes and doubts had worked themselves out before it; it was the centre of the interest of his life; it was the termination of everything that was good and pleasant in it; beyond, there was nothing but waste and darkened sky. (LD 801)

The panoramic scope of this passage suggests that, with his recognition of his true feelings toward and true relationship with Little Dorrit, Arthur Clennam's entire perceptual field shifts and expands, moving, in fact, closer to that of the narrator himself. With this shift, Clennam's perceptions of his entire world are reoriented around Little Dorrit and thus, by extension, around a true and natural standard of value.

With Arthur Clennam's epiphany, many of the novel's explicit tensions are resolved. However, Clennam's mistakes are by no means the only examples of well-intentioned misjudgments in the narrative. In fact, the narrative repeatedly turns upon such miscalculations. For example, Pet Meagles innocently misjudges Henry Gowan and is consigned to a life of married misery and the residents of Bleeding Heart Yard mistakenly think that Casby is their benefactor and that Pancks is a tyrant. As a moral index, then, the figure of Little Dorrit promises a narrative solution to the problem that good characters may mistake false value for true. If characters cannot trust themselves, they can trust Amy; if characters cannot rely on their own moral impulses to guide them, they can, the narrative asserts, rely on the moral feelings, attitudes, and actions of Little Dorrit.

In fact, Amy's uncle, Frederick Dorrit, imagines her in precisely this role when he "protests" to Fanny and the rest of the newly-rich Dorrit family:

> "Where's your affectionate invaluable friend? Where's your devoted guardian? Where's your more than mother? How dare you set up superiorities against all these characters combined in your sister? . . . To the winds with family credit. . . . I protest against pride. I protest against ingratitude. I protest against any one of us here who have known what we have known . . . setting up any pretension that puts Amy at a moment's disadvantage, or the cost of a moment's pain. *We know that it is base pretension by its having that effect*" (emphasis mine, LD 538).

Frederick Dorrit holds up Amy to her family as a touchstone of moral worth and authentic value, just as Arthur Clennam comes to realize later that all that is "good and pleasant" in his own story terminates in her image. Any character who comes in contact with Little Dorrit has the opportunity to reorient his or her valuations of worth according to the standard of integrity she represents. Such characters are, in fact, held responsible by the narrator for their success—or, more often, failure—in recognizing the true value of Amy's character. While the speculation-minded economy of the novelistic society is willing to trade on the appearance of value, the "natural" model of equivalent exchange privileged by the narrator finds each character individually responsible and almost always at fault—compared to Amy Dorrit.

IV

The issue that remains largely implicit within Dickens's novelistic economy of true and natural values is the question of what grounds or marks these "natural" values. If one can measure the value of a tin kettle or a novelistic character by holding it or him up to the light of Amy Dorrit, how does one go on to discuss the source of that value? In other words, what kind of value does Little Dorrit herself embody and represent? Rather than answering these questions directly, Dickens's novel seems to sidestep them slightly, in part by gesturing toward the familiar Victorian ideologies of work and domesticity. Within the novel, the only stable basis for *economic* value seems to be labor or work, which goes under the rubric of duty. Thus, Arthur is on solid economic ground only after he loses his inheritance and can start working for his own capital, as well as maintenance.[34] Not incidentally, this change in Clennam's financial status also coincides with his moral enlightenment at the hands of the laborious Little Dorrit. In fact, Dickens's novel repeatedly blurs the boundaries between economic and moral value around the issue of work. Thus, one of the earliest signs of Amy Dorrit's moral superiority is her commitment to work. When the narrator introduces Little Dorrit as an "inspired" character, he adds specifically that she is "inspired to be something . . . different and laborious" (LD 111). She not only does needlework herself, she also arranges for her sister and brother to be trained in various lines of work. A sign of her brother's moral turpitude, in fact, is that he cannot stick to any one line of work, but rather gets fired or finds excuses to leave one job after another.[35]

While work seems to provide a basis of value within the economic sphere, however, it is not a sufficient base within the moral realm. The novel is filled with characters like the residents of Bleeding Heart Yard who labor hard, yet find no moral transcendence in their work. This narrative message about the limitations of labor is rendered most explicit in Panck's parodic celebration (and finally dismissal) of the philosophy of "keep me always at it" as the "Whole duty of Man in a commercial country" (LD 202). More fundamental to the novelistic economy than labor, then, is the *moral* value that must guide and support one's labor, as well as underwrite any legitimate economic transaction—the moral value inherent in the character of Little Dorrit. But if her value is not fully underwritten by her commitment to work—her "laborious[ness]"—then what is the source or ground of Amy Dorrit's moral ideality?

Significantly, the other word besides "laborious" that the narrator uses to describe the nature of Little Dorrit's inspiration is "different." On the most literal level, this refers to Little Dorrit's difference from her siblings and the other inhabitants of the Marshalsea; but since both her family and the prison community are constructed as microcosms of the larger novelistic community, the word can, by extension, be used to describe her relationship with all of the other non-idealized characters in the novel. That "difference" is in large part Amy Dorrit's moral femininity, as it is for most of Dickens's domestic heroines. Her femininity, however, is more complex than the femininity that grounds Dickens's other heroines, for while it is obviously derived from the femininity of the Victorian "separate spheres" ideology, it is also significantly different from the idealized version of femininity that relies on and celebrates the "angel in the house." Unlike Florence in *Dombey and Son,* for example, Amy Dorrit does *not* remain in the domestic sphere. In fact, for most of the novel, Amy Dorrit does not even have a domestic sphere in which she could remain; instead, she has a room in the Marshalsea prison. Nor does she remain even there; though she attempts to make her father's room domestic, Amy herself leaves that room daily to do needlework in other people's houses. Rather than being isolated from monetary transactions, then, Little

Dorrit's version of femininity involves actively marketing her labor; Little Dorrit must be able to handle money without being tainted by it. In *Little Dorrit,* Dickens attempts to create a femininity that can co-exist with economic value, without being corrupted by or absorbed into the system of such value. This creates its own problem, however, for if it is not her domestic difference that distinguishes and stabilizes Little Dorrit's moral value, what does stabilize that value—the value on which Dickens's entire antispeculation alternative seems to depend?

Ultimately, of course, the answer to this question is that nothing does stabilize this value, because nothing *can* stabilize it. Dickens is trying to find a stable alternative within a set of economic, ideological, and representational systems that are themselves inherently unstable.[36] Dickens himself, however, refused to accept this diagnosis of his own cultural situation, and instead struggled to create in Little Dorrit a reliable index of value. That value, in turn, seems centered on one controlling feeling or motivation—Little Dorrit's absolute and selfless devotion to her father. Virtually all of Little Dorrit's idealized actions are motivated by and centered around her concern for her father, and it is the almost subject selflessness of that concern that seems to ensure her moral purity. Maggie calls Amy "Little Mother" and, like a good mother, her devotion to the family stems from her love for the father of the family. Little Dorrit is at once child and wife to her father, just as she later becomes child and wife to Arthur Clennam—even insisting that Arthur continue to call her by her diminutive, "Little Dorrit," rather than by her Christian name. Even Arthur himself, however, is not allowed by the novel's plot to become Little Dorrit's suitor, and thus compete for her attentions, until *after* her bonds to her original, biological father are severed through his death. Only the close familial bond between father and daughter seems a location of selfless *feminine* devotion sufficient to insure the natural value that Dickens idealizes. Rather than keeping Amy Dorrit contained within the domestic sphere, Dickens takes the paternalist core of domestic ideology and transforms it into an almost untransferable relational bond.

The problem with this bond as a basis for feminine morality, however, lies in the threat of female sexuality—a threat Dickens himself at once denies and acknowledges, dismisses, and defends against. Amy Dorrit may play the role of a mother, but, unlike a mother, she must also remain sexually virginal and pure; for if Amy Dorrit is allowed to exit the domestic sphere and sell her labor, Dickens has to ensure that her labor is never sexualized. The only way to adequately ensure this in the novel, it seems, is to ensure that Amy Dorrit herself is never sexualized. By creating a child-woman heroine and a child-woman bride (with a child-woman name), Dickens attempts to immunize his heroine against the threat of female sexuality. However, the pressure of female sexuality on Little Dorrit's character is in evidence from near the beginning of the novel, manifesting itself in a number of different ways. First, it is parodied through the character of John Chivery and his pathetic attraction to Little Dorrit. This comic subplot enables Dickens to invoke and defuse the threat of Amy's twenty-two-year-old sexuality. At the same time, however, this comic subplot spills over into Little Dorrit's all too serious feelings for Arthur Clennam. When John Chivery addresses her as she muses on the iron bridge, Little Dorrit starts with a look of horrified repulsion that is totally out of character. Embarrassing herself and injuring Chivery, the extremity of her response is a measure of the shock she feels when the gatekeeper's son materializes in the place of her own secret object of desire. Besides this outburst on the iron bridge, almost the only other narrative trace of Amy's desire is her story about the Princess, the little woman, and the shadow. While an obvious metaphor for Amy's own sexuality, the story of repression, self-suppression, and loss constitutes a fairly safe container for the heroine's unchildlike desires. It not only offers narrative reinforcement to the continued suppression of Amy's desires, but also, as a story within a story, it doubly distances those threatening desires from the main action of the novel.

The most dramatic exposure of the threatening pressure of Amy's own sexuality comes early in the novel during her late night encounter with a prostitute. The prostitute first approaches Little Dorrit thinking that she is a child. As a child, Little Dorrit would be immune from the taint of the prostitute's explicit sexuality; she would be able to receive without corruption what the prostitute had to give her (a touch, money, comfort, etc.) and, in receiving, be able to give back to the prostitute a portion of her lost humanity. When the prostitute discovers that Amy Dorrit is a woman, however, and not a child, she recoils as if stung. Even though Little Dorrit begs the woman to "Let me speak to you as if I really were a child," the woman responds:

"You can't do it. . . . You are kind and innocent; but *you can't look at me out of a child's eyes*. I never should have touched you, but I thought you were a child."
And with a strange, wild, cry, she went away (emphasis mine, LD 218).

It is as if Little Dorrit's womanhood acts as a mirror—a mirror that reflects the prostitute's corruption back onto herself. At the same time, Amy Dorrit's very ability to mirror the corrupt female sexuality of the prostitute exposes the taint of sexuality within Amy herself and explicitly links this taint to prostitution—to the trading of women's sexual labor for money. Once Little Dorrit's sexuality is betrayed by this narrative encounter, her relationships to her father and the paternal figure of Arthur Clennam are rendered highly problematic; for if Amy is sexualized, the intensity of her attraction to these older men takes on a sexual edge as well. Because Amy's devotion is also so explicitly childish, her relationship to her father—and by extension to Arthur Clennam as well—takes on the shade of incest. Instead of the father-daughter bond grounding Little Dorrit's femininity, then, that bond itself takes on connotations of perverse sexuality and corrupt female seductiveness.

The novel attempts to protect itself from the incestuous implications of its own representation of femininity in a number of ways, including those I have already discussed. It creates Amy Dorrit as child woman, it frustrates and secretes her desire for Arthur Clennam for most of the narrative, and it tries to defuse the possibility of Amy's sexualization through the comic subplot of John Chivery. Dickens's main strategy for the protection of Little Dorrit, however, is not through her own characterization, but through the representation of other female characters. By locating female sexuality elsewhere—particularly in the painfully comic figure of Flora Casby and the perverse character of Miss Wade—Dickens attempts to ensure the purity of his fictive paragon. In the end, Flora Casby's age and goodheartedness, combined with her comic characterization, enable her to cast off her sexuality and be reintegrated into Dickens's novelistic community. Miss Wade, in contrast, remains a threateningly alien and perverse carrier of female sexuality through to the end of the novel.

Dickens's entire characterization of Miss Wade is a series of effects that exceed the narrative details he provides about her character. To demonstrate that she is the carrier of female sexuality, the narrative offers the explanation of Miss Wade's illicit and loveless affair with Henry Gowan. The energy of Miss Wade's sexual transgressiveness, however, lies not in the relatively banal heterosexual affair with Gowan that is only represented "off-stage" in the novel, but in the implicit, unspoken lesbianism of her relationship with Tattycoram. Likewise, the explanations of childhood trauma and betrayal with which Miss Wade justifies her misanthropy in her autobiographical narrative do not add up to the poisonous air she breathes into all of her social interactions—setting spies on Henry Gowan and Pet Meagles, casting a tangible pall over every room she enters, and, most significantly, spying on and then seducing Tattycoram.[37] All in all, the narrative's characterization of Miss Wade seems designed to draw her perversity in such bold figures that it cannot be overlooked, even as Dickens presents her as simply one among a number of novelistic characters. As a defense against the implications of Amy Dorrit's sexualized femininity, then, the characterization of Miss Wade is so overwrought and overwritten that it virtually cries out that there is something more fundamental than a minor character unsettling the narrative.[38]

Miss Wade's excessive characterization, then, suggests that Dickens senses a serious threat to his narrative resolution and its vision of a moral society. Unfortunately for that vision, what unsettles the narrative is ultimately neither female sexuality nor perverse sexuality more generally; rather, it is something even less definable and containable than sexuality—it is an irresolvable tension between Dickens's desire for a natural basis for individual morality and his sense that any moral ground, even that represented by Little Dorrit, is impossibly hemmed in by threats and qualifications. Just as the call by administrative reformers to ground public government in the private sector was undermined by individual instances of moral turpitude, so Dickens's call to moralize the individual agent so as to cure social ills is undermined by his inability to ground this moralization. The individual agent—in this case, Arthur Clennam as reformed by Amy Dorrit—seems to promise a solution to the administrative reformers, the novelist, and the novelist as administrative reformer. This solution fails, however, because the situation to which all these writers were responding was a crisis in institutional agency—a crisis of the apparently uncontrollable and autonomous actions of supra-individual institutions like the civil service, the stock exchange, Parliament, and "Society." Neither Dickens nor the administrative reformers could see the crisis in these terms; instead, they saw individual men, whether civil service employees or middle-class merchants and professionals, as "responsible," and reformers blamed these men for their failures of duty.

Dickens's novel exposes one thing that remains invisible in the journalistic calls for administrative reform: the capitalist economy, which underlies the individualization of responsibility, is itself an institution. It is an institution, moreover, that problematizes the very solutions it invites by constructing the individual man as a competitive, ever-aspiring and desiring entity—and therefore as inherently unstable and in need of some moral ground. Adapting conventional Victorian ideology, Dickens offers the "different and laborious" Amy Dorrit as the corrective basis of morality for both the individual agent and his institutions. However, given the taint her sexuality confers, she remains as problematic as all other foundational gestures in this novel of moral, governmental, and financial corruption.

NOTES

1. Letter, Charles Dickens to W. C. Macready, 4 October 1855, in *The Selected Letters of Charles Dickens,* ed. F. W. Dupee (New York: Farrar, Straus, and Cudahy, 1960), 219–20.
2. Dickens's desire to find a stable ground on which to base the social and economic system seems, in retrospect, a very conservative reaction to a situation of "groundlessness" that has been largely naturalized by the late twentieth century. Even in the 1850s when Dickens wrote, more radical positions than that adopted by Dickens were beginning to be imagined and embraced. But the hegemonic position of the period from which and for which Dickens (in this instance) wrote

still maintained the need for a stable "ground" on which to base any moral and efficacious social system. My goal in this essay is not to criticize Dickens for his impossible or "naive" attempt to find such a ground, but rather to trace out the specific ways in which he responded to the cultural situation of apparent economic and moral groundlessness.

3. As a moral touchstone or, in Arthur Clennam's words, "vanishing point," Amy Dorrit's role and, ironically, even value, in the novel are almost purely relational. Not only does the figure of Little Dorrit represent a female character who lives her life completely in relation to her family and a small number of friends, but also, and more significantly, "Little Dorrit" represents a moral ideal that is always defined in opposition to moral corruption and perversity. One of the most interesting effects of this role is the phenomenon whereby Amy Dorrit, as heroine, is constantly displaced by the qualities and characters she opposes in any analysis of her character and role in the narrative. When Arthur Clennam looks "back upon his own poor story" and finds that "she is its vanishing point," Dickens himself seems on some level to be acknowledging the ambiguity of his feminine creation. Forever vanishing into and beneath others' narratives—their own poor stories—Amy Dorrit's particular form of heroism makes any analysis of her character necessarily indirect and oblique.

4. See Edward Hughes, "Civil Service Reform, 1853–5," *Public Administration* 32 (1954): 17–51, and Olive Anderson, *A Liberal State at War: English Politics and Economics During the Crimean War* (New York: St. Martin's; London: Macmillan, 1967).

5. The metaphor of legislative and administrative institutions as mechanisms or machinery permeates Victorian thinking and writing about government. The metaphor is found in almost every contemporary article or critique I cite below and even gives its title to one of the articles—"The Machinery of Parliamentary Legislation," *Edinburgh Review,* 99 (1854): 244–82. Martin Krygier discusses and cites examples of the metaphor of administration as machine in "State and Bureaucracy in Europe: The Growth of a Concept," in *Bureaucracy: The Career of a Concept,* ed. Eugene Kamenka and Martin Krygier (New York: St. Martin's, 1979), 17–18.

6. Trey Philpotts has argued that Dickens actually disagreed with the report's call for competitive examination and, further, that Sir Charles Trevelyan was an object of Dickens's satire. Philpott's reading fits with Dickens's general skepticism toward systems—including overly systematic reforms. In uncovering so many interesting historical details about Dickens's involvement with the administrative reform effort, however, Philpotts overlooks the larger ideological issues being contested through the Administrative Reform Association and Dickens's novel. See Trey Philpotts, "Trevelyan, Treasury, and Circumlocution," *Dickens Studies Annual* 22, ed. Michael Timko, Fred Kaplan, and Edward Guiliano (New York: AMS Press, 1993): 283–301.

7. Olive Anderson writes in *A Liberal State . . .* that "Many Politicians openly acknowledged that the real reason why the House insisted upon setting up the Committee . . . was the clamour for it outside Parliament" (50). Some of this agitation was directed at the organization and administration of the nation's

military departments, with a particular call for an investigation of the failures of communication and incompetence that led to the fall of Sebastapol.

8. At the Association's foundational meeting, held in the London Tavern on May 5, 1855, the fifteen hundred persons in attendance passed a series of resolutions that "attribut[ed] the disasters of the war to the inefficient and practically irresponsible management of the Government departments, recommend[ed] as remedy the introduction of 'enlarged experience and practical ability into the service of the State,' and protest[ed] against the aristocratic monopoly and the exclusion from office of able members of the commercial community" (R. A. Lewis, "Edwin Chadwick and the Administrative Reform Movement," *University of Birmingham Historical Journal* 2 [1949–50]: 192–93).

   In addition to the fifteen hundred present at the London Tavern meeting, many hundreds more, including a number of Members of Parliament, were turned away, and an overflow meeting had to be held in the Guildhall. These initial meetings were followed by the compilation of a large subscription list and the establishment of provincial branches of the association. After the opening resolution, the Administrative Reform Movement published three official pamphlets, probably written by Edwin Chadwick.

   Lewis summarizes the three pamphlets as follows:

   The first pamphlet was an exposure of the existing department heads, the "safe men," the do-nothing men, the complacent men. . . . In the second it was described how the legislature, settling recently the best form of government for 150 million Indians, had decided that patronage, private or political, ought to be abolished, that departmental nomination and probation were untrustworthy and that appointment must be thrown open to public competition. . . . The third pamphlet argued the case for open competitive entry and dealt with the objections raised by official critics [such as Sir James Stephen and Sir George Lewis] (Lewis, 195).

   Lewis provides the following citations with his summary: *A.R.A: Official Paper No. 2. The Devising Heads and Executive Hands of the English Government; A.R.A.: Official Paper No. 3. Unfitness of the Present Home Government for the Performance of New and Important Public Duties; A.R.A.: Official Paper No. 4. Appointments for Merit discussed in Official Answers of Official Objections to the Abolition of Patronage.*

9. Charles Dickens, "Speech," Administrative Reform Association Meeting, Drury Lane Theatre, 27 June 1855, printed in *The Speeches of Charles Dickens: A Complete Edition,* ed. K. J. Fielding (Harvester-Wheatsheaf: Humanities P International, 1988), 201.

10. Dickens, "Speech," 207.

11. Dickens, "Speech," 201.

12. Dickens, "Speech," 206.

13. The public/private opposition deployed in the Northcote-Trevelyan Report was between the government as "public" and business, industry, trade, and certain of the professions as "private." In contrast, in the separate spheres or domestic

ideology of Victorian England, the public was considered any activity outside of the home, including business and government, while the private was the domain of domesticity and the home. Dickens makes use of both of these oppositions in *Little Dorrit,* but his analysis differs from that of the administrative reformers precisely on the issue of how natural and stable was the domain of private business and trade.

14. Quoted from Sir Stafford Northcote and Sir Charles Trevelyan, "The Northcote-Trevelyan Report," (signed 23 November, 1853), reprinted in *Public Administration* 32 (1954): 2.

15. The private professional standard which forms the point of contrast to the civil service is described by the report thus:

Those who enter it generally do so at an early age, when there has been no opportunity of trying their fitness for business. . . . This to a great extent is the case in other professions also, but those professions supply a *corrective* which is wanting in the Civil Service, for as a man's success in them depends upon his obtaining and retaining the confidence of the public, and as he is exposed to a *sharp competition* on the part of his contemporaries, those only can maintain a fair position who possess the requisite amount of ability and industry for the proper discharge of their duties. The able and energetic rise to the top; the dull and inefficient remain at the bottom ("Northcote-Trevelyan," 3).

16. See, for example, "A Poor Man's Tale of a Patent," *Household Words* ii, no. 30 (19 October, 1850): 71–73; "Red Tape," *HW* ii, no. 47 (15 February, 1851): 481–84; and "Nobody, Somebody, and Everybody," *HW* xiv, no. 336 (30 August, 1856): 145–47.

17. Party and patronage were corrupting because an elector could be enticed by promises of a "place" to vote for one delegate, when another was more truly "representative" of his politics. Self-interest would be involved in either choice, but in the case of patronage and jobbery, a more immediate and near-sighted version of self-interest dominated.

Note also the relationship between corruption in administrative and legislative government: the latter was corrupt because delegates could use their influence to place electors in lucrative and secure administrative posts. Party politics and aristocratic family, in turn, were the means through which delegates obtained their influence over those appointments.

18. Cyrus Redding, "Administrative Reform," *Colburn's New Monthly Magazine* 107 (1856): 127.

Samuel Morley, the chairman of the Administrative Reform Association, expressed the same sentiment in slightly less moralistic language: "The first advance toward the effectual remedy of the existing evils must spring from a thorough change in public opinion as to relations between members of Parliament and their constituents" (cited in Olive Anderson, "The Janus Face of Mid-Nineteenth-Century English Radicalism: The Administrative Reform Association in 1855," *Victorian Studies* 8 [March 1965]: 238).

19. Anderson, *A Liberal State,* 154.
20. Jurgen Habermas, *The Structural Transformation of the Public Sphere,* trans. Thomas Burger with Frederick Lawrence (Cambridge, Mass.: MIT P, 1989), 87.
21. Dickens, *Selected Letters,* 220.
22. Edgar Johnson, *Charles Dickens: His Tragedy and Triumph,* v. 2 (New York: Simon and Schuster, 1952), 846.
23. Dickens to Forster, *Letters* II, 772, Georgina Hogarth, 5/9/56, quoted in Johnson, p. 889.
24. Johnson, v. 2, p. 846. The most thorough reading that I found of Dickens's original conception and the change in that conception is Harvey Peter Sucksmith's introduction to *Little Dorrit,* ed. Harvey P. Sucksmith (Oxford: Clarendon P, 1979).
25. Jeff Nunokawa, who has written the most suggestive account of *Little Dorrit*'s engagement with the economic problems of Victorian society, sees the economic crisis of the novel as one of appropriation, acquisition, and the inexorable cycle of equivalent exchange. Nunokawa reads the novel's proffered solution to that crisis as the mystified coming together of "true" lovers, as in the case of Arthur Clennam and Amy Dorrit at the end of the novel—a kind of "acquisition" so naturalized as to escape the circuit of exchange. Miss Wade's perversity, in turn, is read by Nunokawa as a condition of poverty that can never naturalize or mystify its appropriative gestures, and thus that threatens to expose the mystified logic of exchange on which the novel's resolution, and English society more generally, depends.

    While I find Nunokawa's reading compelling, it seems inadequately sensitive to the novel's foregrounding of speculation (rather than exchange) as the economic transaction that threatens the larger social fabric. In fact, in a number of passages, Dickens gestures toward equivalent or "fair" exchange of "natural" values as crucial to the solution to the speculative crisis that plagues Victorian society and morality, as well as its economy. Like Nunokawa, however, I identify Little Dorrit as the key to the alternative economy offered by Dickens. Whereas Nunokawa reads Amy Dorrit's relationship with Arthur Clennam as key to the novel's economic problem, though, I read Amy Dorrit *herself,* in her character as touchstone or "ground," as the core of Dickens's imagined alternative social and economic order. See Jeff Nunokawa, *The Afterlife of Property* (Princeton: Princeton UP, 1994), 19–39.
26. For Weiss, in particular, economic crisis and bankruptcy remain a theme, rather than a structure, that underlies all aspects of the problems Dickens takes up in the novel [see Barbara Weiss, *The Hell of the English: Bankruptcy and the Victorian Novel* (Lewisburg: Bucknell UP, 1986), 148–59]. Brantlinger, in *The Fictions of State,* goes further than Weiss in developing a structural analysis of financial crisis and debt in the Victorian novel, but is ultimately more interested in public than private debt, as he is in "the state" and "fiction," rather than the intricate and historically specific ideologies and structures that operate within a given text and between that text and its historical moment [see Patrick Brantlinger, *Fictions of State* (Ithaca: Cornell UP, 1996), 136–84].

27. Charles Dickens, *Little Dorrit* (London: Penguin, 1967), 89. All further citations to the novel are to this edition and will be given parenthetically in the text.
28. Furthermore, the passage links moral imposition and recklessness with the even more negative images of "degeneracy" and "perverted delights." Just as the novel essentially reduces financial speculation to thievery, so the narrative seems to assert that such moral speculation as Gowan's can be reduced to, in essence, degeneracy and perversion. The linkage of degeneracy and perversion to the character of Gowan, in turn, suggests that for Dickens those terms and qualities carry the "taint" of male homoeroticism.
29. In a rare moment of self-assertion and verbalization, in fact, Little Dorrit herself echoes the narrator's critique of Gowan's character with her own, telling Clennam in a letter that

    Owing . . . to Mr. Gowan's unsettled and dissatisfied way, he applies himself to his profession very little. He does nothing steadily or patiently; but equally takes things up and throws them down, and does them or leaves them undone, without caring about them. When I have heard him talking to Papa during the sittings for the picture, I have sat wondering whether it could be that he has no belief in anybody else, because he has no belief in himself (LD 606).

    Of course, the image of cynical carelessness that Amy Dorrit constructs of Henry Gowan is the inverse of her own oh-so-sincere concern and responsibility, and it is these very qualities in her that enable her to see through his own understated self-advertisements.
30. This is a central point of Brantlinger's reading of the realist novel and Victorian capitalism. Brantlinger goes on to argue that there is a historically specific conjunction between the emergence of a literary form—the realist novel-based on the denial of the absence at its very core and the emergence of national economies based on national or public debt. While I think this is a provocative insight, it seems to me overly dependent on the conflation of very different discursive notions of "absence" or "lack." I am more interested here in understanding Dickens's and the administrative reformers' own diagnoses of their society's "lacks," and then tracing this connection between their language and our own critical and analytical terms.
31. Hilton, "Chalmers as Political Economist," in *The Practical and the Pious,* ed. A. C. Cheyne (Edinburgh: Saint Andrew P, 1985), 147.
32. One of the most vivid, even melodramatic, of these passages is Arthur's discussion of his renunciation of love. He tells Little Dorrit, in reference to his lost love,

    "I found that the day when any such thing would have been graceful in me, or good in me, or hopeful, or happy for me or any one in connection with me, was gone, and would never shine again."

    The narrator describes the effect of this statement on Amy Dorrit thus:

    If he had known the sharpness of the pain he caused the patient heart, in speaking

thus! While doing it, too, with the purpose of easing and serving her. . . . O! If
he had known, if he had known! If he could have seen the dagger in his hand,
and the cruel wounds it struck in the faithful bleeding breast of his Little Dorrit!
(LD 402–03).

33. Note also that this failure is described with the same ironic indefinite pronouns
    projected as the novel's original title (''Nobody's Fault'') and which entitle one
    of Dickens's *Household Words* satires on English government (''Somebody, No-
    body, and Everybody'').
34. Here my reading differs significantly from Jeff Nunokawa's, who sees labor itself
    as an unstable form of acquisition. What is acquired by labor, according to
    Nunokawa, has been appropriated—wrested from the circuit of exchange—and
    thus also will be lost to that same circuit. In contrast, I see Dickens as celebrating
    labor, with qualifications, as one ''natural,'' and thus true, source of economic
    value. When the legitimately earned gains of labor are lost in the bursting of the
    Merdle bubble, the reason for these losses is not so much an inexorable circuit
    of exchange as it is the speculative gap at the center of the Victorian finance
    economy or (reading that gap morally) the speculative ambitions and pretensions
    of all those otherwise laborious investors.
35. In this way, Amy's brother is a milder version of the morally degenerate Henry
    Gowan who uses his aristocratic pretensions to avoid what the narrative clearly
    sees as ''honest labor.''
36. While the instability of value could be reduced to a poststructuralist discussion
    of the instability of the sign, my discussion focuses on the more historically
    specific instabilities involved with Dickens's failure to ground value. These in-
    clude not only the capitalist economic system, but also the ideological systems
    that bolstered it, such as the domestic ideology that saw women as an antidote
    to masculine economic and psychological instabilities.
37. In fact, there is even a disjunction between the genre of Miss Wade's autobio-
    graphical history and the title that is attached to it either by Dickens or by Miss
    Wade herself—''The History of a Self-Tormenter.'' While the content of Miss
    Wade's narrative adopts the novelistic mode of psychological realism, the title
    evokes the older, Gothic mode of the psychological grotesque or type. This formal
    disjunction between content and title, then, is another in the series of failures to
    contain or explain the perversity this character exudes.
38. Miss Wade not only highlights, rather than diffusing, the threat of female sexuality
    in the narrative, she also functions as a link between this threat and another threat
    to the narrative's moral vision—the threat of working-class anger. Miss Wade
    literally draws out the working-class anger of Tattycoram. At the same time, as an
    illegitimate child of the middle class, Miss Wade's own anger at her marginality is
    aligned with that of the working classes. Miss Wade, then, is not only threatening
    because she is sexually perverse, but also because she is angry. Here again she
    plays a crucial role as carrier and would-be container of a narrative threat. When
    Tattycoram leaves Miss Wade and returns to the Meagles, she renounces her
    anger. To reinforce this renunciation, Mr. Meagles points to the figure of Little
    Dorrit as a prototype of the graciously, even happily downtrodden. On no occasion

does Little Dorrit react with anger—even internally. Rather, Little Dorrit simply accepts and internalizes her treatment, taking her family's faults upon herself. This situation, combined with the fact that for much of the novel she must work for wages, makes Little Dorrit's structural position remarkably similar to that of the novel's main working-class representative, Tattycoram, and also like that of Tattycoram's perverse double, Miss Wade. The intensity with which Dickens's characterization of Miss Wade insists that *she* is the carrier of both sexuality and anger in the novel suggests that Miss Wade is not only Tattycoram's dark double, but also the even darker double of the novel's heroine, Little Dorrit.

WORKS CITED

Anderson, Olive. *A Liberal State at War: English Politics and Economics During the Crimean War.* New York: St. Martin's P, 1967.

———. "The Janus Face of Mid-Nineteenth-Century English Radicalism: The Administrative Reform Association in 1855." *Victorian Studies* 8 (March 1965): 232–42.

Brantlinger, Patrick. *Fictions of State.* Ithaca: Cornell UP, 1996.

Dickens, Charles. *Little Dorrit.* Ed. John Holloway. London: Penguin, 1967.

———. *Selected Letters of Charles Dickens.* Ed. F. W. Dupee. New York: Farrar, Strauss, and Cudahy, 1960.

———. *Speeches of Charles Dickens: A Complete Edition.* Ed. K. J. Fielding. Harvester-Wheatsheaf: Humanities P International, 1988.

———. "A Poor Man's Tale of a Patent." *Household Words* ii, No. 30 (19 October 1850): 71–73.

———. "Red Tape." *Household Words* ii, No. 47 (15 February 1851): 481–84.

———. "Nobody, Somebody, and Everybody." *Household Words* xiv, No. 336 (30 August 1856): 145–47.

Habermas, Jurgen. *The Structural Transformation of the Public Sphere.* Trans. Thomas Burger with Frederick Lawrence. Cambridge, Mass.: MIT P, 1989.

Hilton, Boyd. "Chalmers as Political Economist." *The Practical and the Pious.* Ed. A. C. Cheyne. Edinburgh: Saint Andrew P, 1985.

Hughes, Edward. "Civil Service Reform, 1853–5." *Public Administration* 32 (1954): 17–51.

Johnson, Edgar. *Charles Dickens: His Tragedy and His Triumph,* Vol. 2. New York: Simon and Schuster, 1952.

Krygier, Martin. "State and Bureaucracy in Europe: The Growth of a Concept." *Bureaucracy: The Career of a Concept.* Ed. Eugene Kamenka and Martin Krygier. New York: St. Martin's, 1979.

Lewis, R. A. "Edwin Chadwick and the Administrative Reform Movement." *University of Birmingham Historical Journal* 2 (1949–50): 178–200.

"Machinery of Parliamentary Legislation." *Edinburgh Review* 99 (1854): 244–82.

Northcote, Sir Stafford, and Sir Charles Trevelyan. "The Northcote-Trevelyan Report" (signed 23 November 1853). Reprinted in *Public Administration* 32 (1954): 1–16.

Philpotts, Trey. "Trevelyan, Treasury, and Circumlocution." *Dickens Studies Annual* 22. Ed. Michael Timko, Fred Kaplan, and Edward Guiliano (New York: AMS, 1993): 283–301.

Redding Cyrus. "Administrative Reform." *Colburn's New Monthly Magazine* 107 (1856): 127–35.

Sedgwick, Eve. *Between Men: English Literature and Male Homosocial Desire.* New York: Columbia UP, 1985.

Sucksmith, Harvey P. "Introduction." In *Little Dorrit.* Oxford: Clarendon P, 1979.

Weiss, Barbara. *The Hell of the English: Bankruptcy and the Victorian Novel.* Lewisburg: Bucknell UP, 1986.

Dickens, the Virgin,
and the Dredger's Daughter

Robert R. Garnett

*With Dickens, sexual and religious desires were never entirely distinct.
His erotic and idealistic impulses merged naturally in his fascination
with the feminine. With the catalyst of Mary Hogarth's death early in
his career, he developed a highly spiritualized personal religion embodied in the heroines of his early novels, icons of feminine purity and
innocence like Rose Maylie of* Oliver Twist. *The shining perfections of
these paragons reflect a prim and sterile idealism, but over the years
his feelings grew more complex, and the heroines of the later novels
begin to betray a moral ambiguity reflecting increasingly ambiguous
impulses in Dickens himself. Lizzie Hexam of* Our Mutual Friend *expresses this complexity most fully. As a daughter of the London Thames,
she emerges from an insistently muddy and carnal background—pollution, decay, and drowning; but, though she partakes of the river's darkness, her dark sensuality mysteriously informs and enriches her moral
excellence. With Lizzie, Dickens's rarefied feminine ideal acquired a
body, and became a woman with both a physical and moral nature.*

"Dickens and sex is an unpromising subject," one critic has remarked—by
"sex" meaning Dickens's fictional women (Carey 154). What is unpromising
about the subject, however, is not the women themselves, but the tendency
of critics to discuss them as realistic characters, or as flawed attempts at
realism; often joined, moreover, with an absorbing interest in the actual

women on whom they might have been modeled. Such literal readings misconstrue the women of the novels, especially the heroines. Critical comments like "the biggest gap in his achievement consists in his failure to portray even once, with any kind of fullness or understanding, a normal sexual relationship" approach Dickens's fiction with wrong expectations, and make strangely banal demands of it, as if a novel's highest achievement were to provide useful case studies of "normality" for a textbook on marriage and the family (Carey 154). His female characters were never intended to serve as model partners in "a normal sexual relationship"; their primary relationships are not with the males of the novels at all, but with Dickens himself. A Giotto may paint a Madonna, a Rossetti may create a "stunner," a fashion illustrator may sketch a mannequin of preternatural willowiness—in each case it would be obtuse to complain that the portrait does not resemble a middle-class wife of normal moral or physical endowments. Just as Dickens's friendly feelings for John Forster, say, or Wilkie Collins, were dwarfed by his far more intense feelings for Mary Hogarth and Ellen Ternan, his fictional heroines, too, are charged with his strongest and most complex emotions, both religious and erotic.

The heroines, in fact, enable us to penetrate the surface of Dickens's public religion and confident opinions, and glimpse deeper impulses, aspirations, and questionings; and they reveal a notable development in his feelings over the years, as he moved from an earnest adoration of otherworldly innocence and purity to an awareness of the mysterious, ambiguous interdependence of spirit and flesh. His grief for Mary Hogarth and his fascination with Ellen Ternan are the most striking biographical events along this journey. But the fictional heroines illuminate the imagination which was predisposed to respond so ardently to these two young women, and suggest how Dickens's long, "invisible" involvement with Ellen Ternan led him into unfamiliar moral territory, where the ethereal and the erotic merged, and the idealized, spiritualized femininity he worshiped took on human flesh.

With Dickens, sexual and religious longings were never entirely distinct, although he would have been reluctant to acknowledge the connection. His nature was both strongly erotic and strongly idealistic, but these apparently divergent tendencies converged in his fascination with the feminine. His women characters express Dickens's most compelling needs and desires, but those needs and desires grew increasingly ambiguous, and the later heroines exhibit a moral complexity which embodies more complex feelings in Dickens himself. The shining perfections of his early paragons reflect a prim and sterile idealism; by the time of *Our Mutual Friend*'s Lizzie Hexam—darkly sensual but morally pure—Dickens's rarefied feminine ideal had acquired a body, and become a woman with both a physical and moral nature.

Dickens and sex, largely understood, is a particularly promising subject.

1.

It is Dickens and religion that would seem to be a discouraging topic. One of the most enduring and intense of human concerns was, it often appears, almost a blank to him. Michael Slater's *Dickens and Women* is twice as long as Dennis Walder's *Dickens and Religion,* and the only surprise in this disproportion is that it is not greater; the novels evince a keen interest in women and very little in religion—religion in any formal sense, at least.

Although pious sentiments crop up often enough in Dickens's fiction, he expended little real thought or imagination on spiritual reflection, and his theology seems hardly to exist. *The Life of Our Lord,* his simplified and desacralized children's version of the Gospels, served well enough as Dickens's own version, too. He variously distrusted, disliked, or detested both dissenters and papists, while the Established Church simply bored him, like young David Copperfield falling asleep during Sunday morning services in Blunderstone. Restless, active, and practical, Dickens was not by nature or education disposed to otherworldly meditations, and his indifference was exacerbated by ignorance and Podsnap, Gunpowder-Plot prejudices. As glimpsed in the novels, his Christianity is a thin compound of warm feeling, rational benevolence, and lingering, edifying, pathetic deaths accompanied by winged angels and snippets from the New Testament.

"What people don't realize is how much religion costs," Flannery O'Connor once observed. "They think faith is a big electric blanket, when of course it is the cross" (354). The electric blanket aside, this aphorism well describes Dickens's attitude. Religion seemed admirable to him as a soothing and uplifting consolation, a balm for bereavement and other tribulations of mortality. He had no concept of Christianity as a mystery; as a sacramental marriage of the natural and the divine; as a passion, penance, or sacrifice; as—in the words of T. S. Eliot's Magus—"Hard and bitter agony for us, like Death, our death" ("Journey of the Magi"). Christ's sojourn in the wilderness, for example, was by Dickens's reckoning not a trial of mortification and temptation, but an interlude for "praying that he might be of use to men and women, and teach them to be better, so that after their deaths, they might be happy in Heaven"—a pious idea, but not remotely suggested by the New Testament accounts (*Life of Our Lord* 24). The fiction invariably treats pulpit religion as a bully and a fraud, as (for example) with *Bleak House's* Chadband. Dickens's God was a deity of good feeling and mercy; divine judgment had no place in either his temperament or his cosmology. He strongly disapproved of the jealous, retributive Old Testament God. ". . . I would never refer any one—but especially a child—to the Old Testament when I have the New Testament and its one great figure, for the illustration of every conceivable moral lesson," he wrote to Angela Burdett Coutts in 1855 (*Letters* 7:577). He could bring himself to like God only in the person of Christ, and a Christ with no edges at that: "No one ever lived, who was so good, so kind, so gentle, and so sorry for all people who did wrong, or were in any way ill or miserable, as he was," he asserted in *The Life of Our Lord* (11). The disruptive, monitory Christ—"Suppose ye that I am come to give peace on earth? I tell you, Nay; but rather division"—does not figure in Dickens's Christology (Luke 12:51). His dabbling in Unitarianism, moreover, suggests that he had no very strong conviction of Christ's divinity. *The Life of Our Lord,* for example, omits any awkward reference to the Incarnation or the Holy Spirit's begetting of Christ: "His father's name was Joseph, and his mother's name was Mary," Dickens writes, and leaves it at that (13).

Such religious inanition seems at first glance one of his major weaknesses as an artist, not simply because his nominal religion itself was so vapid, but because it suggests that he possessed scarcely any religious sensibility or spiritual awareness at all. "What a Dream it is, this work and strife, and how little we do in the Dream after all!" he wrote to his friend Macready in 1858, but this happened to be an exceptionally unsettled year for Dickens, and such modesty and detachment are uncharacteristic (*Letters* 8:531). He hardly ever doubted his own wisdom, competence, or importance, and he was seldom much impressed by anyone else's; like Mrs. Skewton's hired footman in *Dombey and Son,* his "organ of veneration was imperfectly developed" (413).

Yet despite his skepticism, his robust self-confidence, and his strenuous worldliness, and despite the bland and soupy quality of his professed Christianity, he had immortal longings, though they found no home in any church, and no voice in any creed of dogma. His concept of the highest Good took the form of a sublime feminine benevolence—"The notion of some infinitely gentle/Infinitely suffering thing" (as T. S. Eliot wrote in "Preludes"). Even Dickens's Christ is feminine in his softness, and a few of his male characters—Joe Gargery, for example—have "the touch of a woman," but generally speaking, Dickens preferred his femininity in female shape, and his religion followed suit (*Great Expectations* 138). He could detect comedy in a thousand corners of life, but he could perceive holiness only in the glow of a pure, earnest, compassionate, and affectionate young woman. His first profound religious experience was prompted by the death of his young sister-in-law Mary Hogarth, when he was 25.

2.

Mary Hogarth's death was the catalyst for an earnest, ardent mythmaking which began immediately with the creation of *Oliver Twist*'s Rose Maylie.

Yet Rose and her successors do not originate so much in Mary herself, or any other specific woman in Dickens's life, as in his worship of the feminine principle, as he imagined it. Failing to find in Christianity a divinity to inspire him, he had to invent his own, and needing an object on which to fix his fervent, even mystical devotion to the feminine, he seized on the luminous memory of Mary Hogarth. His need for a mythic virginal goddess preceded her, and the goddess he created soon superseded her. If, as he claimed, he dreamed of Mary every night for nine months after her death, by the end of that time he certainly knew his dream vision of her better than he had known Mary herself, the actual girl.

He was inclined to believe that his dreams of Mary had mystical origins: "I should be sorry to lose such visions for they are very happy ones—if it be only the seeing her in one's sleep—I would fain believe too, sometimes, that her spirit may have some influence over them, but their perpetual repetition is extraordinary" (*Letters* 1:366). And subsequently, the most mystical, or nearly mystical, moments in Dickens's life came in association with Mary Hogarth. Visiting Niagara Falls during his American tour in 1842, he was moved to unusual (for him) religious awe. "It would be hard for a man to stand nearer God than he does there," he wrote to Forster:

> There was a bright rainbow at my feet; and from that I looked up to—great Heaven! to *what* a fall of bright green water! The broad, deep, mighty stream seems to die in the act of falling; and, from its unfathomable grave arises that tremendous ghost of spray and mist which is never laid, and has been haunting this place with the same dread solemnity—perhaps from the creation of the world.... I can only say that the first effect of this tremendous spectacle on me, was peace of mind—tranquillity—great thoughts of eternal rest and happiness—nothing of terror. (*Letters* 3:210–11)

In this transcendent mood, his thoughts inevitably reverted to Mary, as if he sensed her spirit hovering in that "tremendous ghost of spray and mist" which haunted the place with such dread solemnity. Politely, he expressed a wish that Forster could be there with him, but then confessed: "I was going to add, what would I give if the dear girl whose ashes lie in Kensal-green, had lived to come so far along with us—but she has been here many times, I doubt not, since her sweet face faded from my earthly sight." Why the spirit of Mary Hogarth should have been sightseeing at Niagara Falls is not altogether clear, but it is evident that for him, hers was the human face of perfect beatitude, the natural and inevitable image of his most intense otherworldly longings: "peace of mind—tranquillity—great thoughts of eternal rest and happiness."

An even more striking occasion of Mary's mystical presence was Dickens's "curious dream" in Italy in 1844, more than seven years after her death.

Again he confided in Forster: "In an indistinct place, which was quite sublime in its indistinctness, I was visited by a Spirit. I could not make out the face, nor do I recollect that I desired to do so. It wore a blue drapery, as the Madonna might in a picture by Raphael; . . . I knew it was poor Mary's spirit" (*Letters* 4:196). Attempting to embrace the Spirit, he was rebuffed:

> . . . I wept very much, and stretching out my arms to it called it "Dear." At this, I thought it recoiled; and I felt immediately, that not being of my gross nature, I ought not to have addressed it so familiarly.   (*Letters* 4:196)

Even in the ghostly world of his dream, the dreaming Dickens regards spirit and "gross nature" as radically incompatible and mutually impenetrable; the spiritual "recoils" from physical embrace, the ethereal abhors matter. Though deeply sympathetic, the Spirit of Mary wants no truck with Dickens's flesh-and-blood body, preferring to keep their relationship rarefied, spirit to spirit like Milton's angels: "Easier than air with air, if spirits embrace,/Total they mix, union of pure with pure/Desiring . . ." (*Paradise Lost* 8:626–8). Perfect love—such as Mary Hogarth's compassionate love for him (at least in his dream), and his adoring love for her—is entirely a spiritual intercourse, Dickens assumes, in which bodies are impediments rather than instruments; it is not simply different from carnal desire, but excludes it.

Apologizing to the Spirit for his forwardness, Dickens requested a token of its authenticity, and then, to detain it, inquired: "What is the True religion?" The Spirit hesitating in reply, he prompted it by suggesting his own vague, nondenominational creed: "You think, as I do, that the Form of religion does not so greatly matter, if we try to do good?" When the Spirit failed to ratify this helpful suggestion, Dickens proposed what must have been, to his waking self, a dreadful alternative: ". . . or perhaps the Roman Catholic is the best? perhaps it makes one think of God oftener, and believe in him more steadily?' The Spirit assented:

> "For *you*," said the Spirit, full of such heavenly tenderness for me, that I felt as if my heart would break; "for *you*, it is the best!" Then I awoke, with the tears running down my face and myself in exactly the condition of the dream.

Whether or not this advice was sound, Dickens—despite his tears (and unlike Scrooge after his nocturnal vision)—did not act on it; indeed, some of his most virulent anti-Catholic diatribes erupted during his sojourn in Switzerland only two years later.

In its mundane aspects, the dream narrative is very characteristic of Dickens—in its mixture of powerful sentiment, business-like pragmatism, and self-absorbed lack of consideration for his wife—for after feeling "as if my heart would break" and waking in tears, he did not hesitate to wake Catherine and insist that she listen to him recount the dream and memorize it for purposes of later verification: "I called up Kate, and repeated it three or four times over, that I might not unconsciously make it plainer or stronger afterwards." Even within the dream itself, Dickens was skeptical enough to demand that the Spirit provide proof of its authenticity: "Oh! give me some token that you have really visited me!"

But the interest of the narration goes beyond these evidences of his daytime personality. Dickens once professed himself a student of dreams: ". . . I have read something on the subject [of dreams], and have long observed it with the greatest attention and interest," he wrote in 1851, and went on to argue that dreams may reflect "the subject closely occupying the waking mind . . . in a sort of allegorical manner" (*Letters* 6:276). Even without straining for allegorical (or psychoanalytic) meaning, however, one may detect, or at least suspect, pregnant ambiguities in this dream of Mary Hogarth. It was both poignant and comforting, and yet at the same time troubling in its Catholic tendencies and trappings, not to mention the Spirit's specifically Catholic recommendation: a vision he might relate to his wife and his closest friend, Forster, but never to his public. Dickens wanted to believe the vision genuine, and at the same time he attempted to demystify and rationalize it, attributing it (in his letter to Forster) to the stimulus of recent thoughts and incidents. And more than six years later, referring to a dream about "a very dear young friend" who had died, he further reduced the vision to a quaint anecdote: "I was living in Italy, and it was All Souls' Night, and people were going about with Bells, calling on the Inhabitants to pray for the dead.—Which I have no doubt I had some sense of, in my sleep; and so flew back to the Dead" (*Letters* 6:277). Nothing of the dream's mystical force emerges from this prosaic explanation (which, despite its confident "no doubt" tone, seems to be factually inaccurate as well).[1]

And yet, whether "a dream, or an actual Vision!" the experience powerfully affected him: "I was not at all afraid, but in a great delight, so that I wept very much," he told Forster; the Spirit was "full of such heavenly tenderness for me, that I felt as if my heart would break" (*Letters* 4:196). It was one of the relatively few times in his life that he felt himself in the immediate presence of, and in communication with, the Divine, which for Dickens naturally assumed the form of a young woman—Mary Hogarth, inevitably, but a Mary Hogarth strangely conflated with the Virgin Mary. Dennis Walder observes of Dickens, "If he could never accept Mariolatry, he was nevertheless subject to a lifelong yearning for some female image of spirituality, of personal guidance and redemption" (11). But though Dickens might be horrified by Roman Catholic Mariolatry, his own religion in its most transcendent and intense form was unquestionably an idiosyncratic Mariolatry. If he ever heard of it, he would have been scandalized by the dogma of the Immaculate Conception enunciated by Pius IX in 1854, but his own private dogma of Mary Hogarth's perfection, established even earlier, was similar enough: "I solemnly believe that so perfect a creature never breathed. . . . She had not a fault" (*Letters* 1:259).

Strong-willed, ambitious, and driven, Dickens craved the complementary qualities of an idealized femininity: softness, tenderness, sympathy, selfless and yielding devotion. The Spirit of Mary Hogarth "was so full of compassion and sorrow for me . . . that it cut me to the heart" (*Letters* 4:196). He naturally tended toward goddess worship. His benevolent, demythologized Christianity, for all its earnestness, wholly lacked the passionate yearning with which he reached out to embrace the Spirit of Mary. Where his personal faith overlapped with generic Protestantism, he was content to accept, or at least tolerate, the latter; where his Mariolatry deviated from orthodoxy, the former took precedence. Dickens was not one to reverence authority, ecclesiastical or otherwise; he was willing to subscribe to Christianity so far as it conformed to his own private emotional world; but no further.

The Spirit's gentle but decisive rejection of a merely ethical religion—Dickens's hopeful idea that "the Form of religion does not so greatly matter, if we try to do good"—suggests that he himself suspected the spiritual and emotional limitations of such a bare rational creed, of its inability to satisfy his own excitable imagination and demanding temperament. He needed more than just good feeling and uplift; he needed a deity to adore. In the Peschiere, in Genoa, where he dreamed of Mary in 1844:

> . . . there is a great altar in our bedroom, at which some family who once inhabited this palace had mass performed in old time; and I had observed within myself, before going to bed, that there was a mark in the wall, above the sanctuary, where a religious picture used to be; and I had wondered within myself what the subject might have been, *and what the face was like.*
>
> (*Letters* 4:196).

What was missing over the altar was probably a crucifix or a painting of Christ, but Dickens supplied the lack characteristically—with an image of Mary Hogarth. He worshiped the virgin, if not the Virgin. Ironically, his private religion found its closest Christian parallel in the devotional customs of the Roman Church to which he was, by long and strong prejudice, fiercely hostile.

3.

His aspirations toward sanctity are fictionally personified in the series of virtuous maidens beginning with Rose Maylie. Rose is the prototype Dickens heroine, setting (in a profusion of semicolons) the pattern for all the later icons of his religion:

> The younger lady [Rose] was in the lovely bloom and spring-time of woman-hood; at that age, when, if ever angels be for God's good purposes enthroned in mortal forms, they may be, without impiety, supposed to abide in such as hers.
>
> She was not past seventeen. Cast in so slight and exquisite a mould; so mild and gentle; so pure and beautiful; that earth seemed not her element, nor its rough creatures her fit companions. The very intelligence that shone in her deep blue eye, and was stamped upon her noble head, seemed scarcely of her age or of the world; and yet the changing expression of sweetness and good humour; the thousand lights that played about the face, and left no shadow there; above all, the smile; the cheerful, happy smile; were made for Home; for fireside peace and happiness.   (194)

Although in appearance a beautiful young woman, Rose is, in essence, ethe-real; not of earth or flesh. Her lovely body is only a concession to her temporary sojourn among the "rough creatures" of mortality. Dickens's gaze is focused on her radiant moral excellence; such physical description as he offers is either metaphorically fuzzy—"the thousand lights that played about the face"—or merely rhapsodic cliché. The notion of Rose as an angel in mortal form is a poetic conceit, but she is nonetheless so far above mankind in its fallen condition that she seems misplaced in her human body; for however enchanting in its springtime bloom the body is nevertheless the home of carnal appetites, desires, and corruption. Rose's slight figure suggests her minimal participation in the flesh, and when she falls ill and nearly dies, it is as if her soul were contemplating an early escape from the leaden drag of mortality. Despite Dickens's own energetic participation in the material and secular world, he assumed a radical disjunction between the corruptible realm of the human—of "mortal forms" and "rough creatures"—and the higher, purer regions of angels and spirits and whatever other immaterial beings he might have imagined.

Even "enthroned in mortal form," Rose seems to float several inches off the ground. At seventeen, she hovers on the threshold of womanhood: physi-cally and morally mature, she is still virginal, precariously balanced between childhood innocence and sexual initiation. Rose stands at the apogee (for Dickens) of feminine experience; the years to come can bring only decline. With marriage will come sexual knowledge and parturition: even the male paragon Harry Maylie is one of those "rough creatures" of earth. In fictional terms, prospective husbands are necessary adjuncts for young heroines, but in Dickens's religion of the virgin, actual husbands represent the Fall. Wives and mothers are well enough in their way, and young brides better yet, but Dickens's real passion—spiritually speaking—is vestals. Someday Rose will be a household angel, but only as a figure of speech; right now, at seventeen, she is a real angel.

The spirit of Rose Maylie is revived in Little Nell and continues in such characters as Ruth Pinch, Florence Dombey, Agnes Wickfield, Esther Summerson, and Amy Dorrit. Probably the culminating figure in this series is *David Copperfield*'s Agnes, and Dickens is explicit about her significance. If we judge Agnes by realistic standards, her announcement of Dora's death by pointing heavenward (which David seizes on so avidly as an image of her sanctity) seems a pious affectation; but if we recognize her as a religious icon, as a visible image of the holy, the meaning of her gesture becomes clear. It is not really Agnes pointing up, but Dickens himself directing us to her heavenly provenance and meaning, just as medieval painters signified the Holy Spirit by a dove, or saintliness by a gilded halo. Despite his *Household Words* attack on Millais's 1850 painting *Christ in the House of his Parents,* Dickens shared with the Pre-Raphaelites not only their moralistic and romantic bent, but also their taste for symbolism and iconography.

Writing of *Oliver Twist* in 1950, Graham Greene proposed that a writer's "whole career is an effort to illustrate his private world in terms of the great public world we all share" (429). What needs and desires of Dickens's private world do characters like Rose Maylie and Agnes Wickfield translate into the public language of character and action? What does his fascination with and reverence for such heroines reveal about his religious impulses? It is evident that he sympathized with their vulnerability as orphans or virtual orphans, cherished their sexual innocence and purity, and admired their key-jingling domestic proficiency. Above all, however, he adored them as overflowing fountains of gentleness, sweetness, motherly nurture, sisterly affection, service, generosity, fidelity, and self-sacrifice. They assuage and absorb the troubles of those they love; and, as if to emphasize the purity of their devotion, the beneficiaries of their love are frequently undeserving, if not worthless. The heroines are saintly, even Christ-like, in their willingness to suffer for others, in their renunciation of all self-interest, let alone self-assertion. They are passionately sympathetic—not carnal—lovers; a Dickens heroine surrenders her will as unreservedly as a more worldly paramour would yield her body.

Though as human beings they seem too altruistic to be plausible, sometimes too meek to be admirable, and occasionally too perfect even to be likeable, as a recurrent fantasy the heroines answered an emotional desideratum in Dickens, providing him with an imaginative refuge from the world's hard, restless, aggressive, predatory, egocentric, and even demonic energies and cravings—some of which seem characteristic of Dickens himself. He was scarcely ascetic or mystical; we rightly associate him with ambition, dynamism, melodrama, and noise, not to mention the vigorous virility that produced ten children and led to the Ellen Ternan affair. Yet his sexually bland heroines seem to represent a wishful sanctuary even from erotic energies. It is otherwise almost inexplicable that a man so fascinated by and attracted to women should repeatedly celebrate female characters so distinctly lacking in sensuality and allure. Far from being sexually delectable, as one critic argues, Dickens's early heroines—those before the Ellen Ternan era—are with few exceptions "as tempting as wax fruit" (Ingham 28–38; Tomalin 85). They attract him not despite their unnoticeable, insubstantial bodies, but because of them.

In the crowded concourse of Dickens's characters—male and female, weak and strong, good and bad—the heroines remain unsullied by sexual experience, untempted, unwavering in virtue, unchallenged as moral cynosures. Their passivity, frequently censured, results not from weakness, but from their calm repose at the center of the novels' centrifugal energies. As with Crashaw's St. Theresa, "Love's passives are his activ'st part." The heroines do not have to act, because—morally speaking—they are already where they should be; they need not involve themselves in the hurly-burly to triumph, because the triumph eventually comes to them, drawn by the quiet gravitational force of their goodness. The restless activity of the novels subsides in their tranquillity; they conquer by their excellence, not by their exertions. The heroine whom critics most love to hate, *David Copperfield*'s Agnes, is the best example of this invincible power of moral serenity; in the course of the novel she does almost nothing but sit and wait, and yet in the end she vanquishes not only the gross evil of Uriah Heep, but the wayward energies and "undisciplined heart" of David himself. The transcendent good embodied in such heroines is a sacrificial, suffering good; it nurtures but does not agitate; it stays indoors and waits for the prodigals to return home; it prevails by affection, not by assertion. Because of them, the world of Dickensian heroines has an inevitable tendency toward moral order.

Dickens never lost faith in his private religion of the virgin. Begotten in his childhood, transfigured by the death of Mary Hogarth, the beatific ideal of the young and loving virgin beat deeply in his heart of hearts. The vestal heroines persist to the end, or nearly to the end, of his fiction. They were an ineradicable part of him; to jettison them would have been a kind of spiritual suicide, leaving his fiction emotionally hollow. And so long as the heroines of invulnerable goodness and virtue prevail, the moral world of the novels is unambiguous and optimistic. The virtuous characters may confront obstacles, villains, and disappointments, but they are never beset by moral uncertainties. The early Dickens had little tragic sense, little awareness that life might throw up emotional tangles and moral complexities to defy the powers of purity and goodness.

4.

Dickens's own life resembled a three-volume novel: first his childhood and youth, shadowed in the early chapters of *David Copperfield*, featuring his heroic rise from debtors' prison and blacking factory to the spectacular success of *Pickwick*. Then came two decades of imperial triumph, the *pax dickensiana,* during which the Mary Hogarth heroines flourished; and yet, with accumulating omens of discontent and restlessness in his life, and his marriage decaying, the heroines also began to come under stress. And finally there was the Ellen Ternan era, commencing with her revolutionary advent in 1857 and lasting to the end of his life with their invisible, or nearly invisible, affair.

His relationship with his beloved Nelly is, of course, meagerly documented, but it seems clear enough that his love for her was very unlike his reverence for the memory of the vestal Mary Hogarth, and he needed somehow to reconcile the obvious conflict between his devotion to a chaste feminine ideal, glowing with innocence and sexual purity, and his darker passion for the fascinating young actress. In his last dozen years, his Mary Hogarth religion was not abandoned, but deepened and transformed.

Late in 1857, several months after meeting Ellen Ternan, Dickens wrote to his confidential friend Mrs. Watson:

> I wish I had been born in the days of Ogres and Dragon-guarded Castles. I wish an Ogre with seven heads (and no particular evidence of brains in the whole lot of them) had taken the princess whom I adore—you have no idea how intensely I love her!—to his stronghold on top of a high series of Mountains, and there tied her up by the hair. Nothing would suit me half so well this day, as climbing after her, sword in hand, and either winning her or being killed.
>
> (*Letters* 8:488)

A characteristic Dickensian fancy—in its fairy-tale machinery, its humor, its hyperbole, its violence, and not least its high romantic aspiration: chivalric love will inspire him to alpine feats of valor and self-sacrifice. In fact, however, Nelly Ternan was neither fairy tale princess nor chaste disembodied spirit, but a young woman very much alive in the flesh. "Realities and idealities are always comparing themselves together before me, and I don't like the Realities except when they are unattainable—*then,* I like them of all things," he told Mrs. Watson. It might be an exaggeration to call Ellen Ternan a conversion experience for Dickens, but she unquestionably complicated his long-held Marian religion. The physical reality of her desirability, and his sharp desire for her, challenged the ethereal religion to which he had faithfully subscribed for twenty years, through an apostolic succession of angel-heroines. Nelly became a second icon on his altar, a new and very dissimilar divinity drawing him—not up to mountaintops—but down into illicit desire, secrecy, scandal, guilt, and almost certainly adulterous consummation.[2] Dickens was a popular novelist, not a moral philosopher, but his later fiction betrays a struggle between two radically divergent feelings: his ardent adoration of the suffering virgin, and his erotic love for the young actress.

Our Mutual Friend's Lizzie Hexam reveals how his moral philosophy—if that is the right term—grew more complex during the Ellen Ternan era. In many respects Lizzie conforms to the well-established pattern of Dickensian heroines: in her youth and purity, in her devotion to her unsavory father and ingrate brother, in her reforming, redemptive influence on Eugene Wrayburn. In *Dickens, Women and Language,* Patricia Ingham lumps her without interest or distinction among Dickens's "nubile girls," a populous group including (among others) Rose Maylie and Agnes Wickfield (18); while Michael Slater, in *Dickens and Women,* more or less agrees that Lizzie is fairly usual Dickens stuff: "at first sight she appears to be a standard Dickens heroine in every respect except that of social class"; and further examination confirms that she "is not a character likely to hold the modern reader's interest for her own sake." Although "she plays a much more active part, even to the extent of rescuing the hero by her physical prowess, than is at all customary for a melodrama heroine," she nonetheless remains "essentially a melodramatic creation," "an idealized character . . . fatally lacking in any sort of emotional or intellectual complexity" (284–86). That Lizzie, the uneducated daughter of a Thames waterman, speaks almost perfect middle-class English is routinely cited as damning evidence of her merely conventional characterization.

But Lizzie is not so predictable and simplistic a character as all that. What is distinctive about her is her ambiguous, mermaid duality, her union of the pure, radiant virgin and the murky, dangerous river. She is an idealized heroine in the Mary Hogarth line, but her moral vitality emerges from river slime and corpse-dredging. Rose Maylie springs from an edenic rural setting: "The rose and honeysuckle clung to the cottage walls; the ivy crept round the trunks of the trees; and the garden-flowers perfumed the air with delicious odours"(*Oliver Twist* 215). By contrast, we first encounter Lizzie Hexam helping her father salvage drowned bodies which rise, in no very pretty condition, from the bottom muck of the Thames; "Pharaoh's multitude that were drowned in the Red Sea, ain't more beyond restoring to life" than Gaffer's latest recovered corpse, as Lizzie's brother Charlie picturesquely points out (61). Gaffer himself is frequently likened to a vulture. Lizzie is a daughter of the Thames and of every dead and rotten thing in it: not Spenser's "sweet" and "silver streaming" Thames, but the large open sewer of mid-Victorian London. Whereas Rose Maylie seems a product of immaculate conception, wearing human flesh like a lovely but superfluous outer garment, Lizzie Hexam is intimately involved with the flesh; all the drowning and the corpses of *Our Mutual Friend,* its insistent references to death and decaying flesh, emphasize her immersion in the world of corruptible matter, her non-ethereal nature. There is nothing at all idealized about her close connection with—her origins in—the foul river and the corpses it swallows and disgorges, just as there was nothing very idealistic in Dickens's unholy fascination with the corpses, often of drowning victims, that he loved to ogle in the Paris morgue.

The sinister Thames of *Our Mutual Friend* is, like those corpses, strangely, grimly fascinating, a kind of seductive moral whirlpool. It threatens and allures: allures because it is threatening, threatens because it is alluring:

> Not a sluice gate, or a painted scale upon a post or wall, showing the depth of water, but seemed to hint, like the dreadfully facetious Wolf in bed in Grandmamma's cottage, "That's to drown *you* in, my dears!" Not a lumbering black barge, with its cracked and blistered side impending over them, but seemed to suck at the river with a thirst for sucking them under.   (219)

Lizzie shrinks from the river and the sodden bodies it offers up: ". . . In the intensity of her look [watching her father search for bodies] there was a touch of dread or horror" (43). When her father hauls in a corpse, Lizzie hoods herself to avoid seeing it. "It's my belief that you hate the sight of the very river," he accuses her, and she replies with polite understatement: "I—I do not like it, father" (45). Lizzie's delicacy asserts that she possesses the same maidenly and lady-like feeling as earlier heroines. When Rose Maylie, for example, learns from Nancy that there is such a thing as vice, she recoils in incredulous horror: " 'What dreadful things are these!' said Rose, involuntarily falling from her strange companion" (267); and Agnes Wickfield, too, would react to the noisome river and corpses with revulsion, just as she would shrink from a sexual proposition from Uriah Heep.

But Lizzie herself recognizes that, like it or not, she is a product of the river, and the river remains a part of her, and not a small part. As Lizzie's father reminds her, "The very fire that warmed you when you were a babby, was picked out of the river alongside the coal barges. The very basket that you slept in, the tide washed ashore. The very rockers that I put it upon to make a cradle of it, I cut out of a piece of wood that drifted from some ship or another" (45–46). The river runs through Lizzie's veins as it does not run—or we can scarcely imagine it running—in the veins of Rose or Agnes. Rivers are a favorite Dickens metaphor for the inexorable flow of life toward death, but the Thames of *Our Mutual Friend* is very different from the vague river on which little Paul Dombey, for instance, floats down toward the eternal sea. Lizzie's river is no cloudy metaphor, but an actual, grim agent of destruction and dissolution: ". . . everything so vaunted the spoiling influences of water—discoloured copper, rotten wood, honey-combed stone, green dank deposit—that the after-consequences of being crushed, sucked under,

and drawn down, looked as ugly to the imagination as the main event''
(219–20). It suggests the muddy undercurrents of human life, its elements of
crudeness, mortality, and corruption, its kinship with the slime and ooze, its
involvement in sweat, lust, and violence. It lies at the antipodes from maidenly
innocence and otherworldly detachment.

And yet for all her virginal virtues, Lizzie is strangely drawn to the river.
''To please myself, I could not be too far from that river,'' she remarks, but
adds with curious ambiguity, ''I can't get away from it, I think'' (278).
Circumstances chain her to the river; but in the shadow of this ostensible
meaning lurks a hint of some inner compulsion. The river is, figuratively,
within her, and whether she wishes to or not, she cannot get away from the
dark currents of her own being. Dickens emphasizes her sensual, erotic nature
by repeated references to her gypsy coloring. ''A dark girl of nineteen or
twenty'' (43), Lizzie has a ''rich brown cheek'' (70). Wrayburn remarks:
''. . . that lonely girl with the dark hair runs in my head'' (210). Seen though
a window, she appears in a framed, fire-lit tableau of drowning victims and
dark sensuality, muted by sorrow:

> It showed him the room, and the bills upon the wall respecting the drowned
> people starting out and receding by turns. But he glanced slightly at them,
> though he looked long and steadily at her. A deep rich piece of colour, with
> the brown flush of her cheek and the shining lustre of her hair, though sad and
> solitary, weeping by the rising and the falling of the fire. (211)

Her sorrow softens her sexual allure without diminishing it; perhaps even
enhancing it. And as with *Hard Times*'s Louisa Gradgrind, Lizzie's habit of
gazing at the hearth suggests her passionate intensity, the glowing embers
serving as an emblem of her own sexual warmth.

Lizzie's greatest danger is not the obsessive attentions of Bradley Headstone and Eugene Wrayburn, but her own strong attraction to Wrayburn,
which is immediate and disconcertingly apparent. When he first arrives at
the Hexams' to inspect a freshly recovered corpse, she departs in embar-
rassment when he stares at her, instead: ''One of the gentlemen, the one who
didn't speak while I was there, looked hard at me. And I was afraid he might
know what my face meant'' (70). Dickens leaves ''what my face meant''
ambiguous: ostensibly she fears that her guilty countenance will betray her
father's corpse-robbing, but what she may be more anxious to conceal from
Wrayburn is her unwilling responsiveness to his blunt amorous interest.

Despite his barely disguised lust and doubtful intentions, and despite her
own ardent feelings, Lizzie idealizes Wrayburn: ''. . . his lightest touch, his
lightest look, his very presence beside her in the dark common street, were
like glimpses of an enchanted world . . .'' (465). And both Dickens and
Wrayburn, in turn, make fitful attempts to idealize Lizzie, eulogizing her

sterling qualities. Wrayburn, for example, calls her a "self-denying daughter and sister," and Dickens as narrator describes her as "pure of heart and purpose" (286–87). But it is neither her pure heart nor saintly self-denial which fascinates and compels her suitors; the violence of Headstone's passion suggests the sexual nature of his compulsion, and Wrayburn admits to his own "bad intentions": "I have wronged her enough in fact; I have wronged her still more in intention" (808). Lizzie may not design to allure; when Headstone tells her, "you are the ruin—the ruin—the ruin—of me," she can honestly reply, "I have never meant it," just as she has said of the river, "It's no purpose of mine that I live by it still" (452–53, 278). Yet she cannot escape her own sexual attractiveness—nor, one suspects, would she really wish to—any more than she can escape the attentions of Wrayburn and Headstone, or they can divert themselves from her.

Headstone's obsession takes him to criminal extremes, but there is nothing unnatural in his desire itself, which both he and the narrator liken to irresistible elemental forces—fire and wind and storm:

> . . . in certain smouldering natures like this man's, that passion [love] leaps into a blaze, and makes such head as fire does in a rage of wind, when other passions, but for its mastery, could be held in chains.   (396)

> "No man knows till the time comes, what depths are within him. . . . To me, you brought it; on me, you forced it; and the bottom of this raging sea," striking himself upon the breast, "has been heaved up ever since."   (454)

Wrayburn's urbane languor is also dissolved by sexual urgency. "If there is a word in the dictionary under any letter from A to Z that I abominate, it is energy," he remarks early in the novel, apparently too sunk in elegant ennui to exert himself even in pursuit of casual conquests, but his sleeping energies are quickly wakened by his first glimpse of Lizzie, so that the difference between him and Headstone seems more a matter of style than nature (62). Hardly anything could be less ethereal than the sexual compulsion which creates this fatal triangle. Headstone tells Lizzie, "You draw me to you" (454); Wrayburn similarly tells her, "I can't go away. . . . You don't know how you haunt me and bewilder me" (759–60). "She must go through with her nature, as I must go through with mine," Wrayburn says of Lizzie and himself (764–65). All three are under the sway of desire, Lizzie not least.

Her character greatly enriches the virginal, idealized religion of which the Mary Hogarth heroines were the saints and emblems in the early novels. *Our Mutual Friend* acknowledges that even the most exalted human love is grounded in earth; that love's spiritual ascent involves a descent into the labyrinth of the hungry, corruptible flesh. Unlike *David Copperfield*'s Agnes, who points up, and only up, Lizzie Hexam points up *and* down. Lionel

Trilling argued that we "understand Little Dorrit to be the Beatrice of the *Comedy,* the Paraclete in female form," and the same might be argued of all of Dickens's earlier heroines (65). But these analogies do not fit Lizzie very comfortably. Her disturbing acquaintance with the river's depths has given her a taste of forbidden knowledge—forbidden, at least, to heroines like Agnes Wickfield and Amy Dorrit. Lizzie's mixture of purity and eroticism suggests the tangled chiaroscuro of love's mixed desires and ambiguous motives, which made Dickens as uneasy as they made her.

Sex and guilt generally go together in Dickens. From Bill Sikes to Bradley Headstone, he associated strong erotic feeling with violence, crime, and murder. Eugene Wrayburn drinks in guilt simply by looking at Lizzie. After spying on her in the Hexams' waterside windmill house—set amid "slimy stones," "rank grass," and "pretty hard mud"—he reports himself feeling like "Guy Fawkes in the vault and a Sneak in the area both at once," and takes a drink of burnt sherry to assuage his conscience:

> "Pooh," said Eugene, spitting it out among the ashes. "Tastes like the wash of the river."
> "Are you so familiar with the flavour of the wash of the river?" [Mortimer inquires].
> "I seem to be to-night. I feel as if I had been half drowned, and swallowing a gallon of it." (212)

Despite her uncompromised virtue, even Lizzie feels guilty. Learning that her father is suspected of murdering John Harmon, she is oppressed by dread, though certain of his innocence and certainly innocent herself: "As she came beneath the lowering sky, a sense of being involved in a murky shade of Murder dropped upon her; and, as the tidal swell of the river broke at her feet without her seeing how it gathered, so, her thoughts startled her by rushing out of an unseen void and striking at her heart" (114). As she broods by the river, her thoughts drift downstream: "And as the great black river with its dreary shores was soon lost to her view in the gloom, so, she stood on the river's brink unable to see into the vast blank misery of a life suspected, and fallen away from by good and bad, but knowing that it lay there dim before her, stretching away to the great ocean, Death" (115). The imagery of the dark river, combined with the sentence's awkward syntax and rhythm, suggests Lizzie's uncertainty about the source of her dread—and perhaps Dickens, too, was uncertain. It has something to do with murder and death, but it goes far beyond the crime of which Lizzie's father is suspected. It is a nameless guilt springing from unfathomed sources in her psyche, and it has more to do with her own sexual feelings than with any actual or alleged sins of her father.

But while the river is an insistent image of pollution, drowning, and guilt, it also nourishes Lizzie's rich sensuality. She is virginal and sexually pure, but she knows the river; she is innocent in deed, but not in impulse or desire. And Dickens realizes that Lizzie's impulses and desires are vital, in ways that earlier heroines have been anemic. The virtue of her sensuality appears in her contrast with Bradley Headstone's admirer, the schoolmistress Miss Peecher: "Small, shining, neat, methodical, and buxom was Miss Peecher; cherry-cheeked and tuneful of voice. A little pincushion, a little housewife, a little book, a little workbox, a little set of tables and weights and measures, and a little woman, all in one" (268). There is little of the dark Thames in Miss Peecher; her character and her life are prim, tidy, clean, and reasonable. Most of the terms used to describe her might be applied with equal justice to Agnes Wickfield or Esther Summerson, Dickensian heroines of the highest order, and yet now, in the case of Miss Peecher, such constricted domestic virtues are mocked. The repetition of "little" stresses the diminutive extent of her world, the narrow range of her emotions and experience. Her innocence is not a virtue but a failure to engage with life, an ignorance of its murky underwater depths. Lizzie has helped to haul up many drowned corpses, and Wrayburn nearly becomes one of them—they both know the river intimately. Miss Peecher has not even got her feet wet.

The currents of desire are dangerous, of course. Bradley Headstone drowns in the river, and unlike Wrayburn, he stays drowned; his figurative drowning is enacted literally in his fatal struggle with Riderhood beside the Thames lock. When Riderhood insists, "I can't be drowned," Headstone replies, "I can be! . . . I am resolved to be." But in fact, he has already drowned. His final words vengefully invite Riderhood to taste the same agonies of longing and passion that he has suffered: "Come down!" he cries, and together they sink to "the ooze and scum behind one of the rotting gates" (874).

Deadly to Headstone, immersion in the river revives Wrayburn, however. His near drowning in the Thames, when assaulted by Headstone, is symbolically a cleansing, baptismal experience, emblematic of moral rebirth and initiation into a higher love. Lizzie is both his death and his salvation; Wrayburn is spiritually transformed by her love. To Bella Wilfer "did Mr Eugene Wrayburn impart that, please God, she should see how his wife had changed him!" (883). But this happy reformation has come about only because he first desired the river-dredger's daughter. He could not have been saved unless he had first "drowned" in desire. Such sexual urgency could hardly be more different from, for example, David Copperfield's dilatory amorous drift toward his "sister" Agnes.

In the apparently incongruous elements of Lizzie Hexam's character—her radiant virtues, her erotic nature, the "ooze and slime" of the Thames, and its drowned corpses—*Our Mutual Friend* integrates opposite impulses in Dickens, his reverence for a lofty feminine ideal and his very earthly passion for a specific young woman. Both the ideal and the fallen are fused in Lizzie:

she is the earthly incarnation of the Mary Hogarth divinity. Dickens himself, in the last chapter, moralizes Wrayburn's reformation as a triumph of the regenerative power of Lizzie's love and virtue: his "feelings of gratitude, of respect, of admiration, and affection" defeat the low and baneful influence of "Society"(891). But while this neat *sententia* reaffirms Dickens's usual populist sentiments, along with the ideals of his Mary Hogarth religion, *Our Mutual Friend* also reveals an unexpected sacramental awareness, a recognition that the created world is impregnated with sacred potential; that transcendent love begins in the passionate, corruptible flesh: "Soule into the soule may flow,/Though it to body first repaire." Thus Donne in "The Extasie," and though for many good reasons we do not usually associate him with Donne, Dickens too had come to muse on the mysterious interdependence of soul and flesh: "Loves mysteries in soules doe grow,/But yet the bodie is his booke."

NOTES

1. The editors of the Pilgrim Edition of Dickens's letters point out that he is unlikely to have dreamed this dream any time near All Souls; they place the incident sometime in late September (*Letters* 4:197n).
2. Peter Ackroyd writes: "All the engagement of his nature, all the idealism and veneration, were elicited only by the innocent young girl or young woman; and, since this is the tone that Dickens always adopted towards Ellen Ternan, it seems almost inconceivable that theirs was in any sense a 'consummated' affair" (Ackroyd 916). This is an interesting speculation, but the presumption must be that their affair was consummated in the usual way.

WORKS CITED

Ackroyd, Peter. *Dickens.* New York: HarperCollins, 1990.

Carey, John. *The Violent Effigy.* London: Faber and Faber, 1973.

Dickens, Charles. *David Copperfield.* Ed. Nina Burgis. Oxford: Clarendon P, 1981.

———. *Dombey and Son.* Ed. Alan Horsman. Oxford: Clarendon P, 1974.

———. *Great Expectations.* Ed. Margaret Cardwell. Oxford: OUP, 1994.

———. *Letters.* Ed. Madeline House, Graham Story, Kathleen Tillotson et al. Oxford: Clarendon P, 1965–.

————. *The Life of Our Lord*. 1934. Reprint, Philadelphia: Westminster Press, 1981.

————. *Oliver Twist*. Ed. Fred Kaplan. New York: W. W. Norton, 1993.

————. *Our Mutual Friend*. Ed. Stephen Gill. Harmondsworth: Penguin, 1971.

Greene, Graham. "The Young Dickens" in Norton *Oliver Twist*, 426–32.

Ingham, Patricia. *Dickens, Women and Language*. Toronto: U of Toronto P, 1992.

O'Connor, Flannery. *The Habit of Being*. Ed. Sally Fitzgerald. New York: Random, 1979.

Slater, Michael. *Dickens and Women*. Stanford: Stanford UP, 1983.

Tomalin, Claire. *The Invisible Woman*. 1990. Reprint, New York: Random, 1992.

Trilling, Lionel. "Little Dorrit." In *The Opposing Self*. New York: Viking, 1955.

Walder, Dennis. *Dickens and Religion*. London: Allen & Unwin, 1981.

News from the Dead: Archaeology, Detection, and *The Mystery of Edwin Drood*

Lawrence Frank

As Dickens's uncompleted, last novel, Edwin Drood *responds not only to Darwin's* Origin of Species, *but also to Austen Henry Layard's* Discoveries at Nineveh *and to Charles Lyell's* Antiquity of Man. *The narrative rejects traditional antiquarianism through its denial of prehistory, for it offers a sustained meditation on the nature of historical knowledge; the problems posed by fragmentary and negative evidence; and the conditional status of all historical reconstructions, including those offered in detective novels. In the novel, Lyell's discussion of the Temple of Jupiter Serapis in his* Principles of Geology *is implicitly offered as the model for acts of reconstruction engaged in by historians, by fictional detectives, and by readers of mysteries. Appropriately, the fragmentary novel, and by implication every text, becomes an archaeological relic that demands interpretation even as it defies it.*

I.

In 1863 two articles appeared in Charles Dickens's weekly *All the Year Round,* one entitled "How Old Are We?"—a review of Charles Lyell's recently published *Geological Evidences of the Antiquity of Man* (1863); the other, "Latest News from the Dead," an evocative discussion of those "dead

---

and buried cities that it is one of the labours of the living in our day to disentomb'' (473). The two unsigned articles can be seen to be premonitory: they anticipated the mystery posed by Dickens's death on June 9, 1870, after his completion of six of the proposed twelve monthly numbers of *The Mystery of Edwin Drood* (1870). More radically than the other novels Dickens lived to complete, the fragmentary *Edwin Drood* becomes news from the dead, inviting various responses to riddles that remain to this day, responses that seek to solve the mystery of the disappearance of Edwin Drood on a stormy Christmas morning. Such speculations are founded upon various evidence—Dickens's Memorandum Book, his working notes for the novel, the manuscript, and surviving page proofs—and upon the testimony of people like John Forster, Dickens's literary executor, Charles Dickens, Jr., and Dickens's daughter, Kate Perugini, each of whom claimed to have been privy to Dickens's plan for ending the novel.[1]

For us, *Edwin Drood* becomes an archaeological relic that both demands and resists those interpretations that we bring to it. Appropriately, the status of such interpretations becomes a central preoccupation within the novel itself. As a piece of detective fiction, *Edwin Drood* necessarily deals with the nature of evidence, the reconstruction of past events, and the solution to a crime that may, finally, never have been committed: we simply are never to know if Edwin Drood is alive, or dead; the personal effects—an engraved watch, a chain, and a stick-pin—recovered from Cloisterham Weir would seem, undoubtedly, to be his; but they remain mute, unresponsive to the interpretations that various characters in the novel bring to them.

Dickens had, of course, dealt with such issues both in *Bleak House* (1852–53) and in *Little Dorrit* (1855–57). In seeking out the law-writer whose handwriting Lady Dedlock has apparently recognized, Mr. Tulkinghorn will engage in an archaeological excavation of the past. He will be led to Krook's Rag and Bottle Warehouse, that repository of bones, clothing, bottles of various sorts and, more importantly, of those personal and legal documents that might provide a clue to the past if someone like Tulkinghorn can reconstruct it from the fragmentary evidence he turns up. In the double narrative of the novel, Dickens was already exploring various ways of rendering the past intelligible, in the process meditating upon a universe filled with seeming coincidences that may, or may not, attest to some providential design. In *Little Dorrit,* Arthur Clennam returns to England after the death of his father, obsessed with his father's watch that he regards as a token his mother is to understand (47). The old, silk watch-paper, worked in beads with the letters, ''D.N.F.'' (349), becomes a hieroglyphic text pointing to the past, and to the circumstances of Arthur Clennam's birth. With the passing reference to Giovanni Battista Belzoni (31), the Italian strongman turned collector of Egyptian antiquities for Henry Salt and the British Museum, the narrative reveals its own archaeological preoccupations and the need to reconstruct the past through evidence that does not, and cannot, speak for itself. "Do Not Forget!" (*Dorrit* 350) becomes an appropriate motto both for *Bleak House* and *Little Dorrit*, indicating a past that is not to be forgotten lest it reassert itself destructively in the present. Written before the *Origin of Species* (1859) and the *Antiquity of Man*, the two novels anticipated the archaeological perspective informing Charles Darwin's discussion of transmutation and Charles Lyell's argument for the reality of human prehistory: Dickens fully appreciated the problematic nature of any reconstruction of the past. Years before turning to *Edwin Drood*, he possessed a sophisticated awareness of using the historical imagination to explain the present through the excavation of the past.[2]

Appropriately, the events narrated in *Edwin Drood* occur primarily in Cloisterham, an "ancient English Cathedral Town" (1), that is presented originally as an antiquarian curiosity. Yet, early on, the novel asserts a relationship between the emerging discipline of archaeology and detection: it offers a prolonged meditation upon historical knowledge and the solutions toward which the genre of detective fiction drives.[3] Both become historical disciplines engaged in reconstructing the past through fragmentary, inevitably inadequate, evidence. *Edwin Drood* shares the sophistication of the 1863 review of Lyell's *Antiquity of Man*. In the novel, as in "How Old Are We?", there is a concern with issues central to Lyell's attempt to demonstrate, in the face of prevailing opposition, the existence of prehistoric peoples, the pre-Adamites so abhorrent to Christian orthodoxy. Like the discipline of prehistoric archaeology, the novel confronts the problematic nature of evidence, the art of reconstructing in narrative form the inaccessible past, and the challenges posed by the phenomenon of negative evidence. Throughout, the novel would seem implicitly to dramatize, even to recapitulate, a transition from an established antiquarian perspective to a truly archaeological one, a transition in Victorian Great Britain from a prevailing consensus among men of science and gentlemen amateurs to a new consensus emerging in the 1860s that would sweep away the traditional biblical chronology to open up an abyss of time that obscures human origins altogether. All of this is acknowledged in the final paragraph of "How Old Are We?": "The issue of all these researches [into the antiquity and ancestry of man] is, in the opinion now held by geologists, that although man, whose traces are found only in the post-tertiary deposits, is geologically a new comer upon earth, his antiquity is, nevertheless, much greater than chronologists have hitherto supposed" (37). Such an observation challenges the antiquarian confidence in Baconian empiricism and in a providential chronology; it undermines one form of historical imagination and introduces another form destined, perhaps, to supersede it and to become available to a general reading public not only through works of geology and archaeology, but through detective fictions like the *The Mystery of Edwin Drood.*[4]

II.

In *Edwin Drood*, the congenial optimism of the nineteenth-century antiquarian is suggested, only to be parodied, in the opening description of Cloisterham. In the history of the town the novel honors a philological and antiquarian model, following the successive peoples, with their differing languages, that once inhabited the spot. Cloisterham, "a fictitious name," has been "once possibly known to the Druids by another name, and certainly to the Romans by another, and to the Saxons by another, and to the Normans by another; and a name more or less in the course of many centuries can be of little moment to its dusty chronicles" (14). The history of Cloisterham is founded upon surviving edifices and on documents that point backward in time as far as the Celts, who were believed to have inhabited England in the period immediately preceding the Roman occupation. It looks forward to another time and to future inhabitants whose language may not be the English spoken and written in the Cloisterham of the 1840s.[5] The novel captures the cadences and the spirit of Richard Chenevix Trench's *On the Study of Words* (1851) in which language is "the great, oftentimes the only, connecting link between the present and the remotest past, an ark riding above water-floods that have swept away or submerged every other landmark and memorial of ages and generations of men" (93). For Trench the philologist becomes a figurative geologist engaged in the study of "moral and historical researches": "You know how the geologist is able from the different strata and deposits, primary, secondary, or tertiary, succeeding one another, . . . to arrive at the successive physical changes through which a region has passed . . . to measure the forces which were at work to produce them, and almost to indicate their date. Now with such a composite language as the English before us, . . . here too are strata and deposits, not of gravel and chalk, sandstone and limestone, but of Celtic, Latin, Saxon, Danish, Norman, and then again Latin and French words." Anyone with the "skill to analyze the language might re-create for himself the history of the people speaking that language" (94–95).

On the Study of Words reveals Trench's confidence in the enduring spoken word: its imperishable nature is "borne witness to by the present language of [the British] people, on which language the marks and vestiges of great revolutions are visibly and profoundly impressed, never again to be obliterated from it" (94). For "beyond all written records in a language, the language itself stretches back . . . [,] a far more ancient monument and document than any writing which employs it'' (93). His enthusiasm for the spoken word as a reliable form of ''fossil history'' (17) permits Trench to shrug off the other implications of his geological figure of speech: both for Charles Lyell in the *Principles of Geology* (1830–33) and Darwin in the *Origin of Species,* the geological record was to remain an imperfect annal, marked by significant blanks, by missing pages, chapters, and volumes. Yet, Trench's geological analogy remains illustrative and unproblematic.[6] His attitude, so representative of the Anglican establishment, seems to inform the history of Cloisterham, that ''ancient city . . . so abounding in vestiges of monastic graves, that the Cloisterham children grow small salad in the dust of abbots and abbesses . . .; while every ploughman in its outlying fields renders to once puissant Lord Treasurers, Archbishops, Bishops, and such-like, the attention which the Ogre in the story-book desired to render to his unbidden visitor, and grinds their bones to make his bread'' (14).

Such passages in *Edwin Drood* will, finally, parody in a nuanced way not only someone like Trench, but those antiquarians who incorporated a philological model into their accounts of Britain. The history of Cloisterham echoes accounts of the past from the time of the Celts to the conversion of the Anglo-Saxons that was seen to mark the founding of the modern British nation. In *The Celt, The Roman, and the Saxon,* first published in 1852, Thomas Wright provided a characteristic account of British history. In his preface to the second edition of 1861, Wright observes, ''There is hardly a corner in our island in which the spade or the plough does not, from time to time, turn up relics of its earlier inhabitants, to astonish and to excite the curiosity of the observer, who, when he looks to an ordinary history of England, finds that the period to which such remains belong is passed over with so little notice'' (v). Wright then proposes ''to give a sketch of that part of our history which is not generally treated of, the period before Britain became Christian England—the period, indeed which, in the absence of much documentary evidence, it is the peculiar province of the antiquary to illustrate. Every article which . . . is turned up by the spade or the plough, is a record of that history, and it is by comparing them together, and subjecting them to the assay of science, that we make them tell their story'' (v-vi). Although he acknowledges the fact of those ''centuries which present little more than a blank in our ordinary annals'' (vi), Wright is possessed of a confidence that he shares with Trench. He acknowledges the incompleteness of the written record; he seems wary of traditional lore. Yet, he is sure that he can, indeed, offer a reliable account of the past. He will begin with the Celts and the Druids, with a primeval period that antiquarians claim immediately preceded the Roman presence in Britain: his is a strategy shared with others who, in their Christian orthodoxy and their commitment to the status quo in Victorian Britain, seek to truncate time and to deny a prehistoric age that would subvert the biblical account of human history.[7]

Throughout *The Celt, the Roman, and the Saxon,* Wright touches upon topics relevant to the narrative of *Edwin Drood.* He deals with the history of the names of contemporary British towns and cities, following the lead of Trench with his concern for words as fossil history. He mentions the various names of Rochester—Bremenium, Durobrivæ, Hrofes-ceaster—anticipating the history of the town fictionalized as Cloisterham.[8] Wright devotes page upon page to Roman funeral monuments and to their Latin inscriptions, foreshadowing the preposterous Mr. Sapsea and the self-serving epitaph to be inscribed upon the monument to his dead wife. He discusses Roman and Saxon burial customs, including both cremation and the later, more common, interment of bodies in sepulchral chests and stone sarcophagi along with the personal effects of the dead. At one point he writes of a stone sarcophagus in the York museum, quoting an antiquarian blessed with a Dickensian name, a Mr. Well-beloved: "On removing the lid, the coffin appeared to be about half filled with lime. . . . The lime having been very carefully taken out, the lower surface presented a distinct impression of a human body. . . . A very small portion of the bones remained; sufficient, however, to indicate that they were those of a female. . . . The lime . . . having been carefully scraped away, the remnants of a lady's ornaments were brought to light" (311–12). Such a passage could well become grist for the mills of those who argue that John Jasper has, indeed, murdered his rival, Drood, placing the corpse in a Cathedral crypt to be eaten away by quicklime, leaving untouched the tell-tale ring that Drood may have had in his possession on the last night on which he was seen.[9]

These are tantalizing facts. But the significance of *The Celt, the Roman, and the Saxon* for *Edwin Drood* involves, more interestingly, the antiquarian ethos that the novel will reject in its promotion of the archaeological perspective that was to inform a new scientific consensus in the 1860s and to provide a model for the act of detection.[10] The novel implicitly challenges Wright's confidence that he can subject various forms of evidence "to the assay of science" and make them tell "their story" (vi). It will raise questions about the developmental, progressive model of British history promoted in the decades prior to Darwin's *Origin* and Lyell's *Antiquity of Man.* The novel will subvert Wright's belief in a providential history that reveals God's plan for the British people and a British empire that was to rival, and to outlast, that of Rome. Even the belief in the continuity between Saxon Britain, with the "municipal constitutions" (443) of its purportedly independent towns, and Victorian Britain will be parodied, particularly Wright's claim that such towns "hold a very important place in the history of social development . . . to which we owe that due mixture of Saxon and Roman that forms the basis of modern civilisation" (455).[11]

Such claims underlie Wright's hostility to theorizing and his dismissal of the Danish three-age model of human history. Two years after Lyell publicly proclaimed the fact of human prehistory before the British Association for the Advancement of Science in 1859, Wright can attack "the system of archæological periods which has been adopted by the antiquaries of the north. . . . It is true that there may have been a period when society was in so barbarous a state, that sticks or stones were the only implements with which men knew how to furnish themselves; but I doubt if the antiquary has yet found any evidence of such a period" (vii). In the service of a biblical chronology and a providential history, Wright later concludes, "The most probable view of the case seems to be, that the mass of our British antiquities belong to the age immediately preceding the arrival of the Romans, and to the period which followed" (82).

Wright promotes a dogmatic antiquarianism to preclude the union of natural history and human history that Lyell would seek to forge two years later in the *Antiquity of Man*.[12] But in its final paragraphs the *Celt, the Roman, and the Saxon* introduces an element of uncertainty that belies the claims Wright has insistently made. He turns to a discussion of inscribed stones found in Wales and Cornwall, apparently belonging to "the period following immediately after that of the departure of the Roman legions." The inscriptions are in Latin, but "the names are apparently Celtic" (461). The inscription on one such stone in Wales "was evidently written by one who spoke Latin corruptly; but its greatest singularity is the circumstance that the inscription is cut on the back of an older inscribed stone, dedicated to the emperor Maximinus; and although the pure Roman inscription is written in lines across the stone, the later inscription is written, like those found in Cornwall, lengthways." Apparently, several stones had "a cross at the top, so that there can be no doubt of the people to whom these belonged being Christians" (462). With the interpretation the book ends, asserting the continuity between Celtic, Roman, and Christian Britain and offering a history that is documented and intelligible. But with its multiple inscriptions, the fragmentary stone becomes a figurative palimpsest: it reveals the existence of trace upon trace leading forever backward in time and inducing historical vertigo.

With its unintended implications, Thomas Wright's discussion of the stone suggests how the narrative of *Edwin Drood* can resist Victorian antiquarianism, with its faith in providence and progress, and mock those like the Reverend Septimus Crisparkle whose world may well be circumscribed by the Alternate Musical Wednesdays that he attends. The novel insistently chides those who would argue that a providential design governs British history and leads to the glories of the Victorian era: "A drowsy city, Cloisterham, whose inhabitants seem to suppose, with an inconsistency more strange than rare, that all its changes lie behind it, and that there are no more to come. A queer moral to derive from antiquity, yet older than any traceable antiquity" (14). The reference to those traces that antiquarians like Thomas Wright pursue so assiduously mocks their project. Not only may history have no traceable beginning, there is no end to history, the telos of which has apparently led to the British empire and to those like Edwin Drood who complacently talks of those "triumphs of engineering skill" that are "to change the whole condition of an undeveloped country" (21) like the Egypt that awaits him. His condescension reveals the condition of most of those associated with Cloisterham.

Edwin Drood dismisses any claim to progress, particularly if providential design has led to the insipid world of Minor Canon Corner where the reverend Mr. Crisparkle now resides with his quaint, elderly mother: "Swaggering fighting men had had their centuries of ramping and raving about Minor Canon Corner, and beaten serfs had had their centuries of drudging and dying there, and powerful monks had had their centuries of being sometimes useful and sometimes harmful there. . . . Perhaps one of the highest uses of their ever having been there, was, that there might be left behind, that blessed air of tranquillity which pervaded Minor Canon Corner, and that serenely romantic state of the mind . . . which is engendered by a sorrowful story that is all told" (39–40). The days, weeks, and months to pass will prove how illusory is the tranquillity of Minor Canon Corner and the belief that history is a "pathetic play that is played out" (40). In the process, the novel explores the problematic nature of the evidence, documentary and otherwise, that a Thomas Wright subjects to "the assay of science": for every artifact "turned up by the spade or the plough" does not tell its own story (vi), but is coerced into meaning by those who examine it.

As the Cloisterham children "grow small salad in the dust of abbots and abbesses, and make dirt-pies of nuns and friars" and as the "ploughman [grinds the] bones" (14) of the long-dead members of the clerical hierarchy, they blithely destroy relics of the past. Even those relics that do survive pose a challenge to the antiquarian: "In the midst of Cloisterham stands the Nuns' House; a venerable brick edifice whose present appellation is doubtless derived from the legend of its conventual uses" (15). There may, in fact, be no proof that the building had once been a nunnery. Rather, its origins and the transformations it may have undergone through the centuries remain shrouded in myth and conjecture. It can only puzzle the historian, just as others in the future may be puzzled as they contemplate a "resplendent brass plate" from the nineteenth century, "flashing forth the legend: 'Seminary for Young Ladies. Miss Twinkleton'." (15). Just as the inscribed stone in Wales defies Thomas Wright's interpretation, the Nuns' House resists attempts to reconstruct its history: the ironic legend proclaiming its current use can not tell its own story, either in the present or in the future.

Edwin Drood transforms monuments to the past into figurative texts that retain an irresolvable ambiguity. The novel begins to demonstrate a sophisticated geological and archaeological awareness, first in the depiction of the

Nuns' House, later in its introduction of the "mysterious inscription" over the portal to Mr. Grewgious's chambers in Staple Inn, located near "the most ancient part of Holborn," where the man who is Rosa Bud's guardian both works and lives. In its apparent simplicity, the inscription reads, "J $\begin{matrix} P \\ T \\ 1747 \end{matrix}$"
(88). The novel will return to the inscription with a curious insistence. Grewgious himself has never "troubled his head about [it], unless to bethink himself at odd times on glancing up at it, that haply it might mean Perhaps John Thomas, or Perhaps Joe Tyler" (88–89).[13] The narrative toys with the inscription, playing whimsically, it would seem, upon its possible meanings. In choosing his niche in life, Grewgious has settled down "under the dry vine and fig-tree of P.J.T., who planted in seventeen-forty-seven" (89), an observation that invokes the family trees and genealogies of antiquarianism, but also the language tree of Victorian philology and, perhaps, the Tree of Life of Darwin's *Origin of Species*. As Grewgious entertains Drood on the night he entrusts the lad with the ring once belonging to Rosa Bud's mother, he emphasizes the solemnity of the moment with a special wine: "If P.J.T. in seventeen-forty-seven, or in any other year of his period, drank such wines—then, for a certainty, P.J.T. was Pretty Jolly Too" (93). The evening ends as Grewgious addresses his image in a looking-glass: "There are such unexplored romantic nooks in the unlikeliest men, that even old tinderous and touch-woody P.J.T. Possibly Jabbered Thus, at some odd times, in or about seventeen-forty-seven" (99).

Like the Nuns' House, the corner house in Staple Inn has become a figurative document or manuscript from which a chronology and a history, however whimsical, are to be constructed. But the narrative insists that the inscription cannot be made to "tell [its] story," refuses to become "a record of . . . history" (Wright vi). All the verbal playfulness with the inscription draws attention to the fact that an order has been imposed upon the inscribed characters that is not sanctioned by the triangular inscription in which no letter possesses an indisputable priority. The various renderings of J $\begin{matrix} P \\ T \\ 1747 \end{matrix}$ arbitrarily order the letters that could be arranged in other ways and suggest other interpretations. The renderings seem to contextualize the letters by connecting the date with the erection of the building, with a purportedly historical personage, and with an historical era. Inevitably, the inscription remains mysterious, enigmatic, potentially without meaning, a reminder of the perils of creating accounts from ancient edifices, in whatever condition, and from the inscriptions on them. For in the "little nook" called Staple Inn there is "a little Hall, with a little lantern in its roof: to what obstructive purposes devoted, and at whose expense, this history knoweth not" (88).[14]

III.

The Mystery of Edwin Drood has become a special kind of history, one that does not lay claim to omniscience. The status of the narrative is more fully revealed later in the novel after Drood's disappearance. The suspected Neville Landless has removed himself rom Cloisterham to rooms in the vicinity of Staple Inn. Mr. Grewgious, suspecting John Jasper of *something,* has been on the lookout for the choirmaster who persecutes Landless by spying on him in his London retreat. In pondering the significance of what he knows and what he suspects, Grewgious finds himself, on one particular night, gazing at the stars ''as if he would have read in them something that was hidden from him'': ''Many of us would if we could; but none of us so much as know our letters in the stars yet—or seem likely to, in this state of existence—and few languages can be read until their alphabets are mastered'' (160).

The passage signals the transition from an antiquarian concern with Latin, Saxon, and English inscriptions to other written languages, Egyptian hieroglyphics and Assyrian cuneiform, whose alphabets and grammars had only been deciphered in recent decades. Rosa Bud has poutingly expressed her distaste for all things vaguely Middle Eastern by dismissing ''Arabs, and Turks, and Fellahs, and people.'' She professes to hate the pyramids and Miss Twinkleton's lectures on ''tiresome old burying-grounds! Isises, and Ibises, and Cheops, and Pharaohses; who cares about them? And then there was Belzoni or somebody, dragged out by the legs, half choked with bats and dust'' (21). Rosa's petulance serves to establish early on the preoccupation in *Edwin Drood* with British imperialism and with that provincialism that will reveal itself as pure racism in Mr. Sapsea's and Mr. Honeythunder's denunciations of Neville Landless.[15]

But other issues are suggested in Rosa's irreverent reference to Giovanni Battista Belzoni. In his popular *Narrative* (1820), Belzoni described several of his Egyptian exploits. One was his discovery in 1818 of the concealed passage in the second pyramid of Giza that led to the burial chamber of Rosa's tiresome Cheops. More important perhaps was Belzoni's rediscovery in 1817 of the buried temple of Abu-Simbel. In gaining access to the temple, Belzoni became perhaps the first European in a thousand years to see its interior. Later visitors were to find Greek graffiti in the temple, carved into the Egyptian statuary by soldiers around 59 BC, some 1700 years after the temple had been built. To visit Abu-Simbel was to become a ritual for those archaeologists who were to displace the antiquarians: Heinrich Schliemann was to make the requisite visit in 1888, only two years before his death.[16]

Belzoni engaged in the collection of Egyptian antiquities and rediscovered Abu-Simbel in a time before the appearance of an archaeological awareness.

As an adventurer and collector—some would see him as a grave-robber—he lacked the kind of sophisticated perspective suggested by the moment in which Mr. Grewgious contemplates the stars as if they were some hieroglyphic or cuneiform script as yet undeciphered and untranslated. For many Victorians the moment would conjure up the dispute over priority in the decipherment of the Rosetta stone, involving Britain's Thomas Young and Jean-François Champollion.[17] More specifically, readers of *All the Year Round* might be reminded of "Latest News from the Dead." Its opening paragraph celebrates the archaeological feats of recent years, pointing particularly to the decipherment of Egyptian hieroglyphs and of Assyrian cuneiform: "Old Egypt is delivering up fresh secrets of her dead, at Thebes and elsewhere . . . Nineveh and Babylon, having been in the hands of such resurrectionists as Mr. Layard, Sir Henry Rawlinson, and others, are left at peace for a short time" (473). By 1863 any news from Nineveh and Babylon might be seen as old news. For the feats of Layard and Rawlinson belonged to the 1840s and 1850s when the two achieved fame, Layard for excavation of sites he identified with the Biblical Nimrud and Nineveh and Rawlinson for the decipherment of the Assyrian cuneiform.[18] Austen Henry Layard had begun his excavations near Mosul in November, 1845. His account of his work at Nimrud was published in 1849: *Nineveh and its Remains* was an immediate sensation. Later, Layard and Dickens were to become friends. Dickens supported Layard's successful candidacy for a seat in Parliament, where he served in the late 1850s and throughout the 1860s. Earlier, in 1853, Dickens met up with Layard on a visit to Rome and Naples: together, the two climbed Mount Vesuvius.[19]

In his various books Layard evokes the sense of mystery and wonder surrounding his discovery of a high Assyrian civilization almost lost to human memory. In an introduction to the 1849 American edition of *Nineveh and its Remains,* Edward Robinson captures the nature of the wonder aroused by a figurative resurrectionist like Layard. Robinson distinguishes "the classic lands of Greece and Rome" whose monuments and inscriptions have been known for centuries from the "hoary monuments of Egypt . . . [that] have presented to the eye of the beholder strange forms of sculpture and language . . . mute for so many ages." Even more wonderful has been the recovery of Nimrud and Nineveh "whose greatness sank when that of Rome had just begun to rise": here we "have to do, not with hoary ruins that have borne the brunt of centuries in the presence of the world, but with a resurrection of the monuments themselves." He concludes, "It is the disentombing of temple-palaces from the sepulchre of ages; the recovery of the metropolis of a powerful nation from the long night of oblivion" (1:ii-iii).

It is from Edward Robinson's "long night of oblivion" that Victorian Cloisterham, whose monuments and inscriptions would seem "to have been known for centuries,'' will be resurrected as if by one of the fabled archaeologists of "Latest News from the Dead." The town will be transformed from a place of only antiquarian interest into an archaeological site as mysterious and foreign as Herculaneum, Pompeii, and Layard's Nineveh. It will become a formerly buried city, disinterred to yield its secrets to an uncomprehending world. When, on the evening of John Jasper's midnight ramble through the Cathedral with Stony Durdles, the ever-complacent Dean asks if the choirmaster plans "to write a book about us," he responds, "I really have no intention at all, sir, . . . of turning author or archæologist. It is but a whim of mine" (100). Whether the excursion is merely a whim or part of a plot to kill Edwin Drood and to conceal his corpse in a Cathedral crypt is beyond anyone's ability to know. But in Jasper's excursion with Durdles, Cloisterham and the Cathedral are metamorphosed into a domestic version of the excavated Nimrud that Layard described in *Nineveh and its Remains* and in the abridgement, the *Popular Account of Discoveries at Nineveh* (1851), that Dickens owned.[20]

    In the abridged account of his excavations at Nimrud, Layard retains a De Quinceian set-piece from *Nineveh and its Remains* in which he seeks to suggest the dream-like splendor of the Assyrian city that he has discovered in a mound near the city of Mosul. It is a place akin to the Southern Asia of De Quincey's dreams in the *Confessions of an English Opium-Eater* (1822), a place totally foreign to the British imagination, unknown even to the Bedouins who "have lived on these lands for years" (294). In the words of Sheikh Abd-ur-rahman, perhaps only apocryphal, his "father, and the father of [his] father, pitched their tents here . . . and none of them ever heard of a place under ground" (294). The sheikh can only proclaim, "Wonderful! Wonderful!'', a response that Layard seeks to evoke in his British readers by conducting them upon an imaginary tour of the "subterraneous labyrinth" where one encounters "colossal winged figures: some with the heads of eagles, others entirely human, and carrying mysterious symbols in their hands": "To the left is [a] portal, . . . formed by winged lions. . . . Beyond this portal is a winged figure, and two slabs with bas-reliefs; but they have been so much injured that we can scarcely trace the subject upon them '' (307). Farther on, "among these scattered monuments of ancient history and art, we reach another doorway, formed by colossal winged bulls in yellow limestone" (308). Layard moves on to other galleries and chambers, "examining the marvelous sculptures, or the numerous inscriptions that surround [him]" (310). He has created a phantasmagoric experience, suggesting that we may be "half inclined to believe that we have dreamed a dream" and that some, "who may hereafter tread on the spot when the grass again grows over the ruins of the Assyrian palaces, may indeed suspect that [he has] been relating a vision" (311). An archaeological experience induces a new awareness of unimagined realms and an appreciation of the evanescent status of the evidence that attests to them.[21]

Ironically, it is an awareness that Dickens had already captured in his descriptions of Rome in *Pictures from Italy* (1846). In describing his visit to the Eternal City early in 1845, over six months before Layard began his dig near Mosul, Dickens manages to transform Rome into yet another buried city quite as wonderful as the Nimrud of Layard, as it rises out of the "undulating flat" of the Roman Campagna. From afar he sees "innumerable towers, and steeples, and roofs of houses, . . . and high above them all one Dome": "It was so like London, at that distance, that if you could have shown it me, in a glass, I should have taken it for nothing else" (*Pictures* 364).

In the transforming mirror of Dickens's imagination Rome becomes a figurative Herculaneum, Pompeii, Nineveh, or Babylon, one of the disinterred cities later to be celebrated in "Latest News from the Dead." It is a city of desolation, with the Coliseum, the Forum, and ancient temples offering a vision of ruin upon ruin. Beneath its streets lie the catacombs, "quarries in the old time, . . . afterwards the hiding-places of the Christians. These ghastly passages . . . form a chain of labyrinths, sixty miles in circumference." The "great subterranean vaulted roads" (386) become a city beneath a city, suggesting the world of a barely imaginable past beneath contemporary Rome. In the streets of modern Rome "you pass by obelisks, or columns: ancient temples, theatres, houses, porticoes or forums: it is strange to see, how every fragment, whenever it is possible, has been blended into some modern structure, and made to serve some modern purpose. . . . It is stranger still, to see how many ruins of the old mythology: how many fragments of obsolete legend and observance: have been incorporated into the worship of Christian altars here; and how . . . the false faith and the true are fused in a monstrous union" (398).

Dickens's Protestant suspicion of Roman Catholicism cannot prevent him from perceiving the Eternal City as a rich De Quinceian palimpsest. His experience seems to culminate as he and his party return at night from an excursion on the Campagna, an "unbroken succession of mounds, and heaps, and hills, of ruin." The Campagna becomes "a Desert, where a mighty race have left their footprints in the earth from which they have vanished" (396). As early as 1845, Dickens has prepared to engage in a revery that bespeaks a complex archaeological awareness:

> To come again on Rome by moonlight, after such an expedition, is a fitting close to such a day. The narrow streets, devoid of footways, and choked, in every obscure corner, by heaps of dung-hill rubbish, contrast . . . with the broad square before some haughty church: in the centre of which, a hieroglyphic-covered obelisk, brought from Egypt in the days of the Emperor, looks strangely on the foreign scene about it. (397)

The moon "gushes freely" through the "broken arches and rent walls" of the Coliseum whose stones have been used to rear other "ponderous buildings"; while an "ancient pillar, with its honoured status overthrown, supports a Christian saint: Marcus Aurelius giving place to Paul, and Trajan to St. Peter" (397).

Dickens responds to Rome with the eye of the geologist and the archaeologist, recognizing the existence of ancient Egypt, the rise and fall of imperial Rome, the emergence of a Christian Rome under Roman Catholic dominance; he even acknowledges the mundane present in "the little town of miserable houses" where "the Jews are locked up nightly, when the clock strikes eight" (397). He has presented a multilayered past, a stratified archaeological site that, like Layard's Nimrud, demands excavation and has at its center an obelisk engraved with hieroglyphs to be deciphered and translated.

The perspective suggested in *Pictures from Italy* and in Layard's abridged *Discoveries at Nineveh* provides a context in which to consider John Jasper's moonlight excursion with Stony Durdles. The outing should not be seen primarily as evidence that Jasper is plotting to kill Edwin Drood and to conceal his corpse in a Cathedral crypt, even though the "unaccountable expedition," as if to a foreign land, leads Jasper and Durdles by a mound of quick-lime that is, in the words of the mason, "quick enough to eat your bones" (103–04). Rather, the Cloisterham through which they move has become an archaeological site: its various edifices contain vestiges of the past in "fragments of old wall, saint's chapel, chapter-house, convent, and monastery" (14). There is even "a piece of old dwarfwall" (104), another relic of the past, behind which Jasper pauses to spy upon Mr. Crisparkle and Neville Landless. Then he and Durdles pass out of Minor Canon Corner to enter the Cathedral precincts where "a certain awful hush pervades the ancient pile, the cloisters, and the churchyard" (105). They descend into the Cathedral crypt where Durdles discourses of the "old-uns," those "buried [magnates] of ancient line and high degree" (29) whose corpses may have turned to dust. They leave the crypt, beginning their ascent to the great tower, stopping on "the Cathedral level" where "the moonlight is so very bright . . - . that the colors of the nearest stained-glass window are thrown upon their faces." Durdles opens the door to the tower staircase, holding it for Jasper "as if [he is] of the grave" (107). The two explorers toil up "the winding staircase," pausing at different stages, at places that include "low-arched galleries" from which they glimpse "the moonlit nave," while above them "the dim angels' heads upon the corbels of the roof [seem] to watch their progress" (107–08).

Durdles and Jasper reenact the experience that Dickens has had of Rome by moonlight; they enter a realm like that of the excavated Nimrud, a realm of dream that reveals the enduring nature of the past. As the two attain the

Cathedral tower itself, they look down on Cloisterham, "fair to see in the moonlight: its ruined habitations and sanctuaries of the dead, at the tower's base: its moss-softened red-tiled roofs and red-brick houses of the living, clustered beyond: its river winding down from the mist on the horizon, as though that were its source, and already heaving with a restless knowledge of its approach towards the sea" (108). A spatial journey has become a temporal one: there is a movement from the sepulchral depths of the Cathedral that suggests not only a medieval past, but the dust and soil prior to its erection, and the dust to which the Cathedral may return. Durdles and Jasper have moved through strata of human time, rising to the tower and to a prospect of present-day Cloisterham, so confident that all change lies behind it. As in Dickens's depiction of the broad square in Rome, with the obelisk and the statuary, a complex synchronic and diachronic reality has been suggested, a rendering of human time indebted to philology, geology, and an archaeology that has opened new vistas of time through the excavation of "dead and buried cities that it is one of the labours of the living in our day to disentomb" ("News from the Dead" 473).

IV.

But, as Cloisterham's "river [winds] down from the mist on the horizon, as though that were its source" (108), an even more profound sense of the past has been suggested, a past extending into epochs that far predate the time of Roman Britain, a time before the literate societies of Egypt, Babylon, and Assyria. For Victorians living in the 1860s and 1870s, such mists were now associated with a preliterate world prior to that of the Celts: they were mists of time through which archaeologists were just beginning to peer. For an antiquarian like Thomas Wright, such a period was not only shrouded in impenetrable mists, fog, and shadow, rather, such a period had never existed. Even in the second edition of *The Celt, the Roman, and the Saxon,* Wright could deny that worked flints demonstrated the reality of prehistoric times. In defense of a traditional chronology, Wright argues that worked flints must be either the product of metal tools in the Roman era or, even worse, forgeries of the present (71). However, throughout the 1860s and 1870s a consensus was forming about human prehistory. In 1875 William Gladstone would introduce Heinrich Schliemann to the London Society of Antiquarians in language that had become conventional and, to many, unexceptionable: "When many of us who are among the elders in this room were growing up, the whole of the prehistoric times lay before our eyes like a silver cloud covering the whole of the lands that, at different periods of history, had become so illustrious and interesting; but as to their details we knew nothing. . . . Now we are beginning to see through this dense mist and the cloud is becoming transparent, and the figures of real places, real men, real facts are slowly beginning to reveal to us their outlines'' (quoted in Daniel and Renfrew 46). Gladstone, of course, was referring to Schliemann's quest for Troy, but his words suggest that like-minded people, even the devoutly Christian, had accepted prehistory as a reality, an assumption that John Lubbock, now Lord Avebury, could question as he promoted the reality of human prehistory in the seventh edition, posthumously published, of his classic *Prehistoric Times* (1913).[22]

Perhaps, for readers of *All the Year Round,* such mists had first been parted by the review of Charles Lyell's *Antiquity of Man* (1863). ''How Old Are We?'' begins by praising Lyell as ''one of the soundest and most reasonable of geologists'' (32) and proceeds to offer an approving summary of a book that sought, in the face of opposition from scriptural literalists, antiquarians, and others, to demonstrate the fact of human prehistory. The review ends by endorsing Lyell's argument for the antiquity of man: ''The issue of [recent research] is, in the opinion now held by geologists, that although man . . . is geologically a new comer upon earth, his antiquity is, nevertheless, much greater than chronologists have hitherto supposed'' (37). Traditional chronologies of human history, based on varying interpretations of scripture, were swept away to reveal a past that defied the prevailing common sense of the early nineteenth century and offered a new view of human origins.[23]

Those readers of *All the Year Round* who might have turned from ''How Old Are We?'' to the *Antiquity of Man* itself would have found in its pages not only an argument for the fact of human prehistory, but the demonstration of a methodology for reconstructing the past, a methodology to be replicated in detective fiction, particularly in *Edwin Drood.* In his book Lyell proceeds to establish human antiquity by reviewing recent discoveries in submerged prehistoric lake villages in Switzerland, Ireland, and elsewhere. He recounts his visits to excavation sites in England and on the Continent, where worked flints had apparently been found in association with the fossil remains of extinct mammals. In the process Lyell knowingly dramatizes the complex assumptions with which he works.

From the start Lyell understands the reluctance of those like a Thomas Wright to accept human prehistory: ''I can only plead that a discovery which seems to contradict the general tenor of previous investigations is naturally received with much hesitation'' (68).[24] Such hesitation is both religious and psychological in its basis. But it also reflects the nature of the evidence with which Lyell must work. Earlier in the *Principles of Geology* (1830–33), and here again in the *Antiquity of Man,* Lyell stresses the ''fragmentary nature of all geological annals'' that he examines, producing gaps ''in the regular sequence of geological monuments bearing on the history of man'' (207–08). Both the geological and archaeological records become an ''interrupted series of consecutive documents'' so that it is difficult to construct ''any thing like a connected chain of history'' (208). As he pursues the evidence that he needs in ''the dark recesses of underground vaults and tunnels, which may have served as places of refuge or sepulture to a succession of human beings and wild animals'' (94), Lyell becomes a self-conscious detective in a mystery novel: at one point, in discussing the effects of glacial action, he observes how difficult it may be to read the geological and archaeological records ''without having the ice-clue in his mind'' (139). In interpreting the incomplete annals that constitute such records, he must deal with fragmentary evidence, even with figurative pages erased by glacial action. He must confront the problem posed by the skepticism of a Thomas Wright who sees worked flints as forgeries, or of others who dismiss them as accidents of natural processes. Perhaps more daunting, Lyell acknowledges the challenge of the ''negative fact'' (151): all too often, there are no fossilized human skeletons, whole or fragmentary, to be found in association with the flint instruments and with the fossilized remains of extinct mammals: ''Instead of its being part of the plan of nature to store up enduring records of a large number of the individual plants and animals which have lived on the [earth's] surface, it seems to be her chief care to provide the means of disencumbering the habitable areas . . . of those myriads of solid skeletons of animals'' (146).

Here Lyell strikes a note to be heard throughout the *Antiquity of Man:* ''In our retrospective survey, we have been . . . obliged, for the sake of proceeding from the known to the less known, to reverse the natural order of history, and to treat of the newer before the older'' (*Antiquity* 108). With these words Lyell clarifies the practices of the geologist, the palaeontologist, and the archaeologist. He identifies the nature of the various historical disciplines that move from fragmentary evidence in the present to a complex reconstruction of the past. He is setting forth the program of the *Antiquity of Man* as he deals with flint tools, fossilized animal bones, and geological formations to demonstrate to the skeptical the reality of human prehistory. He also reminds his readers of the *Principles of Geology,* in which he has sought to demonstrate the nature of geological changes over vast periods of time: ''As examples of such [geological] changes . . . which have become accessible to human observation, I have adduced the strata near Naples in which the Temple of Jupiter Serapis at Puzzuoli was entombed'' (45).

In referring to the Temple of Jupiter Serapis, Lyell suggests that his discussion of the temple in volume one of the *Principles of Geology* has become a model for the practice of the historical disciplines of geology and archaeology. He does so with confidence, relying upon the authority of William Whewell, master of Trinity College, Cambridge, and philosopher of science, who turned in his three-volume *History of the Inductive Sciences* (1837) to Lyell's discussion of the Temple of Serapis as exemplary of ''those researches in which the object is, to ascend from the present state of things to a more ancient condition from which the present is derived by intelligible causes'' (3:481). Such sciences include philology, geology, archaeology and, by extension, those acts of detection in which it becomes necessary to reconstruct past events from fragmentary evidence surviving into the present.

Whewell goes on to clarify the nature of such palaetiological sciences, as he calls them. They involve ''inquiries concerning the monuments of the art and labour of distant ages; . . . examinations [into] the origin and early progress of states and cities, customs, and languages; as well as . . . the researches concerning the causes and formations of mountains and rocks, the imbedding of fossils in strata, and their elevation from the bottom of the ocean. All of these speculations are connected by this bond—that they endeavour to ascend to a past state of things, by the aid of the evidence of the present'' (3:482). Implicitly, philology and historical archaeology offer a methodology and a characteristic language for the geologist and palaeontologist who become readers of literal and figurative documents. For Whewell, it is Georges Cuvier who becomes a representative figure, '' 'the geologist [as an] antiquary of a new order' '': ''The organic fossils which occur in the rock, and the medals which we find in the ruins of ancient cities, are to be studied in a similar spirit and for a similar purpose. Indeed, it is not always easy to know where the task of the geologist ends, and that of the antiquary begins'' (3:482). The study of the history of the earth and that of the history of humankind merge into one coherent discipline governed by similar practices.

Whewell proceeds by observing, ''It is more than a mere fanciful description, to say that in languages, customs, forms of society, political institutions, we see a number of formations superimposed upon one another, each of which is, for the most part, an assemblage of fragments . . . of the preceding condition'' (3:484). The palaetiological sciences—those ''sciences [which] might be properly called *historical*'' (3:486)—study a past embodied in the form of ''the ruined temple [that] may exhibit the traces of time in its changed level, and sea-worn columns; and thus the antiquarian of the earth may be brought into the very middle of the domain belonging to the antiquarian of art'' (3:482–3). The temple to which Whewell alludes is Charles Lyell's ''Temple of Jupiter Serapis, near Puzzuoli'' (3:483). In invoking Lyell's discussion of the Temple, he confers upon it the status of a classic, the model for the reconstruction of the past. However, Lyell's account of the Temple becomes the foundation for a subtle, yet potentially radical, historiography beyond the ken of the conventional antiquarian or even the sophisticated Natural Theologian. His discussion of the Temple of Serapis becomes an epistemological and narratological tour de force, an exemplum for the practice of the historical disciplines, that reveals the indeterminate nature of the reconstructions such disciplines offer.

Significantly, the frontispiece to volume one of the *Principles* is not an illustration of some geological wonder, as is the case in volumes two and three, but an engraving of the Temple of Jupiter Serapis, a Roman ruin on the Bay of Baiae in the vicinity of Naples and the once-buried cities of Herculaneum and Pompeii with which it becomes associated. The frontispiece announces Lyell's strategy: throughout the three volumes of the *Principles,* he will turn to philological, linguistic, and archaeological figures of speech, illustrating how to read the history of the inanimate and animate worlds. Such a history, freed of the strictures imposed by scriptural literalism, can be seen to have been written in a hieroglyphical script that geologists and palaeontologists had only recently deciphered. Fossil shells, particularly those of various molluscs, become figurative characters; properly read, they reveal the earth's history over vast periods of time.[25]

As a monument to a former age, the Temple of Serapis may be approached as a figurative document inscribed by nature's own hand. Its periodic subsidence beneath and re-elevation above the waters of the Mediterranean demonstrate the unending cycle of subsidence and elevation that, for Lyell, prevails over the earth's surface, a cycle that refutes the claims of scriptural literalists and British catastrophists: the history of the Temple is designed to document the processes of geological change that, within an appropriate time scheme, will explain the submergence of continents and the elevation of the Alps and the Andes without recourse to catastrophic events or divine intervention.[26]

Before turning to the discussion of the Temple of Jupiter Serapis, Lyell observes, "Buildings and cities submerged for a time beneath seas or lakes, and covered with sedimentary deposits, must in some places, have been re-elevated to considerable heights above the level of the ocean" (1:448). This, in part, has been the fate of the ruin whose history Lyell sets out to reconstruct. All that can be seen of it now are three erect, but broken columns, the pavement that supports them, and the remnants of toppled columns of African breccia and granite. From these remains Lyell reconstructs the original edifice: "The original plan of the building could be traced distinctly; it was of a quadrangular form, seventy feet in diameter, and the roof had been supported by forty-six noble columns" (1:452–53). Yet, Lyell must acknowledge an unresolved issue: "Many antiquaries have entered into elaborate discussions as to the deity to which this edifice was consecrated; but [a] Signor Carelli . . . endeavours to show that all the religious edifices of Greece were of a form essentially different—that the building, therefore, could never have been a temple—that it corresponded to the public bathing-rooms at many of our watering-places" (1:453). The plan of the original building may be reconstructed, but its real nature and use may, perhaps, never be determined. All such remains become the subject of dispute; interpretations must rely on other evidence that the antiquarian or the archaeologist chooses to bring to bear upon the problem. For even if the building were a temple, so Carelli claims, "it could not have been dedicated to Serapis,—the worship of the Egyptian god being strictly prohibited at the time the building was in use, by the senate of Rome." Nonetheless, Lyell wryly defers to the antiquarians to designate "this valuable relic of antiquity by its generally received name" (1:453).

The dispute over the name of the structure and its use alludes to the heated debates over the status and meaning of fossils, whether they are to be seen as sports of nature or the remains of dead, perhaps extinct, organisms.[27] Yet, Lyell's archaeological analogy points to the elusive nature of all fragmentary evidence. He is in the process of transforming the Temple of Jupiter Serapis into an incomplete text to be deciphered and read as he turns "to consider the memorials of physical changes, inscribed on the three standing columns in most legible characters by the hand of nature" (1:453). He proceeds to interpret the hieroglyphic cavities produced in the columns by marine molluscs when the temple was partially submerged in the Mediterranean. From his readings of the various signs on the columns, Lyell provides a relative chronology of the subsidence and re-elevation of the coast on which the temple stands: "As the temple could not have been built originally at the bottom of the sea, it must have first sunk down below the waves, and afterwards have been elevated" (1:454). Just as marine fossils atop mountains attest to the origin of the mountains beneath the sea in ages long past, the history of the temple offers an index to the "alternate elevation and depression of the bed of the sea and the adjoining coast during the course of eighteen centuries" (1:455).

But a relative chronology cannot be satisfying. Lyell sets out to establish an absolute chronology for the subsidence and re-elevation of the Temple of Serapis in order to illustrate further his own vision of cyclical geologic time and the incremental workings of geologic change. He consults a variety of texts, the first of which is the temple itself: "It appears, that in the Atrium of the Temple of Serapis, inscriptions were found in which Septimus Severus and Marcus Aurelius record their labours in adorning it with precious marbles" (1:456). If the temple had originally reflected the influence of the Greek colonizers of Pompeii and Herculaneum, the Romans of "the third century of our era" had adapted it for their own uses, leaving their Latin inscriptions for later generations to read and to puzzle over. Lyell now invokes literal documents, some written "in the imperfect annals of the dark ages" (1:456), before the emergence of a truly historical awareness. Written perhaps in medieval Latin, they record events in 1198 and 1488 which may have caused the subsidence beneath the Mediterranean of the tract upon which the temple was built. Lyell then turns to letters written, presumably in Italian, by a Signor Falconi and a Pietro Giacomo di Toledo that record the 1538 eruption of Monte Nuovo and the re-elevation of the sunken coast and the appearance, so Falconi writes, of *"the newly discovered ruins"* (1:457) of the temple.

As he proceeds, Lyell necessarily relies on documents written in different centuries, presumably in two languages and perhaps in a variety of dialects; some of the documents—the letter by Pietro Giacomo di Toledo—do not even mention the temple itself. From these documents of varying reliability Lyell creates a context for the figurative text of the Temple of Serapis. The history of the temple—if temple it has ever been—remains a narrative, chronologically and causally ordered, about an edifice whose nature and uses throughout the centuries remain undetermined and, finally, beyond determination. No one more fully relishes the nature of his interpretations than Lyell himself. In concluding his discussion of the temple, Lyell adds, "In 1828 excavations were made below the marble pavement of the Temple of Serapis, and another costly pavement of mosaic was found, at the depth of five feet or more below the other. The existence of these two pavements at different levels seems clearly to imply some subsidence previously to all the changes already alluded to.... But to these and other circumstances bearing on the history of the Temple antecedently to the revolutions already explained, we shall not refer at present, trusting that future investigations will set them in a clearer light" (1:458–59). Such investigations might reveal yet another pavement beneath the two already discovered. The study of the temple may well produce an infinite regress, revealing pavements beneath pavements, figurative texts beneath figurative texts, transforming the Temple of Jupiter Serapis, years before the *Suspiria de Profundis* (1845), into a De Quinceian palimpsest, awaiting future revelations.[28]

The *Antiquity of Man* becomes Lyell's discussion of the Temple of Jupiter Serapis writ large. In its pages Dickens—and perhaps those readers of the celebratory "How Old Are We?" who turned to it—would have found, not only a model for William Whewell's palaetiological sciences, but for the various acts of detection that occur in *The Mystery of Edwin Drood*. In the *Principles,* marine fossils and cavities in the columns of the Temple of Serapis become figurative signs; in the *Antiquity of Man,* worked flints and other human artifacts also become figurative writing found in "the pages of the peaty record" (112) or in bone caves transformed figuratively into "sepulchral vault[s]" (192). They offer fragmentary evidence by which to reconstruct a human past before written records. Once again, Lyell encounters the inherent ambiguity of the evidence that he presents: for worked flints, "so irregular in form as to cause the unpractised eye to doubt whether they offer unmistakable evidence of design" (379), may be dismissed by those like Thomas Wright who are opposed to the idea of human prehistory. Even if someone were to accept such flints as human artifacts, there remains the vexing fact that, all too often, Lyell has found such relics only in association with the fossil remains of extinct elephants, rhinoceroses, and cave-bears. There are no human skeletal remains, intact or fragmentary, to demonstrate the coexistence of human beings with extinct mammals.

Inevitably, Lyell observes, "the thread of our inquiry into the history of the animate creation, as well as of man, is abruptly cut short" (206). Geology and archaeology lead into a maze: there is no narrative thread by which such historical disciplines may penetrate to an ever-receding center.[29] This is the difficulty with which any practitioner of a palaetiological science is faced. William Whewell recognizes that such disciplines that "travel back towards the origin, whether of inert things or of the works of man," treat events "as connected by the thread of time and causation" (*History* 3:488). But the figurative maze which Whewell and Lyell invoke may be transformed into the labyrinth of human motivation and consciousness. For Whewell the "palætiological sciences," dealing with "the past causes of events," lead to a "moral palaetiology," the study of the human in a larger sense. Such disciplines offer a "ready passage" from "the world of matter to the world of thought and feeling,—from things to man" (3:486–87).

The historical disciplines provide a ready passage into the maze that constitutes the heart of detective fiction, the labyrinth of human motivation and consciousness, to be negotiated by "the thread of time and causation." It is the maze into which the characters in *Edwin Drood* move when they attempt to reconstruct the events that have led up to the disappearance of Drood on the stormy Christmas morning when he has last been seen by Neville Landless. All of those concerned in the fate of Edwin Drood, John Jasper among them, become practitioners of a "moral palætiology," amateur detectives engaged in a geological and archaeological endeavor that will lead to those literal and figurative annals whose radical imperfection has been most tellingly evoked by Charles Darwin in the *Origin of Species* (1859). Self-consciously following Lyell's *Principles,* Darwin observes, "I look at the natural geological record, as a history of the world imperfectly kept, and written in a changing dialect; of this history we possess the last volume alone, relating only to two or three countries. Of this volume, only here and there a short chapter has been preserved; and of each page, only here and there a few lines. Each word of the slowly-changing language, in which the history is supposed to be written, being more or less different in the interrupted succession of chapters, may represent the apparently abruptly changed forms of life, entombed in our consecutive, but widely separated formations" (316). Darwin here turns to an extended philological figure of speech to emphasize the radical imperfection of the geological record upon which a history of species can be based in an attempt to fend off opponents to evolutionary hypotheses. In the same way Lyell stresses the incompleteness of the archaeological record in the *Antiquity of Man* with a full awareness of those reluctant to accept the fact of human prehistory.[30]

The elaborate figures of speech to which Lyell and Darwin resort suggest the problematic nature of any historical discipline working with fragmentary evidence from another time. They can return to us Mr. Grewgious contemplating the stars: for "none of us so much as know our letters in the stars yet—or seem likely to, in this state of existence—and few languages can be read until their alphabets are mastered" (160). The future remains closed to the characters in the world of *Edwin Drood;* for them, the past exists in the form of mutilated texts written in languages whose alphabets are difficult if not impossible to master. Living in an unspecified decade after Lyell's *Principles of Geology,* but prior to the publication of the *Origin of Species* and the *Antiquity of Man,* they become engaged in attempts to reconstruct the past, to arrive at a history that has been forged "among the mighty store of wonderful chains that are for ever forging, day and night, in the vast iron-works of time and circumstance" (118).[31]

Perhaps the one missing link in the chain exists in the form of the articles—the gold watch, the chain, and the stick-pin—that Septimus Crisparkle has found in Cloisterham Weir. The articles, especially the watch engraved with the initials, E.D., become figurative monuments from the realms of geology and archaeology by which to reconstruct a temporal chain of events. Like the geologist and the archaeologist, the would-be detectives of Cloisterham confront a fragmentary text, akin to the worked flints found in association with mammal bones, but unaccompanied by human remains: for Edwin Drood's personal effects do not lead to the recovery of his corpse. In spite of the efforts of John Jasper and others in dragging the river, nothing is to be found: "All the livelong day, the search went on; upon the river . . . ; upon the muddy and rushy shore. . . . Even at night, the river was specked with lanterns, and lurid with fires." The searchers explore "remote shingly causeways near the sea, and lonely points off which there [is] a race of water . . .; but no trace of Edwin Drood [revisits] the light of the sun" (136); he is lost in Edward Robinson's "long night of oblivion" (Robinson, introductory note, 1:ii).

The people of Cloisterham are met with the fact of negative evidence, unable to prove that Edwin Drood is actually dead, the victim of an accident or of foul play. Yet, with a parochialism that barely masks their racism, the townsfolk can be manipulated by John Jasper and led by Mr. Sapsea's distrust of Neville Landless's "Un-English complexion" (135) to turn their suspicions upon the young man so recently arrived from Ceylon, an island associated in the British imagination with their own version of the Indian subcontinent.[32] With John Jasper's help, Mr. Sapsea has created a context, one informed by the values of British imperialism, in which a collective attempt to reconstruct the past occurs. As detectives, the people of Cloisterham become practitioners, unwittingly, of William Whewell's moral palaetiology. They first try to establish a relative chronology and, then, an absolute one with causal implications. To account for what *must* be Drood's jewelry, the townspeople create a narrative akin to that offered by Lyell in his discussion of the Temple of Jupiter Serapis. They organize the various meetings between Drood and Neville Landless, beginning with the night on which the two have almost come to blows, into a coherent chronology. Ignorant of John Jasper's obsession with Rosa Bud, they postulate a beginning that is necessarily arbitrary and suspect, as elusive as the mosaic pavements of the Temple of Serapis.

Into their account, the characters weave Septimus Crisparkle's report of Landless's admiration for Rosa Bud, as well as the information about the broken engagement and Drood's plan, according to Rosa, to await the arrival of Mr. Grewgious before leaving Cloisterham. These events precede the Christmas Eve dinner attended by Jasper, Drood, and Landless that leads, if Landless is to be believed, to the midnight walk along the river and the parting of the two young men at the Minor Canon's door, after which Drood was to return to the Gate House rooms of Jasper. When the town jeweller identifies the engraved watch as "one he had wound and set for Edwin Drood, at twenty minutes past two" on Christmas Eve, any gaps in the narrative would seem to be filled: "It had run down, before being cast into the water; and it was the jeweller's positive opinion that it had never been re-wound. This would justify the hypothesis that the watch was taken from [Drood] not long after he left Mr. Jasper's house at midnight, in company with the last person seen with him, and that it had been thrown away after being retained some hours" (144). The incomplete chronology would now seem to be complete, without any missing links in the chain of events. It would seem no longer to be a relative chronology, but an absolute one, crucial events associated with specific times. As detectives the people of Cloisterham have engaged in "researches in which the object is, to ascend from the present state of things to a more ancient condition, from which the present is derived by intelligible causes " (Whewell 3:481).

But the hypothesis, like one in any of William Whewell's palaetiological sciences, remains at best an interpretation of fragmentary evidence, including Drood's personal effects and the negative fact that there is no corpse. The account has been worked out within the context of a provincial fear of the foreign Neville Landless who becomes the object of the prejudices of British imperialism: "Before coming to England he had caused to be whipped to death sundry 'Natives'—nomadic persons, encamping now in Asia, now in Africa, now in the West Indies, and now at the North Pole—vaguely supposed in Cloisterham always to be black, always of great virtue, always calling themselves Me, and every body else Massa and Missie" (143). The passage may well satirize a belief in the noble savage that is condescending and misconceived in a time before the Great Mutiny of 1857–58 and the Jamaican uprising of 1865. Yet it suggests how such parochialism may become transformed so that the apparently submissive native, "supposed . . . always to be black," may be demonized into a savage brute who must be controlled by agents of the Crown, for his own good.[33]

Such prejudices become pervasive; they obstruct other possible interpretations of the evidence that the townspeople consider. So, it is not clear how the good people of Cloisterham would respond to information that they might dismiss as untrue or unthinkable. They have produced an account satisfying to everyone but the laconic Mr. Grewgious and those remaining loyal to Neville Landless, including Mr. Crisparkle and Helena Landless. From the start Helena has understood John Jasper's obsession with Rosa Bud and the extremes to which it might lead. But she is from Ceylon, possessed of an awareness quite foreign to the world of Cloisterham. Grewgious, alone, has watched as Jasper has collapsed into "a heap of torn and miry clothes" (138) upon learning of the broken engagement after the futile search for Drood's body. Perhaps Grewgious connects that episode with the fact that the ring he has entrusted to Drood is not among the personal articles that Crisparkle has recovered from Cloisterham Weir. He may be able to use such a negative fact to create an alternative account of Drood's disappearance.

But, in its fragmentary form, *Edwin Drood* provides information that neither Helena Landless, Mr. Grewgious, nor anyone else currently in Cloisterham possesses, including the old codger, Mr. Datchery, who arrives in town to conduct yet another investigation into Drood's disappearance. No one knows of the chance meeting on Christmas Eve, before he joins Landless and Jasper, between Drood and the old woman who, only later, will be identified by Deputy as "Er. Royal Highness the Princess Puffer" (214). As he talks with the woman, Drood notes that "a curious film passes over her, . . . 'Like Jack that night!' " (126), during their earlier dinner at the Gate House when Jasper has confessed that he has "been taking opium for a pain—an agony—that sometimes overcomes [him]" (10). Drood learns that the old woman smokes opium too and that Ned is a "threatened name. A dangerous name" (127). Yet, he resolves to say nothing of the meeting to Jack, "who alone calls him Ned" (127), until the following day. Drood has the opportunity to play detective, to engage in an act of moral palaetiology. No one can know if he creates his own harrowing narrative out of the fragments of evidence that have been presented to him: a narrative by which to glimpse Jasper's complex motives and his ambiguous passion for Rosa Bud. He may well be prepared for his return to the Gate House after his midnight ramble along the river with Neville Landless. If Jasper awaits Drood's return, under the influence of the opium to which he turns for relief, no one can reconstruct the bizarre midnight struggle, if any, that may have occurred in Jasper's rooms.[34]

For the knowledge to which acts of detection in *The Mystery of Edwin Drood* drive is never of the future, but only of the past: in the universe of Charles Darwin's *Origin of Species* and of Charles Lyell's *Antiquity of Man,* such knowledge involves the reconstruction of events not witnessed, always based upon fragmentary and ambiguous evidence. In the course of the novel, Edwin Drood has had the opportunity to engage in a moral palaetiology, to play detective. But, so too has the reader who has been invited to scrutinize and to rewrite the generally accepted account arrived at by the people of Cloisterham. In this way *Edwin Drood* engages us in the act of constructing interpretations, internalizing the practices and the worldview of those historical disciplines that can be seen to culminate, to the dismay of Charles Lyell and defenders of Natural Theology, in the *Origin of Species.* Darwin demands of his readers an understanding of the nature of the historical imagination, as the unsigned, 1860 review of the *Origin* in *All the Year Round* recognizes. The reviewer knowingly repeats, almost to a word, a passage central to Darwin's long argument: "We are no longer to look at an organic being as a savage looks at a ship—as at something wholly beyond his comprehension: we are to regard *every production of nature as one which has had a history;* we are to contemplate every complex structure and instinct as the summing up of many contrivances, each useful to the possessor, nearly in the same way as when we look at any great mechanical invention as the summing up of the labour, the experience, the reason, and even the blunders of numerous workmen" ("Natural Selection" 299, emphasis added). With these words, as the reviewer understands, the world of William Paley's *Natural Theology* (1801) and of the argument from design has been swept aside: we are now all to be seen as creatures of history in a non-teleological universe.[35]

In this context, *Edwin Drood* offers a performance of how to read the world. The methodology suggested in the novel and the worldview implicit in it can be grasped through the reader's participation in an act of interpretation demanded by the disappearance of Edwin Drood and by the fragmentary status of a novel that Dickens did not live to complete. The narrative does not insidiously infect us with Gabriel Betteredge's detective fever, as D. A. Miller's brilliant reading of Wilkie Collins's *The Moonstone* in his *The Novel and the Police* (1988) would suggest. Nor does it exist to police consciousness, to impose the normative values of a Septimus Crisparkle, although the novel would seem to do so in identifying John Jasper as a "horrible wonder apart" that students of the criminal intellect "perpetually misread" (175). For Jasper, too, exists within an historical situation to which the novel points and through which he may be understood to some degree. Rather, *Edwin Drood* dramatizes a method of making sense out of apparently indecipherable events, of ordering into narrative form that which can disconcert, puzzle, even paralyze. In a universe no longer intelligible according to a literal reading of Scripture or to

William Paley's Natural Theology, the narratives of the historical disciplines initiate new paradigms in which many of us continue to find solace.[36]

V.

But, such solace is illusory, always to be tempered by an awareness of the stubborn ambiguity of the fragmentary evidence with which any practitioner of an historical discipline must work. Like the geological and archaeological monuments for which it comes to stand, the Temple of Jupiter Serapis invites and resists interpretation, always pointing to elusive mysteries at the center of history. In his reluctant movement toward an acceptance of Charles Darwin's transmutation theory, Charles Lyell returns in the *Antiquity of Man* to the tenuous nature of the evidence with which the geologist and the palaeontologist must work: "When we reflect, therefore, on the fractional state of the annals which are handed down to us, and how little even these have as yet been studied, we may wonder that so many geologists should attribute every gap in the past history of the organic world, to catastrophes and convulsions . . ., or to leaps made by the creational force from species to species" (449). Here Lyell renews his attack upon the catastrophists, even as he hints at a rejection of the doctrine of special creation. He knows that the fact of negative evidence cannot be used to refute Darwinism, even as it cannot be used to deny the reality of human antiquity.[37]

Yet, in the *Antiquity of Man* Lyell fails to follow the logic of his own argument and to heed his own warnings both about the misuse of the negative fact—the fossils to confirm the Darwinian hypothesis may well be found—and, more significantly, about the dangers of teleological speculations. He cites Darwin: "Progression . . . is not a necessary accompaniment of variation and natural selection. . . . One of the principle claims of Mr. Darwin's theory to acceptance is, that it enables us to dispense with the law of progression, as a necessary accompaniment of variation" (412). Nevertheless, Lyell concludes the *Antiquity of Man* by repeating Asa Gray's claim that the Doctrine of Variation and Natural Selection do not weaken the foundations of Natural Theology, as he engages in—a teleological speculation: "The supposed introduction into the earth at successive geological periods of life,—sensation,—instinct,—the intelligence of the higher mammalia, bordering on reason,—and lastly the improvable reason of Man himself, presents us with a picture of the ever-increasing dominion of mind over matter" (506).

Ironically, Lyell himself anticipates those who might yield to the "materialist tendency" (506) and see in such a progression, real or imagined, an inevitable development informed only by natural law. In 1863 he could foresee the evolutionary anthropology that, in the books of E. B. Tylor and James

Frazer, were to promote a purely naturalistic account upon a Comtean, rather than a Darwinian, vision of human development.[38] In *Primitive Culture* (1871) and in *The Golden Bough* (1890), Tylor and Frazer were to remain oblivious to Lyellian warnings about the inadequacy of the annals—geological, archaeological, or anthropological—upon which any historical discipline must rely. In their confident rationalism, Tylor and, later, Frazer ignored the possibility that progression is not a necessary accompaniment of historical change. In the opening chapter of *Primitive Culture,* Tylor establishes the assumptions that form the foundation of his classical evolutionism: "The condition of culture among the various societies of mankind, in so far as it is capable of being investigated on general principles, is a subject apt for the study of laws of human thought and action. On the one hand, the uniformity which so largely pervades civilization may be ascribed . . . to the uniform action of uniform causes: while on the other hand its various grades may be regarded as stages of development or evolution, each the outcome of previous history, and about to do its proper part in shaping the history of the future" (1:1). With his Eurocentric parochialism, Tylor—and Frazer after him—will create a hierarchy of societies, each representing a stage in the evolutionary progress toward the reign of the positive. It is with remarkable self-confidence that Tylor concludes *Primitive Culture:* "To impress men's minds with a doctrine of development, will lead them in all honour to their ancestors to continue the progressive work of past ages, to continue it the more vigorously because light has increased in the world, and where barbaric hordes groped blindly, cultured men can often move onward with clear view. It is a harsher, and at times even painful, office of ethnography to expose the remains of crude old culture which have passed into harmful superstition, and to mark these out for destruction. Yet this work . . . is not less urgently needful for the good of mankind. Thus, active at once in aiding progress and in removing hindrance, the science of culture is essentially a reformer's science" (2:453). E. B. Tylor, the Comtean positivist with a "materialist tendency," has returned to the teleology of an antiquarian like Thomas Wright who offers in *The Celt, the Roman, and the Saxon* a providential history of Britain. As the practitioner of yet another historical discipline, Tylor reconstructs the barbaric past, even as it supposedly persists into the present in the form of those savages and peasant folk whom he treats as living fossils. In doing so, Tylor relies on documentary evidence, often provided by the agents of the British Empire, that he fails to treat with appropriate skepticism.

Appearing in 1870, in the year before the publication of *Primitive Culture, The Mystery of Edwin Drood* repeats the warnings of Lyell's *Antiquity of Man,* hinting always at the unreliability of fragmentary evidence found in literal and figurative documents; it anticipates the dangers of a naive teleology, whether that of the pompous Mr. Sapsea or the real-life E. B. Tylor, ever in the grips of an unexamined provincialism and an undisguised racism. The fragmentary novel reveals that it is impossible to know the ends of history: it points to the conditional nature of all historical knowledge through an awareness of "the fractional state of the annals which are handed down to us" (Lyell, *Antiquity* 449) and of the perils of self-serving teleologies. In *Edwin Drood* the Nuns' House has become a Dickensian version of the Temple of Jupiter Serapis. With its legendary and elusive origins, it endures in and through time, accruing new uses and new meanings that never quite pass away, but that elude understanding. The novel *will* call attention to the limits of historical knowledge, to the "little Hall [in Staple Inn] with a little lantern in its roof: to what obstructive purposes devoted, and at whose expense, *this history* knoweth not" (88, emphasis added). The novel *will* remind us of the reality of chance and necessity, the unpredictable nature of the future, as Edwin Drood and Rosa Bud suddenly decide to end their engagement, to "change to brother and sister from this day forth" (114). At that moment Drood has in his possession the ring of Rosa's dead mother, entrusted to him by Mr. Grewgious. He decides not to tell Rosa of the ring and to return it to Grewgious upon his next visit to Cloisterham. Decisions that could not have been anticipated will produce consequences that are never to be known: for "among the mighty store of wonderful chains that are for ever forging, day and night, in the vast iron-works of time and circumstance, there was one chain forged in the moment of that small conclusion, riveted to the foundations of heaven and earth, and gifted with invincible force to hold and drag" (118).

Charles Dickens was himself to become caught up in an unpredictable chain of events, "for ever forging, day and night, in the vast iron-works of time and circumstance." On the evening of June 8, 1870, having "put a flourish to the end of the last chapter of the sixth number of *The Mystery of Edwin Drood,* exactly the halfway point of the novel" (Kaplan, *Dickens* 554), he was stricken at dinner and collapsed, unconscious. With his death on the following morning, he bequeathed to us the fragmentary *Edwin Drood,* the testament to the "fractured state of the annals which are handed down to us" (Lyell, *Antiquity* 449). Akin to fossil remains, to worked flints, and to ruined edifices inscribed in foreign characters that may defy translation, the novel dramatizes the difficulties—epistemological and narratological—upon which it meditates. Whatever has happened to Edwin Drood in the early hours of that Christmas morning—whether he has been murdered, suffered some fatal or deeply injurious accident, or spirited himself away—remains beyond our capacity to know. His disappearance poses an archaeological mystery as puzzling as that posed by the Temple of Jupiter Serapis or by Cloisterham itself, that ancient city "so abounding in vestiges of monastic graves," a city in which "fragments of old wall, saint's chapel, chapter-house, convent, and monastery, have got incongruously and obstructively built into many of its houses and gardens'' (14).

The fragmentary status of *Edwin Drood,* accidental as it is, forever obscures whatever design Dickens may have had for its ending. Nevertheless, like Charles Lyell's provocative discussion of the Temple of Jupiter Serapis, the novel comments on those seemingly completed edifices such as *Bleak House* and *Little Dorrit* to which reconstructions of the past become so central. It reminds us that assumptions about their coherence of design and meaning must remain tentative, merely speculations about the meanings of texts whose ambiguous status, like that of the Temple of Serapis, defies our attempts to interpret them. Any interpretation of a *Bleak House* or of a *Little Dorrit* remains as inconclusive as those attempts to resolve the mystery of Edwin Drood's disappearance. It is important to remember that *Bleak House* points to its own fragmentary status in the dash with which Esther Summerson's narrative closes without ending; *Little Dorrit* comes to its apparent close with a central act of reconstruction incomplete, for Arthur Clennam marries Amy Dorrit, still in ignorance of his own past. The fragmentary *Edwin Drood* attests to the purely conjectural nature of interpretation, another palaetiological discipline that may lead, perhaps inevitably, to an infinite regress.

Each of us who reads *The Mystery of Edwin Drood* becomes a hypothetical visitor to a figurative Cloisterham, now an archaeological curiosity like "the dead and buried cities that it is one of the labours of the living in our day to disentomb" (473), that offers us—"News from the Dead." Like Belzoni's Abu-Simbel, Layard's Nimrud, and Dickens's Rome, with the "hieroglyphic-covered obelisk" in the square fronting a "haughty church" (*Pictures* 397), Cloisterham will challenge any would-be excavator. The buildings of Edwin Drood's time may no longer stand in their entirety. Perhaps the monument erected by the honorable Mr. Sapsea to the memory of a wife wise and humble enough to have married him is no longer intact; it may be in fragments, its inscriptions defaced by time, barely discernible, and written in an alphabet and a grammar of a dead language. The inscriptions become enigmatic signs for a traveler to contemplate, someone not unlike the inquisitive Mr. Davis of *Pictures from Italy.* Dickens's fellow Englishman had "a slow curiosity constantly devouring him, which prompted him to do extraordinary things, such as taking the covers off urns in tombs, and looking in at the ashes as if they were pickles—and tracing out inscriptions with the ferrule of his umbrella, and saying, with intense thoughtfulness, 'Here's a B you see, and there's a R, and this is the way it goes on in; is it?'' ' (378).

Poking at inscriptions he can barely decipher, disappearing into sepulchres, Mr. Davis serves as an apt warning to anyone who would definitively resolve the mysteries posed by *Edwin Drood* and those fractured annals, literal and figurative, left to us by the hand of time. We should never forget the comic anxiety of Mrs. Davis and her party that Mr. Davis might well become lost in the labyrinth of his antiquarian preoccupations: "This caused them to scream for him, in the strangest places, and at the most improper seasons. And when he came, slowly emerging out of some sepulchre or other, like a peaceful Ghoul, saying 'Here I am!' Mrs. Davis invariably replied, 'You'll be buried alive in a foreign country, Davis, and it's no use trying to prevent you!' " (378). Fair warning to all practitioners of those historical disciplines to which a detective novel like the fragmentary *Edwin Drood* introduces us, for the past is, indeed, a foreign country where "they do things differently."[39]

NOTES

1. For the account book of *All the Year Round* and, where available, the names of the authors of unsigned articles, see Oppenlander. For a discussion of the history and publication of *The Mystery of Edwin Drood,* see Cardwell xiii–1.
2. For discussions of these issues, see Lawrence Frank, "*Bleak House,* the Nebular Hypothesis, and a Crisis in Narrative"; and "*Pictures from Italy*: Dickens, Rome, and the Eternal City of the Mind."
3. For a recent discussion of the rise of the novel in England, see McKeon 25–128; for discussions of detective fiction as a genre, see Ousby; and Todorov 42–52.
4. My reading of *Edwin Drood* is indebted throughout to Philippa Levine, particularly, 70–100; and Van Riper, particularly 74–183. For discussions of the dissolution of the myth of Adam, see Greene 221–339; and Rossi 267–70.
5. For the dating of the events in *Edwin Drood,* see Jacobson 83.
6. For a discussion of Richard Chenevix Trench, see Aarsleff 230–47.
7. In *The Amateur and the Professional* Philippa Levine quotes Richard Mercer Dorson's claim in *British Folklorists* that Wright "perfectly [typifies] the early Victorian antiquary-scholar" (14). Although there is no evidence that Dickens owned *The Celt, the Roman, and the Saxon,* he did have in his library copies of three other works by Wright. See Stonehouse 120.
8. For a discussion of Rochester and the books to which Dickens may have turned for its history, see Jacobson 49–50.
9. See Cardwell xiii–xiv; and Jacobson 126–27.
10. For discussions of these issues, see Schnapp 275–314; and Van Riper 117–43, 184–221.
11. For discussions of the idea of progress, see Bowler; and Levine, *Amateur* 70–100.
12. See Schnapp, 286, 314.
13. For a discussion of Staple Inn and the inscription, see Jacobson 108–10.
14. For the relevance of this passage to the discipline of intellectual history, see LaCapra 23–71.
15. For discussions of imperialism in general and of British imperialism in the nineteenth century, see Barrell; Brantlinger; Said, *Culture* and *Orientalism;* and Suleri.

16. For discussions of Belzoni's life, see Wills and Hoare 548–52; and Mayes; for Schliemann's visit to Abu-Simbel, see Traill 267–83.

17. For discussions of the decipherment of the Rosetta stone and the controversy involving Thomas Young and Champollion, see Irwin; Iverson; and Wood.

18. For an account of excavations in Mesopotamia, see Lloyd.

19. For an account of Layard's life, see Waterfield; for discussions of the relationship between Layard and Dickens, see Cotsell; Kaplan, *Dickens* 296, 330–31; and Metz.

20. Dickens owned several of Layard's works: see Stonehouse 71.

21. See Rossi 85–101.

22. For discussions of the establishment of human prehistory, see Daniel; Daniel and Renfrew; Grayson; and Van Riper.

23. For three classic accounts of the subversion of a prevailing common sense, see Gillispie; Greene; and Rossi.

24. Throughout I shall be quoting from the third edition of the *Antiquity of Man* (1863), the edition Dickens himself owned: see Stonehouse 75.

25. See Lyell, *Principles* 3:1–2:"As the first [geological] theorists possessed but a scanty acquaintance with the present economy of the animate and inanimate world, and the vicissitudes to which these are subject, we find them in the situation of novices, who attempt to read a history written in a foreign language, doubting about the meaning of the most ordinary terms; disputing, for example, whether a shell was really a shell."

26. For discussions of geology in nineteenth-century Britain, see Gould; Laudan; Porter; Rupke; and Wilson.

27. For a discussion of the argument over the status of fossils throughout several centuries, see Rudwick.

28. My interpretation of Lyell's discussion of the Temple of Jupiter Serapis and of *Edwin Drood* has throughout been influenced by recent discussions of archaeology: see, especially, Hodder.

29. See Miller, *Ariadne's Thread* 1–27.

30. Darwin's *Origin of Species* was reviewed in *All the Year Round* in two articles: see "Species," *All the Year Round* 2 June 1860:174–78; and "Natural Selection," *All the Year Round* 7 July 1860:293–99. For discussions of Darwin and Victorian fiction, see Beer; and Levine, *Darwin* 119–76. For a relevant discussion of Dickens and detective fiction, see Hutter.

31. For speculations on the setting and time of the events in *Edwin Drood,* see Jacobson 49–50, 83, and 149.

32. For relevant discussions of nineteenth-century British attitudes toward India and the East, see Brantlinger; Frank, "Dreaming the Medusa"; Said, *Culture* and *Orientalism;* and Suleri.

33. See Brantlinger; and Jacobson 137.

34. For representative psychological readings of *Edwin Drood,* see Frank, *Dickens* 187–237; Herst; Kaplan, *Mesmerism;* Sedgwick 161–200; and Thomas 219–37.

35. See Hutter 136–37; "As we move from *Bleak House* to *The Mystery of Edwin Drood,* the detective function becomes yet more complex because Dickens' view of writing and of perception itself becomes more sophisticated. The novelist is

now less omniscient. . . . Dickens' novels of the 1860s, like those of Wilkie Collins, are particularly concerned with questions of epistemology: . . . the explication of a mystery becomes less important than the *process* of perception and solution.''
36. At this point I am clearly responding to Foucault, *Discipline and Punish,* and to D. A. Miller, *The Novel and the Police.* I am suggesting that fiction, particularly detective fiction, can introduce new ways of making the universe intelligible and that ''culture'' may not be as hegemonic as Foucault and Miller suggest. I am using a variety of works to inform my argument: se Bakhtin; Iser; Kuhn; and McKeon 25–128. For a recent critique of Foucault, see Barrish.
37. For discussions of these issues, see Gillespie 1–40; Rudwick 164–17; and Van Riper 117–83.
38. For discussions of Victorian anthropology in its various forms, see Stocking, *Victorian Anthropology* and *After Tylor.*
39. I am responding to Lowenthal xvi and to the title of his book that alludes to L. P. Hartley's *The Go-Between.* For a recent discussion of the relationship of the present to the past, see Kincaid 3–58.

WORKS CITED

Aarsleff, Hans. *The Study of Language in England, 1780–1860.* Princeton: Princeton UP, 1967.

Bakhtin, M. M. *The Dialogic Imagination: Four Essays.* Trans. Caryl Emerson and Michael Holquist. Ed. Michael Holquist. University of Texas Press Slavic Ser. 1. Austin: U of Texas P, 1981.

Barrell, John. *The Infection of Thomas De Quincey: A Psychopathology of Imperialism.* New Haven: Yale UP, 1991.

Barrish, Phillip. ''Accumulating Variation: Darwin's *On the Origin of Species* and Contemporary Literary and Cultural Theory.'' *Victorian Studies* 34 (1991): 431–53.

Beer, Gillian. *Darwin's Plots: Evolutionary Narrative in Darwin, George Eliot and Nineteenth-Century Fiction.* London: Routledge and Kegan Paul, 1983.

Belzoni, G[iovanni Battista]. *Narrative of the Operations and Recent Discoveries within the Pyramids, Temples, Tombs, and Excavations in Egypt and Nubia; and of a Journey to the Coast of the Red Sea, in Search of the Ancient Berenice; and Another to the Oasis of Jupiter Ammon.* London, 1820.

Bowler, Peter, J. *Fossils and Progress: Paleontology and the Idea of Progressive Evolution in the Nineteenth Century.* New York: Science History Publications, 1976.

Brantlinger, Patrick. *Rule of Darkness: British Literature and Imperialism, 1830–1914.* Ithaca: Cornell UP, 1988.

Cardwell, Margaret. Introduction. *The Mystery of Edwin Drood.* By Charles Dickens. Oxford: Clarendon, 1972. xiii–1.

Charles Dickens' Book of Memoranda: A Photographic and Typographic Facsimile of the Notebook Begun in January 1855. Ed. Fred Kaplan. New York: New York Public Library, 1981.

Collins, Wilkie. *The Moonstone.* Ed. J. I. M. Stewart. London: Penguin, 1987.

Cotsell, Michael. "Politics and Peeling Frescoes: Layard of Nineveh and *Little Dorrit.*" *Dickens Studies Annual: Essays on Victorian Fiction.* Ed. Michael Timko, Fred Kaplan, and Edward Guiliano 15 (1986): 181–200.

Daniel, Glyn. *A Hundred and Fifty Years of Archaeology.* Cambridge: Harvard UP, 1976.

Daniel, Glyn and Colin Renfrew. *The Idea of Prehistory.* 2nd ed. Edinburgh: Edinburgh UP, 1988.

Darwin, Charles. *The Origin of Species by Means of Natural Selection or the Preservation of Favoured Races in the Struggle for Life.* Ed. J. W. Barrow. New York: Penguin, 1985.

De Quincey, Thomas. *Confessions of an English Opium-Eater. The Collected Writings of Thomas De Quincey.* Ed. David Masson. Vol. 3. London, 1897. 209–449.

———. *Suspiria De Profundis. The Collected Writings of Thomas De Quincey.* Ed. David Masson. Vol. 13. London, 1897. 331–69.

Dickens, Charles. *American Notes and Pictures from Italy.* Oxford Illustrated Dickens. Oxford: Oxford UP, 1987.

———. *Bleak House.* Ed. George Ford and Sylvère Monod. New York: Norton, 1977.

———. *Little Dorrit.* Ed. Harvey Peter Sucksmith. Clarendon Dickens. Oxford: Clarendon, 1979.

———. *The Mystery of Edwin Drood.* Ed. Margaret Cardwell. Clarendon Dickens. Oxford: Clarendon, 1972.

Dorson, Richard Mercer. *The British Folklorists: A History.* Chicago: U of Chicago P, 1968.

Foucault, Michel. *Discipline and Punish: The Birth of the Prison.* Trans. Alan Sheridan. New York: Pantheon, 1977.

Frank, Lawrence. *Charles Dickens and the Romantic Self.* Lincoln: U of Nebraska P, 1984.

———. "*Bleak House,* the Nebular Hypothesis, and a Crisis in Narrative." Society for Literature and Science Annual Meeting. Radisson Bel-Air Summit Hotel, Los Angeles.3 Nov. 1995.

———. "Dreaming the Medusa: Imperialism, Primitivism, and Sexuality in Arthur Conan Doyle's *The Sign of Four.*" *Signs: Journal of Women in Culture and Society* 22.1 (1996): 52–85.

———. "*Pictures from Italy:* Dickens, Rome, and the Eternal City of the Mind." *Il Confronto Letterario* 14 (1997):239–55.

Frazer, James G. *The Golden Bough: A Study in Comparative Religion.* 2 vols. 1890. Rpt. as *The Golden Bough: The Roots of Religion and Folklore.* 2 vols. New York: Avenel, 1981.

Gillespie, Neal C. *Charles Darwin and the Problem of Creation.* Chicago: U of Chicago P, 1979.

Gillispie, Charles Coulston. *Genesis and Geology: A Study in the Relations of Scientific Thought, Natural Theology, and Social Opinion in Great Britain, 1790–1850.* Cambridge: Harvard UP, 1951.

Gould, Stephen Jay. *Time's Arrow, Time's Cycle: Myth and Metaphor in the Discovery of Geological Time.* Cambridge: Harvard UP, 1987.

Grayson, Donald K. *The Establishment of Human History.* New York: Academic, 1983.

Greene, John C. *The Death of Adam: Evolution and its Impact on Western Thought.* Ames: Iowa State UP, 1959.

Hartley, L. P. *The Go-Between.* London: Hamish Hamilton, 1953.

Herst, Beth F. *The Dickens Hero: Selfhood and Alienation in the Dickens World.* New York: St. Martin's, 1990.

Hodder, Ian. *Reading the Past: Current Approaches to Interpretation in Archaeology.* New York: Cambridge UP, 1986.

"How Old Are We?" *All the Year Round* 7 Mar. 1863:32–37.

Hutter, Albert D. "Dismemberment and Articulation in *Our Mutual Friend.*" *Dickens Studies Annual: Essays on Victorian Fiction.* Ed. Michael Timko, Fred Kaplan, and Edward Guiliano 11 (1983): 135–75.

Irwin, John T. *American Hieroglyphics: The Symbol of the Egyptian Hieroglyphics in the American Renaissance.* New Haven: Yale UP, 1980.

Iser, Wolfgang. *The Implied Reader: Patterns of Communication in Prose Fiction from Bunyan to Beckett.* Baltimore: Johns Hopkins UP, 1974.

Iversen, Erik. *The Myth of Egypt and Its Hieroglyphics in European Tradition.* Copenhagen: Gec Gad, 1961.

Jacobson, Wendy S. *The Companion to* The Mystery of Edwin Drood. London: Allen and Unwin, 1986.

Kaplan, Fred. *Dickens: A Biography.* New York: William Morrow, 1988.

————. *Dickens and Mesmerism. The Hidden Springs of Fiction.* Princeton: Princeton UP, 1975.

Kincaid, James R. *Child-Loving: The Erotic Child and Victorian Culture.* New York: Routledge, 1992.

Kuhn, Thomas S. *The Structure of Scientific Revolutions.* 2nd ed. Chicago: U of Chicago P, 1970.

LaCapra, Dominick. *Rethinking Intellectual History: Texts, Contexts, Language.* Ithaca: Cornell UP, 1983.

"Latest News from the Dead." *All the Year Round* 11 July 1863:473–76.

Laudan, Rachel. *From Mineralogy to Geology: The Foundations of a Science, 1650–1830.* Chicago: U of Chicago P, 1987.

Layard, Austen Henry. *Nineveh and its Remains: With an Account of a Visit to the Chaldæan Christians of Kurdistan, and the Yezidis, or Devil-Worshippers; and an Enquiry into the Manners and Arts of the Ancient Assyrians.* 2 vols. London, 1849.

————. *Popular Account of Discoveries at Nineveh.* New York, 1854.

Levine, George. *Darwin and the Novelists: Patterns of Science in Victorian Fiction.* Cambridge: Harvard UP, 1988.

Levine, Philippa. *The Amateur and the Professional: Antiquarians, Historians and Archaeologists in Victorian England, 1838–1886.* Cambridge: Cambridge UP, 1986.

Lloyd, Seton. *Foundations in the Dust: The Story of Mesopotamian Exploration.* New York: Thames and Hudson, 1980.

Lowenthal, David. *The Past is a Foreign Country.* Cambridge: Cambridge UP, 1985.

[Lubbock, John], Lord Avebury. *Prehistoric Times: As Illustrated by Ancient Remains and the Manners and Customs of Modern Savages.* 7th ed. London: Williams and Norgate, 1913.

Lyell, Charles. *The Geological Evidences of the Antiquity of Man.* 3rd ed. London, 1863.

————. *Principles of Geology.* 3 vols. Chicago: U of Chicago P, 1990–91. Rpt. of *Principles of Geology, Being an Attempt to Explain the Former Changes of the Earth's Surface, by Reference to Causes Now in Operation.* 3 vols. 1830–33.

Mayes, Stanley. *The Great Belzoni.* London: Putnam, 1959.

McKeon, Michael. *The Origins of the English Novel, 1600–1740.* Baltimore: Johns Hopkins UP, 1987.

Metz, Nancy Aycock. "Little Dorrit's London: Babylon Revisited." *Victorian Studies* 33 (1990): 465–86.

Miller, D. A. *The Novel and the Police.* Berkeley: U of California P, 1988.

Miller, J. Hillis. *Ariadne's Thread: Story Lines.* New Haven: Yale UP, 1992.

"Natural Selection." *All the Year Round.* 7 July 1860:293–99.

Oppenlander, Ellen Ann. *Dickens' All the Year Round: Descriptive Index and Contributor List.* Troy, NY: Whitson, 1984.

Ousby, Ian. *Bloodhounds of Heaven: The Detective in English Fiction from Godwin to Doyle.* Cambridge: Harvard UP, 1976.

Paley, William. *Natural Theology; or Evidences of the Existence and Attributes of the Deity. Collected from the Appearances of Nature.* 3rd ed. London, 1803.

Porter, Roy. *The Making of Geology: Earth Science in Britain, 1660–1815.* New York: Cambridge UP, 1977.

Robinson, Edward. Introductory Note. *Nineveh and its Remains: With an Account of a Visit to the Chaldæan Christians of Kurdistan, and the Yezidis, or Devil-Worshippers; and an Inquiry into the Manners and Arts of the Ancient Assyrians.* By Austen Henry Layard. Vol. 1. New York, 1849. i–viii.

Rossi, Paolo. *The Dark Abyss of Time: The History of the Earth and the History of Nations from Hooke to Vico.* Trans. Lydia G. Cochrane. Chicago: U of Chicago P, 1984.

Rudwick, Martin J. S. *The Meaning of Fossils: Episodes in the History of Palaeontology.* 2nd ed. Chicago: U of Chicago P, 1985.

Rupke, Nicolaas A. *The Great Chain of History: William Buckland and the English School of Geology (1814–1849).* Oxford: Clarendon, 1983.

Said, Edward W. *Culture and Imperialism.* New York: Knopf, 1993.

———. *Orientalism.* New York: Pantheon, 1978.

Schnapp, Alain. *The Discovery of the Past.* Trans. Ian Kinnes and Gillian Varndell. New York: Harry N. Abrams, 1997.

Sedgwick, Eve Kosofsky. *Between Men: English Literature and Male Homosocial Desire.* New York: Columbia UP, 1985.

"Species." *All the Year Round* 2 June 1860:174–78.

Stocking, George W., Jr. *After Tylor: British Social Anthropology, 1888–1951.* Madison: U of Wisconsin P, 1995.

———. *Victorian Anthropology.* New York: Free Press, 1987.

Stonehouse, J. H., ed. *Catalogue of the Library of Charles Dickens and Catalogue of the Library of W. M. Thackeray.* London: Picadilly Fountain Press, 1935.

Suleri, Sara. *The Rhetoric of English India.* Chicago: U of Chicago P, 1992.

Thomas, Ronald R. *Dreams of Authority: Freud and the Fictions of the Unconscious.* Ithaca: Cornell UP, 1990.

Todorov, Tzvetan. ''The Typology of Detective Fiction. *The Poetics of Prose.*'' Trans. Richard Howard. Ithaca: Cornell UP, 1977. 42–52.

Traill, David A. *Schliemann of Troy: Treasure and Deceit.* New York: St. Martin's, 1995.

Trench, Richard Chenevix. *On the Study of Words: Lectures Addressed (Originally) to the Pupils of the Diocesan Training-School, Winchester.* 9th ed. New York, 1863.

Tylor, Edward B. *Primitive Culture: Researches into the Development of Mythology, Philosophy, Religion, Language, Art, and Custom.* 7th ed. 2 vols. New York: Brentano's, 1924.

Van Riper, A. Bowdoin. *Men among the Mammoths: Victorian Science and the Discovery of Human Prehistory.* Chicago: U of Chicago P, 1993.

Waterfield, Gordon. *Layard of Nineveh.* London: John Murray, 1963.

Wellbeloved, Charles. *Eburacum: or York Under the Romans.* York, Eng., 1842.

Whewell, William. *History of the Inductive Sciences, from the Earliest to Present Times.* 3 vols. London, 1837.

[Wills, W. H. and Mrs. Hoare]. ''The Story of Giovanni Belzoni.'' *Household Words* 1 Mar. 1851:548–52.

Wilson, Leonard G. *Charles Lyell: The Years to 1841:The Revolution in Geology.* New Haven: Yale UP, 1972.

Wood, Alexander. *Thomas Young, Natural Philosopher: 1773–1829.* Cambridge: Cambridge UP, 1954.

Wright, Thomas. *The Celt, the Roman, and the Saxon: A History of the Early Inhabitants of Britain, down to the Conversion of the Anglo-Saxons to Christianity.* 2nd ed. London, 1861.

Copy-Book Morals: *The Woman in White* and Publishing History

Sundeep Bisla

The exchange of the two women in white in Wilkie Collins's narrative may be regarded as a covert representation of Collins's anxieties about the piracy of his works by mid-nineteenth-century American publishers. Collins appears to be lobbying against the lack of "copy-book morals" (here read literally, as a lack of publishing morals) evident in the contemporary American custom of reprinting English books. One failing in D. A. Miller's analysis of Collins's "novel" is the wish to read the exchange of narratorial control effected by Count Fosco's seizing and inscribing himself into Marian Halcombe's diary as solely a figurative "raping" of her rather than as also what, on a literal level, it is—the theft of a text. In addition, the many instances of "closeting" evident in Collins's narrative might not only be thematizing those sensational closeting of gender/genre instabilities that interest Miller but they might also, on a more mundane level, be simply representing the closeting of texts.

> "What an extraordinary people you are!" cried Martin. "Are Mr. Chollop and the class he represents, an Institution here?... Are bloody duels, brutal combats, savage assaults, shootings down and stabbing in the streets, your Institutions! Why, I shall hear next, that Dishonour and Fraud are among the Institutions of the Great Republic!"
>
> The moment the words passed his lips, the Honourable Elijah Pogram looked round again.

"This morbid hatred of our Institutions," he observed,
"is quite a study for the psychological observer."
—*Martin Chuzzlewit*

I

Nothing more boring—or, indeed unmarketable, it would seem (from John Sutherland's experienced perspective[1])—than inquiries into the quotidian life of books. In *The Times Literary Supplement* he concludes a review—entitled with suggestive ambiguity "What Sells Best, and Why"—of Lee Erickson's latest effort in this realm of theoretical apostasy with a question which goes to the heart of many a literary-critical project: what sells best, and best *sells,* in the market of *literary* studies. The answer would seem to be, anything *but* publishing history.

> Like other good research in the field, *The Economy of Literary Form* raises the question, is "publishing history" a viable subject in its own right? Can it do more than supply useful prefaces to great literary works . . . or great literary figures? . . . There are, in the 1990s, no departments of publishing history and few job opportunities. The PhD student who wants to eat would be better advised to stick to literary theory or gender studies.   ("What Sells" 27)

Job opportunities being limited at all levels of the Anglo-American literary studies market, and space for new theoretical approaches being necessarily more so, the question posed by a somewhat dispirited Sutherland is, understandably, not just one of academic, but indeed of physical, survival. The irony in his words rests in the paradox that while publishing history, the study of the market forces affecting fiction, has not yet reached its full potential as itself a saleable commodity at the institutional level, part of the reason for that lag appears to be that "the market" is more than ever coercively controlling—disciplining and punishing those who need it perhaps?—the output of literary scholars, ironically ensuring there's not a publishing historian around just at the moment you really need one.

However, leaving aside this meta-disciplinarity, a matter for a different plane of investigation—for a different genre, if not indeed generation—we might instead hazard a more tangential response to Sutherland's "left-handed" challenge to academia to find room where there appears to be ever-pressingly less and less room. Rather than simply tacitly adopting his dispirited outlook upon the viability of the practice of "publishing history" per se, as the gloom generally surrounding the job market invites us to do,[2] we might, quite unfashionably, assert that publishing history, in a general sense, is (to a certain extent—admittedly, the nature and "shape" of that extent being of no small significance) what our more interesting literary and gender theorists have been *doing* all along. It is no coincidence, not just one obsession among others, that Jacques Derrida continues to come back in his writings to the questions of the perils of "dissemination" and the mechanics of copyright.[3] Consider as one example this quotation from *"La parole soufflée"* on the dangers inherent in speaking or writing: "Artaud knew that all speech fallen from the body . . . immediately becomes stolen speech. . . . Theft is always the theft of speech or text, of a trace. . . . But the theft of speech is not a theft among others; it is confused with the very possibility of theft, defining the fundamental structure of theft" (*Writing* 175). In a similar manner, and for a similar reason, it would seem theft of *meaning* "defines" the fundamental structure of *language*; hence, the impossibility of a project such as J. L. Austin's repeated attempts at making a rigorous distinction between performatives and constatives in his lectures on *How to Do Things with Words*.[4]

This evocation of a possible consanguinity between "literary theory" and "publishing history," a point of course inviting a great deal more elaboration, will however have to remain a cursory one, as at this point this essay, having other concerns in mind, must leave the question to one side—opening itself up undoubtedly to a return of (how appropriate) "the repeatable," of iterability[5]—turning instead now to consider that other path along Sutherland's road to academic success and survival, the similarities and dissimilarities between "publishing history" and "gender studies." However, to accept unthinkingly these two entities as pointedly distinct, as Sutherland's naming them with two different labels would seem to suggest, would be to deny too many other possibilities: for example, that one might *enable* the other, or that both might be nothing at all, that they might exist nowhere but in the mind of John Sutherland. It would be precipitately to give in to a fatally estranging insularity of perspective akin to that isolationism of thought which had so concerned Dickens as a possible natural outgrowth of mid-nineteenth-century nationalisms:

> It is more or less the habit of ever country—more or less commendable in every case—to exalt itself and its institutions above every other country, and to be vain-glorious. . . . Out of the particularities thus engendered and maintained, there has arisen a great deal of patriotism, and a great deal of public spirit. On the other hand, it is of paramount importance to every nation that its boastfulness should not generate prejudice, conventionality, and a cherishing of unreasonable ways of acting and thinking, which . . . are ridiculous or wrong.
>
> ("Insularities" 1)

Dickens goes on to associate this particular state of mind with the peculiar geographic situation of England: "We English people, owing in a great degree to our insular position . . . have been in particular danger of contracting habits which we will call for our present purpose, Insularities'' (1). Today, in our ever-increasingly "globalizing" world, it is even more of a scandal than it might have been for Dickens & Co. when, consummate cosmopolites that we are, we are found out to have been unfoundedly perpetuating similar "insularities." Understandably, then, in my attempt at replying to Sutherland, I find myself unable to accept the terms of his argument without somewhat skewing beforehand the inquiry to come. Therefore, I must make clear here that the following will be a comparison of two *interpretations*—and at that not at all necessarily distinct ones—before, if this is possible, any attempt has been made to subsume them within the disarticulative ranks of specific *disciplines*.

At this point, a return of Derrida would seem ever more improbable (or, to adopt a Freudian outlook, ever more *probable*) given the fact that the critic I will be turning to now is one who makes quite clear his discontent with those, by 1988 when his book was published, all too prevalent and all too predictable readings undercutting and ignoring—unjustifiably blanching through an ill-advised leeching-procedure it would seem—examples of undeniably rubicund and culturally efficacious certainties, carceral and otherwise, which might have been operative within English Victorian culture—those predictable interpretations in our critic's opinion being ones which instead too uncritically make recourse to an at-one-time popular, routinized strategy of highlighting "the disseminal operations of language, narrative, or desire" (Miller, *Novel* xi). I will be considering, with respect to Collins studies, D. A. Miller's revolutionarily revitalizing essay *"Cage aux folles:* Sensation and Gender in Wilkie Collins's *The Woman in White,''*[6] an essay which, while it may be judged by many an exemplary effort in "gender studies," would by no one (least of all John Sutherland, at least at this moment) be mistaken for a contribution to "publishing history." In (at this point only potential) counterpoint, I will be offering an interpretation of my own which, while it might look at first like "publishing history,''[7] will hopefully not have grown so begrudgingly enamoured of that badge of honor, of its membership amid the ranks of the academically under-appreciated, as to be unable to take account of the debts it nevertheless still owes to those who practice more successful—and perhaps more successfully—"disciplines."

Our skepticism with regard to pre-set distinctions will also apply to our analysis of Miller's essay. Far from allowing him to reside content in his sureties and certainties—perhaps most of all in his surety and certainty to be not practicing deconstruction, to have left Derrida and all that quite safely far behind—that is, far from allowing his distinctions and distinctiveness to solidify into the appearance of a truth which we dare not afterwards question, we will, if we are to get anywhere, need to treat those assertions with a fair degree of skepticism. The first of Miller's proposals which we will have to question will be his fundamental one: that the narrative of *The Woman in White* propagates a general and unconscious hermeticism and carcerality. In order to assess whether Miller's self-professed gamble with Foucault's panopticism in *The Novel and the Police* pays off, we will have to look at that point in Collins's narrative where, according to Miller, this carcerality most explicitly comes to the forefront, that scene in which Count Fosco reads Marian Halcombe's diary after she has fallen into a fever-heralding swoon. Miller finds this scene to be, indeed, seems to catch it in the act of being, an incarceration—to be more precise, a *double* incarceration. We will have to ask if it truly is such, if it truly is a scene effectively concluding the novel's subversiveness with its introduction of a violently corrective policing—as an enthusiastically applied, perhaps over-enthusiastically applied,[8] Foucauldianism might find—or whether it is perhaps the point when the narrative is at its most *anti*-carceral. Indeed, we will have to ask if this scene is not instead the point when the narrative fissures at its center opening up as a result of having represented allegorically the theft of its book form, thus piercing through from within and thereby causing to rupture—or being pierced through from without and thereby allowing to rupture—any would-be hermetic seal which had been on the point of closing as it becomes an allegory of its own reading gone wrong, as it gives in to the fundamental uncontrollability of language, the trace, which always already had been threatening it.

While *The Woman in White* (1860) undeniably sets in motion a carceral rhetoric, our fundamental skepticism will not rest content with Miller's carcerality-for-carcerality's-sake type of argument. Yes, the police, in one form or another, are anywhere and everywhere in *The Woman in White,* as they are also in *The Moonstone,* but why exactly are they there? Why are the book's ever-increasingly exact and exacting narrative dynamics necessary? What is calling this pervasive policing into being? Could this will towards universal (perhaps the more appropriate word here would be "trans-Atlantic") control be simply another lock-step facet of a purportedly Foucauldian world gone over in various ways to the disciplinarians, or might this instance of disciplinarity, propagated by this particular narrative (but not perhaps solely by it), indeed be a reaction to a world which at the time was not disciplined enough? Is *The Woman in White* perhaps deploying its carceral rhetoric in a consciously reactive, situation-specific—as opposed to unconscious and culturally-pervasive—manner? And is it doing so in order perhaps to defend against a world filled with international intrigue, a world at one level populated by fictional Italian Counts who steal your letters, your diary, even your woman in white, the moment you are not looking, and populated at another by real Yankee publishers who spirit away your profits, your plot (your *Woman in White*), the food from your mouth (anything that's not tied down?) the moment you allow the trace to leave your body or your home?

Could it be that what Miller sees in his chapter on *The Woman in White*
(and indeed throughout *The Novel and the Police,* that book dealing for the
most part solely with three very successful, and very successfully pirated,
English writers—Dickens, Trollope, and Collins—writing in this period of
American "anti-policing") as a uniform carcerality is called into being, and
split down its middle (as would necessarily, then, also be Miller's book) by
language's fundamental uncontrollability? Could it be that Miller might be
indebted (albeit only to a certain extent and in a certain manner needing to
be mapped out) to Jacques Derrida—or even, how truly shocking for at least
John Sutherland, if not also for Miller, to Simon Nowell-Smith among other
publishing historians? While pursuing this aspect of our response to Sutherland's challenge we need to be prepared to find that the *success* of the undeniable carceral manipulations at work in *The Woman in White* might perhaps
be circumscribed by and predicated upon an a priori and a posteriori fundamental *failure. The Woman in White,* I will be arguing, is less about the
disciplinary "securities of language and perception"[9] or even the disciplinary
securities of a "normal" sexuality than it is about the specific problems these
various disciplinary norms are reactively deployed to address; that is, this
book and its narrative are specifically concerned with the fundamental insecu-
rities of dissemination in general and of the mid-nineteenth-century publishing
trade in particular.

When in his analysis of *The Woman in White* Miller discusses "the police,"
he is, except in the instance of viewing the Count as jailer, often quite thorough and quite persuasive; it is only when he writes of "the novel" that he
gets into real trouble. Miller is correct, to an extent, to defend the disciplinary
sureties of the Victorian world against the undecideabilities of much late
twentieth-century literary critical practice. The mid-Victorian era was as-
suredly an era intensely concerned with, among other matters requiring disciplining, the issue of finding a means, both at home and abroad, of effectively
counteracting the loss of a Benjaminian type of "aura" to which writing was
subject. Not the least of the age's defences against this vulnerability of writing
to "theft," in its various forms, was that system of legal regulations called
copyright—buttressed of course by various moral rhetorics (those profoundly
carceral, Dickensian oratories written in the key of *against mis-*): that against
plagiarism, or mis-appropriation; that against mis-quotation; that against
"mis-interpretation"; and that against "non-relevance" or mis-application
of critical acumen, to name but a few. However, what happened when this
system broke down or found itself rendered ineffectual? When the British
body-politic found the extent of its dominium to be, quite shockingly, insuffi-
cient to contain all the intrigue? What happened when a foreign country—even (or especially) one only relatively recently established in its

foreignness—refused to recognize English copyrights? Should the critic reading this undisciplined situation find there to be at work in the fictional reactions to it a culturally productive disciplining deployed by the violated English authors nevertheless? Surely only if he or she were to be focussing too close to home, that is, too close to England. Or rather should one find in that too late policing a feeble attempt at closing the gate after the horse had bolted? Can we speak of control when faced on one level with the absolute lack of it and on another with the after-the-fact reactive excess of it? Should we not rather see both of these situations as signs of things being quite fundamentally—as well as quite sensationally—"at large"?

We can only formulate this question, however—if we have first of all avoided too hastily collapsing the level of the book with that of the narrative—a distinction which the ambiguous term "the novel" cannot help but hide from view. We might if we were feeling clever take a metacritical perspective on our own essay and ask whether gender studies had not taken center stage already, as one might be tempted to ask, the woman in white as conduit between men once again?[10] While the adoption of this self-conscious perspective is laudable, not the least because it breaks us out of a too common tendency towards critical insularity (and its fellow traveller, an insularity of criticism), the form in which this question is expressed, a form imitating Miller's rhetoric, is too careless. We must not let terms become solidified into immovable objects, least of all the central object of our study; therefore, it is important, plodding along carefully, to unpack this instance of clever rhetoric and to notice that the shape of that "conduit" is less one linking automatically two men discussing an all-too ambiguously defined "novel" than it is one which moves along certain specific circuits within, through, and even around the "text," that is, through the *narrative level* and beyond it to the *book level*.[11] But then who can be blamed for perhaps missing this distinction when presented with a narrative about a "woman in white" encasing, or caging, itself within a book entitled *The Woman in White,* as the similarity in name could only serve to work towards the goal (indeed almost as if this were the purpose behind the design) of obscuring, indeed perhaps even of collapsing, it?

The tenor of Sutherland's comments in the rest of his review would seem to imply that surrounding, halo-like, any publishing-history-oriented endeavor is a worthiness of purpose which should not be gainsaid. That worth would however seem to be one which continues to escape the appreciation of most academics. This lack of critical enthusiasm is not very surprising. I grant that publishing history seems at first to offer very little with regard to materials of interest, just the prospect of seeing one or several inert books laid out in front of one. Only a few details would seem to be available to analysis, and those, if not too insignificant to matter, then most certainly not very intriguing—just covers, cover pages, title pages, fly leaves, illustrations, type-face variations, textual revisions, typographical errata, repaginations, publish-ing details, and perhaps the consistency of the leaves, the binding, and the stitching. Not (currently) the most saleable of inquiries, to say the least. Nevertheless, to see only these aspects of publishing history is to forget its object of study's more traditionally valorized and far less corporeal element. To sentence publishing history to the *assignation à résidence* of the *covering* of the narrative is to forget that that covering's enclosed narrative itself is, has in fact always been, embedded in the flotsam and jetsam of commercial relations, both between individuals and between nations. It is to forget that even from publishing history's elevated perspective, the narrative has always also been open to being read. And it is with this elevation that the real value of the approach is disclosed, as, reading from the as-yet fairly novel point of view that this new discipline would seem to offer, the publishing historicist is in a position to deploy critical acumen from a more detached, more emanci-pated, perspective than is usual when faced with the coercively controlling climate of narratological or ideal-reader-oriented intransigence symptomatic of much of today's literary criticism. This critical elevation is of course of no small significance in the project of reading a novel like *The Woman in White*, a novel—as Miller so incisively demonstrates in his prefatory discus-sion of its "sensationalism" (*"Cage"* 146–56)—excessively concerned with the readerly domain, with what its readers are feeling and with who its readers are. The task of taking account of the individual reader's situation being of central concern in this case, the critic cannot be "taking things personally," cannot be seeing him- or herself in the role of "ideal reader." He or she, ideally, then, should be situated, if anywhere, in the meta-readerly perspec-tive. Reading already from this detached perspective, the publishing historicist thus finds him- or herself in an excellent position to take account of this particular novel's specific anxieties about the interpenetrations perpetrated between the narrative-level and book-level "realities" (a binary of special significance to the publishing historicist). He or she thus arrives, by a different route, at the position already occupied by those theorists who had been ex-panding the too constrictive domain of narratology. In the case of *The Woman in White*, publishing history's zoom-in towards the narrative complements and overlaps with gender theory's zoom-out from within.

Therefore, it comes as no surprise that Miller's essay should advance our interests to a certain extent. Insofar as he declines to take up the habit of consciously or unconsciously giving in to what we might call (acknowledging academia's tendency to unreasonably follow modes) the "narrative carcer-al"—a critical passivity of which the more affectively disposed reader-re-sponse criticisms or orthodox New Criticisms might be considered to be the culmination[12]—Miller reassembles critical perspective at a safe, less sensa-tionalized, distance. Through skillful recourse early on in his essay to an assertion taken from Margaret Oliphant's contemporary review of sensation novels: "The reader's nerves are affected like the hero's" (qtd. in *"Cage"* 153), he progresses beyond the aridity of simply reading the narrative, thereby in essence elevating his reading beyond the limitations of the normal critic-to-narrative relations. Refusing the lure of tacitly contracting to see himself in the place and role of ideal reader, the critic who might otherwise had been reading merely about the hero now has license to "read" the readers reading about, and being affected like, that hero; specifically, in Miller's case, he has license to study the book's tumultuous plot's incitements of gender-turbulence within those readers.

Miller's disarmingly successful reading explores the more remarkable scenes of sensation in the story. It enters the narrative at those points where the essay might find the narrative to be attempting to break free of its own constraints by overthrowing its narrator—if not indeed also the constraints of Miller's reading itself. (Anne overthrows our narrator Hartright's self-possession with her touch from behind him; Fosco throws open our hereto-fore-narrator Marian's—and reader's—heretofore sacrosanct diary; and Marian throws back more forcefully our narrator Hartright's gaze). In these scenes, the touching of the necessarily male[13] reader by a feminine nervous-ness—quite masterfully implicated by Miller with Daniel Paul Schreber's experience of undergoing a "feminizing [of the] constitution via the nerves" (*"Cage"* 161)[14]—sets off in that reader what Miller terms a "homosexual panic." The disequilibrium of the male reader's gender-identification, as well as his counteractive panic, are the products of his having undergone the nerve-racking shocks which the reading of the narrative elicits. Miller rigorously explores the implications, for him necessarily gender-based ones, of these turnings-upon the heretofore privileged and inviolable narrators, and by ex-tension upon the readers: recall: "the reader's nerves are affected like the hero's."

In each of the scenes which Miller discusses in detail, the narrative can be seen to be attempting to break free of the narrative carceral. It can be seen to be attempting to position itself at that long-view on itself, the taking on of which view, when considered to be allegorically representing a swift ascent towards the situation of the book's reader holding the book or weekly periodi-cal in his or her hands, compromises so many of the supports of our modern-day criticism's usual ideal-reader-oriented narratological analyses. Therefore, Miller must adopt a new lexicon with which to talk about this potentially eruptive sensation narrative. That lexicon which he chooses orbits around—appropriately for an inquiry concerned with avoiding anachro-nisms—an old formulation, one hailing from Collins's century, Karl Ulrichs's formulation casting (and caging) the male homosexual as a person exhibiting symptoms of the woman inside or "the woman-in-the-man." Miller argues,

through a virtuoso reading of Walter Hartright's panic at being touched on
the shoulder at night by Anne Catherick on the road near Hampstead Heath,
that the narrative's dual projects of recapturing this particular woman escaped
from the asylum and the male reader's need to exert control over his nervousness, that femininity inside to which the novel quite intemperately will
nevertheless continually be bringing him to consciousness, are linked in the
novel's generalized desire to keep "the woman" bound. Appropriately,
Miller has qualified Ulrichs's ambivalently valedictory woman-in-the-man
formulation beforehand. Not only does it participate in a misogynistic cultural
strategy of incarcerating females, Ulrichs's construction also participates in
the homophobic caging or self-closeting of the homosexual: "Meant to win
a certain intermediate space for homosexuals, Ulrichs's formulation in fact
ultimately colludes with the prison or closet drama—of keeping the 'woman'
well put away—that it would relegate to the unenlightened past" (*"Cage"*
155).

This rescinding of the release-order suggested by Miller's teleological
phrasing here, his laying stress upon the "ultimate" loss of the legible "intermediate" space for homosexuals, foreshadows, it would seem, Miller's subsequent carceral interpretation[15] of the progression of the entire narrative of
The Woman in White. It is not only Walter Hartright who has to make recourse
to a "violent counteraction," a panicked self-enforced recloseting, when the
feminine nervousness inside threatens to break free (as he does when he
"tightens his fingers round 'the handle of [his] stick' " in order to "reaffirm"
his ostensible-but-threatened gender identification (*"Cage"* 152)); the novel
as a whole would, according to Miller, also seem to need to proscribe in its
latter half what it had in its reckless earlier sections practiced.

This attendant closing-off of the once viable transgressive space, this policing of the previously undisciplined zone, reaches its most impressive, and
oppressive, extreme for Miller at a specific moment in the story: the shocking
Marian-Fosco encounter that takes place at the end of Marian's diary narrative. The effacement near the mid-point of the story of Marian as narrator by
Fosco's insinuating himself into her diary after she has fallen into a delirium
at the end of an eavesdropping adventure—literally an eaves and dropping
adventure—is for Miller a moment when the narrative as a whole, censuring
itself through the preaching and practicing of what he characterizes as an
"aversion therapy," a brutal shift towards heterosexuality and therefore a
containment of that panic which the narrative had established in its first half,
fundamentally transforms in theme and genre, altering from "immoral"—to
use a contemporary characterization Miller borrows from the Victorian reviewers—sensation novel to newly-converted representative of the commonplace, average, Victorian domestic novel. Punning on the narrative's apparent
"straightening" out, Miller writes,

Foremost on the novel's agenda in its second half is the dissolution of sensation in the achievement of decided meaning. What the narrative must most importantly get straight is, from this perspective, as much certain sexual and gender deviances as the obscure tangles of plot in which they thrive. In short, the novel needs to realize the normative requirements of the heterosexual menage whose happy picture concludes it. This conclusion, of course, marks the most banal moment in the text, when the sensation novel becomes least distinguishable from any other kind of Victorian fiction.   *("Cage"* 165)

The Marian-Fosco scene's radical alteration of perspective, the usurpation of narratorial control which it recounts and the consequent viewing of the situation from the other side (of the oceanic gender-gap) which it effects, reproduces, then, the path of Ulrichs's ultimately collusive formulation, the change in narrators being a local rendering of the larger movement of the novel's plot from the genre of sensation fiction to that of Victorian domestic fiction, from the genre of homosexual panic to the genre of heterosexual violence. The established paradigms of homosexual panic and the woman-in-the-man reach their logical conclusions, and collusions, when the narrative, coming to close off that intermediate space in which homosexual panic had once found haven, finally, successfully does what it had only been threatening to do in the Walter-Anne scene, that is, when it finally, successfully "jumps out of its skin," the more effectively to be able to turn back upon itself and slap on the normative cuffs. Thus, according to Miller, we have homosexual panic countered and contained by the traditional story of heterosexuality. Indeed, that it is in this case a violent heterosexuality is all the more understandable as this "rape," to use Miller's term for Fosco's act, elaborates an earlier-introduced, and quite unpersuasive, discussion in Miller's essay of reading-as-usual being a figurative "raping" of the text, with the exception, somehow, in the case of sensation fiction, in which case the act of reading becomes necessarily a figurative being-raped. As marking the transfer, then, of readerly identification from the figuratively raped Marian Halcombe to the figuratively raping Count Fosco, the scene, as interpreted by Miller, is *doubly* marking—as a conforming to genre specifications both with regard to reader-manipulation as well as with regard to content (tumultuous sexuality being replaced by strict heterosexuality)—the transition from sensation fiction to "normal'," or more properly normalized, fiction. Describing this transformative and self-transforming scene and the shifting identifications effected by it, Miller holds,

It is *not only*, then, that Marian has been "raped" ... We are "taken" too, taken by surprise, which is itself an overtaking. We are taken, moreover, from behind: from a place where, in the wings of the ostensible drama, the novelist disposes of a whole plot machinery whose existence ... we never suspected. ... To being the object of violation here, however, there is an equally disturbing alternative: to identify with Fosco, with the novelistic agency of violation. *For the Count's postscript only puts him in the position we already occupy. Having just finished reading Marian's diary ourselves, we are thus implicated in the sadism of his act, which even as it violates our readerly intimacy with Marian reveals that "intimacy" to be itself a violation.* The ambivalent structure of readerly identification here thus condenses—as simultaneous but opposite renderings of the same powerful shock—homosexual panic and heterosexual violence.   (*"Cage"* 164; italics added)

"Having just finished reading Marian's diary ourselves, *we* are thus implicated in the sadism of his act" the "we" here for the first time in Miller's essay includes Miller himself.[16] The founding stance of his essay, Miller's foundational meta-discursive perspective upon the reader, is lost as the result of a mediation through Fosco's sequential-but-simultaneous identifications first with Miller and then with the reader. When the narrative jumps outside itself, and beyond or "behind" the reader, emblematized by Fosco's temporally circumscribing the reader and thus "taking" him—to be experienced of course as if we were the female Marian (hence the conjunctive "not only . . .") rather than our male reader selves—by surprise, we have the introduction of a reader of the reader, the position Miller already occupies. Then, as Miller demonstrates, the reader himself turns to "identify with" Fosco (now becoming the one taking instead of any longer surprisingly being the one taken) and, through these Fosco-engineered disarticulations, we have the reader coming to touch the critic who had until then been reading the reader.

As after this point in the narrative Miller is simply reading the "same old story" of the Victorian heterosexual couple-to-be overcoming their various impediments, we might consider him to be putting into practice a logic learned from his earlier reading of the Walter-Anne scene. Every drop of sanguinity in his inquiry freezing as the carcerally-minded, panic-suppressing reader comes out to touch his position, Miller would seem to "catch" here a contagious homosexual-panic panic, an urge to normalize, for what would seem to be transferred in this encounter is an urge towards containment and the restriction of a discourse of, and a discoursing upon, homosexual panic. There is however as less facetious way of characterizing this reversion to the norm of Miller's interpretation. It is not surprising that Miller's inquiry should begin to see the same old Victorian novel other critics encounter, for, having lost as he has the critical distance upon which many of his innovations were founded, Miller has simply moved back into the position he had originally, with the help of Oliphant, broken free from at the beginning of his essay. In effect, it is not surprising that he should read, reading as he now does from the same old perspective, the same old story.

Here it would seem Oliphant gives way to Foucault. Understandably, as who wants a dusty Victorian novelist and reviewer as your theorist when you can have a modern French philosopher instead. At this point Foucauldian panopticism and gender theory come together in a viewing of the heterosexual coupling as not only an interlocking but also as a locking of the Slammer door, as the elevated perspective—which had until then been operative, if often only in the background—of Miller's inquiry is tacitly jettisoned. The puzzle-piece-locking which apparently goes on here between Fosco and Marian would seem to circumscribe and extinguish quite effectively the intermediary reader, causing him to disappear in a puff of smoke, so that we are hereafter left with simply the critic-as-usual, with the critic reading *The Woman in White* from the perspective of ideal-reader.

I would argue, however, that gender theory's bodily-bias and Foucauldian panopticism's carceral bias, more than the dictates of the narrative, are bringing about the controlling paradigm of Miller's reading of this scene. Miller is imposing this reversion before the fact, before the demands of the text dictate that he do so—if indeed they ever do so at all. The "fall" of Miller's perspective, his relinquishment of his hard-won freedom of critical vantage-point, comes too soon; it is more forced than fortuitous, and I believe it causes his reading to mistake the character of not only the fundamentally non-conservative (in various senses of that word, non-traditional, non-hermetic) usurpation occurring here but also the character of the rest of the just as fundamentally non-conservative narrative to follow. As I will attempt to show, we do not have from this point onwards an at-one-time shocking narrative, contented in the knowledge of having finally succeeded in its "wish to abolish itself" (*"Cage"* 165), now simply propounding the sureties and certainties of good-old Victorian morality and honor—not to mention good-old Victorian wedded bliss. Similarly, locally, we do not here in the scene of Fosco's reading Marian's diary so much a complementary foreclosure, just one more example of that well-worn, inclosive, psychological body-economy of a call being responded to by its fitting, and "proper," answer—an "X" by its anti-"X" (Fosco as simply providing the lack of the lack)—as we do the supplanting of one entity (the narrative stage) by a wholly other one (the book stage), one working according to the dictates of a wholly alien moral system.

The conception of the heterosexual duo's coupling as a type of lack meeting its complementary fulfillment would seem to be, at this point and hereafter, controlling Miller's interpretation, and thereby working in no small part to bring about his reading of the text's present and subsequent instances of "reverting to the norm." The crescendo of shocks in this scene: Marian's diary being violated (how horrible), Fosco being disclosed as the violator of it (of all people), and we readers *identifying* with Fosco (how truly scandalous), is one which Miller, in a premature turn to decrescendo, or rather anti-crescendo, is too quick to silence. The suggestiveness of the scene is cancelled by Miller, or temperamental maestro, in mid-escalation, ending for all intents and purposes only half-way through its proper course, at the point of Marian's violation. Indeed, the reader's homosexual panic in the first half of the scene (apparently caught when the reader had been put in the position of Marian) *governs* Miller's interpretation of the second half, thus not allowing for any more panics or any panics of other kinds when the reader finds himself undergoing the stigma of identifying with (perhaps penetrating the position of or being penetrated by) the Count himself divorced from his relation to Marian: an identification which would certainly seem excellent fodder for Miller's discussion—not to mention being more in line with his initial paradigm of the shocking meeting between Hartright and Anne Catherick on Hampstead Heath, as here Fosco comes figuratively to touch the reader on the shoulder as they both stand upon the same theoretical plane.

This focus upon the path Miller might have taken had he kept reading as usual is suggested by a hint dropped—"broache[d] obscurely, in the blind spot of 'nonrecognition' " (*"Cage"* 184)—by Miller's essay itself. There is no clear textual reason for Miller's having stopped the interpretation here—specifically, that is, *before* the reader had reached the position of Fosco. There is nothing positively motivating or even negatively justifying this arrest in reading—to which, albeit reluctantly, a point of Miller's own bears witness, for, as he notes, after this scene, "[s]hocks decline 'dramatically' " (*"Cage"* 165), that is, they do not positively *stop*. Therefore, I believe we are justified in supposing the scene's purported carcerality to be solely the result of the pre-convictions of the Foucauldianism *sans réserve* being practiced here, not the result of any narrative thematics specifically necessitating the sudden recoil. On the contrary, as the rest of the narrative will make clear, what was necessary at this point was Miller's having continued *reading*, that is, interpreting, if not quite in the same manner then at the very least certainly from the same elevation as previously.

Instead, however, we have the *disciplinarial* imposition of a carceral Foucauldian paradigm which fundamentally distorts the scene. Miller's foreclosive interpretation models beforehand the text as he would have that text be. For Miller, the latter part of the scene can only be interpreted as a containment, as the *closing off* of the earlier stage of panic, and not as itself a new stage of panic. His reading is thus insufficiently detached to "get straight" the implications of Fosco's crime. Fosco, as the practitioner/enforcer of a coercive heterosexuality, would seem to be here for Miller the grand determinate negator of what had gone before, the hostile pharmacologist—a role he actually assumes on occasion in the story—advancing upon us with a spoonful of an "antidote," or anti-dose, for an earlier case of transitory homosexuality. The reader's movement towards the position of that immoral villain is one which Miller never truly lets take place as we never quite come to identify with Fosco himself, only with Fosco as rapist of Marian, that is, as Marian's counter. The *method* of Miller's essay is therefore contained by his essay's *design*. Miller's over-arching argument that the encounter between Marian and Fosco comes to be incarcerated within the "traditional" cage of hetero-sexual violence, comes too quickly and too effectively to control his local interpretations, those interpretations having until this point been based on sticking with the movements of the text, a text in the latter part of this scene suggesting other (scandalous-as-ever) possibilities to the still suitably-detached critic. The containment exhibited at this point is more the one ef-fected by Miller's circumscribing, inward-moving, carceral critical perspec-tive—supported in its project by his predisposition to explore the psychological dimension, thus positing beforehand that the inquiry will stay inside, more specifically, will trace a revolution around, the insular bounds of an individual consciousness (presumably that of the author)—than it is one potentially manifest in what he characterizes as the narrative's circumscribing, inward-moving, normative project. The scope of his inquiry is at this point limited by his willed retorsion, both backwards and downwards, away from the position of Fosco, a retorsion which is not only looking ahead to the conclusions of his inquiry but also looking backwards to the debt owed to the "gender" or "theory" (read, carceral) aspects of this reading he has undertaken in the name of "gender theory."

Our literary critic's having, as I said, replaced at this point his more applica-ble theorist, Oliphant, with his less applicable one, Foucault, this is necessarily the point at which "gender theory" and "publishing history" part ways. Miller's enforced turn back towards Marian results in an effacement of the "lettered" aspects—in this narrative detailing in every other scene the sealing, burning, copying, signing, forging, dreaming, burying, substituting, violating, questioning, or composing of texts—of the count's crime of reading, leaving to resonate only the physical elements of the equivocal (and mesmerically sensational) metaphor of "rape" with which he characterizes the count's crime. However, one does not have to follow Miller in his reductive simplifi-cation of the scene along the lines of a body-logic in which Fosco supplies Marian's "lack," or indeed also of the complementary genre-logic which leaves us with the once-sensation-novel-reader now reading the non- or anti-sensation (domestic) novel.

When Miller writes, "To being the object of violation here, however, there is an equally disturbing alternative: to identify with Fosco, *with the novelistic agency of violation,*" (emphasis added) we need not follow him in allowing the sensationalism of his final clause to overpower or efface the significant ramifications of the identification taking place *apart from* the count's having become "the novelistic agency of [Marian's] violation." What might it mean, quite simply, to "identify with Fosco"? Despite Miller's significant invest-ment of rhetorical and critical ingenuity in establishing Marian as the gravita-tional center of the interactions taking place in this scene, these efforts are not enough to completely obscure the scene's explosive, expansive, and indeed expatriate, elements. Indeed, the outward and upward movement of the reader identifying with Fosco, that shocking distention which carries her into the circumscriptive region of the beyond-narrative, would seem seriously to put in question Miller's *carceral* characterization of the scene. For, in essence, nothing's boring inwards here. Rather the narrative—as though enacting a scene from *The Night of the Living Dead*—is exhuming or exiling itself outwards, as it erupts into the book level. *Viewed from a sufficiently detached perspective,* the supplanting in the scene is found to be not so much an inwardly collapsing, conservational, carceral compulsion as an outwardly everting event or *escape.* That is, it is not so much an author-centered, psychological redisciplining (calling forth Miller's two-parts-making-a-whole, conclusive/collusive structuring) as it is an "externally" focussed, readership-centered, usurpation—one founded upon the conceptualization of the book's readership as two distinct groups: British versus American, "good" versus "bad," readers.

Fosco's illicit reading (and hence the identification with him by the reader) is not a fundamental shift at the level of genre but rather one at the level of perspective. We do not have in this scene a generic (or genericizing) reversion to the norm, but rather a taking of the earlier warnings announced by the narrative to their dreaded conclusions or horizons: a *radicalization,* as opposed to normalization, of the sensational aspects of the narrative. Miller's focus in this scene upon the apparently conservative "straightening out" of the reader misses the radical alteration of perspective, as perspective, experienced by that reader, as the, to this point, fundamentally carceral world of the narrative transforms into the fundamentally anti-carceral one of the book. The no longer fog-bound reader of this sensationally shocking scene, finding herself newly plopped down in Kansas, might well breathlessly intone, "I'm not in London anymore," as we have here a radical break out of the carceral modality (as indeed we should have also out of the carceral critical mentality, as the narrative-turning-to-book here is leaving behind Miller's hermetic body- and prison-metaphors—or at least their constrictive charge) as now it would seem *the criminals were running the institutions.* Hence, we have upon the introduction of Fosco in this scene, quite to the contrary of Miller's analysis, a novel which has become *increasingly* threatening, indeed more than ever before, to British Victorian norms, rather than a novel, or its author, coming back into line with the majority of its, or his, contemporaries.

However, this radicalization, being itself based more in the realm of publishing history than gender theory—based, that is, in issues further removed from the gravitational pull of the narrative carceral than Miller's parabolic interpretation (the literary critical interpretation we have which nevertheless comes closest to doing this text justice) is in a position to take account of—it is necessarily a radicalization which would tend to go unnoticed in the current critical climate. Fosco's crime is less sexual than textual. The illicit reading of Marian's diary is the moment when the purportedly-caged reader's subjection to the narrative floats most forcefully to the surface of the story—and quite shockingly (indeed for all England-bound interpretations quite impossibly)—beyond, shifting around the center-point of the text, diary/book. As Fosco's "rape" is the unauthorized reading of Marian's diary, the narrative at this point necessarily lays particular stress upon the materiality of that text. At the end of the scene, we learn that we have Fosco's "strict sense of propriety"[17] to thank for his having restored Marian's diary to her desk so that she might pass it along through verbal transcription, at the end of a veritable assembly-line of book production, to Walter Hartright, our general editor, so that we might now be reading it. It is a literal rather than sexual criminality which interpolates the reader of this scene, leading one to suspect that the "closet" one makes recourse to in this novel might be more one which offers protection from criminals attracted to texts than protection from unstable gender identifications or the evincing of the markers of proscribed sexualities. I will return to this point later. While Miller reads the narrative from the Marian-Fosco encounter onwards (with the exception of an interesting, if somewhat self-undermining, discussion of the bonds among the Brotherhood) as simply a reversion to "that same old story" of the closing, and closeting, heterosexual love-match deferred, I see Fosco's crime itself as a culminating act which is the eventuation, rather than the determinate negation or counteraction, of the previously ever-threatening crime alluded to (and simultaneously warned against) by the shocks coming prior to it. Walter Hartright's unwitting "crime" of helping Anne Catherick escape re-confinement is a mis-recognition of the nascent lesson—here learned all too late—to keep women or their texts closeted in order that they should not meet up with men not so exemplarily moral as Hartright.

It is this textual crime of Fosco's which the subsequent individual narratives of the story will all work to condemn, to a greater extent perhaps than they will work to condemn his more audacious crime of substituting Laura for Anne, Anne for Laura. Having passed through the sensationalized vale (or perhaps heath) of soul-making—recall the count's advice to Marian to avoid the "storms of life" by dwelling in the "valley of Seclusion" (457)—without having learned the lesson that would have averted Fosco's crime, the narrative will thereafter subject itself, and its reader, to a re-education garbed in a style more common to Collins's day. After Fosco's crime of reading the diary, the reader will be subjected to an education which will have moved from the realm of the body, an education on the nerves, to the realm of the spirit, a morality tale or allegory, a shift in character but not in substance, as both the shocks in the first half and the exactions of moral retribution in the second come to lobby for the same thing, the closeting of texts.

The most fundamentally disturbing aspect of the shock produced by the scene of Fosco's reading I would argue is that shock which inheres in finding our good selves put in the situation of the immoral count by an author with whom we had thought we were on friendly terms. Offering, myself, a formulation as magisterially unfounded and unfoundable as Miller's assertion that we should view sensation fiction to be an essentially unique form of fiction with respect to a raped/raping dichotomy of reader identifications, I assert that the reader of any fiction (except in cases of obviously antagonistic relation such as that of the mid-nineteenth-century American reader of *Martin Chuzzlewit*) always considers him- or herself to be, in the opinion of the author, a good reader. In the reading of any novel the reader, always assured in her belief that there exists a degree of good faith between herself and her author, assumes, along the lines of an unspoken contract, that the author is, if not quite on her side, then at least not inveterately suspicious of her and certainly not actively antagonistic towards her. (In a similar manner, the average twentieth-century critic, so often reading from the position of "ideal" (read, angelic) reader, does so as well.) The reader always considers herself to be the "good reader"—consonant with Collins's interpreters consistently considering the reader of this novel to be the individual English (that is, fundamentally "good") reader.[18]

The absolute horizon for the good reader, therefore, is the situation of the "bad" reader. When the assumed good faith between herself and the author is violated there occurs an "ambivalent structure of readerly identification" indeed ("*Cage*" 164). Being thrown into the "bad" perspective by being made to move from identifying with the virtuous Marian—both the position occupied empathically by the good reader and allegorically by the author—to identifying with the villainous Fosco, that unexpected casting of the iniquitous (self-repressedly iniquitous, that is) reader in the role of the villain which announces bad terms to be existing between author and reader, causes that startling shock heard round the Anglo-American literary world that along with the others generated by this novel served to inaugurate the genre of sensation fiction, that shock which Miller, too-constrictively, is intent upon characterizing as simultaneously homosexual panic and its containment. Quite simply—as might be hoped with regard for the moral health of any society—the Fosco-like "raping" reader is not the "morally upright," that is, successfully "cured" or "curing," reader of marriage-plot fiction but rather the immoral-as-ever American reader still out to get her fiction at a cut-rate price, only one now projecting her voracious desire for texts (or, more properly, having her desire projected) into even the space of the narrative she consumes.[19]

The schizophrenia of the identifications prompted by the scene of Fosco's reading Marian's diary is therefore more geographic than gendered—more trans-Atlantic—since *The Woman in White* turns out to be a suppressed allegory, simultaneously published in both Britain and America,[20] subliminally lobbying against the American practice of pirating British works.[21] The nineteenth-century American readers who had been obtaining their reading material if not for "free," as far as payments to the author went, then for lower-than-English rates (leaving the British author feeling like exploited labor) should have felt quite at home with the story's crossing over from Marian to Fosco, for allegorically this shift represents the book's crossing of the Atlantic Ocean. They should not have been shocked to be put in Fosco's position, but of course were, since the novel does not immediately represent itself as a copyright allegory. (Even if it had, they probably would still have been shocked, as one seldom acknowledges one's own iniquity, as, for example, in the epigraph it is the characteristically British "morbid hatred" Pogram comments upon and not the charge of an inveterate American dishonorability.) Indeed, instead of shock while reading the Marian-Fosco scene the American readers, those other Victorians, should have felt a twinge of recognition, because what Fosco is illicitly doing, Collins implies, to Marian's text is what they have been doing, immorally if not quite at that time criminally, for years to the texts of British authors.

The Woman in White is a textual monument to what in the British authors' view was American avarice. That Collins, in order to make a certain segment of his readership feel the iniquity of its government's policies and to strengthen its moral fiber through a subliminal education in British honor—remembering of course that the author was not able to control the composition of his audience[22]—should have put all his readers in the position of a character perpetrating the grossly dishonorable act of reading another character's diary, understandably at that time shocking, and still so to an extent. Collins's novel therefore should be considered a text in which the American public is continually undergoing an aversion therapy, but an aversion therapy different in kind from that suggested by Miller, that is, one designed to shame them out of their immoral practice of pirating British works. A secondary effect of this castigation was that the honorable British readers were subjected to a moral testing and re-solidification which they did not need,[23] but an education which, most likely in Collins's opinion, would have proven worthwhile anyway, and which predictably has elided itself in the thinking of the critics as simply another example of that well-established, generic, Victorian British preoccupation with honor.

Along this line, the latter half of the novel would seem to be obsessed with the question of acting, or not acting, honorably. It is perhaps in this sense and when viewed from a solely British perspective, then, that we might say that *The Woman in White* begins in its latter half to take on the guise of the same old Victorian story. However, firmly to conclude this is to fall victim to a misrecognition potentially on the order of taking a lady in white for a woman in white. Like so many of Collins's recourses to common Victorian conventions, this recourse to honorability is one which has a specific allegorical purport, giving it a character and goal fundamentally different to, more trans-Atlantic than, that which might repose in the recourse to honor made by other Victorian authors. The honor Collins promotes is not so much an uncomplicated British honor directed towards British readers in order to cure the almost valorizingly highlighted ills of their green and pleasant land (as many Collins critics would have it) as it is an antidote offered in the hopes of curing American dishonorability in that so very foreign and yet somehow homely Victorian "Counterworld," to adopt and expand the horizons of Knoepflmacher's term, across the Atlantic.

In 1880, when Collins closed his polemical protest "Considerations on the Copyright Question" with the farewell, "Good-by for the present, Colonel. I must go back to my regular work, and make money for American robbers, under the sanction of Congress" (618), he had already been selling quite well (with and without "special arrangement") in America. He was at this time in his career, then, understandably concerned about the issue of the lack of an international copyright agreement. A few years earlier in the winter of 1873–74 he had embarked on a reading tour of America and during his last reading engagement, on 27 February 1874, in the spirit of Dickens's trip of 1842, had upset some members of his Boston audience by bringing up this sore point in Anglo-American literary relations (Ashley 102). But even in 1859, as an as-yet only moderately successful author, Collins had several reasons for resenting the lack of legal protection for British works in America, not the least of which being the issue, albeit relatively small-scale, of remuneration. Collins was losing money to American publishers, money which on moral grounds he believed should be coming his way rather than going theirs. Because of the lack of an Anglo-American copyright agreement—an effective litero-legal black-hole which went unplugged until the passage in the Senate of the Simmonds Bill in 1891 (Clark 181)—American publishers had no legal constraints preventing them from publishing British works, and indeed some historians hold that they were in fact encouraged to do so by a clause in the Copyright Act passed by the first Congress in 1790.[24] While there had informally come into being a system of "trade-courtesy" among the more prominent American publishers,[25] the fairly generous amounts paid by a publisher for advance sheets, which not only allowed him to get a jump on any "unofficial" pirates but also allowed him to claim the work as his, hopefully sacrosanct, property among the bigger houses, were not quite enough, in Collins's —and his even more aggrieved friend Dickens's—opinions, to successfully mitigate the loss in profits.[26]

Briefly, before we look at The Woman in White itself, we might cite a few nascent attempts at allegorical lobbying against the mind-set of those copy-right infringers across the ocean in the works written just prior to 1859. Collins's first full-length novel to be simultaneously serialized trans-Atlan-tically was the one written just before *The Woman in White, The Dead Secret,* which ran in both *Household Words* and *Harper's Weekly* from January to June 1857 (Ashley 52). In that novel, we discover Collins making explicit his feelings about the unwillingness of the Americans to recognize British copyright, for we find one of his characters upholding what must have seemed at that time to anyone but a British author trained as a lawyer, as Collins was, to be quite excessively fastidious copyright principles. When Rosamond Frankland, née Treverton, naively asserts her wish to pay her uncle Andrew's duplicitous servant Shrowl five pounds for a copy, taken from the "Rare. Only six copies printed," *History and Antiquities of PORTHGENNA TOWER,* of the plan of the Treverton family home, the key to solving the mystery of the location of the elusive Myrtle Room which contains the secret referred to in the book's title, her husband Leonard has to shame her into a proper understanding of the intricacies involved in honoring copyright.[27] She com-plains, "What harm are we doing, if we give the man his five pounds? He has only made a copy of the Plan: he has not stolen anything" (*DS* 221). However, the blind Leonard, sensitive to copyright issues to an unusual de-gree, protests against his wife's "reason[ing] like a Jesuit," emphatically replying, "He has stolen information, according to my idea of it" (*DS* 221). Of course, Rosamond will get the plan in the end, and just as implacably that "theft of information" will be her undoing as copyright infringers seldom go unpunished throughout Collins's works—a retributive guarantee which, while it may not hold true for his novelette *A Rogue's Life,* nevertheless certainly does for *The Woman in White.*

At the end of *A Rogue's Life* (1856), a story also appearing in both *House-hold Words* and *Harper's Weekly,* Doctor Dulcifer, the coiner and last "em-ployer" of the Rogue, having escaped the Bow Street runners sent to capture him, successfully flees to America and there adopts a profession which Collins even at this early age of his career must have loathed; remaining consistent with prior practice, the unregenerate Dulcifer ends up engaging in a different form of theft in the New World, "editing a newspaper in America" (*RL* 188). Old File, his accomplice in the English counterfeiting operation, serves as his publisher. Many nineteenth-century American newspaper editors having been unrepentant "re-printers" of English texts,[28] Dulcifer is cast by Collins in the iniquitous situation of having turned his already tainted hand to, in essence, if not quite a different type of forgery, then certainly a different type of thievery, or false "circulation"—at least in English moral terms, if not American legal ones—on the other side of the Atlantic.

Thus we find the relationship between villainy and American publishing to be established quite early in Collins's career, in fact, even before he had

begun selling well unauthorizedly in the Wild West. Therefore we must look
for some other motivation for Collins's interest in copyright besides a purely
monetary one. After duly acknowledging the danger involved in taking fiction
for fact, I suggest that there was apparently a Collins family "tradition" of
opposing the attenuation of payments to the artist resulting from false wares
being circulated on the market.[29] Early in *A Rogue's Life* we find a passage
which suggests that piracy had most probably been a prominent issue throughout Collins's lifetime for it might have indirectly affected the payments his
eminent painter father, William Collins, R. A.—perhaps referred to in the
following passage's allusion to the "famous artists of the English school"
—received for his paintings. The Rogue's championing of the wronged contemporary English artists turns into a discoursing upon the evils of the nobles'
lack of an ability to discriminate between the good and the bad, the original
and the forgery, when buying Old Masters:

> The unfortunate artist had no court of appeal that he could turn to . . . For one
> nobleman who was ready to buy one genuine modern picture at a small price,
> there were twenty noblemen ready to buy twenty more than doubtful old pic-
> tures at great prices. The consequence was, that some of the most famous artists
> of the English school, whose pictures are now bought at auction sales for
> fabulous sums, were then hardly able to make an income. They were a scrupu-
> lously patient and conscientious body of men, who would as soon have thought
> of breaking into a house, or equalising the distribution of wealth, on the high-
> way, by the simple machinery of horse and pistol, as of making Old Masters
> to Order. They sat resignedly in their lonely studios, surrounded by unsold
> pictures which have since been covered again and again with gold and bank-
> notes by eager buyers at auctions and show-rooms, whose money has gone into
> other than the painter's pockets—who have never dreamed that the painter had
> the smallest moral right to a farthing of it.   (*RL* 41–42)

Disclosing the vast number of forgeries out on the market thus was one way
to help the struggling contemporary artist, working in either paints or pens,
to put food on his table. For Collins, it was a moral imperative to find a
means of educating the connoisseur as to the difference between an original
and a copy of an Old Master, consonant with instructing the reader as to
which copy of the woman in white, or perhaps that should be *The Woman in
White,* was the Fair(lie) copy and which the bad.

Evidence from the currently available Collins correspondence suggests that
the section from *A Rogue's Life* discussed above was written in response not
only to the imminent repeal of the Stamp Act of 1819, which since that time
had made cheap newspaper piracies impossible, but also to the piracy in early
1855 of a painting by Collins's (and his father's) good friend, the painter E.
M. Ward:

The whole question of protection of the interests of authors as well as artists in their own works, is coming before the public—in connection with the taking off of the Newspaper Stamp, which will enable any scoundrel who starts a low paper to steal articles from good papers—or *whole books* with perfect impunity, as the act now stands—just in fact as the scoundrel stole your name and sold his copy of your picture with it. If nothing else will do, the authors must have a *League* and the artists must join them. Parliament and hereditary legislators don't care a straw about us or our interests—we must somehow make them care.[30]

Collins, as the vehemence of this letter would imply, was dedicated to making people care about piracy. Four years later, in a manner similar to that adopted in *The Dead Secret,* he would again be fictionally lobbying, but in that commercially more successful instance his pen would be focussing upon (as it had at the end of *A Rogue's Life*) an international perspective, as that fantasized "League" of British authors transformed into an Italian Brotherhood[31] and the grandiloquent Doctor Dulcifer returned to England in the form of an even more grandiloquent Italian Count.

The "postmodern" introduction of a synecdochic representation of a text within that text's narrative, exemplified by Fosco's "rape" of Marian's diary, the stand-in for Collins's book, has many literary antecedents, a famous example being Cervantes's Part II of *Don Quixote,* published some ten years after the first half of that story. In the Prologue to Part II, Cervantes tilts against one Avellaneda of Tordesillas, the writer of a false *Second Part of the Exploits of Don Quixote de la Mancha* which appeared while Cervantes was still writing his version of the continuation of the story. Cervantes acerbically replies to one of Avellaneda's gibes, stating, "Tell him also that I do not give a farthing for his threat to deprive me of profit by means of his book . . ." (*Don Quixote* 469; translation modified) ["'Dile tambien que de la amenaza que me hace que me ha de quitar la ganancia con su libro, no se me da un ardite . . ." (*Ingenioso Hidalgo* 77)]. In Chapter 72 of Cervantes's continuation we find Don Quixote encountering a character apparently moonlighting from doing service in Avellaneda's "false history," and the scene of Cervantes's Don Quixote taking up the false Second Part of the history and calling it to task for mistaking the name of Sancho Panza's wife, Teresa Panza (*not* Mari Gutierrez), in chapter 59, is a quite amusing example of the assertion of precedence (or would that be "historical truth"?) in fictional creations (voiced by a fictional creation no less) at a time when there was no copyright law. What is needed, Cervantes has one of his characters say, is of course a law which would prevent such things happening by reserving the right to the first chronicler, Cervantes's own persona: "were it possible, there should have been a law [*se habia de mandar*] that no one should dare to write of the affairs of the great Don Quixote except Cide Hamete, his first historian [*su primer autor*]; just as Alexander decreed that no one should paint him except Apelles" (*Don Quixote* 854, *Ingenioso Hidalgo* 349).

One is prompted to wonder what might have happened had Don Quixote not heeded prudence and changed his planned trip to the jousts in Saragossa upon being told that the false Quixote had been (or rather would be), indeed, had in a sense always already been, there. Had the two Don Quixotes met up at Saragossa or anywhere else along the course of their travels during this war for profits between their creators, we might have had a pre-playing of the plot of *The Woman in White,* that story in which two women who look alike are moved here and there as if they were chess pieces in a struggle between two men who end up eventually having "writing-business to transact" (607), and who themselves in their turn are just standing in as relatively minor players, as individual author and publisher, in a much larger political conflict bridging the Atlantic and orbiting around issues of inter-jurisdictional relations (*not* those between Madrid and Tordesillas or even those between Italy and England) and questions of the translatability of virtue, character, and national honor—or should that be honour?: *se habia de mandar* indeed.

II

"I warn all readers of these lines that Miss Fairlie's inheritance is a very serious part of Miss Fairlie's story . . ." (149): quite serious; though not in the way in which the lawyer Gilmore presumably intends. *The Woman in White,* this narrative which is the proleptic allegorical representation of its book form's future sojourn among the immoral (but nevertheless unfortunately sovereign) Americans, from its first page onwards, is a case without a court, a legal case being brought instead to the judgment of its (trans-Atlantic) readers: "As the Judge might once have heard it, so the Reader shall hear it now" (5); "the story here presented will be told by more than one pen, as the story of an offence against the laws is told in Court by more than one witness" (5). Laura Fairlie's inheritance—as well as the permissions exacted by Walter Hartright to publish the various narratives he collects—serve as the allegorical stand-ins for the rightful remuneration due to an author as compensation for the pains he or she has taken in his or her literary labors. Naturally, the more readers those pains serve to amuse, the greater should be the payments accorded. However, when this linear progression in royalties inexplicably sputters, as a result of being immorally siphoned off by men who have done nothing to earn their profits—at least Avellaneda had gone to the trouble of constructing his own narrative—but steal someone else's story while their government quite unashamedly looks the other way, not only is the self-righteous novelist quite reasonably angered, but things not surprisingly tend to take on a rather sinister cast.

A degree of villainy is created for which only as grandly amoral a villain as the foreign—and I stress the Count's alienness—Count Fosco can serve as avatar, for does not Collins himself remind us that only the heretofore undomesticated ("Gently, Mr. Hartright. Your moral clap-traps have an excellent effect in England—keep them for yourself and your own countrymen, if you please" (604)) foreigner can move so easily beyond the pale of common English morality: "I thought the crime too ingenious for an English villain, so I pitched upon a foreigner" (Yates 591). Fosco's international, or more properly beyond-English, "ingenuity" is of the same order as that exercized by the allegorical Native American chief who is himself utilized so pointedly at the beginning of Collins's article "Considerations on the Copyright Question." This protest opens with a parable, a "little anecdote," which bears a striking methodological resemblance to *The Woman in White*: the anecdote is a fictional allegory of copyright infringement. It is set in the early days of North American settlement by the Dutch and recounts the "theft" by an Iroquois chief from a Dutch settler of a watch "made by [the Dutchman] and containing special improvements of his own invention" ("Considerations" 609). When requested to return the watch, the chief refuses, saying, "Possibly your watch is protected in Holland. . . . It is not protected in America. There is no watch-right treaty, sir, between my country and yours" ("Considerations" 610). Collins ends the parable with the key to its decipherment: "[t]he prototypes of modern persons have existed in past ages. The Iroquois chief was the first American publisher. [The Dutchman] was the parent of the whole European family of modern authors" ("Considerations" 610). Here we have Collins, by characterizing the American publishers as more-native-than-the-Native-Americans in their "lawlessness" and "savage" immorality, coyly taking to its extreme a pervasive rhetoric of American republicanism and sovereignty which was being used throughout the century to support the American publishers' contention of feeling like absolute foreigners, consistent with those taunts of "moral-clap-traps" aimed by Fosco at Hartright, in the face of British understandings of honor and civility.[32]

Besides casting the copyright infringer as "other," with respect to British morals and British nationality, Collins attempts in *The Woman in White* to emphasize the helplessness of the text which that infringer violates by metaphorically representing it as a child, or a vacuous, child-like female. If one imagines works of fiction to be the brain-children of their authors (as does Collins in the preface to his earliest short story collection *After Dark* (1856): "[Readers] may depend on the genuineness of my literary offspring . . . they are not borrowed children" (v)), then the narrative would seem to agree with Count Fosco when he says of Laura, that women "are nothing but children grown up" (330). It is not surprising, then, that the Count should have earlier ridiculed Laura's naive moral sentiments as being fit only for a child's hand-writing primer. He remarks, "My dear lady . . . those are admirable senti-ments; and I have seen them stated at the tops of copy-books" (235). Indeed, the American publisher whom Fosco represents would presumably ridicule in a similarly belittling manner (and so does[33]) any attempt at ascribing a simple moral schema of good-versus-bad—Percival Glyde's label for this schema is "copy-book morality" (235)—onto the nineteenth-century Anglo-American "copy-book" system, or to use a less childishly literal, more tradi-tional term, the publishing trade. These "copy-book morals" which the so-phisticated Fosco so urbanely deprecates as "comfortable moral maxims" (236) and which he so manifestly lacks will prove more astute than he had given them credit for when—in the scene at the opera in which he self-incriminatingly flees from an uncomprehending Professor Pesca—the other-wise accomplished equanimity which had allowed him to bring off the auda-cious plot of the substitution of one woman (or *Woman*) for another is so thoroughly overthrown, thereby teaching him, as himself the case in point, the moral and literal lesson that indeed crimes *do* "cause their own detection" (235). Laura's cipher-like vacuousness, which has been remarked by many critics, Miller included—"The same internment that renders Laura's . . . mind imbecile . . . fits her to incarnate the norm of the submissive Victorian wife" ("*Cage*" 172)—may indeed mark her as the quintessential Victorian wife, but it also serves as analogue to that fundamentally uncontrollable transfer-ability (what Derrida in "Signature Event Context" and elsewhere calls "iterability"), and therefore fundamental vulnerability to violation, which characterizes writing (or indeed any form of expression), thereby quite effec-tively highlighting her allegorical status as the stand-in for the inanimate book which is in danger of being pirated; that is, when the allegory has been demystified, Collins's Angel in the House is disclosed to be rather the book in the closet.

Laura's doppelganger, being a character of similarly little substance, the plot's center-piece, the substitution of Anne Catherick, the Woman in White, for Laura Fairlie, can be considered to be enacting the central move in the drama of literary piracy. We learn near the end of the book that Laura and Anne are actually half-sisters, Anne being the offspring of an affair between the now-deceased Mr. Philip Fairlie and the maid of a friend. Fairlie's having published two copies of himself—in the Shakespearean sense of printing copies of oneself[34]—one legitimate and one not, has led to the possibility of his estate being shifted away from its proper course. In the end it will be Walter Hartright who takes over the task of reassembling—literally, in the narratives he gathers—and re-establishing the single, proper line of descent. And it is a curiously filial, rather than sexual or monetary, interest—"The sad sight of the change in her from her former self, made the one interest of my love an interest of tenderness and compassion, which her father or her brother might have felt, and which I felt, God knows, in my inmost heart'' (464)(—which he displays in his quest for the re-establishment of Laura's claim to her proper identity and her proprietary rights over the family lands. Hartright will be the one who has successfully controlled the possibility of the loss of property and coin opened up by Mr. Fairlie's hither-thither (the pun in this case being appropriate) "dissemination."[35]

Walter's interests not remaining Platonic for very long, the novel "reverts" (to use Miller's term) to both the heterosexual domestic story and the story of the successful re-establishment of the rights and lineage of the proper—as Marian Halcombe's cheering introduction on the last page makes clear—"*Heir of Limmeridge*" (643). But this apparent reversion is in actuality not a return to any sort of Victorian "norm." Rather, it is a turn to an idealized, and at that time decidedly abnormal, Victorian utopia in which British authors would no longer be subject to the threat of American piracy. The assurance held out by the narrative's seeming to have turned to a norm in this domestic ending is partly the result of the "double negative" situation of this particular narrative's acting as subversive agent among an audience of subverters themselves—and therefore appearing to valorize norms. (Can we really characterize this complicated, but nevertheless intelligible, situation as simply "carceral"?) Once again offering an instance of Collins's systematic strategy of redeploying common Victorian conventions for his own ends, of offering up the same form hiding a different content, the narrative ends with what would appear to be the most conventional of conclusions.[36] The story ends with a cheery "domestic" situation which on the surface looks like, but is actually only a clever allegorical imitation or doppelganger of, the usual—"banal" is the term Miller uses, obviously having mistaken the sense of Collins's ending for that of one of Thackeray's or Trollope's[37]—Victorian domestic tableau of heterosexual-couple-with-child. However, this tableau should not be seen as simply a reversion to Victorian conventionality but rather also as a bit of Collinsian wish-fulfillment: in the merging, in the person of the infant heir, of the *Fair(lie)-copy* of the Woman in White and the *Hart-right* we find Collins advocating the hopeful symbolic re-establishment if not within the American reader of a fair heart then at least within her legal system of his claims to his Copy-right.

Hartright's disclosure of Percival Glyde's crime, in that more celebrated "copy-book" instance of the narrative, highlights the connection between women and books upon which Collins's allegory is in part relying. Glyde is described by Hartright, in a characterization resonating with Fosco's earlier crime, as having "usurped" a "whole social existence" (521). One might recall here Hartright's earlier distress at Laura's having been rendered, as a result of the almost total success of Fosco's machinations, "socially, morally, legally—dead" (421). The success of Glyde's mirroring crime, his carefully planned forgery of the registering of his parents' marriage in the register at Old Welmingham, is overthrown by the existence, unknown to him, of a "legitimate" copy at Knowlesbury. That other copy renders "illegitimate" that one upon which Glyde has (to borrow a phrase Hartright uses to describe the effects of incarceration upon Laura) "set [his] profaning marks" (443). The existence of the other copy, like that of the other woman, renders his crime, in effect, a crime of substitution. The parallel in the crimes is further heightened by Glyde's ultimate incarceration within the vestry. The false baronet having been one of the two principal agents in the story responsible for the incarceration of women in madhouses, it is appropriate that he should himself die locked within—incarcerated as a result of the "hampering" of an old lock on an old door—an asylum of his own, in the dilapidated vestry housing the "marked" copy as the room around him begins to burn.

Through this re-presentation to us of Fosco's crime of substituting women in Glyde's crime of substituting books, the narrative therefore suggests not simply that books can stand in for women but that women can stand in for books—a quite significant allegorical transformation in a story recounting the redirection, through the substitution of those women, of legacies, as one is then prompted to wonder whether the story might not also be recounting the redirection of literary profits.

True to his name, Hartright throughout the story acts the perfect English gentleman, thus also serving as the perfect agent of moral instruction for those readers across the ocean so much in need of it. After Glyde's death, Walter, considering that he would have, had Glyde lived, been in a position to blackmail him with the threat of the disclosure of Glyde's secret illegitimacy and his usurpation of a legacy that was not legally his, decides that properly he could have done only one thing: "In common honesty and common honour I must have gone at once to the stranger whose birthright had been usurped—[and] I must have renounced the victory . . ." (539). Common honesty and common honor are here meant to signify not just an English honor but at the least an Anglo-American one—if not indeed a universal honor—as Collins's disseminal hopes for this book are that it might imbue each of its readers with that same sense of common honesty and honor repeatedly exemplified in Hartright's good actions and almost too-upstanding-to-be-believed moral rhetoric. A drama of grand dimensions is being played out here, since one could imagine, the rightful heir being thoroughly absent and even unknown in the immediate context, that someone in Hartright's position, with a Laura to resurrect, might be tempted to blind himself to the bad karma which might inhere in choosing the path of suppressing the correct heir's rights. (And what is *The Moonstone* if not an exploration of this same bad

karma—specifically as it is manifested in the Indian "Brotherhood's" exacting a (seemingly) Indian rather than English form of vengeance according to
the dictates of a (seemingly) Indian rather than English form of honor?) And
yet Hartright chooses the strictly honorable path, implying that the Americans
should do the same, despite any possible adverse effects which might eventu-
ate with respect to their base monetary or fundamentally non-justifying national (and, in the case of their Anglo-influenced conceptions of "honor,"
unjustifiably nationalistic) interests.

This rhetoric of honorability deployed in the latter half of the narrative is,
from the standpoint of lobbying against piracy, at least as important as, perhaps in fact more important than, Hartright's and the Italian Brotherhood's
eventual exactions of reparations and/or blood from the villains which conclude the story. The sub-plot of the moral instruction of the reader is, if
anything, rendered more forceful near the end of the novel by the unhampered
mobility, especially across international borders, of the Brotherhood. We
should recall here Fosco's cosmopolitan insistence upon the nation-specific
and nation-bounded nature of virtue:

> Here, in England, there is one virtue. And there, in China, there is another
> virtue. And John Englishman says my virtue is the genuine virtue. And John
> Chinaman says my virtue is the genuine virtue. And I say Yes to one, or No
> to the other, and am just as much bewildered about it in the case of John with
> the top-boots as I am in the case of John with the pigtail.   (237)

The ubiquitous nature of the providential vengeance wreaked by the Brotherhood's agents—and "agents" will certainly be the operative word in the
works of those authors writing in Collins's wake and living in just as interna-
tionally intriguing times: Buchan, Fleming, Le Carré, among others—is designed to suggest that, contrary to appearances, there does indeed exist a
uniformity of virtue, a commonality of morals, everywhere. The novel dreams
that the category of bad readers which has, before the narrative's beginnings
and throughout its course, been allowed to come into being through a lack of
policing, will be reassimilated by some (admittedly paranoid and panoptic,
the man with the scarred cheek having been eavesdropping amazingly coincidentally in the right place at the right time) inter-national, indeed supra-
national, Brotherhood. The Brotherhood thus in the end brings into being
what initially had been the narrative's, what we might call in counterpoint to
Miller's characterization, pre-"primal scene" desire: a positing in its opening
gambit that there could be established a domesticity everywhere, through
Professor Pesca's sheer energetic willfulness if nothing else.

The narrative had covertly attempted to establish this universal "domesticity" when our secret operative of the association, at the "starting-point of
the strange family story[38] which it is the purpose of these pages to unfold,"

had answered the door—no "accident," despite Walter's off-hand pronouncement to the contrary—when Walter had rung at his mother's and sister's cottage home: "I had hardly rung the bell, before the house-door was
opened violently; my worthy Italian friend, Professor Pesca, appeared *in the
servant's place*" (7; emphasis added). This appearing in the domestic's place
is not the only assumption of a domestic role attempted by Pesca: "The ruling
idea of his life appeared to be, that he was bound to show his gratitude to
the country which had afforded him an asylum and a means of subsistence,
by doing his utmost to turn himself into an Englishman" (7). The Brotherhood
will at the end of the narrative successfully complete this task broached at
its beginning by its member Pesca, only on a much larger, in fact universal,
scale. Its implacable non-restrictability, serving to allegorically represent a
domesticity everywhere (and a domesticatability of everything), will be the
deus ex machina resorted to finally (if you can't bring the Americans to
the legal system,[39] bring the legal system—or League of Authors—to the
Americans) by this narrative intent upon establishing one system of honor
across the entirety of the Anglo-American literary domain.

III

When Count Fosco is not stealing women or their texts, he is writing a text
of his own, an act which necessarily renders him vulnerable to the same
crime he himself has perpetrated. This self-undermining act is only a replaying (from the anomalous situation however of the bad publisher now taking
a turn as author) of the self-undermining act of writing, in the mid-nineteenth
century, a potentially best-selling English novel and then publishing it. One
pictures here a red flag being waved in front of a bull. To know that an
international dispute is going on at the time and to send one's narrative out
into the arena nevertheless, an arena filled with inveterate publishers—and
patriotic republicans, the difference between the two not being very much, if
at all, in evidence—is to know beforehand what is going to happen to that text.
It is, in essence, to have previously defused—through an act of diffusion—any
charges of Freudian "censorship" (the hiding, and hoarding, of the secret),
Foucauldian discipline, or Millerian belated "re-education" of the homosexual—indeed any and all theories of containment—which the psychological
observer might have been waiting to offer.
  Open-minded foreigner that he is, the Count naturally has an ambivalent
attitude towards the question of the ownership of his written confession, the
penultimate narrative in this novel composed of a series of narratives. In it,
he exhibits a tension which both acknowledges the vulnerability of his writing
to theft and paradoxically claims ownership of that writing at the same time.

While writing the confession the Count is more aware than anyone that he is in fact opening himself up to being vulnerable to the same theft he had perpetrated overtly in the initial theft of Marian's diary, what we might call her "characters," and to that later one he had perpetrated covertly in a type of replaying of the earlier crime in the switching of Laura's *character* for Anne's[40]—of perhaps having his writing, his "characters" stolen from him. Recall his tacit allusion to the etymological tie between "character" and "type": "Percival! Percival! . . . Has all your experience shown you nothing of my character yet? I am a man of the antique type!" (336). A regulatory provision in the Count's confession working against this vulnerability, this inherent portability of the character of one's characters, is the metaphoric conflation of his writing with land.[41] This conflation could be applied as well to our earlier discussion of Philip Fairlie's estate being re-established in its proper course as his wayward "dissemination" is countered, for in that instance the possibility that "Laura Fairlie" could be applied to the wrong person makes possible the loss of the Limmeridge estate. The Count avails himself of the rhetorical maneuver of conflating writing with land when he claims his writing as his legacy: "Receive these fervid lines—my last legacy to the country I leave for ever" (629). Appropriately, what is passed along in this "legacy" is of course another legacy, the chance for Hartright's and Laura's son to become "one of the landed gentry of England" (643). However, the Count has earlier in his confession acknowledged that anxiety which goes along with allowing writing, to quote Derrida, "to fall from the body," when he offers a particular scene, that of his carrying Anne Catherick's clothes to the house where Laura Fairlie lay drugged by him, freely, on a sort of international trade model, to the public domain: "What a situation! I suggest it to the rising romance writers of England. I offer it, as totally new, to the worn-out dramatists of France" (626). The Count well might be repaying an intellectual debt here, for we are reminded of Fosco's description of the "innocent follies" of his early literary life when he "ruled the fashions of a second-rate Italian town, and wrote preposterous romances, on the French model, for a second-rate Italian newspaper" (260). The sophisticated visitor to England—our resident alien with respect to both the English Isle and the narrative[42]—thus evinces in his confession not only what might be seen as a domestic desire to exert ownership over his writing but also what might be seen as a foreign concilement to that writing's (indeed any and all writing's) inherent tendency to become alienated from its primary "owner."

The Count's confession would thus seem to be divided on the question of the ownership of texts in a way which was also true of classic copyright cases. The Count being a character in a narrative allegorizing a British author's dispute with his American readers, this resemblance is not surprising, for, in the famous English copyright cases *Tonson v. Collins* (1762), *Millar v. Taylor*

(1769), and *Donaldson v. Becket* (1774), it was also a matter of the English, particularly the London booksellers, dealing with a recalcitrant "other," the Scottish booksellers and their "illegal" reprints.[43] The count's duelling rhetoric of a free-trade-in-ideas versus a lines-as-legacy mentality suggests that he understands quite well the tensions involved in controlling the text which has passed beyond a border, be that border a national boundary or merely the gap between pen tip and page. While Fosco implies he would wish to establish a paternal, familial control over these lines of his, as his legacy, he also understands that their having fallen from his body necessarily leaves them open to theft, or perhaps to common ownership.

There is a tension here between keeping the text for oneself and allowing it to exit from the safe domesticity of the author's brain, a tension memorably characterized in *Tonson v. Collins* in the argument of Joseph Yates—seven years later to preside as a Justice of the Court of King's Bench in the famous case of *Millar v. Taylor.* In 1762 then-Counselor Yates argues,

> I allow, that the author has a property in his sentiments till he publishes them. He may keep them in his closet; he may give them away; if stolen from him, he has a remedy . . . But from the moment of publication, they are thrown into a state of universal communion.
>
> (*English Reports* 96:185, qtd. in Rose, *Authors* 77)

Yates reasserts and expands upon this logic in his famous and influential dissenting opinion in *Millar v. Taylor.* The implication of the tension in the Count's narrative is that, paradoxically, the author who would rather not perish as author had better not publish—a different take on a phrase coming into common parlance in our own age, "publish *and* perish." Indeed, that author would do better to keep his text in the closet or self-incarcerated in the domestic asylum. But, on the other hand, there is another option which Collins's narrative proposes: the author, when he does publish, has only to make certain beforehand to have established that each person with whom his text might come into contact recognizes the same principles of the ownership of intellectual property that he does, therefore, in a sense, not really having allowed it to leave the closet even as he has allowed it to venture forth out of the home.

This universality of the honoring of copyright is just what *The Woman in White* as narrative—not content with simply diverting the world but believing the point is to change it also[44]—is trying to bring about, even, or rather *especially,* as it, anti-carcerally carceral as ever, in its book form haplessly falls "victim" to the American pirates. A "native production" bringing a curse along with it? (*The Moonstone* 112). The narrative's ultimate moral can be nothing else than that there *is,* counteracting Fosco's assertions to the contrary (237, 604), an ultimate sense of universal justice. It is no accident that by the end of *The Woman in White* the reader sees quite clearly which, or whose, type of virtue is wrong. For the common goal of the two halves of the book has been to teach her through the incursions they have made respectively into her nervous and moral systems that there is more than one way to establish a commonality of virtue, if not through the reinforcement—via disconcerting, sensational shocks—of the threat of the possibility of coincidentally meeting up with some agent of retribution coming around any and all corners—or turnings of the page—then perhaps through a morality tale in which the reader is made to read of herself continually committing her crime—and continually *paying* for it.

To return to our framing discussion: Miller's essay ends with the quite persuasive claim—consistent as it is with the well-established view of the Victorians as excessively concerned with issues of sexual propriety—that the closet-drama played out in *The Woman in White* has exhibited its effects on into the twentieth-century, specifically in our present age's "homophobic virulence in response to AIDS" ("*Cage*" 189). This claim for a trans-historical space for the homosexual closet implies the establishment of an ontological privilege for this particular closet extending back at the least to the mid-nineteenth century. This privileging would tend to deny a place to other "closets" which might also have had cultural currency at the time, such as the one suggested by Joseph Yates, that bedroom in which one might keep one's manuscript safe from violation. It would tend to suppress—or repress—any and all other motivations for wishing to control the typographical traces (or shocked gasps of surprise and denial) one lets fall from one's body.

A central aspect of my argument has been the recontextualization of this closet in, or more appropriately around, Collins's novel. Miller's need not remain the only interpretation of the narrative's closet-dramas, even while it might remain one of the most authoritative. I have attempted to show that for the critic situated in the meta-readerly perspective—helped along in my endeavor to maintain this perspective by my having been for a good part of my essay reading a critic reading *The Woman in White*—the closet one makes recourse to in this novel is not only that one in which one hides one's at first eruptive and then subsiding proscribed sexuality, but also the one in which one hides one's manuscript or book from the potentially non-paying, potentially dishonorable readers.

There is, it should be noted, fundamentally no real conflict between my interpretation and Miller's. My essay merely proposes a different frame for the narrative's anxious closetings so ably and so engagingly brought forth by Miller. But to acknowledge this intellectual "debt" is also in a sense to take a gamble, as it is an acknowledgment which risks allowing the difference between the two interpretations to possibly become obscured through vague terminology. While "gender studies" (or what we have decided to call such) and "publishing history" (ditto) may indeed intersect, overlap, enable one another, and Sutherland's dispiritedness at academia's blindness may indeed be at base uncalled for, it is nevertheless important that we note that this interanimation and mutual enabling follow specific paths or circuits. Therefore, discourse about "conduits" matched with clever recourse to bodily metaphors in order to speak about interpretations, as well as books or language, which are certainly not "bodies"—or at least not exclusively so[45]—is eventually going to end up being unhelpful at best and distortive at worst. Indeed my mention of an "interanimation" is itself distortive. It is not that my interpretation of *The Woman in White* and Miller's discussion of the novel's closet-dramas mutually enable one another in some sort of simple here-to-there-and-back-again type of relay, but rather that the closet-dramas *in the narrative,* being not ends in themselves, are the means by which Collins attempts to counteract that drama occurring, so to speak, "off-stage," the uncloseting-drama *of the book.* The undeniable sureties of Collins's narrative written of by Miller are founded upon and directed against that fundamental lack of surety involved in the attempt at the control of language. We might, while keeping the form, change the content of one of Miller's assertions, thereby altering his contention that "[m]ale security in *The Woman in White* seems always to depend on female claustration" ("*Cage*" 166) to read, "*authorial* security in the narrative of *The Woman in White* seems always to depend on *textual* claustration." While my interpretation owes a great deal to Miller's, that debt is not a vague one situated along the level of the "conduit" but rather one situated at the particular levels of narrative and book.

A new "dialogism" emerges to complement the "monologism" which Miller finds to be operative in two of Collins's novels. While it may indeed be true at one level, to quote Miller summarizing Foucault, that a "new type of power . . . begins to permeate Western societies from the end of the eighteenth century" (Miller, *Novel* 17), it is also at another level true that at this time a world, or globalizing economy, comes into being marked by a new degree of authorial *powerlessness.* In other words, the police certainly do show up, but so do the pirates. And in this case we should note that it is most definitely an instance of the pirates calling forth those police and not vice versa. In the specific instances of Collins and of Dickens, their would-be rosy conception of their international reading community is a conception continually harried by the specter of large-scale American piracy. Thus while the "monologism" of Collins's and Dickens's narratives may become increasingly strident, indeed while the "everyday middle-class world," the ostensibly "extralegal" domain in which they in large part locate, and localize, their stories, may indeed take on an increasing policing function (Miller, *Novel* 3), this compensatory, even over-compensatory, carcerality is called into being by the existence of a more general "dialogism" circumscribing and permeating those narratives. In other words, this carcerality is called into being in reaction to the aggravating situation of Marian's world of domestic *privacy,* the world of the narrative, coming to be circumscribed and kidnapped, or indeed at certain significant points called out of itself, by the world reading the book, by Fosco's world of international *piracy.*

With regard to the lines making up *The Woman in White,* and of the trace in general, the only certainty we can have is that of being fundamentally uncertain; as Derrida, commenting upon Austin's repeated failures at successfully imposing policing categories (specifically the labels "performative" and "constative") upon utterances, suggests: "If the police are always waiting in the wings, it is because conventions are by essence violable and precarious . . . " (*Limited* 105; translation modified). The question to be asked, finally, is why the need for all these police, both official and unofficial, in the first place? If the police are there, what is it that they have come, albeit everineffectively, to control? In *The Novel and the Police* do we not find at a particular point of its exposition (the Marian-Fosco encounter) a scene offering to us the drab prospect of the return of that same old "ritual" of reading of which Miller, and many others, have by that time had quite enough: that "easy" demonstration that "the various decorums that determine a work of literature, from within as well as from without, are exceeded by the disseminal operations of language, narrative, or desire"? (Miller, *Novel* xi). In Miller's fascinating book, almost lost amid all the clever turns of phrase and shockingly original readings, do we not find in the turn to the scene of Count Fosco's reading of Marian's diary, a very "boring" scene indeed? Perhaps in more ways than one. Do we not have here, yet once again, the "resurfac[-ing] at the very site of its apparent containment" of the motivation for all the policing in the first place? (Miller, *Novel* xi). And is that motivation not just the gross lack of "copy-book morals" on the part of the villains of this story, Percival Glyde and Count Fosco, but also that ever-threatening piracy by the Americans, that fundamental iterability of language, and quite simply those so aggravatingly irrepressible "disseminal operations of language, narrative, [book,] or desire"? Finally, are we not faced in *The Woman in White* with a situation in which, instead of being effectively policed or policeable, lines (both literal as well as genealogical) quite simply do, as they ever will continue to, cause their own defection?

IV

Hard-to-discipline indebtedness attaches not just to the reading but also to the writing of *The Woman in White.* Victorian England's emphasis on virtue, "proper" civility, and honor when read in the context of publishing history cannot help but be found to be indebted to an extent to the lack of honor of the Americans. The influence on the English public of Walter Hartright's moral rigidity is derived from the wish to make the Americans feel ashamed of their lack of good breeding, ashamed of their lack of an ability to discriminate in selecting their reading matter. Not only the sensations generated by *The Woman in White,* but also its carceral psychology, its undercurrent of restraint, of wishing to keep the text safely in the bosom, the woman in the asylum or home, and even perhaps the woman-in-the-man safely hidden or the homosexual in the closet, all owe their formation to the American pirates. In a sense, Collins may have had a legitimate grievance against the pirates, but in voicing it, he incurred an intellectual and structural debt which, if English copyright law in the later 1700s had not decided to focus predominantly upon the words used, the "form of expression" as opposed to the "content,"[46] might have rendered the situation, in that imaginary Anglo-American Court of Justice to which *The Woman in White* is addressed, to add insult to injury, the *American pirates v. Collins* rather than the other way around.

Going further, were it today, in the arena of theoretical approaches, a question of the idea, of the "sentiment," rather than the form of expression—assuming for the moment the two could somehow be practically and consistently disengaged from one another[47]—in other words, were it today a question of the concept as opposed to the name, John Sutherland's complaint with which we began this essay would be rendered completely unfounded, assuming, that is—albeit unrealistically—that under those circumstances he still found need to voice it. In a world such as that one, one operating according to the dictates of a different copyright mentality entirely, a world in which labels necessarily would have ceased to be so all-important, to the extent that the presence or absence of the label "theory," not to say "gender," would have ceased to affect the saleability, as Sutherland believes it does in this surface-obsessed world of ours, of one's argument we might legitimately ask him, what it should matter that an approach such as the one practiced by an essay which explored a narrative's and author's anxious closetings resulting from that author's inability to pre-prescribe a safe future path for his writing after it had left his hand might happen somewhere along the line of its life to come to be labelled literary theory, or gender theory, or new historicism, or postcolonial theory, or new criticism, or feminist theory, or cultural studies, or even publishing history. After all, when all is said and done, if I might be allowed—as they say so tellingly in *this* world, if not in that one—to coin a phrase, what's in a name?

NOTES

Funding for the research and writing of this essay was provided by an Overseas Postgraduate Research Scholarship from the Government of Australia and an International Postgraduate Research Award, from the University of Sydney. Penny Ingram, Deirdre Coleman, William Maidment, and Simon Petch kindly read drafts.

1. See his "Publishing History" and *Victorian Novelists.*

2. For one entry into what appears to be a growth area in the academic literary market see Nelson.

3. See *Dissemination,* esp. 95–117 and 287–366; "Signature, Event, Context" in *Limited* 1–23; "Limited Inc a b c . . ." in *Limited* 29–110; and "Psyche: Inventions of the Other."

4. See the three essays in *Limited Inc.:* "Signature, Event, Context," and its extended reiterations "Limited Inc a b c . . ." and "Afterword: Toward an Ethic of Discussion."

5. Lest I should appear to be distorting Derrida's argument, I must make clear that iterability for him "does not signify simply . . . repeatability of the same, but rather alterability of this same . . ." and "iterability is at once that which tends to attain plenitude and that which bars access to it. Through the possibility of repeating every mark as the same it makes way for an idealization that seems to deliver the full presence of ideal objects . . . but this repeatability itself ensures that the full presence of a singularity thus repeated comports in itself the reference to something else, thus rending the full presence that it nevertheless announces. This is why iteration is not simply repetition" (*Limited* 119 and 129).

6. In *Novel* 146–91. Subsequent citations to this essay will be to this printing and will be given parenthetically in the text as *"Cage."*

7. Sutherland would presumably not agree with my adoption of this name for the approach I am here practicing as in a review of Mark Rose, *Authors and Owners; Susan Stewart, Crimes of Writing* (Durham: Duke UP, 1994); and Martha Woodmansee and Peter Jaszi, eds., *The Construction of Authorship,* he makes the point, "We do not, I think, have a label for the kind of hybrid legal-literary-critical approach embodied in these three books . . ." ("Copyright Disaster" 4).

8. Justifying—albeit equivocally, as an intellectual debt to Foucault which nevertheless remains an "intellectual gamble"—his own inquiry, Miller points out that a peculiar reticence is evident in *Discipline and Punish:* "perhaps the most notable reticence in Foucault's work concerns precisely the reading of literary texts and literary institutions, which . . . are never given a role to play within the disciplinary processes under consideration" (Miller, *Novel* viii). Perhaps Foucault, more interested in his other work in "literary institutions" that Miller's statement might indicate, was reticent for a reason, for as Robert Darnton points out, "books . . . do not respect limits, either linguistic or national. They have often been written by authors who belonged to an international republic of letters, composed by printers who did not work in their native tongue, sold by booksellers who operated across national boundaries, and read in one language by readers who spoke another" (47). As my essay can quite easily trace its genealogy back

to Foucault's remarkable "What is an Author?" the text which has done more
to prompt the recent resurgence of interest in copyright and the construction of
authorship than any other, I must point out that I am not arguing with Foucault's
analyses, simply with Miller's having taken them into regions where Foucault
was motivated to remain reticent—in my opinion appropriately reticent, given
the fact that almost every legitimate publishing center in the late eighteenth and on
into the nineteenth century had its Brussels, Vienna, or Boston, among others—its
undisciplined pirating double—to contend with.

9. Miller, *Novel* 54. I import this phrase from Miller's essay on *The Moonstone* in
   order to have a chance to highlight the similarly excessively constricted horizon
   of his reading of that novel. In that instance, his interpretation, adopting what
   we might call a "strategy of *localizing the investigation*" (Miller, *Novel* 36;
   emphasis Miller's), reads *The Moonstone* as fundamentally a "monological"
   novel governed by the disciplinary norms of English detection. Ignoring the, in
   this case, overtly thematized international frame, Miller therefore discounts the
   "dialogism" circumscribing that domestic detective work evidence by the task
   of recovery undertaken by one violated culture (in this particular case India)
   against another "immoral" one (in this case England).

10. Besides "*Cage*," esp. 186–90, see Sedgwick for another version of this type of
    argument, clothed in a different form of expression.

11. I am attempting here to make a start at following Darnton's lead: "By its very
    nature . . . the history of books must be international in scale and interdisciplinary
    in method. But it need not lack conceptual coherence, because books belong to
    circuits of communication that operate in consistent patterns, however complex
    they may be" (47).

12. For an example of the former see Poulet.

13. Miller holds that the narrative in general assumes its reader to be male. I would
    dispute this point to an extent. Although it may be true that the reader is assumed
    to be male (or rather, to be more precise, to be sexually interested in women) by
    Walter Hartright, our "master narrator who solicits the others' narratives and
    organizes them into a whole" ("*Cage*" 153, n. 5), this particular supposition
    cannot be made to extend also to the narrators of the many narratives which
    Hartright does not himself author.

14. In Miller's capable hands Walter Hartright's shocking meeting of Anne becomes
    a truly Freudian and/or Schreberian "bring[ing] together." Cf. Freud 42.

15. I mean to suggest by this ambiguous phrase a carceral predisposition exhibited
    not solely by the trajectory of *the object* of Miller's interpretation, but also—per-
    haps more so—by the trajectory of *that interpretation* itself.

16. My interpretation of this scene and of Miller's interpretation of it benefitted from
    discussion with Penny Ingram.

17. *The Woman in White*, ed. Sutherland, 344. All further references, unless otherwise
    noted, will be to this printing—the "younger" of the twin printings used for this
    essay—and will be cited parenthetically in the text.

18. Following in the tradition of Knoepflmacher who asserts that Collins gives a
    "fuller hearing than any of his English predecessors to the antisocial voice of
    the [English] Rebel" (366–67), the latest in the line of solely-Anglo-oriented

interpretations sensing a particular non-Englishness to be at work in *The Woman in White* and endeavoring to make that alienness comment back upon a split English psyche is Schmitt's article in which the author argues for seeing a schizophrenic distanciation to be imposed by the novel upon its unquestionably English reader which the narrative then works to finally recuperate. It is my contention that the signs of "apparent subversiveness" or "Un-Englishness" which Schmitt and others find in the novel are actually signs of the American pirates imposing themselves upon Collins's psyche and text.

19. Peter Brooks was the first to suggest that we can find traces within the narrative of a certain internalization of *The Woman in White*'s readers' desires. However, his is also an insular world of "good," as yet unfallen, solely English readers: "*The Woman in White* . . . kept the English reading public in thrall . . . Collins's representation of readers and writers constantly scribbling and constantly reading one another, even when they weren't meant to, suggests an image of the popular serial novel as a prelapsarian age of unlimited storytelling and the unlimited consumption of story" (169–70).

20. Sutherland's edition of *The Woman in White* obligingly gives us Collins's own description of the publishing history of his novel from the head of the manuscript, now, somewhat appropriately, held in the United States, institutionalized in the Pierpont Morgan Library: "[*The Woman in White*] was first published, in weekly parts, in 'All the Year Round'. . . . During the same period it was periodically published in New York, U.S. (by special arrangement with me) in 'Harper's Weekly' " ("Appendix A: The Composition, Publication, and Reception of *The Woman in White*" 647). Here we find Collins parenthetically giving voice to the worry that during this period his novel could have been published, quite legitimately as far as American law was concerned, in the States *without* "special arrangement" with him—as indeed it was.

21. While the narrative was in large part based on the case of Madame de Douhault, I will in what follows not only be dealing mainly with Collins's peculiar additions to the story, for example, the other woman—briefly mentioned in the case and then only posthumously as "le corps d'une autre personne" (Méjan 3:229)—becoming a focus for the story and honorability becoming a major theme, but I will also be implicitly suggesting why Douhault's story should have initially appealed to Collins at this fraught moment in publishing history.

22. This inability to control dissemination was the problem in the first place.

23. The Copyright Act of 1842 had done wonders for stemming within England the piracy of British works, through the policing effects of clauses such as clause 15:"Remedy for the Piracy of Books by Action on the Case," and clause 23:"Books Pirated shall become the Property of the Proprietor of the Copyright and may be recovered by Action" ("An Act" 409, 412). The Act prompted the undertaking of such cases as *Dickens v. Lee* (1844), that one concerning the attempted piracy of "A Christmas Carol."

24. The double negative structuring of Section 5, that manifestly unrestrictive stricture, of the 1790 Copyright Act held: "[N]othing in this act shall be construed to extend to prohibit the importation or vending, reprinting, or publishing within the United States, of any map, chart, book or books, written, printed, or published

by any person not a citizen of the United States, in foreign parts or places without the jurisdiction of the United States'' (rptd. in Patterson 198). Nowell-Smith writes of this section that it was ''a quite unnecessary provision, it might be thought, since in any case such books [published abroad by non-citizens] could not obtain copyright. But if unnecessary it was an encouragement to American publishers to reprint popular English books without the author's consent and without remunerating him. In fact the law was designed to benefit United States citizens—authors, publishers, and printers—and to penalize the subjects of the kingdom from which the states had successfully revolted'' (18–19). Kaplan and Brown point out that when the American copyright law was revised in 1831 and 1870 the clause was retained (799). Thus, for one hundred years, it remained, when viewed from the perspective of the English authors, what we might call an effective thoroughly ''un-policing'' policing statute.

25. See Patten 97–98 and Charvat 313. Mott, *American Magazines* 386, offers several examples of the breakdown of this system.

26. Late in his career, in a letter to a friend written just before his second trip to America, Dickens asserted: ''For twenty years I am perfectly certain that I have never made any other allusion to the republication of my books in America than the good-natured remark—'If there had been an international copyright between England and the United States, I should have been a man of very large fortune instead of a man of moderate savings' '' (Anonymous, ''A Letter by Dickens'' 209–10). Collins was not so ''good-natured'': ''It has been calculated, by persons who understand these matters better than I do, that for every reader in England I have ten readers in the United States. How many unauthorized editions of this one novel of mine—published without my deriving any profit from them—made their appearance in America? I can only tell you, as a basis for calculation, that *one* American publisher informed a friend of mine that he had 'sold one hundred and twenty thousand copies of "The Woman in White.' '' He never sent me sixpence'' (''Copyright Question'' 618). Patten argues that ''all things considered'' *in actuality* Dickens was not hard done by by this system (342). Kappel and Patten make a similar point: ''[I]f one looks at the record of American publishers and Dickens with a neutral eye, one sees a fairly respectable history, despite . . . the refusal of Congress and the American people to enter into any form of reciprocal convention covering literary properties'' (32). Appeals such as these for retrospective analyses of the ''actual'' situation should not distract us from the more pertinent issue here, that of the contemporary subjective impressions, in the minds of these authors, of this system and of the American pirates.

27. The narrative has laid the ground earlier by pointedly explaining to us Shrowl's reasoning in making a copy rather than stealing the plan outright. Shrowl chose to make ''the best copy he could of the Plan, [intending] to traffic with that, as a document which the most scrupulous person in the world need not hesitate to purchase'' (*DS* 206). He had not reckoned, however, upon Leonard Frank-land. Or for that matter, Walter Hartright, for, Collins's *The Woman in White* would seem to suggest, with its ever-increasing stress upon honor, rather than that ''we can never be paranoid enough'' (''*Cage*'' 164), that we can never be scrupulous enough—or perhaps that should be, paranoid enough about our scrupulosity.

28. See Mott, *American Magazines* II:128–30. Mott elsewhere recounts the story of the American "giant," a newspaper of larger-than-average proportions, *Brother Jonathan* printing in 1842 an "extra" which consisted of the entire text of Dickens's *American Notes,* advance sheets of which had been obtained by bribing a London pressman (*Golden Multitudes* 82).

29. Indeed, the tradition might well have gone a fair way back in the Collins family history. Peters holds that Collins's grandfather's book *Memoirs of a Picture*—a fictional work based on his life as a fairly unsuccessful picture dealer in which he condemns the then-rampant practice of picture forgery—was a "direct inspiration" for *A Rogue's Life* (12).

30. Collins, letter to E. M. Ward, 20 March 1855, in Coleman 41–42.

31. It is no mere coincidence, one suspects, that Collins in dedicating *The Woman in White* to Bryan Waller Procter, the poet-lawyer, should have characterized himself—calling up in the context of the subsequent narrative the image of a British Brotherhood, an underground London literary secret society out to exact vengeance—one of Procter's younger "brethren in literature" (2).

32. One anonymous reviewer for the, at that point in its history, rabidly anti-international-copyright *Democratic Review* not surprisingly emphasizes, repeatedly, the distance between the two nations: "[The British author] has no reason to complain, if in *another country,* the *antipodes* perhaps of his own, and a *totally distinct* political organization, his work is reproduced, for the benefit of a *new* population, without any injury to any of the rights or interests of his secured by law *at home.* . . . [T]o this *foreign* nation it is a question of expediency whether or not to grant him, to any greater or less extent, a privilege of copyright; and . . . actually in the case of the present demand upon our government on behalf of English authors, the preponderance of the expediency—an expediency coincident with the moral right of the matter—is against its concession" (Anonymous, "Note," 615; emphases added).

33. See for example the argument of Henry C. Carey, the Philadelphia publisher: "Read *Bleak House,* and you will find that [Mr. Dickens] has been a most careful observer of men and things . . . He is in the condition of a man who had entered a large garden and collected a variety of the most beautiful flowers growing therein, of which he had made a fine bouquet . . . [yet he] insist[s] that he is owner of the bouquet itself, although he has paid no wages to the man who raised the flowers" (20, 25).

34. "Thou shouldst print more, not let that copy die" (Sonnet II: 14).

35. In this sense, the drama between Walter Hartright and Anne Catherick on Hampstead Heath has always already taken place, for their meeting and Walter's vacillating as to whether or not to let her go (the act which symbolically re-enacts Phillip Fairlie's sin of letting himself go) is simply a replaying of the moment of Anne's conception.

36. Elaine Showalter, anticipating Miller's focus upon Collins's "conventionality," writes, "Like Dickens, Collins inevitably ends his novels with sentimental happy marriages of patient woman and resolute man, marriages whose success is validated by the prompt appearance of male offspring" (163).

37. Having halted at the surface-reading of this scene, Miller would seem to have forgotten the fundamental lesson of the novel, that just as the clothes don't necessarily make The Woman, the conventions don't necessarily make the "Victorian."

38. We might recall here the pun being set in operation—in contrast to that contained in a title such as *Dealings with the Firm of Dombey and Son, Wholesale, Retail, and for Exportation—by Collins's subtitling The Evil Genius* (1886) "*[A] Domestic* Story." That story is on one level patently a domestic story, being the recounting of the break-up of a marriage and happy home. However, it is also a domestic story on another level, as is signalled by Collins's having the lawyer Sarrazin at one point in a dinner conversation advert to the issue of American piracy: "[T]heir government forgets what is due to the honor of the nation. . . . The honor of a nation which confers right of property in works of art produced by its own citizens, is surely concerned in protecting from theft works of art produced by other citizens" (115). (This reference is to a pirate American edition of the novel.)

39. With respect to Collins's opening pronouncement that "the Law is still, in certain inevitable cases, the pre-engaged servant of the long purse" (5), see Chapter XI in Barnes, "Bribery, or the Necessary Expenses of Congressional Action: November 1851-February 1853," in which he details Bulwer's and Dickens's failed attempts, around the time Collins was first coming to know them, at collecting the funds necessary to turn the serious attention of Congress towards an Anglo-American copyright agreement.

40. Note that Fosco formulates his plan of duplicitous substitution immediately after he has berated Percival for the latter's failure in his over-heated attempts at securing his wife's *signature* on the contract loaning her fortune to her husband. Instead of one kind of "character," then, they will take another. Also, recalling that the labels on the clothes the count causes Laura to be dressed in effectively bring about the transformation in identities—characters equalling character, as the nurses at the asylum peremptorily testify: "Look at your own name on your own clothes. . . . There it is, in good marking ink . . . Anne Catherick, as plain as print!" (436)—the count's theft of identity, like his theft of Marian's diary, would seem to be at its basis a textual one.

41. On the conflation of text and land, especially in the case of *Millar v. Taylor,* see Swartz. See also my dissertation's chapter on *Basil:* "The Manuscript as Writer's Estate: [Wilkie Collins's] *Basil* [1852] and the Early-Victorian Copyright Act."

42. The count's ambivalent situation as what I am calling a "resident alien" with respect to the narrative has already been quite consummately demonstrated for us by Miller in the passage from page 164 analyzed above.

43. While *Tonson v. Collins,* unlike the other two cases, was not a litigation directly pitting an English against a Scottish bookseller, but rather a trumped-up collusion between two English booksellers, nevertheless, at issue was Benjamin Collins's (no relation to Wilkie) offering for sale Scottish reprints of English works, which works, as a result of the age's less than sure and certain stance on the proper interpretation of the Statute of Anne of 1710, were at the time in copyright flux.

As Mark Rose points out, at a certain level the eighteenth-century literary-property debate "was a commercial encounter, played out in the form of a national contest between England and Scotland, in which a deeply entrenched establishment was challenged by outsiders" (*Authors* 92).

44. In this sense we might say that the "realism" which the sensation novel is so often found by contemporary reviewers to be lacking is more than made up for, at least in this case, by a grandly propagandistic, fundamentally political, "practicalism" or hyper-realism.

45. I would mention here a remark made by Vice-Chancellor J. L. Knight-Bruce in *Prince Albert v. Strange* (1849) when discussing the protection of literary property from "invasion": "this class of property, by nature not corporeal at all, or not exclusively corporeal, require[s] to be defended against incorporeal attacks, and not at all or not exclusively against bodily assaults" (*Prince Albert* 312).

46. Writing of the important discussion of copyright in William Blackstone's *Commentaries on the Laws of England* (1766)—Blackstone having been Joseph Yates's adversary in *Tonson v. Collins*—Rose points out that the conception of "property" in intellectual works was divested by Blackstone of its till-then traditional stress upon the ideas or sentiments themselves and that stress reinvested in the specific words used to express those sentiments: "[U]nder pressure from Yates's rejection of the notion that ideas might remain property once published ... Blackstone significantly shifted the conception of literary property from ... 'sentiments' to the conception of the essence of the property as a fusion of idea and language. ... Not ideas alone, but the expression of ideas: this, to put Blackstone's point in the familiar modern form which it anticipates, was what copyright protected. ... The bearer of meaning through which the writer's ideas were realized was language. Clothed in words, which Blackstone treated as if they were a kind of substance, the writer's sentiments became property" (Rose, "The Author in Court" 228).

47. Judge Learned Hand, approaching the elusive boundary from the direction opposite to Blackstone, points out that theories or precedents are no help in the practical matter of locating this line in copyright cases: "[A]s soon as literal appropriation ceases to be the test, the whole matter is necessarily at large ... but there is a point in this series of abstractions where they are no longer protected, since otherwise the [writer] could prevent the use of his 'ideas,' to which, apart from their expression his property is never extended. Nobody has ever been able to fix that boundary, and nobody ever can" (278–79).

WORKS CITED

"An Act to Amend the Law of Copyright [1st July 1842]." *Statutes of the United Kingdom of Great Britain and Ireland, 5 & 6 Victoria, 1842*. London: Her Majesty's Printers, 1842. Cap. 45; 404–15.

Anonymous. "A Letter by Dickens on International Copyright." *The Dickensian* 5 (1909): 209–10.

Anonymous. "Note" on "The International Copyright Question: Protest Against the Doctrine of the *Democratic Review* Thereon." *The United States Magazine and Democratic Review* 12 (1843): 614–16.

Ashley, Robert. *Wilkie Collins.* London: Arthur Barker, 1952.

Barnes, James J. *Authors, Publishers, and Politicians: The Quest for an Anglo-American Copyright Agreement 1815–1854.* London: Routledge & Kegan Paul, 1974.

Bisla, Sundeep. *The Borderless Word: The Fictions of Wilkie Collins and the Victorian Copyright Debates.* Diss. U of Sydney, 1999.

Brooks, Peter. *Reading for the Plot.* New York: Knopf, 1984.

Carey, Henry C. *Letters on International Copyright.* [1853]. 2nd ed. New York: Hurd & Houghton, 1868.

Cervantes Saavedra, Miguel de. *The Adventures of Don Quixote.* Trans. J. M. Cohen. Penguin Classics. London: Penguin, 1950.

———. *El Ingenioso Hidalgo Don Quixote De La Mancha: Parte Segunda.* Madrid: D. Miguel de Burgos, 1826.

Charvat, William. *The Profession of Authorship in America, 1800–1870.* Ed. Matthew J. Bruccoli. Columbus: Ohio State UP, 1968.

Clark, Aubert J. *The Movement for International Copyright in Nineteenth Century America.* Westport, Conn.: Greenwood Press, 1960.

Coleman, William Rollin. *The University of Texas Collection of the Letters of Wilkie Collins, Victorian Novelist.* Diss. U of Texas at Austin, 1975.

Collins, Wilkie. *After Dark.* Vol. 21 of *The Works of Wilkie Collins.* London: Chatto & Windus, 1885–93.

———. "Considerations on the Copyright Question." *International Review* 8 (1880): 609–618.

———. *The Dead Secret.* Vol. 4 of *The Works of Wilkie Collins.* London: Chatto & Windus, 1885–93.

———. *The Evil Genius: A Domestic Story.* New York: M. J. Ivers & Co., 1886.

———. *The Moonstone: A Romance.* Ed. J. I. M. Stewart. Penguin Classics. London: Penguin, 1986.

———. *A Rogue's Life: From his Birth to his Marriage.* Vol. 15 of *The Works of Wilkie Collins.* London: Chatto & Windus, 1885–93.

———. *The Woman in White.* Ed. Harvey Peter Sucksmith. Oxford World's Classics. [1980] Oxford: Oxford UP, 1992.

———. *The Woman in White.* Ed. John Sutherland. Oxford World's Classics. Oxford: Oxford UP, 1996.

Darnton, Robert. "What is the History of Books?" *Reading in America: Literature and Social History.* Ed. Cathy N. Davidson. Baltimore: Johns Hopkins UP, 1989. 27–52.

Derrida, Jacques. *Dissemination.* Trans. Barbara Johnson. Chicago: U of Chicago P, 1978.

———. *Limited Inc.* Trans. Samuel Weber and Jeffrey Mehlman. Ed. Gerald Graff. Evanston, Illinois: Northwestern UP, 1988.

———. "Psyche: Inventions of the Other." Trans. Catherine Porter. In *Reading De Man Reading.* Ed. Lindsay Waters and Wlad Godzich. Minneapolis: U of Minnesota P, 1989. 25–65.

———. *Writing and Difference.* Trans. Alan Bass. Chicago: U of Chicago P, 1978.

[Dickens, Charles.] "Insularities." *Household Words,* 13 (19 January 1856): 1–4.

Dickens v. Lee (1844). *The Jurist.* Vol. 8:Part 1. 183–86.

Freud, Sigmund. "Psychoanalytic Notes on an Autobiographical Account of a Case of Paranoia." *Standard Edition.* Ed. and Trans. James Strachey. London: Hogarth Press, 1953–74. 12:12–79.

Hand, Learned. Decision in *Nichols v. Universal Pictures Corp.* 45 Fed. Cas. 2nd Circuit 119. Rptd. in Kaplan and Brown. 276–82.

Kaplan, Benjamin, and Ralph S. Brown, Jr., eds. *Cases on Copyright.* 2nd ed. Mineola, N.Y.: Foundation Press, 1974.

Kappel, Andrew J., and Robert L. Patten. "Dickens' Second American Tour and His 'Utterly Worthless and Profitless' American 'Rights'." *Dickens Studies Annual* 7 (1978): 1–33.

Knoepflmacher, U. C. "The Counterworld of Victorian Fiction and *The Woman in White.*" In *The Worlds of Victorian Fiction.* Ed. Jerome H. Buckley. Cambridge, Mass.: Harvard UP, 1975. 351–69.

Méjan, Maurice. "Affaire de Madame de Douhault," vol. 3:5-ff., and "Suite de L'Affaire de Madame de Douhault," vol. 6:5–92. *Receuil des Causes Célèbres.* 2nd. ed. Paris: 1808–1814.

Miller, D. A. "*Cage aux folles:* Sensation and Gender in Wilkie Collins's *The Woman in White.*" In his *Novel.* 146–91.

————. *The Novel and the Police*. Berkeley: U of California P, 1988.

Mott, Frank Luther. *Golden Multitudes: The Story of Best Sellers in the United States*. New York: Macmillan Co., 1947.

————. *A History of American Magazines, 1850–1865*. Vol. 2 of *A History of American Magazines*. Cambridge, Mass.: Belknap, 1957.

Nelson, Cary, ed. *Will Teach for Food: Academic Labor in Crisis*. Minneapolis: U of Minnesota P, 1997.

Nowell-Smith, Simon. *International Copyright in the Reign of Queen Victoria*. Oxford: Clarendon Press, 1968.

Oliphant, Margaret. "Sensation Novels." *Blackwood's Edinburgh Magazine* 91 (1862): 565–74.

Patten, Robert L. *Charles Dickens and His Publishers*. Oxford: Clarendon Press, 1978.

Patterson, Lyman Ray. *Copyright in Historical Perspective*. Nashville: Vanderbilt UP, 1968.

Poulet, Georges. "Criticism and the Experience of Interiority." Trans. Catherine Macksey and Richard Macksey. In *Reader-Response Criticism: From Formalism to Post-Structuralism*. Ed. Jane P. Tompkins. Baltimore: Johns Hopkins UP, 1980. 41–49.

Prince Albert v. Strange (1849). *English Reports* 64:293–321.

Rose, Mark. "The Author in Court: *Pope v. Curll*. (1741)" In Woodmansee and Jaszi. 211–29.

————. *Authors and Owners: The Invention of Copyright*. Cambridge, Mass.: Harvard UP, 1993.

Schmitt, Cannon. "Alien Nation: Gender, Genre, and English Nationality in Wilkie Collins's *The Woman in White*." *Genre* 26 (1993): 283–310.

Sedgwick, Eve Kosofsky. *Between Men: English Literature and Male Homosocial Desire*. New York: Columbia UP, 1985.

Shakespeare, William. Sonnet 11. *The Riverside Shakespeare*. Ed. G. Blakemore Evans et al. Boston: Houghton Mifflin, 1974. P. 1751.

Showalter, Elaine. *A Literature of Their Own*. Princeton: Princeton UP, 1977.

Sutherland, John. "The Great Copyright Disaster." *The London Review of Books* 17:1 (12 January 1995): 3–4.

————. "Publishing History: A Hole in the Centre of Literary Sociology." *Critical Inquiry* 14 (1988): 574–89.

————. *Victorian Novelists and Publishers.* London: Athlone Press, 1976.

————. "What Sells Best, and Why." *The Times Literary Supplement* (31 May 1996): 27.

Swartz, Richard. "Patrimony and the Figuration of Authorship in the Eighteenth-Century Literary Property Debates." *Works and Days* 7:2 (1989): 29–54.

Woodmansee, Martha, and Peter Jaszi, eds. *The Construction of Authorship: Textual Appropriation in Law and Literature.* Durham, N.C.: Duke UP, 1994.

Yates, Edmund. "Mr. Wilkie Collins in Gloucester Place." *Celebrities at Home.* 3rd Series. 1879:145–46. Rptd. in Wilkie Collins. *The Woman in White.* Ed. Sucksmith. Appendix C: 588–94.

Gaskell's *Ruth* and Hardy's *Tess* as Novels of Free Union

Jeanette Shumaker

When first published, both Gaskell's Ruth and Hardy's Tess of the D'Urbervilles *(1891) stirred controversies about how Victorians should deal with so-called "fallen women." Like* Ruth *and* Tess, *neglected nineteenth-century novels about free union—such as Amelia A. Opie's* Adeline Mowbray *and W. Francis Barry's* The New Antigone—*contain conflicting narratives of female rebellion and repentance. Whereas the heroine of the liberationist narrative proclaims her right to a free union, the reformed heroine of the penitential narrative endorses the conventional morality that regards as "fallen." The ideological disparities between liberationist and penitential narratives cause unrealistic contortions in the plots of Opie's and Barry's novels of free union. Using the theories of Michel Foucault and M. M. Bahktin to examine such disjunctions between narratives creates an understanding of the plot ruptures that critics decry in* Ruth *and* Tess, *as well as an awareness* of the underlying cultural conflict over female sexuality. Although much has been written about Ruth *and especially* Tess, *their ties to novels of free union have not previously been discussed.*

When first published, both *Ruth* (1853) and *Tess of the D'Urbervilles* (1891) stirred controversies about how Victorian society should deal with so-called "fallen women." Like *Ruth* and *Tess,* neglected nineteenth century novels about free union—such as Amelia A. Opie's *Adeline Mowbray* (1805) and W. Francis Barry's *The New Antigone* (1887)—contain conflicting narratives of female rebellion and repentance. During the radical narrative, the rebellious heroine rejects the double standard, demanding the sexual freedom allowed to men. When she comes to see her rebellion as sinful, the narrative of her penance begins. Whereas the heroine of the liberationist narrative proclaims her right to a free union, the reformed heroine of the penitential narrative endorses the conventional morality that regards her as "fallen." The ideological disparities between liberationist and penitential narratives cause unrealistic contortions in the plots of Opie's and Barry's novels of free union.[1] Examining such disjunctions between narratives creates an understanding of the plot ruptures that critics decry in *Ruth* and *Tess*, as well as an awareness of the underlying cultural conflict over female sexuality. Although much has been written about *Ruth* and especially *Tess*, their ties to novels of free union have not been discussed.[2]

Why are Opie's and Barry's novels rarely read, and why is *Ruth* regarded as Gaskell's weakest novel? Readers of our post-1960s era may find it difficult to empathize with the pained ambivalence of nineteenth-century novels of free union and to tolerate the resulting tensions in their plots. The ambivalence of such novels may also annoy us because, according to D. A. Miller, "closure remains a powerful ideal" (280). Our cultural distance from these novels augments the aesthetic reasons for why *Ruth* is often dismissed, and for why Opie's and Barry's novels are ignored, whereas the more radical *Tess* is admired. *Tess* diverges from the ambivalence of the earlier novels to argue that the "fallen woman" is pure. However, at times the plot of *Tess* becomes as unrealistic as those of the earlier novels, for the same reason—ambivalence about the rights and nature of women. The collisions between penitential and liberationist narratives in *Ruth, Adeline, Antigone*, and, to some extent, *Tess* represent their authors' internal arguments over whether heroines should have the sexual freedom that even nineteenth-century feminists only rarely claim for women. The conflict between narratives makes not only *Tess* but the lesser-known novels into intriguing documents of the century's struggle over female chastity. Although the penitential narrative fills most of the pages of each novel, the memorable parts of *Adeline, Antigone*, and *Ruth* are their radical opening chapters. These utopian openings prepare for a more concerted attack on Victorian notions of female chastity in *Tess*. Gaskell's and Barry's brief endorsements of the sexual liberation associated with Shelley and Blake show the persistence of radical notions during the Victorian age that enabled such ideas to resurface in novelists such as Hardy during the fin de siècle.

Michel Foucault's *History of Sexuality* allows us to recognize the sexual radicalism throughout *Adeline, Ruth*, and *Antigone*, despite their apparent disavowal of it during their penitential narratives. Foucault argues that nineteenth-century culture heightens pleasure and desire through verbalizing the struggle to repress them. Such repression creates 'perpetual spirals of power and pleasure'' (45). Pleasure associated with desire is felt most intensely in the absence of sexual behavior. In this situation, the confession of repressed desire becomes its fulfillment. By enforcing confession and penance, Victorian novels enact the century's titillating drama of negativity that Foucault describes as "anti-energy" (85). By "anti-energy," Foucault means that the struggle to repress desire drains characters of their vitality, turning them into obedient, weakened beings. At great personal cost, characters confess their secrets of desire. In the novel of free union, the penitential narrative transforms the active sexuality seen in the liberationist narrative into discourses of confession and repression. This is a Foucauldian shift that preserves the radical impetus by denying it, since the repudiation of sexuality entails a continuing obsession with it. As a result, the heroine's sexual conflict intensifies during the penitential narrative, rather than abating as might be expected.

What makes the heroine of the novel of free union interesting is her exhausting, continuous struggle to repress her desires so that she will not "sin" again. Drawing on Foucault, John Kucich argues in *Repression in Victorian Fiction* that Victorian protagonists often earn heroic stature through their ability to repress. That is so for the penitent heroine of the novel of free union. She transforms her sexuality into verbal self-laceration that earns her a higher place in Kucich's hierarchy of repression than is held by those who condemn her. The heroine regrets her affair, but without it, she would have nothing to define her new virtuousness against; her penitential narrative requires a liberationist subtext to provide drama and prurient interest. The reformed heroine's "improper" desires persist, but she shapes them into words—into the "truth" of her sinfulness. Through this strategy, she avoids repeating the actions that constituted her "sin." Paradoxically, successful penance depends upon the continuing inner conflict seen in the shadowy liberationist narrative buried within the penitential one.

Another way in which liberationist tendencies survive during the penitential narrative can be seen through the lens of M. M. Bakhtin's dialogism. Dialogism posits that novels contain multiple voices that represent ideological positions in conversation with each other: no voice (or position) defeats the others, but rather, the dialogue continues throughout the novel. Such dialogue may be external—between characters—or internal—between a single character (or narrator) at two different times (427). "Heteroglossia" includes the multitude of contexts and conditions that determine novelistic speech; according to Bakhtin, a "diversity of voices and heteroglossia enter the novel" (300), making each novel singularly new. Free-union novels fit Bakhtin's description of heteroglot fictions that "orchestrate" their themes through multiple voices and circumstances (263).

With its moral and other distinguishing characteristics, the penitential narrative may be seen as a subgenre of fiction. Bakhtin argues that many genres

may be included in a novel; each genre that a novel includes imports its own
conventions and language (320). The conventions of the penitential narrative
dominate the second half of novels of free union, but the reader's memory
of the earlier liberationist narrative calls the conventions of penance into
question. The radical voice that is submerged during the middle of *Ruth,
Adeline,* and *Antigone* reverberates long afterwards, questioning the conservative moral of the penitential narrative. Such conflicted novels dramatize the
period's debate about female sexual freedom that Opie, Barry, and Gaskell
seem to intend for the radicals to lose, but unconsciously, may wish them
to win.

Unlike Opie's, Barry,'s and Gaskell's novels, *Tess* never silences the radical
voice. Although Tess learns to see herself as "fallen," the narrator reminds
us repeatedly that she is not, interrogating accepted definitions of proper
womanhood. Hardy's ironic narrator mocks the stilted ideology held by Tess's
peers, and often, by Tess herself. However, feminist critics note that the
narrator sometimes enters into the essentializing discourse that supports the
stereotyping of women as "fallen" or "pure" which is supposed to be the
novel's complaint. That the narrator sometimes supports the patriarchal, penitential narrative through essentializing Tess constitutes a Bahktinian flip from
one ideological position to another. Such flip-flops of voice and position mark
the limits of the narrator's radical ideology. However, these flip-flops may,
as Bahktin argues, be part of an author's strategy for questioning socially
accepted points of view (312–13). I believe that is the case regarding the
inconsistent narrator of *Tess*.

Bahktin describes all speaking characters in novels as "ideologues" to at
least some degree; he notes that "an ideologue must defend and try out his
ideological positions" (333). The label of ideologue fits the narrator as well as
Tess and her peers in regards to their views of female purity. The discrepancy
between the narrator's view of Tess as a "pure" child of nature and her
peers' view of her as "impure" questions the conventions of the "fallen
woman's" penance seen in the latter volumes of *Ruth, Adeline* and *Antigone*.
The dislocation between the early liberationist and latter conservative parts
of *Ruth, Adeline,* and *Antigone* becomes a dislocation between a generally
radical narrator and generally conservative characters in *Tess*. Gaskell's, Barry's, and Opie's narrators do criticize characters for being intolerant of the
reformed "fallen" heroine, yet these narrators regard the heroine's past as
sinful, unlike Hardy's narrator. Through Hardy's deviation from the conservative narrator of the earlier novelists, the struggle between radicalism and
conservatism that many critics see as *Ruth*'s failure becomes *Tess*'s triumph.

To understand how the evolution from the ambivalently moralistic *Ruth* to
the ambivalently Godwinian *Tess* occurs, I shall first describe the conventions
of the novel of free union seen in *Adeline* and *Antigone*. These four novels

span more than eighty years, yet although changes happened regarding women's rights and roles, the novels are strikingly similar in terms of their structural ruptures that reflect underlying ideological conflicts. These similarities suggest that the struggle over female "purity" that perplexed Mrs. Opie at the start of the century continued throughout the century. By the 1890s, the class and gender barriers that the debate about female chastity represented were eroding more quickly than at the century's beginning.

Daughter of a philanthropic doctor, Mrs. Opie rejected William Godwin's offer of marriage. She did marry a successful painter who died two years after she wrote *Adeline Mowbray. Adeline* may have been inspired by the life of Mary Wollstonecraft, according to Liz Bellamy and Roxanne Eberle. Eberle regards the novel as a vindication of Wollstonecraft written in response to Godwin's memoirs that revealed her sexual adventures; Eberle also argues that the novel critiques Godwinian free love for being unrealistic due to the pervasiveness of "destructive male desire" (130).

Adeline's mother is a forerunner of Dickens's Mrs. Jellyby who neglects her daughter except for teaching her radical notions. A hypocrite, Mrs. Mowbray will not forgive her daughter for living with Glenmurray, a radical intellectual. But Mrs. Mowbray does forgive her new husband, drunken Sir Patrick, for attempting to seduce Adeline. As is typical in novels about free union, Glenmurray wants to marry Adeline to shield her from disgrace, but she repeatedly refuses because to accept would be to act against her faith in free love. The unmarried couple is happy except for being pained at the many insults Adeline receives from men and women alike during their travels. Soon after Adeline bears a dead child, Glenmurray becomes ill and dies, leaving her penniless because legally his property could not go to a woman who was not his wife. To support herself, Adeline opens a school. It fails because of her "stained" reputation. Harassed by poverty and seducers, Adeline agrees to marry Berrendale, the friend that Glenmurray long ago advised her to wed in the event of his death. Unfortunately, Berrendale turns out to be a greedy bigamist with little affection for Adeline and the daughter that Adeline bears him. Nevertheless, Adeline does not leave Berrendale for a free union with the kind colonel to whom she is attracted. Instead, as is typical in novels about free union, she disavows her radicalism; Adeline says that even though awful marriages like hers exist, "the mass of happiness and virtue is certainly increased" by the institution (vol. 3, 149). The novel ends with the reconciliation of dying Adeline and her remorseful mother, who adopts Adeline's daughter.

If Opie had wanted to vilify free union, would it not have been more effective to give Adeline a stereotypically virtuous husband and an ignoble seducer? For *The Father and Daughter* (1801), Opie created such a seducer: she knew how. Gary Kelly writes of *Adeline* that "the reader who wishes to find in the 'official text' a covert subversive text may do so . . . a readership who could see a model relationship between woman and man in the relationship between Adeline and Glenmurray . . . just as they could see a model relationship . . . in the relationship between Mary Wollstonecraft and William Godwin, the originals who could, very easily, be read into Opie's tale'' (''Amelia'' 11). In Wollstonecraft's unfinished novel, *Maria: or the Wrongs of Woman* (1798), the heroine leaves her libertine husband for a free union with a good man. *Maria* reverses the pattern of *Adeline,* which begins with its heroine's free union with a good man and ends with her commitment to her marriage to a selfish man. Can Adeline's repentance be seen as reasonable, given that her lover treated her kindly while her husband treated her cruelly, to the point of practicing bigamy, which makes their marriage void? Opie portrays Adeline as self-denigrating to prove that she is not vain. Adeline is a precursor of Ruth and Tess, ''pure'' despite her ''fall'' that is portrayed not as a sin, but as a natural, joyous event. In addition, Adeline's longsuffering penance that calls her society's prejudices into question creates the pattern for the disturbing penances of Ruth and Tess.

Adeline Mowbray pioneers the convention (also seen in *Ruth*) that a friend should convert the ''fallen'' heroine. Mrs. Pemberton, a Quaker, befriends Adeline even though she regards Adeline as sinful. Mrs. Pemberton plays the role that the Bensons play in *Ruth*—that of leading the heroine to God, and, as a result, forcing her to regard her past with shame. In contrast with *Tess,* both *Adeline* and *Ruth* are, in their latter volumes, novels of conversion. But they resemble *Tess* in containing a social critique that, at least for modern readers, may overshadow their religious messages. Soon after the publication of *Ruth,* G. H. Lewes wrote that the moral of Gaskell's novel was that respectable women must help ''fallen'' ones; since then, many critics have agreed with Lewes (269). Opie can be seen as making a similar argument—not necessarily for reclaiming the penitent woman like Gaskell does, but, like Hardy, for disdaining those who ostracize her. Consistent with this message of openness, the religious message of both *Ruth* and *Adeline* is anti-Calvinistic. Adeline, like Ruth, is generous, loving, and honest throughout the novel. Adeline forgives those whose rejections of her are described in a vivid and exhaustive way that displaces the novel's religious message with pointed social criticism. Unlike Berrendale, who appears to be respectable but is not, Adeline appears disreputable but actually deserves respect. Like *Ruth* and *Tess, Adeline* criticizes the double standard for forgiving exploitative men like Berrendale while excessively punishing idealistic women such as Adeline and her ''fallen'' mulatto servant. That Adeline's penance may be seen as inappropriately severe suggests that the novel questions the rules of gender and class that the heroine violated.

Echoing Adeline, Hippolyta in Barry's *The New Antigone* was raised by a radical, atheist parent to see ''the two sexes equal and free'' without marriage (vol. 2, 54). And like Glenmurray, Hippolyta's lover tries to convince her to marry him, but she will not. Hippolyta says to Rupert that "true marriage is the union of heart with heart. . . . Custom is nothing" (2.61). Accidentally witnessing a religious service causes Hippolyta to see herself as "fallen"; she confesses to a priest, leaves Rupert, and enters a nunnery in Spain. As she later melodramatically explains to Rupert, "I must do penance with Magdalene . . . [free union] made me unfit to be any man's wife" (3.245). Hippolyta then convinces Rupert to return to the wife whom he had married while experiencing amnesia during a fever caused by Hippolyta's desertion of him (!!!). Hippolyta's sacrifice causes Rupert's wife to say of Hippolyta: "Is she not the noblest woman on earth?" (289).

The disjunction between the liberationist and the penitential narratives forces Barry's plot into implausible, melodramatic twists that show the author's ineffectual attempts to valorize repentance. According to Pierre Macherey, such disjunctions are typical of didactic novels: "When it [philosophy] is filtered through the modes of narrativity specific to literature, the attempt to rationalize that characterizes philosophical speculation and gives it homogeneity and logic is transformed into a lacunary, jerky exposition" (234). As a Catholic priest, Barry argues for the appropriateness of Hippolyta's conversion by suggesting that her work as a nun serves the unfortunate; Rupert is happy with his wife; Hippolyta's father's secret son happily converts; and her father is about to follow suit by converting also.

Unfortunately, however, Barry's attempt to argue against free union in the latter part of his novel ruins the plot because he creates inconsistencies with the first half. Through the unbelievably quick conversion of Hippolyta once she is exposed to the Church, Barry implies that Hippolyta believed in free union because her father had kept her ignorant of God. But the unintentional message of Hippolyta's conversion is to criticize ascetic religion for making Hippolyta into a self-flagellating nun. As a quintessential Victorian depiction of repression and masochistic asceticism, the novel prefigures *Tess* and recalls *Ruth*. As in those two novels, Barry's heroine's guilt seems unearned and, therefore, tragically wasted, much like Adeline Mowbray's. Hippolyta becomes a Foucauldian robot, a tireless social worker whose efforts to repress her sexual side slowly kill her, as they do Charlotte Brontë's diligent missionary, St. John Rivers. Since Hippolyta's guilt over deviating from her culture's standard of female purity seems misplaced, her guilt calls that standard into question. *Antigone* also criticizes the double standard that makes Hippolyta see herself as too "stained" for marriage whereas her lover Rupert is not. Hippolyta's dedication to the poor recalls Ruth's, and, of course, Hester Prynne's. These "fallen" heroines redeem themselves by conforming to the Victorian convention that angel women soften capitalism's ravages through philanthropy. Through her big heart, the Victorian free-love martyr creates a new, higher standard of purity that is independent of female chastity, as the early nineteenth-century "fallen woman" tried to do in *Adeline*. The portrayals of Adeline and Hippolyta as preachy paragons show how novels of free union mimic the conventions of the Evangelical novel to make their heroines acceptable to Victorian readers. In doing so, Barry and Opie partially undo their invention of unconventional women.[3]

Like Barry and Opie, Gaskell privileges the penitential narrative, endorsing the class and gender structures it supports. However, Gaskell's liberationist narrative is sufficiently memorable to enable subversive readings of *Ruth,* as is also possible with *Adeline* and *Antigone.* In contrast with the earlier novels, *Tess* privileges the liberationist narrative. However, Hardy sometimes conforms to the conventions of the penitential narrative that promote Victorian stereotypes such as the asexuality of Tess as an angelic wife.

Unlike Tess, Ruth is vibrantly sexual during the liberationist narrative. Although the liberationist narrative of *Ruth* is much shorter than the novel's narrative of repentance, it has the rhetorical advantage of coming first. In contrast with *Ruth, Adeline,* and *Antigone,* the liberationist narrative of *Tess* is never contradicted by the narrator of the penitential narrative. The narrator continues to reiterate Tess's purity during the penitential narrative. Thus, *Tess* avoids the abrupt shift in the narrator's point of view between the liberationist and penitential narratives of the earlier novels. The reiteration of the heroine's purity makes *Tess* a more consistently radical novel than *Ruth, Adeline,* or *Antigone.*

The order of the narratives in *Tess* is more complex than in the earlier novels, which begin with a liberationist narrative and end with a penitential one. In *Tess,* the heroine pays for her rape and her subsequent joyless affair before either her liberationist or her penitential narrative begins: she endures the ignominy of being pregnant, and the sorrow of losing her baby. These sad events create a narrative of social criticism that protests Tess's senseless suffering, not a narrative of her repentance. This disturbing prelude is appropriate to a novel that will question the ideology of class and gender that requires the repentance of the hard-working heroine. The liberationist narrative finally begins in Talbothays, but soon ends with Tess's confession on her wedding night. The liberationist idyll does not reappear until Angel forgives Tess for her affair with Alec and also for murdering him. Tess's penance, which she only occasionally rails against, starts when Angel rejects her on their wedding night, then dominates the rest of the novel. By the time the penitential narrative concludes the novel with Tess's execution, her sufferings are staggering. The unjust weight of Tess's suffering not only makes a strong statement about class and gender prejudices, but forces the lengthy penitential narrative to endorse the brief liberationist narrative much more obviously than it does in *Ruth, Adeline,* or *Antigone.*

It is part of Hardy's revision of the conventions of novels of free union that Tess does not experience the joy in her affair that Ruth, Adeline, and Hippolyta do. The reason for this is that Alec rapes Tess. After their encounter in the Chase, Tess submits briefly to a joyless relationship with Alec, feeling that he has already appropriated her body anyway. Though Tess is an unrecognized aristocrat, she also belongs to the tradition of the raped working-class girl who appears in Barrett Browning's *Aurora Leigh* (1857): the effects of Tess's membership in this tradition are to make Angel's rejection of Tess even more despicable, and to make Tess appear asexually "pure" despite her affair.

But Tess's lack of passion for Alec also makes passionate Ruth seem to be more of a revolutionary heroine that we might expect—or less of one, if we recall, with Patsy Stoneman, that Ruth spends much of her life regretting her adolescent sexual passion. On the contrary, Tess's passion for Angel is less a corporeal one than the spiritual one expected of a Victorian middle-class wife who worships her husband as a god. Tess's reunion with Angel at the end of the novel is drained of sexuality by his deathlike state and her temporary madness; exhausted after murdering Alec, Tess is Angel's nurse and he, hers. Tess must conform to the asexual ideal of her era to prove that she is the "pure woman" of the novel's subtitle. If Hardy had dared to be as radical as Gaskell and the free-love novelists in their early chapters, he could have made Tess's rape a seduction, allowing Tess to have sexual passion for both Alec and Angel while remaining "pure." But since Gaskell, Opie, and Barry do not maintain their radicalism throughout their novels, it may be unrealistic to expect Hardy to confront Victorian notions about female chastity more directly than he did.

Both *Tess* and *Ruth* employ pastoral elements that legitimize female sexual freedom. The liberationist portion of *Ruth* has the stylistic advantage of being written more compellingly than the rest of the novel in a pastoral language rarely found in Gaskell's realistic fiction.[4] The pastoral depiction of Ruth ends after nine chapters when Bellingham (later called Donne) abandons her. Tess's pastoral narrative does not start until she meets Angel, and it returns when Angel and Tess are reunited near the novel's end.

Pastoral discourse repeatedly links both Ruth and Tess to nature. Nature reflects their emotions and succors them when no human will, as many critics have noted.[5] When Ruth is the naive, sensitive sprite of the pastoral opening, she feels deeply about nature but has not yet learned to reflect. Hilary Schor compares the Ruth of the early chapters to the piquant heroines of Wordsworth's ballads. The heroine who is deceived into a false marriage in Caroline Norton's *Lost and Saved* (1863) is described in an expansive way that also fits Ruth and Tess, as well as Adeline and Hippolyta: "She enjoyed more, she suffered more, she felt more, than a great proportion of her fellow-creatures" (vol. 1, 56). Like the Promethean hero of the Romantic period, such a woman is vulnerable because of her unusual powers, yet is also to be admired for them. Gary Kelly sees Adeline in this way as the heroine of a novel of passion (*English* 185). *Ruth* and *Tess* can be seen as outgrowths of the novel of passion that was popular during the Romantic period. The pastoral elements in both *Ruth* and *Tess* elevate the liberationist narrative and its passionate heroine beyond conventional morality, making the penitential narrative seem inappropriately earth-bound.

Within the context of the radical narrative, being associated with nature validates "natural" passions that are prohibited by an "unnatural" society. Adeline and Hippolyta make such arguments, as did the Romantic writers to whom their creators are indebted. However, Ruth and Tess are too "naturally" unsophisticated to verbalize these arguments. The depiction of Tess as unintellectual essentializes her in a sexist manner, according to Penny Boumelha. Nevertheless, Tess's nearly unshakable naivete is crucial to the novel's attack on the double standard that considered "fallen women" to be wily Duessas rather than heroines of Romantic poetry.

Ruth, unlike Tess, outgrows her naivete during the penitential narrative. That Ruth's intellectual skills grow during her penance supports the appropriateness of her reform. Late in the novel, Ruth out-argues Bellingham/Donne during the climax of the penitential narrative that Gaskell makes into a feminist and Christian Bildung. On the contrary, the peak of Tess's eloquence occurs when she confesses to Angel at the close of the liberationist narrative. Her inability to convince him that her sexual experience means what his does leads to her suicidal arguments that he condescendingly dismisses in the same way he had dismissed her logical disagreement with the double standard. Angel's prejudices effectively silence Tess for most of the rest of the novel; it is he and his culture who essentialize her as "natural" female victim, marginalized into dumb horror. During the penitential narrative, Tess does not send her heartfelt letters of complaint to Angel until too late, nor does she dare to speak to Angel's family. The arguments that she makes to Alec against his religion are mere repetitions of Angel's. Like an automaton, she follows what she deems to be Angel's instructions to kill Alec: Alec's murder is the tragic result of the cruel penance that destroyed what little self-esteem she had. Tess's growing silence and inability to think for herself during the penitential narrative prove that Hardy regards her penance as unjust and destructive, whereas Ruth's development of eloquence and wisdom justify her penance from Gaskell's perspective.

It is Angel who launches the unfair penitential narrative, as soon as he realizes he is living a narrative of free union. That realization comes from his erroneous belief that Tess is the "natural" wife of Alec, making Tess's legal marriage to Angel bigamy. The liberationist narrative is one that could have developed had Angel transcended his sexist beliefs. At the novel's end, the liberationist narrative reappears when Angel returns to Tess, stimulating her to kill Alec, and thus, indirectly, herself. Through causing this sequence of destruction, Angel shares the conventional seducer's role of ruining the heroine's life with Tess's rapist, Alec; this role is occupied in *Ruth* solely by Bellingham. Even though Angel never sexually seduces Tess, his emotional seduction of Tess causes her much more pain after he betrays her than Alec's rape ever did. Angel's emotional seduction of Tess also leads her to murder Alec. The true "fall" in the novel is thus Angel's, as many critics have noted. When Angel unnecessarily destroys his and Tess's Edenic happiness with his severity, he supports the novel's critique of chastity being seen as the supreme female virtue. Angel brings the liberationist narrative to a grotesque culmination through murder and execution in *Tess*. Through choosing a penitential narrative over a liberationist narrative of forgiveness for past sexual "sins," Angel creates a tragedy that criticizes middle-class prejudices.

In novels by Opie, Barry, and Gaskell, "fallen" heroines escape the tragedy that must befall Tess for the narrator to be able to condemn her penance. Instead, Opie's, Barry's, and Gaskell's heroines face a trial of their new conservatism which they overcome. *Ruth*'s most difficult temptation comes ten years after her seduction when she meets Bellingham/Donne, and he proposes at last. After resisting the attraction that his voice rekindles, Ruth refuses him because she no longer respects him. Tess is never tempted to sell herself to Alec in the way that Ruth is tempted to return to Bellingham as his mistress or wife. Tess's temptation is to adhere to her loyalty to Angel to the point of starving her family; such a cruel double bind allows Tess to appear "pure" despite her unwilling return to Alec. That the sacrifice required of Tess is both revolting and grotesque—selling herself to Alec to save her mother and siblings from hunger—suggests Hardy's disagreement with the prejudice against the working-class, "fallen" heroine that consigns her to prostitution permanently. *Tess* takes the free-union novel's convention of temptation to a shocking climax. In doing so, *Tess* makes its narrative of penance a monstrosity.

The penitential narrative in novels of free union criticizes those who, like Angel, unfairly reject the heroine. In Hardy's novel, Farmer Groby and the respectable folk of Marlott condemn Tess, whereas in Gaskell's novel it is Ruth's employers (a seamstress and a businessman, Bradshaw) and Bellingham's mother who condemn her. According to Judith Walkowitz, dressmakers like Ruth were thought to augment their meager wages through occasional prostitution: however, "experts" questioned whether such women had time for prostitution after sewing for fourteen hours a day (14). Mrs. Bellingham links seamstresses with prostitutes when she ignores Ruth's evident devotion to her son, seeing her as a live-in prostitute. Mrs. Bellingham also seems to share the view of Evangelical reformers that prostitutes, especially occasional ones, led respectable men like her son astray (Walkowitz 34). Bradshaw fears that Ruth's corruption contaminated his children during the years that she was their governess. Bradshaw says, "I saw her daily—I did not know her" (347). He uses the language of sexual knowledge—to know a woman—to deny Ruth's goodness because of the forbidden knowledge that she possessed, that sexual knowledge which, according to Foucault, Victorians regarded as central. Bradshaw's daughter, Jemima, disagrees that Ruth is corrupt and regrets her jealousy of Ruth.

Jemima's disinterested defense of Ruth is part of Gaskell's attempt to vindicate Ruth. Vindicating Ruth continues through showing Bradshaw as "fallen" because of his pride and ambition. After his son disgraces him by embezzling money, Bradshaw stops condemning Ruth. Bradshaw worries that he himself corrupted his son through the ambitiousness that Bradshaw hid under an austere front. He sees that his lifelong sin of egotism is much more serious than Ruth's brief fling. Angel is Bradshaw's counterpart in learning that he is far more flawed than the heroine ever was. Unlike Opie and Barry, Hardy and Gaskell double their penitential narratives to include both "fallen" men and women. This doubling rebukes the attitude that the "fallen" heroine is necessarily more corrupt and corrupting than respectable men.[6]

Ruth expands this inversion of the status of the respectable and the "fallen" when the heroine nurses her community during a dangerous epidemic. Echoing the heroines of Opie's and Barry's novels, Ruth lives up to the self-sacrifice expected especially of "disreputable" women. As in *The Scarlet Letter* (1850) and Wilkie Collins's *The New Magdalen* (1873), the "fallen" heroine is acceptable as a nurse when supervised by a male physician, although she would not be allowed to be a wife or teacher. Perhaps defeating others' physical disease was thought to quell her moral disease. Or perhaps nursing was so dangerous and so necessary that anyone was welcome.[7] Through being a competent and kindly nurse, Ruth regains much of the status she had lost through scandal. Tess is never allowed a similar reconciliation with her community. Whereas Gaskell imagines popularity for Ruth that exceeds even that of Hester Prynne in her community, Hardy creates a nightmare of wasted penance and ever-deepening disgrace because forgiveness comes to the heroine too late. Through such machinations, Gaskell validates the penitential narrative, whereas Hardy condemns it as horrifying.

The aspect of *Ruth* that is inconsistent with Gaskell's endorsement of penance occurs during the last section of the novel, when Ruth nurses her faithless seducer. Ruth's willingness to nurse Bellingham suggests that she may not have gotten over her love for him. He kills her through infection as he had earlier killed her potential to become a wife.[8] The sexual exploitation of working-class women and the prejudice that enables it are the ethical diseases that Ruth's community suffers from as much as Tess's. However,

Ruth's willingness to nurse Donne comes partly from loyalty to him as her son's father and partly from her commitment to charity, not from romantic passion. In her generosity beyond the ties of convention or deserving, the heroine echoes the Biblical Ruth, supporting Gaskell's religious narrative of penance.

Through his vanity and arrogance Donne misinterprets Ruth's disinterested motives, claiming her as "My Ruth" (444). "My" shows that Donne still regards her as his own pet or slave whom he values because of her sacrifice for him. If he were truly grateful, however, he would not assume that he deserves her love. The fact that Bellingham sports a new name suggests not only the instability of his identity, but his deceitfulness as a master of the discourse of love associated with the poet Donne. Like Alec D'Urberville, Bellingham/Donne believes that after he has sex with a woman she belongs to him forever. In refusing to marry her seducer or have him support their son, Ruth defies Bellingham's ownership. Yet Ruth nurses him partly out of recognition of an indissoluble tie between them, implying that she either assents to his view of herself as permanently his or regards him as permanently her charge. Ruth embraces the risk of disease with only a slight shrinking, as though it were her fate to be his victim, like a battered wife returning for more abuse. In this sense Ruth's sacrifice for her seducer contradicts her hard-won independence, making her penitential narrative less of a feminist Bildung than it might have been.

Tess's sacrifice for Angel is much more disturbing than Ruth's for Bellingham—involving as it does a murder to fulfill the conditions that Angel had said would convince him to take Tess back. Tess is far more independent of Alec than of Angel, believing the latter to be her ruler in the patriarchal sense of husband. Ruth does not assent to such a definition with Bellingham, although he attempts to impose it. From a feminist point of view, Ruth's emotional distance from her seducer, which remains even while she nurses him, gives her penitential narrative plausibility and a certain dignity. On the other hand, Tess's lack of independence from Angel brings her penitential narrative into question. Angel taught Tess to use the double standard and class prejudice to unfairly denigrate herself; since Tess cannot see that the conventions of the penitential narrative lead her to unjust self-accusations, her penance itself becomes questionable.

In contrast with the more radical Hardy, Gaskell has her heroine's penance culminate in triumphant selflessness, much as Opie and Barry do. Like Ham in *David Copperfield*, Ruth dies saving her enemy. While Ham longs for death, however, Ruth does not. She longs to live for her son. A female Christ figure, Ruth sacrifices herself to save a soul whom she knows is base. For as Christ died for sinners, forgiving those who hurt him, Ruth dies for the sinner who hurt her most. Tess also is associated with the crucified Christ, and

Angel and Liza-Lu with Christ's disciples, as critics have noted.[9] But Tess's association with Christ is more complex than Ruth's, for Tess murders her rapist whereas Ruth saves her seducer. Yet the effect of both linkages to Christ is similar—to draw readers' attention to the unfair treatment of the ''fallen'' heroine that leads to her martyrdom as the capstone of the penitential narrative. In Ruth's case, the linkage to Christ strengthens the religious dimension of Gaskell's penitential narrative, as well.

A sentimental deathbed scene at the climax of novels of free union builds sympathy for their socially unacceptable heroines. Dying, Ruth sings without recognizing those around her, reminiscent of Ophelia in her crazed, betrayed innocence. Ruth's distance from reality fits the convention of femininity being linked to death through the fragmentation of madness. Pent up so long by self-restraint, Ruth finally expresses herself, oblivious of others' needs for once. Through this freedom, Ruth transcends the boundaries of her Madonna role to enjoy the process of dying. Ruth's oblivion seems a reward for her suffering, but it is a pathetic one that belittles her heroism, leaving an impression of her as a victim, rather than as the steadfast survivor that she was during most of the penitential narrative. The ambiguity about how much Ruth remains a victim versus how much she triumphs through her penance is the novel's central conundrum. Such ambiguity demonstrates the difficulty that Victorians like Gaskell had in believing that a woman's fall can ever be unambiguously fortunate. The ambiguity undercuts Gaskell's lengthy penitential narrative and reinforces her brief free-love narrative.

Ruth's beauty as a corpse is equally ambiguous; it can be read as an endorsement of either the Christian or the liberationist narrative. Victorians equated the tranquillity seen in dead Ruth's facial expression with a spirit on its way to heaven. In death, Ruth's beauty, which troubled her in life, is finally a blessing. To the Bensons, it is a sign of her saintliness. But not to Bellingham; his misreading of her is tied to his erotic view of her body, living or dead—a view that would have shocked Ruth. Even in death, as in dying, Ruth cannot achieve the coherently virtuous and inspirational identity that she desired.

A Christian reading of Ruth's death would consider it a triumph of her spirit over the forces that could have corrupted her but did not. Yet Ruth's insanity conflicts with the notion that her death reinforces the penitential narrative. Felicia Bonaparte argues that madness makes Ruth's sainthood less plausible. Critics find it unbelievable that steadfast Ruth could go mad. Perhaps Gaskell wants us to regard Ruth as undergoing the visionary madness of a medieval mystic. But Ruth's madness lacks the coherence that such a visionary state implies.

Unlike the death of Richardson's Clarissa, Ruth's does not reform her seducer. Bellingham feels that in offering to marry Ruth, and later, in offering to support her orphaned son, that he has "done my duty" (450) "for my youthful folly" (449). His calling their affair a "folly" demonstrates his denial of both the magnitude of the pain that he caused Ruth, as well as the affair's religious dimension as sin. Through her Christian faith, Ruth braves a world in which she knows that right rarely prevails. However, since Ruth's self-sacrifice does not transform Bellingham, its usefulness is brought into doubt in another weakening of Gaskell's penitential narrative.[10]

Ruth's death, like Tess's, is a quasi-suicide that further erodes Gaskell's penitential narrative. Margaret Higonnet notes that female suicides in works by women usually have an open-ended quality (79–81). Ruth's has such an ambiguous character. Critics speculate that Gaskell made Ruth embrace a "fallen woman's" traditional fate—death—to try to placate readers who were angry about Ruth's happiness with the Bensons (Gaskell xi). But Ruth's death seems an unjust punishment because she has already suffered and re-pented a "sin" that the first nine chapters present as "natural." As Anderson writes, "The ending of the novel must be seen as Gaskell's failure to work through her competing accounts" (131). The novel's ending thus unexpect-edly reinforces the argument made by its liberationist beginning. The injustice of Ruth's death stimulates the reader's rage at the ostracism of "fallen women"; the execution of Tess creates a similar effect.[11] Such a reading of *Ruth* sees it as a forerunner of the more radical *Tess*. The ending of *Ruth* is even more torn than is the rest of the novel between the religious meaning associated with the penitential narrative and the social criticism associated with the liberationist narrative.

Tess, like Ruth, goes mad before her death, but more violently, putting Hardy's penitential narrative in a more disturbing light than Gaskell's. Bona-parte argues that Ruth's madness preserves her demon. Ruth's demon is the rebellious side that dominates her during the liberationist narrative, then re-cedes when the ideal mother of the penitential narrative emerges. On her deathbed, maddened Ruth does not recognize her son, as her demon reap-pears.[12] Gaskell's short story, "The Poor Clare," provides a bridge from the touching madness seen in *Ruth* to the demonic paroxysm seen in *Tess*. The heroine of "The Poor Clare" suffers from a curse that creates a demonic double who acts maliciously and flirtatiously without the heroine's consent. Whereas Ruth's mad double refuses to fit the ideal mother role to which Ruth had devoted herself, Tess's mad double stabs Alec in a revenge forbidden to angelic wives. Later, Tess is horrified at what she has done. Her arrest while lying on an altar at Stonehenge suggests that she is being sacrificed to an ancient double standard. Ann Mickelson writes that it is "an ironic ending which speaks eloquently of the lack of even a rough egalitarianism for women in society" (123).

That Tess must be martyred to indict the penitential narrative and promote the liberationist narrative explains her murder of Alec, which some critics find unbelievable. Some critics likewise find it hard to believe that Tess's frenzied murder of Alec leaves Tess innocent, much as Ruth's madness does.[13] Tess's murderous demon takes over, ironically, as a result of Angel's insistence upon female chastity (Butler 212). Hardy may have shared the Victorian belief in the weakness of the female will that Janet Oppenheim describes: "At the heart of all medical attitudes towards women's nerves, health, and character was the presumed weakness of the female will. It was implicit in the notion of woman as a creature who reacted rather than initiated, whose feelings dominated her intellect" (181). If Tess is seen as merely reacting to prolonged abuse by Alec and Angel when she lives with Alec and then kills him, her "purity" is preserved. However, the mindlessness of Tess that this interpretation implies is disturbing. J. Hillis Miller identifies the subversiveness of Tess's incorruptible purity thus: "To be led by a new 'sentiment' of human worth or meaning to call the 'impure' the 'pure' may lead to an overturning of the usual relations of possession and dominance in society" (83). Tess must remain pure at whatever cost for the liberationist narrative to defeat the penitential one, allowing radicalism to prevail. That the necessity for Tess's purity creates implausibility in characterization and plot is an example of how ideological imperatives mar novels of free union.

Tess kills Alec through an inspiration that comes like "a shining light" (377) in a parody of religious conversions like Ruth's and Hippolyta's; Tess's murder of Alec thus repudiates the Christian worldview that underlies the penitential narrative. The murder of Alec is not the only instance in Hardy's novel when Victorian religion is obliquely criticized for upholding the notions of gender and class that ruin Tess. Timothy Hands writes that "In Tess's contemplated suicide, the self-denying instinct of the devotee approaches the extremity of a perversion" (68). Hands sees a critique of asceticism in *Tess* that I believe is more blatant than those made by the excessive self-punishments of Ruth, Adeline, and Hippolyta. Alec, too, participates in Hardy's critique of asceticism through his brief conversion into an evangelist who glories in masochistic self-denial. For Tess, self-suppression leads to a madness that has a religious flavor, while the religious passions of Ruth and Hippolyta carry a tinge of insanity.

All of these heroines' penitential narratives utilize Gothic horror to question whether the "fallen woman" ought to turn ascetic. Michelle Masse argues that the drama of the Gothic genre comes from its heroines' struggle to see their unnaturally masochistic relationships with men as fitting the feminine norm. Tess does view masochistic relationships as normal, except when she leaves or attacks Alec and when she writes a blaming letter to Angel. Tess's worship of Angel is her religion, and as such, is the source of her masochistic asceticism. For pious Ruth, Hippolyta, and Adeline, the case is different. When reading against the grain of Gaskell's, Opie's, and Barry's penitential narratives, we see that traditional religion is criticized for causing the "fallen woman's" masochistic asceticism. More disturbingly, Hardy's novel blurs religion and patriarchal love to show that both depend on the humiliation of women that characterizes the Gothic.

As critics such as Amanda Anderson and Nina Auerbach argue, the struggle over female chastity seen in nineteenth-century fiction signifies more than an attempt to control women's bodies. In Victorian novels, issues of gender and class are intertwined, as many critics have noted. Auerbach examines Victorian anxiety about the power of women, including "fallen" ones. She argues that the fluidity of women, which at times is portrayed as a demonic ability to elude the markers of class and gender, is nonetheless celebrated throughout Victorian literature and art. With less optimism, Anderson points out that anxiety about the "fallen woman's" transformations reveals a deeper cultural unrest over social mobility (2, 198). Starting out as a respectable woman, the "fallen woman" lowers her status through exhibiting the active sexuality that only the "lowest" working-class women are supposed to possess. The "fallen" heroine can temporarily recover or enhance her class and gender status through deceit, as do Ruth and Tess. But after the revelation of her falsehood, the "fallen" heroine is punished to enforce the laws of class and gender that are sanctified by their link with truth. As a part of her punishment, the "fallen" heroine must die to quell cultural anxiety over the fragility of class barriers that she has exposed and exploited.

The heroines of Opie's and Barry's novels, like Ruth and Tess, become working women who die literally or figuratively (in Barry's novel, it is the latter, through the heroine's retreat to a convent). The "fallen woman" becomes a symbol of failed social climbing. This is so even when, as in Tess's case, she is simultaneously seen as working woman and decayed aristocrat: both positions are marginal compared to the middle-class position that she could have taken as Angel's wife. When a novel endorses the "fallen" heroine's penance, it sanctifies the barriers of gender and class that she violated. This is so even when a novel such as *Ruth* criticizes the severity of particular Christians towards the "fallen" heroine. When a novel like *Tess* questions the appropriateness of the heroine's penance, however, then the class and gender barriers that the "fallen woman" has broken remain permanently ruptured.

Tess is blatantly anti-penitential, although it contains discordant overtones that endorse the essentialism sometimes supported by its narrator. Despite these overtones, *Tess* critiques the system of class and gender that dooms its heroine. However, *Ruth, Adeline* and *Antigone* give as mixed messages about Christian penance as they do about free love. The hesitations in Gaskell's, Barry's, and Opie's novels dramatize the courage of Hardy in rebelling against standard notions about "fallen women," but also show that Hardy was not the first novelist to depict free union idyllically. These brief utopian depictions, as well as the lengthy masochistic narratives that complement them, constitute a Foucauldian transformation of sexual desire into impassioned words that interrogate hierarchies of class and gender. The ambivalence of Opie's and Barry's minor novels creates thematic richness as well as structural weaknesses; without ideological struggle *Ruth* and even *Tess* would be as predictable as Grant Allen's once popular, didactic novel of free union. *The Woman Who Did* (1895).[14] Bahktin's dialogism allows us to value *Adeline, Antigone, Ruth,* and *Tess* for their ideological conflicts. Not only women's sexual freedom is at stake, but the fluidity of class and gender which that freedom represents. The ideological biases of each author strain the believability of the plots of even such classics as *Tess,* as they do to a greater extent in the splintered novels of Opie, Barry, and Gaskell. Analyzing and acknowledging the conflicts between the liberationist and penitential narratives of these novels reveals both the novels' appeal as reflections of contemporary ideological battles and their implausibility because of their authors' predilections about how the battles should end.

NOTES

1. Other free-union novels include George W. M. Reynolds's *Mary Price: The Memoirs of a Servant Maid.* (1853), Matilda Houstoun's *Recommended to Mercy* (1862), Richard Jefferies's *Restless Human Hearts* (1875), George Gissing's *Denzil Quarrier* (1892), and Sarah Grand's *The Heavenly Twins* (1893). I don't discuss these because the free-union tale is merely a subplot. Novels of free union that lack the split between free love and penitential narratives include George Meredith's *One of Our Conquerors* (1891), Frank Moore's comical *I Forbid the Banns* (1893), Joanna E. Wood's *The Untempered Wind* (1894), George Meredith's *Lord Ormont and His Aminta* (1894), Grant Allen's *The Woman Who Did* (1895), and H. G. Wells's *Ann Veronica* (1909), as well as short stories by George Egerton in *Discords* (1894). Kate Chopin's *The Awakening* (1899) could be regarded as an American free-love novella. The Lady Dedlock subplot to Dickens's *Bleak House* (1852–3) and William Morris's "Defence of Guinevere" (1858) might also be read in light of free-love conventions.
2. Critics such as A. S. Whitfield have linked *Ruth* with *Tess* before in ways I do not cover (142); see also Rosemarie Bodenheimer (159), Nina Auerbach (168–72), Felicia Bonaparte (91), Peter Stiles (58–66), and Gail Cunningham (30).
3. Although Opie's and Barry's somewhat eccentric heroines may be of interest today, would they interest feminists of their time? Sandra Stanley Holton writes that the most radical feminists hated marriage, preferring free union (211), unlike the majority of feminists. Elaine Showalter explains why mainstream feminists rejected free union. By the 1890s, according to Showalter, male radicals often

favored it, but female radicals worried about pregnancy, childraising, and sexually transmitted diseases, regarding celibacy as a more effective rebellion against patriarchy than free union. As Frank Mort writes, ''In polemicizing for celibacy and spinsterhood, feminists were challenging the growing sexualization of all women in medicine, psychology, and the work of male sexual radicals'' (139). (See also Sheila Jeffreys.)

4. See Bodenheimer and Schor.
5. See Uglow (330), Michael Ponsford (490), and Anne Z. Mickelson.
6. Contemporary audiences were shocked by Gaskell's sympathetic portrayal of Ruth, and especially by the Bensons' lie to prevent Ruth from becoming an outcast (Easson 200/329). Gaskell suggests that the Bensons' white lie is far more justified than the damaging lies that prejudices towards ''fallen women'' create. See John Kucich's *The Power of Lies.*

    And see R. A. York for a discussion of how having a secret makes characters interesting and significant in Victorian novels (63). As outsiders with secrets, Ruth and Tess could have been included in York's gallery of ''sensitive and unsure'' heroines and heroes (154).
7. Martha Vicinus describes the development of nursing as a profession during the nineteenth century. In the 1850s, nurses performed servants' tasks: they cleaned the floors of wards, prepared their patients' food, had little time off, and slept in the ward or dormitory (86). Such a lowly position was less respectable than the governess role that Ruth held when the Bradshaws thought she was a widow.
8. See Helena Michie (56).
9. See Henry Kozicki (158) and John A. Anonby (18).
10. Opie, Gaskell, and Hardy adhere to the myth that ''fallen women'' must die. But in reality, Walkowitz observes that prostitution—a more ''disreputable'' career than that of any of the heroines discussed—''was a transitional stage'' for Victorian working-class women who generally moved into more respectable positions such as wife, servant, or seamstress by their mid-twenties (15).
11. See Dianne F. Sadoff.
12. See Auerbach, also.
13. See Mary Jacobus (46) and Lynn Parker.
14. The popularity of Allen's novel may have stemmed from its denial that female passion exists. Allen's heroine is dedicated to one man, as convention dictates; and her passion for this lover is more spiritual than physical. Thus, Allen's ''fallen'' heroine fits Victorian notions of the Angel in the House to a startling degree.

WORKS CITED

Anderson, Amanda. *Tainted Souls and Painted Faces: The Rhetoric of Fallenness in Victorian Culture.* Ithaca: Cornell UP, 1993.

Anonby, John A. "Hardy's Handling of Biblical Allusions." *Christianity and Litera-ture* 30.3 (1981): 13–26.

Auerbach, Nina. *Woman and the Demon.* Cambridge: Harvard UP, 1982.

Bahktin, M. M. "Discourse in the Novel." *The Dialogic Imagination: Four Essays.* Trans. Caryl Emerson; trans. and ed. Michael Holquist. Austin, U of Texas P, 1981. 259–422.

Barry, W. Francis. *The New Antigone.* 1887. New York: Garland, 1976.

Bellamy, Liz. *British Women Writers.* Ed. Janet Todd. New York: Continuum, 1989. 515–16.

Bick, Suzann. "Take Her Up Tenderly," *Essays in Arts and Sciences* 18 (1989): 17–28.

Bodenheimer, Rosemarie. *The Politics of Story in Victorian Social Fiction.* Ithaca: Cornell UP, 1988.

Bonaparte, Felicia. *The Gypsy-Bachelor of Manchester.* Charlottesville: UP of Vir-ginia, 1992.

Boumelha, Penny. *Thomas Hardy and Women: Sexual Ideology and Narrative Form.* New Jersey: Barnes and Noble, 1982.

Butler, Lance St. John. *Victorian Doubt.* London: Harvester, 1990.

Crick, W. A. *Elizabeth Gaskell and the English Provincial Novel.* London: Macmil-lan, 1975.

Cunningham, Gail. *The New Woman and the Victorian Novel.* London: Macmillan, 1978.

Easson, Angus, ed. *Elizabeth Gaskell: the Critical Heritage.* New York: Routledge, 1991.

Eberle, Roxanne. "Amelia Opie's Adeline Mowbray: the Libertine Gaze." *Studies in the Novel* 26.2 (Su 1994): 121–52.

Foucault, Michel. *The History of Sexuality.* Vol. 1, trans. Robert Hurley. New York: Vintage, 1980.

Gaskell, Elizabeth. *Ruth.* 1853. London: Dent, 1984.

Hands, Timothy. *Thomas Hardy: Distracted Preacher?* London: Macmillan, 1989.

Hardy, Thomas. *Tess of the D'Urbervilles.* 1891. New York: Bantam, 1984.

Higonnet, Margaret. "Speaking Silences: Woman's Suicide," *The Female Body in Western Culture,* ed. Susan Rubin Suleiman. London: Harvard UP, 1985. 68–83.

Holton, Sandra Stanley. "Free Love and Victorian Feminism: the Diverse Matrimo-
nials of Elizabeth Wolstenholme and Ben Elmy." *Victorian Studies* 37.2 (1994):
199–222.

Jacobus, Mary. "Tess, the Making of a Pure Woman." *Modern Critical Interpretations: Tess of the D'Urbervilles.* Ed. Harold Bloom. New York: Chelsea House,
1987., 45–60.

Jeffreys, Sheila. *The Spinster and Her Enemies: Feminism and Sexuality, 1880–1930.*
London: Routledge, 1985.

Kelly, Gary. "Amelia Opie, Lady Caroline Lamb, and Maria Edgeworth: Official and
Unofficial Ideology." *Ariel* 12.4 (October 1981) 3–24.

———. *English Fiction of the Romantic Period 1789–1830.* London: Longman, 1989.

Kozicki, Henry J. "Myths of Redemption in Hardy's *Tess of the D'Urbervilles.*"
Papers on Language and Literature 10 (1974): 150–58.

Kucich, John. *The Power of Lies: Transgression in Victorian Fiction.* Ithaca: Cornell
UP, 1994.

———. *Repression in Victorian Fiction.* Berkeley: U of California P, 1987.

Macherey, Pierre. *The Object of Literature.* Trans. David Macey. Cambridge: Cambridge UP, 1990.

Masse, Michelle. *In the Name of Love: Women, Masochism, and the Gothic.* Ithaca:
Cornell UP, 1992.

Michie, Helena. *The Flesh Made Word.* New York: Oxford UP, 1987.

Mickelson, Anne Z. *Thomas Hardy's Women and Men: the Defeat of Nature.* New
Jersey: Scarecrow, 1976.

Miller, D. A. *Narrative and Its Discontents.* Princeton: Princeton UP, 1981.

Miller, J. H. "Repetition as Immanent Design." *Modern Critical Interpretations: Tess
of the D'Urbervilles.* Ed. Harold Bloom. New York: Chelsea House, 1987. 61–86.

Morgan, Rosemarie. *Women, Sexuality, and the Novels of Thomas Hardy.* London:
Routledge, 1988.

Mort, Frank. *Dangerous Sexualities.* London: Routledge, 1987.

Opie, Amelia. *Adeline Mowbray: or the Mother and Daughter.* 1805. New York:
Garland, 1974.

Oppenheim, Janet. *Shattered Nerves: Doctors, Patients, and Depression in Victorian
England.* New York: Oxford UP, 1991.

Parker, Lynn. "Pure Woman and Tragic Heroine?" *Studies in the Novel* 24.3
(1992): 273–81.

Ponsford, Michael. "Thomas Hardy's Control of Sympathy in *Tess of the D'Urbervilles.*" *Midwest Quarterly* 27.4 (1986): 487–503.

Sadoff, Dianne Fallon. "Looking at Tess." Higonnet, Margaret ed. *The Sense of Sex: Feminist Perspectives on Hardy.* Urbana: U of Illinois P, 1993. 149–71.

Schor, Hilary. "The Plot of the Beautiful Ignoramus: *Ruth.*" *Sex and Death in Victorian Literature.* Ed. Regina Barreca. London: Macmillan, 1990. 158–77.

Shelston, A. J. "*Ruth:* Mrs. Gaskell's Neglected Novel." *Bulletin of the John Rylands University Library of Manchester* 58.1 (1975): 173–92.

Showalter, Elaine. *Sexual Anarchy: Gender and Culture at the Fin de Siecle.* New York: Viking, 1990.

Stiles, Peter. "Grace, Redemption, and the Fallen Woman: Ruth and Tess." *Gaskell Society Journal* 6 (1992): 58–66.

Stoneman, Patsy. *Elizabeth Gaskell.* Brighton: Harvester, 1987.

Uglow, Jenny. *Elizabeth Gaskell: A Habit of Stories.* Boston: Faber, 1993.

Vicinus, Martha. *Independent Women: Work and Community for Single Women.* Chicago: U Chicago P, 1985.

Walkowitz, Judith R. *Prostitution and Victorian Society.* Cambridge: Cambridge UP, 1980.

Whitfield, A. S. *Mrs. Gaskell.* London: Routledge, 1982.

Wickens, G. Glen. "Sermons in Stones." *English in Canada* (1988): 184–203.

York, R. A. *Strategies and Secrets: Communication in the Nineteenth-Century Novel.* Rutherford: Fairleigh Dickinson UP, 1994.

New Historicizing Dickens

William J. Palmer

This theoretically focused survey of Dickens criticism (principally book-length studies) pursues two goals. On one hand, it is a history of the critical application of the New Historicist theoretical approach to reading literary texts (specifically the novels of Dickens). Beginning with a pre-history of historicist forays into both Dickens criticism and Victorian cultural studies in the 1950s and 1960s, this survey maps the evolution of the New Historicist approach to reading Dickens's fiction over the decades of the 1970s, 1980s, and 1990s.

On the other hand, this survey is also a history of the definition of New Historicist theory itself. Briefly examining the philosophical and theoretical models of New Historicist thinkers such as Foucault and Bakhtin, it goes on to examine the accommodation of those theories to the acts of critical reading and discourse by theorists such as Hayden White and Dominick LaCapra, the articulation of those theories and discourse strategies for applied literary criticism especially by Renaissance scholars such as Stephen Greenblatt and Louis Montrose, the codification of these applied criticism techniques by editors such as H. Aram Veeser, and finally the burgeoning application of New Historicist theory and discourse strategies to the novels of Charles Dickens. Yet, while this survey is a history, it ends on a futurist note. It attempts to extrapolate the direction that New Historicist readings of Dickens's fiction might take in the future.

Dickens Studies Annual, Volume 28, Copyright © 1999 by AMS Press, Inc. All rights reserved.

Major Swindon: "What will History say?"
Gen. Burgoyne: "History, sir, will tell lies as usual."
            —*The Devil's Disciple.* George Bernard Shaw

"There's more to it. There's always more to it. This is what
history consists of. It's the sum total of all the things they
aren't telling us."
                                    —*Libra,* Don DeLillo

Everyone knows what (and who) the paradigm for a historical novelist is: Sir
Walter Scott, the Scottish master of historical narrative. He was as equally at
home and at ease in nineteenth-century Scotland and England as in the heavily
armored Middle Ages or the kilted and dirked seventeenth and eighteenth
centuries. Everyone also knows that at times the greatest, most popular, nineteenth-century novelist, Charles Dickens, invaded Sir Walter's turf and took
a stab at writing historical novels. Witness his two quite similar novels of
revolution, *Barnaby Rudge* and *A Tale of Two Cities.*

But Dickens and the venerable Sir Walter Scott were two very different
types of historical novelists. Scott defines the traditional historical novel
where the real events of historical time and place provide a romantic backdrop
and a picturesque, often sublime, setting for individual intrigues and heroic
action. For Scott, history was driven by romantic heroes like Quentin Durward
and Rob Roy. For Dickens, the historical novel took on a much different
caste, anchored itself in the working classes, and concerned itself with the
politics of revolution as opposed to Scott's consistent politics of restoration.
In other words, if Scott is the paradigm for a traditional, romantic, historical
novelist, then Dickens (in all of his novels, not just the two above mentioned)
is the model for the New Historcist novelist (even though that specific theoretical description did not even come into existence until the late twentieth
century).

Restoration vs. Revolution

If (as Hayden White argues in *Metahistory*) traditional history (especially
of the nineteenth century) was written in terms of a romantic master text
driven by heroes, charismatic figures of mythic proportion, or if (as Michel
Foucault and Mikhail Bakhtin argue) traditional history was written in terms
of a power-centered research model and tended to ignore the many other
voids outside of the hub of power, those voices forced to the margins of social
and political life, then the novels of Walter Scott, though they sometimes
focus on characters who reside outside of the corridors of power (such as

Rob Roy, or Jennie Deens in *The Heart of Midlothian*), are centered on the courts and castles, courtrooms and counting houses of the powerful and rich.

If Scott must plead guilty to all of the excesses of traditional historicism (romanticism, power-centeredness, master textuality), Dickens seems most of the time to be just the opposite in his presentation of the historical scene in his novels. The ultimate social realist of the nineteenth century, Dickens consistently ironizes the romantic view of things by contrast to the oppressive texture of his London slum world. The opening of *Bleak House,* for example, presents an ongoing contrast between the exaggerated language of romantic mythologization and the dark squalor of the utterly elemental social reality of the mid-Victorian London landscape. The opening chapter of *Bleak House* is like the first twenty minutes of Steven Spielberg's historical war film *Saving Private Ryan.* It is a starkly realistic overture to history, a collection of previously ignored images that thickens and deepens our sense of historical truth whether it involves the D-Day Invasion of Normandy or Victorian London in the fog and rain. Scott's traditional historical fiction of restoration versus Dickens's New Historicist fiction of revolution: Which gets closer to the truth? Which tells fewer lies?

The postmodernist New Historicist project of Michel Foucault, Mikhail Bakhtin, Hayden White, Stephen Greenblatt, Louis Montrose, Dominick La-Capra and many others has proven itself especially congenial to the immersion into and representation of the nineteenth-century history of change, reform, class conflict, and existential survival that dominates the fiction of Charles Dickens. When the goals of the New Historicist literary theoretical project are spelled out, they are strikingly similar to the goals of social realism that emerge from the plots, characters, and style of Dickens's novels.

Where New Historicism strives for a "thickening" (to use Clifford Geertz's term) of the historical text, Dickens's novels consistently expand their social concerns to the histories of the homeless poor, the working classes, the marginalized of Victorian society. Where New Historicism emphasizes a verticalizing of the historical text as opposed to the horizontal and linear story of history based upon major, often cataclysmic, events and very powerful people. Dickens's novels also penetrate deeply into every class, every working group, every level of Victorian society. Whereas the traditional historical novel is written in accordance with a master text of history (romantic, heroic, power-based), the New Historicist fiction of Dickens delves into the subtexts of history, decenters the historical focus to those on the margins of the historical event (such as the poor, women, the politically disenfranchised). Whereas Scott's novels use history as a setting, a landscape for the creation of stories, Dickens's novels reverse that process and actually employ their stories in an examination of how history works, an analysis of history itself as a dynamic process functioning on a number of different levels and within a complex set of interacting contexts. To appropriate Hayden White's term, Dickens's novels are also "metahistories," histories about the writing of history. In fact, over the course of his full career, Dickens formulates a clear and present philosophy of history which places him in a theoretical relation to the whole body of historical discourse that Scott never even presumed to court.

Verticalizing History

But the New Historicist project is not merely Revisionist (an approach to the writing of history that focuses heavily upon economic factors) nor arrogantly dismissive of traditional history. New Historicism strives by the act of verticalizing history to represent and examine the relationships between the power-centered classes and the marginalized population that together form the dynamic of history. For a New Historicist novelist like Dickens in a novel of social history like *Bleak House,* it is the relationship of the aristocratic Dedlocks to the members of the middle-class (like Esther Summerson) and to the marginalized poor (such as Nemo the scrivener and Jo the crossing sweep) that drives the historical representation of Victorian England. In *Bleak House* social history is consistently verticalized as the reader (guided by two very different narrators) moves constantly up and down between the levels of society and bears witness to their fatal and/or productive interactions.

Dickens, then, is indeed writing decentered, verticalized, from the margins fiction which thickens the novel project to include new characters, settings, issues and metaphors all of which in turn define him as a writer most congenial to the applications of New Historicist critical theory and methodology.

The Archaeological, Diffusive Methodology

That is, indeed, what the New Historicist project is all about and how it works. It is simultaneously both a theory of history and a methodology for rewriting and reinterpreting history. While the theory of New Historicism poses the most interesting questions and explores hitherto suppressed or ignored approaches to the composition of historical texts (both master texts and subtexts), the methodology that this new form of historicist thinking generates is equally important. The research methodology of the New Historicist emphasizes

(1) the archaeological unearthing of new documents and archives hitherto suppressed or ignored in the writing of master-text traditional history (such as the letters of midwestern black women or the reservation reports of Bureau of Indian Affairs agents);

(2) the exploration of the impact of what Dominick LaCapra calls the "instruments of diffusion" (such as historical novel portrayals of history) upon the mass or popular perceptions of history;

(3) the employment of new analytical or interpretational techniques, such as those of literary criticism, for the re-reading and re-interpretation of the extant texts of traditional history.

Thus the theory which was generated out of dissatisfaction with the exclusivity and narrowness of the traditional historical method with its illusory rationale of objectivity in turn has generated a New Historicist methodology which opens up and verticalizes the research tools of the New Historicist. New History is being created now out of very different sources and documents under a new definition of the very concept of "archive."

However, the New Historicist project is not only concerned with unearthing, expanding, recording and interpreting the hitherto suppressed (or just ignored or unheard) voices participating in the historical process. New Historicism is also not only concerned with recognizing and defining the competing subtexts of history. And, the New Historicism is not only involved with exploring the margins of the historical process. New Historicism certainly embraces all of these social and political and textual agendas as they appear to a greater or lesser extent in historical documents (Hayden White would call these "chronicles") including (to use Dominick LaCapra's term again) all of the different "instruments of diffusion" that purvey the stories of history to a mass audience. These "instruments" could include novels, poems, plays, newspaper reportage, films, music, theater, and television. New Historicism is interested in all of these issues and methodologies, but it is also powerfully focused upon the historical functioning of language.

The Discourse of History

Beyond all of the realist socio-political interactions which are essential to the decentering and verticalizing of historical thought, the New Historicism is very much about the discourse of history: How it is written; where its information is obtained; who is writing it; what biases influence it; how its language works; and what contingencies and contexts influence that language. In this sense, the New Historicist is as much concerned with the style of history as with its substance because the New Historicist knows now that in fact the style actually is the substance. It is this parallel consciousness of the interactive relationship between styles and substance on the New Historicist's part that has built a methodological relationship between the historian and the literary critic/theorist (a necessary relationship most strongly emphasized in the works of Dominick LaCapra).

The interpretive methods of literary criticism and critical theory serve the New Historicist project in two distinct ways. First, literary criticism and critical theory (especially the postmodernist techniques of deconstruction and cultural studies) help to re-read and re-interpret the extant historical master texts and diffusion mechanisms, thus giving the New Historicist direction as to what has been suppressed or left out or simply overlooked by those master texts of traditional, power-centered history. But second, literary studies also embrace New Historicism in their equal interest in the discovery of new subtexts (suppressed texts or overlooked texts or submerged texts or competing, deconstructive texts) which serve to "thicken" the historical text when placed in conjunction with the extant, traditional, oft-interpreted master text.

Thus, New Historicism is very much about the discovery of history and the new textuality which results from the interpretive study of that discourse. All of the most prominent New Historicist theorists, from Michel Foucault and Mikhail Bakhtin to Hayden White and Dominich LaCapra to Stephen Greenblatt and Louis Montrose and Clifford Geertz to familiar Dickensian critics such as Brooke Thomas and Deirdre David, are involved with the ways in which the language of historical discourse hides subtexts, pushes agendas, proselytizes biases, and imagologically creates themes and patterns of historical expression.

The term that Hayden White uses most prominently in *Metahistory* to describe these subtextual stylistic encodings of the traditional historian's non-objectivity or anti-objectivity and to expose history's inevitable and invincible subjectivity is the term "emplotment." For White, all historical discourse is emplotted with submerged tropes which express thinly disguised ideological agendas beneath the surface of professionally objective historical texts. White's "tropics of discourse" are the icebergs of traditional history which rise up from beneath the surface of the historical text and wreck its illusion of objectivity. These emplotted styles, tropes, narratives and agendas expose the one-dimensionality of the power-centered master narratives which dominate the alleged linear objectivity of traditional historical writing. For White, traditional history professed an ideal of objectivity that it could never obtain because of the limited research sources (obtained from those in power) that it employed and because it was betrayed by the very language that it was expressed in, a language subtextually emplotted with all sorts of self-referential and self-exposing tropes of subjectivity and political/ideological agenda creation.

Following the stylistic emphases of Hayden White in the discussion of historical textuality, Dominick LaCapra (in books like *History and Criticism* and *Rethinking Intellectual History*) emphasizes the need for historical discourse to employ the methods of literary critical discourse in order to understand the contexts of interpretation. In *History and Criticism* LaCapra writes "that historians have much to learn from disciplines such as literary criticism and philosophy" (the comfort zones of Foucault and Bakhtin) "where debates over the nature of interpretation have been particularly lively" (9–10). LaCapra is especially interested in how interdisciplinary texts such as the philosophical writings of Wittgenstein, Sartre, Marx, and Bakhtin, and literary texts such as novels, can contribute to ways of rethinking our historical consciousness. Taking his key from Georg Lukacs, LaCapra argues that since "the novel was *the* genre of the bourgeois epoch," historians should be closely attuned to its representations of the cultural, social, economic, and political history of the eighteenth and nineteenth centuries in western European history. Historians should read novels and novelists should interpret history LaCapra argues, and the New Historicists of the 1980s and 1990s have focused upon this dialogic relationship between the two closely allied disciplines.

Following the theoretical lead of these philosophical rhetoricians of historical discourse, applied historicist critics such as Stephen Greenblatt, Louis Montrose, Clifford Geertz, Brook Thomas, and Deirdre David demonstrated the dialogical relationships between history and literature. For these practicing New Historicists, the theater, the novel, a historical period's poetry, became moving vehicles on a crowded two-way street of historical, social, literary contextuality. Social, intellectual, and cultural history opened new doorways for the reading of old literature, and literature, especially the most popular class-based forms such as Elizabethan theater and the new genre of the novel, helped to fill in the gaps in the linear story of history and facilitated the verticalizing of the hitherto horizontal master text of history.

Especially in the short lifespan of the novel genre from the eighteenth century to the present, fiction was constantly historicizing itself. The traditional historical novel methodology of Sir Walter Scott was one modus operandi, but what the New Historicists realized was that all novels are involved in one way or another in the contextualizing of the historical moment. History is always encoded within the fictional act because that act is always involved with the time and the place, the people and their culture, the society and its discontents. History is always engaged not only with the historical moment of which it writes, but more importantly with that in which it is written. Thus, a historical novel about the French Revolution can and must also be read as a cautionary historical warning of the potential for revolutionary excess in Dickens's present-day England of the late 1850s.

The Instruments of Diffusion

What LaCapra and Dickens and the New Historicists in general also certainly realized was that very few members of the mass audience of any culture actually read the work of professional historians. The mass reading audience may read digested versions of historical discourse as filtered through the tabloid press, but more probably the mass audience receives its versions of history through the McLuhanesque vehicles of popular culture: fiction, the movies, television, popular music, tabloid journalism. Through these "instruments of diffusion" history in all its humanness and intricacy comes to life, is represented, and is interpreted for the mass audience. There was no more eyes-wide-open participant in the mass dissemination of historical interpretation than Charles Dickens, no writer more conscious of the power of the many nuances of historical discourse, no writer more convinced that the mass representation of a verticalized social history could actually contribute to changing the world. If Dickens had lived in the late twentieth century, he might not have been a novelist, might not have presented his messages, his view of history to his mass audience via language. He probably would have been a socially conscious rock star like Bob Dylan (what else is "Blowin' in the Wind" if not a marginalized commentary upon history?) or an historically obsessed film *auteur* like Steven Spielberg or Oliver Stone. Perhaps the best argument for LaCapra's "instruments of diffusion" theory at the end of the twentieth century is the compromise that has been struck between the professional historian and the mass dissemination of history by the cable television existence of *The History Channel* or the vast popularity of the historical television series of a documentarian like Ken Burns.

The History Wars

But such compromises between traditional history writing and the New Historicism have not always been struck. New Historicism has been a willing combatant in the "Culture Wars" of the 1980s and 1990s. Within the historical community all sorts of different battle lines have been drawn both in reaction to and in support of the concepts of New Historicism. One professional historian characterized the alarming departures from conventional history writing of the New Historicism as "McHistory"—all "special sauce, lettuce, cheese, pickle on a sesame seed bun" (see Engelmann). Another writes that "most academic historians have come to think of themselves as soft social scientists, analysts of politics, cultures, and society. They interpret, explicate and explain" (See Goodman). As well as these irascible verbal brickbats, the New Historicism has opened deeper chasms in the historical community, a small civil war within the more global culture wars. Feeling that both the venerable American Historical Association and The Organization of America Historians have sold out to the New Historicists, a new conservative group, The Historical Society, has been formed to try to take the writing of history back to "the good old days" (see Leatherman). Perhaps the most notorious of the revisionary skirmishes is that between the traditional historians of the American west (following in the hoofprints of Frederick Jackson Turner) and the New Westies (led by Patricia Ireland) who are most aggressively applying the tenets of New Historicism to this highly popular regional focus of American history. In *History and Criticism* Dominick LaCapra predicted exactly this sort of ideological combat within the historical community when he wrote:

> One prominent feature of this discussion and institutional context in the modern period has been a marked split between (and within) elite and popular cultures accompanied by the emergence of a commodified "Mass culture" or "culture industry" that has alienated certain cultural elites and threatened to appropriate both older and newer forms of popular culture.

Dickens and Metahistory

If Dickens were alive and writing in the 1990s, he would have charged right in like the Light Brigade to this combative discussion of the sources, the subjects and the very philosophy of history. In his novels he consistently took the representation of social history one step further into the philosophical realm of metahistory. Like late twentieth-century novelists such as Don De-Lillo, John Fowles, E. L. Doctorow, Graham Swift, and A. S. Byatt, Dickens's fiction consistently involves itself in a self-referential meditation upon the nature of history itself. If metahistory is history about the writing of history and metafiction is fiction about the writing of fiction, then Dickens is a meta-historical novelist. He is a novelist for whom the very nature of history and the intricacies of writing history become a theme in itself within his novels. Taken together (or separately to a lesser degree) Dickens's novels build a coherent philosophy of history which serves as a commentating subtext to the historical actions, characters, and themes of his fiction. As his characters go about their lives, engage in their small revolutions, Dickens also is consistently extrapolating the meanings of history and articulating its philosophical ideas. "It was the best of times, it was the worst of times," he writes, and his vision is embodied in that famous opening of *A Tale of Two Cities*. History for Dickens is a constant dialectic flux, a deconstructive series of critical oppositions which define the historical consciousness.

Dickens's vision of history is perhaps best represented in the words of Gaffer Hexam addressed to Rogue Riderhood as they bob in their boats on the Thames at midnight in the opening scene of *Our Mutual Friend*. Gaffer's words capture the important interrelationship between time, history and change: "We have worked together in time past, but we work together no more in time present nor yet future'' (*Our Mutual Friend,* 1,1). For Gaffer Hexam, the interpretation of the past has given him direction for action in both the present and the future. For Charles Dickens, this same sense of history as an interactive continuum which, once understood, can serve as a guide for human action lies at the center of his personal philosophy of history as expressed in his novels.

Dickens's philosophy of history strongly subscribes to both the doctrine of perfectibility of the late eighteenth-century philosopher/novelist William Godwin and the theories of evolution of the Victorian biological community culminating in the work of Charles Darwin. From Godwin, Dickens took the humanist ideas of natural goodness and perfectibility. From all of the scientists who preceded Darwin in the nineteenth century Dickens took the ideas of constant flux and the necessity of historical progress in order to survive, as an individual, as a community, as a society, as a nation, as a species. As David Halberstam, the new journalistic social and cultural historian of the late twentieth century, recently stressed, ''our job is not just to give you today, but to remind you, and prepare the way for the future with reminders of the past. We are custodians of the past as well as the future.'' Like Halberstam, Dickens saw the present as a fulcrum of history, a balance point between the past and the future. Dickens's novels are always self-referentially aware of their own historical agenda. Dickens consistently examines the socio-cultural history of the past and the present in his fiction as a means of giving his popular reading audience some historical sense of direction for the future. *Hard Times* is one of Dickens's clearest examples of the novel as warning, the novel as cautionary signpost of what lies ahead if the present course is not altered.

Thus, Dickens, as a social and cultural historian in his novels, is always acutely aware of the New Historicist principles of giving voice to the marginalized of society (such as Poor Jo in *Bleak House* or Stephen Blackpool in *Hard Times*), of thickening and verticalizing the representation or the narrative of history that he is presenting (as in *Barnaby Rudge* and *Our Mutual Friend* where he portrays those novels' societies from the bottom up), and of decentering the master texts of Victorian history by the creation of dialogically competing subtexts which are at times startlingly modern and even postmodern (such as his ongoing meditations upon the essential evolving nature of History itself within his own history).

Dickens and New Historicism

The actual practice of New Historicism as a critical stance in relation to fiction, film, theater, popular culture, whatever, is a three-fold interpretative act. It involves, first, questioning; then, rendering; then finally, layering the historical text. But even as this re-contextualizing is taking place the New Historicist must also remain self-referentially aware of the philosophical med- itation upon history itself which swims beneath the surface of the thematic action of the text. In other words, the New Historicist project balances its interpretation between the traditionally historical, the New Historical and the Metahistorical. The New Historicist project, the very existence of a philosoph- ical concept of a "New Historicism," has always been a compromise between the past (traditional history, traditional historicist methodology), the present (New Historicism), and whatever metahistorical subtexts or metatexts or sty- listic emplotments emerge from historical texts. Metahistory is like the science fiction concept of "parallel universes." A New Historicist literary critic can read the linear, surface text of a novel's action or characterization, its dramatic master text. But a New Historicist critic must also read vertically. The New Historicist critic must read down into a novel's subtexts as well as into the parallel world of a novel's metatext (its self-referential meditation upon its own composition, its own sense of its historical existence). New Historicism has always been a compromise: between past readings of history and newer ones that emphasize New Historicist principles; between past methodologies of historical research and present more inclusive, less power-centered ones; between the traditional. Romantic, linear style of writing history and the New Historicist verticalized style of decentered historical discourse. But, though somewhat prickly at times, the New Historicist project has always been a thoughtful compromise that asserts that New History always builds upon past work, thickens and verticalizes it, never discards it.

Of all the Victorian novelists, Dickens's fiction invites the application of the New Historicist project. First of all, Dickens's novels constantly question past history, challenge the power-centeredness of the past and the present, raise dialogic oppositions to traditional historical views of subjects as dispa- rate as the French Revolution, the New Poor Laws, the Chancery Law system, the Utilitarian factory system, or Victorian literacy and the Ragged Schools. Secondly, Dickens's novels render or fill in the representation of history by giving voice to the marginalized members of the society which the master text of power-centered traditional history may have intentionally excluded or merely overlooked as inconsequential. And thirdly, Dickens's fiction always offers the opportunity for a vertically layered reading of history. In setting, character and theme, his novels represent the Victorian age and the historical consciousness of that age from the bottom up, from the point of view of the marginalized, sometimes utterly invisible (witness Nemo in *Bleak House*), lower classes to the power-centered ruling classes. Joseph Conrad wrote: "Fiction is history, human history, or it is nothing. . . . A historian may be an artist too, and a novelist is a historian, the preserver, the keeper, the expounder, of human experience'' (*Notes on Life and Letters*). And Albert Camus wrote: ''A novel is never anything but a philosophy expressed in images.'' Dickens practiced both of their theories of the novel as well as those of the New Historicists throughout the writing of his fiction. Fiction as history, fiction as philosophy, fiction as marginalized voices speaking out, fiction as dialogic subtexts offering cautionary visions of the future, fiction as metatext formulating a philosophy of history, fiction as Dickens's mass market vehicle for all of these different kinds of socio-cultural meditations upon the Victorian age, fiction was Dickens's way of creating a new history to replace the traditional historical narratives which he (and many others in his age and in ours) perceived as too limited, too restricted in their forays in the direction of their truth.

If Dickens, then, is one Victorian novelist who is utterly receptive to the New Historicist critical approach, how does a critic go about applying that approach to the Dickensian canon? What does a Dickens critic have to do, first, to prepare oneself to New Historicize, and then to execute that New Historicization upon Dickens's fiction?

A New Historicist Dickensian How-To

In the 1990s age of Martha Stewart, The Frugal Gourmet, and Tim the Tool-Man Taylor, there is nowhere that the theoretical mantra of ''How-To'' is chanted more fervently than in the academic temples of literary criticism. The different sects of ''How-To'' circle one another warily, sometimes coming together to chant and dance, at other times wandering off into the solitary wilderness to meditate. How do you deconstruct a text? How do you study culture in a text, or a text in culture? How do you feminize or genderize or post-colonialize or Marxize or New Historicize a text? In a postmodern world, these theoretical, methodological questions tend to overshadow the rather fragile existence of the text itself. The comparison of the postmodernist critic to Tim the Tool-Man Taylor, the comical television Mr. Fixit who (on the sit-com *Home Improvement*) more often destroyed it than fixed it, is not really that farfetched. Tim the Tool-Man consistently used a sledgehammer to kill a fly, ran tremendous amounts of horsepower or electrical current through his power tools to the point that they would either explode or crash or catch fire thus destroying the very object that the tool was being employed to fix (as well as often destroying itself). Sometimes, it seems, that is what postmodernist critical theory does to the texts it encounters.

New Historicism can certainly be prone to this sort of overkill if it loses sight of its basic principles or gets out of synch with the text it is trying to historicize. So how should a New Historicist critic approach a text? With a revved-up power saw or a flyswatter? Or should the New Historicist critic just settle down and calmly find out what the text is made of, remove its outer shell and carefully probe its inner workings, its competing power sources, its intricate stylistic circuitry? In doing this, the New Historicist critic brings to bear upon that text all of the historical, theoretical, and critical tools in the New Historicist tool box. Yet, the New Historicist critic must be careful not to break the text down until all the proper historical connections have been made.

New Historicism functions in terms of a clearly articulated philosophy and methodology which needs to be studied and mastered before the critic starts working upon a text. Texts are too fragile to withstand too much postmodernist fixing, too fragile to withstand too many postmodernist powertools. Thus the first rule of the New Historicist project is a cautionary one: Don't fall into the same trap that closed on the early deconstructionists and Marxists; don't get carried away with your power. If we are to believe Joseph Conrad, history is always present in a novel, and if we are to believe Albert Camus, so is philosophy. The convergence of history and philosophy and literary texts (or any "instrument of diffusion") is one of the central concerns of the New Historicist project, but a critic must be very careful and knowledgeable about how he or she goes about accomplishing that convergence.

In order to New Historicize a text (any text, not just Dickens's), a critic must first know the philosophical, ideological, methodological principles which underlie the whole project of New Historicism. First read Foucault: *The Order of Things, The History of Sexuality, Discipline and Punish, Power/ Knowledge*. Then read Bakhtin: *The Dialogic Imagination, Rabelais and His World*. Next read Hayden White: *Metahistory, Tropics of Discourse*. Finally read Dominick LaCapra: *History and Criticism, Rethinking Intellectual History*. These are the primary ideological works of the New Historicism. They need to be read in depth, cover to cover, annotated, diagrammed, memorized. These are the works that give a New Historicist critic credibility, philosophical substance, a theoretical vocabulary, a way of thinking about texts, a way of thinking about society and culture—hell! a way of thinking about life.

After reading these major theorists, it is extremely useful to read the work of the theoretical commentators on these philosophical theorists. Renaissance scholars Stephen Greenblatt and Louis Montrose were instrumental in the early days of New Historicism in the 1980s in defining both the theory and the methodology of New Historicist literary practice. The work in both essays and books of Brook Thomas, Herbert Lindenberger, Patrick Brantlinger, Wesley Morris, Marlon Ross, Alan Liu, and Jonathan Arac is focused on the defining and refining of various aspects of the ideology and methodology of the New Historicism. One collection of essays, *The New Historicism* edited by H. Aram Veeser, is an excellent source for sampling the work of these commentators upon the seminal works of Foucault, Bakhtin, White and LaCapra. Of course, there are other contributing theorists to the New Historicism to be considered such as Fredrick Jameson, Frank Lentricchia, Walter Benjamin and Clifford Geertz, but one cannot read everything (or perhaps one can) and these theorists while they touch on the New Historicism have generally taken their work in different directions.

New Historicism and the Novel Genre

Once one has absorbed the theory on the levels of both the philosophers and commentators, the New Historicist literary critic can focus on the particular genre in question. In the case of the novel genre, the New Historicism has a strong argument for its application in the work of some of the early novel theorists such as Ian Watt. His *The Rise of the Novel* defined the beginnings of this particular modern genre in the early eighteenth century in England as directly related to the rise of a capitalist middle class who, through their powers of marketing and the development of technology, would change the whole structure of English society in the extremely short span of about eighty years at the end of the eighteenth and the beginning of the nineteenth century. Watt's socio-cultural genre work provides a bridge between traditional historical views of the novel genre as representative simply of an individual author's reaction to and representation of a particular time and place and the New Historicist's approach to the genre as a type of writing particularly designed and adapted to express the views and liberate the voices of those members of a capitalist society who had not previously been included in the settings, subject matters, and themes of other types of literary writing such as the classical romance or Augustian poetry due to the modes of production that those genres served. For the New Historicist, Margaret Anne Doody's attempt to rewrite the history of the novel genre in *The True Story of the Novel,* arguing that the genre is more than two thousand years old with its roots in ancient Greek prose epics, is a challenge not just to the history of the genre but to the genre as based upon history, as finding its voice in the concentration of some particular historical situations which demanded a unique voice and style. Margaret Anne Doody's version of the novel genre emphasizes its beginnings in the ritual and mythology of Ancient Greece. The New Historicist version of the novel genre, while quite certainly overly Anglocentric, does however emphasize its beginnings in the social change and the desire for realism of a specifically historical epoch.

Many fine New Historicist genre studies of the 1980s and 1990s have built upon Watt's pre-New Historicist sensibilities. One of the most interesting (and Foucaultian) of these genre studies is D. A. Miller's *The Novel and the*

Police which, taking its cue from *Discipline and Punish,* sees the very need for policing as New Historicist evidence that the novel genre consistently deals with a disordered decentered world. Miller argues that the novel genre project as defined by Ian Watt and others is intent upon producing a "stable, centered subject in a stable centered world" for the newly empowered middle class "is inevitably doomed to failure" (Miller, xi) because it suppresses so many other voices (texts) which lie outside of the master text which the police are empowered to protect. John Kucich in *Repression in Victorian Fiction* follows a similar Foucaultian path. "The impulse behind this book" Kucich writes, "is an attempt to redefine behavior in certain novels that has been ahistorically tied to fear, guilt, or avoidance as, instead, a nineteenth-century strategy for exalting interiority. This exaltation is not of a public or active kind; keeping the term *repression* helps preserve the sense of a self-conflictual, self-divided interiority that withdraws from the spheres of action and speech (pace Michel Foucault)" (2). Kucich goes on to show how for the Victorians *repression* is "the ideological instrument that actually produced a certain historical subject. . . the nineteenth-century cultural decision to value silenced or negated feeling over affirmed feeling, and the corresponding cultural prohibitions placed on display. . . . Arthur Clennam's willingness to play the part of 'nobody' " (3). Taking Foucault as his model, Kucich's theory of repression goes right to the heart of Victorian life as well as examining new ways of reading some of the major Victorian novelists, Dickens included. Society and the novel, culture and the novel: the New Historicist approach when it is successful creates both a historical interpretation and a unique new approach to the critical reading of literary texts. In the work of Miller and Kucich, the two objectives—understanding of the age and understanding of the texts—go hand in handcuffs.

But New Historicism is also inter-theoretically conversant with other postmodernist approaches to reading novels. Deborah Epstein Nord in *Walking the Victorian Streets* succeeds powerfully in historicizing in terms of Foucauldian definitions of sexuality the situation of women as figures of feminist representation in nineteenth-century England. "In the Victorian dialectic of disconnection and contagion," Nord writes, "the figure of fallen female sexuality shifts from marker of individuality and alienation to agent of connection and of disease both physical and social" (8). Defining the nineteenth-century novelist as a verticalizing force and a voice for the marginalized of society, Nord writes that the "novelist-spectator took on the task of representing the poor and the outcast as features of middle-class experience and of illustrating the invasion of disease and disgrace into the homes of the respectable" (2).

New Historicism as a critique of discourse strategies (as defined by Hayden White in *Metahistory*) finds expression in Jan B. Gordon's *Gossip and Subversion in Nineteenth-Century British Fiction.* For Gordon, "gossip is the (often) studied resistance to propriety—the ownership of discourse imagined to be self-same or identical'' (xii). This ''resistance to propriety'' is the kind of discursive subversion that realizes, as the New Historicist does, ''that there are always other stories to be told. And even when the gossip gives us a new account—to combine narrative and economic metaphors—it often strikes the reader as something he either already knew or *should have known''* (xiv). For example, Gordon's reading of Dickens's *Bleak House* stresses that the ''outside weather with which *Bleak House* commences clearly has as its corollary an interior, discursive climate wherein an opaque 'wall' of writing shuts out the still, small voice of advocacy as surely as the implacable sheets of London fog obscure the noonday sun'' (155). Fittingly, Gordon's chapter on Dickens and *Bleak House* studies the power-centered (in Chancery) control of information which is subverted by all of the competing voices of the socially marginalized that populate the novel.

Deirdre David's *Rule Britannia: Women, Empire and Victorian Writing* also begins with the invocation of the opening of *Bleak House,* but she evokes that ''historical moment'' in 1852 to compare the situation in the Victorian age to a similar ''historical moment in 1952, in the seedy suburbs of a city little changed from Dickens's London'' where given ''Britain's class-bound society, the age was more austere for some than for others, just as, in *Bleak House,* the 'ill-favoured and ill-savoured' neighborhood that houses the Smallweed family differs significantly from the St. Albans countryside that surrounds the quaint coziness of Bleak House itself'' (xi). For David, the New Historicist project is as much about the twentieth-century present as about the Victorian past. ''In writing this book,'' she emphasizes very much in the vein of Frederick Jameson or Homi K. Babha, ''I have always had in mind the way fictional and non-fictional texts produced during the Victorian period construct, in part, the material reality of a historically transformed fruit and vegetable stall in South London'' (xiii). Deirdre David's study of female subalternity in Victorian historicist writing, in Macauley as well as in Dickens, looks at a evolving nineteenth-century literature which consistently expresses a discomfort with ''domestic despotism purchased with imperial wealth'' (45) as is the case in Dickens's *Dombey and Son* in the relationship between father and daughter.

What all of these genre critics hold in common is their approach to the socio-cultural themes of late eighteenth and nineteenth-century fiction from the model of New Historicist thought. All focus upon the verticalizing of historical discourse via the liberation of the voices of the panoptically repressed and marginalized members of society as represented in those texts. All focus upon the emplotted agendas of the discursive style of these novels. And, all find in these texts fully delineated philosophies of history which illuminate the progress of socio-cultural discourse with the Victorian age serving as a fulcrum of a history of ideas beginning in the rise of capitalism and imperialism in the eighteenth century and progressing into the twentieth century. Not coincidentally, all place the novels of Charles Dickens at the very center of this evolution of New Historicist discourse.

Dickens: The Pre-History

What follows is meant to be a brief history of the New Historicizing of Dickens's fiction. However, as is the case in any exercise in historiography, the points of demarcation cannot always be conveniently dated and catalogued. The New Historicizing of Dickens's fiction, for example, cannot be simply relegated to those works of the 1980s and 1990s which post-dated Stephen Greenblatt's coining of that term. Just as the philosophy of Existentialism was preceded by thousands of years of philosophical inquiry into the identity of the individual (going back to the "know thyself" of the Greeks) before Sartre named it in the 1940s, and just as Darwin's theories of evolution and natural selection were preceded by decades of biological research in the Linnean model by predecessors like Lyall, the New Historicizing of Dickens has a rich pre-history.

The Doctor Spock of the New Historicizing of Dickens and the Victorian novel is Richard Altick, His *The English Common Reader* which is subtitled "a social history of the mass reading public. 1800–1900," though published in the late 1950s, is still one of the most valuable research tools that any Dickensian or student of the nineteenth-century novel can consult. Though Altick's *The English Common Reader* pre-dates the New Historicism of the 1980s by almost 25 years, the historical research questions that Altick asks are quite similar in their verticalizing intent and their consciousness that the reading public and those who wrote for that reading public were acutely aware of the marginalized condition of a large percentage of their readers. In the 1960s and 1970s, Altick follows *The English Common Reader* with a succession of social histories, all of which took the same verticalized approach, analyzed how popular literature and performance art formed Victorian culture: *Lives and Letters: A History of Literary Biography in England and America* (1965), *Victorian Studies in Scarlet* (1970), *Victorian People and Ideas* (1973), and *The Shows of London* (1978). Dickens, of course, was never far from the center of any of these studies. In 1983, Altick's former students from Ohio State University presented him with a festschriften perceptively titled *Victorian Literature and Society* (1983). Usually such tributes are given to senior major professors or mentors who have reached the end of long and fruitful careers. But in this case, Altick's students were a bit premature. To paraphrase Mark Twain, Altick's festschriften was no more than an indication that "the reports of my death have been greatly exaggerated."

In 1991, Altick published *The Presence of the Present* which, as was always his style, bears the descriptive subtitle "Topics of the Day in the Victorian Novel." Fittingly, this brilliant compendium of New Historicist research begins with the words "Looking back." "Looking back," Altick begins, "I realize that the idea of this book originated many years ago, when I first discovered the pleasures of reading Victorian literature, especially fiction, alongside contemporary documents of Victorian life and the steadily increasing number of social historians of that period" (vii). In *The Presence of the Present,* Altick's introduction begins with a quote from the first page of the first issue of the famous Victorian Magazine *Punch: "Punch* . . . makes the most of the present, regardless of the past or future" (1). That New Historicist [in]sensibility of the interrelatedness of time and history, the New Historicist research interest in what Altick terms "topicalities," which are often the best signs and encoded texts for the understanding of the interests of marginalized social voices, and the New Historicist conviction that the literature of the day is built upon these indicators of the vertical layering of socio-cultural relationships, make *The Presence of the Present* one of the true power tools in the New Historicist's tool box. And Dickens dominates Altick's book. Any number of cultural "topicalities" are brought to bear to support new readings of all of Dickens's novels. *The Presence of the Present* belongs in every Victorian New Historicist's and every Dickensian's library.

If Altick is the consulting authority for all of the Dickensian New Historicists, there are also a great many other Dickens critics of the fifties, sixties, and seventies who tinkered with concepts of history, who examined popular "instruments of diffusion," who made connections between "topicalities" and representation in their readings of Dickens's novels. Altick in *The Presence of the Present* acknowledges his own predecessors in the business of vertically historicizing Dickens's fiction: "the historical approach to this great body of literature" Altick writes, "is, of course, not new. The topicality of Dickens's novels, in particular, has been impressively revealed by a succession of scholars inspired by the pioneer work, a generation ago, of Humphry House, Kathleen Tillotson, and John Butt" (1).

Of Altick's generation of Dickensian historicists, Ross Dabney prefigures the work of Deirdre David in *Love and Property in the Novels of Dickens* (1967). Dabney focuses upon what he terms a Dickensian "obsession," the way Dickens links the gestures and poses he detests—casual superiority, negligent aristocratic self-indulgence—as well as particular vices—sexual immorality, selfishness, cruelty, meanness with money—into a complex whose natural and characteristic expression seems to be a proclivity for marrying, or trying to make others marry, for money" (27). Grahame Smith in *Dickens, Money and Society* (1968) goes one step further than Dabney and prefigures the New Historicist emphasis upon discourse strategies that lies at the center of Hayden White's work. Writing of Dickens's fiction, Smith argues that the very richness of the comedy stems partly from the exaggerations by means of which a recognizable social reality is inflated into a grotesque parody of itself. Language plays a part in all of this, but it is a language that reflects, in however distorted a manner, the everyday world'' (5). For Smith, ''the Dickens problem presents itself essentially as a question of fictional form which is related to the analysis of society'' (8).

Two prominent 1980s Dickens critics take similar and complementary historicist views of the engagement of Dickens's novels with the evolving social history of his place and time. Alexander Welsh in *The City of Dickens* (1971) and F. S. Schwarzbach in *Dickens and the City* (1979) both evidence the growing consciousness of postmodernist theoretical approaches to the reading of Dickens's social thematics which were just beginning to assert themselves in that decade. Welsh writes: ''Charles Dickens lived through and reacted to an experience of the city that is in many respects continuous with our own'' (3). Schwarzbach echoes him by declaring that ''[m]odern life is city life'' (1) and ''as any student of the social history of the Victorian period knows, when one turns to specialized studies to check the accuracy of Dickens's observations, as often as not, Dickens is quoted as the leading witness on that very matter'' (2). For both of these Dickens critics, the interaction of literary representation and social history is a complex dynamic which demands both keen observation of social reality and the interpretive skills of the social theorist. ''History affords ample evidence of this process,'' Welsh writes. ''Modern scientific descriptions of the city pretend to owe more to direct observation than to past interpretations; the city is conceived as a set of interrelated problems in contemporary finance, engineering, politics, and psychology, and the persons responsible for the analysis of these problems are called 'city planners,' as if they dealt only with the future. But the description of some of the problems is ancient, and especially to be found in . . . literature'' (4). For Welsh, ''[t]o describe Dickens's description of the city is to study this process. . . . He worried about what went on there, and the old ways of grasping what went on were confounded by historical change'' (4). Schwarzbach defines his study of Dickens's fiction in similar terms, terms that both Hayden White and Dominick LaCapra would surely applaud: ''I have found it necessary to move beyond those areas of study to which literary criticism recently has confined itself, and to bring to bear upon the central problem insights derived from the disciplines of history, social history, sociology and psychology, as well as from the close study of the texts themselves'' (4). Thus, at the dawning of the formation of a formal, named ''New Historicist'' school of postmodernist thought, a significant number of Dickensian literary critics were already involved in exploring this relationship between Dickens's fiction and the theoretical re-conception of historical criticism of the postmodernist age.

The New Historicist Dickensians

After 1980 and the naming of New Historicism as a recognized school of theoretical literary criticism. Dickens's fiction became one of the most prominent sites for the exploration of the themes of verticalizing history and of liberating marginalized voices. New Historicist critics were also acutely aware of the metahistorical possibilities of texts and searched for encoded philosophies of history emplotted in the stylistics of literary productions. The diversity of postmodernist theoretical approaches to interpretation opened all sorts of discursive possibilities to a new generation of Dickens critics attracted to the social, political, cultural encodings of his novelistic style.

Following the lead of Raymond Williams, James M. Brown in *Dickens: Novelist in the Market-Place* (1982) argues that the "relation between the novel and society in Dickens's mature work is not simple and passive, as is implied in many reflection theories of the documentary type. It is a complex relationship in which the novelist's critical vision of social reality is mediated through both literary conventions and his affiliation to class values" (4). In *Dickens and the Social Order* (1985), Myron Magnet examines the often truculent and repressive conservatism of Dickens, a decidedly disciplinary and panoptic set of social tendencies which go against the grain of the commonly accepted "Father Christmas" image of Dickens which has been so long accepted by the Dickensian critical establishment. "This cluster of attitudes," Magnet writes, "constitutes a coherent structure of belief and feeling rather than a set of quirky, unexamined prejudices. Such views, moreover, are not extrinsic to Dickens's novelistic achievement but instead are embedded in the grain of his artistic imagination" (4). Magnet's book gives Dickensians a new, disturbing and very different view of Dickens's relations to the marginalized classes of Victorian England and underscores the complexity of his fiction's dialogic representation of those marginalized classes. Pam Morris in *Dickens's Class Consciousness: A Marginal View* (1991) employs "Mikhail Bakhtin's analysis of the novel as a inherently dialogic form always engaged in a polemical relation with dominant voices of its era" which offers "a means of historicizing texts dynamically, erasing that mechanistic gap between fiction on the one hand and its 'background' on the other" (ix). Morris follows Bakhtin's theoretical lead into a discussion of the margin/center, servant/master relationships that dynamically form so many of Dickens's novels.

Like Deirdre David, Suvendrini Perera takes yet another postmodernist path, that of post-colonial and subaltern studies, in *Reaches of Empire* (1991) which deals with the literary inscription of Imperialism upon English society by a succession of nineteenth-century novelists with the heaviest emphasis placed upon the fiction of Charles Dickens. In a similar vein to the work of both David and Morris, Gail Turley Houston in *Consuming Fictions: Gender, Class and Hunger in Dickens's Novels* (1994) specifically aligns her work with the New Historicism:

> New Historicist methodology offers luxuriant permission to bring any and all "texts" into the student's reading of a culture as one unravels the ways the culture shapes those texts while attending to the warp by which those texts have shaped the culture as well. My own interest in the material culture that constructed Victorian gender and class results in what I hope will be construed as a "thick description" of the range of ideologies (including medical, economic, and alimentary implicit and explicit in the term *consumption.* (xiv)

As did Myron Magnet, John Schad, editor of a collection of essays titled *Dickens Refigured: Bodies, Desires and Other Histories* (1996), has brought together a number of essays which argue a less liberal, more disciplinary, Dickens. Taking his cue from Jonathan Arac and D. A. Miller, Schad's collected essays "locate in Dickens perspectives that distance and indeed police the eccentric, or marginal" (1) as they are found emplotted in the Dickens style. The section on "Dickens and History" in Schad's collection includes articles by Linda Shires, John Lucas, and Diane Elam which examine Dickens's self-referential relation to different kinds of history (personal, cultural, social, national) inside of specific novels (*David Copperfield, Bleak House, Little Dorrit*). Catherine Waters in *Dickens and the Politics of the Family* (1997) also looks at one of the darker sides of Dickens's personal history, how his own family and the breakup of his marriage is inscribed upon the representation of the Victorian family in both Dickens's early work (influenced by his own dysfunctional family and his own family-abandoned childhood) and his later work (after the break-up of his marriage and the Ternan liaison).

Murray Roston goes in yet another New Historicist direction in *Victorian Contexts: Literature and the Visual Arts* (1997) where he quotes Stephen Greenblatt on his first page as an entry into his extended study of the relationship between Victorian literature, with a strong emphasis upon Dickens's fiction, and Victorian visual art's representation of social history. Roston characterizes his own work as a "synchronic, cross-media exploration" intent upon "locating aspects of Victorian literature within the changing contexts of the painting, architecture, and decorative arts of the time, in order, by such comparison, to identify the contemporary impulses to which these media were reacting" (5).

Thus, the New Historicizing of Dickens's fiction may be initially in the preparation—the reading of the philosophers and commentators, the reading of the genre historicists, the reading of the prior New Historicizers of Dickens's fiction—but is ultimately in the perception and immersion and imagination of the Dickens critic in the dynamic relationship between a complexly verticalized history and Dickens's intricately emplotted texts. This essay has attempted a number of things in support of this dynamic relationship. It has tried to introduce the philosophical/theoretical/critical model which provides the foundation for a New Historicism. It has tried to conduct a "how-to" workshop for critics entering upon the New Historicist adventure (to steal a metaphor from Richard Altick). And it has tried to examine the major texts of both New Historicist theory and practice as well as of the New Historicizing of the novels of Charles Dickens. But perhaps most of all, it has tried to pay tribute to a fascinating group of philosophers and scholars who progressively, building carefully upon one another's work over a period of almost fifty years, have given us a new sense of both history and criticism, a new approach for the reading of historical texts, a new consciousness of the multi-layered qualities of historical style and language, and an exciting forum for the interdisciplinary exchange of historical, literary critical, cultural, and social discourses. To paraphrase the rock-and-roll enthusiasm of my youngest daughter, "History Rules!"

WORKS CITED

Altick, Richard. *The English Common Reader.* Chicago: U of Chicago P 1957.

———. *Lives and Letters.* New York: Knopf, 1965.

———. *Victorian Studies in Scarlet.* New York: Norton, 1970.

———. *Victorian People and Ideas.* London: J. M. Dent and Sons, 1973.

———. *The Shows of London.* Cambridge, MA: the Belknap Press, 1978.

———. *The Presence of the Present.* Columbus: Ohio State UP, 1991.

Brown, James M. *Dickens: Novelist in the Market-Place.* Totowa, NJ: Barnes and Noble Books, 1982.

Bakhtin, Mikhail. *The Dialogic Imagination.* Austin: U of Texas P, 1981.

———. *Rabelais and His World.* Bloomington: Indiana UP, 1984.

Conrad, Joseph. *Notes on Life and Letters.*

Camus, Albert. *Lyrical and Critical Essays.* New York: Knopf, 1968.

Dabney, Ross. *Love and Property in the Novels of Dickens.* Berkeley and Los Angeles: U of California P, 1967.

David, Deirdre, *Rule Brittania: Women, Empire and Victorian Writing.* Ithaca and London: Cornell UP, 1995.

Doody, Margaret Anne. *The True Story of the Novel.* New Brunswick, NJ: Rutgers University Press, 1996.

Dickens, Charles. *Barnaby Rudge.*

———. *David Copperfield.*

———. *Bleak House.*

———. *Hard Times.*

———. *Little Dorrit.*

———. *A Tale of Two Cities.*

——— *Our Mutual Friend.*

DeLillo, Don. *Libra.*

Engelmann, Larry. "McHistory." Paper Delivered at *National Conference on the Teaching of the Vietnam War.* Washington, D.C.: April, 1988.

Foucault, Michel. *The Order of Things.* New York: Vintage, 1973.

———. *The History of Sexuality.* New York: Pantheon, 1978.

———. *Discipline and Punish.* New York: Pantheon, 1978.

———. *Power/Knowledge.* New York: Pantheon, 1980.

Gordon, Jan B. *Gossip and Subversion in Nineteenth-Century British Fiction.* New York: St. Martin's Press, 1996.

Geertz, Clifford. *The Interpretation of Cultures.* New York: Basic, 1973.

Goodman, Thomas. "Telling the Stories of Narrative History." *The Chronicle Higher Education.* 14 August 1998.

Houston, Gail Turley. *Consuming Fictions: Gender, Class and Hunger in Dickens Novels.* Carbondale: Southern Illinois UP, 1994.

Halberstam, David. Lecture at Purdue University. 5 October 1997.

Kincaid, James R. and Kuhn, Albert (Eds.). *Victorian Literature and Society.* Columbus: Ohio State UP, 1983.

Kucich, John. *Repression in Victorian Fiction.* Berkeley and Los Angeles: U of California P. 1987.

Leatherman, Courtney. ''Saying Their Field is in 'Disarray,' Historians Set Up a New Society.'' *The Chronicle of Higher Education,* 8 May 1998.

LaCapra, Dominick. *Rethinking Intellectual History.* Ithaca: Cornell UP. 1983.

———. *History and Criticism.* Ithaca: Cornell UP, 1985.

Morris, Pam. *Dickens's Class Consciousness: A Marginal View.* New York: St. Martin's 1991.

Magnet, Myron. *Dickens and the Social Order.* Philadelphia: U of Pennsylvania P, 1985.

Miller, D. A. *The Novel and the Police.* Berkeley and Los Angeles: U of California P, 1988.

Nord, Deborah Epstein. *Walking the Victorian Streets.* Ithaca: Cornell UP: 1995.

Palmer, William J. *Dickens and New Historicism.* New York: St. Martin's 1997.

Perera, Suvendrini. *Reaches of Empire.* New York: Columbia UP, 1991.

Roston, Murray. *Victorian Contexts: Literature and the Visual Arts.* New York: New York UP, 1997.

Schad, John (ed.). *Dickens Refigured: Bodies, Desires and Other Histories.* Manchester and New York: Manchester UP, 1996.

Schwarzbach, F. S. *Dickens and the City.* London: Athlone, 1979.

Smith, Grahame. *Dickens, Money and Society.* Berkeley and Los Angeles: U of California P, 1963.

Spielberg, Steven. *Saving Private Ryan.* 1998.

Scott, Sir Walter. *Rob Roy.*

———. *The Heart of Midlothian.*

Shaw, George Bernard. *The Devil's Disciple.*

Thomas, Brook. ''Preserving and Keeping Order by Telling Time in *Heart of Darkness*'' in H. Aram Veeser (ed.). *The New Historicism.* New York: Routledge, 1989.

Veeser, H. Aram (ed.). *The New Historicism.* New York: Routledge, 1989.

Waters, Catherine. *Dickens and the Politics of the Family.* Cambridge: Cambridge UP, 1997.

Watt, Ian. *The Rise of the Novel.* Berkeley and Los Angeles: U of California P, 1957.

Welsh, Alexander. *The City of Dickens.* Oxford: Clarendon P, 1979.

White, Hayden. *Metahistory.* Baltimore: Johns Hopkins UP, 1973.

———. *Tropics of Discourse.* Baltimore: Johns Hopkins UP, 1978.

Recent Dickens Studies: 1997

Elisabeth G. Gitter

A survey of writing about Dickens published in the United States in 1997 reveals a sobering reality: few major university presses are publishing scholarly books devoted to him—or to any other single author. Smaller presses have become the most important outlets for monographs on nineteenth literature. The good news for Dickensians is that both general-interest and specialized academic journals continued to publish a diverse and original array of worthwhile articles. Also heartening was the appearance of several excellent new editions of Dickens's work. Writers about Dickens in 1997 took a variety of approaches: their work reflected the influence of feminist theory in all its forms, queer theory, new historicism, and innovations in cultural studies. Foucault was the most frequently cited theorist, but Bakhtin, Adorno, Barthes, Williams, and Lukács were also influential. Historicist studies abounded, and there was strong interest in Dickens as both creator and purveyor of a mass-market narrative product.

Simon Gray's mordant *Breaking Hearts* is narrated by Professor Helena Twiscombe, distinguished Dickens scholar and "PhDrunkard." Author of three bulky but elegant critical tomes, Twiscombe has descended into a permanent condition of hallucinatory, bottle-in-the-top-drawer-and-two-more-squirreled-away alcoholism. After a lifetime devoted to the "great man,"—both to the body of his work and the "immense largeness of his soul"—Twiscombe has been put out to pasture by her academic colleagues, a living-dead bunch of pension-fixated, "bloated elves" who, she claims, are not really stupid about anything except the books they teach (4, 12, 13).

Sobered by Professor Twiscombe's fate, I have approached this year's stack of writing about Dickens with the gin bottle locked away, but the key not too well hidden. Gray's Twiscombe reminds us all too pointedly of what fun Dickens would have made of Dickensians: listening to a colleague's "imbecilities and dead ideas," she moans, "Charlie D., Charlie D . . . come and look at this lot." (30).

Trends

If Dickens were indeed to come and look at this year's lot, he might be more alarmed than amused to observe that fewer university presses than ever are interested in publishing books about him. As William Galperin reminds us in his thoughtful survey of recent writing about the nineteenth century, the scholarly publishing industry is changing—and keeping an ever more relentless eye on the bottom line. In response to economic pressures, many university presses have, as Galperin puts it, "simply left the scene" (878). This year, among major university presses, Harvard, Princeton, Yale, Chicago, Cornell, Johns Hopkins and University of California published nothing on or directly relating to Dickens. Only Cambridge published more than one Dickens monograph; Oxford, Duke, Vanderbilt, Kentucky, and Northern Illinois each published only one. Scholars who wrote on Dickens relied primarily on small presses and on St. Martin's, which continues to be an important—perhaps the most important—outlet for academic writing on the nineteenth century. Only three critical books published in 1997 were devoted solely to Dickens; the rest were multiauthor studies, usually organized around a single theme. While thematic approaches, when they are not too rigidly coercive, can uncover exciting connections among disparate authors and texts, the dwindling number of scholarly Dickens books is, obviously, cause for concern.

The good news for Dickensians is that journals continue to be hospitable to their work. In 1997 interesting articles appeared in numerous general-interest academic journals as well as in the indispensable *Dickens Quarterly* and *Dickensian. (Dickens Studies Annual* got a bit behind schedule and did not publish a 1997 volume, but will catch up in 1998.) Also heartening was the publication of several excellent new editions of Dickens's work.

Critics in 1997 most often characterized Dickens—the author and the man—as contradictory, inconsistent, duplicitous, and subversive. To help make sense of all the doubleness and ambivalence they uncovered, the writers under review used a variety of theoretical approaches. Feminist theory in all its forms was influential; queer theory and recent scholarship on the body also shaped many discussions. Historicist studies, postmodern and otherwise, abounded, and there was considerable interest in Dickens as both creator and purveyor of an emerging mass-market narrative product. Foucault, apparently inexhaustible, was the theorist of choice for a number of studies. Despite rumors to the contrary, Freudian, Jungian, Kleinian, and Marxist theory are, if not fashionable, then at least undead. Barthes and, to a lesser extent, Bakhtin, Adorno, Raymond Williams, and Lukács were frequently cited this year; deconstruction as an approach is thriving, but Derrida *ipse* was seldom mentioned. "Empire" appears, unaccountably, to have declined as a topic of critical interest. The most sophisticated writers gracefully combined a variety of theoretical approaches and resisted the temptation to squeeze exuberant Dickensian texts into tight theoretical corsets.

* * *

In preparing this survey, I have done my best to read all the books and scholarly articles written about Dickens that were published in print in the United States in 1997, with the exception of dissertations, most reviews, and children's editions; I am grateful to Trevor Packer for helping me get hold of the books that I needed. In the interests of keeping to a reasonable length, I have not chosen to review everything that I read. A few 1997 books did not reach me in time to be included; I regret those as well as any inadvertent omissions. My focus has been on critical writing; I have paid attention only to the more noteworthy new editions of Dickens's work.

Although publications on Dickens in 1997 did not lend themselves to easy categorizing, I have organized them under what I hope are useful headings. The topic most frequently discussed was Dickens and the family: a surprising number of critics were interested in his representations of women and children and the domestic world. Other thematic discussions were concerned with ethics, representations of time and history, and the development of a Victorian reading public. Of Dickens's individual works, *Bleak House* was the subject of the most intense critical attention in 1997, but articles on a number of his other novels were also published, as well as some important studies of his journalism. Under the heading, "Mostly for Fun," I have listed a few works that seem to have been written as much for enjoyment as for edification.

Women, Children, and the Family

Of the many fine books about Dickens in 1997, *Angels and Absences: Child Death in the Nineteenth Century,* by Laurence Lerner, was my favorite. I had thought that Garrett Stewart had put the subject of child deaths to final rest in his magnificent 1984 *Death Sentences: Styles of Dying in British Fiction,* but Lerner has managed to unearth a fresh set of questions. His point of departure is a consideration of real deaths in the nineteenth century; from there he surveys poems about deaths of children, reading them primarily as strategies of consolation. Dickens is the central figure of the book, especially, inescapably, as the creator of the deaths of Paul Dombey and Little Nell.

Lerner uses his inquiry into Dickens's famous child deaths as the occasion for theoretically sophisticated explorations in several directions. He is interested in traditions of representation of childhood and definitions of the uncertain and erotically-charged boundary between child and adult. Since the dying Victorian child was often represented as an angel, Lerner, with illuminating comparative references to Goethe, discusses the nature and function of belief in angels in an increasingly skeptical age. Examining Dickensian representations of child deaths also allows Lerner to ruminate on the nature of pathos: how it is achieved and its relationship to Dickens's much-discussed theatricality and political anger.

Angels and Absences offers a variety of pleasures. It is not only a sophisticated work of criticism, but also an informal anthology of writings about child death: Lerner reprints dozens of little-known letters of condolence, journal entries of bereaved parents, epitaphs, and memorial poems. The book is illustrated with an interesting but somewhat random collection of examples of Victorian deathbed-scene paintings, cemetery sculpture, and representations of Paul and Little Nell. Readers will especially admire—and at times be moved by—Lerner's witty, elegant, and thoughtful prose; smoothly integrating history and fiction, he meditates on death and loss, the nature of bereavement, and the power and appeal of Dickensian sentimentality.

On a related subject, a useful companion to *Angels and Absences* is *Suffering Mothers in Mid-Victorian Novels,* by Natalie J. McKnight, who points out that when children died, Victorian mothers were often told to blame themselves. McKnight quotes a passage from an 1858 issue of *The British Mother's Journal* that would have made a grim but fascinating footnote to Lerner's book:

> On [mothers'] shoulders lies the greater part of the blame [for infant mortality]—we fill the churchyards, and send babies a short cut from the cradle to the grave—we kill them by our bad management. (8)

Like Lerner, McKnight is interested in the differences between reality and fiction. Drawing upon medical manuals, women's magazines, and conduct books, as well as representations of the maternal Queen Victoria, she explores the origins of the Victorian ideal of motherhood, the historical effects of that ideal, and the role of fiction in reflecting, subverting, and reinforcing it.

In her amusingly titled chapter on Dickens, "Making Mother Suffer, and Other Fun in Dickens," McKnight surveys his numerous representations of "bitchy" maternal types (37). "Bitchy" is not, perhaps, *le mot juste,* and the explanation McKnight offers for Dickens's tendency to create and then punish bad mothers (his bad mother is at the root of it all) may strike some readers as both predictable and facile. While McKnight may be accused of playing a little too fast and loose with feminist psychological theory, she does offer a brisk and spirited survey of both angelic and monsterous Dickensian moms.

In *Victorian Testatments: The Bible, Christology, and Literary Authority in Early-Nineteenth Century British Culture,* Sue Zemka takes a more theoretically sophisticated approach to Dickens's idealized mothers. Zemka argues that in the first half of the Victorian period, when religious authority and practice were weakening, traditional religious faith was increasingly replaced by a celebration of spiritual individualism and the nuclear family, and childhood and femininity began to be represented as sacred categories. While pointing out that Dickens, like other early Victorian writers, used images of childhood and femininity as "vehicles of a secular gospel of feeling," Zemka emphasizes that his idealized representations are continually undermined by an "almost compulsive" exploration of half-hidden tensions and contradictions (120).

Zemka rests her case on an imaginative choice of three textual sources: *The Life of Our Lord, Dombey and Son,* and Dickens's letters to Angela Burdett Coutts on the topic of the reform of "fallen women." Beneath the surface clarity of moral vision and authorial stance, Zemka finds signs of a "mimetic confusion of the emotions and attributes which supposedly separate the cast of characters involved": distinctions are blurred between Dickens and his Christ, between Dickens's Christ and his women and child characters, between Dickens and his readers, and between Dickens and the prostitutes he desired to reform (122). In straddling the boundary between entertainment and edification, Dickens manages to register both the "ideological facade" of a sentimental culture and the contradictions which that facade conceals.

When it comes to taking aim at contradictions behind sentimentalized domestic facades, Dickens's own family life of course makes a tempting target, and in 1997 a few critics (including McKnight and Pool) could not resist joining the reproachful chorus. In *Dickens and the Politics of the Family,* Catherine Waters, too, adds her voice to the general scolding. Waters's response to Dickens's caddish treatment of his wife unwittingly echoes that of one of Simon Gray's more inspired creations in *Breaking Hearts:* Professor Twiscombe's colleague and nemesis, Horatia the Corrector. The formidable and humorless Corrector, whose "special favorite hate" is Twiscombe's beloved Charlie D., has drawn up a lengthy bill of particulars against the novelist:

She starts with the marriage, his marrying one sister and then falling in love with the younger one, moving her into his menage, when he adored, adored, *adored* her, and there was poor Catherine, the wife, the third party, watching this male monster of heterosexuality worshipping her little sister while being bored and irritated by herself, his actual wife, whose only fault, *only fault* was that she was clumsy, fell over things, was pretty stupid and couldn't speak coherently in public (in other words, a shame and a disgrace of a wife). And then the younger sister collapsing, dying, and Charlie D. making a meal of it, sobbing, making memorials and monuments to her, and Catherine, the wife, can you imagine? . . . What it was like to be Catherine, the wife, with this husband who insulted her by grieving over her dead sister, while at the same time she herself was producing children, some of them corpses.   (28)

Worse yet, according to the Corrector, have been Charlie D.'s political crimes. Not limiting himself to the oppression of the women in his own household, he has had a hand in the oppression of the working classes by promulgating the middle class values that have imprisoned them.

Alas, the Corrector has anticipated the thesis of Waters's *Dickens and the Politics of the Family*. It is rotten luck indeed for a scholar to have her argument turn up as the object of a parody by Simon Gray—and also a hint that perhaps the argument suffers from predictability.

Like the Corrector, Waters uses the rupture of Dickens's own family life as a starting point for her examination of the family's "inescapably political" function as a construct in Dickens's writing (12). Her purpose is to explain the "puzzling gap" between Dickens's reputation as "the purveyor of cosy domestic bliss" and his fascination with the fractured and unhappy families portrayed in most of his fiction. Combining feminist, Foucauldian, and new historicist methodologies, Waters makes the familiar claim that Dickens's novels are "enabling representations in the Victorian social economy" (27). His depictions of families, whether those families are blissfully harmonious or grotesque, perform the function of normalizing middle-class domestic ideology and (here's where the Corrector chimes in again) enforcing middle-class authority.

Although Waters's thesis is stale, her book has many virtues. She makes a strong case for a historical shift in Dickens's novels "away from an earlier stress upon the importance of lineage and blood"—a stress that is clearest in *Oliver Twist*—and toward "a new ideal of domesticity assumed to be the natural form of the family" (27). In one of the book's most original chapters, Waters traces this historical shift in Dickens's Christmas scenes, from *Pickwick*, through the Christmas books, to *Great Expectations*. Bringing relevant historical information to persuasive readings of particular scenes and passages, she succeeds, despite her reductive thesis, in describing and defining the development of a discourse of domesticity in a range of Dickens's writings.

In her chapter on Dickens in *Vessels of Meaning: Women's Bodies, Gender Norms, and Class Bias from Richardson to Lawrence,* Laura Fasick is also interested in sentimentality and the domestic sphere. Building on recent scholarship of the body, Fasick undertakes a well-researched examination of what she argues are complex Victorian attitudes toward women as consumers and providers of food. Fasick questions the overly simple claim that Victorians in general—and Dickens in particular—glorified the figure of the abstinent, inappetent, obsessively nourishing female. The delicate, slender Amy Dorritts and Esther Summersons are idealized, Fasick argues, not because they lack appetite or exhibit bodily control for its own sake, but because they offer an abundance of psychic and spiritual nourishment. Abstinence, unless it is in the service of others, is suspect; Dickens's most angelic heroines, in fact, are associated with a genuine appreciation of the pleasures of cayenne pepper and a pennysworth of pickles.

To make her case, Fasick provides a brief, lively catalog of withholders and providers of nourishment, from Mrs. Joe to the jelly-making Esther, pointing out that the true monster of Victorian literature is not the passionately appetitive woman, but the one "whose passion is to deny and castigate others' various appetites," (73). However, she fails to explain completely why Esther—to be Esther—must be too delicate to digest the rich food that she cheerfully prepares for the enjoyment of others, or why Amy Dorrit never gets to pop a leftover pickle in her own mouth.

Another interpreter of female body language is Mary Ann O'Farrell, who devotes a chapter of *Telling Complexions: The Nineteenth-Century English Novel and the Blush* to an ingenious reading of Rosa Dartle's tell-tale scar in *David Copperfield*. In her witty interpretation of the blush in the nineteenth-century English novel, O'Farrell uses Foucault selectively, flexibly and at times even playfully, with a Barthesian twist, to trace a progression from the confessional and self-monitoring blushes in Jane Austen to the liquid, bottled product of cosmetic commerce.

O'Farrell builds on earlier work by Helena Michie and Audrey Jaffe (both of whom have discussed the role of the scar in establishing identity in Dickens's novels) in arguing that Rosa Dartle's identity "seems to lie precisely in insinuation, in a kind of flirtation with legibility that wants, finally, to refuse legibility" (89). For O'Farrell, Rosa Dartle's unstable, hybrid mark—part blush, part scar—resists a symbolic interpretation. Because the blush is "a site of anxiety for Dickens (about class, about women, about the body, and about significatory excess)," he transforms the ostensibly legible blush, in Rosa Dartle's case, into a lurid scar, and, in the process, moves from Austenian manners to melodrama (82). While for some writers (and readers) blushes and scars may hold out the promise—or reinforce the presumption—that the body and the character are in some sense legible, O'Farrell argues that Rosa Dartle's blush/scar exemplifies Dickens's ambivalent and intermittent commitment to bodily legibility.

O'Farrell's consideration of Rosa Dartle's blush/scar widens into a broader discussion of the relationship of skin color and texture to race and social class. By looking for blushes, O'Farrell notices some fascinating patterns: for example, the difference between the intermittent, legible signalling of the delicately blushing cheek of Clara Copperfield, and the unvarying—and therefore illegible—classed redness of Clara Peggotty, whose face must be read as always unblushing or always blushing. I also recommend, but in a short review cannot do justice to, O'Farrell's complex readings of Little Em'ly's seemingly upperclass ability to blush; of the white, then red, finger marks that David leaves on Uriah Heep's red cheek; and of Rosa Dartle's desire to brand Emily's face.

Although O'Farrell's discussion is focused primarily on *David Copperfield,* her analysis of Dickens as an ambivalent marker of bodies has implications for many of his other novels as well. Her project in this book was to present a survey of legible bodies in the nineteenth novel, but I cannot help wishing, on behalf of Dickensians, that she had extended (or, in the future, that she will extend) her meditation on Dickensian marked bodies beyond *David Copperfield* to his other novels. A detailed examination of *Bleak House,* in particular, would be especially welcome from so skilled a reader of body language.

Ethics

Like many of the other 1997 writers on Dickens, Dominic Rainsford, in *Authorship, Ethics and the Reader: Blake, Dickens, Joyce,* is interested in tracing a progressive historical shift in Dickens's novels. In most other respects, however, he differs from them. In particular, he takes issue with poststructuralist approaches that "neglect or suppress the ethical force of literature" (8). He does not, however, simply long to return to a naive Leavisite ethics of literature. Agreeing with Geoffrey Galt Harphan that it is at their ethical intersection that theory, including poststructuralist theory, becomes humanized and that literature becomes conceptually interesting, Rainsford wants to locate and describe that intersection as it is revealed in the "writing authors" of narratives by the historical authors, Blake, Dickens, and Joyce. (Nature-lovers who are drawn to the book by the picture of a brooding John Muir on the dust jacket should be forewarned; Muir is not among the writers mentioned in the text.)

Rainsford claims that any writing that shows human beings interacting must lend itself to his ethics-oriented approach, but he singles out Blake, Dickens, and Joyce because their works clearly and strongly show the sense of crisis in moral authority that intrigues him. He sees each of the three as becoming increasingly embroiled "in ethical questions raised by the act of describing, through literature, social and individual ills which paralleled the experience of real people," and as reflecting this increasing embroilment "through increasingly troubled versions of implied authorial presence" (3). The idea of the author, as it is conveyed to the reader in the text, becomes a "microcosm" or "synecdoche" of the real world problems that engaged and troubled the three historical authors. By presenting themselves as ambiguous, disturbing, or subversive presences in their novels, Blake, Dickens and Joyce, Rainsford argues, stimulate a more questioning and skeptical—and therefore higher—level of ethical thought: "they encourage the reader to be wary, in a world of fragmentary self-knowledge, of any author's, or even any reader's, assumption that he or she is on the right side, doing the right thing" (3).

With Catherine Waters, Rainsford recognizes that Dickens is, on one level, always vindicating Victorian middle-class domestic values. For Rainsford, however, to focus on this aspect of Dickens is to miss most of the complexity and texture of the novels. What interests him is how and why Dickens develops an authorial presence that in a variety of ways disrupts his ostensible Victorian bourgeois agenda. Rainsford sees in Dickens, as in Blake and Joyce, a progression and intensification of efforts to subvert that agenda through an increasing use of "morally dubious intimations of himself as author and as private individual" (100). Dickens's linguistic playfulness and his humor; the complex and subversive strategies through which he questions his protagonists' virtue, likens them to villains, or dissolves their identities; the quirkiness and oddness of some of Dickens's characters and imagery; and the simplistic endings that fail to resolve the complex problems raised by the novels are examples of Dickens's disruption of the "ethical surface" of his plots.

Rainsford's prose is dense and often graceless, but he reads closely and pays meticulous attention to language. His use of Blake as a kind of touchstone is one of the most interesting features of his chapters on Dickens. At times, however, it is hard to swallow his argument, primarily because he asks us to accept a small logical leap every time he claims that a particular characteristic of a text serves a larger ethical purpose. For example, Rainsford enlists qualities that other critics have attributed to Dickens's occasional lapses as a writer—flat characters, inconsistencies, dull patches in his plots—as evidence of a disruptive authorial presence. Through an intriguing but not always persuasive argumentative sleight of hand, Rainsford thus transforms novelistic sows' ears into ethical silk purses.

In the interest of finding examples of Dickens's casting doubt on his own moral authority, Rainsford is occasionally guilty of oversimplifying complex tropes and complicated characters. He asserts, for example, that Rosa Dartle is "painfully coarse" as a literary conception, "supposedly a woman of obsessive passion, but in fact a Gothic harpy and irredeemable lunatic, with her Captain Ahab-like symbolic disfigurement'' (141). While a reading of this kind may advance Rainsford's argument, it discourages the sort of rich and nuanced interpretation that Mary Ann O'Farrell brings to her discussion of Rosa Dartle.

Time, History, and Historicisms

Can Jane Eyre Be Happy? is the delightful sequel to John Sutherland's popular *Is Heathcliff a Murderer?,* his first volume of puzzles in classic fiction. Once again, Sutherland takes up the questions that really (but often secretly) vex readers of English fiction. He asks, for example, why Robinson Crusoe finds only a single footprint, where Fanny Hill keeps her contraceptives, and whether Daniel Deronda is circumcised. For readers of Dickens, Sutherland has three posers: what does Mr. Pickwick retire from?; why is Fagin hanged and why isn't Pip prosecuted?; and, finally, how good a swimmer is Magwitch?

Sutherland's strategy is to use his seemingly straightforward historical "puzzles'' as invitations to more interesting and wide-ranging speculations. The baffler about Pickwick, a man "entirely without a *curriculum vitae*'' before 12 May 1827, turns into a more answerable and intriguing question: why did Dickens create Pickwick as a man without a past (48, 50)? In the case of Fagin, who under the criminal law of the 1830s was not guilty of a capital crime, the initially narrow legal/historical question opens up a more searching inquiry: why do readers feel a kind of "savage pleasure'' at the thought of Fagin's excessive punishment? How does Dickens create a rhetoric of hate that makes us concur in the "peal of joy'' that goes up when Fagin is hanged (59)? In wondering at Magwitch's impossible athletic feat of swimming to shore from the hulks through the current-ridden Thames estuary in winter, fully clothed and in irons, Sutherland is able in just a few pages to explore a series of fascinating related historical questions: what did the Victorians know about swimming? What was their attitude toward the water? How and when was swimming transformed from an activity about which early Victorians (including Dickens) knew almost nothing into a familiar recreation?

In *Dickens and the New Historicism,* William J. Palmer also provides an abundance of useful facts about Victorian life and culture. His central chapter, "Dickens and Shipwreck,'' for example, anchors Dickensian shipwrecks and metaphors of shipwreck in a wealth of erudite detail about the historical perils of sailing ("the full-rigged ship remains about the most dangerous vehicle ever invented by man''); the financial and social costs of shipwreck (as many as two hundred underwriters under the Lloyd's umbrella might insure a single

voyage); the incompetence of many ships' crews and masters (they tended
to be both drunk and unschooled in navigation); and journalistic treatments
of shipwrecks (51–53). Tracking shipwreck as a plot device and as a metaphor
for financial ruin, revolution, and psychological and social upheaval, Palmer
argues that in shipwreck imagery "Dickens found a metaphor for his age"
(100).

Palmer's theoretical claim is that Dickens anticipated the work of new
historicism by acknowledging and describing the verticalized, nontraditional
cultural history that exists "beneath the horizontal line of factual historical
events" (3). An unbashed Dickens enthusiast, Palmer believes that Dickens
was acutely aware that "history cannot just bull its way toward the future,
ignorant of the culture, marginalized voices, modes of expression, and subtexts that lie beneath, and contribute to" the master texts of history (4).
Palmer's Dickens looked at traditional histories with a new historicist's skeptical eye; gave voice to the poor, the powerless, and the marginalized; explored the movement of history from eighteenth-century "ports of order"
into the chaos of the unstable Victorian world; and understood intuitively the
new historicist's project of representing history in a way that historicizes
time itself.

The two most substantial chapters of the book—the one on shipwreck and
another on the influence of George Lillo's domestic tragedy, *The History of
George Barnwell*—are particularly good; even readers who are dubious about
Dickens's prescient commitment to a new historicist project will find them rewarding.

Because she does not see Dickens as a genius with a unique historical
vision, Elizabeth Ermath would, I think, disagree with Palmer's approach. In
The English Novel in History, 1840–1895, she notices, as Palmer does, that
Dickens resists a linear, "horizontal" representation of time. For Ermath,
however, Dickens reimagines the construction of time not because of some
special intuitive understanding of history, but because, like other novelists of
the period, he did not fully subscribe to the historical convention that historical time *is* time. Dickens's novels, Ermath argues, exemplify a more general
nineteenth-century rhetorical shift away from simple, picaresque narrations.
In his early novels, Dickens, like other writers of the 1840s, constructed
history in terms of the temporal patterns of the pilgrim's progress or conversion narrative; after 1850, along with Trollope and Eliot, he allowed the
providential plot pattern to fade (but not disappear), and more fully exploited
conventions of narrative realism to reveal a more complex vision of the
social world.

The weakness in Ermath's argument as it pertains to Dickens is that,
although his narrative patterns of course changed and developed during his

career, his novels in many ways resist chronological schematizing. For example, Ermath claims that after 1850 a temporal version of a single-point perspective system became the commanding narrative convention in Trollope, Eliot, and the post-*Dombey* Dickens. This may be more or less true in general, but fails to recognize the full significance of the inventiveness and variety of the late Dickens's most un-Trollopelike rhetorical strategies. Certainly one could argue that the narrative perspectives in Eliot, Trollope, and the late Dickens are, in most important ways, more different from one another than they are alike.

Dicken's Victorian Readers

Daniel Pool's *Dickens' Fur Coat and Charlotte's Unanswered Letters: The Rows and Romances of England's Great Victorian Novelists,* a sequel with another catchy but somewhat misleading title, is, like Sutherland's *Can Jane Eyre be Happy?*, intended to be read for (serious) pleasure by a general audience. Pool's style in this latest book is as breezy and information-packed as it was in his earlier volume, *What Jane Austen Ate and Charles Dickens Knew.* This time Pool constructs a gossipy history of novel publishing in the nineteenth century, interweaving stories about the major writers of the period with tales of publishing rivalries.

For most of the book, Dickens is the central figure: Pool argues that although we may think that the Victorian novel was the product of a group of authors—Thackeray, the Brontës, George Eliot, and Trollope—in reality "it was at the outset the work of a single, driven, tormented genius"—Charles Dickens—who created "a whole new way of writing fiction and describing society" (5). Pool sees Dickens not only as the "quintessential Victorian self-made man," but also as the prototype of the modern celebrity novelist, "one of the first willing victims of the new celebrity culture that the mass media made possible" (186). While knowledgeable Dickensians may find some of Pool's claims a bit overstated and some of the historical and biographical territory that he covers too familiar, they will admire his knack for telling a good story.

Inevitably, *The Pickwick Papers* figures prominently in Pool's account of Dickens's development as a popular, professional serial novelist. Jonathan Grossman provides a useful and detailed supplementary discussion in "Representing Pickwick: The Novel and the Law Courts." Grossman's argument is that the story of Pickwick in itself conveys a story of *Pickwick;* the transition of Dickens's work from fragmentary narrative sketches into the form of the Victorian novel takes place, Grossman claims, at the trial of Pickwick. To the extent that they call attention to the author's powers of creation,

Pickwick's visits to the law offices and the courts are less about Dickens's critique of the law than they are about the establishment of the middle-class, professional author in the Victorian period.

Jennifer Hayward, in *Consuming Pleasures: Active Audiences and Serial Fictions from Dickens to Soap Opera,* takes a more panoramic look at serial fiction. As the title promises, this book has panache; it is also informed by a lively intelligence and good scholarship. Hayward's project is to examine serials ranging from *Our Mutual Friend* to *Terry and the Pirates* and *One Life to Live.* She attempts not only to describe the formal qualities of serials, but also to understand viewer/text relations in a mass-market culture that, as Pool points out, arguably began with Dickens.

Hayward tackles Dickens through *Out Mutual Friend,* which she claims to present as a "case study" in the development of the mass serial. Her discussion rightly begins with the technological innovations and social and economic developments that made the production and marketing of the nineteenth-century mass serial possible, but her real interest is in the readers of serial fiction: she looks at how a mass audience was transformed into a reading community and, acknowledging the difficulties, she tries to assess the effect of serials on readers. Finally, she examines the effects of readers' demands on Dickens, who was both a manufacturer of narrative for a vast, faceless audience and, as he insisted, involved in an intimate, interactive relationship with his public. With all these issues in mind, and using reviews, contemporary news stories and events, Dickens's manuscript notes, number plans, and revisions, as well as the novel itself, Hayward presents a detailed and compelling account of the relationship of the serialized *Our Mutual Friend* to its demanding, complaining, impatient, and adoring readers.

In "Dickens, Theater, and the Making of a Victorian Reading Public," Deborah Vlock in effect calls into question Hayward's focus on Dickens as a writer of mass-produced serials. Hayward and Vlock agree that Dickens's readers were a community, but Vlock sees them above all as a community forged by a common experience of the theater. Novelists like Dickens, Vlock argues, assumed that their readers were immersed in the culture of the theater; that they had a shared familiarity with theatrical stereotypes and tropes; and that they read novels with "an acute awareness of theatrical presence" (165). With the fervor of a true believer, Vlock exhorts us to read Dickens aloud, so that we, too, can develop an ear for his various theatrical voices and thus acquire an "authentic" Victorian relationship to his texts.

A useful addendum to Vlock's article is "Dickens's Military Men," in which John Reed traces the portrayal of military figures in the novels to familiar stereotypes that Dickens's readers would have recognized from the stage. Reed offers a chronological survey of the novels, identifying some of these stock stage characters: the amorous army officer, the bluff sea captain or Jolly Tar, the *miles gloriosus.* While noting their theatrical roots, Reed reminds us that Dickens developed his military characters in his own original way, and that he always favors the unpretentious, humble, and undervalued, the common seaman over the boastful or corrupt officer.

Journalism

In his fascinating *Dickens's 'Young Men': George Augustus Sala, Edmund Yates and the World of Victorian Journalism,* Peter D. Edwards has uncovered a wealth of unpublished material on two of the most interesting of the Bohemian "little Dickenses" who wrote for *Household Words* and/or *All the Year Round.* Although a number of young men assisted Dickens during the 1850s, Edwards has chosen to focus on Sala and Yates not only because of the accessibility of important manuscript and other little-known material by and about them, but also because both were influential and representative figures in the Victorian cultural scene. As the impecunious and undereducated sons of actors, both the raffish Sala and the more sober Yates had strong social, cultural, and political ties to Dickens. Although Yates and Sala went on to have long and colorful careers after they worked with Dickens, Edwards makes a compelling case that the private lives and professional careers of these two protean, energetic, and interconnected journalists have much to tell us about Dickens and the unconventional journalistic circles in which he and his "young men" travelled.

Edwards's book is a model of meticulous scholarship and scrupulous (but never tedious) attention to detail. He has mined the massive collections of Sala and Yates papers and writings and brought to light the most valuable nuggets. (My favorite of these these is Yates's parodic swipe at Matthew Arnold, "Stanzas from an Atlantic Steamer," in which Yates imagines Arnold in the throes of seasickness on his way to America in 1883.) Weaving together accounts of Yates's and Sala's lives and writings, Edwards has produced a concise narrative that is both engaging and rich with detailed information. Dickensians will especially appreciate the unusual portrait of Dickens that emerges from the observations of the "little Dickenses" and their circle; seeing him through their eyes provides some of the surprise and pleasure that, as Edwards remarks, we experience when we view Hamlet from the point of view of Rosencrantz and Guildenstern in Tom Stoppard's play (3).

If Michael Hollington plans to develop and expand his substantial two-part article, "Dickens, *Household Words,* and the Paris Boulevards," he will no doubt profit from Edwards's research on Sala's experiences in Paris. In his wide-ranging and provocative discussion, Hollington investigates the critical response of Dickens and other *Household Words* writers to Paris in the 1850s, a period when the city, in the process of "Haussmannization," was undergoing a painful transition toward modernity. Sala and Dickens, knee-deep in mud, both witnessed the triumph of the forces of cleanliness and progress, as paving stones were replaced by macadam, and the medieval city's muddy streets gave way to the boulevards of the new Paris.

Hollington's energetic argument goes in a number of directions. He shows that Dickens's Parisian persona has much in common with Baudelaire's: both represent themselves as detached observers of the urban spectacle, *flâneurs* who casually stroll the Paris boulevards in search of visual experiences. At the same time, like Baudelaire, Dickens lamented the passing of paving stones and winding, narrow streets. But, Hollington argues, Dickens's *flânerie* was also uniquely Dickensian, fraught with anxiety and ambivalence. In the urban theater of Paris, Dickens could not bear the idea of being a spectacle himself. Moreover, likening Paris to a Vanity Fair, he and his *Household Words* writers saw the sights of the city as hiding both scandal and social injustice.

A major difficulty in discussing representations of Paris in *Household Words* and *All the Year Round* is uncertainty about whether some of the articles were written by Dickens or by one of his "young men," a number of whom were in Paris in the 1850s and '60s. Hollington sidesteps this problem when he is unsure of authorship, referring to *Household Words* writers generically. John M. L. Drew, in "Charles Dickens, Traducteur? A New Article in *All the Year Round*," directly confronts the uncertain authorship of at least one such anonymous Parisian article. Using biographical evidence, Drew makes the case that although Dickens's stylistic hand is not obvious in "Dress in Paris," an article based on Eugène Pelletan's *La Nouvelle Babylone,* Dickens himself was the author/translator.

Studies of Individual Works

Bleak House

With its narrative complexities and duplicated images, *Bleak House* inspired some of 1997s most theoretically rich writing. As part of a broader argument that gossip is a synecdoche for the consumption of plots, Jan B. Gordon devotes a chapter of *Gossip and Subversion in Nineteenth-Century British Fiction: Echo's Economies* to a semiotic reading of *Bleak House.* Since Gordon is fond of puns and parentheses, it is safe to assume that the subtitle, *Echo's Economies,* is a warning that the reader will be drawn into metatextual labyrinths of the kind favored by the eponymous Italian theorist (*ecco* Eco's echoes).

Gordon's lengthy, demanding, and ingeniously argued discussion of *Bleak House* is concerned with showing how language functions in—and within—the novel to put all utterances—gossip, rumors, scraps of paper, forgeries and "authentic" documents—on the same plane. He argues, for example, that Esther Summerson's diary—an instance of a "third-order discourse" (i.e., repeated from another which is contained within yet another)—not only exemplifies the many concentric interiorities in the novel (Nemo's garret behind Krook's ragshop; the original will behind the copy), but also legitimizes "a political or inscriptive authorlessness" (234). With all utterances in the novel reduced "to a kind of 'free' indirect discourse," the State can function as the recipient and source, the distributor and reproducer, of all information (235). Or, to put it perhaps too simply, by the end of *Bleak House* almost everyone works for Inspector Bucket.

In "Double Exposure: Arresting Images in *Bleak House* and *The House of Seven Gables,* Ronald Thomas, too, investigates how copying and reproducing become tools for social discipline. Focusing on the evolving technology of nineteenth-century photography, Thomas pays particular attention to the relationship of Lady Dedlock's painted portrait, contained in the privacy of her own home, to her commodified photographic image, printed in a magazine for all to see. Thomas rehearses the familiar argument that duplication and reproduction consolidate the power of the State, as embodied in Inspector Bucket; the detective, with his unerring, cameralike eye, fixes the identity of the criminal in our midst.

If postmodern life imitates art, it should not be surprising that there is yet another article on reproduction and duplication in relation to *Bleak House.* Along with Gordon and Thomas, Eleanor Salotto is interested in the uses of mimicry, copying, and identity, although her take on the subject is through a feminist lens. Weaving together discussions of mimicry, masquerade, and copying, Salotto constructs an imaginative and theoretically rich reading of Esther's narrative, which, she argues, participates in the demolishing of a stable notion of feminine identity (333). Salotto's Esther resists decoding; through the use of mimicry and masquerade (including drag), Esther ironizes her representation of herself and thus refigures her identity. In addition to enjoying Salotto's other sophisticated readings, fans of O'Farrell's *Telling Complexions* will be pleased to find that Salotto also offers an intriguing discussion of Esther's scar as a disruptive marker (336).

Kathleen Blake's "*Bleak House,* Political Economy, Victorian Studies," can be read as a corrective to Foucauldian readings of *Bleak House* that overemphasize the role of Inspector Bucket as the agent of an oppressive, panoptical modern state. Blake tartly reminds us that Dickens's utilitarianism was Bentham's, not Foulcault's, and that "it is most ill-considered and anti-historical" to associate Chancery with the institution of the modern police, as D. A. Miller does. While Foucault's (and Miller's) Panopticon stresses one-way surveillance, in Bentham's more benign Panopticon there is openness to public scrutiny and accountability: "abuses can be known, criticized, and reformed" (3). Blake argues that because many critics have ignored what Bentham actually wrote, they have overlooked the close equivalence between his and Dickens's critiques of Chancery, and have therefore misread and miscast Dickens as an out-and-out foe of utilitarianism.

One of the most provocative sections of Blake's article is the concluding section, "Political Economy and Victorian Studies," in which she speculates about why Victorianists on both the political left and the right have chosen to see *Bleak House* simply as a critique of political economy and to overlook the areas of agreement between Dickens and the utilitarians. Blake spares neither Leavis nor Altick, and Gertrude Himmelfarb comes in for a brisk scolding, too. For their own idealogical reasons, many Victorianists, Blake argues, have refused to recognize that in attacking Chancery "Dickens aligns himself with utilitarianism in the open and in good faith." (17).

A Christmas Carol

We may have thought that Dickens was merely a great novelist, but in "The Primitive Keynsianism of *A Christmas Carol*" Lee Erickson seeks to demonstrate that Dickens also had the makings of world-class economist. Erickson argues that Dickens had an "intuitive solution" to the financial depression of 1843 and a proto-Keynsian grasp of the importance of financial liquidity and consumer spending. Fiscally conservative readers may rest assured, however, that there are limits to Dickens's Keynsianism: Erickson tells us again what we always knew—that Dickens believed not in government programs to stimulate the economy, but in personal good will and generosity.

David Copperfield

In " 'The Reader Whom I Love': Homoerotic Secrets in *David Copperfield*," Oliver S. Buckton makes ingenious use of the concept of autobiographical space, the narrative theory of Philippe Lejeune, and Judith Butler's analysis of gender identity, to reveal the homoerotic threads that are woven into the historical and textual fabric of *David Copperfield*. Buckton makes the case that the confidential relationship between Dickens and his friend and biographer, John Forster, both underlies and explains the confusion between autobiography and fiction that characterizes readings of the novel. Buckton's claim is that Dickens's intimate friendship with Forster, who made suggestions and listened to his ideas as Dickens was writing *David Copperfield*, engendered the novel; to complete an autobiographical work, Dickens required the participation of his reader/biographer/friend.

Buckton is interested not only in the homoerotic aspects of the novel's composition, but also in revealing the gendered significance of "the disciplined heart." David's melancholia, Buckton argues, is evidence of his renunciation of same-sex desire in the interests of the worldly accomplishment and heterosexual union required for formal narrative closure. By locating traces of lost or renounced objects of desire that are concealed within the narrative and that "covertly" direct its trajectory, Buckton unclosets *David Copperfield* as a narrative of gendered identity (217).

Buckton's article is theoretically sophisticated, complex, and imaginative, and his readings of homoerotic scenes in the novel, especially those involving Uriah Heep, are provocative, if controversial. I have some reservations, however, about Buckton's depiction of the intimate friendship between Dickens and Forster during the time of *David Copperfield*'s composition. Much of the sense of their relationship at this period comes not from Dickens, but from Forster's *Life of Charles Dickens,* which Forster wrote under the shadow of Dickens's later emotional abandonment. While Dickens certainly relied on Forster for advice, the depth and intensity of Dickens's emotional commitment to Forster—as opposed to Forster's to him—is open to question. It would be interesting in the future to read more from Buckton on the complicated, shifting, ambivalent Dickens-Forster friendship.

Buckton argues that a disciplined heart in *David Copperfield* is one that desires correctly. This is certainly true, but many readers have wondered why the correct object of David's desire has to be Agnes, that "legless angel of Victorian romance," as George Orwell put it (Garnett 213). For these anti-Agnes readers, the explanation of David's melancholia may have more to do with her sexless dreariness than the renunciation of same-sex desire. In "Why Not Sophy? Desire and Agnes in *David Copperfield*," Robert Garnett takes up the problem of Agnes. He understands that Emily, Rosa Dartle, and Dora are hopelessly flawed, but he wonders why, instead of Agnes, the domestic, virtuous, and vivacious Sophy (or one of her domestic, virtuous, and vivacious sisters) could not be the correct Mrs. Copperfield. The answer, Garnett argues, is that *David Copperfield* must be read as a religious pilgrimage, a "spiritual aeneid" that leads David toward "beatific detachment" from the world (215). The proper spiritual guide for pilgrim David is the serene, static, and spiritualized Agnes; Sophy and her sisters are too lively and delightful to fill the role of Beatrice or to personify Augustine's Continence.

Garnett's reading of *David Copperfield* strikes me as improbably allegorical. It is noteworthy, however, that although his methodology and interpretation are completely different from Buckton's, Garnett too emphasizes renunciation and the repression of desire.

Peter O. Arnds begins *Wilhelm Raabe's "Der Hungerpastor" and Charles Dickens's "David Copperfield": Intertextuality of Two Bildungsromane* with a disarming disclaimer: Wilhelm Raabe—also known as "the German Dickens"—is little known outside of Germany. Indeed, Arnds confesses, Raabe is little known even inside Germany. Nobody, in fact, reads Raabe anymore; to young Germans he is at most a slightly familiar name, while old Germans remember him only vaguely from the days when his *Kinderbücher* were still required reading in the schools. Moreover, Arnds admits, Dickens and Raabe have little in common: for starters, Dickens aimed to entertain his readers; Raabe, on the other hand, is relentlessly "ponderous."

Daunted neither by Raabe's obscurity nor by the tediousness of his prose, Arnds resolutely embarks on his project, which is to establish an "intertextual link" between the much-loved *David Copperfield* and the rightly-forgotten *Der Hungerpastor*. In composing his Bildungsroman, Raabe evidently lifted plot, characters, and, chunks of text ("linguistic material," as Arnds more delicately puts it) from Dickens, and Arnds's goal is systematically to uncover and describe all these borrowings. To elevate this potentially pedestrian comparison of parallel texts, Arnds erects an extraordinarily complex theoretical structure. His writing is so difficult to follow, however, (English, perhaps, is not his first language), that it is only possible to guess what that structure might be. A sample of Arnds's perplexing prose will suffice: "A close reading reveals the nature of the subtext's consistency. Rather than occurring randomly, the passages in which Dickens text echoes form a pattern in *Der Hungerpastor* that clearly proves that Raabe intended to write a Bildungsroman" (8).

Arnds is methodical—if at times incomprehensible—in his approach, but he is not completely honest with his readers. Those who persevere will begin to figure out, after a hundred pages or so, that Raabe fell into obscurity in postwar Germany not because his writing was ponderous but because of its embarrassing antisemitism. Arnds wants to argue, as others have done, that the red-headed Uriah Heep is a Jew in disguise, and that Raabe's satanic Jewish villain, Moses, is a Heepian offspring; this argument, whatever its merits, ignores the more pervasive truth that the antisemitism of *Der Hungerpastor* has a nastiness all its own. Moses, the irredeemably depraved Jew, is a particularly repellent example of a stock figure in German antisemitic literature; responsibility for him cannot be laid at Dickens's door.

Dombey and Son

Lisa Surridge is an eloquent exponent of 1997's most frequently argued position: that Dickens's representations are ambivalent and contradictory. In "Domestic Violence, Female Self-Mutilation, and the Healing of the Male in *Dombey and Son*," Surridge charts a middle course between two familiar critical positions, arguing that *Dombey and Son* is neither simply a celebration of the nurturing and healing power of the feminine nor a covertly misogynistic text of hatred and fear, populated by monstrous, castrating women. Focusing on the female characters who are the objects of either male-inflicted violence or self-laceration, Surridge claims that while the novel indeed "re-centers the feminine in the domestic and patriarchal house," it does so "in a manner which perpetuates the pattern of female self-abnegation" by relying for resolution on the wounded female body (78). Referring to Dickens's number plans and the Browne illustrations as well as to the published text, Surridge makes a convincing case for the ambivalence of a novel that vindicates the feminine by explicitly celebrating women's power to nurture, while at the same time subtextually supporting male domestic violence and hatred of women.

Great Expectations

The year 1997 was a surprisingly quiet for work on *Great Expectations*. The most noteworthy articles were all comparative: "Love in the Garden: *Maud, Great Expectations,* and W. S. Gilbert's *Sweethearts*," by Alan Fischler; "The Trappings of Romance in *Jane Eyre* and *Great Expectations*" by Anny Sadrin; and " What Shall I Say I am—to-day?': Subjectivity and Accountability in *Frankenstein* and *Great Expectations*," by Jay Stubblefield.

Fischler's wide-ranging study is the most ambitious of the three. He begins his discussion of the garden setting in *Maud, Great Expectations,* and *Sweethearts* with a general consideration of how literary depictions of the garden were bound to change after the "depredations" of Charles Lyell and Charles Darwin. The traditional image of the garden as a sacred place—the locus of innocence, the fall into sin, and the final redemption—could not, Fischeler argues, withstand the "intellectual onslaught" of Victorian scientific discourse (765). Positioning the three texts under discussion chronologically, in relation to the publication of Lyell's *Principles of Geology* and Darwin's *Origin of the Species,* Fischler does not go so far as to claim that Dickens is a Darwinian novelist or that *Great Expectations,* published a year after *Origin of the Species,* alludes directly to Darwin's work. Fischler argues, rather, for a nonspecific, diffuse influence. He recognizes—as other critics have—that while Dickens uses the garden in *Great Expectations* as the traditionally symbolic setting for the Christian allegory of Pip's life, the novel's Christianity is random, residual, and contradictory. Fischler thinks that the influence of *Origin of the Species* may help explain—in a general way—why Dickens produced a novel in which "Christian symbols retain their presence but have lost their point" (774).

The two other comparative articles on *Great Expectations* make modest claims. Sadrin acknowledges that the narrative strategies of *Jane Eyre* and

Great Expectations are altogether different, but manages to find a basis for some interesting comparisons using the terms of A. J. Greimas's *Sémantique structurale.* Stubblefield sees in *Great Expectations* a more complex and morally developed revision of Shelley's portrayal of the relationship between creator and creature, but seems to forget that he is comparing a Romantic apple to a Victorian orange.

In "Mr. Jaggers at the Bar," Daniel Tritter not only makes the point that Jaggers is the only lawyer in Dickens's oeuvre to specialize in criminal law, but also offers useful background on the hierarchical structure of the legal profession in Dickens's day.

Hard Times

Good news for students of *Hard Times!* With the publication of Margaret Simpson's superb *Companion to "Hard Times,"* readers will no longer have to bother turning to endnotes. More importantly, they will find in Simpson's thorough, learned, and entertaining volume a wealth of information—more than mere endnotes could ever provide. Especially useful for scholars are the links Simpson makes between the serialized portions of *Hard Times* and articles on similar topics that appeared simultaneously in *Household Words.* The longer notes are really short historical essays; even the most knowledgeable readers will profit from Simpson's detailed discussions of factory legislation and trade union activity of the period. The volume is also full of delightful bits of Victoriana: the history of lending libraries, nineteenth-century circus acts, the evolution of clown costumes, recipes for walnut ketchup and scalding rum and butter, the dangers of fire-damp, the origins of India Pale Ale.

Little Dorrit

Daniel Novak's "If Re-collecting Were Forgetting: Forged Bodies and Forgotten Labor in *Little Dorrit*," is a theoretical tour de force. Novak uses his dense and tightly argued Marxist/Lukácian reading of *Little Dorrit* as the occasion for a wider exploration of the uses of synecdoche in Dickens. Challenging Dorothy Van Ghent's famous argument that parts of the body in Dickens stand for the whole person, Novak makes the more complicated claim that Dickens uses synecdoche to enlist the body into "artfully performing both the metonymic labor of narrative and the metaphoric work of capital." Novak's point is that an ambivalent Dickens does this "in order to manage, contain, and forget the fluid, commodified body whose specter haunts his texts" (22). Novak does not limit his analysis to *Little Dorrit* or even to Dickens's oeuvre: using a Marxist/Lukácsian lens, Novak interrogates the trope of synecdoche itself. His claim is that bodily synecdoche, through which the whole exists as an "invisible backdrop of reference" for the part, is a forgery, "a bluff of unity" in the service of capitalist consciousness (3).

While Marxist analysis may seem a bit passé, Novak carries it off with wit and originality. He makes convincing connections between the cut-and-pasted bodies of the Merdles and the forged bank notes that Merdle produces; offers useful comments on Dickens as both a fragmenter of bodies and a "master consolidator"; and, most importantly, encourages a rethinking of the meaning and uses of synecdoche in Dickens's writing.

One of the few critical works in 1997 to address the effect of the British Empire on Dickens's writing is "The Opium Trade and *Little Dorrit:* A Case of Reading Silences," by Wenying Xu. Like Novak, Xu is interested in exposing textual repressions and interrogating elisions. The silence that invites Xu's attention is the blank history of Arthur Clennam's twenty years in China. Xu argues that by focusing on this significant silence, we will be able to see "an imperialist ideology historically at work": in failing to fill in the blank of those mysterious years, Dickens in effect dismisses China as a place without specificity or reality, and thus participates in the concealments of the "disorders" that permeated the Sino-British relationship (54).

One of these specific "disorders" was the opium trade, and Xu argues that Arthur and his father may well have been directly or peripherally involved. Xu assembles a fair amount of circumstantial evidence to make the case: the East India Company trade monopoly; laws governing how and where independent merchants could operate in China; the expanding Chinese market for opium; the Clennam family's feelings of guilt; Arthur's disgusted abandonment of money-making; and of course the textual refusal to name the family business. The historical material that Xu marshals is fascinating, but some of the textual readings seem strained. There is little evidence, for example, to support interpreting the illegitimate birth of Arthur as symbolizing "the sin that the Clennams committed in China" (59). It is not necessary, however, to go along with all of Xu's arguments in order to appreciate this intriguing investigation of *Little Dorrit*'s silences.

Martin Chuzzlewit

In " 'I Rise With Circumstances'; Making It in Dickens's *Martin Chuzzlewit,*" Martin Jay Dessner provides a historical context for the attempts of the characters of *Martin Chuzzlewit* to move up socially and economically. Through a survey of the novel's characters, Dessner shows that as the old system of patronage and favor was replaced by a more entrepreneurial economy, and as the professions were redefined and reconfigured, the Pecksniffs, Mrs. Gamps, and John Joblings of the world could use their ability, enterprise, or talent for self-promotion to enter new professions or to make their fortunes in new ways.

Our Mutual Friend

Thomas Syd, like many readers, regrets the decline of Bella Wilfer from a "fine brave spirit" into a "sweet commodity," a 'self-effacing doll" in the Harmon doll's house (8, 17). In " 'Pretty woman, Elegantly Framed': The Fate of Bella Wilfer in Dickens's *Our Mutual Friend,*'' Syd argues that in the novel Dickens protests the re-formation of Bella Wilfer by her moral monitors. Syd's unfashionable view is that the domestic diminishment that Bella and Lizzie Hexam suffer represents a repressive Victorian social system that Dickens himself condemns.

A Tale of Two Cities

Syd sticks up for the domesticated Bella Wilfer; Garnett justifies Agnes Wickfield; Salotto ironizes Esther Summerson: 1997 was a big year for defenses of Dickens's house angels. In her elegantly written article, " 'The world within us': Jung and Dr. Manette's Daughter," Wendy Jacobson keeps up the redemptive work. By rereading Lucie Manette's character in Jungian terms, Jacobson hopes to find Lucie a more "interesting creation" than she has generally been thought to be (95). In her elegantly written essay, Jacobson very sensibly argues that it is not useful simply to dismiss Lucie as a failed realistic figure; rather, she should be understood as an "anima"—a mythic presence who, in opposition to the demonic Madame Defarge, brings light and integration to the shattered personalities inhabiting this dark novel.

Mostly for Fun

The Proverbial Charles Dickens, by George B. Bryan and Wolfgang Mieder advertises itself in the *Dickens Quarterly* as "The Ideal Reference Source for Dickens Scholars." I must confess, however, that I had a bit of trouble figuring out how one might *use* this delightful book, except for fun. And fun it is to leaf through the exhaustive key-word index to proverbs in Dickens's writing. The book begins with a brief introductory essay reminding us how clever Dickens was at setting off rhetorical fireworks, proverbial and otherwise. The rest of the volume is taken up by the index of proverbs, proverbial expressions, proverbial comparisons, and wellerisms. I can imagine some clever Dickensians using this list to invent a parlor game—just the sort of thing Dickens himself would have enjoyed.

The Dickensian always offers an assortment of articles that are as entertaining as they are instructive. This year I particularly enjoyed John Cosnett's "Charles Dickens and Sleep Disorders." It turns out that Dickens knew and wrote about them all: insomnia; hypersomnia (that's what Joe, the Fat Boy had); and parasomnia, or abnormal sleep (the restless leg syndrome suffered by Twemlow, for example). I won't make the inevitable joke about Cosnett's essay being a cure for the disorders it discusses, since in fact he is a concise and lively writer.

Noteworthy Editions

Under the general editorship of Michael Slater, the Everyman Dickens series is progressing toward completion. *American Notes* and *Pictures from Italy* have come out together with the Samuel Palmer illustrations in a volume edited by Leonee Ormond; this inexpensive edition would be useful, I imagine, in a course on Victorian travel writing. Also for this series, Peter Mudford has edited *"Master Humphrey's Clock" and Other Stories*, with illustrations by George Cruikshank, George Cattermole, and Phiz (H. K. Browns). Mudford's chronologically arranged edition offers an attractive alternative to the Penguin *Selected Short Fiction:* the Everyman collection has fewer selections than the Penguin, but contains the complete "Master Humphrey's Clock." Mudford's concise introduction and notes are excellent.

Dickens's *Selected Journalism, 1850–1870,* edited by David Pascoe for Penguin, reprints a generous selection of seventy-two articles from *Household Words* and *All the Year Round*. Pascoe has organized the pieces thematically under appealing categories such as "Insularities," "Sleep to Startle Us," and "Amusements of the People," and has supplied headnotes to each article describing its textual provenance. As is usual with Penguin's new editions, there are fine notes, a bibliography, and a Dickens chronology.

The Oxford World Classics *David Copperfield,* edited in 1982 by Nina Burgis, has been reissued with a new introduction by Andrew Sanders. This new edition continues to use the 1981 Clarendon edition text, based on the first one-volume edition with errata slip. Sanders's introduction gracefully weaves the requisite biographical information with a reading of the novel that emphasizes its themes of insecurity, impermanence, and transience. In this edition the relevant passages from Section 2, Book 1, of Forster's *Life of Charles Dickens* have been added to the appendices, which also include Dickens's preface to the 1867 edition, an account of the trial titles for *David Copperfield,* Dickens's working plans for the numbers, and excellent explanatory textual notes. The editors have also provided a map of London in the 1820s and, as in the other editions in this series, a Dickens chronology and illustrations.

"A Last Retrospect"

Trey Philpotts begins his thorough and incisive "Recent Dickens Studies: 1996" in *Dickens Studies Annual* with a *cri du coeur:* "Enough already!" Understandably appalled by the "overwhelming volume" of writing on Dickens, Philpotts wonder how much of it—especially the portion that is trivial, banal, under-researched, and poorly written—is simply "grist for the publication mills."

I share Philpotts's satiety—and his concern. Nevertheless, just as he did last year, I have had the satisfaction of finding a number of critical works that were of real interest and value. While Simon Gray's *Breaking Hearts* has put an end to my patience for simplistic Foucauldianism, it has not soured me on the best Dickens scholarship. Among 1997's critical bright spots were O'Farrell's *Telling Complexions,* Zemka's *Victorian Testaments,* and Edwards's *Dickens's 'Young Men.'* I profited especially from the cluster of excellent studies of *Bleak House.* Several articles—particularly those by Novak, Blake, Salotto, Hollington, and Buckton—showed promise of transformation into worthwhile book-length projects. And reading Lerner's *Angels and Absences* was the purest pleasure.

At the end of his life, De Toqueville wrote triumphantly, *"Je n'ai jamais fait de ma vie un article de revue"* (Ticknor 239). On the one hand, I envy him (among other things) his resolve; on the other hand, I would not have missed the humbling, exasperating, tiresome, and unexpectedly rewarding experience of surveying a year's work on Dickens.

WORKS CITED

Arnds, Peter O. *Wilhelm Raabe's "Der Hungerpastor" and Charles Dickens's "David Copperfield": Intertextuality of Two Bildungsomane.* New York: Peter Lang, 1997.

Blake, Kathleen. "*Bleak House,* Political Economy, Victorian Studies." *Victorian Literature and Culture* 25 (1997): 1–22.

Bryan, George, and Wolfgang Mieder. *The Proverbial Charles Dickens.* New York: Peter Lang, 1997.

Buckton, Oliver S. " 'The Reader Whom I Love': Homoerotic Secrets in *David Copperfield,*" *ELH* 64.1(1997): 189–222.

Cosnett, John. "Charles Dickens and Sleep Disorders." *Dickensian* 93 (1997): 200–204.

Dessner, Lawrence J. " 'I Rise With Circumstances': Making It in Dickens's *Martin Chuzzlewit*." *Dickens Quarterly* 14 (1997): 146–53.

Dickens, Charles. *American Notes and Pictures from Italy*. 1842 and 1846. Ed. Leonee Ormond. Rutland, VT: Everyman/Charles Tuttle, 1997.

———. *David Copperfield*. 1849–50. Ed. Nina Burgis. NY: Oxford UP, 1997.

———. *"Master Humphrey's Clock" and Other Stories*. Ed. Peter Mudford. Rutland, VT: Everyman/Charles Tuttle, 1997.

———. *Selected Journalism, 1850–1870*. Ed. David Pascoe. NY: Penguin, 1997.

Edwards, P. D. *Dickens's 'Young Men': George Augustus Sala, Edmund Yates and the World of Victorian Journalism*. Brookfield, VT: Ashgate, 1997.

Erickson, Lee. "The Primitive Keynsianism of Dickens's *A Christmas Carol*." *Studies in the Literary Imagination* 30 (1997): 51–66.

Ermath, Elizabeth Deeds. *The English Novel in History, 1840–1895*. NY: Routledge, 1997.

Fasick, Laura. *Vessels of Meaning: Women's Bodies, Gender Norms, and Class Bias from Richardson to Lawrence*. DeKalb: Northern Illinois Press, 1997.

Fischler, Alan. "Love in the Garden: *Maud, Great Expectations,* and W. S. Gilbert's *Sweethearts*," *Studies in English Literature* 37 (1997): 763–81.

Galperin, William. "Recent Studies in the Nineteenth Century." *Studies in English Literature* 37(1997): 877–964.

Garnett, Robert R. "Why Not Sophy? Desire and Agnes in *David Copperfield*." *Dickens Quarterly 14* (1997): 213–31.

Gordon, Jan B. *Gossip and Subversion in Nineteenth-Century British Fiction*. New York: St. Martin's, 1996.

Gray, Simon. *Breaking Hearts*. Boston: Faber and Faber, 1997.

Grossman, Jonathan H. "Representing Pickwick: The Novel and the Law Courts." *Nineteenth-Century Literature* 52 (1997): 171–97.

Hayward, Jennifer. *Consuming Pleasures: Active Audiences and Serial Fictions from Dickens to Soap Opera*. Lexington: U of Kentucky, 1997.

Hollington, Michael. "Dickens, *Household Words* and the Paris Boulevards." 2 parts. *Dickens Quarterly* 14 (1997): 154–64; 199–212.

Jacobson, Wendy. " 'The world within us': Jung and Dr. Manette's Daughter." *Dickensian* 93 (1997): 95–108.

Lerner, Laurence. *Angels and Absences: Child Deaths in the Nineteenth Century*. Nashville, TN: Vanderbilt UP, 1997.

McKnight, Natalie J. *Suffering Mothers in Mid-Victorian Novels.* New York: St. Martin's, 1997.

Novak, Daniel. "If Re-Collecting Were Forgetting: Forged Bodies and Forgotten Labor in Little Dorrit." *Novel* 31 (1997): 21–44.

O'Farrell, Mary Ann. *Telling Complexions: The Nineteeth-Century English Novel and the Blush.* Durham: Duke UP, 1997.

Palmer, William J. *Dickens and the New Historicism.* NY: St. Martin's, 1997.

Philpotts, Trey. "*Recent Dickens Studies: 1996.*" *Dickens Studies Annual* 27 (1998): 307–63.

Pool, Daniel. *Dickens' Fur Coat and Charlotte's Unanswered Letters: The Rows and Romances of England's Great Victorian Novelists.* NY: HarperCollins, 1997.

Rainsford, Dominic. *Authorship, Ethics and the Reader:* New York: St. Martin's, 1997.

Reed, John R. "Dickens's Military Men." *Dickens Quarterly* 14 (1997): 139–45.

Sadrin, Anny. "The Trappings of Romance in *Jane Eyre* and *Great Expectations.*" DQ 14(1997): 69–91.

Salotto, Eleanor. "Detecting Esther Summerson't Secrets: Dickens's Bleak House of Representation." *Victorian Literature and Culture* 25 (1997): 333–52.

Simpson, Margaret. *The Companion to "Hard Times."* Westport CT: Greenwood, 1997.

Stewart, Garrett. *Death Sentences: Styles of Dying in British Fiction.* Cambridge: Harvard UP, 1984.

Stubblefield, Jay. " 'What Shall I Say I Am—To-day?': Subjectivity and Accountability in *Frankenstein* and *Great Expectations.*" *Dickens Quarterly* 14 (1997): 232–42.

Surridge, Lisa. "Domestic Violence, Female Self-Mutilation, and the Healing of the Male in *Dombey and Son*," *Victorians Institute Journal* 25 (1997): 77–104.

Sutherland, John. *Can Jane Eyre Be Happy? More Puzzles in Classic Fiction.* NY: Oxford UP, 1997.

Syd, Thomas. " 'Pretty Woman, Elegantly Framed': The Fate of Bella Wilfer in Dickens's *Our Mutual Friend.*" *Dickens Quarterly* 14 (1997): 3–23.

Ticknor, George. *Life of William Hickling Prescott.* Philadelphia: Lippincott, 1875.

Thomas, Ronald. "Double Exposures: Arresting Images in *Bleak House* and *The House of Seven Gables.*" *Novel* 31 (1997): 87–113.

Tritter, Daniel F. "Mr. Jaggers at the Bar." *Dickens Quarterly* 14 (1997): 92–107.

Vlock, Deborah M. "Dickens, Theater, and the Making of a Victorian Reading Public." *Studies in the Novel* 29 (1997): 164–90.

Waters, Catherine. *Dickens and the Politics of the Family.* Cambridge: Cambridge UP, 1997.

Xu, Wenying. "*The Opium Trade* and *Little Dorrit:* A Case of Reading Silences." *Victorian Literature and Culture* 25 (1997): 53–66.

Zemka, Sue. *Victorian Testaments: The Bible, Christology, and Literary Authority in Early-Nineteenth Century British Culture.* Stanford: Stanford UP, 1997.

Vocation and Production: Recent George Eliot Studies

Alicia Carroll

The study of George Eliot has changed dramatically since the last great wave of Eliot scholarship in the 1980s. Now, as then, changes in critical perceptions of Eliot mirror recent revolutions in contemporary literary criticism and theory. Indeed, signaling Eliot's importance to the canon of nineteenth-century literature, her works are touchstones in much of the most politically avant criticism on Victorian literature. Recent George Eliot scholarship is as likely to be postcolonial or queer as it is to be historicist or feminist. And this new work complements a new image of the novelist herself, who is re-envisioned in a number of new biographical works and by the riveting Monument to the Memory of George Eliot: The Autobiography of a Shirtmaker, *Edith Simcox's newly published diary account of her friendship with and her desire for Marian Evans. To the established debates over Eliot's feminism and political conservatism then, have come questions about her representations of empire and race, of desire between men, and of desire between women. Moreover, to the standard representations of, for example, a diffident George Eliot who leaned heavily upon a ministering George Henry Lewes, have come vivid portraits of George Eliot the serial novelist who was actively engaged with her reading public. Much of this new work is nothing short of brilliant, inspired with that spirit of vocation that vitalizes Eliot's novels themselves. Much, of course, is not. An equally strong element of production for the sake of production drives Eliot scholarship today and we now have an Eliot mill that is perhaps all too active. But overall in Eliot studies, the world has come knocking,*

and not just the academic world. Eliot has also come alive in the press,
on television, and on the internet in the past ten years; these areas,
in addition to the new criticism and primary works, are discussed in
this essay.

At the turn of the twenty-first century, the study of George Eliot has become
an industry which is marked, not always at once, by vocation and production,
two Victorian ethics which Eliot herself held dear. The work which followed
the 1980 centenary seemed to bear the mark of vocation as Eliot particularly
defined it. Like individual St. Theresas, such inspired studies as Suzanne
Graver's *George Eliot and Community,* Dorothea Barrett's *Vocation and Desire,* Margaret Homan's *Bearing the Word,* or Nina Auerbach's *Woman and
the Demon,* each found its ''epos'' in the reform of the canon and the rein-
statement of George Eliot to her rightful place there (*Middlemarch* 1). But
like Dorothea Brooke, a new generation of Eliot scholars lives in a more
prosaic time, and the need to produce, created by an ever increasingly competitive job market and tenure standards, has resulted in an Eliot mill which has
churned out hundreds of articles and many, many books published in the
1990s alone. The inspired study, the creative and original work, surely exists,
but it is now a more precious commodity. In writing this essay on recent
Eliot studies then, I do not attempt comprehensiveness. Rather, from the mass
of production I wish to identify major trends and developments in Eliot
studies, to see where we have come since the centenary, and to identify in
particular some of the controversies which will accompany Eliot scholarship
into the new millennium.

Entering the field almost concurrently with the reclaiming of Eliot herself,
a burst of theoretical possibilities has opened Eliot studies to the variety of
critical perspectives which have revolutionized the profession in recent years.
Where Eliot scholarship was once dominated by those interested in the history
of ideas, the position of women, or in Eliot as a field of study unto herself,
now the study of George Eliot is also very popular amongst scholars focusing
not on author or period, but on literary theory and the study of culture.
Postcolonial studies, studies of race, the gender study that is referred to as
''queer theory,'' and theoretical (as well as materialist) feminism now com-
prise major forums of Eliot scholarship, and the impact of this work will be
controversial and long lasting. In addition to these new readings of Eliot,
there are several contributions to the primary literature which, now accessible
to a wide audience, will change the way in which future generations approach
Eliot. These are, among others, Eliot's journals which will be published in
1999, and the remarkable journal of Eliot's admirer Edith Simcox, *A Monument to the Memory of George Eliot: The Autobiography of a Shirtmaker.* In

the 1990s Eliot scholarship was to be energized by the production of such material. Finally, George Eliot has also become a lively presence in popular culture: in the press, on the Internet, and on television as well, like Dickens and Austen, Eliot has recently attracted a wide contemporary audience. This essay will first discuss the new primary works, then the criticism, and finally, the representation of Eliot in the press and on the Internet.

While Eliot's notebooks and journals have long been available in library collections like the Beinecke, only in the 1990s have many of them been published in their entirety. Having this material readily accessible is more than a convenience; it is likely to change the nature of Eliot studies which are already becoming more interested in the intersections between Marian Evans's life and her fiction. Obviously, the journals which will become available in 1999 and are not accessible for review here, will be a tremendous contribution to the field. However, there is more to discuss here, like the extraordinary diary of Edith J. Simcox.

Edited by Constance M. Fulmer and Margaret E. Barfield, Edith J. Simcox's *A Monument to the Memory of George Eliot: Autobiography of a Shirtmaker,* (New York: Garland, 1998), is arresting reading for the scholar who has struggled to get to know George Eliot through her own words or through those of her biographers. The intimacy of the diary is striking, and I felt a kind of thrill as I read Simcox's lucid prose: "I was ushered in without hesitation. They were together sitting reading" (4). We enter into this private home with Simcox and her narrative provides us with many glimpses of Marian Evans amidst her circle of friends, with Lewes, in conversation, and finally, as a friend negotiating a difficult friendship with a woman who was in love with her. Although this is the diary of a radical Victorian thinker and activist who is noteworthy in her own right, the diary will undoubtedly be read by Eliot scholars for glimpses of the novelist. And these are there in abundance.

For example, in her passion for Marian Evans, Simcox records (purportedly) her every word. Many conversations contain information Marian Evans would not divulge as George Eliot. She tells Simcox that "every writer was *ipso facto* a teacher.—and educational influence—on his readers—and the lightest poetaster would not escape the weight of attendant responsibilities" (22). There are also disturbing discussions of Evans's feelings toward her own gender whom she cannot value, she says, as she values men:

> Then she said—perhaps it would shock me—she had never all her life cared very much for women—it must seem monstrous to me—I said I had always known it. She went on to say, what I also knew, that she cared for the womanly

ideal, sympathized with women and liked for them to come to her in their troubles, but while feeling near to them in one way, she felt far off in another—the friendship and intimacy of men was more to her. Then she tried to add what I had already imagined in explanation, that when she was young, girls and women seemed to look on her as somehow "uncanny" while men were always kind.   (117–18)

While this is, of course, mediated through Simcox who seems to have already anticipated these responses, it is nonetheless extraordinary, not because of its apparent misogyny, but because of the image of the young Marian Evans who was clearly ostracized by the majority of her own sex. This information surely informs our understanding of Eliot's difficult relation to women's suffrage; there seems to have been very personal rationales behind her politics. Simcox's diary also gives us reports of what Marian Evans was reading and thinking, of how she survived the ordeal of George Henry Lewes's death, of her marriage to "the fatal Johnny" Cross (19), and of her death. Students of Victorian culture will be captivated by this carefully annotated, utterly frank work which speaks over the distance of time as if that were no distance at all. Edited by Constance M. Fulmer and Margaret E. Barfield (in an unfortunately small font), this work will become central to the next generation of Eliot scholars.

Another invaluable contribution is Jane Irwin's edition of *George Eliot's Daniel Deronda Notebooks* (Cambridge: Cambridge P, 1996). This is an impeccably edited work which provides a full scholarly textual apparatus which will be of great help to the Eliot scholar. The book is divided into two parts. First is the Berg Notebook which contains notes and quotations from Homer and Pindar, then notes on Jewish learning from the Talmud to the Kabbalah. The second part consists of the Pforzheimer Notebooks which contain notes on Hebrew literature, Sheakespeare, Jewish festivals and life, Bacon, Rabelais, Cambridge University life, and the History of Music. Here we can see the density of Eliot's learning, the process of the acquisition of knowledge itself. As the editor argues, the accessibility of these notebooks will alter future readings of *Daniel Deronda,* particularly post-colonial readings: "Before concluding that her Jewish learning made her an advocate for the Zionist cause, so that she 'deserted her own vocation and spoilt her novel,' readers of *Daniel Deronda* might well inform themselves about her acquisition of that learning. Her researchers . . . will reveal 'the place of creative power' in an area of the novel which lies outside the experience of most of us who have not been or are not Jews" (xli-xlii). This is a wonderful tool for Eliot scholars.

The early 1990s also brought Eliot scholars two small but crucially important books. First, the portable *Selected Essays, Poems, and Other Writings,* published in paperback in 1990 by Penguin Classics. While the large *Collected*

Essays, edited by Thomas Pinney had been available for twenty years, having the major essays and poems collected in one place is a welcome relief and will make Eliot studies more accessible to both the professional scholar and to the student of Eliot. The essays are not eclectic, but include Eliot's classics "The Natural History of German Life," "Silly Novels by Lady Novelists," and "Woman in France: Madame de Sable." The reviews include Eliot's revealing comments on Thomas Carlyle, Stowe, Margaret Fuller and Mary Wollstonecraft, and Goethe. Important excerpts from Eliot's translations of Feuerbach and Strauss appear, along with excerpts from the poems *Armgart, The Spanish Gypsy,* and gratefully, all of the "Brother and Sister Sonnets." Among the "other writings" is the George Eliot-Fredric Harrison Correspondence. Edited by A. S. Byatt and Nicholas Warren, this (as my own well-worn copy attests) is a very useful book.

The year 1992 brought another paperback collection of the critical writings. The *Selected Critical Writings,* is edited by Rosemary Ashton (New York: Oxford UP, 1992), and includes only a wide selection of Eliot's criticism, translations, reviews, and annotated excerpts from "The Sad Fortunes of the Reverend Amos Barton," *Adam Bede* and *Felix Holt* (the "Address to Working Men"). This collection is also scrupulously edited and annotated and provides a fuller representation of Eliot's writings on art, religious thought, and literary criticism than the Penguin. It is a very helpful, and very handy, portable edition.

Also appearing are new editions of Eliot's novels. A new *Middlemarch* appears in the Oxford World Classics series, 1997. This contains an introduction by Felicia Bonaparte that is wonderfully written. The text is a reproduction of the 1986 Clarendon edition. It contains an updated Selected Bibliography, a chronology, and explanatory notes. It is edited by David Carroll. In the same series is a new *Silas Marner,* 1996, edited and with an introduction by Terence Cave. The copy text is the second edition of 1861, from an 1868 edition which has been collated with the first edition and the cabinet edition of 1878. A Clarendon edition of the novel is currently in progress. We also have a new *Romola* based on the Clarendon edition, with full scholarly notes and edited well by Andrew Brown. An annotated critical edition of *The Mill on the Floss* is a welcome book. It is also based on the Clarendon and it is edited by Carol Christ. The critical selections include Victorian contemporary responses to the novel, and most welcome, the readings of our own contemporaries, including Mary Jacobus, Margaret Homans, and Deirdre David. There are two new editions of *Felix Holt,* from the Penguin Classic series, edited by Lynda Mugglestone, 1995, and for the Everyman Paperback series, edited by A. G. van den Broek. Finally, we even have a new *Collected Poems* and rarer, a new edition of *Impressions of Theophrastus Such.* Fully annotated and edited by Nancy Henry, this edition will be useful to Eliot scholars.

The major books on Eliot include several biographies which reflect the diversity of contemporary approaches to the genre itself. To the biographer, Eliot presents some particular issues. Her creative life seems divided into two distinct periods: the years of translation and periodical writing and editing followed by the years of novel writing. From a late twentieth-century feminist perspective, her liaisons with men like John Chapman, George Henry Lewes, and John Cross present a problem of representation. Finally, despite the mass of journals, letters, essays, and novels George Eliot left behind, she is quite difficult to pin down, to get to know. Recently, we have had both traditional and innovative attempts at writing the life of Eliot.

Rosemary Ashton's *George Eliot: A Life* (London: Hamish Hamilton, 1996), is a traditional biography which seeks to present the whole person, not the figure expurgated by John Cross or compressed by Gordon Haight. Yet, Ashton faces a task here which she did not face in her superb biography of George Henry Lewes. That is that a mass of material has already been written on Eliot's life, and Ashton's vision is comprehensive, but not substantially different than what has come before. She agrees with Eliot's fundamental conservatism and her dependence on George Henry Lewes as both have previously been identified. The thrill of constructing the novelist and chasing her own vision, as she was free to do in her biography of Lewes, then, does not inform this book. However, as straightforward biography it is undoubtedly more complete than Haight, more insightful in its literary analyses than Redinger, and indeed, it pays much more attention to the role the novels played in Eliot's life. This biography is well researched and well written. Yet it is not ground breaking or epoch making.

The biographical and critical book which dominates recent Eliot studies, and which is likely to dominate Eliot studies for some time to come, is Rosemary Bodenheimer's *The Real Life of Mary Anne Evans* (Ithaca: Cornell UP, 1994). Any review of recent Eliot studies must start with this work which, by reading her letters, gives us an unprecedented way of reading Eliot, the work and the life. It is a major achievement in both literary criticism and literary biography, and perhaps in its emphasis on writing as an act of self-creation, even in postmodern literary biography.

What is most significant about *The Real Life* is the intelligence with which it addresses the conjunction of Eliot's life, letters, and fiction. Valuing letters less as "gossip," than as creative writing itself, Bodenheimer asserts "a respect for the writerly fictionality of letters" and a need to read Victorian letters "against the prevailing social codes of letter writing which [Eliot] has both absorbed and marked in her own way" (20). As she identifies, through careful analysis, the writerly quality of these letters, Bodenheimer produces a "study of the narrative gestures that most deeply characterize" George Eliot (21). This is a way of reading that many Eliot scholars have been seeking. It allows us to ask questions about, for example, the ways Eliot "transforms personal fictional conflict," or the extent to which "limits of the fictional imagination [are] determined by what we can learn of her relations with the social and moral codes that shape her letters" (21). It is through just such questions that Bodenheimer determines "the recurring activities of form or style, the patterns of response and assertion" with which Eliot "negotiated between public and private worlds" (21). Examining the period Eliot referred to as the "Holy War," Bodenheimer argues that the conflict with the adolescent Marian Evans's father over churchgoing "became a story that commandingly patterned the thought of George Eliot" (67). Bodenheimer notes the initial boldness of these letters, the exit of stilted adolescent prose, and the entrance of Evans to "newly unapologetic performances of herself" (68). She also notes here the development of the organic metaphor for change which begins "a long and troubled George Eliot discourse in which the life of plants figures the human potential for social evolution" (77). Ultimately in Evans's retreat from full rebellion in the Holy War letters, Bodenheimer locates the pattern which was to mark Eliot's canon: "When she became a writer, her messages to the world found their irresistible truth less in the liberation of free enquiry than in a perpetual repetition of the bold setting forth and the chastened return which marked the trajectory of her Holy War" (84).

According to Bodenheimer, the need to take positions which would shock and appall her family, friends, and the world at large, was the story of Marian Evans's life. The Holy War over churchgoing with her father was followed by much more serious breaches of convention: Eliot's alliance with George Henry Lewes and her marriage to John Cross. Here as well, *The Real Life* breaks new ground, seeing the liaison with Lewes less as a "liberating choice of an 'outlaw' sexual situation," than as the "inventive fire" which drove Eliot again and again to dramatize "in innumerable variations the gap between her characters' private choices and the fatal or comic misreadings of their communities" (86). Hence, Bodenheimer reads *The Mill on the Floss* as replicating these types of "structures of misunderstanding" rather than looking for autobiography (103). Engaging the problem of misreading and misinterpretation with Maggie Tulliver, Eliot immerses her novel "in dramatizing the helplessly tangled stresses of competing claims which constitute acts of choice" (103).

In her chapter on "The Outing of George Eliot," Bodenheimer also looks at the role Marian Evans's encounters with misrepresentations plays in *The Mill on the Floss*. Indeed, in this excellent book, Bodenheimer is often at her best in discussing that novel which she describes as "a record of the anger generated by that turbulent year of uncontrollable talk" (146). It was the Liggins controversy as well as hurtful betrayals of her pseudonym by old friends like Herbert Spencer that motivated "Gossip burst[ing] into the text of *The Mill on the Floss* like a flood of violence'' (146). The following paragraph with its insights into the novel is representative of both the lucidity of Bodenheimer's writing and the quality of her analytic skills:

> In its focus on the elaborated details of sexual scandal, the representation of gossip (bk. 7, chap. 2) feels like an emanation from a mind well practiced in the projection of nightmarish voices. These voices are rendered neither in imagined dialogue nor in narrative summary but in a collective free indirect discourse that evokes the qualities of fearful fantasy. The speakers are nameless and faceless, but the sound of their—ostentatiously female—voices and the insane logic of their judgment are perfectly audible. Although the narrative irony makes it perfectly clear that ''the world's wife'' is vicious and self-serving, ready to pander to female success and equally happy to kick a fellow woman when she's down, George Eliot's invention of two hypothetical gossip stories instead of one has the side effect of linking gossip more closely with the inner life of its subject. For the two stories told by the narrator on behalf of 'the world's wife' are crass distortions of the two sides of Maggie which are in moral struggle.   (146–47)

Each of Bodenheimer's chapters sheds just such innovative, analytic light on how patterns visible in the letters mark the fiction. Analyzing the letters surrounding Marian Evans's choice to live with George Henry Lewes, her ''outing'' as George Eliot, her struggle to reconcile ambition and womanhood, her relationship with her stepsons, and finally, her resistance to and participation in her own canonization as a great writer and a sage, Bodenheimer brings us not just a new understanding of the letters' impact on the novels, but a new George Eliot. Challenging both the *nouveau* political partisanship of current literary studies and the conservative readings of the past, Bodenheimer aims ''to dissolve monolithic notions of George Eliot's teaching and ideology by suggesting how they emerge from dynamic reactions and counter reactions within her emotional economy'' (266). The conflict of representation between the liberations of the life and the sacrifices of the fiction, then, is recorded in the letters which document a ''creative activity of remorse'' and a ''tendency toward self-revising analysis'' which ''fueled the fictional elaboration of a whole range of perception,'' resulting in creative ''interrogations'' of for example, gossip in *The Mill on the Floss* and *Middlemarch,* or ''of ambition and mentorship in *Daniel Deronda*'' (266). Bodenheimer's book will set the standard of Eliot scholarship for many years to come.

George Eliot: An Intellectual Life (New York: St. Martin's, 1990), also a kind of biography of the mind by Valerie Dodson, adds to our understanding of Eliot's reading and her engagement with ideas. Dodson is concerned with Eliot as an ''intellectual turned novelist'' (1). Therefore its focus is not on the novels but on the shaping of the mind which conceived them. Dodson represents first the major issues involved in the ''philosophical debates'' in

Eliot's England. She then follows Eliot's role in that debate through her study and through her non-fictional prose. Dodson's book is helpful to students of Eliot and Victorian culture. But it will not replace the serious scholar's return to the original sources.

Finally, Reprint Services has made available John Cross's *George Eliot's Life*. This book will be useful to have for those who are interested in the role Cross played in constructing an image of George Eliot and a mythology of her life.

Several major books on George Eliot have contributed to the field in the nineties, and one such is Carol A. Martin's *George Eliot's Serial Fiction* (Columbus: Ohio State UP, 1994). On the little discussed topic of Eliot as a serial writer, this work reminds us of Eliot's encounters with the genre and its impact on her career. Indeed, Martin does envision serial fiction as a genre unto itself and details the difficulties Eliot encountered when writing realism within its confines. Where the genre demanded cliff hangers, delicate heroines, and sensationalist plots, Eliot was developing her habits of "careful psychological presentation of character, strong narrative control, and detailed contextualizing" (Martin 51). According to Martin, however, Eliot learned a great deal from serial conventions, becoming more attentive to drama by the end of her first serial project, *The Scenes of Clerical Life*. She also learned how to sidestep conventions, developing strategies for resisting the advice (and the anxiety) of her first publisher, John Blackwood.

Martin argues that between "Amos Barton" and "Janet's Repentance," Eliot came to balance dramatic action, psychological inquiry, and realist, socio-political inquiry in her work in part because she was also balancing the expectations of serial readers with her own "determination not to alter what she consider[ed] essential" (92). By the end of her career, Eliot had learned to incorporate serial conventions to her advantage as a novelist. Her use of "sensation" for example "gradually became more sophisticated, she rarely exploits the dramatic ending in a way that interferes with her focus on character and theme" (263). Indeed, in her accommodations to the serial format rearranging chapters in Middlemarch, for example, Eliot "gained an interna symmetry and a new depth and subtlety" (263). In Martin's hands this interac tion between audience expectations, editorial expectations, and artistic integ rity is lively and informative, helping us to remember the context in whicl Eliot's fiction developed, and helping to remind us that the business of pub lishing clearly impacted on the work of writing.

Martin's reading of *Romola,* for example, places that novel in a new con text. *Romola's* "landscape of the conscience" is "especially incompatible,' she argues, with installment publication whose readers "looked for a mor traditional story of love thwarted, woman deceived" (151). Eliot's resistanc in *Romola* "of passion, jealousy, and other perils and rewards of love tha delighted Victorian readers in sensation fiction'' (152), is an important precursor to the later masterpieces *Middlemarch* and *Daniel Deronda.* The resistance of serial sensationalism has never been considered as playing such a large role in Eliot's work and the results are intriguing. For example, Martin argues that serialization plays a role in the organization of each novel and proves that Eliot was not " 'above' the influence of newspaper criticism'' (187). Martin reveals that alterations to the manuscript of *Middlemarch* "were made in direct response to public opinion'' (187). The bi-monthly half-volume mode of the serialization of *Middlemarch* and *Daniel Deronda* accommodates Eliot's organic structure and development of plot and character better, Martin points out, than the chapter serialization of *Romola.* More importantly, Martin shifts her focus from the well-known examples of Eliot's difficulties with negative criticism, to her interactive response to positive ones. Because Eliot responded to readers appreciative of Dorothea Brooke, "Eliot and Lewes realized that the original plan to leave her out of Book II and hence out of readers' sight for four months would be a mistake'' (190). *Daniel Deronda,* on the other hand, is proof of "Eliot's refusal to conform'' to the popular demands of serial readers (259). Not every one of Eliot's novels was serialized of course, and this compromises Martin's study a bit. She often speculates on books which were not serialized. While it is useful to know that both *Adam Bede* and *The Mill on the Floss* were considered too controversial for serialization, it is less useful to hear that *Silas Marner,* also not serialized, "could have been, in Maga, almost a fourth scene from clerical life'' as it "lends itself most readily to the serial format'' (95).

The major contribution of this study is its continual refinement of our idea of George Eliot. Previously, we have been led by biographers and scholars to focus on Eliot's diffidence and her inability to tolerate bad reviews. Martin sketches less the shrinking artist than the working writer actively engaged with her public, "retain[ing] her own vision and yet benefiting] from the reactions of publisher and public'' (264). The perspective is valuable.

A smaller book which also addresses George Eliot and the world of Victorian publishing is Susan Rowland Tush's *George Eliot and the Conventions of Popular Women's Fiction* (New York: Peter Lang, 1993). This offers a comparative study of Eliot's major novels and their less well known counterparts, those "silly novels'' Eliot critiques in her famous essay. Tush bases her thesis on the idea that Eliot's "Silly Novels by Lady Novelists'' was not a misogynist tract, but rather "a personal credo of what female fiction ought to be, and her challenge is directed as much to herself as to any other woman writer'' (4). Reading *Adam Bede, The Mill on the Floss,* and Middlemarch against conventional novels like *The Old Grey Church, The Enigma,* and *Adonijah, A Tale of Jewish Dispersion,* Tush argues that without knowing these novels ourselves, we cannot see Eliot's innovations, parodies, and perhaps, her radicalism. This is a good point and although this book is occasionally awkwardly written, it is useful for Eliot scholars and Victorianists.

All of the major books written on Eliot in the 1990s share a desire to expand our knowledge of her life and her times as well as the impact of our own culture on the act of interpreting. The trend to contextualize is clear in one of the first books written on Eliot in this decade. In J. Russell Perkin's *A Reception-History of George Eliot's Fiction* (Ann Arbor: UMI Research P, 1990), the author addresses this problem of historical "restoration." One cannot, he argues, " 'restore' a text as one restores a painting, as though the critical tradition were so many layers of varnish which need only to be cleaned away for access to an ontologically pure work of art" (17). We can, however, become "aware of the historical nature of our interpretations" (18). Perkin identifies the splits in Eliot criticism between visions of "Eliot the novelist (or 'artist') and Eliot the philosopher or intellectual" (19). Written at the end of the 1980s, the book calls for a reclaiming of literary history and a rejection of "the Yale School's mode of criticism" whose "hermetic quality" ignores the "contextual, intertextual, and interdiscursive nature of meaning" in literary works" (148).

Such contextual work was to be done in innovative ways in the 1990s. David Carroll's *George Eliot and the Conflict of Interpretations* (Cambridge: Cambridge UP, 1992) is among the first of works in this decade to examine not the influence of the history of ideas on Eliot, but the impact of a "crisis of interpretation" which afflicted the history of ideas itself in the nineteenth century (xii). Decidedly and gracefully, Carroll acknowledged both his debt to and his differences from earlier Eliot scholars. His work is engaged less with the question of influence or affinities, more with the difficulties Victorians faced in locating a "scheme of meaning" or a "coherent" or systematic "view of the world" which would not dissolve under the act of interpretation (1). Carroll argues that a "crisis of interpretation" accompanies Victorian hermeneutics, spreading from "a body of rules for the translation and understanding of ancient texts, biblical and classical, to the recognition that interpretation was a foundational activity in which everyone was inescapably involved" (3). Utterly detached from literary theories such as deconstruction, Carroll argues through an historicized conception of hermeneutics that Eliot's fiction represents in a "vivid, almost apocalyptic, sense that traditional modes of interpretation—making sense of the world—were breaking down irrevocably" (4). Each novel then is envisioned as moving toward an "inevitable episode, the contradiction, the gap which disconfirms its hypothesis" and enacts the crisis of interpretation (4).

Carroll reads all the major novels in this study. Some high points include his reading of *Adam Bede* which envisions the novel as a conflict of pastoral "theodicies" between Dinah Morris's "Christian masterplot in the rural Arcadia of Hayslope" (77) and Hetty Sorrel's "classical vision" of a pagan world of luxury" (81). Within these narratives of salvation and desire, "the other theodicies of Hayslope are defined and assessed" (83). Carroll offers that ultimately "there is no worldview, theodicy, calculus, or theory, which can explain away that central discontinuity of life which is registered as suffering" (104).

Carroll's chapter on *Middlemarch* is also a deliberate attempt to take Eliot scholarship one step beyond the study of the novel's "apparently totalising images—the web, the text, the pier-glass, the organism" which are less dependable than they seem, "trapped in their own metaphoric nature" (235). "An essential ingredient of the epic scope of *Middlemarch* is the representative nature of—various and subtly inconsistent theories of life—major characters are by definition, those whose world-views are in the process of being formed, challenged, or dismantled" (241). Throughout the chapter Carroll balances these world views with "actual conditions of nineteenth-century society" (272). The novel offers only a "temporary salvation" which makes "tolerable the gap between a character's world view and the facts of life of which provincial martyrdom consists" (272). This study of the conflict of interpretations in the novels welcomes a more ambiguous, less unified Eliot than we had envisioned in the past.

In addition to single-author studies on Eliot, some comparative studies have also complicated both the assumptions and the methodologies of the past. One such is Nancy L. Paxton's *George Eliot and Herbert Spencer: Feminism, Evolutionism, and the Reconstructing of Gender* (Princeton: Princeton UP, 1991). The importance of this study lies in the light it sheds on the difficulties which evolution theory posed for George Eliot's feminism. Because evolutionary theorists like Spencer and Darwin were taken so seriously by Victorian intellectuals, including Eliot herself, their insistence upon the biologically ordained inferiority of women was powerfully destructive to the concept of equality between the sexes. Paxton's argument in this carefully-researched book is twofold: she seeks to prove that Herbert Spencer's anti-feminism "profoundly influenced" and facilitated the exchanges between science and medicine in both England and America in the nineteenth century, "helping to change permanently the ways Victorians wrote about women, gender, sex, and motherhood" (8). Paxton examines the challenges George Eliot poses to the gender politics of evolutionary theory in her fiction. Describing this as an "archeological effort," Paxton aims to "recover a lost chapter in the history of sexuality by articulating the voice of feminist resistance as it finds expression" in Eliot's treatment of nature, women, gender, female sexuality, motherhood, feminist ambition, and desire (9).

Paxton's study then progresses methodically through the novels, reading each against one of Spencer's scientific tracts. One of her most powerful chapters is on *Adam Bede* and Eliot's critique of both Darwin's and Spencer's sentimental view of "Mother Nature." In this novel which takes orphaned children, incompetent mothers, and infanticide as its focus, and as a fact of human society, Eliot creates an evolved world in which "nature and women present themselves ambiguously; an accurate assessment of either demands that all the traditional associations likening women and nature be reexamined" (47). By reading the disastrous maternity of the beautiful Hetty Sorrel against Spencer's argument for the scientific importance which the personal beauty of women plays in natural selection, Paxton proves that Eliot's novel "warns the reader about the difficulties of reading women's outward appearance as a sign of Nature's 'intentions,' or of deducing the 'nature' of all women from the relatively few examples one encounters in one's own life" (47).

It will not be news to anyone that *The Mill on the Floss* is deeply engaged with evolutionary theory, producing that problematic mix of breeds, Maggie Tulliver and her brother Tom. However, Paxton's discussions of nature and education in the novel are fresh and insightful. She argues that Tom Tulliver's school days offer a critique of education as the utilitarian Spencer envisioned it; Tom studies by rote and cannot interpret the classics because his teaching has been merely quantitative. Only when Maggie and Philip "reinterpret the texts for him in terms he can understand" does Tom appreciate them (80). Significantly, Paxton discusses Maggie Tulliver as a direct response to theories of Victorian evolution which held women's sexuality as their "primary allure" and motherhood as their "supreme function" (82). Rejecting both the role of temptress and of mother, Eliot's Maggie shows her resistance to biological determinism. Paxton's book also offers an ingenious and important study of gender reversal and maternity in *Silas Marner*. Finally, she takes on the issue of women's suffrage in *Felix Holt*, theories of origin and knowledge in *Middlemarch*, and civilization and degeneration in *Daniel Deronda*. This is the best kind of historical work on a major Victorian author and a major Victorian issue. Always questioning the politics at play between Spencer's theories and Eliot's fiction, Paxton's book is a lively dialogue which finally incorporates the role gender plays in Eliot's representations of evolution theory.

Also concerned with evolutionary theory and its impact on Victorian novelists is George Levine's article "By Knowledge Possessed: Darwin, Nature, and Victorian Narrative" (*New Literary History,* Spring 1993). Levine argues that "the ideal of objectivity to which science professed allegiance parallels in [Victorian] fiction the persisting story of self-abnegation for the sake of truth, often at the expense of both knower and known, protagonist and lover, who frequently must die either literally or figuratively for their efforts" (364). This article ends with a short epilogue on George Eliot which ought to be required reading for anyone studying the practice of literary criticism.

Another comparative study is important because it redefines the genre of comparative study itself. This is Alison Booth's *Greatness Engendered: George Eliot and Virginia Woolf* (Ithaca: Cornell UP, 1992). After reading it one has two reactions. One asks oneself why no one thought to do this before. One also finishes this book with a sense of optimism for the future of literary studies. Linking these two great women writers, "palace spies" who wrote within the "great tradition" to voice their "subtle but radical dissent" (i), Booth's book pursues not the influence of Eliot on Woolf, but the "study of an ideal of feminine influence . . . that both authors incorporated in their texts with much equivocation" (3). The tensions that Booth locates within each writer, of the desire for greatness and the will to self-sacrifice, of "a nostalgia for separate spheres and for an essential, inborn gender" (3), are then beautifully laid out in a series of chapters which juxtapose the two and their major works.

Confined as many of us are on a day-to-day basis by periods and movements, I find this book a tonic. Knowing the difficulty in studying one great writer, I find this careful study of two an achievement. Confessing her initial preference for the Victorian period, and her prejudice against Modernism—"modernists were formalists and elitist experimenters" (x)—Booth soon came to qualify her "love" for George Eliot while she developed a "passion" for Woolf (xi). Both emotions come through in this book and they are matched with a wide historical, cultural, and biographical knowledge and a finely tuned power of analysis. The latter is not reserved solely for the two authors but for "critical and canonical standards as well" (21). "Throwing light" on the feminist tradition as it was in part established by Woolf and Eliot, "also challenges the categories that have recently been imposed on feminist theory" (21). While she calls for an "eclectic method," Booth's approach is arguably materialist feminism in the "Anglo-American," rather than the "French psycholinguistic school" (21).

Booth's study begins with a chapter on Eliot, Woolf, and feminism. She finds that while the two writers share a skepticism for empirically defined notions of gender and the confinement of women in the "greenhouse" of domesticity (51), "they still retained the ideal of feminine selflessness as though it were the quality of mercy to soften the 'justice' or injustice of a deterministic, masculinist world" (51). She explores the inherent biographical and narrative paradox of the will to subordinate the feminine self with authorial greatness. She argues that for both women writers the problem of a gendered voice mattered deeply. Claiming greatness, Eliot spoke as a man, and to Woolf, eschewed feminine "charm." Woolf regretted the loss of sex in "Eliot's manliness" of style (83). Seeking "omniscience," however, she too warned that "manifest womanhood can be 'fatal' to the writer and her text" (83).

Booth also studies both women as historians of common life, heroism, and the selfless ideal, but her best chapters juxtapose the novels *Romola* and *Orlando, Felix Holt* and *The Years,* and *Daniel Deronda* and *Between the Acts.* Ultimately, Booth envisions Woolf as able to successfully "dispute the interdependence of artistry, authority, and masculine identity" even as in her own authorship she "strove to complete as her heroines were unable to do, the story of George Eliot herself" (284). Throughout, this story of the impact of gender on greatness never loses touch of the particularities of each author. Dense and well-researched, *Greatness Engendered* is also beautifully written and contains an element lately more rare than a tenure-track line: original thinking.

What is wanted in a comparative study is some real dialogue between two writers; conclusions ought to be drawn whether these reflect affinities between writers or whether these suggest how both are engaged with the representation of similar phenomenons. *George Eliot and George Sand* by Daniel Vitaglione (New York: Peter Lang, 1993), promises to fulfill this agenda, but ultimately does not. Vitaglione juxtaposes the pair and places them in historical and ideological contexts, showing convergences and divergences on religion, politics, art, and the position of women. His book contains summaries of historical context which may be helpful to students, although quotations from the French are not offered in translation. But there is no real guiding dialogue here between the two authors, nor are there any in depth analyses of texts which might reveal an interplay between Sand's idealism and Eliot's realism.

In the 1980s, Eliot was initiated into what is now called queer theory through her inclusion in Eve Kosofsky Sedgwick's landmark study *Between Men* which includes a chapter on *Adam Bede.* Kathryn Bond Stockton's *God Between Their Lips: Desire Between Women in Irigaray, Bronte, and Eliot* (Stanford: Stanford UP, 1994), may be to lesbian studies in particular what Sedgwick's was to gay studies in general. This is a controversial and provocative book which, like its title, significantly places Irigaray as its central theorist through which Bronte and Eliot might be read. Indeed, this book takes a delight in theory which is rare in traditionally conservative Eliot studies. "Post-structuralist feminists," argues Stockton, "are the new Victorians (3). They "write their own versions of a *spiritual* materialism that remarkably echo Victorian discussions of bodies and God" (8). Eliot scholars who are annoyed by such elisions between centuries may be outright offended by the confidence of some of Stockton's more provocative statements, such as "The figure of the hymen is crucial to *Middlemarch*" (170). Stockton's arguments may privilege her theoretical position to an extent that may cause some readers concern for the loss of the author at hand. For example, Stockton's vision of George Henry Lewes seems to distort grossly his role in Eliot's life. At one point he is pictured as "busy dining out on the invitations that came with her renown" (185). At the beginning of their liaison, Lewes was, of course, much more well known as a writer and intellect than Marian Evans was. From all extant evidence their relationship seems to have been mutually supportive, not exploitive. There is an attempt to displace Haight, moreover, which is rather after the fact. Since Redinger and even Gilbert and Gubar's work on Eliot, Haight's depictions of Marian Evans's relationships with John Chapman and Lewes have been problematized. Stockton writes that "We have seen the way in which Haight's biography draws its boundaries as Haight fashions the manly author and the womanly woman. He does not see, in the story he tells, the tangled relations between a woman's work and her desire" (192). Gordon Haight of course was writing his biography more than thirty years ago. But by 1994, Stockton is preaching to the converted on this issue. At any rate, what is needed at this point is a feminist elucidation of the role which Eliot's liaisons with Chapman and Lewes *did* play in the creation of George Eliot. References to Haight dominate here. Indeed, engaged so closely with Irigaray, Stockton does not engage those Eliot scholars who have worked on this issue.

Stockton's most controversial reading, however, involves *Middlemarch*. Her analysis of Dorothea Brooke's displacement from the feminine by her participation in the male project of political economy, her "*religious act of sexual renunciation*" [emphasis Stockton's], and her analysis of Rosamond Lydgate's domestic work as an activity that "goes toward producing herself as a luxury" are perceptive readings. (202). Most interesting, Stockton argues that "spiritual experience can nurture (and intensify) sexual desire" (231). On the phenomenon of Will Ladislaw's femininity, Stockton suggests the possibility "that the feminine aspect of Will mediates to Dorothea her perception and enjoyment of the erotic gaze of women" (232).

Committed to political readings, however, Stockton can only see Dorothea Brooke's marriage to Will Ladislaw as either "cementing" her "into marriage" where she "clutch[es] her bourgeois privilege or, alternately, as a place from which Dorothea Brooke is seeking "autoerotic relations" with Rosamond Lydgate which "caress[es] their desire in the midst of their marriages" (242). It is the final scene between Rosamond and Dorothea, not the lightening bolt between Will and Dorothea, that Stockton finds to be the novel's climax (242). The latter is merely an echo of the former. For Stockton, Dorothea Brooke is ultimately a martyr, emblem of a "cultural visibility" denied to women (249). At the end of her book, I am left impressed with her analyses of scenes between women, their mirroring and echoing throughout the novel. She is particularly effective at analyzing language in scenes between women where, for example, she locates "St. Theresa's ecstasy . . . the wound and the jewel of a feminine fracture" (243). Yet, I am also left wondering how Stockton might reconcile the bogeys of "bourgeois marriage" and the "domestication of women" in the social realist novel with woman's, and not the least with Marian Evans's pursuit of sexual pleasure with men. In the novels, the narrative pursuit of Will Ladislaw, like the pursuit of Arthur Donnithorne, Tito, Daniel Deronda, or Stephen Guest, looks very much like the pursuit of pleasure, rather than the echo of it, to me. At any rate, the fact that woman's desire is so complicated by issues of gender, power, economics, race, and class, and perhaps especially by Eliot's status as a woman writing as a man, should necessitate that further work be done on the subject of woman's desire in Eliot's fiction.

Certainly, the moral Eliot, the high-minded novelist of the midlands, is more conflicted and more complex than many readers have been lead to believe. Whether she is just as conflicted as *avant* queer theorists argue, is another question. Jeff Nunokawa's radical study of *Silas Marner*, "The Miser's Two Bodies: Silas Marner and the Sexual Possibilities of the Commodity," (*Victorian Studies*, Spring 1993), is another queer reading of George Eliot's fiction which this time looks at "agitation" in scenes which may assert "an illicit desire between men" (281). "What could be simpler than *Silas Marner's* support for family values?" Nunokawa asks (273). This opening sets the tone of the article which also seems concerned with Eliot's inordinate "sense of propriety" (277)and her "propaganda campaign on behalf of familial propriety," as well as her "efforts to propagate an aversion for other kinds of congress" (275). One wonders, however, how if scenes between Silas and Eppie or Daniel and Mordecai might compare to those between Oliver and Fagan, for example, and the extent to which Eliot's sense of propriety is different from that of other Victorian novelists. Nunokawa may accomplish motivating many people who read *Silas Marner* in high school to read it again, as they should. But, if he wants to be convincing in reading Daniel Deronda's physical reactions to Mordecai as the "homosexuality" of Daniel Deronda "that never quite surfaces as explicit theme [but] is embodied in a homophobic unease" (281), he will have to articulate that implicit homophobia more clearly. Nunokawa lists his evidence as follows: "The aversion inspired by Mordecai's 'spasmodic grasps,' 'eager clasps,'" his 'thin hand pressing [Deronda's] arm tightly': 'Deronda coloured deeply, not liking the grasps'; 'Daniel [rose], with a habitual shrinking which made him remove his hand from Mordecai's." (281)—each of these is an interesting excerpt, however, Nunokawa needs to articulate more clearly why each is particularly homophobic. Additionally, each scene of agitation or aversion might be matched by a scene describing Deronda's retreats from Gwendolen Harleth or Mirah Lapidoth—retreats which have also traditionally been read as motivated in part by the intensity of Deronda's attraction to each female character. In a novel which begins, moreover, with one of the most famous depictions of qualified heterosexual attraction in English fiction: "Was she beautiful or not beautiful? And what was the secret form which gave the dynamic quality of her glance? . . . Why was the wish to look again felt as coercion, and not as longing in which the whole being consents?'' (1), it seems strange to focus so exclusively on Deronda's attraction to the intensely other, Mordecai. Mordecai is a spectral representation of a vibrant spirituality in a dying body. His grasps are halfway from another world, and his spirituality, attractive but also alien and frightening, seems acquisitive. Deronda represents a threatened Englishness, and one wonders how much of this is ''homophobia,'' how much xenophobia? Questions which involve the whole picture need to be asked in order to arrive at a plausible reading. Nunokawa's article will prompt thought on homophobia in Eliot's work, yet, many Eliot readers will have difficulty with the clearly politically driven thesis.

Another book on representations of sexuality in nineteenth-century fiction also has a clearly articulated political agenda, to locate representations of the desirous woman who is here figured as heterosexual in Eliot's fiction. Judith Mitchell seeks women as desirous subjects in *The Stone and the Scorpion: The Female Subject of Desire in the Novels of Charlotte Bronte, George Eliot, and Thomas Hardy* (Westport, CT: Greenwood, 1994). This is a feminist study which seeks to locate the female subject of desire in some major Victorian novels. For ''if such a construct as a female subject (as opposed to object) of desire is possible, she should certainly be found among'' their heroines, Jane Eyre, Maggie Tulliver, Gwendolen Harleth, Tess Durbeyfield, and Sue Brideshead (2). Mitchell must grapple in her chapters on Eliot with the question of the extent to which Eliot's realism mirrors or participates in the erotic domination and objectification of women. She must also grapple with ''a theory of desire that seem[s] especially masculine, in that it was triangular, competitive, and de-emphasized the position of the object or third term of the triangle'' (3). Mitchell challenges the very duality of the terms ''subject/object'' and their ''power-based hierarchy''—the dualities which are often represented in Eliot's novels in gendered terms. Referring to literary, psychoanalytic, and visual theorists, Mitchell studies the polarization of desire from Milton's reluctant Eve to Brontë's *Shirley*, to Freud, to *Fatal Attraction*, and she prefaces this with a clearly articulated political statement against the silencing of female desire.

Mitchell explores the duality of Eliot's novels which are at once so infused with erotic metaphor and so devoid of erotic action. She finds that throughout Eliot's career she moves progressively closer to creating a genuinely desirous woman subject, only to fail with Gwendolen Harleth in *Daniel Deronda*. Eliot ultimately shares that novel's title characters' embrace of the spirit over the flesh so much so that she cannot endure a character ruled by desire or passion. Moreover, Eliot's narrator, Mitchell asserts, gazes upon women as objects and endorses ''transcendence'' (153). ''The look of desire in George Eliot's novels, then is ineluctably male. Her female characters never look desirously at males, and they are ideally unaware that they themselves are looked at constantly'' (91). This is a good point. However, male characters are also often subjected to the gaze of the narrator. A long description of Adam Bede prefaces the novel itself, as the long description of Daniel Deronda rowing on the Thames prefaces his meeting with Mirah. Deronda sits for his portrait by the Meyrick girls. An inclusion of men as objects of a female author's gaze would make this study even more intriguing.

Some of Mitchell's most interesting analyses combine gaze theory with film theory. For example, as the "look of desire" is "so immensely important in the relations between women and men in George Eliot's novels," it has the same impact in the novels as close-ups have in film (97). Such moments resonate with an erotic charge that clearly motivates action, but have little to do with the desire of the woman pictured. For example, Hetty Sorrel, a sensuous spectacle in the dairy making butter, never has an erotic desire of her own for Arthur Donnithorne. Maggie Tulliver, who is minutely pictured and described many times in the novel does a terrible battle between her desire for Stephen Guest and her passion for spiritual purity. "This disassociation of the erotic from passion, in fact lies at the heart of George Eliot's dilemma in *The Mill on the Floss,* and militates against the genuine feminist thrust of the narrative" (109). In *Middlemarch* and *Daniel Deronda,* Mitchell argues that Eliot focuses on "the power politics of the domination/submission hierarchy" (122), and helpfully discusses Dorothea Brooke who is so in command of herself at other times, and who yet seems unconscious of both sexual desire and revulsion. Mitchell argues that Gwendolen Harlelth seems "frigid" (135), however, that frigidity is certainly wed to her loveless marriage? But on the erotics of gaze between Gwendolyn and Deronda, Mitchell is quite good. This is an important chapter on Eliot which not only places her representation of her desirous woman in a historical continuum, but offers probably our best understanding of Eliot's conflicted renunciation of desire to date.

Among works which study both the position of women and the role of class in Victorian culture is another article on the representation of desirous women, Margaret Homan's "Dinah's Blush, Maggie's Arm: Class, Gender, and Sexuality in George Eliot's Early Novels." This is a major article which seeks to define George Eliot's representations of desirous women within—or without—the paradigm established by Nancy Armstrong in *Desire and Domestic Fiction.* If there Armstrong locates two paradigms: "the replacement of a monstrous sexual woman by a domesticated one" and the phenomenon of the "middle-class woman civilizing aggressive males," Eliot, Homans argues, conflates both (157). Homans focuses on the class battles reflected in *Adam Bede* and *The Mill on the Floss* where Dinah's blush and Maggie's "humiliation" at Stephen Guest's attempt to kiss her arm "identif[y] the sexual woman with the angelic and proper middle class ideal" (176).

Also intensely concerned with class is Elizabeth Langland's *Nobody's Angels: Middle-Class Women and Domestic Ideology in Victorian Culture.* Langland takes on *Middlemarch* to explore Eliot's avoidance of the domestic realm and the "always feminized and marginalized domestic detail" in the novel (208). Just like the canon which was to claim *Middlemarch,* that novel itself "relegates to an inferior status" almost any "engage[ment] with domesticity" (208). Langland's thesis in this study which includes the analysis of etiquette texts, novels by Dickens, Gaskell, and Oliphant, as well as the diary of a domestic servant Hannah Cullwick, pursues the simultaneous construction of "an angelic image of middle-class women" and "in a corollary movement, [the] essential[izing] of working and lower class women as merely bodies, sexual and physical machines" (212). Langland finds the disappearance of labor in *Middlemarch* and the thrusting of Dorothea's plot on the foreground of the novel to be participating in the creation of a class gap which still troubles feminism: "For middle-class feminism was built upon the assumption that another class existed to perform menial labor, and working-class women were constructed to bolster and facilitate the middle-class project" (208). Indeed, Langland clearly finds Eliot and *Middlemarch* complicit in the crime of class domination and canon formation. Her focus on what is not in *Middlemarch*—the presence of women who swept Dorothea's blue-green boudoir or cooked the soup dribbled by Casaubon—provokes an alarming awareness of the extent to which that novel's exclusive focus on the upper middle-class characters qualifies it for serious study. *Adam Bede* which Langland does not discuss here, after all, is an extraordinary novel in which women's work and an inter-class love triangle dominate the narrative. That early realist, pastoral narrative has never held the place of *Middlemarch* in the great tradition. Langland is convincing as she argues the role which domesticity, or its absence, plays in canonization. Occasionally Langland is too sweepingly authoritative as she refers to a generalized conception of George Eliot, who is represented only through *Middlemarch* here, and her language is too often rife with jargon. However, the chapter on *Middlemarch* is provocative and will provoke further discussion on the role domestic duty plays in Eliot's fiction and in canon formation itself.

Indeed, gender studies constitute a majority of the articles published on George Eliot in 1990s. These are simply too numerous to review here, but a good number require mention because they make a significant contribution to the field. Beginning with the most recent, these include Sarah Gates's "The Sound of the Scythe Being Whetted': Gender, Genre, and Realism in *Adam Bede*" (*Studies in the Novel,* Spring 1998). Here Gates "would like to propose a way to add gender to the study of genre and realism, in a reading that accounts for the particular descriptive tropes and plot trajectories assigned by generic convention to the 'masculinity' and 'femininity' that are each needed for closing scenes of stable domesticity'' (20). Kate Flint studies Eliot's use of the first-person male narrator in ''Blood, Bodies, and The Lifted Veil'' (*Nineteenth-Century Literature,* March 1997). Andrew Dowling studies marriage laws in '' 'The Other Side of Silence': Matrimonial Conflict and the Divorce Court in George Eliot's Fiction'' (*Nineteenth-Century Literature,* December 1995). Examining Eliot's poetry, Susan Brown has written on ''Determined Heroines: George Eliot, August Webster, and Closet Drama by Victorian Women'' in *Victorian Poetry* (Spring 1995). On women who give gifts and their meaning, Steven Dillon has written ''George Eliot and the Feminine Gift'' (*Studies in English Literature,* Autumn 1992). Also on marriage, Joanne Long Demaria has written ''The Wondrous Marriages of *'Daniel Deronda'*: Gender Work, and Love'' (*Studies in the Novel,* Winter 1990). Two articles look at Eliot's response to great male authors: Diana Postlewaite in ''When George Eliot Reads Milton: The Muse in A Different Voice'' (*ELH,* Spring 1990) and ''*Middlemarch* and George Eliot's Female (Re)vision of Shakespeare'' by Marianne Novy (*JEGP,* January 1991). On mothering, Diana Postlewaite has also written ''Of Maggie, Mothers, Monsters, and Madonnas: Diving Deep in *The Mill on the Floss.*'' (*Women's Studies,* March 1992). A major article which appeared in *PMLA,* Susan Fraiman's ''*The Mill on the Floss,* the Critics, and the *Bildgunsroman*'' (January 1993), clearly seeks to rewrite our earlier visions of Eliot and the *bildungsroman.* Finally, in ''George Eliot's Pulse'' (*differences: A Journal of Feminist Cultural Studies,* Spring 1994), Neil Hertz studies Eliot and authorship and argues that, for example, Hetty Sorrel's and Armgart's transgressions function as allegories of Eliot's own fantasy of transgression as a woman writer. All commit ''crimes'' which are like writing and must be redeemed by writing. This is a small sample of the mass of published articles on Eliot and gender in the nineties.

Since Edward Said's influential reading of *Mansfield Park* in *Culture and Imperialism,* readers of the British novel have learned to look for the other at the heart of England's empire. And while George Eliot will always reign as *the* novelist of the midlands, today readers perceive that she is rarely there alone. Indeed, Eliot has now been reclaimed as one of the most sophisticated internationalists of the Victorian period. Post-colonial critics are now turned especially towards *Daniel Deronda* and the question of empire-building raised by the main character's departure ''for the East'' at the novel's end. Patrick Brantlinger's essay in *Victorian Studies,* ''Nations and Novels: Disraeli, George Eliot, and Orientalism'' (Spring 1992), is now instituted as a classic essay of postcolonial studies.

For Eliot studies, this essay began the scrutiny of *Daniel Deronda* as a novel that problematically interrogates imperialist ideology through a paradoxically "romantic version of 'orientalism' [which] oppose]s] rather than support[s] the stereotyping that would identify one's nation and race as superior to others'' (258). Arguing against Eagleton, Brantlinger locates Eliot's nationalism as—even if "analogous to the public realm of self-serving individualism in private life'' (Graver 242)—also a "nationalism that clashes with merely provincial, merely English, narrowness, including the social Darwinism that served as ideological prop for the so-called new imperialism of the late nineteenth-century'' (271). While Eliot may not ultimately escape "the ideological circle of nationalism-imperialism-racism,'' Brantlinger argues, she none the less "expresses the desire to infuse'' those "seemingly inevitable ideologies ... with a cosmopolitanism that looks beyond'' provincial English and British jingoism (273).

Later readers have often been less charitable toward Eliot's novel and more recently it has been embroiled both in the real politics of the middle east as well as in gender politics. For example, in *PMLA,* Bruce Robbins, the author of "Death and Vocation: Narrativizing Narrative Theory'' (January 1992), argues that Daniel Deronda's vocation is doubly exclusive, achieved at "the expense of a strong-willed woman, Gwendolen Harleth. And even without the events of the late 1980s in the Occupied Territories, it would be hard not to remember that his Zionist mission—what Edward Said calls the 'Jewish equivalent of an Oriental pilgrimage,' excludes and marginalizes Harleth as much as Zionism has continued to exclude and marginalize the Palestinians'' (Robbins 44).

Reina Lewis, in *Gendering Orientalism: Race, Femininity, and Representation* (New York: Routledge, 1996), agrees. Lewis's thesis argues, with the majority of post-colonial critics, that Eliot's novel is Orientalist despite its claims to "fellowship'' with the Jewish people (Eliot *Letters* VI 301–02). Lewis stakes out familiar ground when she argues "that the development of Jews as a signifier of otherness for English society reinforces, despite its attempts to challenge, naturalized ideologies of racial difference'' (192). More interesting is Lewis's examination of Victorian readings of *Daniel Deronda* and the way in which "fluctuating theories of racial identity were read into the book by both Gentiles and Jews'' (Lewis 192). Lewis argues that *Daniel Deronda* actually played an important role in the national identity of Anglo-Jewry and that the novel's reception "was a central moment in the formation of Diaspora identities'' 9192). Lewis then attempts to shed light on the role which *Daniel Deronda* has played in the formation of culture itself.

This is also the focus of Susan Meyer in her important book, *Imperialism at Home: Race and Victorian Women's Fictions* (Ithaca: Cornell UP, 1996). Like Anita Levy's influential *Other Women,* Meyer's book examines links between British women and other races. Her two chapters on Eliot focus on *The Mill on the Floss* and on *Daniel Deronda.* In the former, Meyer focuses on the darkness of Maggie Tulliver; in the latter, on "Gwendolen's desire for freedom and escape [which] is enacted through Deronda's discovery of his Jewish identity" (27). Meyer selectively attends less to Victorian domestic fiction's alliances with imperialist ideology, more to "the fact that the social positioning of various writers of the domestic novel in nineteenth-century Britain put them in a different relation to the project of empire" (9). Allying racial darkness and female rebellion, Meyer locates an important source of tension in *The Mill on the Floss* and she is eloquent on the novel's painful ending. The "nut brown" Maggie is pictured as an almost "savage" biological throwback, one which will be "annihilated" by "pink and white English conformity," commerce, and progress (156). "Only those who are the most fitted to this society will survive, while the rest are the unfavoured races of mankind. This is a fact the novel at once laments—and presents as immutable" (156). Likewise, in *Daniel Deronda,* Meyer studies the problem of plot in which "a British woman is compared to people of oppressed racial groups, and in which the narrator is critical of British racial domination" (167), but in which as well a Jewish exodus from Europe is advocated. Meyer ultimately argues that Gwendolen is sacrificed in the novel which ushers "the strong selves of women" out at its end (194). Meyer's work possibly sets the standard for feminist, postcolonial studies. Her analyses are carefully historicized while her writing is consistently elegant.

Katherine Bailey Linehan has also written on *Daniel Deronda* in her article "Mixed Politics: The Critique of Imperialism in *Daniel Deronda*" (*Texas Studies in Literature and Language,* Fall 1992). Linehan was among the critics in the early nineties to question Eliot's treatment of empire in her novel. Arguing that Eliot is essentially conservative, depending on a conservative vision of nation, patriarchy, and race, Linehan suggests that Eliot is trapped by her conservatism even as she advocates escaping it. My own article on *Felix Holt,* "The Giaour's Campaign: Race and Desire in Felix Holt" (*Novel,* Winter: 1997), is concerned with orientalism in Eliot's novel.

The majority of postcolonial work on Eliot, however, maintains its focus on *Daniel Deronda.* In his study on Judaism, *Constructions of 'the Jew' in Literature and Society: Racial Representations 1875–1945* (Cambridge: Cambridge UP, 1993), Bryan Cheyette also includes a study of *Daniel Deronda* that is informed both by postcolonial theory and by recent writings on the construction of race. Again, looking at the otherness constructed within English society, Cheyette examines a series of canonical British writers who place "racial representations at the centre of literary production" (xi). In his study, Cheyette manages to balance a formidable knowledge of history and theory with a keen reading of Eliot's novel. Placing her in the context of Matthew Arnold and Trollope's representations of race, Cheyette argues that "Just as Arnold's sense of 'culture' attempted to transcend racially differentiated Jews, Eliot's persona [in "The Modern Hep! Hep! Hep!"] emphasizes both a higher 'affinity' with 'the Jews' and at the same time, their 'superlative particularity' '' (43). Cheyette is good on Eliot's ambivalence towards Judaism and its people, agreeing with recent examinations of *Daniel Deronda* which problematized Eliot's once unimpeachable reputation for tolerance. But Cheyette connects that particular representation of Judaism with a generic question about representation itself. *Daniel Deronda* is ''a fruitful example of the realist novelist going beyond the doctrine of liberal realism in order to represent the ultimately unknowable Semitic 'other' '' (42). After a detailed, even intimate, reading of the novel, Cheyette argues that ''Eliot's 'experimental' post-realist novel . . . does not pursue the issue of gender in relation to historical change, but instead, foregrounds an ambivalent Semitic discourse which was intended to provide an alternative vocabulary of 'the nation', to that of a materialist liberalism which would help renew a society whose future direction was ever-more fraught with uncertainty'' (53). This is an important chapter for Eliot scholars and makes a valuable contribution to readings of *Daniel Deronda* and race. I wish only that Cheyette might have written more on Eliot and that he might—throughout his study—have refrained from the use of quotations around terms like ''race,'' ''culture,'' and ''other.'' Surely we are all aware of the constructed nature of such terms by now.

Another work on George Eliot and the construction of nations is remarkable for what it leaves out. Bernard Semmel's *George Eliot and the Politics of National Inheritance* (New York: Oxford UP, 1994), makes no references to any of the work done in the 1980s or later on the idea of nations and novels. His approach is both textual and biographical, arguing that Eliot's canon represents a ''trauma of disinheritance'' (15). As industrialism began to dominate the nation, so did a ''bloodless cosmopolitanism'' replace ''insular patriotism and a naive pride in the national character'' (14–15). As one of the book's organizing principles, Semmel aligns this national loss with Eliot's personal loss of ''the loving security of her early years as her evolving religious opinions and flouting of social conventions alienated her father and brother whom she loved'' (15). Semmel then follows the impulse in Eliot's novels to focus on issues of inheritance—both familial and national—of free will and determinism, of positivism and compromise, and finally on disinheritance and the metaphor of race. Deeply engaged with Eliot's contemporaries like Herbert Spencer, Comte, and Feuerbach, Semmel's study is equally disengaged with thinkers of our own century here. Semmel uses terms like ''race'' and ''blood'' without considering their own political ramifications or the current controversy over Victorian appropriations of other peoples like Jews or Gypsies as metaphors. Nor does Semmel engage with any of the feminist ramifications of this study which considers the tensions between Eliot's conservatism and radical flouting of convention. Had such considerations been made here, Semmel would have contributed much more to Eliot studies.

Deeply engaged with theory, Julian Wolfrey's chapter on George Eliot in *Being English: Narratives, Idioms, and Performances of National Identity from Coleridge to Trollope* (SUNY Press, 1994) is perhaps the antithesis of Semmel's book. Wolfreys also focuses on *Daniel Deronda*, which he describes as "a story about national Being and the dialectic between "national families' felt by the eponymous hero." (130). Deronda "acts against the ideology of Englishness" and is "caught by the paradoxes of identity" (130). Ultimately, Deronda is removed to "that imaginary space of nationhood as alterity and symbolic force that the Englishness of the text cannot accomodate" (150). This book questions easy historical and generic assumptions in interesting ways which are informed by the latest critical theory. The chapter on Eliot is perhaps one of the most *avant* discussed here, and it contributes to the vitality of post-colonial work on Eliot.

Finally, a small body of work is developing on Eliot's internationalism. Barbara Hardy writes on "Rome in *Middlemarch:* A Need for Foreignness" in the journal devoted to the study of Eliot and Lewes, *George Eliot and George Henry Lewes Studies* (September 1993). Hardy argues that "Rome in *Middlemarch* is an opening for foreignness that stands for George Eliot's Europeanism and internationalism, and for Marian Evans's discontent with the English provincial Midlands" (1). John Rignall's collection of essays on *George Eliot and Europe* (Vermont: Ashgate, 1997), also contributes widely to our understanding of Eliot and the European community. Until recently viewed, almost nostalgically and exclusively as the "novelist of the midlands," Eliot is here envisioned more accurately as urbane and cosmopolitan. The volume begins with its best essay, a tantalizing glimpse into the soon to be published journals by their editor. Focusing on Eliot's travel journals in particular, Margaret Harris in "What George Eliot Saw in Europe: The Evidence of Her Journals" convincingly argues for the sophistication of this writing appearing now in its fully restored form. "Their piecemeal publication," she argues, "has distracted attention from the craft of their construction" (2). If in the travel writing we see Eliot the scholar whom we well know, we also now see an informal Marian Evans, picnicking with "wine and Keats" or finding in Weimar "a glass of cold water from a pump by the roadside delicious as nectar" (5, 6). We see what does not appear in Eliot's formal essays like "Recollections of Weimar." We also see the dynamic person that Cross and Haight left out of their biographies.

This volume also offers significant post-colonial essays. Hans Ulrich Seeber discusses "cultural synthesis" (17) in *Middlemarch* while Derek Miller discusses "allegories of empire" (113). There are contextual historical studies on continental education, on the Renaissance, Greek scholarship, and comparative anatomy. As well, there are comparative studies of Eliot and Tolstoy, Victor Hugo, Balzac, Proust, and de Staël. This collection contains sixteen essays which will be useful to scholars who wish to understand Eliot's connection to things European. As the study of novels becomes more and more concerned with questions of nation and empire, our full understanding of Eliot's travel experiences and her affinities and divergences from her European predecessors and contemporaries will become more and more valuable. This volume is an important contribution to the field.

Theoretical works on narrative in George Eliot have not dominated the Eliot scene in the '90s as they did in the '80s. J. Hillis Miller has written an article on the nature of otherness and misreading in Eliot, entitled "The Road on the Other Side of Silence: Otherness in *Middlemarch*" (*Edda*; vol. 3:237–45, 1995). He argues that "Thinking by analogy . . . [in reading the novel, the reader sees] "one person as like some other person and then [we] literalize that similarity" (237). "For Eliot, the misreading of another person is a salient example of the fatal and fateful mistake of literalizing metaphor" (237).

Michael M. Boardman has also turned to the study of narrative and is concerned with the phenomenon of innovation in his book *Narrative Innovation and Incoherence: Ideology in Defoe, Goldsmith, Austen, Eliot, and Hemingway* (Durham, NC: Duke UP, 1992). In his chapter, "Eliot, the Reader, and Parable," Boardman argues that each Eliot novel is an innovation in its combination of story and moral, mimesis, and ideology. "To the extent that Eliot's are unified, it is the unity of equivalent parts working to the same end and not . . . a hierarchical relationship of subordination" (111). "The central paradox of the novel's form is that what is originally intended as a substructure takes on the magnitude of an independent exemplum that then, by virtue of its interaction with the main action, converts that action into Eliot's most powerful representation of female oppression" (145).

Also on narrative theory is Siward Atkin's "Free Indirect Style and the Rhetoric of Sympathy" in *Perspectives on Self and Community in George Eliot: Dorothea's Window,* (Lewiston, NY: Edwin Mellen 1997), edited by Patricia Gately, Dennis Leavens, and D. Cole Woodcox. This collection includes essays by Barbara Hardy and Felicia Bonaparte on enclosure and history, respectively, given at an Eliot conference early in the 1990s.

In this age of cultural studies, single-author psychoanalytic studies of George Eliot have also not proliferated. One psychoanalytic work, however, *The Transformation of Rage: Mourning and Creativity in George Eliot's Fiction* (New York: NYU, 1994), by Peggy Fitzhugh Johnson, is influenced by a variety of psychoanalytic theorists, from Freud to Bowlby. This book envisions George Eliot's career as a creative response to the loss of her parents. Examining Eliot's "personal conflicts and her denial of aggression in her characters," Johnson looks for patterns in the novels which may be "manifestations of the mourning process" (4). Johnson examines parental loss in *Adam Bede* for example. The banishment of Hetty and the convenient marriage of Arthur and Dinah, she suggests, reflects "the author's fear of the aggressive impulses coming from within herself" (39). In *The Mill on the Floss,* Johnson argues that Eliot fails "to separate her own life from her heroine's" (67). Eliot is "justifying her own pattern of behavior" through Maggie's elopement (67). Johnson is particularly interesting on "narcissistic rage" and aggression turned inward. Even those readers who, like myself, avoid psychoanalytic readings of dead authors, will find these analyses provocative. They offer yet another wrinkle in what we know is the conundrum of Eliot's reticence and repression in writing the lives of women.

Alan D. Perlis in *A Return to the Primal Self: Identity in the Fiction of George Eliot* (New York: Peter Lang, 1989), has written a psychoanalytic study which sees Eliot's "protagonists as partial individuals who are distortedly shaped by the force of their egoism" (i). The study charts familiar territory (the influence of Wordsworth particularly) and does not engage extensively with recent criticism.

General and introductory studies of George Eliot are alive and well, perhaps too well, producing from the Eliot mill a great many general studies or collections of essays. However, my concern here is with the introductory works which engage with the last wave of Eliot scholarship. For example, John Peck's casebook on *Middlemarch* (New York: St. Martin's, 1992), is exactly what we have needed in the 1990s: a collection of the new classics. Here are readings of the novel by Terry Eagleton. J. Hillis Miller, D.A. Miller, Suzanne Graver, Sally Shuttleworth, Kathleen Blake, and Gillian Beer. This is an important collection for undergraduate and graduate students who will also be exposed through this book to a variety of ways of reading. It is also a convenient collection for scholars.

Likewise, the MLA's new *Approaches to Teaching Middlemarch* (New York: MLA, 1990), will be useful to both experienced and new teachers of Eliot's great novel. Edited by Kathleen Blake, this work allows us to look over the shoulders of some of the finest Eliot scholars as they consider teaching *Middlemarch*. Elizabeth Deeds Ermath, J. Hillis Miller, Suzanne Graver, Carol Martin, and Alison Booth are here, among others. Each presents not a dry pedagogy but a creative and innovative practicum that I find invigorating.

Linda K. Robertson has written a new study, *The Power of Knowledge: George Eliot and Education* (New York: Peter Lang, 1997), which scholars and students will find useful. The focus is particularly on the influence of both gender and class on education, and the presentations of education in Eliot's work. On *The Mill on the Floss* in Twayne's Masterwork Series, Rosemary Ashton has written *The Mill on the Floss: A Natural History,* (Twayne 1990), which includes one chapter on Eliot's use of scientific language in the novel, and then goes on to devote a chapter to each of the novel's major issues: realism, tragedy, love and duty, structure. The book also includes biography of Eliot and a chapter on the state of education in Eliot's day. Students will find this book very useful. A more general study, *George Eliot* (Plymouth, England: Northcote House, 1997), by Josephine McDonagh, begins very traditionally with basic biographical information that sometimes has the air of myth. But it goes on to develop several chapters on specific themes in the novels. "Regeneration: The Uses of the Family" has particularly good readings of *Romola* and *Felix Holt.* Undergraduates should find these chapters useful. Likewise Alan W. Bellringer's *George Eliot* (New York: St. Martin's, 1993), is a basic introduction which concludes with a brief review of Eliot criticism. Karen L. Pangallo has edited *The Critical Response to George Eliot* (Greenwood, 1994), which collects a sample of Victorian and contemporary responses to Eliot's novels. However, the contemporary selections are often obscure; certainly none are classics on individual novels. This struck me as anomalous in light of the book's definitive sounding title. By the same editor is *George Eliot: A Reference Guide 1972–1987* (Boston: G. K. Hall, 1990). This guide includes very useful abstracts as well as bibliographical information.

Web sites can also sound alluring, but as yet, the two most significant Eliot web sites need major expansion. The journal *George Eliot-George Henry Lewes Studies* has devised its own web site, with contents pages for its current and back issues. It also provides links to other sites, but none yet offers the information an Eliot scholar, or even an undergraduate student might be seeking. The journal site looks quite professionally done, and hopefully it will be expanded to include conference information for scholars or on-line articles, perhaps a chat site for teachers, more photographs, etc. Their address is: *http: //www.personal.psu.edu/faculty/k/a/kaw16/Eliot.htm.* Also of interest is a site maintained by Mitsuharu Matsuoka, a professor at Nagoya University. This site is updated consistently and provides many useful links to things Victorian and to things of interest to college professors, such as links to English department home pages, etc. The address of this site is: //lang.-nagoya-u.ac.jp/-matsuoka/. This site and some other information will also come up with any George Eliot search on the World Wide Web. However, we are still waiting for a really useful Eliot site to be achieved.

The nineties brought several new film adaptations of George Eliot's novels, but only the BBC's "Middlemarch" caused a sensation. Perhaps the best thing about the six-part 1994 PBS "Middlemarch" was not the series itself, but the amount of impassioned writing which it produced. Described by critics as everything from a "well-meaning, even loving translation of [Eliot's] text" to an "abortion," the series shows an excruciating attention to the details of its period setting (Knoepflmacher 52; Knowles 54). But it is less than slavish to Eliot's novel. In this version of *Middlemarch,* for example, the beauty of

the sets can obscure the very prosaic ordinariness of Middlemarch the community. The latter becomes envisioned as one grand vista after another and
Middlemarch's narrowness, its "spots of commonness" become difficult to
discern amidst the great parks and gardens.

It is hard to resist reviewing the series "Middlemarch," and it seems
almost everyone has. In order to avoid writing an entire review essay on
"Middlemarch" reviews, I am confining myself to only two selections which
cover the central issues raised by the series. The first is a collection of short
reviews "*Middlemarch* on TV—A Symposium," and the second is Louis
Menand's "Eliot Without Tears." The symposium, published in *George Eliot-George Henry Lewes Studies* (September 1994) collects a lively group
of essays. Menand's article is a lucid and eloquent comment not just on
Middlemarch, but on the novel and culture as well as on the powers and
limitations of word and image respectively.

"*Middlemarch* on TV" certainly affirms the fact that George Eliot scholars
take both their *Middlemarch* and its exegesis very seriously. Much as these
scholars may try to assure that they approached the series without suspicion
("I *liked* it," insists one), few can allow the film to displace or even approximate their own visions of the novel (Wallace 65). Although Anne D. Wallace
disavows a desire for some "mythical accuracy to an original," she echoes
the criticisms of most: "The BBC's *Middlemarch* implicitly promotes an
addiction to utopian pastoralism, a blindness to history, a regressively conservative attitude toward women and marriage. Besides this twentieth-century
television story, George Eliot's nineteenth-century novel appears veritably
subversive" (Wallace 66). U. C. Knoepflmacher is the most charitable, reminding us that the series "caused hundreds to scurry to a text they had long
ignored" (47). The series as well provided him with "something fresh . . . affinities [he] had never pondered" between, for example, Raffles and Ladislaw,
which he saw juxtaposed in the film as both "bohemian enemies of smug
complacency" (51). Sebastian D. G. Knowles finds no room for praise, however. What may have been a "success" is ruined by the series's bungled
ending which reports neither the marriage of Dorothea and Will, nor the birth
of their son. Knowles finds this tantamount to an "abortion," and his review
is a rant, "a demand that the makers of this mini-series never be allowed to
make another one" (54, 53). The value of this symposium, and of Menand's
review, is not just that each is a defense of why the novel matters, but that
each is concerned with articulating why the novel matters in a culture such
as ours which is so wedded to the visual image and so committed to sentimen-
talizing the past.

Indeed, Louis Menand's review "Eliot Without Tears" (*New York Review
of Books,* May 12, 1994), begins as a film review but ends as a critique of
culture itself. Along the way it eloquently articulates what matters about

George Eliot and perhaps what matters about the genre of the novel itself. Menand comments on the critical nature of the loss of the narrator's voice in the film version, for example, by demonstrating the nuances of a narrative moment. "Miss Brooke had that kind of beauty which seems to be thrown into relief by poor dress." Arguing that film cannot fully represent the construction of Dorothea as "an epic figure" from just such "nearly subliminal effects created" by the sentence's "juxtapositions" of her beauty and the plainness of her dress, Menand locates what the film sacrifices (5). Later Menand discusses the alteration which bothers Eliot scholars the most, the removal of the storm scene from the final encounter between Dorothea and Will Ladislaw. In the film the former is transformed from a terrifying electrical storm to a sunny English garden. Menand notes that in the original the visceral force of the storm literally throws the lovers together in terror. It reduces them to frightened children and it echoes the novel's early reference to St. Theresa of Avila and her brother; both are images of "maturity confronting, as though a child all over again, the wonders of a world both fallen and new" (7). This is, Menand reminds us, "*the* epic image in English: it closes *Paradise Lost,* and it closes Wordsworth's *Prelude*" (7). But the thunderstorm scene struck the series' makers as "only a cliche" and they have let it go by" (7). This is an acute reading of George Eliot and the value of the written word. It is also an acute reading of contemporary culture which seems unaware of its own touchstones. A George Eliot scene is interchangeable with one from Forster. It is, after all, the garden that takes precedence.

The BBC "Middlemarch" prompted several essays on the importance of Eliot which make very pleasurable reading. These include Mary Gordon's personal reflection "George Eliot, Dorothea and Me: Reading (and Rereading) *Middlemarch,*" which appeared in *The New York Times Book Review* (May 8, 1994). Sally Beauman, writing in *The New Yorker,* comments on the novel and reflects on the uniqueness of Eliot's position as a serious woman writer in the Victorian period ("Encounters with George Eliot," April 18, 1994). Not related to *Middlemarch,* but similar in tone and style is the witty piece by A. S. Byatt and Ignes Sodre, "The Dislikable Gwendolen," in *The Times Literary Supplement* (October 6, 1995). These essays reflect the living nature of Eliot's work. For the weary academic, they can often be invigorating or even better, fun.

On that note, I come to the conclusion of this essay. I began by speaking of the spirit of vocation and the need for production which have worked together to produce a mass of Eliot scholarship within the last ten years. From the mass of production, the diversity of Eliot studies is striking. The field has undoubtedly been glutted, but also revitalized—again—in the nineties, now becoming more specialized, and more political. Having now progressed beyond the project of restoration and canonization which began with the centenary, indeed, with the deconstruction of canon formation which is now popular, the tack of Eliot criticism may even have shifted from revival to critique. One thing is sure in the next millennium, as representations of culture, of sexuality and gender, and of nation and race are contested throughout literary studies, George Eliot will be a central figure in the debate.

Wilkie Collins Studies: 1983–1999

Lillian Nayder

This survey examines the scholarship devoted to Collins since 1982, reviews recent editions of his fiction as well as biographical studies, and identifies and discusses trends in Collins criticism. The essay is divided into five parts: "Collins and the Police," "Collins, the Gothic, and Sensation Fiction," "Collins and Gender," "Collins and Empire," and "Collins, Narrative Structure, and Narrative Strategies." The survey concludes with a bibliography that lists more than 200 works, including editions, biographical and critical studies, and dissertations. Among the subjects discussed are the canonization of Collins, and the ways in which his status as Victorian rebel has been questioned and his cultural significance and aims redefined. Also discussed are the influence of Foucault on Collins scholarship, the growing interest in historical and cultural approaches to Collins's fiction, and the contributions of Collins scholarship to Victorian studies, particularly the examination of gender and class ideologies.

The fortunes of Wilkie Collins, as determined by literary critics over the last fifteen years, largely reverse those of Collins's own illegitimate characters, whose disreputable origins and marginal status are revealed during the course of his novels. In *The Woman in White,* Sir Percival Glyde is exposed as a man with "no more claim to the baronetcy and to Blackwater Park than the poorest labourer who worked on the estate" (521), and Magdalen Vanstone learns that she has "no name" in the novel of that title. But the name of

---

Dickens Studies Annual, Volume 28, Copyright © 1998 by AMS Press, Inc. All rights reserved.

Wilkie Collins has become increasingly well known to general readers and to students of literature, and his claim to artistic renown has been secured, despite his lowly literary origins in the sensation school of English fiction.

The recent BBC productions of *The Woman in White* (1997) and *The Moonstone* (1996) demonstrate the continued popularity of Collins's best-known works, and Collins scholarship still centers on these two titles. Yet virtually all of Collins's writings have now become a legitimate subject of academic discussion, with book-length studies from Yale and Oxford that broadly cover his career, articles on the early and late fiction in refereed journals and collections, nearly a dozen of his novels marketed as World's Classics, and a "definitive" biography from Princeton University Press that includes an Appendix on the just published *Ioláni*. Much of Collins's lesser-known work has recently become available: for example, a complete collection of his short fiction appeared in 1995, and two volumes of his letters are forthcoming in 1999. These publications testify to Collins's growing academic legitimacy, which is due, in part, to changes in the field of literary studies, as critics have become less concerned with the intrinsic or "timeless" value of literature and more interested in the ideological work that it performs. But whether his novels are defended as canonical "masterpieces" or used to explore the contradictions and complexities of Victorian culture, Collins has emerged from the shadow of the "inimitable" Charles Dickens and come into his own.

With the publication of Andrew Gasson's *Wilkie Collins: An Illustrated Guide* (1998), readers now have available an encyclopedia of information about Collins and his works that rivals those devoted to Dickens and Dickensiana. Beautifully illustrated, with alphabetically arranged entries describing fictional characters and works as well as publishers, friends and associates of Collins, Gasson's *Guide* is an important new resource, particularly because of the bibliographical information it provides. Collins scholars have yet to pay much attention to the manuscripts of his novels, although the textual notes to some recent editions briefly describe them, and William Baker's comparison of the holograph manuscript of *No Name* with its serial parts suggests how valuable such scholarship can be. More attention has been paid to the complex publishing history of Collins's fiction—particularly his late novels—thanks largely to the efforts of Graham Law, and both Anne Lohrli and Catherine Peters set the bibliographical record straight by identifying misattributions to Collins.

The bibliographical work on Collins is heartening, yet it does not fully register the boom in Collins scholarship since the mid-1980s. As the sheer number of books, articles, and dissertations focusing on Collins suggests, his significance to Victorian studies is steadily growing. Since 1982, graduate students have written more than three dozen dissertations that include Collins, eleven of them devoted solely to his fiction. Perhaps most importantly, Collins's novels are central to new theories of the novel and to current examinations of Victorian gender and class ideologies. Whether Marxist, Foucaldian, or feminist in their methods, critics often turn to Collins's fiction to expose what they see as the workings of Victorian culture.

Because of the quantity of material published on Collins since 1982, the discussion that follows is not comprehensive, and mentions only a portion of the works listed in the Bibliography. Rather than reviewing each and every study, this essay identifies and discusses major trends in Collins criticism. It picks up where Kirk Beetz's article on "Wilkie Collins Studies, 1972–1983" left off, and its Bibliography includes a number of essays dating from 1983, but omitted by Beetz. My discussion of critical studies follows a descriptive analysis of recent editions of Collins fiction, and sections on Collins's letters and on biographical studies, and it is divided into five parts: "Collins and the Police"; "Collins, the Gothic, and Sensation Fiction"; "Collins and Gender"; "Collins and Empire"; and "Collins, Narrative Structure, and Narrative Strategies." The Bibliography itself is divided into the following sections: Editions; Letters; Biographical Studies; Publishing History and Bibliographical Studies; Collections of Critical Essays; Books on Collins; General Studies; Studies of Individual Works; Collins and Dickens; Comparative Studies; and Dissertations.

Editions

In his 1984 review of Collins studies, Beetz noted that Collins scholarship has "long been hampered by the unavailability of authoritative texts" (333). There is still no definitive edition of Collins's complete works, and readers continue to rely at times on the unannotated and incomplete AMS edition of *The Works of Wilkie Collins* in 30 volumes (1970), itself a reprint of the 1900 edition published by Peter Fenelon Collier. However, more than a dozen scholarly editions of individual novels have been published in the 1980s and 1990s—by Oxford University Press, Broadview Press, and Penguin—in addition to the unannotated editions of Collins's fiction now available from Sutton and Dover, eliminating some of the difficulties that have faced Collins critics in the past.

This section focuses solely on English language editions of Collins's works. However, dozens of editions of Collins's novels have appeared in translation since the mid-1980s, particularly in Russia, where a collected edition in ten volumes and another in five volumes were published in 1992, in addition to thirteen editions each of *The Moonstone* and *The Woman in White* between 1987 and 1992. For a detailed discussion of Collins's works in translation and his international reception and popularity, see Kirsten Hüttner, *Wilkie Collins's "The Woman in White": Analysis, Reception and Literary Criticism of a Victorian Bestseller* (1996).

Perhaps the most striking evidence of Collins's newfound academic legitimacy is the decision of Princeton University Press to bring out an edition of Collins's first and hitherto unpublished novel *Ioláni; or, Tahiti as it was. A Romance,* written in 1844 and rejected by Longmans and Chapman and Hall in 1845. Edited by Ira B. Nadel, *Ioláni* has appeared in the spring of 1999. Twenty-five years after writing this novel, Collins described it as a work in which his "youthful imagination ran riot among the noble savages, in scenes which caused the respectable British publisher to declare that it was impossible to put his name on the title-page" ("Wilkie Collins" 279), and few critics are likely to argue for its intrinsic literary merit. Nonetheless, *Ioláni* has considerable importance as the novel written at the outset of Collins's literary career and will no doubt add to our understanding of his artistic development. What little is written about the work to date suggests that it provides an interesting counterpoint to his later novels, particularly those concerned with cultural and racial differences and the process of empire building. Unlike *The Moonstone,* which begins with the British conquest of Seringapatam and considers the consequences of that act in England and India, *Ioláni* claims to represent Tahitian culture "as it was." Despite his reference to the "noble savages" in the novel, however, Collins does not idealize the aboriginal culture but foregrounds the barbarism of Ioláni, the high priest of the Areoi, who fathers a child by the heroine, Idia, and then attempts to sacrifice both to the gods. Drawing on the work of the missionary William Ellis, Collins represents the "savage" practices of the Tahitians in *Ioláni,* particularly infanticide, and appears to provide a rationale for European colonization. At the same time, he treats the persecution of Idia as his major theme, anticipating his portraits of Englishwomen victimized by their male relations, and formulating the theme that pervades his later fiction: the barbarism of patriarchy.

While Collins's first novel has now been published in a scholarly edition, two of his late novels (that is, novels of the 1880s) have recently appeared in such form, published by Broadview Press—*The Evil Genius,* edited by Graham Law (1994), and *Heart and Science,* edited by Steve Farmer (1996). Each of these Broadview editions contains an excellent Introduction and useful Explanatory Notes (footnotes, in Farmer's case), Appendixes, a Chronology and a Select Bibliography, as well as a Note on the Text that explains the publishing history of the novel and provides details of its serialization.

Law bases his text of *The Evil Genius* on the 1900 Collier edition, describing textual variants in his Notes, and he reprints contemporary documents that pertain to the novel in his Appendix, including contemporary reviews and divorce court reports. His Introduction is divided into sections on marriage law, women and family, and Victorian publishing practices, and usefully combines biographical, literary, and cultural analyses. Law contrasts the "comedy and realism" of *The Evil Genius* with the "mystery and melodrama" of Collins's earlier fiction, particularly *The Woman in White,* and its "narrative economies" with the "multiple plotting and multiple narration" of preceding novels (9), a change in narrative form that he associates with "developments in contemporary publishing" (25). Law discusses the "curious combination of the radical and the conservative" (7) in Collins's thinking—the tensions between his "liberal view" of marriage "as an equal partnership" and his acceptance of the sexual double standard on adultery (12). In "his own life choices," Law argues, Collins challenged Victorian domestic ideology "by consorting irregularly with 'unrespectable' women" rather than by "positively exploring the concept of marriage as a partnership, based on legal and social equality" (16), and in *The Evil Genius* he expresses "indignation at the image of women as sexual outcasts" but does not encourage them "to stand side by side with men in public life" (17).

Steve Farmer bases his text of *Heart and Science* on the 1883 Chatto & Windus three-volume edition, while also indicating the novel's original divisions in monthly parts, and he includes two photographs of the autograph manuscript at the University of Texas at Austin. His Appendixes contain contemporary reviews, material from the Victorian debate over vivisection, letters written by Collins that pertain to the novel, and a list of its serial divisions. In his Introduction, Farmer discusses the literary status of Collins's late fiction—his "long-hidden gems" (8)—and argues for the artistry of *Heart and Science,* noting its thematic and structural connections to Collins's best-known novels as well as its innovations. He recounts the vivisection controversy on which Collins bases the novel, outlines its critical reception, and describes its serialization in the *Belgravia.*

Heart and Science is also available in an unannotated edition from Sutton, publishers who have recently brought out most of Collins's novels of the 1880s, each with a brief biographical note—*Jezebel's Daughter, The Black Robe, "I Say No", The Guilty River,* and *The Legacy of Cain*—reviving works that are virtually unknown to Collins's readers. Dover has published an unannotated but nicely illustrated edition of *Blind Love* (1986), Collins's final novel, completed by Walter Besant after Collins's death, and their editions of *Hide and Seek, The Dead Secret, The Haunted Hotel,* and *Tales of Terror and the Supernatural* are still in print. But the Broadview editions, with their Introductions, Notes, and Appendixes, are especially well suited to classroom use, and are most likely to develop a new audience for Collins's late fiction: those "other" novels that, in Farmer's view, "deserve individual recognition" (7).

The recognition that Collins *has* received over the past fifteen years is largely due to those at Oxford University Press, who have made available nearly a dozen of his novels as attractive and well-edited "World's Classics." In order of Collins's composition, the Oxford editions include: *Basil,* edited by Dorothy Goldman (1990); *Hide and Seek,* edited by Catherine Peters (1993); *The Dead Secret,* edited by Ira B. Nadel (1997); *The Woman in White,* edited by John Sutherland (1996, 1998); *No Name,* edited by Virginia Blain (1986, 1998); *Armadale,* edited by Catherine Peters (1989); *The Moonstone,* edited by Anthea Trodd (1982, 1998); *Man and Wife,* edited by Norman Page (1995); *Poor Miss Finch,* edited by Catherine Peters (1995); and *The Law and the Lady,* edited by Jenny Bourne Taylor (1992). Each of these editions contains a useful Introduction, Explanatory Notes, a Bibliography and Chronology, and a Note on the Text.

Goldman bases her text of *Basil* on the revised 1862 edition published by Sampson Low rather than the 1852 edition published by Bentley, and she describes some of the more significant textual variants in her Notes. In her Introduction, Goldman argues that *Basil* anticipates the sensation novels of the 1860s, and she discusses its relationship to Collins's other early works, including his short fiction. She describes the novel's mixture of romance and realism as well as Collins's use of doubles, analyzing his subtextual treatment of sexuality and the relationship between text and subtext. In Goldman's view, Collins uses the novel to reveal "the hidden sexual tensions within Victorian culture," "bring[ing] to the surface hidden pressures, repressed motives, and secret beliefs" (xi, xvii).

Catherine Peters bases her text of *Hide and Seek* on the 1861 edition published by Sampson Low, for which Collins substantially revised the 1854 edition published by Bentley. "Though Collins often changed the text of his novels when they were republished," Peters observes, "his alterations to *Hide and Seek* are greater than those he made to any other novel" (xxiv). In her Note on the Text, Peters briefly describes the condition of the autograph manuscript at the Pierpont Morgan Library, and she provides some textual variants in her Explanatory Notes, including a number of lengthy passages omitted by Collins in 1861. She also addresses these revisions in her Introduction, in which she contrasts the first half of *Hide and Seek* with the second, describing the novel as a work in which Collins was "at a crossroads" (vii), ready to try his hand at domestic comedy rather than melodrama and to temper his social criticism to gain "public acceptance" (ix). Peters considers Dickens's influence on the novel and Collins's inversion of "Dickensian themes" (xiii), recounts the novel's mixed reception, describes its autobiographical "sub-text" (xxi), and discusses the metaphoric significance of the heroine's deafness, which she ties to Collins's theme of social marginalization. Rather than considering the relation between the heroine's physical handicap and Collins's critique of gender constructions, which promote the deafness and muteness of the "ideal" Victorian woman, Peters asserts that Collins's "sympathies were always with the disadvantaged," whom he felt "were not intrinsically different from their more fortunate neighbors" (xvii). For Peters, *Hide and Seek* "is a novel about affection, especially family affection, and the distortions caused by the lack of it," and "families, natural and acquired, dominate" it (xvi). Yet Collins, "this most untypical of Victorian writers," criticizes the often joyless "nuclear family," and suggests that children's love does not come naturally but "must be earned" (xvi–xvii).

Like Peters, Ira B. Nadel discusses Collins's "fascination with physical handicaps" (xxi) in his Introduction to *The Dead Secret*—in this case, the blindness of Leonard Frankland—as well as Collins's concern with mental illness, and he identifies the heroine, Rosamond Treverton, as "one of Collins's earliest strong-minded and active heroines," a prototype of Marian Halcombe in *The Woman in White* (xxii). Nadel notes that the reading, writing, and action of Collins's female characters "structure the novel," and he describes Sarah Leeson as "the Other" in its cast—"threatening, unknown, dangerous" (xxii). Nadel touches on a host of interesting points, but without developing any at length: these include Collins's fascination with exchanged identities and with secrecy, especially "hidden texts" (xxiii); his sense of the theatrical and its importance to the novel; his debt to Dickens; and his use of setting and Gothic conventions. With such issues at hand, the attention Nadel devotes to "factual sources" for Porthgenna Tower seems a bit misdirected. Nonetheless, he makes his readers aware of significant issues raised by the novel, aptly characterizes it as a "transitional" work (ix), and shows how it anticipates the themes and characters of Collins's later fiction. Nadel's text of *The Dead Secret* is based on the 1861 edition published by Sampson Low.

John Sutherland's Oxford edition of *The Woman in White* replaces that of Harvey Peter Sucksmith (1980). Whereas Sucksmith based his edition on the serialized version in *All the Year Round* to capture "the original spirit of the novel," "conceived and written as a serial" (Sucksmith xxii), Sutherland bases his text on the 1861 edition published by Sampson Low. However, Sutherland points to significant textual variants in his Notes, where he also indicates the original serial divisions, and in Appendix A he discusses the composition, publication, and critical reception of the novel, reproduces the poster from Collins's stage adaptation of *The Woman in White,* and includes a fascimile of its opening page in *All the Year Round.* Appendix B explains Collins's sources for the novel, and Appendix C provides a chronology of the narrative, "assembled from internal evidence" (663). In addition, Sutherland reprints Collins's 1860 Preface in his end matter. All of this material makes the Oxford edition much more useful than the Penguin, edited by Julian

Symons (1974, 1985), which has very limited notes, a badly outdated bibliography, and virtually no information about the publishing history of the novel. Sutherland's Introduction is as useful as his Appendixes, and foregrounds the sensationalism of *The Woman in White,* which he relates, in part, to the unconventionality of Collins's own life, particularly his sexual relationships with Caroline Graves and Martha Rudd. At the same time, Sutherland calls attention to the artistry of the novel, its "forensic" techniques and its "vindication of circumstantial evidence" (xvi). Sutherland discusses its legal sources and literary antecedents as well as its influence on Victorian writers, and he demonstrates that the novel "reverberates" with topical concerns (xix), including the wrongful incarceration of Rosina Bulwer by her famous husband, the baronet Edward Bulwer Lytton, in an English lunatic asylum in 1858.

Virginia Blain bases her text of *No Name* on the 1864 edition published by Sampson Low, describing some of Collins's more significant revisions in her Explanatory Notes and her Note on the Text, listing the original serial divisions, and describing the holograph manuscript at the King's School, Canterbury. The information she supplies on textual variants and publishing history is more extensive than that provided by Mark Ford in the Penguin *No Name,* also based on the 1864 edition, and her Notes are more numerous than his, although both editors gloss many of the same references. Ford's Introduction emphasizes the originality of *No Name* within the Collins canon: its avoidance of Gothic and exotic elements, for example, and its early disclosure of "the book's single secret" (viii)—the illegitimacy of the Vanstone sisters. In Ford's view, Collins uses the illegitimacy of the sisters as well as Magdalen's remarkable talent at role playing to expose the constructedness of social identity, which "may be borrowed, invented, dismantled or buried" (ix). Ford describes the theatricality of both the novel and its heroine, and sees Collins questioning "moral absolutes" (ix) and "prevailing [social] codes and structures" (xvi). Ford identifies the "uninhibited" and "unscrupulous" Magdalen as "one of Victorian fiction's most radical subversives" (x), and suggests that the socially acceptable alternatives embodied by the more conventional female figures in the novel are no more convincing or satisfying than Magdalen's own reformation in its final pages.

Like Ford, Blain considers the importance of plotting to *No Name*—a mark of Collins's artistry as well as a mode of social critique—and discusses Dickens's "galling interference" (xi) with the novel, Collins's marketing strategies, and his difficulties adapting the work for the stage. Blain examines the importance of role playing in *No Name,* and argues that Collins uses doubles to "deconstruct" the "binary oppositions of melodrama" (xiv) and to show that all women, even those who seem antithetical, are placed in a similar position and forced to depend upon men. According to Blain, Collins reworks social stereotypes in the novel, and uses the heroine's illegitimacy to criticize gender norms: "Illegitimacy, with its connotations of allowing no legal inheritance or possession of property, no given social class, no status as a responsible person in the eyes of the law, no legal name, serves here as an evocative and subversive metaphor for the position of all women as non-persons in a patriarchal and patrilineal society" (xix). While acknowledging that Collins "shrank from allowing [Magdalen] to win a victory entirely on her own terms" (xx), Blain characterizes him as a "subversive" (xv) who "comes much closer to a true sympathy with the plight of women in Victorian society than Dickens ever did" (xix), and she contrasts *No Name* with *Bleak House,* the illegitimate Esther Summerson with Magdalen, who "refuses to take upon herself any guilt for her position" (xx).

Catherine Peters uses the 1869 edition published by Smith, Elder as the basis for her text of *Armadale,* comparing it to earlier editions. In her detailed Note on the Text, she describes the publishing history of the novel, the state of the holograph manuscript at the Huntington Library, and Collins's dramatic adaptations, noting that his play *Miss Gwilt* depicts Lydia Gwilt as a "stereo-typed female victim" (xxvii) rather than a victimizer. Her Explanatory Notes provide an interesting description of Ozias Midwinter from the *Cornhill* serial that Collins "toned down" for the volume edition (820), and a lengthy pas-sage from the manuscript that Collins omitted from the serial. Peters quotes from Collins's pertinent letters as well as annotating literary and topical references. She describes the composition of *Armadale* in her Introduction, and places the novel in biographical context. She also details the critical response of reviewers offended by Miss Gwilt, and the mixed reaction to the novel's elaborate plotline. In Peters's assessment, Collins's treatment of Allan Armadale's dream "subverts" rational explanations, encourages "a reliance on the prophetic," and anticipates Jungian mythology (xxi–xxii). Peters char-acterizes *Armadale* as "a harsh novel" similar to *Basil* in its "unrelieved intensity" (xii), a work in which Collins responds to marriage law reform by examining "the conception of the family" and "the position of women" (xiii). Identifying the topical concerns that inform the novel, including the status of the "fallen" woman and the abuses of private asylums, Peters examines its major themes—"biological and psychological inheritance" (xvi) and "questions of identity" (xvii). In *Armadale,* unlike Collins's other novels, men rather than women "struggle to identify themselves" (xviii), Peters argues: "it is a woman, Lydia Gwilt, who stands out as the character with a steady identity" (xix), and whose imagination, plotting, and disillusionment represent Collins's own (xx).

John Sutherland's Penguin edition of *Armadale,* like Peters's, is excellent, and contains an interesting and informative Note on the Manuscript as well as a Note on the Text, and an Appendix on Collins's dramatic versions of the novel, which describes the differences among *Armadale, Armadale: a Drama in three Acts* and *Miss Gwilt.* Sutherland bases his text on the *Cornhill* serial, adding the Dedication, Foreward, and Appendix that Collins wrote for the 1866 two-volume edition. In his Notes, Sutherland explains references, describes source material, and provides a host of passages, some quite lengthy, from the manuscript: some crossed out, some presumably cut in the proof stage, and some reworked. He also identifies passages added at the proof stage, and cites variants among editions. Generally speaking, these Notes are very useful and reliable, but in comparing Mr. Bashwood's love for Lydia Gwilt to Dickens's for Ellen Ternan, Sutherland mistakes Ellen Ternan's age; she was eighteen and not twenty seven when she and Dickens met in 1857 (699).

In his Introduction, Sutherland discusses *Armadale* as both a sensation and a detective novel, and describes Collins's interest in the technological innovations of his day. He considers Collins's use of "headline stories" (ix), including the Yelverton bigamy case, recounts the story of the novel's composition, and characterizes it as a work "obsessed with illness" as well as "fate, congenital doom and inherited blight" (xii). Examining the detective figures in *Armadale,* including the private investigator, Sutherland notes the many acts of "espionage" committed in the novel (xiv). He recounts Lydia Gwilt's history, noting its "tantalizing gaps" (xviii), and describes the hostility directed at her and at the sensation novel generally by reviewers. He sees the sympathetic figure of Ozias Midwinter as Collins's answer to Thackeray, whose portrait of Woolcomb in *Philip* was "virulently racist" (xx), and argues that Collins represents a "fraternal embrace of black and white" in the friendship of Midwinter and Armadale. Sutherland compares the rivalry between Lydia Gwilt and Neelie Milroy to that of Caroline Graves and Martha Rudd, the two women in Collins's own life, and connects "the fatality theme" in the novel to the "religious austerity of Wilkie's father" and to Collins's own hope that "life's outcome is not necessarily ordained" (xxiv–xxv).

Steve Farmer's edition of *The Moonstone* is forthcoming from Broadview Press in 1999; judging from his edition of *Heart and Science,* it should prove most useful. In 1992, Knopf published *The Moonstone,* edited by Catherine Peters, as a volume in Everyman's Library. Although Peters does not identify the edition on which her text is based or provide any explanatory notes, she includes Collins's Prefaces of 1868 and 1871, a Select Bibliography, and a Chronology. In her introduction, Peters describes Collins's sources for *The Moonstone,* its composition, and its literary influence, and she analyses the subtexts that give the novel "a deeper significance" (v). According to Peters, Collins offers a "symbolic commentary on the theme of possession" in *The Moonstone,* "putting in question the concepts of value and ownership," particularly the "ownership" of India by the British, while also investigating the idea of self-possession: "If neither our emotions, nor even our actions, are under our conscious control, the safe boundaries of existence waver and dissolve" (xiv). Peters sets Collins apart from most of his contemporaries in his "sympathetic" portrait of the "gentlemanly Brahmins" (xviii, xxi), and argues that he questions "racial and imperialist stereotypes" in his novel (xix). Collins's sympathy extends to the other social outcasts in *The Moonstone,* Peters suggests, especially to Rosanna Spearman, who reveals Blake's "unconscious guilt" in her letter to him, and who has "access to levels of meaning that the conventional English world does not dream of" (xxii).

In 1984, Signet published *The Moonstone,* with the text taken from the 1871 revised edition published by Tinsley, and with an Introduction by Frederick R. Karl. This edition includes the Prefaces of 1868 and 1871, a very brief Textual Note, and an outdated Selected Bibliography, but no explanatory notes. Karl's Introduction provides biographical information on Collins, reviews his literary career, describes his relationships with Dickens and Reade, and considers his debt to the Gothic and his contribution to the genre of detective fiction. Karl characterizes Collins as a "rebellious" novelist interested in the " 'underclass,' " and *The Moonstone* as a text "made up of commentary by those who are usually in secondary positions in Victorian fiction" (1–2). Collins's use of multiple narration allows him to give "credence to the views and feelings of the lower classes in general and the servant classes in particular" (9), Karl argues. By contrast, the imperial theme of the novel appears largely inconsequential in Karl's view, despite Collins's concern with the Indian Mutiny of 1857 and his "interest in Indian questions" (10). To Karl, the British colony simply provides a variant on the Gothic locale: "Its mysteriousness [and] inflammability . . . furnish the background that once belonged to castles, remote areas, winding passageways, Mediterranean-type killers, and medieval premonitions" (11). Karl considers Collins's ties to Vidocq and Poe as well as his connection to Walpole, and discusses *The Moonstone* as a detective novel that reveals Collins's "concern with forms of order" and his optimistic belief "in solutions and resolutions" (20).

The Moonstone is also available from Oxford and Penguin, in editions that date from 1982 and 1966 respectively, and that were briefly reviewed by Beetz in 1984. The Penguin *Moonstone* is edited by J. I. M. Stewart, its text based on the revised edition of 1871. Stewart includes the Prefaces of 1868 and 1871 and a short Note on Sources, but no textual notes or bibliography of critical studies. His Introduction provides biographical information about Collins, characterizes his novel as a "perfectly plotted" work, praises his ability to create atmosphere and "delineate character" (7–8), and describes his thematic and structural use of criminal trials and records. Stewart also recounts Collins's friendship with Dickens and their interest in melodrama. Not surprisingly, Stewart's Introduction is badly outdated, particularly in its account of Collins's "ability to portray women with . . . fidelity" (9) and in his sense of Collins as a "rebel" (21) who lacks "originative instinct" and "failed to break clear into any imaginative world authentically his own" (20), a failure he attributes, in part, to the influence of Charles Reade after Dickens's death.

Like Stewart, Trodd bases her text of *The Moonstone* on the 1871 revised edition and includes Collins's two Prefaces, but she also provides a brief Note on the Text that describes the most significant changes in Collins's revised edition, a Bibliography, and useful Explanatory Notes on references, sources, textual variants, and the original serial divisions of the novel. In her Introduction, Trodd compares *The Moonstone* to *The Woman in White* and *Armadale,* describes the novel's critical reception, and considers its narrative construction. She argues that the plot emphasizes "male teamwork" and she asserts that "women's moral and social identity is not an issue" in the novel (xiii)—a questionable claim that Trodd's own comment on the "abnormal and enforced silence" (xiii) of the female characters belies. Trodd considers the significance of Sergeant Cuff's errors, which suggest "the dangers and limits of the detective police as they then figured in the public consciousness" (xv), and she compares him to other detective figures in Victorian fiction. Trodd finds Collins "superior . . . to xenophobia" in his treatment of the Indians yet she characterizes his critique of imperialism as "half hearted" (xviii), and notes the largely suppressed treatment of class conflict in the novel as well: "The text gestures at [class] resentment, but leaves it totally unglossed" (xx). In Trodd's view, *The Moonstone* is "a masterpiece of equivocation" (xxi) that reflects "Collins's desire to return to respectability after the back streets of *Armadale*" (xx).

Norman Page bases his text of the Oxford *Man and Wife* on the 1870 edition published by F. S. Ellis. He provides a brief Note on the Text, a Select Bibliography, and Explanatory Notes on Collins's references and sources. In his Introduction, Page questions the way in which Collins's life and works have been divided into phases of achievement and decline, and he argues that *Man and Wife,* like the other novels of the 1870s, "share[s] many of the qualities of its better-known predecessors" (viii), combining "social purpose" with the elements of sensation fiction (xxiii). Page focuses on Collins's two social concerns in *Man and Wife*—the institution and laws of marriage and the cult of athleticism—noting that Collins uses them to reveal what he perceives as the deficiencies of his culture. Page finds Collins's treatment of marriage and "what it entails for women" both "courageous and modern" (xii, ix), and he accounts for Collins's concern with athleticism by explaining its relation to oppressive gender constructions, anti-intellectualism, and "the philistinism" that permeates "national life" (xvii). Page describes Collins's frank treatment of sexuality in the novel but also notes the association between sexuality and villainy. He sees a tension between "fatalism and free will" in the work (xxi), and feels that it "undergoes a generic transformation" in the third volume (xviii), as a comedy of manners becomes a sensation novel dominated by the "disturbing" Hester Dethridge, a figure who points to "a substratum of the uncanny and the inexplicable beneath the rational surface of a world of evidence, deduction, and proof" (xix).

For her text of *Poor Miss Finch,* Catherine Peters uses the 1875 edition published by Chatto & Windus. She includes a Note on the Text, which briefly describes the holograph manuscript at Princeton, a Select Bibliography, and Explanatory Notes detailing Collins's references and sources. In her Introduction, Peters discusses the significance of blindness, the central theme of *Poor Miss Finch,* and what Collins represents as the advantages of that condition, which liberates his heroine from social constraints: "In her easy familiarity with her darkened world she is an Eve before the Fall, eager for greater experience, but vaguely aware that the adventure of sight has its disadvantages" (xii). Peters outlines the philosophical and scientific discussions of blindness that Collins used as sources for his novel, and she explains its publishing history, its unfavorable critical reception, and its current neglect, which she attributes to its "spider's web of improbabilities" (xvi). Describing *Poor Miss Finch* as a novel that is "persistently undervalued" (vii), Peters praises its use of doubles and its "odd disjunctions," which give the work the "magic resonance" of a myth or folktale (xvii).

Jenny Bourne Taylor bases her text of *The Law and the Lady* on the 1876 one-volume edition published by Chatto & Windus. She includes a detailed Note on the Text, a Select Bibliography, an Appendix reprinting materials relevant to Collins's difficulties with the *Graphic,* and Explanatory Notes on references, sources, and textual variants. In her Introduction, Taylor explains Collins's sources for *The Law and the Lady* (particularly the case of Madeleine Smith), discusses the novel's publishing history, and considers Collins's interest in new modes of publication that "cut . . . across conventional distinctions between high and popular literary forms" (xiii). She complicates the standard critical view of Collins's literary decline, and shows how *The Law and the Lady* "mingles and amplifies . . . the concerns and conventions" of the earlier novels in "bizarre" and "disturbing" ways (ix). As Taylor notes, Collins again considers the relationship between power and interpretation, the workings of the conscious and the unconscious, and the problem of female identity in marriage, yet he "takes greater risks" in addressing these subjects than he had previously (x). Although Collins's novel is "not exactly . . . a feminist detective story," it represents the identities of wives as "tenuous and indeterminate" (xiv), recognizes the sexual desires of women, and parodies traditional conceptions of gender.

In addition to the numerous editions of Collins's novels just described, two annotated editions of his short fiction have appeared in the 1990s—Norman

Page's Oxford edition of *Mad Monkton and Other Stories* and Julian Thompson's *Wilkie Collins: The Complete Shorter Fiction,* published by Carroll & Graf. As his title suggests, Thompson includes all of the twelve stories edited by Page in his own collection, along with thirty-six others. For some stories, the two editors use different titles, depending on the particular versions they reprint. Each provides a Note on the Text and an Introduction. Thompson reproduces the stories as they appeared in the first edition in which they were collected, or (for uncollected stories) in the original periodical source, and he supplies a headnote for each story, detailing its publishing history and offering a brief critical commentary. Page does not describe his editorial principles as clearly as Thompson does, but he explains that, in the case of stories substantially revised for republication, he has chosen to reprint the original versions. Additional information on textual variants and on the sources of texts would be welcome. Page provides information on publishing history and references in his Explanatory Notes, and includes a Select Bibliography and Chronology. His Introduction is much more substantial than that of Thompson, and it describes Collins's short works as "interesting in their own right" yet also important as "small-scale explorations of themes, situations, and characters, and even small-scale experiments in techniques, that recur in his full-length fiction" (viii). As Page notes, Collins uses his short fiction to test the limits of various subgenres, and to play with and "subvert" the conventions of Gothic tales, ghost stories, and detective stories (viii).

The Letters

The forthcoming publication of *The Letters of Wilkie Collins,* in two volumes edited by William M. Clarke and William Baker, marks a turning point in Collins scholarship, as a substantial selection of Collins's correspondence will become available to readers and critics for the first time. Scheduled for release in June 1999, the letters range from 1838 to 1889, and are divided into ten sections. The two volumes contain a total of 591 letters (a number of which are summarized) out of the approximately 2,000 extant, from private collections as well as holdings at numerous institutions, including: the Pierpont Morgan Library; the New York Public Library; the Humanities Research Center, University of Texas at Austin; the Houghton Library, Harvard University; the Department of Special Collections, University of California, Los Angeles; Princeton University Library; the Lilly Library, Indiana University; the Beinecke Rare Book and Manuscript Library, Yale University; University Library, University of Illinois at Urbana; the Huntington Library; the Boston Public Library; the Bodleian Library, Oxford University; Stanford University Libraries; the Folger Shakespeare Library; the British Museum; the Mitchell

Library; Columbia University; University of Iowa Libraries; and the Leeds University Library. The editors provide an overview for each section and a brief headnote for each letter, as well as a Chronology, various Indexes, and a detailed Introduction. Written by a novelist who valued his privacy, these letters will enable critics to develop, if not to redefine, their current understanding of Collins. Despite the absence of letters to Caroline Graves and Martha Rudd, Collins's correspondence will illuminate his political and religious views, his personal and professional relationships, and his working methods.

In the meantime, a number of critics have published articles on Collins's correspondence, bringing to light previously unpublished material. In "Charles Reade, Wilkie Collins, and Marcus Clarke," P. D. Edwards discusses two unpublished letters dating from the 1870s, written by Collins to Clarke, who adapted *The Moonstone* for the Australian stage. Keith Lawrence examines two unpublished letters from the Huntington Library, written by Collins to Edward Smyth Pigott in 1852—letters that, in Lawrence's view, "emphasize Collins's distrust of established churches" while also revealing "his acceptance—at least during his early and middle years—of certain fundamental Christian doctrines, centered in the divinity of Christ" (392–93). William M. Clarke develops a very different image of the novelist in his analysis of Collins's "teasing marital correspondence" with a teenage girl, Nannie Wynne, examining letters Collins wrote between 1885 and 1888, and in which he "fantasized the joys and sorrows of marriage" (31) by addressing Miss Wynne as if she were his wife. Concluding, as did Miss Wynne's mother, that there was probably " 'no harm' " in the correspondence, Clarke suggests that the letters typify Collins's "teasing" yet "open-handed" relations with women: "After a lifetime of deliberately avoiding the marital state, he finally lived it through a twelve-year-old girl and a friendship which her mother found surprising but not disturbing" (35).

Biographical Studies

The surprising elements of Collins's life are the focus of Clarke's important biography, *The Secret Life of Wilkie Collins,* first published in 1988 and revised in 1996. The husband of Collins's great-granddaughter, née Faith Dawson, Clarke draws on the resources of the family, including personal recollections and ephemera, to illuminate Collins's *"menage à trois"* of more than twenty years, and his relationship with Martha Rudd, with whom he adopted the surname "Dawson" and had three illegitimate children.

Less interested in Collins "as a writer" than with "Collins, the man" (xv), Clarke begins with Collins's death and the reading of his will, and then turns back to his family history, childhood and youth, assessing his relationships with his parents and also with Dickens. Clarke devotes the second half of his study to Collins's relationships with Caroline Graves and Martha Rudd, and to the families he established with his two mistresses. Clarke provides a fascinating account of Collins's romantic entanglements and his role as a father. He usefully demystifies the "legends" surrounding Caroline Graves as the original "woman in white" (91), reveals Collins's ability to make his "last, and perhaps best, mystery" (xii) out of his own private life, and details the unfortunate consequences that Collins's refusal to marry had on his children, who "never lost the consciousness of who they were and why they were different" (186). As Clarke astutely shows, Collins's "unorthodox" attitudes towards sex and marriage put his children at a considerable disadvantage, giving them a sense of "fundamental unacceptability" (187), and harming Caroline's daughter Harriet as well: "The tight control exercised by Wilkie Collins over his plots was hardly paralleled in his private life. He meant well. His openness, candour, and strength of will enabled him to choose a lifestyle at variance with the habits of his time. But . . . Martha's children, particularly Marian and Hettie, found it difficult to cope with the circumstances he had produced; and Harriet and *her* children ultimately suffered from the environment he and Caroline had created" (204).

Clarke's fascinating and informative account of Collins's "secret life" supplements the 1991 biography that has quickly overshadowed it—Catherine Peters's *The King of Inventors: A Life of Wilkie Collins.* Insofar as a biography can be considered "definitive," Peters's study falls into that category, demonstrating a thorough and remarkable knowledge of Collins's life and works, drawing on an extensive body of unpublished material from more than a dozen archives, filling in many gaps in earlier biographies, and presenting an insightful portrait of Collins as a man "haunted by a second self" (1) and "determined" on "unconventionality" (3). Writing in a lively and engaging style, Peters recounts Collins's family history and happy childhood, his education and employment at a tea merchant's firm in the Strand, and his turn to a writing career. She provides a detailed and compelling account of Collins's changing relationship with Dickens as well as his "secret connections" (187) with Caroline Graves and Martha Rudd, and the "role" he assumed as Martha's "husband," "Mr. Dawson" (297). Peters considers the contrasts between the plotlines that Collins constructed for his novels and his own behavior, which she uses to address the moral complexities of his position. While acknowledging Collins's insensitivities and his talent for keeping the women in his life "firmly in [their] place" (299), she is careful "to do Wilkie justice" (300) by recognizing the family responsibilities he willingly assumed and by describing his social idealism.

Unlike Clarke, Peters is as interested in Collins the writer as she is in

Collins the man, and discusses his journalism, dramas and fiction in detail, providing important information about the publishing history of his works. Although her readings are not as detailed or as complex as those provided by some critics, they provide a basic introduction for readers unversed in Collins scholarship, and nicely complement her analysis of Collins's life experiences. Peters's biography supersedes those of Nuel Pharr Davis (1956) and Kenneth Robinson (1951, 1974), and is a must for anyone interested in working on Collins or understanding the man behind the literary works.

In addition to these two major biographies, a number of articles on Collins's relationships with particular friends, and on the ties between his life and works, have been published in recent years. These include Sue Lonoff's account of Collins's friendship with Edward Lear, Catherine Peters's analysis of Collins's friend Frances Dickinson, Andrew Gasson's and P.D. Edwards's examinations of Collins and Edmund Yates, and R. C. Terry's discussion of reminiscences about Collins. A second article by Peters, on the "independent women" in Collins's life and writings, is particularly interesting, and addresses the "contradictory impulses" (12) of his fictional portraits of women and his real-life relationships with them. Noting that Collins dramatizes gender transgressions among his heroines yet ultimately returns them to their proper place, Peters raises a crucial question about these "shifts": "Are they an artistic loss of nerve, or a measured assessment of the true options available to women?" (12). As the following sections make clear, Collins's fiction consistently generates such questions, as critics grapple with the contradictions that inform his novels and with Collins's complex aims in writing them.

Critical Studies

Collins and the Police

In the 1970s and early 1980s, Collins was largely valued by literary critics as a "dissident moralist" (Meckier 104) who questioned the Victorian proprieties, explored "forbidden territories" (Hughes 144), and constructed an anarchic yet appealing "counterworld" (Knoepflmacher 353) in answer to stifling social conventions. However, the 1982 publication of *Corrupt Relations*—the work of Richard Barickman, Susan MacDonald, and Myra Stark—suggested the complexities of Collins's position by revealing the "strategies of indirection" (112) with which he voices, and qualifies, his dissent. With the publication of D. A. Miller's *The Novel and the Police* in 1988, the portrait of Collins the rebel was not merely qualified but revoked, and replaced with the image of Collins the social disciplinarian. While many critics continue to argue for the subversiveness of Collins's fiction, they now do so in circumspect ways, put on their guard by Miller's Foucaldian readings of *The Woman in White* and *The Moonstone.*

Drawing on Foucault's *Discipline and Punish,* Miller argues that Collins's novels serve a policing function despite their seeming lawlessness, and uphold rather than subvert Victorian gender and class norms. Thus in *The Woman in White,* Collins appears to violate gender boundaries in his portraits of manly women and womanly men, but ultimately restores his transgressive characters to their proper place, eliciting a homophobic response from his (male) readers by giving them a case of female "nerves," and demonstrating the need for strict gender definitions. In *The Moonstone,* similarly, Collins writes a novel in multiple voices, from a range of class positions, appearing to embrace democratic ideals. Yet the dialogism of the novel proves to be a ruse, in Miller's view, and gives narrative form to a disciplinary power that is diffuse and lacks a definable center.

Miller's readings have generated considerable interest in Collins over the past decade, have placed his best-known works at the center of an important new theory of the novel, and have given Collins criticism a sophisticated and theoretical turn. Miller's revisionary portrait of the novelist provides a useful counterpoint to the work of earlier critics who took Collins "the rebel" at his word. Those critics who pointedly "ally" themselves with Miller—Cannon Schmitt, for example (291)—approach Collins's vaunted rebelliousness with a healthy degree of skepticism, and generally argue that claims for Collins's "subversiveness" are, at best, "partial[ly] valid" (Schmitt 284).

However, Miller's Foucaldian readings of Collins have their own limitations, and fail to acknowledge the complexities of Collins's position, as their gaps or omissions suggest. In discussing *The Moonstone,* for example, Miller mentions neither the Prologue nor the Epilogue, the narrative framework that dramatizes the British theft of the sacred Hindu diamond and its eventual restoration, which critics sometimes cite as evidence of Collins's anti-imperial stance. Miller's claims that *The Moonstone* is monological and that, "in every crucial case, all readers . . . pass *the same judgment*" (53), are among his most tenuous. As those who teach the novel know, *The Moonstone* consistently generates interpretive conflicts about criminality and guilt, and is *designed* to do so, and few would uncritically accept Miller's pat description of the solution to the crime (significantly, one cannot speak of *the* crime, since the diamond is stolen repeatedly in the course of the novel): "The diamond has been stolen not by Rachel or Rosanna (whose suspicious behavior is only intended to screen Franklin Blake, the man they love and think has stolen it), but by Godfrey Ablewhite, who needs ready cash to pay off his debts" (41). Although Miller identifies Godfrey Ablewhite as *the* thief, Colonel Herncastle is guilty of this crime as well, and Collins refers to him as the "Honourable John," the nickname of the East India Company.

Furthermore, the "hero" Franklin Blake, though provided with an excuse for his own theft of the diamond, is not exonerated as fully or neatly as Miller asserts. As Elizabeth Rose Gruner notes in her thoughtful article on family secrets in *The Moonstone,* "we establish that Godfrey is both a philandering debtor and a thief, but we never really establish that Franklin is neither" (138). For all their brilliance, Miller's readings overlook these ambiguities and hence prove reductive, excluding potentially subversive material from consideration and denying the possibility of genuine resistance or critique on Collins's part.

For reasons such as these, Miller's readings have themselves been questioned and reworked by critics, including those most clearly influenced by his work. Thus Cannon Schmitt, in an argument about the construction of English nationality in *The Woman in White,* shares Miller's skepticism about the subversiveness of the novel but complains that Miller's reading "confirms one type of subject and one type of politics endlessly," lacks "historical grounding," and "enforc[es] a regime of the same" (291). Schmitt reminds us that "for Foucault discourse works not merely to ensure the reproduction of the same . . . but to harness subversion in order to produce difference" (291). Citing M. M. Bakhtin rather than Foucault, Lillian Nayder takes issue with Miller's claim that *The Moonstone* is monological, and makes a case for the dialogism of the novel by reading it against Defoe's *Robinson Crusoe.* And Laurie Langbauer applies Miller's interpretive strategies to Miller himself, pairing him with "the heroes in [Collins's] texts" (234) in her critique of "men in feminism," and arguing that Miller—like Walter Hartright—treats women as "a conduit of power between men" (231). Using feminism and "insights about gender" to establish the "dominance" of the Foucaldian over "other male-defined schools of criticism," Miller privileges the homosocial, Langbauer asserts, "preserves" the misogyny that he ironically "ventriloquizes," and excludes women from the critical debate in which he engages with other men, as they "maneuver for institutional power" (231–32).

Whether or not we accept Langbauer's assessment of Miller and his will-to-institutional power, there is little doubt that "criticism inspired by Foucault" has "assert[ed] its . . . dominance" (Langbauer 231) in Collins studies, as in literary studies generally, in recent years. Yet Collins critics continue to read detection in various ways—historical, psychoanalytic, and formalistic—and to represent Collins as a social critic as well as a social disciplinarian, a writer as anxious to expose class and gender inequities as he is to justify them. In "Family Secrets and the Mysteries of *The Moonstone,*" for example, Gruner casts Collins as the detective who investigates and exposes the "criminal underpinnings" of the Victorian family (139), representing domestic privacy as a troubling form of secrecy required of its members, particularly women (133). Reading *The Moonstone* against the Road murder case of 1860, Gruner finds "a scathing commentary on the Victorian family in Collins's selective recapitulation of the details of the case" (128), and argues that Collins uses his novel to indict the "ideology of the domestic sphere" (128), especially "the social pathology of female silence" (133). In Miller's view, Sergeant Cuff is dismissed by Lady Verinder because his services are redundant—because the family already has its own system of surveillance in place. But for Gruner, Cuff fails because "there are family secrets which the police cannot penetrate—secrets not, perhaps, worse than murder or theft, but more difficult to reveal" (140).

In her insightful book, *Domestic Crime in the Victorian Novel,* Anthea Trodd anticipates Gruner's analysis in her own discussion of *Basil,* a novel in which "middle-class domesticity is, indeed, the real crime to be discovered" (103). At the same time, Trodd places Collins in a more defensive posture than Gruner does. In Trodd's view, Collins both expresses and quells his anxieties about class boundaries, the sanctity of the home, and the relation between the public and the private spheres when he represents uneasy encounters between policemen and ladies in his fiction—between Sergeant Cuff and Rachel Verinder in *The Moonstone,* for example—a recurring motif in novels of the 1860s: "At the end of [*The Moonstone*], the sanctity of the home is re-established, the detective beaten gently back to his proven areas of competence, the spectre of [the Road murder case] laid" (29). Trodd's argument is all the more important because the class anxieties that Collins embodies in his policemen are often overlooked by critics who valorize the detective's knowhow—by Beth Kalikoff, for example, who acknowledges that Cuff is "fallible" (125) yet characterizes him as "a worthy police detective," "sharp, psychologically attuned . . . and truly professional without being ruthless" (124), and who compares his techniques to those of Collins himself.

In her reading of family secrets in *The Moonstone,* Gruner briefly notes that Collins not only exposes "the hypocrisy and criminality of the Victorian family" but also "quietly reinscribes [Rachel Verinder] in the system" he investigates through her marriage to Franklin Blake (140). Collins's tendency to both criticize and reinscribe the inequities he represents in his fiction is more fully considered in a number of works on detection in his novels. In *Dead Secrets: Wilkie Collins and the Female Gothic,* perhaps the most significant critical study of Collins to appear in the 1990s, Tamar Heller examines the "detective work" performed in *The Moonstone* and its significant "gaps and silences," arguing that the novel "is Collins's great cover up" and "simultaneously expresses and suppresses the ideological and generic tensions that had animated his fiction from the beginning of his career" (142–43). On the one hand, Heller explains, the novel uses the theft of the moonstone to expose the connections among "types of domination" (143), providing a "radical reading of British culture" (145). On the other hand, it "papers over the traces of its own exposé," and the recurring motif of "buried writing" attests to this erasure (143). Identifying Ezra Jennings as a figure for Collins, Heller sees the detective's decision to take his writings with him to the grave as "a synedoche for the novel's tendency at once to diffuse its social criticism and to draw attention to its own self-censorship" (144). Although the emphasis Heller places on "containment" in *The Moonstone* may itself contain the subversiveness of that novel, her reading is brilliant and her book eloquently written and argued, a must for anyone interested in Collins.

What Heller terms the "ideological doubleness" (163) of Collins's detective fiction is the subject of several critical essays, including "Investigating Social Boundaries," chapter 2 of *Wilkie Collins*. Here, Nayder focuses on Collins's representation of amateur detectives, middle-class women and working-class men who themselves become objects of scrutiny in *Hide and Seek, The Dead Secret* and *The Law and the Lady,* violating overly restrictive class and gender norms in the course of their investigations, but eventually returning to their proper, subordinate places as the novels draw to an end: "each of these works questions the assumption that gender and class distinctions are grounded in nature, while also treating sexual differences and class distinctions as innate and naturally determined" (42). In a related discussion of "Wilkie Collins, Detection, and Deformity," Teresa Mangum considers the implication of female detection for the form of detection fiction—the interrelation between "gender and genre" (285) in *The Law and the Lady*—arguing that Collins's novel investigates gender norms and "exposes the deforming constraints of domesticity" but also "represse[s]" or "manages" the anomalous and aberrant (302); its conclusion both "conforms to gender conventions" and "reiterates the arbitrariness and cruelty of 'norms' " (303). In Mangum's view, the anomaly of the female detective produces "formal aberrations" in the "masculinist plot" of the novel (286), and the deformed figure of Misserimus Dexter, described by Collins as a "half-man," embodies the "de-forming" effects of the female sleuth "bent on straining gender codes" (293, 295), while also diverting attention "from the social and fictional freak of the novel's title—the female detective" (296–97).

The double-edged quality of Collins's detective novels—their tendency to both critique and reinscribe, expose and repress—is a subject that interests psychoanalytic critics as well as feminist ones. As an "investigation of the unconscious," Janice M. Allan explains, *The Moonstone* "is a fundamentally divided text . . . devoted to a study of the always already divided nature of the self" (186), and "explores, without resolving, the oppositions which support Western metaphysics: presence/absence, speech/writing, consciousness/unconsciousness, and through the exploration of inside/outside, the very basis of opposition itself" (192). The internal divisions of the self in *The*

Moonstone are discussed most cogently by Ronald R. Thomas, in his analysis of Blake's "missing dream" (in *Dreams of Authority*), the repressed truth about the theft that must be discovered and reenacted to complete the story. The novel's "real goal . . . is not the recovery of stolen property (which never happens) but the recovery of the thief's memory of his missing dream," a recovery that leads to Collins's *real* revelation: "that the self is a combination of selves" (210), and the mind "fundamentally divided against itself" (216). Godfrey Ablewhite is not the only character to lead a double life—all Collins's figures must, since an "unknown 'second self' " is "inscribed in every human consciousness" (218). In Thomas's view, Collins's achievement lies in his recognition of the "dynamic struggle" between "censorship and desire" (213) and his ability to display "the tactics of censorship" (218)—tactics that are political as well as personal. The theft of the moonstone expresses "personal sexual desire" but also "British colonial domination": "the disappearance of the stone from the novel is a denial of this disagreeable political truth as well as a personal denial" (205). As a psychoanalytic critic, however, Thomas subordinates the political to the personal in his analysis of *The Moonstone*: in generalizing about "every human consciousness" and the " 'dangerous individual' " inscribed within it, and in psychologizing crime, Thomas downplays the historical issues of racial exploitation and imperial injustice insofar as Collins represents them, as he does in using the British raj as a metaphor for the mind—"an empire divided against itself" (205).

While Thomas considers the psychological divisions revealed by Collins in anticipation of psychoanalysis, others consider the generic and epistemological divisions that underlie his detective novels. In *The Secret Theatre of Home,* Jenny Bourne Taylor reveals Collins's "cognitive juggling" in *The Moonstone,* a novel that "conjure[s] with countervailing yet collusive paradigms, paradigms which . . . cannot be brought into interpretative alignment" (176): "Of all Collins's novels, *The Moonstone* is the clearest case of a story 'in a state of continual contradiction with itself,' and that contradiction is crucially shaped by the process of interplay and transformation between the models of the unconscious in the text and those which implicitly frame it" (205). Alexander Welsh considers the rivalry between circumstantial evidence and personal testimony in *The Moonstone*—"Bruff versus Cuff," as he puts it (228)—and suggests that Collins gives precedence to "personal responses to an event" rather than to events themselves in his investigation of experience and truth (200–01). Placing his faith in "personal acquaintance" instead of "chains of circumstance," Collins "criticize[s] and finally override[s] the business of detection": "Paradoxically, his model work is an antidetective novel"(228–29).

Peter Thoms arrives at a similar conclusion about *The Moonstone* in *Detection and Its Designs,* through very different means—by considering detective fiction as "an inherently self-reflexive form" that calls attention to "the constructedness of its narratives" and to the defensive motives behind their construction (1). Describing detection as a form of concealment in *The Moonstone,* an enterprise that "peels away but covers over, scrutinizes but fails to see" (106), Thoms argues that Franklin Blake "seeks to escape investigation by conducting an investigation that advertises his respectable self" and "proclaims his innocence by displacing his guilt onto another": "In the slow construction of the story . . . we find not a statement of truth but an evasion of it. Blake's editing and narration emerge from his desire to control his self-image, a motive that marks his story-making as a repressive act, a blinkered vision, an anxious journey to a solution that will end speculation and effectively conceal the guilt and doubleness of his character" (6–7). For this reason, Thoms suggests, Collins encourages his readers to "counter . . . the interpretive work of the detective" (8). Because Thoms is a self-described "close read[er]" who leaves the discussion of "ideologies of gender, class, race, etc." (12) to other critics (and one wonders to what his dismissive "etc." refers), his analysis of detection has its limitations, and tends to level important social distinctions among Collins's characters, all of whom must "justify [their] behavior" (103) and "conceal a disreputable self" (111) in Thoms's view. Nonetheless, his analysis of *The Moonstone* is original and, at times, persuasive, even as it depoliticizes Collins's story.

In a more rigorously historical study, W. David Shaw examines the conflict between "interpretive scrutiny" and "radical faith" in *The Moonstone,* comparing its rival "theories of criminal detection" to the rival "theories of history" expressed by David Friedrich Strauss and H. T. Buckle, and arguing that "every attempt . . . to combine these two contradictory views of history—the Hegelian and the positivist—precipitates a crisis in representation" in the novel (289). Contrasting Ezra Jennings, Collins's "heroic thinker," to Cuff (the Strauss of the novel) and to Bruff (its Buckle), Shaw valorizes Jennings's "negative capability" (292), the source of his detective abilities and his powers of historical reconstruction. In a related discussion that draws on Shaw's work, Jessica Maynard considers Collins's use of the Madeleine Smith case in *The Law and the Lady* and describes the Scottish verdict of "Not Proven" as a "failure in binary judgement" (187). Discussing the problem of evidence and the use of contingencies in Eustace Macallan's trial—the need for "imaginative identification" as well as "inductive reasoning" to reconstruct the past (194)—Maynard sees Collins's heroine "mov[ing] away from forms of reading that legislate for closure" (193), a movement that marks, in part, her resistance to definitions of her proper sphere. Refusing to end the story "properly," Valeria Macallan suspends revelation, withholding the truth from her husband and from the public, and "retain[ing] the 'not proven' she set out to dispel" (193).

Whereas Welsh, Shaw and Maynard address the epistemological tensions in Collins's detective fiction, others discuss its generic divisions—Heller, for example, who considers "the tension in [*The Moonstone*] between the genres of detection and the Gothic" (149–50), a division that falls along the lines of gender, with Collins appropriating and revising the Gothic fiction of "his female predecessors" in the new "male-dominated detective novel"(143). Martin Priestman discusses the relation between the "pure" form of detective fiction and the dense content of the three-volume Victorian novel which "valuably clogs the . . . 'reading for the plot' " in *The Moonstone* (34), Ronald R. Thomas categorizes *The Moonstone* as a "transitional text between the two subgenres" of sensation and detective fiction ("Wilkie Collins and the Sensation Novel" 502), and Mark M. Hennelly, Jr. argues for "the compatibility of detective and Victorian fiction" (46), which "meet" in that novel and "share many concerns" (26): "Victorian mainstream fiction discovered not a crosscurrent but a tributory in detective fiction," Hennelly argues, since both "embark on journeys of philosophical discovery, explore the dialectic between objective and subjective truth, and examine the psychological dilemma of the divided self," and counterpoint "domestic norms with perverse, often exotic alternatives either from undesirable alien cultures or from undesireable scapegoats within the dominant culture" (26–27).

Although his language ties the "exotic" with the "perverse" and "undesirable," Hennelly argues that Collins associates the moonstone with renewal and illumination, valorizing Hindu beliefs and using them to criticize English materialism and rationality (29–30): "the insular Victorians . . . must integrate what they see as Indian (or lunar) values into their own petrified culture" (42). Such views are contested by those who see detective fiction as the literary arm of the British Raj, who connect the genre with British hegemony and the enterprise of empire-building, and who question the status of *The Moonstone* as an "anti-imperial text" (Roy 657). For example, Ashish Roy describes "the detective program" as one that supports "the imperial imagination," characterizing detective tales as "instruments of reason, reading mystery as logical justification for surveillance of the other." "By its special, detective programming of conventional ruptures like inside/outside, domestic/alien, sacred/profane, or familiar/uncanny in the intersection of its Indian and English plots," Ashish writes,"*The Moonstone* produces a *mythos* entirely consonant with arguments for empire" (657).

Roy's argument is anticipated by Thomas, who considers the connections among detective fiction, the developing "science" of criminal anthropology, and the "emerging political crisis" over "imperial conquest" (235) in "Minding the Body Politic." Comparing Collins's *The Moonstone* and Doyle's *The Sign of Four,* Thomas argues that "the criminal psychology and the imperial politics implied in these texts collaborate with the emerging scientific theories of criminal physiology . . . to contain and sublimate contemporary political events for which there seemed to be no evident justification'' (235). Thus Collins acknowledges the crimes committed in the name of empire in *The Moonstone* only to obscure them, in part by attributing Blake's theft of the diamond to the ''disorienting influence'' of opium, a drug that profitted the British but that Collins uses to ''represent the subversive and vengeful forces from the colonies that threatened to penetrate the mind of the mother country and its body politic as well'' (237). Approaching *The Moonstone* from a different angle than he does in *Dreams of Authority,* Thomas now suggests the *primacy* of the political in the novel. Reading it in the context of the Indian Mutiny (1857), he identifies Herncastle's theft of the diamond as the ''primal'' or ''originary'' crime of ''colonial conquest'' that is displaced and obscured by Collins's turn to ''sexual allegory,'' ''romantic intrigue,'' and ''physiological determinants'' of behavior (238–41).

Collins, the Gothic, and Sensation Fiction

In the 1980s and 1990s, as in the 1860s, critical attention has focused on Collins's status as a sensation novelist and on his ties to the literary tradition that haunts sensation fiction: the Gothic. Heller devotes her excellent book on Collins to his relation to ''the female Gothic,'' a subversive tradition that dramatizes the victimization of women and the abuses of patriarchy, and that explores the possibilities of feminine subversion. As Heller demonstrates, Collins both associates himself with the female Gothic, which provides him with ''a way of being a social critic'' (8), and distances himself from it in order to establish his professionalism as a male writer. Thus his fiction repeatedly ''evades[s] the full implications of a feminist critique,'' as acts of ''feminine transgression'' become ''the dead secrets of the text'': ''Collins' novels, in fact, are often paradoxically Gothic plots that end with the containment of the Gothic as the site of subversion and literary marginality'' (8).

Although her argument lacks the range and depth of Heller's, Alison Milbank makes some of the same points about Collins's relation to the Gothic in *Daughters of the House,* published in the same year as *Dead Secrets.* Casting doubt on feminist readings of Collins, Milbank argues that he produces variations on ''the female Gothic'' in *The Woman in White* and *The Moonstone,* yet abandons or discredits the plot of female escape in both works. Milbank distinguishes Collins's ''female Gothic'' from what she considers his sensation fiction—novels such as *No Name* and *Armadale,* which more closely approximate ''the male Gothic'' in her view. Although these novels contain aggressive female figures who ''invade'' homes (rather than attempting to escape from them, as the heroines of ''the female Gothic'' do), Collins's ''errant women act only to reinforce Victorian sexual ideology''

(14). Not only do they "collapse into passive conformity" by the novels' end; they serve Collins's "erotic aims" (14), as objects that "provide male erotic pleasure" (26). "The pleasures of a Collins 'sensation' novel are therefore Sadean in nature" (15), Milbank claims.

A number of articles of varying quality discuss Collins's use of Gothic conventions, although none achieve the complexity of Heller's analysis. In an article that covers some of the same ground as *Dead Secrets*, Cyndy Hendershot considers Collins's use of "Gothic doubling" and his "negative appropriation" of the Gothic heroine in *The Woman in White*, citing the novel's "masculinization" of Marian Halcombe (who "acts as a phallic woman" and participates in "the homosocial economy"), the violation and co-option of her "discourse" by Hartright and Fosco, and the eventual "domestication" of her character (127, 129). Hendershot also traces the Victorian detective figure back to the heroine of Gothic tradition, who explores her surroundings in search of truth. Stephen Bernstein considers the Gothic setting of Blackwater Park in *The Woman in White*, through which Collins "inscribe[s] a highly concentrated, at times iconically allegorical, narrative into the very surroundings in which his characters function" (291). With its sinister opacity, Blackwater Park suggests the value of "transparency," "visibility," and the panoptical for Collins as well as "the desire for a deepened understanding of individual subjectivity" (293–94). Distinguishing between Collins's realistic novels and his visionary short fiction, which she feels has not received adequate critical attention, I. I. Burova examines Collins's use of the supernatural in "Mad Monkton," revealing his debt to the Gothic and to Shakespearean tragedy. By contrast, Nick Rance argues that Collins domesticates the Gothic in his early short story, "A Terribly Strange Bed," associating terror with objects that are homely and British, despite the story's Parisian setting, and prefiguring his sensation fiction of the 1860s, in which living people are "more disturbing than . . . mere ghost[s]" (5).

As Christopher Kent notes in his essay on "Probability, Reality and Sensation in the Novels of Wilkie Collins," we should resist the temptation "to dismiss the sensation novel as unreal" (259). Examining Collins's concern with the *nature* of reality, Kent argues that Collins's sensation novels represent reality as a subjective phenomenon, as a product of plotting, and as "a construct undergoing significant change" in his day, "a change which entailed a redefinition of the boundaries of probability and possibility" (260) in response to the science of statistics, theories of determinism, accounts of spiritual phenomena, and the turn to the sensational in the press. Although Collins's sensation fiction "affronted [everyday] reality" with its focus "on the aberrant," we should remember that "Victorian novelists and their critics assumed that the novels of their day would be read by posterity as social history" (259).

Indeed, the realistic and historical concerns of Collins's sensation novels—their origins in contemporary debates over marriage law reform and human psychology, among other topical issues, and their mode of addressing mid-Victorian anxieties about class and gender—largely preoccupy those who have written on the subject in recent years. In "Wilkie Collins and the Origins of the Sensation Novel," for example, John Sutherland associates the "innovations" of *The Woman in White* and its "evidentiary technique" with the concerns manifested in the Police Act of 1856 and the Matrimonial Causes Act of 1857, and with the issues raised by the 1856 trial of the "Rugeley poisoner," William Palmer, particularly "the status of circumstantial evidence" (256). In a complex and original book devoted to Collins's use of nineteenth-century theories of psychology, *In the Secret Theatre of Home,* Jenny Bourne Taylor situates Collins's sensation fiction in a broader historical context, and considers the ways in which his novels assimilate, resist, and transform "a contradictory set of contemporary discourses . . . about consciousness and identity, about the social formation of the self, about the workings of the unconscious and the interlinking of the mind and the body, about the problematic boundaries between sanity and madness" (2). As Taylor explains, Collins exploits "the narrative possibilities of contemporary theories," challenges and reaffirms their "ideological meanings" (26), and both undermines and affirms "a gendered, middle-class subjectivity" (26) in his novels, as his characters struggle for narrative control. She accounts for the decline in Collins's late fiction, in part, by describing how the rival theories on which Collins draws narrowed down to one "dominant discursive model" in the 1870s and 1880s—that of "degeneration" (211).

Taylor outlines the theories of consciousness and social identity that "shape the cognitive parameters of Collins's fiction" and that he "appropriated and transformed as narrative strategies" (19)—most notably, the concept of the "moral management" of insanity. She adds complexity to her analysis of the novels by focusing on the "points of dissonance" within this paradigm, which allow for resistance to "dominant meanings" (30). Her conception of discipline and management is thus more nuanced than D. A. Miller's in *The Novel and the Police,* and Taylor herself explains that she wants to avoid the "monolithic implications" of Foucaldian-inspired analysis (30). Her readings of Collins focus on the "dissonances" that characterize nineteenth-century theories of the mind as well as Collins's own novels: on the "ideological incoherence" of *Basil* (92), a novel that "merges notions of constructed and inherited identities" (93); and on the unstable and conflicting definitions of madness and self-control for women in *The Woman in White,* which uses the concept of moral management as a framework yet "continually transform[s]" its meaning (130). In *No Name,* Taylor argues, the narrative voice "undercuts the sources of its own ideological coherence," and reveals "the impossibility of representing a coherent female subjectivity" (134) at the same time that it brings various models of subjectivity to bear on the heroine. In Taylor's view, Collins takes the sensation novel to its limits in *Armadale,* a work in which "there are no stable oppositions between self and other, reality and imposture . . . nothing but displacement" in plots that hinge on "a name without an identity" (152–53).

Taylor's response to *The Moonstone* and its solution to the diamond's theft foregrounds ambiguity and "the shifting and provisional nature of evidence" (202), and is considerably less pat than Miller's Foucaldian reading or Thomas's psychoanalytic one (in *Dreams of Authority*): "the traces of the past are ambiguous and shifting, there is no focal point from which they can be surveyed, and the physiological experiment that is interpreted as proof is essentially a piece of theatre projected out of a fictional hypothesis which claims the authority of science—an opium-induced re-enactment of an opium-induced action, set up by an opium-dependent doctor" (175). Whereas Heller sees the buried writing in *The Moonstone* as a sign of Collins's own "containment" of subversive material, Taylor argues that the marginal texts within the novel "become central by *remaining* peripheral": "the more embedded and qualified a testimony, the stronger its significance becomes" (180), as Collins uses his narrative structure to illustrate the paradox of the unconscious, its "simultaneous marginality and centrality" (181). Yet the novel presents "competing models of the unconscious" (202), and it also suggests that "marginality is actively constructed"—"rooted in explicit social hierarchies" and "more than simply an analogue of the unconscious mind" (189).

In discussing the interpretive conflicts and the "countervailing . . . paradigms" (176) of Collins's sensation fiction, Taylor presents a portrait of a " 'modern' (even post-modern)" Collins, a sensation novelist who values "play, doubling, and duplicity," who constructs "dialogic and self-reflexive" narratives, and who "breaks down stable boundaries between wildness and domesticity, self and other, masculinity and femininity, 'black' and 'white' " (1). More often than not, however, critics interested in the contradictions of Collins's sensation fiction identify them as uniquely Victorian, the product of class and gender instabilities specific to the 1850s and 1860s.

For example, Jonathan Loesberg sees the contradictions of Collins's sensation fiction as a response to mid-Victorian debates over political reform and class relations in his examination of the "politically charged" (116) structure of *The Woman in White,* "The Ideology of Narrative Form in Sensation Fiction." Loesberg argues that sensation fiction's preoccupation with "identity and its loss"—"a necessary aspect of the suspense that was the aim of sensation narrative"—was shaped by anxieties about "the merging of the classes" often expressed "in the debate over social and parliamentary reform in the late 1850s and 1860s" (117). "Sensation novels evoke their most typical moments of sensation response from images of a loss of class identity" (117), Loesberg notes, yet they structure these images of loss in "narrative[s] of inevitable sequence" (29): "The contradiction in the structure of sensation fiction, then, is that it bases itself upon an element, the image of a loss or shift of class identity, that its thematic explanations of its plot structure, its appeals to various forms of inevitable sequence, must turn around and class as accidental" (130). With a structure at odds with its central themes, *The Woman in White* is characterized by "slippages and dissociations" (134) and expresses "a willed nonseriousness," an attitude that reveals "an ambivalence about the ways Victorians constructed class conflict" (133).

Like Loesberg, Ronald R. Thomas connects Collins's sensation fiction to the class issues of the 1860s in "Wilkie Collins and the Sensation Novel." In Thomas's view, sensation fiction "worked directly on class anxiety and instability" with plots that expose the commercial basis of personal identities and family relations—"acts of commerce, forms of trade, commodities to be bought and sold" (482). While seeming to expose sin and punish excessive class ambition, sensation fiction subverts "conventional values" by revealing "the essential commercialization of the family and of the individual subjects involved in its most intimate transactions" (482). Rather than seeking to preserve traditional class boundaries, Collins's sensation novels show that those boundaries have already been "reconfigured . . . through economic means" (483), and social authority invested "in a new class of 'professionals' " (485), members of a "new aristocracy" (488). Thus in *The Woman in White*, Collins pits his middle-class hero, Walter Hartright, against "villainous aristocratic poseurs" (487), staging his legal and economic triumph over them. In *The Dead Secret*, similarly, Collins identifies lawyers and physicians as members of the "new ruling class," and invests legal and medical discourse with a social authority that "supersede[s] . . . biological facts" (490–91). Aptly, *The Woman in White* "emulates a legal document," while *Basil* "takes the form of a medical file" (497).

Although Thomas speaks of the subversiveness of sensation fiction, he points out that the novels merely reconfigure patriarchy as professionalism, and that Collins's lawyers and physicians "assume the very privilege and power they seem to condemn" (499). As the fate of the Vanstone sisters in *No Name* suggests, "identity . . . is literally composed and executed by . . . professional figures and is subject to their monitoring and control" (492). In Collins's sensation fiction, Thomas goes on to explain, professional authority is "gender[ed]" and "imposed upon female subjects" by men (495). Understood as a response to marriage law reform as well as class redefinition, Collins's sensation novels send a "double message." They can be seen "as part of a growing protest surrounding the larger issue of female political empowerment" but also "as part of a rearguard defense . . . against that protest" (495).

Nayder develops this point in discussing the ties between Collins's sensation fiction and marriage law reform, in a chapter on "Wives and Property in *The Woman in White, No Name,* and *Man and Wife.*" Noting that Collins's sensation novels "represent the private sphere as a place of Gothic strife and suffering" and "dramatize marital strife and domestic horror within the middle-class Victorian home," Nayder describes these works as a response to debates over the laws governing marriage and divorce in England in the 1850s and 1860s, a period during which Collins's readers "became increasingly aware that domestic strife was endemic to their society, and that the victimization of wives by their husbands was a legally sanctioned phenomenon" (72). In Nayder's view, Collins responds to these debates "in a characteristically mixed way" (74). Disappointed by the defeat of the married women's property bill, Collins dramatizes the losses that his heroines endure "when they become wives legally subject to victimization"; alarmed by the passage of the Divorce Act, he expresses "cultural anxieties about the sexual and economic autonomy granted to women": "Indicting the laws governing marriage, Collins demonstrates that women lose their property rights and their legitimacy when they marry, and undergo a type of 'civic death.' But he also suggests that coverture may be a necessary evil, a means of providing for innately dependent women and counteracting the dangers of female emancipation" (74).

In more general terms, Lyn Pykett considers the mixed messages conveyed by Collins's sensation novels in "Wilkie Collins: Questions of Identity," a chapter from *The Sensation Novel,* a volume in a series on "Writers and their Work." As Pykett explains, Collins provides "a critique of Victorian social and moral orthodoxies" in his sensation fiction, and, "articulate[s], explore[s] and interrogate[s] the social and psychological processes by which those orthodoxies were constructed and maintained" (15). Blurring gender boundaries, his novels are "potentially very subversive" but "this subversive potential is (on the whole) contained" (20–21). Focusing on the novels of the 1860s, Pykett discusses Collins's interest in the instability and construction of identity and the family, and his scrutiny and reinscription of social norms, particularly those pertaining to gender and class. Although her general points are familiar ones, her particular readings are often astute, and her chapter provides a thoughtful introduction to Collins's sensation novels and the central issues that they address.

As Melynda Huskey argues in an interesting article on "Embodying the Sensation Heroine" in *No Name,* the blurred gender boundaries to which Pykett refers are literally inscribed on the self-contradictory body of the transgressive heroine, as is the plot of her story: "The sensation heroine's body is like another sensation novel, plotted and prepared with the clues whose importance will be revealed as we connect them rightly to each other and their surrounding novel'' (8). Extending Loesberg's argument that ''images of a loss of class identity'' produce the sensational effect, Huskey demonstrates that the loss of gender identity is equally significant—that ''the sensation novel (and its reader) gets its thrills from the spectacle of a woman on the verge of an irretrievable fall'' (5). Noting that sensation fiction can be ''as punitive and as strict as the strictest parlor moralist could wish'' (6), Huskey points to both the subversive and the conservative strains of Collins's sensation fiction. Collins obscures the line ''between good and wicked women'' (6) and encourages us to sympathize with his criminal heroine, who continually redefines herself and uses her femininity to her own ends. But Collins also ''fixes her, finally, in a single spot'' (10), defining her identity—or lack thereof—according to the law of coverture, and reassuring us that ''the home can be controlled, the family . . . rehabilitated'' (9). ''The sensation heroine survives by defying circumstance, by reserving the right of self-definition. The logic of the sensation novel, however, requires either submission or death from its heroines eventually; they cannot be permitted to resist forever'' (12).

Collins's representation of the sensationalized female body, and the interrelation of gender and class identities in his sensation fiction, are, in part, the subjects of Ann Cvetkovich's ''Ghostlier Determinations: The Economy of Sensation and *The Woman in White*,'' a chapter in *Mixed Feelings.* In this theoretically sophisticated essay, Cvetkovich examines the way in which the ''sensational qualities'' of the novel ''consolidat[e] . . . male power'' while seeming to feminize men (72–73). Cvetkovich argues that Collins's ''sensationalized representations of women,'' which elicit ''nervous reactions'' in Walter Hartright, obscure the material grounds of his class mobility and allow his ''accession to power to be represented as though it were the product of chance occurrences, uncanny representations, and fated events'' (74). In Cvetkovich's view, Collins ''rout[es] Walter's desire and rise to power through the sensational'' (76) not only to obscure the hero's class ambition but also to produce an excess of sensation that seems to emanate from the female body, obscuring the social source of women's value in Collins's own ''version of commodity fetishism'' (90). Much as ''objects become cathected'' in the culture of capitalism, their value misperceived as intrinsic, so Laura Fairlie is endowed with a sensationalized power that mystifies the social determinants of her value and of Walter's desire for her: ''Walter's sensational attraction to Laura Fairlie depends on both the mystification of how, as a marriageable woman, she represents his means to social success, and the mystification of her body as significant in itself rather than as the marker of social relations'' (95). Read in the context of Victorian capitalism, and in relation to fears of dehumanization and ''deaden[ing] affect,'' Collins's sensation novel offers the ''affective experience'' that the reader desires to safeguard his or her ''individual subjectivity'' (94).

Like Cvetkovich, Gloria-Jean Masciarotte compares the "sensationalist logic" of *The Woman in White* to the logic of "the fetish" (95), and explains the excesses of sensationalism, its " 'mechanical' quality" (91), and the emotional "dysfunction" it produces by examining its relation to capitalism, although she interprets this relation differently than Cvetkovich does. With its fragmentary effects and its artificial narrative devices, Collins's sensation novel is "self-interrogating" (112), and "aestheticiz[es]" its own "market production," incorporating "the reader's pleasure into the machinery" (94). In an argument that draws on both Marxist and Freudian analysis, Masciarotte turns to Anne Catherick and "the effect of her determinate absence of story on the structure of the novel" (113). Masciarotte sees the woman in white as an example of "failed production" (116) on the "historical assembly line" (102) that constitutes the patriarchal family—as "a product that refers back to no existing or legally identifiable relation" (114)—and argues that Collins uses her to question the "existing relations of social production," to disrupt "phallic continuity," and to "suggest alternative narrative possibilities around marriage and reproductive histories of differently marked women" (114, 116). The novel concludes with a family tableau that casts the hero, Walter Hartright, as "the outsider," and that defines Laura as "the son's mother, the mother's daughter, the sister's wife, and . . . the sister's sibling" rather than "the man's wife" (122). "Sensationalist family romance," Masciarotte concludes, "refuses to limit itself to the necessary exogamy of patriarchal law" (120) and, in its critique of individualism, "cuts our dutiful hero out of . . . his own *bildungsroman*" (121).

Although she reads the ending of *The Woman in White* very differently than Masciarotte does, Leila Silvana May develops the idea that Collins's sensation novel defies "the necessary exogamy of patriarchal law" and imagines an endogamous union between Marian and Laura in her own analysis of its "sensational sisters." Describing *The Woman in White* as "a treatise on sisterhood" (82), May argues that Collins exploits the "transgressive possibilities" of sisterly love (83), which threatens to undermine the traditional family structure and "establish an autonomous and subversive domain of sororal justice which is able to function both over and above . . . the legitimate structures of authority" (84). While the sisterhood of Anne Catherick and Laura Fairlie undermines class distinctions, the eroticized sororal love between Laura and Marian provides an edenic alternative to patriarchy. Treated as a brother, Walter Hartright is incorporated into their "world of sibling love" (95), in a "family" characterized by "slippage among [its] roles" (96) and the potential for "monstrous sex" among its members (99). Yet Collins ultimately eases the anxieties this family generates by means of the "legitimate heterosexual act" that produces an heir and by domesticating Marian, who becomes "an angel in the house" (100). Idealized among Victorians for its purity and fidelity while also generating fears about "female agency and desire," sisterly passion is treated with "exaggerated" ambivalence in sensation fiction, which "magnifies" the transgressions it represents as well as "the conventionality of its solution" (82–83).

As in discussions of his detective novels, arguments about Collins's sensation fiction are often divided on the question of its subversiveness. While critics such as Pykett and May identify a pattern of social critique and containment in Collins's sensation fiction, others make a stronger case for its radical aims—among them, Nicholas Rance and Thomas Boyle. In *Wilkie Collins and Other Sensation Novelists,* Rance distinguishes between the "conservative sensationalism" of Mrs. Henry Wood and the "radical sensationalism" of Collins and Mary Elizabeth Braddon (1), which reveals "gaps," "contradictions," and "silences" in the Victorian "moral code" (4, 14), and he reads *The Woman in White* and *No Name* against the works of Samuel Smiles, including Smiles's 1857 biography of George Stephenson, entitled *No Name.* Noting that Walter Hartright's encounter with the woman in white challenges his "premises of judgement"—specifically, the moral piety that the good prosper (2)—Rance argues that Collins's sensation fiction deliberately exposes the "contradictions between 'consciously held ideology and emergent experience' " (13) (Rance here uses Raymond Williams's phrase), and dramatizes the inadequacy of "self-help" as well as its sexual double standard of moral goodness. In a chapter on the late fiction that also considers the relationship between *The Moonstone* and *The Mystery of Edwin Drood,* Rance attributes Collins's literary decline to "the changed social climate" of the 1870s, a period of political complacency that led Collins to "a dismayed acceptance of the durability of the *status quo*" (140) and to an interest in "limited" and "oddly random" social missions (150, 153). "The best fiction of Collins," Rance asserts, derives from the 1860s, a decade in which political change seemed "irresistible" (156). Like Rance, Thomas Boyle considers the "subversive implications of the Sensation novel" in *Black Swine in the Sewers of Hampstead* (142). Yet his reading of *Armadale* as "Collins's most ambitiously subversive work" (159)—a "proto-modernist experiment" that "break[s] out . . . of the confines of the novel form" (159–60)—is considerably less persuasive than the readings provided by Rance because it is largely based on a selective close reading of the novel, and fails to acknowledge the complexities and the potential conservatism of Collins's position.

Collins and Gender

Whether critical assessments of Collins focus on his relation to the Gothic tradition, his anxieties about class relations, or his treatment of detection, most consider the ways in which he constructs gender identities and represents gender relations. However, a number of studies focus specifically on Collins and gender, and these, too, are divided on the question of his social aims and views. Some critics follow the lead of Dorothy Sayers, who in 1944 found Collins " 'genuinely feminist in his treatment of women' " (qtd. in O'Neill 3), while others cast him as a patriarch of sorts. The most convincing arguments are often those that acknowledge Collins's inconsistencies—his ambivalent treatment of gender norms and those who violate them—and that discuss the interpretive conflicts to which his representations of gender give rise.

Those critics who see Collins as a radical social critic generally foreground his recognition of gender identities as social constructions—"inadequate categorisations" (O'Neill 64) that serve the ends of an inequitable patriarchal system. In an essay that he concedes is "politically generous" in its "reading of the cultural work performed by [Collins's] sensation novels" (168) (and in which he mistakenly claims that Lydia Gwilt, pardoned by the Home Secretary, was acquitted of murder), Donald E. Hall foregrounds the "gender fluidity" (168) of the characters in such novels as *The Woman in White* and *Armadale*. With their "emphasis on role-playing as the basis for gender identity" (168), and their recognition that "beliefs, roles, and perceptions are . . . historically specific" (174), Collins's works expose the "social construction of masculinity and femininity" (160) and "the foolishness of those individuals who accept such roles as 'reality' " (168). While she notes the "conflicts between radicalism and orthodoxy" (125–26) in his treatment of gender norms, Virginia B. Morris argues that Collins ignores "biological explanations for women's violent behavior" (109) in his sympathetic portraits of female criminals, and instead attributes their violence to their experience of abuse and dependence "in male-dominated Victorian society" (105).

In *Wilkie Collins: Women, Property and Propriety,* a book that ranges widely among Collins's novels, Philip O'Neill considers how Collins formulates the relation between gender stereotypes and "the interests of property." He argues that Collins questions Victorian gender norms by revealing propriety to be "an ideology with a material basis" and by representing reality itself as "a social construction" that "serves and protects the rights of property" (7–8). In *The Fallen Leaves,* the novel that "comes nearest to justifying [a] 'feminist' label" in O'Neill's view, Collins imagines "an alternative sexual code" and reveals "the masculine parameters of culture, of a cultural regime which presents itself as the natural order and conceals its own specific historical formation" (55). In *The Evil Genius,* however, Collins "valorize[s]" masculinity, and his fiction sometimes attributes gender inequities to "the functionings of chance" rather than to "human agency" (213–14). Thus while Collins "shows how notions of gender are constructed in society" (188), "goes some way towards granting women a sense of their own subjectivity and lets them be free subjects rather than the objects of males" (202), "he is not a feminist," O'Neill explains (187): "Collins . . . is more consistent in his social and political analysis than has generally been recognised; but to see this is not to impose upon him, with retrospective hindsight, a neat form of modern political attitude or an unambivalently urged social programme'' (213).

But while O'Neill speaks of Collins's ambivalence, he doesn't seem particularly interested in discussing the contradictions in Collins's work, and often overlooks the ways in which Collins naturalizes social constructions and reinscribes sexual stereotypes in his fiction. In his analysis of *Basil,* for example, O'Neill acts as an apologist for Collins, and explains away the hero's diatribe against ''unnatural'' women who adopt ''bastard-masculine'' opinions by attributing Basil's remarks to Collins's concern with ''appearance and reality,'' and by providing the following gloss: ''Each sex has valuable properties, characteristics which it would be a loss to abandon and nothing will change if women simply act as men'' (84).

In offering this gloss, O'Neill invokes a model of sexual difference that traces gender identity back to its ''natural,'' bodily source—the model that C. S. Wiesenthal and D. A. Miller see operating in Collins's fiction, to an ideologically conservative end. In an essay on *Heart and Science,* ''From Charcot to Plato,'' Wiesenthal discusses Collins's ''conceptual construction of hysteria'' (258) as an affliction of the female brain, heart, and womb—his portrait of women as ''victims of their own ungovernable passions'' (260) and of ''the migratory womb'' (261) that suffocates them and renders them ''smothering mothers'' (265). As Wiesenthal points out, the image of the migratory womb represents the threat of female adultery as well as the displacement of the mother figure, whose absence forces Collins's heroine to relinquish ''matriarchal values'' and ''a distinctly female past,'' and to look to her husband to ''validate'' her identity (264–65).

In his analysis of *The Woman in White,* Miller is less concerned with the malady of hysteria than he is with female ''nerves,'' perceived as a source of contagion among Collins's characters and readers. According to Miller, Collins's sensation novel not only ''address[es] itself primarily to the sympathetic nervous system'' (146); it induces ''panic'' in readers by staging the ''contagion'' of the male body with female ''nervousness''—a contagion represented by adapting the familiar (and homophobic) Victorian formulation of the homosexual: '' 'a woman's breath caught in a man's body' '' (154). Resisting this contagion, the ''antifeminist'' (168) novel abandons its ''grotesque aberrations'' (165), reinstates the ''phallocentric system of sexual difference'' (178), and reclaims the ''integrity'' of the male body (181) by '' 'shutting . . . up' '' the feminine both within and outside male bodies (including such institutional ''bodies'' as marriage and the madhouse [155–56]). Nonetheless, the norms that Collins reinstates may come to appear monstrous to us because of the drastic means through which they are themselves '' 'engendered' in the course of the plot'' (166)—through Hartright's subjection to attack by the Indians of Honduras and through the cretinization of Laura Fairlie.

In an insightful article on the "fashioning" of gender in *The Woman in White,* "The Tell-Tale Surface," Elana Gomel and Stephen Weninger respond to Miller's reading by arguing that "Collins's novel is as much about the clothes as about the body" (29). In their view, Collins's "language of fashion . . . ultimately problematizes both Miller's conclusions and the quasi-biological model of corporeal gender that underwrites it" (29–30). To Gomel and Weninger, the clothes of Collins's characters rather than their bodies serve as "the primary site for the construction of social sexual identity," and thus the language of fashion works at "cross purposes" with "the epistemological drive to discover and unveil" (30). "Clothes function in *The Woman in White* as a locus for the instabilities and tensions that the novel explores: the frightening slippage of all identity, most especially the precariousness of gender and class. It becomes a tool for exploring the issues of nature and artifice, of the biological body and the (im)possibility of its social reading" (30). In a novel that represents the body as a matter of surface rather than depth, and in which "gender is something one shops for" (33), transvestism becomes a sign of "class privilege" and power (43). At the same time, Collins's fashioning of gender calls into question the Freudian model of women as castrated men. Envisioning masculinity as "a masquerade . . . never properly guaranteed by what is 'hidden from view,' " Collins suggests that castration is "a general condition of human corporeality" while also noting that men transform "corporeal instability" into a mode of power by controlling "their own and women's fashioning" (48).

For D. A. Miller, the character of Marian Halcombe embodies the lesbian or "man-in-the-woman," a figure eventually "convert[ed] . . . into the castrated, heterosexualized 'good angel' " (176) of the household; for Gomel and Weninger, she is a figure who understands that "the privileges of a man are the privileges of choosing a disguise" and who consciously manipulates her appearance before being forced back into a corset and crinoline by "the exigencies of the Victorian plot" (49). By contrast, Susan Balée, in "Wilkie Collins and Surplus Women," sees Marian as "a new ideal of woman," a "strong-minded" spinster used by Collins to devalue "the angel in the house" (199). Reading *The Woman in White* as a product of the 1850s—a response to the "social dilemma" posed by surplus women destined to remain single—Balée defines herself against Miller and argues that the novel subverts sexual stereotypes "to promote new icons": "*The Woman in White* actively works to dismantle old myths of sexuality in order to construct new ones that would be of greater use to an economically-altered society" (201–02). In Balée's view, Collins allies his readers with "the masculine woman and the sensitive man" (209), and portrays Laura Fairlie as "a pathetic character" whose inability to support herself reveals the "unfeasibility" of the angelic role for women who must earn a living (204).

Identifying Collins as a writer dedicated to "social reform" (210), Balée provides a refreshing counterpoint to Miller. Yet she, too, tells only part of the story, as her account of the novel's conclusion reveals: "At the novel's close, Marian also seems to be the extra or 'surplus' woman in the household with Walter and Laura and their child, because she is not a member of this nuclear cluster. Collins, however, skews this perception of Marian's redundancy in the family by having Marian—not Laura—holding the baby" (209). If Marian is meant to embody a new icon of womanhood, however, why does Collins represent her as a surrogate mother rather than a wage earner? Balée accounts for the conservatism of Collins's resolution by suggesting that he "did not want to alienate readers," and she reminds us that "the subversiveness is still there," despite "the happy ending" (210). Yet her argument is not as persuasive as it might be if she considered the conservative strains in Collins's own thinking rather than simply holding the audience responsible for them.

Kathleen O'Fallon's representation of *The Law and the Lady* as a feminist novel is even less convincing, and is based, in part, on a misreading of the text. O'Fallon begins by noting "Collins' uneasiness with his own challenges to traditional gender identification" in his fiction, and the mixture of fascination and repulsion he feels for "his strong women" (231). Yet she goes on to characterize *The Law and the Lady* as an exception to the general rule: "if one wants to claim that Collins is a feminist writer, a large part of that claim must rest on this novel" (232). O'Fallon argues that, in Valeria Macallan, Collins "has finally given his readers a heroine who acts effectively without the supervision of a man" (232). However, in claiming that Valeria refuses "to surrender her own identity and take on her husband's" (234), O'Fallon misreads the heroine's action in the opening chapter; after her marriage to Eustace, Valeria mistakenly signs her *married* name in the register, not her birth name, as O'Fallon erroneously asserts (234). As O'Fallon suggests, Valeria's mistake "adumbrates [her] actions throughout the novel" (234)—yet these actions and their implications differ significantly from those described by O'Fallon. In his opening scene, Collins suggests that Valeria is *all-too-willing* to surrender her identity, and he himself compromises the independence of his female detective by contrasting her transgressive means of detecting crime with her traditional reasons for undertaking detective work—to clear her husband's name and make possible their reunion. In discussing Collins's "fallen women," George Watt points out that Collins "vindicat[es]" his transgressive female figures (98) yet does so "on society's terms" (107)—by "uniting them to very respectable husbands" (98). Patricia Frick makes the same point in contrasting the "frankness, boldness, and compassion'' with which Collins represents "female deviants" with his habit of disempowering them in marriage ("Fallen Angels" 343). Although O'Fallon notes that Valeria dedicates herself to "saving [her] marriage" (235), she valorizes this goal without considering its implications for the presumably autonomous heroine. And while she refers to the pregnancy that eventually sidelines the female detective, O'Fallon does not consider what this physiological change in the heroine suggests about either Collins's conception of womanhood or the gender politics of his novel.

Leonora Ledwon provides a more nuanced and persuasive reading of Collins's portrait of womanhood in "Veiled Women, the Law of Coverture, and Wilkie Collins's *The Woman in White*." Like Susan Balée's essay, Ledwon's is historically grounded, and sees Collins responding to problems faced by Englishwomen in the 1850s and 1860s. But unlike Balée, Ledwon takes account of the complexities of Collins's position, arguing that his novel "begins as a radical critique of women's loss of identity under coverture" yet "finally falls back into complacency, reinforcing the ideological assumptions that law should work differently for men than for women" (1). Drawing on Lacanian theory as well as Victorian legal history, Ledwon shows how Collins uses coverture as the "central paradigm" in his novel—the means of exploring the "loss of feminine identity" (1)—and she examines the three "triads" through which Collins criticizes but ultimately justifies the workings of coverture: Percival, Laura, and Anne; Fosco, the Countess, and Marian; and Fosco, Percival, and Hartright. In competing against Percival and Fosco, Ledwon observes, Hartright comes to resemble them, assuming the role of patriarch and using the law to his own ends. As Laura's husband, Walter "covers" his wife by claiming ownership of her; as the editor of the novel, he "covers" the stories of the female characters "by imposing a linear, logocentric speech over lived female experience" (9): "The moral seems to be that coverture is bad with a bad husband but right and proper with a good husband. . . . The final victim of coverture is the novel itself, covered over by the paternalistic law it attempts to critique" (19).

In another analysis of *The Woman in White,* Shirley A. Stave employs "a hermeneutics of suspicion" (287) to collapse the distinction between "good" and "bad" husbands in Collins's novel. According to Stave, Hartright reenacts the crimes of Sir Percival in legitimizing his own social position, and functions as the villain's "psychological double" and "son" (287): "Reading suspiciously, we see both men in dire financial straits; both men marry Laura Fairlie for her money and then imprison her within the house; both men commit forgeries which legitimize their position within society" (297). While this thesis is compelling, some of the evidence Stave uses to support it is not. In her often implausible reading of the novel, Stave accounts for Walter's agitated perception of Laura's resemblance to Anne by claiming that he—like Glyde—understands that he could "come by a fortune" by "swap[ping]" the two women (292–93). Casting doubt on Walter's "canonical " narrative, Stave goes on to suggest that Walter may actually have married Anne Catherick rather than Laura Fairlie, perpetrating his own fraud: "Were Mrs. Vesey to speak, would she identify Walter's wife as Anne Catherick and Walter as a schemer? Must she then also be silenced, as are all the woman in the novel?" (294). As these questions make clear, the conclusions reached through Stave's "hermeneutics of suspicion" are themselves suspicious. Stave is not alone in basing her reading of *The Woman in White* on the "silences" of Collins and his characters. Yet her claims about what has been silenced seem oddly conjectural and idiosyncratic, and are based on "clues" she believes the narrative "betrays" (302) rather than on the historical "realities" that Ledwon and others use to identify and explain the gaps or omissions in Collins's fiction.

Like Ledwon and Stave, Lauren Chattman discusses Hartright's status as the "good" husband of *The Woman in White,* a role that, in Chattman's view, depends on his ability to repress his own "feminine irrationality" (139) by analyzing and controlling that of his wife. Noting the equation of madness with "undomesticated femininity" in Victorian ideology (129), Chattman argues that "the insane domestic woman functions as a cover for the open secret of nineteenth-century middle-class culture, namely, that *all* subjectivity is constructed as irrational during the period" (123). Turning to *The Woman in White,* she charts Hartright's development as a man of reason capable of diagnosing and managing Laura's "symptoms" (136) and of "impos[ing] order on [an] irrational world," a process accomplished by means of his "organizing gaze" as "a visual artist" whose commitment to realism and whose ability to transform "the fantastically gothic into the everyday" (138) mirror Collins's own: "Collins, like his hero, does more than illustrate the horrors of Limmeridge House and Blackwater Park. In the end, his descriptions attempt to rationalize and control the private chaos that he has exposed" (134).

In connecting the construction of masculinity in *The Woman in White* with the conventions and practice of realism, Chattman echoes a number of Collins critics, for whom questions of gender are inseparable from questions of genre. As we have seen, Teresa Mangum connects the "formal aberrations" of *The Law and the Lady* with the anomaly of the female detective. Similarly, Joseph Litvak, in *Caught in the Act,* argues that "gender-confusion" in *The Woman in White* "can be cured only through a resolution of genre-confusion"—by "disowning" theatricality, despite Collins's sense of the "intimate . . . relationship between 'the Novel' and 'the Play' " (130). In an essay on *No Name,* Deirdre David shows how Collins "conflates resistance to dominant aesthetic and sexual ideologies" (186) in that novel, and she ties his "subversion of fictional omniscience'' to ''his liberal sexual politics''—his sympathy for the rebellious Magdalen Vanstone, a ''heroine in search of subjectivity'' (186). Michael Taylor explains what he sees as the ''power-in-weakness'' (294) of Laura Fairlie by reading *The Woman in White* as a ''preposterous romance'' (296), and Cannon Schmitt, in discussing the ''generic hybridity'' (298) of that novel, argues that its ''two narratives''—one Gothic and one real-ist—both ''hinge on . . . the figure of woman'' (302). Represented by Collins ''as surfaces to be inscribed,'' Laura Fairlie and Anne Catherick ''are essen-tial to the destruction and reconstruction of identity in *The Woman in White*'' (303). ''The novel's Gothic narrative,'' which effectively subverts ''the do-mestic, middle-class version of Englishness'' (293), ''depends upon Sir Perci-val Glyde's and Count Fosco's ability to write 'mad' on Anne and then 'dead' on Laura'' (303); the novel's realist *Bildungsroman* depends on Hartright's ability to erase their marks and ''write Laura . . . into his tale of success'' (304–05), a process that makes possible the ''new Englishness'' that Hartright embodies: ''middle-class manliness possessed of the signs of the rural gen-try'' (306).

Diane Elam complicates the idea that Collins's novel ''invites [men] to make their marks on the blank surface of woman'' (Schmitt 303) in her deconstructionist reading of *The Woman in White*. Explaining that Collins's novel ''examines the relationships among the figures of woman, referentiality, and truth'' (50), Elam argues that ''the problem of referentiality and truth'' is ''gender[ed]'' in the text ''not simply because the body of the woman in white is figured as a blank page . . . to be inscribed by the pen of the authorial and authorizing male'' but because ''the woman in white appears as the figure of reference itself, haunting the representational claims of the realist novel and thus upsetting its pretension to present the truth'' (50). Elam points to the textual problems and uncertainties elided by Hartright's ability to iden-tify Anne Catherick and by the neat resolution of the novel—uncertainties produced, in part, by the ''infinite supplementarity of the woman in white'' who, like figural language itself, reveals ''the impossibility of literal, descrip-tive reference'' (55). At times, Elam's analysis seems formulaic, particularly when she uses Collins's text to illustrate Derrida's claims. Nonetheless, her discussion of referentiality and gender is illuminating, and her analysis of the novel's uncertainties provides an interesting contrast to Chattman, suggesting that Collins breaks with the conventions of ''manly'' realism in *The Woman in White*.

While most discussions of gender in Collins's fiction center on the differ-ences between women and men, a number of critics consider the differences among Collins's female figures instead. In her discussion of *The New Magda-len,* for example, Barbara Fass Leavy describes ''folktale types'' of feminin-ity—'' 'The Kind and the Unkind Girls' '' and '' 'The Black and the White

Bride' " (209)—and argues that Collins uses them as a source for his novel, while also inverting the traditional status of these figures. In *The New Magdalen,* Collins makes the "unkind girl" or "black bride" his heroine, demonstrating her value, and exposes the "kind girl" as the deceiver; in so doing, he "reread[s] his fairy tales in light of socialist principles" (220). In her discussion of *No Name,* Helena Michie describes the differences between the Vanstone sisters as a version of sexual difference—"that is, the difference between the fallen and the unfallen, the sexual and the pure woman" (404)—and considers the way in which the "trope of sisterhood" enables writers to examine and contain "a range of stereotypically unfeminine feelings and behaviors" (407–08), including hostility and competition among women. In Michie's view, sisterhood provides a framework in which Collins can explore female sexuality and yet "reabsorb" it "within the teleology of family," since "fallen sisters . . . are frequently recoupable through their sisters' efforts in a way forbidden to other Victorian fallen women" (404).

For Michie, the recognition of differences among women is particularly valuable because it produces "a richer and more complex feminism" than one presupposing "female unity" (408): "if we can rewrite sexual difference to include the difference(s) between women, we can also begin to reframe Simone de Beauvoir's influential notion of the 'other,' and begin to do the work of looking at what 'otherness' might mean if it were applied to women's relations with each other" (404). The meaning of "otherness" among women, insofar as Collins constructs it, is the subject of Lisa Surridge's article on the "unspeakable histories" of *Man and Wife,* an essay that considers the relationship between Anne Silvester and Hester Dethridge, abused women from different social classes. Whereas the story of middle-class Anne comprises the main plot of the novel, the story of the working-class Hester comprises a subplot. Yet Collins intertwines the two, using Hester's experience of domestic abuse to illuminate Anne's sufferings while also containing "brutal marital violence" (105) within the working-class sphere. According to Surridge, the "literary doubling" of Anne and Hester produces "ideologically opposed effects": on the one hand, it suggests the domestic violence that Anne suffers yet her friends deny; on the other hand, it "cleanse[s] Anne of the rage and aggressive independence which characterize Hester's response to abuse" (119). In spite of the "radical implications" of Hester's narration of domestic violence, she "comes to play a conservative role in the text," "deflecting and absorbing the middle-class, wifely heroine's rage, aggression and independence" (120). In a novel that "wars against itself" (121), and in which the recognition of otherness among women serves both feminist and conservative ends, "the heroine's willing suffering is rewarded by marriage to a baronet," while "Hester's rage finds its home in an asylum" (122).

Collins and Empire

More often than not, discussions of otherness in Collins's fiction focus on his representation of racial difference and empire, a subject central to Collins criticism since the 1973 publication of John R. Reed's essay on "English Imperialism and the Unacknowledged Crime of *The Moonstone*." In this essay, Reed points out that Collins opens *The Moonstone* with the bloody military victory in Seringapatam that gave the British their foothold in India, and sets its main action in 1848–49, the years in which the British forcibly annexed the Punjab, arguing that Collins uses the theft of the Hindu diamond to expose "England's imperial depredations" (286). In his view, Collins portrays "the Indian priests" as "heroic figures" and "the representatives of Western Culture" as "plunderers" (283). Reed's argument inaugurated a debate over the imperial politics of Collins's novel—a debate that is ongoing—and his reading remains an influential one. His view that *The Moonstone* tears "the mask of respectability . . . from the British Empire" (285) has been echoed by a number of critics during the past fifteen years. In "Wilkie Collins's 'Little Jewel,' " for example, Patricia Miller Frick argues that *The Moonstone* reveals the Indians "to be morally superior to the English characters"; in her assessment, as in Reed's, the novel contrasts the "sincerity," "loyalty," "persistence" and "truth" of the Hindus with the "doubt and disorder" of their "hypocritical English counterparts" (318). In comparing *The Moonstone* to *The Sign of Four,* similarly, Arthur Liebman and David H. Galerstein contrast Conan Doyle's racist portrait of Tonga with Collins's heroic portrait of the Indian priests—"the most noble characters in the book, far superior in morality and ethical values [to] almost all the English characters" (73).

More frequently, however, Collins critics have sought to qualify and complicate, if not wholly reject, Reed's argument about *The Moonstone*. Just as Collins's status as a social reformer has been called into question by D. A. Miller and others, so, too, has Collins's reputation as a critic of empire. Ashish Roy's interpretation of *The Moonstone* as an "instrument" of "surveillance of the other" (658) is most clearly opposed to Reed's. Drawing on semiotic theory, in an argument that often seems incomprehensible, Roy challenges the novel's "career as an anti-imperialist text" and claims that *The Moonstone* more effectively justifies empire building than *Robinson Crusoe,* by "bring[ing] together a semiotic repertoire that demonstrates the structural cohesion the imperial imagination aimed at but could never quite achieve when challenged on issues of morality and reason" (657).

Like Roy, Robert Crooks identifies the "colonialist logic" of Collins's novel, which he compares to Robert Ferrigno's *The Horse Latitudes*. Asserting that *The Moonstone,* like detective fiction generally, "articulates a fantasy of mastering otherness" (215), Crooks argues that Collins displaces the "heterogeneity within the self" (revealed by Blake's "altered state of consciousness") with the "larger and more threatening alterity" of Hindu India (220). Yet this "alterity" is no sooner asserted than it is denied. Discrediting the other, Collins translates cultural difference into "inferior sameness," using western medicine to rationally explain the mysticism of the Indians, and reducing their subversive activities in England to a "trivial" instance of "organized crime" (221). Pointing to the telling "lapse[s]" in Collins's "explanatory apparatus," Crooks notes that Blake's unconscious behavior is " 'explained' as an effect of opium," yet "the logic of those actions and the mechanism of their exclusion from his memory [are] not explained at all, but only described"; the same is true of the motives of the Indians and the "coherency of the cultural system" in which they operate. Denying subjectivity to the Hindus, and substituting description for explanation, Collins "renders unnecessary, as [he] renders impossible, any interrogation of the legitimacy, inevitability, superiority, and so forth, of the norm against which difference is defined" (221).

For Reed, Collins's frame narrative, set in India, "provide[s] a distance" from which readers can see English society "for what it is"—criminal and rapacious (283–84)—and those critics who identify *The Moonstone* as anti-imperialist often focus on its frame, which dramatizes the theft and restoration of the diamond. Significantly, Crooks relegates his discussion of Collins's Epilogue—and of Collins's "ambivalence" about empire (227)—to an endnote, a strategy that allows him to argue that "the right of the colonizers to whatever they have managed to wrest away [from India] is never challenged" in the novel (220). Indeed, those articles that argue either *for* or *against* Collins's status as a critic of empire inevitably exclude significant details from consideration. On the one hand, Reed suggests that Collins valorizes the partly Eastern character Ezra Jennings because of his otherness, but fails to acknowledge the importance placed on his selfless service to the Englishman, Franklin Blake, in Collins's conception of his heroism. On the other hand, Deirdre David, in *Rule Britannia,* identifies Jennings as a "babulike figure" who performs the functions of an ideal subaltern (124), yet she dismisses the political significance of Collins's Prologue, which she describes as "a fable of individual brutality erased by a subsequent and coherent sequence of individual stories gathered in the cause of a common good" (18). This approach allows her to argue that Collins's plot confirms the "xenophobic perspective" of Gabriel Betteredge: "It *is* foreign Indians . . . who disrupt the social system so dear to Betteredge's imperial heart, who fracture the domestic social harmony secured by half a century of British colonial conquest" (17). In David's view, Collins limits his critique of British imperialism to what she identifies as its outmoded form of military subjugation, already replaced in the 1860s by the "hegemonic" model of which (David claims) Collins approves. Thus she sees Jennings as the product of an empire that rules its colonized peoples "without violent coercion" (145), by means of discipline and education, and with "the acquiescence of subaltern groups" (142): "Jennings's work . . . - reveal[s] him as a colonized figure so trusted by his masters, so purged of the native savagery that flourished at the time of the thuggee gangs, that he can be assigned the labor of cleansing the center of empire itself of its own corruption" (143). By contrast, Barry Milligan sees Jennings as a figure whose " 'internal complaint,' " and whose use and abuse of opium, provide an implicit critique of imperialism, "echo[ing] the ills and palliatives of British India," an empire maintained by means of opium production and opium wars (75).

What sets David's reading of *The Moonstone* apart from others, and also renders its claims problematic, is her notion that Collins represents an imperial rule maintained by means of discipline and acquiescence rather than violent military subjugation, and that the military subjugation of India was, by the mid-Victorian period, a thing of the past. As several critics have pointed out, on the contrary, Collins's novel was inspired, at least in part, by a particularly violent and none-too-distant episode in British imperial history, the Indian Mutiny of 1857. Both Milligan and Hyungji Park place *The Moonstone* in the tradition of Mutiny novels, noting that the threat posed by Collins's Brahmins "is a historically as well as sexually charged one" (Milligan 73). Park develops this point most fully, arguing that Collins's novel conforms to the "master-narrative" of such works, in which the subjugation of the Indians by the British is inverted and sexualized, in representations of "the victimization of Englishwomen by Indian men" (5) and the "chivalric protection of endangered femininity" by Englishmen (1): "The master-narrative that results from the Mutiny," she explains, "figures the Englishwoman as quintessentially the victim—real, imagined, or potential—of the rapacity of Eastern men, a threat that directly calls on Englishmen to rally to their defense" (6).

Park makes a convincing case for the importance of the Mutiny to *The Moonstone,* but unfortunately she does not consider the ways in which Collins subverts as well as invokes the "master-narrative" she describes. Park sees *The Moonstone* as "a monitary tale in which the danger of Indian sexuality is speculatively imported into the country mansions of Victorian society with devastating results" (7), and she argues that the novel "betrays an unqueried absorption of the Mutiny master-narrative of an Englishwoman's victimization by Indian men or forces" (9). Yet the very fact that Rachel's "gem" is stolen by the Englishman to whom she is engaged—and not by the three Indians—indicates that Collins questions the "Mutiny master-narrative" in his novel. Ironically, Rachel is violated by the very man destined to "protect" her, an act that subverts the chivalric ideal and that suggests Franklin Blake's complicity with the novel's villains.

Jaya Mehta makes this point in her excellent and well-balanced analysis of *The Moonstone* and *The Sign of Four,* "English Romance; Indian Violence," an article that deftly negotiates between Collins's critique of imperialism and his suppression of that critique. In Mehta's view, as in Heller's, Blake's theft of the moonstone conflates sexual with colonial exploitation while also dramatizing the "cultural amnesia of the West" (644)—the desire of the British to forget their guilt: "Blake's somnambulate theft of Rachel's diamond refigures the villain Herncastle's crime, and, on a larger scale, replays the English sack of Seringapatam. That Blake steals Rachel's diamond out of 'good' motives, in order to protect her from its theft by the Indians, does not dismantle this allegory . . . [but] anticipates the 'fit of absence of mind' in which, according to John Seeley's *The Expansion of England* (1883), the English dreamily and innocently acquired their empire" (646). Like Park, Mehta sees Collins's novel as a response to the Indian Mutiny, despite "the utter elision" (617) of this event from its plotline. Yet this elision—more aptly described as a *substitution* of the 1799 Seige of Seringapatam for the 1857 Mutiny—actually enables Collins to criticize the imperial practices of his day: "In substituting the Storming of Seringapatam for the Mutiny, Collins chooses the event most sensationalized before the 1857 revolt, yet an event more distant, more equivocal, and hence more susceptible to revisionism than the more recent event. In selecting . . . as the originating event of the narrative, an event in which British aggression and rapacity had encountered some public criticism, Collins . . . presents an inverted parallel to what the British regarded as the notorious Sieges of Cawnpore, Delhi, Lucknow, and Agra, allowing the reader to read the illegitimacy of empire into the antecedents of the unmentioned Mutiny" (620). In a novel that both subverts and reinscribes "imperialist constructs" (645) and that "oscillates unstably between tracking and erasing" (648), the knowledge of empire's "illegitimacy" is "no sooner suggested than forgotten," as Collins rewrites "colonial retribution . . . as colonial violence" (620). Collins's novel "revolves around central and repeated acts of forgetting alternating with incomplete, ambivalent attempts to remember," Mehta explains, as "knowledge—colonial, racial, gendered, class-based—emerges and submerges like clues in the quicksand" (644, 621).

Like Mehta, Milligan and Ian Duncan provide insightful and well-balanced discussions of Collins's treatment of empire, although they formulate the relationship between England and India in *The Moonstone* in very different ways. Milligan considers the "obsessive English fascination with India" (71) in *The Moonstone* and the mixed feelings about the Orient that Collins conveys—the combination of "dangerous Indian threats" and "seductive Indian thrills" (70) in his novel. Representing India and things Eastern as "both thrilling and threatening" (70), Collins shows how the East has invaded and transformed England: "Just as Franklin Blake arrogantly and mistakenly searches *around* himself for the thief of the Moonstone only to find the culprit *inside* himself in the end, so do Britons deludedly locate India in the East only to find that it is after all an inextricable part of their culture at home" (829).

Whereas Milligan emphasizes the hybridity of "Anglo-Indian culture" in *The Moonstone,* Duncan describes the East's resistance to British assimilation and control. In "*The Moonstone,* the Victorian Novel, and Imperialist Panic," Duncan argues that Collins finds in India a "positive alterity" to English cultural identity, "an alien force that breaks in and out of the domestic order, effortlessly eluding a circumscribed agency of detection" (301–02). As represented by Collins, India "exceeds and outlasts British dominion and knowledge," Duncan asserts, calling into question "the Western linear history that guarantees the narrative of imperial progress" (302–03). "Collins's tale does not propound an anti-imperialist sympathy for oppressed colonial peoples, or admiration for a devilish Hindu culture, but neither does it enthrone the imperialist subject-position, the proud seat of world-historical agency . . . Collins resists an ideologically closed justification of empire by grimly but far from mournfully depicting India as a powerful alien origin that constitutes the limit or end of English national historical identity" (300, 319). Rejecting Reed's overly "sentimental" reading of *The Moonstone* and its sympathy for the Indians as well as Roy's "blunt indictment of *The Moonstone* as 'an imperialist text' " (305 n. 15), Duncan argues that Collins "harnessed the imperial panic" produced by the Indian Mutiny "to depict another world triumphant in its darkness" (305) and to prophesy "the public, democratic, history-making vastnesses of a world economy" (300) that destabilizes the English character, a process conveyed through the effects of opium, the imperial commodity that "enthralls the inner subject to an alien, Asiatic identity" (310).

Like Mehta, who feels that Collins's images of struggle in *The Moonstone* represent both "class-based rebellions" and "anticolonial revolts" (623), Duncan argues that the Indian crowd envisioned in Collins's Epilogue conjures up another crowd gathering at home: "the Populace, in the robes of oriental despotism"—"that most alien of collectivities, the people" (318–19). This connection is developed by Nayder in her article on *The Moonstone,* "Robinson Crusoe and Friday in Victorian Britain." Focusing on the ties between colonized Indians and English workers in Collins's novel, Nayder casts doubt on Betteredge's narrative by pointing to the contradictions of his position as a servant who reads his experiences according to those of Defoe's heroic colonist. In Nayder's view, "it is one of Collins's ironies that, in identifying with Defoe's European master, Betteredge overlooks his connection to the exploited native servant": "Collins subtly develops the connection that Betteredge ignores, reformulating *Robinson Crusoe* in such a way that the faithful retainer plays the part of both Crusoe *and* Friday. In so doing, Collins reminds us of what the imperial ideology encourages us to forget—that working-class Englishmen may be masters in India, but they remain servants at home'' (223–24).

While most discussions of Collins and empire focus on *The Moonstone,* Nayder extends this analysis to include *Antonina, Armadale,* and *The New Magdalen* in her book *Wilkie Collins.* In a chapter on ''Reverse Colonization and Imperial Guilt,'' Nayder examines Collins's fictional response to the Indian Mutiny and the Jamaica Insurrection, arguing that his novels dramatize imperial crimes and punish the English for their misdeeds by staging ''the reverse colonization of England by the Creoles and Hindus who invade the home country and threaten to colonize it'' (101). At the same time, Collins assuages his sense of imperial guilt by ''transform[ing] political and cultural differences into those that seem natural and inevitable to his readers'': ''he consistently displaces the rage of exploited natives with that of independent and treacherous women, and at times attributes the outbreak of seemingly racial violence to sexual jealousy and feminist anger instead of colonial oppression'' (101). In so doing, Nayder claims, Collins ''partly obscures the injuries suffered by the conquered peoples and discredits as well as acknowledges their desire for self-rule'' (101–02). Critical of gender inequities, Collins ''calls attention to the enslavement of English wives'' as well as colonized peoples, yet he also suggests that independent women pose a threat to the empire at home (112). Thus in *Armadale,* Collins uses Lydia Gwilt's associate, Dr. Downward, to connect the image of imperial decline and fall with the practice of abortion, tracing an imperial crisis back ''to women who desire to abandon their proper roles'' and ''avoid motherhood'' (113).

In two articles on *The Woman in White,* Nayder and Cannon Schmitt discuss the imperial subplots of that sensation novel. Nayder considers Collins's use of Count Fosco as a mirror image of the British, a foreign invader whose imperial practices and whose association with the tyrannical Austrian empire provide a displaced critique of British imperialism. But as Nayder goes on to show, Collins defends the British empire as well, sending Hartright on an ''imperial mission'' to Honduras that he represents ''as historically innocent and ideologically pure'' (1), a venture that rehabilitates Hartright's manhood and secures his status as a gentleman. Whereas Nayder sees Collins's Italian character Professor Pesca as a ''colonist-in-the-making,'' a figure who exposes the injustice of the Austrian empire by revealing that Italians ''are not a subject race'' (2), Schmitt argues that Pesca embodies ''an essential otherness,'' a conception of nationality as ''immutable'' and racially determined. In Schmitt's view, this idea of the nation keeps Pesca in his place while also identifying the English as ''natural'' rulers (296).

Collins, Narrative Structure, and Narrative Strategies

Critics sometimes approach the question of Collins's political allegiances and his attitude toward the marginal and other by considering the narrative strategies and innovations that characterize his fiction. Defining himself against those who associate the "multiple narration" of Collins's novels with "relative truths" (Sue Lonoff, for example, in her 1982 article on Collins and Browning [143]), Miller argues that *The Moonstone* upholds a "genteel code" (39) and exercizes a disciplinary power by means of a covert mono-logism. "Speaking a master-voice that corrects, overrides, subordinates, or sublates all other voices it allows to speak" (54), the novel achieves the effect of omniscience in the absence of an omniscient narrator. Anthea Trodd makes a related point in *Domestic Crime in the Victorian Novel*, when discussing Collins's servant narrators. Despite the sympathy Collins extends to his housemaids and servants, and his sense of the problems in miscommunication that class differences produce, he discredits servants' tales, Trodd argues. Assigned the dirty work of sensational narration, these working-class figures reveal the secrets from which Collins's heroes turn in disgust. In *The Woman in White*, Hartright rejects the narrative provided by Mrs. Catherick, a retired lady's maid, distancing himself "from the low, degrading world which she inhabits" (84). In *The Moonstone*, Blake refuses to read Rosanna Spearman's letter, asking Betteredge to do so instead, and thus "the reader encounters a narrative of revelations produced by a servant and read in the text only by another servant": "These scenes in which the heroes . . . reject the servant narratives, with their invitation to complicity, represent their fitness as heroes; they are determined to evolve beyond the murky world of the female servants" (85).

By contrast, Pamela Perkins and Mary Donaghy, in their article on "A Man's Resolution: Narrative Strategies in Wilkie Collins' *The Woman in White*," argue that Collins discredits the hero's point of view and casts doubt on the reliability of his narrative. Representing Hartright as an untrustworthy narrator, Perkins and Donaghy find Collins "exposing the inadequacy of the conventional interpretation [Hartright] is trying to impose on his experience" (395), particularly the sexual stereotypes and "social codes" that Hartright promotes but that Collins feels "damage women" (396). As the editor of the other narratives in the novel, Hartright casts his "shadow" over them (396), and may be concealing material, Perkins and Donaghy suggest, pointing to discrepancies between accounts of events that Hartright tailors for particular audiences. Readers should not be "lulled by the apparent objectivity of Walter Hartright's version of events," Perkins and Donaghy warn, or "lose sight of the fact that Walter's voice and opinions are not identical to those of his creator" (392).

In an essay that focuses on Sir Percival and the false narratives he constructs, and that relates the villain's acts of writing to the hero's, Gwendolyn MacDonagh and Jonathan Smith examine the relationship between writing and illegitimacy in *The Woman in White*. Noting that "villainy in the novel . . . often hinges on the construction of false narratives from other narratives and documents" (277) and that "the criminal . . . writes in blank spaces, manipulates documents, [and] composes narratives" (281), they approach Sir Percival's forgery as a narrative act, and consider his ties to both Hartright and Collins as "constructor[s] of narratives" (275). "If villainy fills blank spaces with writing and tells its own story by assembling and arranging documents, then Walter Hartright also behaves villainously" (278), they assert, as does Collins, "whose method of composition resembles Percival's and Fosco's as well as Walter's" (281). Having drawn these connections, MacDonagh and Smith attribute Collins's sense of the illegitimacy of his narrative to the novel's mode of production. As an author of serialized "commodity-texts" (296), Collins battled "to establish serial publication's legitimacy against the triple-decker novel" (287). His treatment of illegitimacy and narration in *The Woman in White* metaphorically dramatizes "the conflicts he experienced in trying to legitimize new modes of narrative production" (288).

Like MacDonagh and Smith, Peter Brooks explores the relation between serialization and narrative technique in *Reading for the Plot,* considering, too, the importance of "filling in . . . narrative blanks" (170) among Collins's characters. According to Brooks, Collins used "the periodization of serial publication to delay, divert, and spin out the narrative" of *The Woman in White,* creating "a nearly epistemological form of suspense" through multiple narration (169). In a novel "filled with readers and the exchange of written texts" (169)—"a veritable utopia of reading and writing" (170)—characters continually reread and reinterpret "evidentiary narratives," pursuing solutions, prolonging suspense, and producing the pleasure associated with "plot for plot's sake" (170). Whereas MacDonagh and Smith suggest that *The Woman in White* is marked by the illegitimacy of the serialized "commodity-text," Brooks identifies the novel as an "almost fetishistic text" that satisfied the "unlimited appetite" of mid-Victorian consumers and that fed the "devouring presses" in an "age of . . . new industrial means and modes of production and distribution"(170). "Collins's representation of readers and writers constantly scribbling and constantly reading one another, even when they weren't meant to, suggests an image of the popular serial novel as a prelapsarian age of unlimited storytelling and the unlimited consumption of story: a world in which narrative, whatever the subject, enormously mattered" (170).

While MacDonagh, Smith and Brooks tie the narrative techniques of *The Woman in White* to mid-Victorian modes of literary production and consumption, Peter L. Caracciolo traces the narrative structure of Collins's fiction to the storytelling tradition of the *Arabian Nights*. Like the *Arabian Nights,* Collins's novels are often structured as "tales within tales," with narrators telling their stories to influence or sway their listeners (148). For Caracciolo, a number of Collins's female narrators recall Scheherazade, as does Collins himself. Faced with publishing deadlines rather than the executioner of the *Arabian Nights,* Collins struggled to produce "each installment [of *The Moonstone*] in Dickens' *All the Year Round,*" a "Victorian Scheherazade dictating his story against the clock" (158).

Unlike those critics who approach Collins's narrative techniques and structures historically, in terms of class relations or Victorian modes of production, Peter Thoms invokes the archetypal criticism of Northrop Frye and the idea of the quest romance in his extended treatment of the structures of Collins's fiction, *The Windings of the Labyrinth.* Thoms describes plotting as both a mode of organizing events in Collins's novels and as "the central drama of his narratives," in which characters "struggle for control of the stories in which they find themselves embedded": "the subject of narrative literally becomes the unfolding of narrative," as "characters confront the impersonal, imprisoning, and often inherited structures of their lives, and attempt to rewrite them in a bid for freedom and identity" (3). In Thoms's view, Collins's characters gain their freedom by becoming "authors" who design their own lives (4), engaging in quests that create structure, "an order that symbolizes the freedom of 'writing' one's own life" (5).

Despite his interest in self-authorship among Collins's protagonists, however, Thoms ties the designs they create to "a providential order" (7). In the process, he portrays Collins as a moralist who endorses a single and traditional set of values, overlooking the conflicting systems of belief and the political complexities that inform such novels as *The Woman in White* and *No Name.* Rather than considering the relationship between narrative authority and class identity, for example, as Trodd does, Thoms speaks of "the human family" (40) in Collins's fiction—"the human community" (97) in which his characters must find their place. "By pursuing love, generosity, and duty," Thoms argues, Collins's protagonists "journey out of . . . a lower, labyrinthine world, where chance seems to predominate, to discover God's ways and to move in rhythm with them" (7). Only in the "troubled, irresolute moods of *Armadale* and *The Moonstone,* " Thoms asserts, does Collins "fail to affirm God's presence and thus to posit a governing order behind the disorderedness of life" (9). Like Miller, Thoms suggests that Collins's rebelliousness has been exaggerated—that it is "only part of the story" (108). But while Miller warns us against Collins as a policeman in plainclothes, Thoms valorizes what he sees as Collins's moral orthodoxy, and does so without considering the class or gender biases of the "virtues" he commends.

As divided in their representations as Collins's own fiction and nearly as voluminous, nuanced and outspoken by turns, Collins studies are in a flourishing state. The 1999 publication of Collins's first novel, *Ioláni,* along with two volumes of his letters, will provide important new material for analysis and discussion. At the same time, new scholarly editions of Collins's works continue to appear—the forthcoming Broadview edition of *The Moonstone* is just one example. While Collins's short fiction has been collected, editions of his journalism and his plays have yet to be published, and would be very welcome. Critics continue to assess and redefine the meaning of Collins's fiction, extending their discussions to include the early and late novels. But Collins's manuscripts deserve attention as well. Most have yet to be examined with the care lavished on the manuscripts of Collins's contemporaries, Dickens in particular.

BIBLIOGRAPHY

EDITIONS

Novels and Novellas

Ioláni; or, Tahiti as it was (1845)
    Ed. Ira B. Nadel. Princeton: Princeton UP, 1999.
Mr. Wray's Cash Box (1852)
The Frozen Deep and Mr. Wray's Cash-Box. Phoenix Mill, England: Sutton, 1996. 73–141.
Basil: A Story of Modern Life (1852)
    Ed. Dorothy Goldman. Oxford: Oxford UP, 1990.
Hide and Seek (1854)
    Ed. Catherine Peters. Oxford: Oxford UP, 1993.
A Rogue's Life (1856)
    Phoenix Mill, England: Sutton, 1991.
The Dead Secret (1857)
    Phoenix Mill, England: Sutton, 1990.
    Ed. Ira B. Nadel. Oxford: Oxford UP, 1997.
The Woman in White (1859–60)
    Ed. Julian Symons. Harmondsworth: Penguin, 1985.
    Ed. John Sutherland. Oxford: Oxford UP, 1996.
No Name (1862–63)
    Ed. Mark Ford. Harmondsworth: Penguin, 1994.
    Ed. Virginia Blain. Oxford: Oxford UP, 1998.
Armadale (1864–66)
    Ed. Catherine Peters. Oxford: Oxford UP, 1991.
    Ed. John Sutherland. Harmondsworth: Penguin, 1995.

The Moonstone (1868)

    Ed. J. I. M. Stewart. Harmondsworth: Penguin, 1866, 1986.

    Ed. Anthea Trodd. Oxford: Oxford UP, 1982, 1998.

    Intro. Frederick Karl. New York: Signet, 1984.

    Ed. Catherine Peters. New York: Alfred A. Knopf, 1992.

    Ed. Steve Farmer. Peterborough, Ontario: Broadview P, 1999.

Man and Wife (1870)

    Phoenix Mill, England: Sutton, 1993.

    Ed. Norman Page. Oxford: Oxford UP, 1995.

Miss or Mrs? (1871)

    Phoenix Mill, England: Sutton, 1993.

Poor Miss Finch (1871–72)

    Ed. Catherine Peters. Oxford: Oxford UP, 1995.

The New Magdalen (1872–73)

    Phoenix Mill, England: Sutton, 1993.

The Frozen Deep (1874)

The Frozen Deep and Mr. Wray's Cash-Box. Phoenix Mill, England: Sutton, 1996.
    1–72.

The Law and the Lady (1874–75)

    Ed. Jenny Bourne Taylor. Oxford: Oxford UP, 1992.

The Two Destinies (1876)

    Phoenix Mill, England: Sutton, 1995.

My Lady's Money (1878)

    Phoenix Mill, England: Sutton, 1990.

The Haunted Hotel (1878)

    Phoenix Mill, England: Sutton, 1994.

The Fallen Leaves (1879)

    Phoenix Mill, England: Sutton, 1994.

Jezebel's Daughter (1879)

    Phoenix Mill, England: Sutton, 1995.

The Black Robe (1880)

    Phoenix Mill, England: Sutton, 1994.

Heart and Science (1882)

    Phoenix Mill, England: Sutton, 1994.

    Ed. Steve Farmer. Peterborough, Ontario: Broadview, 1996.

"I Say No" (1883–84)

    Phoenix Mill, England: Sutton, 1995.

The Evil Genius (1885)

    Ed. Graham Law. Peterborough, Ontario: Broadview, 1994.

The Guilty River (1886)

    Phoenix Mill, England: Sutton, 1994.

The Legacy of Cain (1888)

    Phoenix Mill, England: Sutton, 1993.

Blind Love (1889)

    New York: Dover, 1986.

Short Fiction

Mad Monkton and Other Stories. Ed. Norman Page. Oxford: Oxford UP, 1994.
Wilkie Collins: The Complete Shorter Fiction. Ed. Julian Thompson. New York: Carroll & Graf, 1995.

LETTERS

Baker, William and William M. Clarke, eds. *The Letters of Wilkie Collins.* 2 vols. London: Macmillan, forthcoming (1999).
Clarke, William M. "A Teasing 'Marital' Correspondence with a Twelve-Year-Old." *Wilkie Collins to the Forefront: Some Reassessments.* Ed. Nelson Smith and R. C. Terry. New York: AMS, 1995. 31–36.
Edwards, P. D. "Charles Reade, Wilkie Collins, and Marcus Clarke." *Australian Literary Studies* 11,3 (May 1984): 400–04.
See also General Studies: Lawrence, Keith.

BIOGRAPHICAL STUDIES

Clarke, William M. *The Secret Life of Wilkie Collins: The Intimate Victorian Life of the Father of the Detective Story.* Chicago: Ivan R. Dee, 1988. Rev. ed. Phoenix Mill, England: Sutton, 1996.
Edwards, P. D. "Wilkie Collins and Edmund Yates: A Postscript." *Wilkie Collins Society Journal* (New Series) 1 (1998): 47–49.
Gasson, Andrew. "Wilkie Collins, Edmund Yates and *The World.*" *Wilkie Collins Society Journal* 4 (1984): 5–17.
Ince, Laurence. "Wilkie Collins: The Intimacies and the Novels." *Wilkie Collins Society Journal* 6 (1986): 5–13.
Lonoff, Sue. "Sex, Sense, and Nonsense: The Story of the Collins-Lear Friendship." *Wilkie Collins to the Forefront: Some Reassessments.* Ed. Nelson Smith and R. C. Terry. 37–51. New York: AMS, 1995.
Peters, Catherine. "Frances Dickinson: Friend of Wilkie Collins." *Wilkie Collins Society Journal* (New Series) 1 (1998): 20–28.
————. *The King of Inventors: A Life of Wilkie Collins.* Princeton: Princeton UP, 1991.
Terry, R. C. " 'Myself in the Background and the Story in Front': Wilkie Collins As Others Knew Him." *Wilkie Collins to the Forefront: Some Reassessments.* Ed. Nelson Smith and R. C. Terry. New York: AMS, 1995. 1–10.
See also General Studies: Peters, Catherine.

PUBLISHING HISTORY AND BIBLIOGRAPHICAL STUDIES

Beetz, Kirk H. "Wilkie Collins Studies, 1972–1983." *Dickens Studies Annual* 13 (1984): 333–55.

Clarke, William M. "The Mystery of Collins's Articles on Italian Art." *Wilkie Collins Society Journal* 4 (1984): 19–24.

Law, Graham. "Last Things: Materials Relating to Collins in the Watt Collection at Chapel Hill." *Wilkie Collins Society Journal* (New Series) 1 (1998): 50–58.

———. "The Serial Publication in Britain of the Novels of Wilkie Collins." *Humanitas* 33 (1995): 1–29.

———. "Wilkie in the Weeklies: The Serialization and Syndication of Collins's Late Novels." *Victorian Periodicals Review* 30,3 (Fall 1997): 244–69.

Lohrli, Anne. "Wilkie Collins: Two Corrections." *English Language Notes* 22,1 (September 1984): 50–53.

Peters, Catherine. "Corrigendum to *The Wellesley Index.*" *Notes and Queries* 36 (234),2 (June 1989), 182. Rpt. as "Corrigendum to *Bentley's Miscellany.*" *Victorian Periodicals Review* 23,2 (Summer 1990): 68.

Rude, Donald W. and L. Layne Neeper. "A Unique Copy of the First American Edition of Wilkie Collins' *The Woman in White.*" *Analytical and Enumerative Bibliography* 2,3 (1988): 107–09.

Vann, J. Don. "William Wilkie Collins (1824–89)." *Victorian Novels in Serial.* New York: MLA, 1985. 43–60.

Weedon, Alexis. "Watch This Space: Wilkie Collins and New Strategies in Victorian Publishing in the 1890s." *Victorian Identities: Social and Cultural Formations in Nineteenth-Century Literature.* Ed. Ruth Robbins and Julian Wolfreys. New York: St. Martin's, 1996. 163–83.

See also Biographical Studies: Gasson, Andrew; *No Name*: Baker, William.

COLLECTIONS OF CRITICAL ESSAYS

Pykett, Lyn, ed. *Wilkie Collins: New Casebooks.* New York: St. Martin's, 1998.

Smith, Nelson, and R. C. Terry, eds. *Wilkie Collins to the Forefront: Some Reassessments.* New York: AMS, 1995.

BOOKS ON COLLINS

Gasson, Andrew. *Wilkie Collins: An Illustrated Guide.* Oxford: Oxford UP, 1998.

Heller, Tamar. *Dead Secrets: Wilkie Collins and the Female Gothic.* New Haven: Yale UP, 1992. Ch. 6, "Blank Spaces: Ideological Tensions and the Detective Work of *The Moonstone,*" rpt. in *Wilkie Collins.* Ed. Lyn Pykett. New York: St. Martin's, 1998. 244–70.

Nayder, Lillian. *Wilkie Collins.* New York: Twayne, 1997.

O'Neill, Philip. *Wilkie Collins: Women, Property and Propriety.* Totowa, NJ: Barnes and Noble, 1988.

Rance, Nicholas. *Wilkie Collins and Other Sensation Novelists: Walking the Moral Hospital.* Rutherford, NJ: Fairleigh Dickinson UP, 1991.

Taylor, Jenny Bourne. *In the Secret Theatre of Home: Wilkie Collins, Sensation Narrative, and Nineteenth-Century Psychology.* London: Routledge, 1988. Ch. 5, "*Armadale:* The Sensitive Subject as Palimpsest," rpt. in *Wilkie Collins.* Ed. Lyn Pykett. New York: St. Martin's, 1998. 149–74.

Thoms, Peter. *The Windings of the Labyrinth: Quest and Structure in the Major Novels of Wilkie Collins.* Athens: Ohio UP, 1992. Ch. 2, "Escaping the Plot: The Quest for Selfhood in *The Woman in White,*" rpt. in *Wilkie Collins to the Forefront: Some Reassessments.* Ed. Nelson Smith and R. C. Terry. New York: AMS, 1995. 183–207.

GENERAL STUDIES: ARTICLES AND CHAPTERS

Allen, Brooke. "More than Sensational: The Life and Art of Wilkie Collins." *New Criterion* 12,4 (December 1993): 31–40.

Bedell, Jeanne F. "Wilkie Collins." *Twelve Englishmen of Mystery.* Ed. Earl F. Bargainnier. Bowling Green: Popular, 1984. 9–32.

———. "Wilkie Collins." *British Mystery Writers, 1860–1919.* Ed. Bernard Benstock and Thomas F. Staley. *Dictionary of Literary Biography.* Vol. 70. Detroit: Gale Research, 1988. 85–101.

Caracciolo, Peter L. "Wilkie Collins and the Ladies of Baghdad, or the Sleeper Awakened." *The Arabian Nights in English Literature: Studies in the Reception of "The Thousand and One Nights" into British Culture.* Ed. Peter L. Caracciolo. New York: St. Martin's, 1988. 143–77.

Cooke, Simon. "Action and Attitude: Wilkie Collins and the Language of Melodramatic Gesture." *Wilkie Collins Society Journal* (New Series) 1 (1998): 5–19.

Frick, Patricia. "The Fallen Angels of Wilkie Collins." *International Journal of Women's Studies* 7,4 (September–October 1984): 343–51.

Gates, Barbara T. "Wilkie Collins' Suicides: 'Truth As It Is in Nature.' " *Dickens Studies Annual* 12 (1983): 303–18. Rpt. in *Wilkie Collins to the Forefront: Some Reassessments.* Ed. Nelson Smith and R. C. Terry. New York: AMS, 1995. 241–56.

Hall, Donald E. "From Margin to Center: Agency and Authority in the Novels of Wilkie Collins." *Fixing Patriarchy: Feminism and Mid-Victorian Novelists.* New York: New York UP, 1996. 151–74.

Kent, Christopher. "Probability, Reality and Sensation in the Novels of Wilkie Collins." *Dickens Studies Annual* 20 (1991): 259–80. Rpt. in *Wilkie Collins to the Forefront: Some Reassessments.* Ed. Nelson Smith and R. C. Terry. New York: AMS, 1995. 53–74.

Kucich, John. "Competitive Elites in Wilkie Collins: Cultural Intellectuals and Their Professional Others." *The Power of Lies: Transgression in Victorian Fiction.* Ithaca: Cornell UP, 1994. 75–118.

Lawrence, Keith. "The Religion of Wilkie Collins: Three Unpublished Documents." *Huntington Library Quarterly* 52,3 (Summer 1989): 389–402.

Milbank, Alison. "Breaking and Entering: Wilkie Collins's Sensation Fiction" and "Hidden and Sought: Wilkie Collins's Gothic Fiction." *Daughters of the House:*

Modes of the Gothic in Victorian Fiction. London: Macmillan, 1992. 25–53, 54–79.

Morris, Virginia B. "Wilkie Collins: No Deliverance But in Death." *Double Jeopardy: Women Who Kill in Victorian Fiction.* Lexington: UP of Kentucky, 1990. 105–26.

Nadel, Ira B. "Wilkie Collins and His Illustrators." *Wilkie Collins to the Forefront: Some Reassessments.* Ed. Nelson Smith and R. C. Terry. New York: AMS, 1995. 149–64.

Nenadic, Stana. "Illegitimacy, Insanity, and Insolvency: Wilkie Collins and the Victorian Nightmares." *The Arts, Literature, and Society.* Ed. Arthur Marwick. London: Routledge, 1990. 133–62.

Oulton, Carolyn. "Wilkie Collins—An Interpretation of Christian Belief." *Wilkie Collins Society Journal* (New Series) 1 (1998): 29–43.

Peters, Catherine. " 'Invite No Dangerous Publicity': Some Independent Women and Their Effect on Wilkie Collins's Life and Writing." *Dickens Studies Annual* 20 (1991): 295–312. Rpt. in *Wilkie Collins to the Forefront: Some Reassessments.* Ed. Nelson Smith and R. C. Terry. New York: AMS, 1995. 11–29.

Peterson, Audrey. "Wilkie Collins and the Mystery Novel." *Victorian Masters of Mystery: From Wilkie Collins to Conan Doyle.* New York: Frederick Ungar, 1984. 11–69.

Pykett, Lyn. Introduction. *Wilkie Collins.* New York: St. Martin's, 1998. 1–29.

———. "Wilkie Collins: Questions of Identity." *The Sensation Novel: From "The Woman in White" to "The Moonstone."* Plymouth, UK: Northcote House, 1994. 14–39.

Rance, Nick. "Wilkie Collins in the 1860s: The Sensation Novel and Self-Help." *Nineteenth-Century Suspense: From Poe to Conan Doyle.* Ed. Clive Bloom, Brian Docherty, Jane Gibb and Keith Shand. New York: St. Martin's, 1988. 46–63.

Thomas, Ronald R. "Wilkie Collins and the Sensation Novel." *The Columbia History of the British Novel.* Ed. John Richetti. New York: Columbia UP, 1994. 479–507.

Trodd, Anthea. *Domestic Crime in the Victorian Novel.* New York: St. Martin's, 1989. Passim.

Watt, George. "Mercy." *The Fallen Woman in the Nineteenth-Century English Novel.* London: Croom Helm, 1984. 97–118.

STUDIES OF INDIVIDUAL WORKS

Short Fiction and Journalism

Burova, I. I. "Interpretatsiia sverkh''estestvennogo v·tvorchestve U. Kollinza." *Vestnik Sankt Peterburgskogo Universiteta* 4,23 (October 1994): 82–87.

Farmer, Steve. " 'The Use of Gas in Theatres' or 'The Air and the Audience: Considerations on the Atmospheric Influences of Theatres.' " *Wilkie Collins Society Journal* 6 (1986): 19–26.

Page, Norman. Introduction. *Mad Monkton and Other Stories.* Oxford: Oxford UP, 1994. vii–xxx.

Rance, Nick. " 'A Terribly Strange Bed': Self-Subverting Gothic.'' *Wilkie Collins Society Journal* 7 (1987): 5–12.

Thompson, Julian. Introduction. *Wilkie Collins: The Complete Shorter Fiction.* New York: Carroll & Graf, 1995. vii–xi.

See also Publishing History and Bibliographical Studies: Clarke, William M.

Novels and Novellas

Ioláni

Nadel, Ira B. Introduction. *Ioláni; or, Tahiti as it was. A Romance.* Princeton: Princeton UP, 1999. ix–xxxvii.

Basil

Goldman, Dorothy. Introduction. *Basil.* Oxford: Oxford UP, 1990. vii–xxii.

Schroeder, Natalie E. and Ronald A. Schroeder. "Basil's Dream: The Failure of the Social Moral Paradigm in Wilkie Collins' *Basil.*" *Massachusetts Studies in English* 11, 1–2 (1992): 63–71.

See also Comparative Studies: Millard, Kenneth.

Hide and Seek

Peters, Catherine. Introduction. *Hide and Seek.* Oxford: Oxford UP, 1993. vii–xxiii.

After Dark

Beetz, Kirk H. "Plots within Plots: Wilkie Collins's *After Dark.*" *Wilkie Collins Society Journal* 4 (1984): 31–34.

A Rogue's Life

Ashley, Robert. "*A Rogue's Life:* Who Ever Heard of Frank Softly?'' *Wilkie Collins Society Journal* 6 (1986): 15–18.

The Dead Secret

Nadel, Ira B. Introduction. *The Dead Secret.* Oxford: Oxford UP, 1997. vii–xxv.

The Woman in White

Andres, Sophia. "Pre-Raphaelite Paintings and Jungian Images in Wilkie Collins's *The Woman in White.*" *Victorian Newsletter* 88 (Fall 1995): 26–31.

Ascari, Maurizio. "Più di una penna, più di un testimone: Tecniche narrative in *The Woman in White.*" *Paragone* 43, 32–34 (February–April 1992): 9–27.

Balée, Susan. "Wilkie Collins and Surplus Women: The Case of Marian Halcombe." *Victorian Literature and Culture* 20 (1992): 197–215.

Bernstein, Stephen. "Reading Blackwater Park: Gothicism, Narrative, and Ideology in *The Woman in White.*" *Studies in the Novel* 25,3 (Fall 1993): 291–305.

Brooks, Peter. "The Mark of the Beast: Prostitution, Serialization, and Narrative." *Reading for the Plot: Design and Intention in Narrative.* Cambridge: Harvard UP, 1984. 143–70, 168–70.

Bury, Laurent. "Shutting in, Shutting out, Shutting Up: Variations sur l'enfermement dans *The Woman in White* de Wilkie Collins." *Cahiers Victorienns et Edouardiens* 43 (October 1996): 31–46.

Cvetkovich, Ann. "Ghostlier Determinations: The Economy of Sensation and *The Woman in White*." *Mixed Feelings: Feminism, Mass Culture, and Victorian Sensationalism.* New Brunswick, NJ: Rutgers UP, 1992. 71–96. Rpt. in *Wilkie Collins.* Ed. Lyn Pykett. New York: St. Martin's, 1998. 109–35.

DeCicco, Lynne Marie. "Against Plausibility: Women's Secrets and Legal Propriety in *The Woman in White*." *Women and Lawyers in the Mid-Nineteenth Century Novel: Uneasy Alliances and Narrative Misrepresentation.* Lewiston, NY: Edwin Mellen, 1996. 141–213.

Elam, Diane. "White Narratology: Gender and Reference in Wilkie Collins's *The Woman in White*." *Virginal Sexuality and Textuality in Victorian Literature.* Ed. Lloyd Davis. Albany: State U of New York P, 1993. 49–63.

Gomel, Elana and Stephen Weninger. "The Tell-Tale Surface: Fashion and Gender in *The Woman in White*." *Victorians Institute Journal* 25 (1997): 29–58.

Hendershot, Cyndy. "A Sensation Novel's Appropriation of the Terror-Gothic: Wilkie Collins' *The Woman in White*." *Clues* 13,2 (Fall-Winter 1992): 127–33.

Hüttner, Kirsten. *Wilkie Collins's "The Woman in White": Analysis, Reception and Literary Criticism of a Victorian Bestseller.* Trier: Wissenschaftlicher Verlag Trier, 1996.

Karsten, Julie A. "From Novel to Film: Wilkie Collins's *The Woman in White*." *Wilkie Collins Society Journal* 5 (1985): 15–21.

Langbauer, Laurie. "Women in White, Men in Feminism." *Yale Journal of Criticism* 2,2 (Spring 1989): 219–43.

Ledwon, Lenora. "Veiled Women, the Law of Coverture, and Wilkie Collins's *The Woman in White*." *Victorian Literature and Culture* 22 (1994): 1–22.

Loesberg, Jonathan. "The Ideology of Narrative Form in Sensation Fiction." *Representations* 13 (Winter 1986): 115–38.

MacDonagh, Gwendolyn and Jonathan Smith. " 'Fill Up All the Gaps': Narrative and Illegitimacy in *The Woman in White*." *Journal of Narrative Technique* 26,3 (Fall 1996): 274–91.

Masciarotte, Gloria-Jean. "The Madonna with Child, and Another Child, and Still Another Child . . . : Sensationalism and the Dysfunction of Emotions." *Discourse* 14,1 (Winter 1991–92): 88–125.

May, Leila Silvana. "Sensational Sisters: Wilkie Collins's *The Woman in White*." *Pacific Coast Philology* 30,1 (1995): 82–102.

McEathron, Scott. "Romantic Portraiture: *The Memoirs of William Collins* and *The Woman in White*." *Victorians Institute Journal* 25 (1997): 7–28.

Miller, D. A. "*Cage aux folles:* Sensation and Gender in Wilkie Collins's *The Woman in White*." *The Novel and the Police.* Berkeley: U of California P, 1988. 146–91.

Nayder, Lillian. "Agents of Empire in *The Woman in White*." *Victorian Newsletter* 83 (Spring 1993): 1–7.

Perkins, Pamela and Mary Donaghy. "A Man's Resolution: Narrative Strategies in Wilkie Collins' *The Woman in White*." *Studies in the Novel* 22,4 (Winter 1990): 392–402.

Schmitt, Cannon. "Alien Nation: Gender, Genre, and English Nationality in Wilkie Collins's *The Woman in White.*" *Genre* 26 (1993): 283–310.

Stave, Shirley A. "The Perfect Murder: Patterns of Repetition and Doubling in Wilkie Collins's *The Woman in White.*" *Dickens Studies Annual* 25 (1996): 287–303.

Sutherland, John. Introduction. *The Woman in White.* Oxford: Oxford UP, 1996. vii–xxiii.

———. "Wilkie Collins and the Origins of the Sensation Novel." *Dickens Studies Annual* 20 (1991): 243–58. Rpt. in *Wilkie Collins to the Forefront: Some Reassessments.* Ed. Nelson Smith and R. C. Terry. New York: AMS, 1995. 75–90.

———. "Writing *The Woman in White.*" *Victorian Fiction: Writers, Publishers, Readers.* New York: St. Martin's, 1995. 28–54.

Symons, Julian. Introduction. *The Woman in White.* Harmondsworth: Penguin, 1974, 1985. 7–21.

Taylor, Jenny Bourne. "Psychology and Sensation: The Narrative of Moral Management in *The Woman in White.*" *Critical Survey* 2 (1990): 49–56.

Taylor, Michael. " 'In the Name of Her Sacred Weakness': Romance, Destiny, and Woman's Revenge in Wilkie Collins's *The Woman in White. University of Toronto Quarterly* 64,2 (Spring 1995): 289–304.

See also Collins and Dickens: Litvak, Joseph; Meckier, Jerome; Comparative Studies: Chattman, Lauren; Langland, Elizabeth.

No Name

Baker, William. "The Manuscript of Wilkie Collins's *No Name.*" *Studies in Bibliography* 43 (1990): 197–208.

Blain, Virginia. Introduction. *No Name.* Oxford: Oxford UP, 1998. vii–xxi.

———. "The Naming of *No Name.*" *Wilkie Collins Society Journal* 4 (1984): 25–29.

David, Deirdre. "Rewriting the Male Plot in Wilkie Collins's *No Name:* Captain Wragge Orders an Omelette and Mrs. Wragge Goes into Custody." *Out of Bounds: Male Writers and Gender(ed) Criticism.* Ed. Laura Claridge and Elizabeth Langland. Amherst: U of Massachusetts P, 1990. 186–96. Rpt. in *Wilkie Collins.* Ed. Lyn Pykett. New York: St. Martin's, 1998. 136–48.

Ford, Mark. Introduction. *No Name.* Harmondsworth: Penguin, 1994. vii–xvii.

Horne, Lewis. "Magdalen's Peril." *Dickens Studies Annual* 20 (1991): 281–94.

Huskey, Melynda. "*No Name:* Embodying the Sensation Heroine." *Victorian Newsletter* 82 (Fall 1992): 5–13.

Michie, Helena. " 'There Is No Friend Like a Sister': Sisterhood as Sexual Difference." *ELH* 56,2 (Summer 1989): 401–21. Rpt. in *Sororophobia: Differences Among Women in Literature and Culture.* Oxford: Oxford UP, 1992. 15–50.

Morris, Debra. "Maternal Roles and the Production of Name in Wilkie Collins's *No Name.*" Dickens Studies Annual 27 (1998): 271–86.

See also Collins and Dickens: Litvak, Joseph; Purton, Valerie; Comparative Studies: Caracciolo, Peter L.

Armadale

Boyle, Thomas. "*Armadale:* 'A Sensation Novel with a Venegeance.' " *Black Swine in the Sewers of Hampstead: Beneath the Surface of Victorian Sensationalism.* New York: Viking, 1989. 159–73.

Peters, Catherine. Introduction. *Armadale*. Oxford: Oxford UP, 1991. vii–xxiii.

Sutherland, John. Introduction. *Armadale*. Harmondsworth: Penguin, 1995. vii–xxvi.

Tutor, Jonathan Craig. "Lydia Gwilt: Wilkie Collins's Satanic, Sirenic Psychotic." *University of Mississippi Studies* 10 (1992): 37–55.

Zeitz, Lisa M. and Peter Thoms. "Collins' Use of the Strasbourg Clock in *Armadale*." *Nineteenth-Century Literature* 45, 4 (March 1991): 495–503.

See also Comparative Studies: Caracciolo, Peter L.

The Moonstone

Allan, Janice M. "Scenes of Writing: Detection and Psychoanalysis in Wilkie Collins's *The Moonstone*." *Imprimatur* 1 (Spring 1996): 186–93.

Bury, Laurent. "*The Moonstone:* Le Roman policier comme strip-tease." *Etudes Anglaises* 49, 1 (January–March 1996): 75–80.

Calanchi, Alessandra. "Visite Guidate: La complicità dello scenario domestico in *The Moonstone*." *Paragone* 43, 32–34 (February–April 1992): 28–46.

Caserio, Robert L. "Story, Discourse, and Anglo-American Philosophy of Action." *Journal of Narrative Technique* 17,1 (Winter 1987): 1–11.

David, Deirdre. *Rule Britannia: Women, Empire, and Victorian Writing*. Ithaca: Cornell UP, 1995. 17–20, 142–47, passim.

Duncan, Ian. "*The Moonstone,* the Victorian Novel, and Imperialist Panic." *Modern Language Quarterly* 55,3 (September 1994): 297–319.

Escuret, Annie. "*The Moonstone:* 'J'enquête donc je lis': Lecture Épistémologique." *QWERTY* 5 (October 1995): 129–40.

Frick, Patricia Miller. "Wilkie Collins' 'Little Jewel': The Meaning of *The Moonstone*." *Philological Quarterly* 63,3 (Summer 1984): 313–21.

Gruner, Elisabeth Rose. "Family Secrets and the Mysteries of *The Moonstone*." *Victorian Literature and Culture* 21 (1993): 127–45. Rpt. in *Wilkie Collins*. Ed. Lyn Pykett. New York: St. Martin's, 1998. 221–43.

Hennelly, Mark M., Jr. "Detecting Collins' Diamond: From Serpentstone to Moonstone." *Nineteenth-Century Fiction* 39,1 (June 1984): 25–47.

Jain, Jasbir. "A Deconstructionist Reading of *The Moonstone*." *Rajasthan University Studies in English* 20 (1988): 61–69.

Kalikoff, Beth. "Fiction, 1850–1870." *Murder and Moral Decay in Victorian Popular Literature*. Ann Arbor: UMI Research P, 1986. 97–126.

Karl, Frederick R. Introduction. *The Moonstone*. New York: Signet, 1984. 1–21.

Martin, Françoise. "Le Corps dans tous ses éclats: Maux et mots du corps dans *The Moonstone*." *QWERTY* 5 (October 1995): 159–68.

Mehta, Jaya. "English Romance; Indian Violence." *Centennial Review* 39,4 (Fall 1995): 611–57.

Miller, D. A. "From *roman policier* to *roman-police:* Wilkie Collins's *The Moonstone*." *The Novel and the Police*. Berkeley: U of California P, 1988. 33–57. Rpt. in *Wilkie Collins*. Ed. Lyn Pykett. New York: St. Martin's, 1998. 197–220.

Milligan, Barry. " 'Accepting a Matter of Opium as a Matter of Fact': *The Moonstone,* Opium, and Hybrid Anglo-Indian Culture." *Pleasures and Pains: Opium and the Orient in Nineteenth-Century British Culture*. Charlottesville: UP of Virginia, 1995. 69–82.

Nadel, Ira B. "Science and *The Moonstone*." *Dickens Studies Annual* 11 (1983): 239–59.

Naugrette, Jean-Pierre. "*The Moonstone:* Signes indiens." *Etudes Anglaises* 48,4 (1995): 407–18.

Nayder, Lillian. "Robinson Crusoe and Friday in Victorian Britain: 'Discipline,' 'Dialogue,' and Collins's Critique of Empire in *The Moonstone*." *Dickens Studies Annual* 21 (1991): 213–31.

Park, Hyungji. " 'The Story of Our Lives': *The Moonstone* and the Indian Mutiny in *All the Year Round*." *Negotiating India in the Nineteenth-Century Media*. Ed. Douglas M. Peers and David Finkelstein. London: Macmillan, forthcoming (1999).

Peters, Catherine. Introduction. *The Moonstone*. New York: Alfred A. Knopf, 1992. v–xxiv.

Priestman, Martin. "Freud and *The Moonstone*." *Detective Fiction and Literature: The Figure on the Carpet*. New York: St. Martin's, 1991. 25–35.

Reed, John R. "The Stories of *The Moonstone*." *Wilkie Collins to the Forefront: Some Reassessments*. Ed. Nelson Smith and R. C. Terry. New York: AMS, 1995. 91–99.

Roy, Ashish. "The Fabulous Imperialist Semiotic of Wilkie Collins's *The Moonstone*." *New Literary History* 24 (1993): 657–81.

Shaw, W. David. "The Critic as Detective: Mystery and Method in *The Moonstone*." *Victorians and Mystery: Crises of Representation*. Ithaca: Cornell UP, 1990. 288–99.

Siegel, Shepard. "Wilkie Collins: Victorian Novelist as Psychopharmacologist." *Journal of the History of Medicine and Allied Sciences* 38 (1983): 161–75.

Smith, Muriel. "The Jewel Theme in *The Moonstone*." *Wilkie Collins Society Journal* 5 (1985): 11–13.

Stewart, J. I. M. Introduction. *The Moonstone*. Harmondsworth: Penguin, 1966, 1986. 7–24.

Thomas, Ronald R. "Minding the Body Politic: The Romance of Science and the Revision of History in Victorian Detective Fiction." *Victorian Literature and Culture* 19 (1991): 233–54.

———. "The Missing Dream in *The Moonstone*." *Dreams of Authority: Freud and the Fictions of the Unconscious*. Ithaca: Cornell UP, 1990. 203–19.

Thoms, Peter. "The Detection of Innocence in *The Moonstone*." *Detection and Its Designs: Narrative and Power in Nineteenth-Century Detective Fiction*. Athens: Ohio UP, 1998. 93–120.

Thornton, Sara. "Dealing with *Disjecta Membra:* Strategies of Homogenization and Interment in *The Moonstone*." *QWERTY* 5 (October 1995): 169–76.

Trodd, Anthea. Introduction. *The Moonstone*. Oxford: Oxford UP, 1982, 1998. vii–xxi.

Welsh, Alexander. "Collins's Setting for a Moonstone." *Strong Representations: Narrative and Circumstantial Evidence in England*. Baltimore: Johns Hopkins UP, 1992. 215–36.

See also Collins and Dickens: Meckier, Jerome; Comparative Studies: Coad, David; Crooks, Robert; Kresge, Delphine; Liebman, Arthur; Smith, Muriel; Zander, Andela.

Man and Wife

Ashley, Robert. "*Man and Wife:* Collins, Dickens, and Muhammad Ali." *Wilkie Collins Society Journal* 5 (1985): 5–9.

Crawford, Scott A. G. M. "Wilkie Collins: Master of Melodrama and Critic of Victorian Athleticism." *Aethlon* 5,2 (Spring 1988): 87–96.

Page, Norman. Introduction. *Man and Wife.* Oxford: Oxford UP, 1995. vii–xxiv.

Surridge, Lisa. "Unspeakable Histories: Hester Dethridge and the Narration of Domestic Violence in *Man and Wife.*" *Victorian Review* 22,2 (Winter 1996): 102–26.

See also General Studies: Watt, George.

Poor Miss Finch

Peters, Catherine. Introduction. *Poor Miss Finch.* Oxford: Oxford UP, 1995. vii–xxiii.

The New Magdalen

Leavy, Barbara Fass. "Wilkie Collins' *The New Magdalen* and the Folklore of the Kind and the Unkind Girls." *Wilkie Collins to the Forefront: Some Reassessments.* Ed. Nelson Smith and R. C. Terry. New York: AMS, 1995. 209–25.

See also General Studies: Watt, George.

The Law and the Lady

Mangum, Teresa. "Wilkie Collins, Detection, and Deformity." *Dickens Studies Annual* 26 (1998): 285–310.

Maynard, Jessica. "Telling the Whole Truth: Wilkie Collins and the Lady Detective." *Victorian Identities: Social and Cultural Formations in Nineteenth-Century Literature.* Ed. Ruth Robbins and Julian Wolfreys. London: Macmillan, 1996. 187–98.

O'Fallon, Kathleen. "Breaking the Laws about Ladies: Wilkie Collins' Questioning of Gender Roles." *Wilkie Collins to the Forefront: Some Reassessments.* Ed. Nelson Smith and R. C. Terry. New York: AMS, 1995. 227–39.

Taylor, Jenny Bourne. Introduction. *The Law and the Lady.* Oxford: Oxford UP, 1992. vii–xxiv.

The Fallen Leaves

See Biographical Studies: Gasson, Andrew; General Studies: Watt, George.

Heart and Science

Farmer, Steve. Introduction. *Heart and Science.* Petersborough, Ontario: Broadview P, 1996. 7–27.

Lansbury, Coral. "The Truths of Fiction." *The Old Brown Dog: Women, Workers, and Vivisection in Edwardian England.* Madison: U of Wisconsin P, 1985. 130–51, 133–41.

Wiesenthal, C. S. "From Charcot to Plato: The History of Hysteria in *Heart and Science.*" *Wilkie Collins to the Forefront: Some Reassessments.* Ed. Nelson Smith and R. C. Terry. New York: AMS, 1995. 257–68.

"I Say No"
Kale, K. A. "Yes and No: Problems of Closure in Collins's 'I Say No.' " *Wilkie Collins Society Journal* (New Series) 1 (1998): 44–46.

The Evil Genius
Law, Graham. Introduction. *The Evil Genius.* Peterborough, Ontario: Broadview P, 1994. 7–30.

COLLINS AND DICKENS

Bump, Jerome. "Parody and the Dickens-Collins Collaboration in 'No Thoroughfare.' " *Library Chronicle of the University of Texas* 37 (1986): 38–53.
Burgan, William M. "Masonic Symbolism in *The Moonstone* and *The Mystery of Edwin Drood.*" *Dickens Studies Annual* 16 (1987): 257–303. Rpt. in *Wilkie Collins to the Forefront: Some Reassessments.* Ed. Nelson Smith and R. C. Terry. New York: AMS, 1995. 101–48.
Crosby, Christina. "History and the Melodramatic Fix." *The Ends of History: Victorians and "The Woman Question."* New York: Routledge, 1991. 69–109.
Hollington, Michael. " 'To the Droodstone': Or, From *The Moonstone* to *Edwin Drood* via *No Thoroughfare.*" *QWERTY* 5 (October 1995): 141–49.
Litvak, Joseph. "Dickens and Sensationalism." *Caught in the Act: Theatricality in the Nineteenth-Century English Novel.* Berkeley: U of California P, 1992. 109–45.
Meckier, Jerome. "An Ultra-Dickensian Novel: *The Woman in White*" and "Undoing by Outdoing Continued: *Great Expectations—The Moonstone.*" *Hidden Rivalries in Victorian Fiction: Dickens, Realism, and Revaluation.* Lexington: UP of Kentucky, 1987. 93–121, 122–52.
Purton, Valerie. "Dickens and Collins: The Rape of the Sentimental Heroine." *Ariel* 16,1 (January 1985): 77–89.
See also *Man and Wife:* Ashley, Robert.

COMPARATIVE STUDIES, LITERARY INFLUENCES, AND SOURCES

Bates, Richard. "The Italian with White Mice in *Middlemarch.*" *Notes and Queries* 31 (229), 4 (December 1984): 497.
Böker, Uwe. "Wilkie Collins, Henry James und Dr. Carpenter's 'Unconscious Cerebration.' " *Germanisch Romanische Monatsschrift* 34,3 (1984): 323–36.
Caracciolo, Peter L. "Wilkie Collins and 'The God Almighty of Novelists': The Example of Scott in *No Name* and *Armadale.*" *Wilkie Collins to the Forefront: Some Reassessments.* Ed. Nelson Smith and R. C. Terry. New York: AMS, 1995. 165–81.
Chattman, Lauren. "Diagnosing the Domestic Woman in *The Woman in White* and *Dora.*" *Eroticism and Containment: Notes from the Flood Plain.* Ed. Carol Siegel and Ann Kibbey. New York: New York UP, 1994. 123–53.

Coad, David. "Other in *The Moonstone* and *Dracula.*" *Annales du Monde Anglophone* 4 (October 1996): 33–53.

Crooks, Robert. "Reopening the Mysteries: Colonialist Logic and Cultural Difference in *The Moonstone* and *The Horse Latitudes.*" *Literature* 4,3 (1993): 215–28.

Frick, Patricia. "Wilkie Collins and John Ruskin." *Victorians Institute Journal* 13 (1985): 11–22.

Gates, David. " 'A Dish of Village Chat': Narrative Technique in Sheridan Le Fanu's *The House by the Churchyard.*" *Canadian Journal of Irish Studies* 10,1 (June 1984): 63–68.

Hapke, Laura. "He Stoops to Conquer: Redeeming the Fallen Woman in the Fiction of Dickens, Gaskell and Their Contemporaries." *Victorian Newsletter* 69 (Spring 1986): 16–22.

Huskey, Melinda. "*Twin Peaks:* Rewriting the Sensation Novel." *Literature-Film Quarterly* 21,4 (1993): 248–54.

Kresge, Delphine. "Voix et voies: *The Moonstone* et *The Big Sleep.*" *QWERTY* 5 (October 1995): 151–58.

Kurata, Marilyn J. "Italians with White Mice Again: *Middlemarch* and *The Woman in White.*" *English Language Notes* 22,4 (June 1985): 45–47.

Langland, Elizabeth. "Enclosure Acts: Framing Women's Bodies in Collins's *Woman in White* and Braddon's *Lady Audley's Secret.*" *Beyond Sensation: Mary Elizabeth Braddon in Context.* Ed. Marlene Tromp, Pamela K. Gilbert, and Aeron Haynie. Albany: State U of New York P, forthcoming (1999).

Liebman, Arthur and David H. Galerstein. "The Sign of the Moonstone." *Baker Street Journal* 44 (1994): 71–74.

Millard, Kenneth. "My Father's Will: Self-Determination and Mental Breakdown in *Basil, The Professor,* and *The Ordeal of Richard Feverel.*" *English* 44 (Spring 1995): 25–39.

Schork, R. J. "*Ulysses'* Priesty Penrose." *James Joyce Quarterly* 31,4 (Summer 1994): 563–66.

Smith, Muriel. " 'Everything to My Wife': The Inheritance Theme in *The Moonstone* and *Sense and Sensibility.*" *Wilkie Collins Society Journal* 7 (1987): 13–18.

———. "An Unnoticed Follower of Wilkie Collins." *Notes and Queries* 35 (233),3 (September 1988): 326.

Wiesenthal, C. S. " 'Ghost Haunted': A Trace of Wilkie Collins in Mary Elizabeth Braddon's *Lady Audley's Secret.*" *English Language Notes* 28,4 (June 1991): 42–44.

Wynne, Deborah. "Vidocq, the Spy: A Possible Source for Count Fosco in Wilkie Collins's *The Woman in White.*" *Notes and Queries* 44 (242),3 (September 1997): 341–42.

Zander, Andela. " 'Spot the Source': Wilkie Collins' *The Moonstone* und John Fowles' *The French Lieutenant's Woman.*" *Zeitschrift fur Anglistik und Amerikanistik* 41,4 (1993): 341–48.

See also General Studies: Caracciolo, Peter L.; *No Name:* Michie, Helena; *The Moonstone:* Mehta, Jaya; *The New Magdalen:* Leavy, Barbara Fass.

DISSERTATIONS

Ackershoek, Maryanne. "The Snake With Its Tail in Its Mouth: Constructions of Detective Fiction" [Collins, Doyle, Christie]. Diss. Brown U, 1993.

Balée, Susan Carol. "Sensation Novels of the 1860s: Murder and Madness Everywhere, But Revolution Repressed" [Collins, Reade, Wood, Braddon]. Diss. Columbia U, 1992.

Beaton, Richard. " 'The World Is Hard on Women': Women and Marriage in the Novels of Wilkie Collins." Diss. U of Wales, 1987.

Berry, John Charles. "British Serial Production: Author, Audience, Text." Diss. U of Rochester, 1989.

Carlson, Laurie Beth. "Narrative Experimentation in Four Mid-Victorian Novels" [E. and A. Brontë, Dickens, Collins]. Diss. U of Kansas, 1994.

Case, Alison Austin. "Writing the Female 'I': Gender and Narration in the 18th- and 19th-Century English Novel." Diss. Cornell U, 1991.

Cooke, Simon. "Collins's Vision: Modes of Visual Reading in the Fictions of Wilkie Collins." U of Exeter, 1997.

DeCicco, Lynne Marie. "Uneasy Alliances: Women and Lawyers in the Mid-Nineteenth-Century English Novel" [Dickens, Collins, Eliot]. Diss. Columbia U, 1992.

Dever, Carolyn Marie. "The Lady Vanishes: Psychoanalysis, Victorian Fiction and the Anxiety of Origins" [Dickens, Collins, Eliot, Darwin]. Diss. Harvard U, 1993.

Doucette, Clarice Marie. "Inside the Flickering Flame: Suspense in Wilkie Collins's 'The Woman in White,' Gide's 'Isabelle' and Robbe-Grillet's 'Le Voyeur.' " Diss. Washington U, 1991.

Farmer, Steve John. "Wilkie Collins's Nonfictional Contributions to Mid-Victorian Weekly Periodicals: The Roots of an Unconventional Morality Apparent in the Major Novels of the 1860s." Diss. U of Kansas, 1989.

Grose, Janet Lynne. "The Sensation Novel and Social Reform: Revising Prescriptions of Gender, Marriage, and Domesticity" [Collins, Braddon, Dickens, Eliot, A. Trollope]. Diss. U of South Carolina, 1995.

Hall, Donald Eugene. "The Literature of Threat: Feminism and English Male Novelists, 1840–1870." Diss. U of Maryland, 1991.

Hall, Jasmine Yong. "A Study in Scarlet Letters: Women and Crime in the Works of Arthur Conan Doyle, Mary Elizabeth Braddon, Wilkie Collins, and Charles Dickens." Diss. Boston U, 1990.

Heller, Wendy Tamar. "Wilkie Collins and the Female Gothic: A Study in the Politics of Genre and Literary Revision." Diss. Yale U, 1988.

Holmes, Martha Stoddard. "Fictions of Affliction: Physical Disabilities in Victorian Culture." Diss. U of Colorado, 1996.

Howe, Winona Ruth. "Writing a Book in Company: The Collaborative Works of Charles Dickens and Wilkie Collins." Diss. U of California (Riverside), 1991.

Ledwon, Lenora P. "Legal Fictions: Constructions of the Female Legal Subject in Nineteenth-Century Law and Literature" [Scott, F. Trollope, Collins, Stoker]. Diss. U of Notre Dame, 1993.

Lemmens, Cheryl Ann. "Dark Recesses of the Soul: Victimization in Selected British Fiction from *Clarissa* to *The Collector*." Diss. U of Toronto, 1988.

Maik, Linda L. "The Female 'I': Woman's Voice in Multivoiced Mid-Victorian Novels." Diss. U of Wisconsin (Milwaukee), 1990.

Masciarotte, Gloria-Jean. "Breaking Society's Looking-Glass: The Feminine Subject/ The Sensation Novel/The Textual Difference." Diss. Brown U, 1988.

May, Leila Silvana. "Relatively Speaking: Representations of Siblings in Nineteenth-Century British Literature." Diss. U of California (Berkeley), 1994.

Milbank, Alison. "Daughters of the House: Modes of the Gothic in the Fiction of Wilkie Collins, Charles Dickens and Sheridan Le Fanu." Diss. U of Lancaster, 1988.

Moore, Pamela Lee. "An Insoluble Mystery Is Standing on Your Hearthrug: Investigations of Female Bodies in Sensation Fiction" [Braddon, Collins]. Diss. SUNY (Stony Brook), 1995.

Morris, Debra Sharon. "The Matrilineal in Wilkie Collins's Novels." Diss. Pennsylvania State U, 1994.

Oberhelman, David Dean. "Mad Encounters: Nineteenth-Century British Psychological Medicine and the Victorian Novel, 1840–1870" [Braddon, Collins, Dickens, A. Trollope]. Diss. U of California (Irvine), 1993.

O'Fallon, Kathleen Adele. "No Longer 'Condemned to Narrate': Undefining Wilkie Collins' Fiction." Diss. U of Oregon, 1988.

Otsuki, Jennifer Lynn. "Totalization and the Other: Images of Race and Gender in Victorian Realism" [Thackeray, Collins, Forster]. Diss. U of California (Irvine), 1991.

Poulson, Sally-Ann. "Reversed Perspectives: A Reexamination of the Later Novels of Wilkie Collins." Diss. Warwick U, 1999 (expected).

Rabuck, Donna Fontanarose. "The Other Side of Silence: Performing Heroinism in the Victorian Novel." Diss. Rutgers U, 1990.

Schmitt, Cannon. "Alien Nation: Gothic Fictions and English Nationality, 1797–1897" [Radcliffe, C. Brontë, Collins]. Diss. Indiana U, 1994.

Sherlock, Robin Elizabeth. " 'Fatal Resemblances': Educating the Female Body" [C. Brontë, Collins, Braddon, Wood]. Diss. U of Rochester, 1996.

Shumway, Suzanne Rosenthal. " 'Mad, Bad, and Embruted': Imagining Female Madness in the Structure of the Novel." Diss. U of Texas at Austin, 1991.

Shutt, Nicola Justine Louise. "Nobody's Child: The Theme of Illegitimacy in the Novels of Charles Dickens, George Eliot and Wilkie Collins." Diss. U of York, 1990.

Taylor, Jenny Bourne. "Wilkie Collins and Nineteenth Century Psychology: Cultural Significance and Fictional Form." Diss. U of Warwick, 1987.

Thoms, Peter Gordon. " 'The Windings of the Labyrinth': Quest and Structure in the Major Novels of Wilkie Collins." Diss. Queen's U at Kingston, 1989.

Tutor, Jonathan Craig. "The Psychological and Spiritual Implications of Wilkie Collins's *Armadale*." Diss. U of Mississippi, 1989.

Van Essen, Thomas. "Figuring the Father: The Paternal Thematics of Wilkie Collins." Diss. Rutgers U, 1987.

Williams, Mary Kellen. " 'Leaping Pulses and Secret Pleasures': Inscribing the Wayward Body in Late-Nineteenth Century Fiction'' [Collins, Stevenson, Wilde, Conrad]. Diss. Washington U, 1994.

In working on this essay, I received help and advice from a number of colleagues, and would especially like to thank Tom Hayward, Elaine Ardia, Jane Costlow and Steve Dillon, all of Bates College.

WORKS CITED

Allan, Janice M. "Scenes of Writing: Detection and Psychoanalysis in Wilkie Collins's *The Moonstone.*" *Imprimatur* 1 (Spring 1996): 186–93.

Balée, Susan. "Wilkie Collins and Surplus Women: The Case of Marian Halcombe." *Victorian Literature and Culture* 20 (1992): 197–215.

Barickman, Richard, Susan MacDonald, and Myra Stark. *Corrupt Relations: Dickens, Thackeray, Trollope, Collins, and the Victorian Sexual System.* New York: Columbia UP, 1982.

Beetz, Kirk H. "Wilkie Collins Studies, 1972–1983." *Dickens Studies Annual* 13 (1984): 333–55.

Bernstein, Stephen. "Reading Blackwater Park: Gothicism, Narrative, and Ideology in *The Woman in White.*" *Studies in the Novel* 25,3 (Fall 1993): 291–305.

Blain, Virginia. Introduction. *No Name.* Oxford: Oxford UP, 1998. vii–xxi.

Boyle, Thomas. *Black Swine in the Sewers of Hampstead: Beneath the Surface of Victorian Sensationalism.* New York: Viking, 1989.

Brooks, Peter. *Reading for the Plot: Design and Intention in Narrative.* Cambridge: Harvard UP, 1984.

Caracciolo, Peter L. "Wilkie Collins and the Ladies of Baghdad, or the Sleeper Awakened." *The "Arabian Nights" in English Literature: Studies in the Reception of "The Thousand and One Nights" into British Culture.* Ed. Peter L. Caracciolo. New York: St. Martin's, 1988. 143–77.

Chattman, Lauren. "Diagnosing the Domestic Woman in *The Woman in White* and *Dora.*" *Eroticism and Containment: Notes from the Flood Plain.* Ed. Carol Siegel and Ann Kibbey. New York: New York UP, 1994. 123–53.

Clarke, William M. *The Secret Life of Wilkie Collins.* Rev. ed. Phoenix Mill, England: Sutton, 1996.

————. "A Teasing 'Marital' Correspondence with a Twelve-Year-Old." *Wilkie Collins to the Forefront.* Ed. Nelson Smith and R. C. Terry. New York: AMS, 1995. 31–36.

Collins, Wilkie. *The Woman in White.* Ed. John Sutherland. Oxford: Oxford UP, 1998.

Crooks, Robert. "Reopening the Mysteries: Colonialist Logic and Cultural Difference in *The Moonstone* and *The Horse Latitudes.*" *Literature* 4,3 (1993): 215–28.

Cvetkovich, Ann. *Mixed Feelings: Feminism, Mass Culture, and Victorian Sensationalism.* Brunswick, NJ: Rutgers UP, 1992.

David, Deirdre. "Rewriting the Male Plot in Wilkie Collins's *No Name:* Captain Wragge Orders an Omelette and Mrs. Wragge Goes into Custody." *Out of Bounds: Male Writers and Gender(ed) Criticism.* Ed. Laura Claridge and Elizabeth Langland. Amherst: U of Massachusetts P, 1990. 186–96.

————. *Rule Britannia: Women, Empire, and Victorian Writing.* Ithaca: Cornell UP, 1995.

Duncan, Ian. "*The Moonstone,* the Victorian Novel, and Imperialist Panic." *Modern Language Quarterly* 55, 3 (September 1994): 297–319.

Elam, Diane. "White Narratology: Gender and Reference in Wilkie Collins's *The Woman in White.*" *Virginal Sexuality and Textuality in Victorian Literature.* Ed. Lloyd Davis. Albany: State U of New York P, 1993.

Farmer, Steve. Introduction. *Heart and Science.* Peterborough, Ontario: Broadview P, 1996. 7–27.

Frick, Patricia. "The Fallen Angels of Wilkie Collins." *International Journal of Women's Studies* 7,4 (September–October 1984): 343–51.

————. "Wilkie Collins' 'Little Jewel': The Meaning of *The Moonstone.*" *Philological Quarterly* 63,3 (Summer 1984): 313–21.

Ford, Mark. Introduction. *No Name.* Harmondsworth: Penguin, 1994. vii–xvii.

Goldman, Dorothy. Introduction. *Basil: A Story of Modern Life.* Oxford: Oxford UP, 1990.

Gomel, Elana and Stephen Weninger. "The Tell-Tale Surface: Fashion and Gender in *The Woman in White.*" *Victorians Institute Journal* 25 (1997): 29–58.

Gruner, Elizabeth Rose. "Family Secrets and the Mysteries of *The Moonstone.*" *Victorian Literature and Culture* 21 (1993): 127–45.

Hall, Donald E. *Fixing Patriarchy: Feminism and Mid-Victorian Novelists.* New York: New York UP, 1996.

Heller, Tamar. *Dead Secrets: Wilkie Collins and the Female Gothic.* New Haven: Yale UP, 1992.

Hendershot, Cyndy. "A Sensation Novel's Appropriation of the Terror-Gothic: Wilkie Collins' *The Woman in White*." *Clues* 13,2 (Fall–Winter 1992): 127–33.

Hennelly, Mark M., Jr. "Detecting Collins' Diamond: From Serpentstone to Moonstone." *Nineteenth-Century Fiction* 39,1 (June 1984): 25–47.

Hughes, Winifred. *The Maniac in the Cellar: Sensation Novels of the 1860s.* Princeton: Princeton UP, 1980.

Huskey, Melynda. "*No Name:* Embodying the Sensation Heroine." *Victorian Newsletter* 82 (Fall 1992): 5–13.

Kalikoff, Beth. *Murder and Moral Decay in Victorian Popular Literature.* Ann Arbor: UMI Research P, 1986.

Karl, Frederick R. Introduction. *The Moonstone.* New York: Signet, 1984. 1–21.

Kent, Christopher. "Probability, Reality and Sensation in the Novels of Wilkie Collins." *Dickens Studies Annual* 20 (1991): 259–80.

Knoepflmacher, U. C. "The Counterworld of Victorian Fiction and *The Woman in White*." *The Worlds of Victorian Fiction.* Ed. Jerome H. Buckley. Harvard English Studies 6. Cambridge: Harvard UP, 1975. 351–69.

Langbauer, Laurie. "Women in White, Men in Feminism." *Yale Journal of Criticism* 2,2 (Spring 1989): 219–43.

Law, Graham. Introduction. *The Evil Genius.* Peterborough, Ontario: Broadview P, 1994. 7–30.

Lawrence, Keith. "The Religion of Wilkie Collins: Three Unpublished Documents." *Huntington Library Quarterly* 52,3 (Summer 1989): 389–402.

Leavy, Barbara Fass. "Wilkie Collins' *The New Magdalen* and the Folklore of the Kind and the Unkind Girls." *Wilkie Collins to the Forefront: Some Reassessments.* Ed. Nelson Smith and R. C. Terry. New York: AMS, 1995. 209–25.

Ledwon, Lenora. "Veiled Women, the Law of Coverture, and Wilkie Collins's *The Woman in White*." *Victorian Literature and Culture* 22 (1994): 1–22.

Liebman, Arthur and David H. Galerstein. "The Sign of the Moonstone." *Baker Street Journal* 44 (1994): 71–74.

Litvak, Joseph. *Caught in the Act: Theatricality in the Nineteenth-Century English Novel.* Berkeley: U of California P, 1992.

Loesberg, Jonathan. "The Ideology of Narrative Form in Sensation Fiction." *Representations* 13 (Winter 1986): 115–38.

Lonoff, Sue. "Multiple Narratives and Relative Truths: A Study of *The Ring and the Book, The Woman in White,* and *The Moonstone*." *Browning Institute Studies* 10 (1982): 143–61.

MacDonagh, Gwendolyn and Jonathan Smith. " 'Fill Up All the Gaps': Narrative and Illegitimacy in *The Woman in White.*" *Journal of Narrative Technique* 26,3 (Fall 1996): 274–91.

Mangum, Teresa. "Wilkie Collins, Detection, and Deformity." *Dickens Studies Annual* 26 (1998): 285–310.

Masciarotte, Gloria-Jean. "The Madonna with Child, and Another Child, and Still Another Child . . . : Sensationalism and the Dysfunction of Emotions." *Discourse* 14,1 (Winter 1991–92): 88–125.

May, Leila Silvana. "Sensational Sisters: Wilkie Collins's *The Woman in White.*" *Pacific Coast Philology* 30,1 (1995): 82–102.

Maynard, Jessica. "Telling the Whole Truth: Wilkie Collins and the Lady Detective." *Victorian Identities: Social and Cultural Formations in Nineteenth-Century Literature.* Ed. Ruth Robbins and Julian Wolfreys. New York: St. Martin's, 1996. 187–98.

Meckier, Jerome. "Wilkie Collins's *The Woman in White:* Providence Against the Evils of Propriety." *Journal of British Studies* 22,1 (Fall 1982): 104–26.

Mehta, Jaya. "English Romance; Indian Violence." *Centennial Review* 39,4 (Fall 1995): 611–57.

Michie, Helena. " 'There Is No Friend Like a Sister': Sisterhood as Sexual Difference." *ELH* 56,2 (Summer 1989): 401–21.

Milbank, Alison. *Daughters of the House: Modes of the Gothic in Victorian Fiction.* London: Macmillan, 1992.

Miller, D. A. *The Novel and the Police.* Berkeley: U of California P, 1988.

Milligan, Barry. *Pleasures and Pains: Opium and the Orient in Nineteenth-Century British Culture.* Charlottesville: UP of Virginia, 1995.

Morris, Virginia B. *Double Jeopardy: Women Who Kill in Victorian Fiction.* Lexington: UP of Kentucky, 1990.

Nadel, Ira B. Introduction. *The Dead Secret.* Oxford: Oxford UP, 1997.

Nayder, Lillian. "Agents of Empire in *The Woman in White.*" *Victorian Newsletter* 83 (Spring 1993): 1–7.

———. "Robinson Crusoe and Friday in Victorian Britain: 'Discipline,' 'Dialogue,' and Collins's Critique of Empire in *The Moonstone.*" *Dickens Studies Annual* 21 (1991): 213–31.

———. *Wilkie Collins.* New York: Twayne, 1997.

O'Fallon, Kathleen. "Breaking the Laws about Ladies: Wilkie Collins' Questioning of Gender Roles." *Wilkie Collins to the Forefront: Some Reassessments.* Ed. Nelson Smith and R. C. Terry. New York: AMS, 1995. 227–39.

O'Neill, Philip. *Wilkie Collins: Women, Property and Propriety.* Totowa, NJ: Barnes and Noble, 1988.

Page, Norman. Introduction. *Mad Monkton and Other Stories.* Oxford: Oxford UP, 1994.

———. Introduction. *Man and Wife.* Oxford: Oxford UP, 1995. vii–xxiv.

Park, Hyungji. " 'The Story of Our Lives': *The Moonstone* and the Indian Mutiny in *All the Year Round.*" Typescript. *Negotiating India in the Nineteenth-Century Media.* Ed. Douglas M. Peers and David Finkelstein. London: Macmillan, forthcoming (1999).

Perkins, Pamela and Mary Donaghy. "A Man's Resolution: Narrative Strategies in Wilkie Collins' *The Woman in White.*" *Studies in the Novel* 22,4 (Winter 1990): 392–402.

Peters, Catherine. Introduction and Explanatory Notes. *Armadale.* Oxford: Oxford UP, 1991. vii–xxiii, 819–29.

———. Introduction. *Hide and Seek.* Oxford: Oxford UP, 1993.

———. Introduction. *The Moonstone.* New York: Alfred A. Knopf, 1992. v–xxiv.

———. Introduction. *Poor Miss Finch.* Oxford: Oxford UP, 1995. vii–xxiii.

———. " 'Invite No Dangerous Publicity': Some Independent Women and Their Effect on Wilkie Collins's Life and Writing." *Wilkie Collins to the Forefront: Some Reassessments.* Ed. Nelson Smith and R. C. Terry. New York: AMS, 1995. 11–29.

———. *The King of Inventors: A Life of Wilkie Collins.* Princeton: Princeton UP, 1991.

Priestman, Martin. *Detective Fiction and Literature: The Figure on the Carpet.* New York: St. Martin's, 1991.

Pykett, Lyn. *The Sensation Novel: From "The Woman in White" to "The Moonstone."* Plymouth: Northcote House, 1994.

Rance, Nicholas. " 'A Terribly Strange Bed': Self-Subverting Gothic." *Wilkie Collins Society Journal* 7 (1987): 5–12.

———. *Wilkie Collins and Other Sensation Novelists: Walking the Moral Hospital.* Rutherford, NJ: Fairleigh Dickinson UP, 1991.

Reed, John R. "English Imperialism and the Unacknowledged Crime of *The Moonstone.*" *Clio* 2 (June 1973): 281–90.

Roy, Ashish. "The Fabulous Imperialist Semiotic of Wilkie Collins's *The Moonstone*." *New Literary History* 24 (1993): 657–81.

Schmitt, Cannon. "Alien Nation: Gender, Genre, and English Nationality in Wilkie Collins's *The Woman in White*." *Genre* 26 (1993): 283–310.

Shaw, W. David. *Victorians and Mystery: Crises of Representation*. Ithaca: Cornell UP, 1990.

Stave, Shirley A. "The Perfect Murder: Patterns of Repetition and Doubling in Wilkie Collins's *The Woman in White*." *Dickens Studies Annual* 25 (1996): 287–303.

Stewart, J. I. M. Introduction. *The Moonstone*. Harmondsworth: Penguin, 1986. 7–24.

Sucksmith, Harvey Peter. Introduction. *The Woman in White*. Oxford: Oxford UP, 1991. v–xx.

Surridge, Lisa. "Unspeakable Histories: Hester Dethridge and the Narration of Domestic Violence in *Man and Wife*." *Victorian Review* 22,2 (Winter 1996): 102–26.

Sutherland, John. Introduction and Notes. *Armadale*. Harmondsworth: Penguin, 1995. vii–xxvi, 681–710.

———. Introduction. *The Woman in White*. Oxford: Oxford UP, 1998. vii–xxiii.

———. "Wilkie Collins and the Origins of the Sensation Novel." *Dickens Studies Annual* 20 (1991): 243–58.

Taylor, Jenny Bourne. *In the Secret Theatre of Home: Wilkie Collins, Sensation Narrative, and Nineteenth-Century Psychology*. London: Routledge, 1988.

———. Introduction. *The Law and the Lady*. Oxford: Oxford UP, 1992. vii–xxiv.

Thomas, Ronald R. *Dreams of Authority: Freud and the Fictions of the Unconscious*. Ithaca: Cornell UP, 1990.

———. "Minding the Body Politic: The Romance of Science and the Revision of History in Victorian Detective Fiction." *Victorian Literature and Culture* 19 (1991): 233–54.

———. "Wilkie Collins and the Sensation Novel." *The Columbia History of the British Novel*. Ed. John Richetti. New York: Columbia UP, 1994. 479–507.

Thoms, Peter. *Detection and Its Designs: Narrative and Power in Nineteenth-Century Detective Fiction*. Athens: Ohio UP, 1998.

———. *The Windings of the Labyrinth: Quest and Structure in the Major Novels of Wilkie Collins*. Athens: Ohio UP, 1992.

Trodd, Anthea. *Domestic Crime in the Victorian Novel*. New York: St. Martin's, 1989.

———. Introduction. *The Moonstone*. Oxford: Oxford UP, 1998. vii–xxi.

Watt, George. *The Fallen Woman in the Nineteenth-Century English Novel.* London: Croom Helm, 1984.

Welsh, Alexander. *Strong Representations: Narrative and Circumstantial Evidence in England.* Baltimore: Johns Hopkins UP, 1992.

Wiesenthal, C. S. "From Charcot to Plato: The History of Hysteria in *Heart and Science.*" *Wilkie Collins to the Forefront: Some Reassessments.* Ed. Nelson Smith and R. C. Terry. New York: AMS, 1995. 257–68.

"Wilkie Collins." *Appleton's Journal of Popular Literature, Science, and Art* (3 September 1870): 278–81.

Review Essay: Fin de Siècle

Margaret D. Stetz

New perspectives on the origins of the modern age may be found in five recent scholarly studies and editions, which set late-Victorian fiction writers in the context of changing notions of religious observance, biological science, English and Irish national identity, and authorship as a profession. The volumes under review are Children of the Ghetto, The Oscar Wilde Encyclopedia, Wilde the Irishman, The Shape of Fear: Horror and the Fin de Siècle Culture of Decadence *and* British Literary Culture and Publishing Practice, 1880–1914. *All five books embed figures such as Zangwill, Wilde, and Conrad in a milieu not just of shifting ideas, but of shifting publication practices and audience expectations. Collectively, these works produce a picture of the literary fin de siècle as a uniquely forward-looking period, yet also as one that demonstrated a nostalgic and conservative impulse, especially through its admiration of Charles Dickens and his contemporaries as embodiments of the lost world of the Victorian men of letters.*

As Victorianists, we often take it as a critical truism that "modernity" began not at the start of the twentieth century, but at the close of the nineteenth. Are we guilty of inflating the importance of the period that we study, by describing it as the point of origin for all that was to follow? Or did something genuinely new happen at the fin de siècle that we can identify as heralding a change in daily life and culture in general, as well as in literature and its practice? Where should we look for the signs of change?

For those interested in the history of publishing as one indicator of cultural shifts, a significant date to ponder might be October 1891. In that month, the

English firm of Hodder and Stoughton released the first issue of a periodical called the *Bookman*. Earlier that same year, the novelist George Gissing, alarmed by the movement that he perceived as a new commodification of authorship and of literature, had made the fictional protagonists of *New Grub Street* joke bitterly that the next development should probably be a journal devoted to satire and gossip about the literary world and its doings. But here indeed was a perfectly serious monthly dedicated wholly to the exchange of information about bookselling, bookbuying, book collecting, and publishing in general. It featured articles (some with portraits) on authors living or dead, accounts of financial successes and failures among the provincial dailies, columns about the latest selections at the circulating libraries, a "Young Author's Page" with advice to would-be writers and public evaluations of the individual manuscripts sent in by readers, along with lists of all the latest books published, arranged by category. Like many an earlier literary magazine, it printed both long and short reviews of books and journals; unlike these, it initiated a column known as "Sales of Books During the Month." As the first issue put it, "We propose under this heading to give from month to month statements by representative and leading booksellers of the volumes they have found most popular during the month (15th to 15th)." With that, the bestseller list was born. Watching titles move up and down became a new source of both entertainment and anxiety; the relationship of reading and writing to business became newly visible. The world of literature, at least, would never be the same.

But what has all this to do with the concerns of a scholarly journal titled *Dickens Studies Annual*? At the very moment when a new age was announcing itself, so too was the continued importance of Charles Dickens in that age publicly affirmed. The opening feature of the October 1891 *Bookman,* a column of "News Notes," contained the following paragraph:

> None of the many issues of Charles Dickens, published by Messrs. Chapman and Hall, have pleased better than the "Crown" edition, just completed in seventeen volumes. The whole of the original illustrations are given, and the paper, printing, and binding reflect great credit on the firm. We understand that, in response to a very generally expressed wish, Messrs. Chapman and Hall intend to publish Forster's "Life of Dickens" in the same form. The demand for Dickens increases day by day.   (16)

Clearly, this was a lovely example of publisher's puffery, yet it was also a bit of accurate reporting. Not only was the reading public's demand for Dickens increasing, at the fin de siècle in England, but so were references to and evaluations of Dickens's legacy proliferating.

Throughout the Nineties, these could be found in quite unexpected, as well as in more predictable, places. Into the category of the former fell, for instance, "New Woman" novels—the fiction by and about women who expressed their discontent with traditional hierarchies of gender and with the social and cultural institutions enforcing those hierarchies. In one such work, *A Fair Deceiver* (1898) by Emily Morse Symonds—a cousin of John Addington Symonds, who published as "George Paston"—the tribute came through the back door, by way of a devastatingly satirical portrait of a fin-de-siècle aesthete and Dickens detractor. This rather Oscar Wildean figure was made to grow ever more ridiculous, both in the eyes of the other characters and of the readers, as he launched into an attack, "with a contemptuous ring in his voice," upon his literary predecessor:

> "Dickens is a negligible quantity. Nobody thinks of reading him nowadays, any more than they read Tennyson. In a few years' time perhaps the literary elect will read 'Pickwick' and the 'Idylls of the King' again for the same reason that we now read Landor and Beddoes—because we do not share them with the common herd. I am rather thinking of reviving Dickens myself one of these days by an analytical article. . . . Only I suppose I should have to glance through some of his works, and I should be afraid of spoiling my style." (182)

Even from a very "advanced" and politically active feminist came the message: Those writers who attempted to assert their own modernity by discrediting the achievements of Dickens merely discredited themselves.

This was a sentiment shared, as might have been more readily anticipated, by end-of-the century novelists and critics of a more conservative bent. George Gissing, nostalgic for an age that had appreciated and encouraged Men of Vision, rather than the mere literary tradesmen to be found at the turn of the century, turned with reverence to the subject of Dickens's legacy. As he declared in *Charles Dickens: A Critical Study* (1898),

> It is the privilege of a great writer to put into his work the finest qualities of his heart and brain, to make permanent the best part of himself, and through that to influence the world. In speaking of Dickens's triumphs as an author, I have felt that the most fervent praise could not err by excess; every time I open his books, as the years go on, it is with ever more of wonder, delight, admiration, and love. (227)

Such triumphs, it was implied, were less likely in the current age, when grasping publishers and equally mercenary authors ran the show. To affiliate oneself with Dickens and to laud his accomplishments became a covert way of paying homage to what had supposedly been lost.

Gissing was not the only late-Victorian writer to draw these connections and to be both a disciple of Dickens and an opponent of the new commercialism that dominated publishing in the closing decades of the century. His contemporary, Israel Zangwill (1864–1926), made his feelings clear in the essay "Authors and Publishers," originally issued in the *Pall Mall Magazine* and collected in the 1896 volume, *Without Prejudice,* where he lamented that the publishers have at last abandoned the pretence of being swayed by any but pecuniary considerations in the exercise of their high function. . . . And yet, I confess, my heart shelters a regret for the old style of publisher, as for the old style of author. . . . The publisher as the patron of genius, the nurser of young talent, the re-inspirer of old, the scholar and gentleman, at once the friend and the banker of his authors, makes a pleasing figure. . . . Still, if the publisher would live up to this ideal, his would remain an honorable profession, instead of sinking to a trade. . . . But the trail of business is over the age. . . .

(231–232)

It was perhaps no surprise, then, that Zangwill also looked to Dickens as one of his heroes, as the exemplar of a commercial success that seemingly had been won without sacrifice of quality to the demands of market forces. Yet this hero-worship proved a little surprising nonetheless, for Zangwill was an English-born Jew, who had grown up feeling the heat from the blaze of anti-semitism fanned by the creation of Fagin and incompletely damped by the penning of Riah the Jew. He had every reason to regard the preservation of Dickens's legacy into a new century with some ambivalence, but found cause instead to celebrate it.

The Israel Zangwill that we meet through Meri-Jane Rochelson's introduction to the superb new edition of *Children of the Ghetto,* his 1892 novel, is a complicated, yet appealing figure, with diverse and conflicting allegiances—someone who could identify both with the British past and the Jewish future and vice versa. In another recent account of Zangwill's character—an essay for volume 197 of the *Dictionary of Literary Biography*—Rochelson has presented him as an appreciator of earlier Victorian literary traditions, but also as a Zionist and, for that matter, a feminist. In sympathy with a number of modern political movements, but romantically nostalgic for an ordered world in which elders were treated with reverence and literary forebears respected as models, Zangwill proved a mixture of radicalism and of mainstream English cultural conservatism. The Dickensian inheritance came through most strongly in his advocacy of realism, the mode he regarded, according to Rochelson, "as the highest form of truth." Throughout his turn-of-the-century fiction, "his message," in contrast to that of numerous contemporaries, was "that art must have a message, or at least an ethical rather than a purely aesthetic foundation" (*DLB 197,* 311). The particular ethical messages of his art were unique, however, in being shaped to appeal simultaneously to a dual audience, comprised of Jewish and Christian readers.

Fittingly, Rochelson has produced an edition of Zangwill's best known novel that also addresses the needs of several audiences at once. When it comes to elucidating the many references to Orthodox rituals and religious artifacts that fill *Children of the Ghetto,* Rochelson takes nothing for granted. Thus, in her note on the mention of "phylacteries and praying shawls," she not only provides the names by which these are better known to Jews (respectively, *tefillin* and *tallit, talith,* or *tallis*), but explanations of the objects' origins and functions, for the benefit of non-Jews. Her note goes beyond mere elucidation, however, to become a kind of mini-lecture in social history, as she considers the changing functions of these objects within a changing culture:

> Although today some women are beginning to use both *tefillin* and *tallitot,* they were traditionally used only by men, and certainly that would have been the case in the community described in *Children of the Ghetto.* Use of the tallit by Jewish men in synagogues is and was nearly universal (the exception being in Reform congregations), while today the use of the tefillin is limited to those observant Jews who say daily prayers. (Rochelson, 507–08)

To have said what roles these "phylacteries and praying shawls" played in the late-nineteenth century would, strictly speaking, have sufficed. But by exceeding a purely explanatory function as editor, Rochelson gets closer to the spirit of Zangwill's text. *Children of the Ghetto* is a narrative that chronicles evolution within the Anglo-Jewish community—an almost Darwinian tale of survival through adaptation to new environments and to new circumstances, as seen in the context of both middle-class and working-class families. The position that it shows Judaism inhabiting in modern London might be summed up by using the title of another of Zangwill's minor masterpieces of the 1890s, a short story called "Transitional." Rochelson's editorial additions make clear that both the Jewish religion itself and the culture surrounding it have never been static, and that adjustments to altered circumstances, such as shifts in gender relations and the abandonment of some forms of worship, did not end in Zangwill's day. Her approach emphasizes that the value of the novel, apart from its aesthetic success as an absorbing story of intergenerational conflict, lies in its ability to document a particular moment in the living tradition of Judaism in the West, and that the tradition itself has continued to be a "transitional" one. Though her discussions of religious practices may sometimes refer to those in North American communities, rather than specifically to the habits of British ones, Meri-Jane Rochelson, like Zangwill, keeps her eyes simultaneously on Judaism's past and present and finds interest in uncovering the relations between them.

She also remains alert throughout to the needs of both the Victorian scholar and the less expert reader. This would be a splendid edition for a college classroom, although its price of nearly thirty dollars may be steep for some students' pockets. Rochelson's attention to placing the details of novelistic plot and setting within a frame of social history—connecting, for example, the individual portrait of a "sweater" with the English public's revulsion against the Jewish owners of garment factories, or "sweating establishments," of the 1880s—gives Zangwill's fiction a second level of significance for those who come to it with little background. Her care in deciding what various audiences ought to know (and when they should know it) shows everywhere, never more than in the thoughtful heading to pages 28 to 36 of the introduction, where she warns those who don't wish to be informed of the characters' fates in advance "to read this portion . . . after finishing the novel." Behind all the editorial decisions lies an evident love of Zangwill's text and a wish to give readers of many sorts as rewarding an encounter with it as possible.

Devotion to an author's achievements is also the dominant emotion behind another reader-oriented work of scholarship on the fin de siècle, Karl Beckson's massive *Oscar Wilde Encyclopedia.* In this case, of course, there is no need to introduce the artist to the audience—certainly not now, when film, theater, and mass market publishing, on both sides of the Atlantic, have been swept up in the celebration of Wilde, and when a major public monument to him has just been unveiled in London. If there is any fin de siècle writer who can be seen to occupy, at the end of our own century, the position that Charles Dickens did at the end of the last one, then it is Wilde. It would be no exaggeration to say that "the demand for [him] increases day by day." And just as Dickens became an emblematic figure for those who wished to affiliate themselves with the literary and cultural values of another time, in order to uphold a tradition of "genius" against the pressures of late-Victorian commodification, so Wilde serves now as the figurehead of oppositional cultural politics. Looking back to Wilde and claiming his legacy for oneself has turned into a commonplace act, albeit still a chic one. In Autumn 1998, for instance, the Bravo Network aired a documentary imported from BBC television—a 1997 program written by Michael Bracewell for the "Omnibus" series—in which pop stars such as Neil Tennant of The Pet Shop Boys announced their debt to the style and imagery of self-display that Wilde pioneered.

The *Oscar Wilde Encyclopedia,* alas, is not the place to explore these questions of use and influence. As Karl Beckson writes, somewhat apologetically, in his introduction, "Restrictions on space have necessitated the exclusion of any mention of plays, novels, recordings, and videos based on Wilde's works or life," for that material "would necessitate a second volume" (xi–xii). I'm sure that I am not alone in hoping that Beckson himself will be persuaded to produce that volume; such a companion work seems essential, and the author of the *Encyclopedia* well qualified to undertake it.

There are, of course, obvious ironies attached to the publication of this large and quite expensive reference source. In the 1890s, the name of Charles Dickens was invoked by Gissing and Zangwill to endorse the practice of realism, whereas Oscar Wilde stood for anti-realism—for viewing fiction as the art of stylish lying, owing nothing to actual life. But here, as Merlin

Holland (Wilde's grandson, via younger son Vyvyan) points out in his witty foreword, is an encyclopedia that enmeshes Wilde in a web of facts. This volume is indeed an invaluable aid to those who read and study Wilde, even casually; yet, as Holland reminds us, "the epithet 'useful' " was one of his grandfather's "least favorite words—the uselessness of anything being, for the most part, directly proportional to its attractiveness as far as he was concerned" (ix). And in terms of physical beauty as a book, this *Encyclopedia,* with its merely serviceable format, leaves something to be desired. There would not have been much for Wilde to admire in its crowded, double-columned pages, so sparing with margins, and its grayish-toned reproductions of photographs squeezed cheek-by-jowl on the same pages with text.

But fortunately, Wilde is not the audience for this book; we of the late-twentieth century are, and we are privileged to have it. Perhaps its greatest appeal will be to those who want to know more about the Wilde who participated in the world of late-Victorian journalism and marketing that so distressed novelists such as George Gissing. Beckson has hunted down Wilde's published reviews, signed and unsigned, of contemporary books and plays, read every one of them, and summarized their contents. The result is an utterly fascinating new sense of Wilde's centrality to the literary world of the 1880s and early 1890s—not only as an author or lecturer, but as a working critic and a mainstay of the periodicals. Beckson is brilliant, moreover, in connecting these obscure and seemingly ephemeral pieces to Wilde's better known works, quoting and emphasizing lines that prefigure the epigrams from essays such as "The Critic as Artist" and "The Decay of Lying."

As one might expect, there are enormously helpful entries that provide capsule biographies of many figures of importance in Wilde's life. Lord Alfred Douglas is there, of course, along with an extensive cast of Wilde family members. But so too are the American expatriate and minor poet Stuart Merrill (1863–1915), the stage manager of an 1896 French production of *Salome;* Henry Du Pré Labouchere (1831–1912), whose Amendment to the Criminal Law Amendment Act of 1885 created the legal grounds for Wilde's prosecution; and the photographer Napoleon Sarony (1821–96), who took the famous glamor shots of Wilde on his American tour. Perhaps the one missing figure whose absence we might regret is the "New Woman" writer Ella Hepworth Dixon, a frequent contributor to *Woman's World,* when that magazine was under Wilde's editorship. Beckson supplies an engaging account of the satirical portrait of Wilde in Robert Hichens's *The Green Carnation* (1894), but is silent about the caricatures of Wilde that also featured prominently in Dixon's *My Flirtations* (1892) and *The Story of a Modern Woman* (1894).

Of recent works related to fin-de-siècle fiction, Rochelson's edition of Zangwill and Beckson's encyclopedia devoted to Wilde will probably have the widest-ranging impact. Both encourage the reading of primary texts and extend scholarly knowledge of the late-Victorian period of non-scholarly audiences. But there is much to recommend several other studies of the period that have appeared in the past year, although they direct themselves more predictably to academic readers alone. Not so much ground breaking works in themselves, these books prove most useful when supplementing or correcting existing bodies of knowledge about literature and the literary world at the turn of the last century.

As the title of a new collection of essays edited by Jerusha McCormack indicates, *Wilde the Irishman* sets out to highlight only one aspect of Wilde's identity. Yet Irishness occupies such a central place in that identity and one that has been so long neglected, that the concentration of focus seems justified. Indeed, McCormack asserts that "For the first time since his death, Wilde is being recognized as Irish" (5)—perhaps just a little bit of an exaggeration, considering the attention to Wilde that has long been paid in Ireland itself. Her claim, however, that "Irish" was an unstable category in the nineteenth century and one that Wilde helped to fix is largely true; as she says in her Introduction, "Wilde was inventing Ireland as he proceeded to invent himself, and, in inventing himself, helped to invent what is now modern Ireland" (2). He was, of course, not alone in such simultaneous defining of a self and of the nation at the close of the century. As might have been predicted, there are numerous and lengthy references throughout this volume to W. B. Yeats. Surprisingly, however, other expatriate contemporaries who participated with Wilde in this process of individual and cultural invention are almost wholly ignored by McCormack's contributors. George Moore rates but two brief mentions; "George Egerton" (Mary Chavelita Dunne), the "New Woman" writer whose novel *The Wheel of God* (1898) created one of the earliest images of Dublin street life and Irish Bohemian culture, is nowhere to be found, and neither is Katharine Tynan, the poet of Irish landscapes and domestic life, whose verse Wilde sought out in his role as editor of *Woman's World.*

What we do have in this volume is eclectic, eccentric, and sometimes rather fun in its waywardness. Although the collection has been pitched to an academic readership, not everything here takes the conventional form of the scholarly essay, and not everything adheres closely to the theme of the collection either. Thomas Kilroy has selected a scene from his 1997 play for the Abbey Theatre, *The Secret Fall of Constance Wilde,* in which Constance and Oscar face off in a dialogue shortly before their deaths, but say nothing about Ireland. Derek Mahon writes what is essentially a belated review of Richard Ellmann's biography, emphasizing Ellmann's failure to capture the significance of Wilde as "the apostle of a new way of being" (147), although he does not suggest that this was a particularly Irish-centered way of being.

There is also the text of a brief and graceful speech by the poet Seamus Heaney—a speech, however, that lauds Wilde's role as a destroyer of all categories, rather than as an inventor of the category of Irishness. In other words, a number of the contributions address the subject of *Wilde the Irishman* only by being about Wilde and by having been written by Irishmen.

Still, the academic essays that actually tackle Jerusha McCormack's topic, such as her own "The Wilde Irishman: Oscar as Aesthete and Anarchist," supply some welcome illumination. Owen Dudley Edwards's "Impressions of an Irish Sphinx," for instance, brilliantly interprets the backgrounds and material of Wilde's fairy tales as Irish: " 'The Nightingale and the Rose' is set in a town with a regal court as well as a university, and as such might derive from Dublin with its Viceregal Lodge more naturally than from Oxford" (59). Meanwhile, W. J. McCormack's "Wilde and Parnell" links the artist's deep interest in this most notorious of Irish politicians to the theme of the "guilty double life" (101), which finds its expression in *The Picture of Dorian Gray.*

Among the essays only peripherally related to Irish matters is John Wilson Foster's "Against Nature? Science and Oscar Wilde," which rather stretches the Irish theme by comparing Wilde's positive attitudes toward evolutionary science with those expressed by Yeats. Unfortunately, Foster must take his documentary evidence mainly from Wilde's Oxford notebooks, written at a period when Wilde was working hard to shed his Irish accent, interests, and identity. What Foster discovers, nonetheless, are signs of Wilde's receptiveness to an "evolutionary foundation of his belief in individuality" (120) and ultimately proof of "the importance of science"—of British science, one almost wishes to add perversely—to "Wilde's world view and artistic vision" (118). Using *The Picture of Dorian Gray,* Foster traces the influence of Wilde's readings of Darwin and Clifford. In the character of Dorian himself, he sees a "specimen . . . of devolution; that is, of the descent, rather than ascent, of man—a sociobiological reversion such as Spencer [an Englishman, of course] might have explained" (121).

Wilde occupies a prominent place, too, in Susan J. Navarette's *The Shape of Fear: Horror and the Fin de Siècle Culture of Decadence* and, once again, it is Wilde's Dorian who offers an attractive focus of study. If some fiction writers at the turn of the century, such as Gissing and Zangwill, viewed themselves as realists in an earlier Victorian tradition passed down from Dickens, and if Wilde positioned himself as the champion of anti-realism in response, then surely all would have been surprised to learn that *The Picture of Dorian Gray* has been reclassified here as a realist text. But Navarette explains:

> In the pursuit of a revised Decadence, the creators of fin de siècle horror became anatomists of the imagination, producing horror stories that served as apt metaphors not merely for the society that produced them but for the concept of

horror itself, which was represented far more realistically than even Darwin (whose research had helped to develop models for the scripting of the body, both literally and textually) could have imagined. . . . Decadent horror writers saw themselves not as fantasists but as true realists who depicted not the crude verities of a Thackeray or an Eliot—'the sweepings of a Pentonville omnibus' were all that Wilde could discern in the latter's novels—but rather what Pater had sought to capture in a style that could deliver 'that finest and most intimate form of truth, the *vraie vérité.*'   (44–45)

Echoing John Wilson Foster's perceptions, Navarette finds the novel "much more concerned with materialism, physicality, and scientific determinism than a cursory reading might suggest" (56). Thus for her, "*Dorian Gray* mines scientific theory as it tropes the human body, both as a text of outwardly pleasing aspect (in which ostensibly suppressed maladies and devolutionary promptings are scripted) and as the site of Gothic horrors" (57).

Navarette's broad definition of "Decadent horror" (in the visual arts, as well as in fiction), as concerned with representations of physical degeneration and with anxieties about the shaping influence of the inherited past upon the present, allows her to bring together groups of texts that might not otherwise have appeared in the same study. Wilde's *Dorian,* Henry James's *The Turn of the Screw,* Arthur Machen's *The Great God Pan,* and Beardsley's drawings of grotesque fetuses in evening clothes wind up side-by-side with Joseph Conrad's *Heart of Darkness.* The juxtapositions, in Navarette's capable hands, turn out to be felicitous and unexpectedly convincing. Read as a story of "the horror, the horror" in perhaps a more literal way than usual, Conrad's allegory of European imperialism begins to reveal surprising narrative underpinnings in common with the genre of the supernatural and stylistic features shared with the language of Decadence. For Navarette, Conrad's strategies are those of a deliberately evasive teller of ghost stories, as well as of a post-Paterian artist working through impressionism and suggestion: "Conrad sought to create a stylistic and textual dis-ease. . . . The reader confronts this textual anxiety and, unwittingly, labors from the first to fix fleeting impressions and to fill in the yawning gaps of meaning, thus acting as . . . a coconspirator in the creation of an evolving horror" (226).

Missing, however, from this account is a sense of who the reader was that Conrad wished to address as a "co-conspirator," as well as any discussion of other sorts of anxieties, extra-textual in nature, that complicated the relations between authors and audiences in the late Victorian period. To learn about the broader literary environment in which Conrad was working, one must consult Peter D. McDonald's *British Literary Culture and Publishing Practice, 1880–1914.* There, Conrad is the centerpiece of the first of the book's three long chapters, "Men of Letters and Children of the Sea: Joseph Conrad and the Henley Circle." With McDonald's study, we come back, in a sense, to the original question of what made the end of the nineteenth century "modern" and locate an answer, once again, in the changing world of publishing and in the increasingly self-conscious career of authorship.

McDonald proclaims his debt throughout to Pierre Bourdieu, the structural sociologist, from whom he has borrowed the notion of "the field"—that is, of an explicable system of socio-cultural "positions" existing at any given historical moment, determining "the entire life cycle of the text from writing to reading" (11). In turn-of-the-century England, with which McDonald concerns himself, "the field" comprised not merely the factual business matters of copyright, contracts, royalties, and distribution that underpinned the dealings of novelists with editors and publishers, but non-material notions of legitimacy and status, based on aesthetics, class, and reputation, that determined the relationships both of novelists and of their works to one another, and also of texts to readers and vice versa. McDonald sees the chief "predicaments" of the period as explained by Bourdieu's notion of two oppositions: "the purists versus the profiteers, on the one hand, and the establishment versus the newcomers, on the other" (17). He lines up first Conrad, then Arnold Bennett, and finally Arthur Conan Doyle according to this set of antitheses. But the polarities turn out, in practice, to be the ends of a spectrum with a greater shared middle than might initially appear.

In McDonald's view, Conrad—at least in the 1890s—was a "purist," out to make his reputation as an artist, rather than as a writer for the masses; "achieving the recognition of a 'few select spirits' was his first priority as a newcomer to the literary field" (24). Yet, as McDonald also notes, there was no such thing as pure purist: "Conrad valued the good opinion of recognized peers above all else, but, as he readily acknowledged, 'there is the problem of the daily bread which can not be solved by praise—public or private' " (24). The chapter on Conrad, then, focuses upon how the author deployed style, content, and ideology, in his 1897 novella *The Nigger of the Narcissus,* to negotiate this conflict between purism and profiteering—to gain the appreciation of W. E. Henley, who, as editor of the *National Observer* and later of the *New Review,* ruled an avant-garde circle dedicated to "the cult of the solitary genius" (34), while also advancing his own career as a writer with popular appeal.

The success with which he accomplished this negotiation was incomplete. *The Nigger of the Narcissus* did not, as Conrad had hoped, become a bestseller. But it did win over Henley—whose disciples at the *Observer* had published stinging dismissals of Conrad's previous novels—through its endorsement of "the Henley circle's anti-decadent cult of manliness" (65) and its conservative nostalgia for the values of a less democratic, less "mob"-oriented age. (Henley, it should be noted, was another of those end-of-the-century critics who looked back admiringly to Dickens and to the earlier

Victorians, to revive the image of the robust Man of Vision.) McDonald sees the novel as an "attack on modernity," but an attack driven not so much by deeply held personal convictions, as by Conrad's strategic sense of what the career of "author," in the age of modernity, would require of him: "To this extent, his text illustrates with particular force the complex non-discursive interests, some of which are specifically literary, at stake in any act of writing, and it testifies to the power of the field's structural determination" (66). Even personal ideology could fall into line, if the stakes were high enough.

At the fin de siècle, writers of fiction became aware, as never before, of "the field" and its exigencies and of the need to position themselves in relation to it. Whether "purists" or "profiteers," all were conscious in new ways of their connection to or rejection of a cultural and political milieu that was making demands quite different from those made upon their predecessors, such as Charles Dickens and his contemporaries. Thanks to the recent spate of informative critical works on the period, we are now beginning to recover a sense of precisely what that late-Victorian milieu was and of how individual authors, such as Zangwill, Wilde, and Conrad, moved within it and flourished. As we learn more about this vital moment of change at the end of the last century, surely we can hope to understand better how we got from there to here.

WORKS CITED

Children of the Ghetto: A Study of a Peculiar People by Israel Zangwill. Edited with an Introduction by Meri-Jane Rochelson. Detroit: Wayne State Press, 1998. 528 pp.

The Oscar Wilde Encyclopedia by Karl Beckson. Foreword by Merlin Holland. AMS Studies in the Nineteenth Century, No. 18. New York: AMS Press, 1998. 476 pp.

Wilde the Irishman, edited by Jerusha McCormack. New Haven: Yale University Press, 1998. 205 pp.

The Shape of Fear: Horror and the Fin de Siècle Culture of Decadence by Susan J. Navarette. Lexington: University Press of Kentucky, 1998. 314 pp.

British Literary Culture and Publishing Practice, 1880–1914 by Peter D. McDonald. Cambridge: Cambridge University Press, 1997. 230 pp.

David Copperfield
An Annotated Bibliography Supplement I—1981–1998

Richard J. Dunn and Ann M. Tandy

This annotated bibliography supplements David Copperfield: An Annotated Bibliography *(New York: Garland, 1981) by continuing to describe and evaluate a reasonably complete collection of information about that novel. The first part concerns the text—the novel in progress, textual commentary, editions with new illustrations and/or commentary and criticism, and various adaptations. Chronological ordering of the first part's entries traces the process of the novel's different editions and adaptations. The second, and larger part of the bibliography, lists, alphabetically by author, studies of* David Copperfield—*criticism, literary influences and parallels, teaching and study materials, and biographical discussions. The starting point for most users should be the supplement's index, although the text includes entry-number cross-references, indicated by parentheses (references to items in the 1981 volume are in brackets).*

343

David Copperfield:
An Annotated Bibliography
Supplement I—1981–1998

Richard J. Dunn
and Ann M. Tandy

Contents

Part II. Studies

Preface

How to Use This Bibliography

This bibliography supplements an earlier volume, *David Copperfield: An Annotated Bibliography* (New York: Garland, 1981) and includes entries through early 1998. As in the earlier volume, the entries are numerically listed and indexed. So that annotations may easily cross-reference the 1981 bibliography, the numbered entries are consecutive from that volume, and thus the present work begins with #779. Any cross-reference before #779 is indicated by brackets [ ]; cross-references within the present volume are indicated by parentheses ( ). For ease of use, some materials (such as critical introductions to new editions) are multiply listed as well as cross-listed.

The Table of Contents lists the major divisions of this bibliography, which generally follow the order of the earlier volume, with separate major sections concerning the text and the critical studies. In the text section, primary materials are arranged chronologically to designate the history of the text in progress, of new editions, of new illustrations, and adaptations of various sorts.

The Index, keyed to authors, character names, and central topics and concepts, no doubt will be the starting point for most users, and selective cross-references within numerous entries further identify related commentary.

As with the earlier volume, this is a bibliography of commentary, continuing popular reception and adaptation, as well as of scholarship and criticism concerning *David Copperfield*. For the vast majority of annotations the editors have worked directly with the material described; exceptions are doctoral dissertations for which we have relied upon *Dissertation Abstracts International,* some adaptations either unavailable or well-described by sources we note, and occasional items we have been unable to locate other than by bibliographic citation. As with the previous volume, this bibliography does not include translations or commentary and study in languages other than English.

Introduction

In 1981, *David Copperfield: An Annotated Bibliography* anticipated the appearance that year of a definitive text, the Clarendon Edition [72], but the Pilgrim Edition of *The Letters of Charles Dickens* [1], (779), had not yet included the years most relevant to *David Copperfield*. Major biographical information, consequently, had not increased greatly since the 1950s, and, for Dickens generally and *David Copperfield* in particular, critical commentary was just beginning to include newer theoretical approaches and insights, especially those of feminism and gender studies, new historicism, and psychological criticism. A few earlier studies provided much stimulus to the newer work, most notably J. Hillis Miller's *Charles Dickens: The World of His Novels* [419], James R. Kincaid's *Dickens and the Rhetoric of Laughter* [373], Q. D. Leavis's linking of Dickens with Tolstoy in *Dickens the Novelist* [386], and articles by Robin Gilmour [320] and Robert Lougy [391] on the vital and sometimes troubling nature of memory in *David Copperfield*. Frequently cited by the most recent generations of Dickens critics, these earlier writings took seriously a novel too often regarded as a sweet interlude before Dickens's more acerbic later works and one that for many readers seemed fully to resolve all mysteries and problems of the heart through the hero's success in both writing and marriage. Critical evaluations of the past twenty years have found *David Copperfield* more problematic and more integral to the larger body of Dickens's writings and to the concerns of both society and literature.

As the entries in this bibliography reflect, much recent attention centers on questions of autobiography and heroism, both of which involve self-making, self-articulating, and self-regarding. Earlier attention to these issues seldom passed beyond questions of the CD-DC interface, the extent to which especially the boy David's life was the reworked fragment of Dickens's own, but the focal point has rightly shifted to David as fictional autobiographer and the complications that his gender and class have upon his point of view. Also, there have been a number of increasingly sophisticated psychoanalytic commentaries, expanding and challenging a number of the largely Freudian earlier readings.

Twenty years ago, one might well have been uncertain about whether Dickens scholarship, especially that concerning *David Copperfield,* would readily incorporate feminist, new historicist, Lacanian, or Foucaultean perspectives. Now, as the pages of this bibliography reflect, *David Copperfield* has been reconsidered and resituated both among other Dickens works; see, especially, Alexander Welsh's *From Copyright to Copperfield* (1073) and William Palmer's *Dickens and New Historicism* (1027), and in larger spheres of concern; see especially Mary Poovey's *Uneven Developments: The Ideological Work of Gender in Mid-Victorian England* (1029) and D. A. Miller's *The Novel and the Police* (1014). Three anthologies of recent criticism (897, 898, 1124) and two collections of essays helpful for the teaching and classroom study of the novel (1111, 1127) make available much of this recent work.

The 1981 bibliography displayed the abundance and variety of commentary on the novel, but, in the absence of editions providing access to and assessment of the novel's genesis, composition, serial publication, illustrations, and popular and critical reception, the introduction to that volume gave a brief overview of both novel and bibliography. Now with such complete critical editions as those by Malcolm Andrews (885), J. H. Buckley (903), and Nina Burgis (907), with a superb edition of the Dickens number plans (780), and with new biographies (1133, 1137), the 1981 need for comprehensive introductory materials and commentary has been well met.

The focus of doctoral dissertations concerning *David Copperfield* has undergone a discernible shift. Earlier dissertations, when going beyond contexts of Dickens's other works, linked it with *Tristram Shandy, Sartor Resartus,* or *Jane Eyre* as a fictional autobiography or Bildungsroman, or as one of various works dealing with the transition from childhood to adulthood. The more recent dissertations, many of them the seedbeds of some of the most sophisticated subsequent articles and books, represent a considerably wider scope of criticism involving both *David Copperfield* alone and in conjunction with a wide range of texts. This greater range of topical and generic frameworks includes with romanticism and modernism, fiction as an art of detection, and numerous theoretical perspectives on the formation and representation of the individual. There has been considerable effort to recover Dickens from some of the negative criticism to which he has been subjected, especially concerning his portrayal of women. The dissertations have often taken leads in reading *David Copperfield* against itself, looking at ways in which such elements as the narrating voice and the representation of gender are undermined, revealing not flaws in the novel, as previous critics may have been too prone to identify, but a greater richness than was previously acknowledged.

New to this volume is the subsection, "Teaching and Study Materials," replacing the earlier, more limited listing, "Study Guides and Handbooks."

This section includes classroom editions, discussions of teaching the novel, helpful reference and introductory materials. The section on adaptations has been expanded greatly, largely because of H. Philip Bolton's extensive bibliography, *Dickens Dramatized* (866). The listings of "Subsequent Editions Containing New Introductory or Textual Matter" now specifically include the numerous later illustrators who departed freely in fresh interpretation from both the subjects and the style of the Phiz originals.

Acknowledgments

The Garland Bibliographies, begun with the 1981 *David Copperfield* volume, addressed one of the many needs for providing readers, students, and teachers of the novel with reasonably complete information and commentary about Dickens, his works, and their continuing interest. As the introduction to this new volume indicates and as its pages must show, bibliographers now can readily acknowledge the collaborative efforts of many others who, particularly in regard to *David Copperfield,* have made this bibliography more a celebrative directory than a locator of lacunae. We therefore acknowledge the major accomplishments of editors of the Dickens letters, of the novel's number plans, of well-illustrated/annotated/appended *David Copperfield* editions, of an electronic homepage (including a concordance), and especially of a listing of the novel's many adaptations.

We are grateful to the general editor of the Garland Bibliographies, Duane DeVries, who, with Dickensian persistence, has negotiated a forest of difficulty toward the re-issue of the initial Garland bibliographies and the publication of their updates. Information services and research bibliographic support from the libraries of the University of Washington have eased much of our searching, and for both counsel and content we thank Ms. Helene Williams, humanities research librarian, and Ms. Barbara Grayson, Ms. Cynthia Blanding and their colleagues in the inter-library loan office. Once again David Parker, curator of the Dickens House, has been helpfully responsive to queries, as has also been John Jordan, director of the University of California Santa Cruz Dickens Project. We are grateful for the research funding provided by the University of Washington Graduate School and for the technical assistance of Rob Weller, keeping us both in and on line. For indexing consultation, we thank Vincent Abella.

From its inception, the design and work on this volume has been the collaborative work of the editors, who finish it with relief as well as appreciation for one another's assistance, and they accept responsibility for any omissions or errors.

Part I. Text

DAVID COPPERFIELD IN PROGRESS:
LETTERS, NUMBER PLANS

779. *The Letters of Charles Dickens.* Vols. 5 (1847–1849)—10 (1864–1864).
Ed. Graham Storey et al. Oxford: Clarendon Press, 1981–1998
This meticulously edited, annotated, and indexed edition incorporates
and supersedes all previous collections of Dickens's letters.
Vol. 5 (1847–1849). Eds. Graham Storey and K. J. Fielding. Oxford:
Clarendon Press, 1981.
This volume covers the period of the inception and the first eight
monthly numbers of *David Copperfield*. In their brief preface, the
editors note that this volume's letters include "most of the confidences
about his childhood that Dickens gave to Forster, and Forster's seeing
Dickens's autobiographical fragment" (See letter to Forster, 22 April
1848). Other letters chronicle his searchings for the best title and character names, his receipt of Forster's suggestion concerning the nature
of Mr. Dick's delusion (22 August 1849), the complaint he received
from the original for Miss Mowcher (18 December 1849), various
directions to Phiz about illustrations, reaction to sales, dealings with
translators and adaptors. This volume, in particular, rewards the patient
reader with a sense of how, as the novel continued from month to
month, Dickens not only kept producing new numbers but dealt increasingly with the novel's reception and remained engaged in a number of other activities.
Vol. 6 (1850–1852). Eds. Graham Storey, Kathleen Tillotson, and Nina
Burgis. Oxford: Clarendon Press, 1988.
This volume includes letters for the period of the remaining monthly
numbers and has much information about the reception of the book
and Dickens's reactions to readers. For example, on 13 July 1850, he
stated his pleasure with "a bright unanimity about *Copperfield*," and
said he had "carefully planned out the story, for some time past, to
the end, and am making out my purposes with great care." In 1850

he had initiated *Household Words,* and in April mentioned the "ponderous" labor of it in conjunction with his novel, but thought "to establish it [the weekly magazine] firmly would be to gain an immense point for the future (I mean my future)." In June 1850, he found himself "busy as a bee" with the two major literary projects, but looked forward to visiting the seaside and finishing the book. To Macready he wrote of his desire that "it be as good a book as I hope it will be, for your children's, children's children to read!" As he completed chapters 56 and 57, he wrote Mrs. Watson (to whom he would dedicate the novel), "There are some things in the next Copperfield that I think better than any that have gone before. After I have been believing such things with all my heart and soul—two results always ensue. First, I can't write plainly to the eye. Second, I can't write sensibly to the mind" (24 September 1850).

Review article: A. Welsh, "I Am Transported Beyond the Ignorant Copperfieldian Present," *Modern Philology,* 88 (1991), 292–298. Welsh finds the letters suggesting that in commenting on the death of his infant daughter, Dora Annie, Dickens engaged in "an ill-considered confusion of fiction with daily life."

Volume 7 (1853–1855). Eds. Graham Storey, Kathleen Tillotson, Angus Easson. Oxford: Clarendon Press, 1993.

This volume includes letters concerning Dickens's reunion with the former Maria Beadnell (model for Dora).

Volume 8 (1856–1859). Eds. Graham Storey and Kathleen Tillotson, Oxford: Clarendon Press, 1995.

This volume has several notes mentioning but no letters directly concerning *David Copperfield.*

Volume 9 (1859–1861). Ed. Graham Storey. Oxford: Clarendon Press, 1997.

This volume includes Dickens's statement about rereading *David Copperfield* before beginning *Great Expectations,* and it has a number of letters mentioning his finishing and delivering the public reading version of *David Copperfield* (letters as early as 3–4 February 1855 indicate earlier efforts at a reading version; the first public reading was not until 1861).

Volume 10 (1862–1864). Ed. Graham Storey. Oxford: Clarendon Press, 1998.

The principal mention of *David Copperfield* in these letters concerns Dickens's public reading adaptation, which he finds "more interesting to me than any of the other Readings, and I am half-ashamed to confess . . . what a tenderness I have for it" (10 July 1862). In a series of letters in early January, 1862, Dickens tells correspondents of the actor

Macready's pleasure with the reading "as a piece of Art" and "as a piece of passion and pathos and playfulness." A year later, various letters note the success following a benefit reading in Paris.

780. Stone, Harry, ed. *"David Copperfield."* In his *Dickens' Working Notes for His Novels.* Chicago: University of Chicago Press, 1987, pp. 103–179.

Although the number plans have been long available on microfilm [2] and although they have often been discussed in part or in full, never have they been so readily available or so fully described and discussed. Stone's general introduction, pp. xix–xx, full-sized facsimile of the plans with complementary typographic transcriptions, and introductory commentary to the *Copperfield* plans greatly aid anyone interested in deciphering the originals. Stone also includes Dickens's trial titles in the order they were bound with the manuscript, noting that this was not the order of composition, and he proposes a possible order of composition for the titles. The number plans are also available in several recent editions of the novel (820, 823, 825, 827).

781. *The Charles Dickens Manuscripts: Selected from the Forster and Dyce Collection.* CD–ROM. Primary Source Media: *http: //casenet.thomson.com/psmedia/dknsmms.htm*

Digitized version of the manuscript and corrected proofs [2, 3] self-described as including "Dickens's personal correspondence, autograph manuscript drafts, page and galley proofs and other papers which provide valuable tools for textual study and enhanced understanding of Dickens and his work."

Textual Commentary: Scholarship Concerning Publication, Textual Matters, Character Prototypes, Illustrations

782. Alexander, Doris. "Dance of Death in *David Copperfield*," "Composites in *David Copperfield*," "Two Mothers in Mrs. Micawber," "The Micawbers Fifteen Years Later," "Copperfield Reincarnate." In her *Creating Characters with Charles Dickens.* University Park: Pennsylvania State University Press, 1991, pp. 77–88, 89–98, 99–106, 107–17, 125–37.

This study strives to go beyond mere identification of character originals in order to evaluate the accuracy with which Dickens "penetrated the psychology of his originals and their effect on their world." The *Copperfield* characters/prototypes discussed in these five chapters include: Uriah Heep/Hans Christian Andersen; Agnes Wickfield/Mary Hogarth; Miss Mowcher/Jane Seymour Hill; Rosa Dartle/Hannah

Meredith and also embodying some of the ferocity of Jane Carlyle; Mrs. Steerforth/Mrs. Basil Montagu. Alexander argues that the composite prototypes for Dora were Maria Beadnell, Catherine Dickens, and Mrs. Thomas Talfourd. Mrs. Micawber is Alexander's example of the amalgamation of two personalities to form one character—those both of Dickens's mother and his mother-in-law. Alexander suggests that the Micawbers were themselves prototypes fifteen years later for the Wilfers of *Our Mutual Friend* and that many of the *Copperfield* characters also reappeared in various forms in *Great Expectation*—notably Betsey Trotwood as Miss Havisham. Alexander argues that, like Dora, Estella at least in part originated from Maria Beadnell.
Reviews: K. J. Fielding, *Dickens Quarterly* 9 (1992), 29–32; P. Davalle, *Dickensian* 88 (1992), 117–19.

783. Collins, Philip. "Dickens's Autobiographical Fragment and *David Copperfield.*" *Cahiers victoriens & edouardiens,* 20 (1984), 87–96; 21 (1985), 97.
Prompted by clarifications by Nina Burgis [72] of the date and relation of the Autobiographical Fragment to the novel, Collins explains his basis for thinking that Forster had more of the fragment than he published, that it continued beyond the blacking-warehouse event, and that Dickens had a separate, more extensive version of the fragment than he gave Forster. In the 1985 addendum, Collins suggests that because of inconsistencies in Forster's various remarks about the Autobiographical Fragment, they seem to have confused the editors of the Pilgrim edition of Dickens's Letters. See also Collins's earlier essay on the mixture of autobiographical truth and fiction [262].

784. Dunn, Richard J. "The Clarendon *David Copperfield.*" *Review,* 4 (1982), 97–109.
This review article notes that the extensiveness of newly available materials both facilitated and complicated the editorial work on this edition [72], and it discusses Burgis's handling of problems Philip Gaskell [19, 20] regarded as essential to a definitive edition of *David Copperfield.*

785. Everson, Philip A. "Proof Revisions in Three Novels by Charles Dickens: *Dombey and Son, David Copperfield* and *Bleak House.*" *DAI,* 48 (1987), 279A (Delaware, 1987).
Examining these three novels in terms of their monthly serial publication, Everson looks at the strictly defined physical format of each installment, arguing that often Dickens's proof revisions were not made for aesthetic reasons, as most critics assume, but rather to meet particular length requirements. He focuses on how these last minute revisions affect the work as a whole, creating "new and often inadvertent meanings in the unrevised passages which surround them." He finds that as Dickens's career progressed and his novels became increasingly complex, these proof revisions took on a greater significance.

786. Friedman, Stanley. "Heep and Powell." *Dickensian,* 90 (1994), 36–43.

    Thomas Powell, a friend of Dickens for several years in the mid-1840s, forged and embezzled from Chapman, his employer, and, in 1849, from America, enraged Dickens by denigrating his art and personal character. Friedman's point is that this insult came at a time to affect Dickens's in-progress characterization of Uriah Heep.

787. Gager, Valerie L. " 'The web I have spun': Shakespeareana in *Dombey and Son* and *David Copperfield.*" In her *Shakespeare and Dickens: The Dynamics of Influence.* Cambridge: Cambridge University Press, 1996, pp. 223–44.

    Gager finds in Phiz's "Our Pew at Church" a "deliberate representation" of the Shakespeare monument in Stratford's Trinity Church, and also notes that "The Friendly Waiter and I" illustration contains a poster for *Two Gentlemen of Verona.* See also Gager (940) and Parker (794).

788. Kitton, Frederic G. "Hablot. K. Browne." In his *Dickens and His Illustrators.* London: George Redway, 1899, pp. 102–106.

    Kitton notes that Browne etched all his designs in duplicate and that there are some slight variations in some of the pairs. He finds many of the *David Copperfield* illustrations "marked by a certain hardness and stiffness of treatment" and "deficient in that vigour and deftness of touch of [Browne's] previous work." Also he describes some carelessness on Browne's part, such as his inversion of the beached boat in which the Peggottys live. Kitton does praise Browne's portrayal of Mr. Micawber in illustrations which also greatly pleased Dickens. Kitton mentions that Browne added a frontispiece to the 1858 cheap edition [40] and two vignettes (another version of "Mr. Peggotty's Dream" and Little Em'ly and David by the sea) to the 1858–1859 library edition [41]. The 1981 annotated bibliography for *David Copperfield* incorrectly stated that the library edition had only a single illustration; as Kitton notes it had the two new ones by Phiz.

789. Lutman, Stephen. "Reading Illustrations: Pictures in *David Copperfield.*" In *Reading the Victorian Novel: Detail into Form.* Ed. Ian Gregor. London: Vision Press, 1980, pp. 196–225.

    Lutman begins by discussing the interrelationship of Victorian visual and literary forms, especially that between melodrama and painting and music. Pictorial effects in *David Copperfield* not only cue illustrations but, he believes, are central to the narrative method, for "David has a habit of mind as narrator and hero of picturing certain moments, and other characters, to himself." But the illustrations provide readers with views of David and a sense of the novel different from that provided by the text. Sequentially, Lutman argues, the illustrations create significant visual repetitions and cues to the development of character and direction of the novel. Both as a reading of and as a guide to how to read illustrations, this is a helpful essay.

790. Mikdadi, F. H. "*David Copperfield* in Arabic." *Dickensian,* 75 (1979), 85–93.

Notes that there is no Arabic unabridged edition, and the translations all reflect the cultural and linguistic differences between English and Arabic, often greatly altering the novel's perspective (about the memories of childhood, for example).

791. Moss, Sidney P., and Carolyn Moss. *The Charles Dickens-Thomas Powell Vendetta: The Story in Documents.* Troy, NY: Whitston Publishing Company, 1996, passim.

During the period Dickens was writing *Copperfield,* his nearly ten-year friendship with Powell turned to anger when Powell became hostile toward Dickens in his *Living Authors of England* [196]. The Mosses assemble for the first time all the pertinent documents of the Dickens-Powell relationship, including an excerpt from Stanley Friedman's article about Powell as a model for Heep (786), and noting on several occasions the physical resemblance between the Phiz drawings of Micawber and Powell. In his review of the Mosses' work, Philip Collins questions the plausibility of Powell as a model for either Heep or Micawber. Among works cited, the Mosses include an obituary for Powell—"The Original Micawber," *New York Mirror,* 29 January 1887, p. 9. See [196] for additional commentary on Dickens and Powell.

Review: P. Collins, *Dickensian* 93 (1997), 209–211.

792. Morton, Lionel. " 'His Truncheon's Length': A Recurrent Allusion to *Hamlet* in Dickens's Novels." *Dickens Studies Newsletter,* 11 (1980), 47–49.

This allusion in the account of Micawber's denunciation of Heep is but one of several to *Hamlet* in *David Copperfield* Morton indicates, and they are appropriate because of this novel's and Dickens's persisting fascination with the return of the dead father. See also Gager (940).

793. Myer, Valerie G. "Martha as Magdalen: An Illustration in *David Copperfield.*" *Notes and Queries,* n. s. 43 (1996), 430.

In addition to the picture of the temptation of Eve within the Phiz illustration, "Martha," there is also a picture showing the Magdalen washing Christ's feet, Myer points out. She also notes that the posture within the picture parallels that of Martha in the main illustration.

794. Parker, David. "Our Pew at Church." *Dickensian,* 88 (1992), 46–47.

Parker's key point concerns the onlooker in the illustration's fore-ground; he suggests it is an image of David the narrator, contemplating his earlier life.

795. Reach, Angus. "Town Talk and Table Talk for the Week." *London Illustrated News,* 16 (16 March 1850), 178.

Reach comments briefly on Dickens's change of plan concerning Miss Mowcher: "Is it worth recording . . . a very commonly-made remark touching the last number of Mr. Dickens's serial—to wit that the author has completely altered his views of the *role* Miss Mowcher is to play in the fortunes of David Copperfield? The curious in the construction of novels ought to compare recent numbers."

796. Regul, Lisa. "The Use of Illustrations in *David Copperfield.*" In *Reading David Copperfield* (1127), pp. 209–24.

Regul comments upon a number of the Phiz illustrations, noting common features and themes in them (such as the similar appearances of all the young, beautiful females), and she makes a strong argument for studying the illustrations closely, for they are important both for their relationship to and expansion upon the written text.

797. Rosenblum, Joseph. "Doctor Strong and Doctor Johnson Revisited." *Dickens Quarterly,* 1 (1984), 54–56.

This case for Samuel Johnson as the model for Strong Rosenblum bases on the Johnson portrayed in John Forster's *Life and Adventures of Goldsmith,* a book Forster dedicated to Dickens. Rosenblum notes linguistic similarities between Forster's Johnson and the Dickens character. On the Johnson prototype, see also [278, 648].

798. Williams, William A., Jr. *Concordance to David Copperfield.* Electronic, 1998. *http: //209.150.140.216/cgi-bin/letty.pl*

This concordance also may be reached through The Dickens Page (1120).

799. Winterich, John T. "How This Book Came to Be." In the 1937 Heritage Press edition, pp. ix-xvi (814).

This preface begins with a series of Thackeray's comments about *Copperfield,* characterizing them as "a compound of generosity and spite," but noting that there seemed no surviving record of Dickens's reaction to *Pendennis,* which also was appearing serially. Winterich mentions some, but not all, of Dickens's trial titles, noting that the word "personal" persisted in them. Also he lists a number of character prototypes, observing that "the penalty of borrowing even an occasional personality from reality" is that an author may be thought to have so derived all of his characters. Winterich concludes by providing the whole of the preface to the Charles Dickens Edition.

OTHER DICKENS WORKS BEARING ON *DAVID COPPERFIELD*

800. Longley, Katharine M. "Charles Dickens and the Doom of English
Wills." *Journal of the Society of Archivists,* 14 (1993), 25–38.
Longley points out that *Household Words* articles concerning the bad
handling of historical records (see "The Doom of English Wills,"
Household Words, 28 September 1850) included mention of David
Copperfield's experiences when articled to a proctor.

SUBSEQUENT EDITIONS CONTAINING NEW INTRODUCTIONS
OR ILLUSTRATIONS

801. *David Copperfield.* Boston: Hurd and Houghton, 1869, 4 vols. in 2.
Reprints Phiz illustrations with additional illustrations by F. O. C.
Darley and John Gilbert. A Fireside Edition (c1870) of Dickens's
Works uses the same text with fewer illustrations in an oddly assembled paper cover set of 109 parts.
802. *The Personal History of David Copperfield.* Household Edition. London: Chapman and Hall, [1872]; New York: Harper, 1872.
With a portrait of Dickens and 61 illustrations by Frederick Barnard,
this was an extensively illustrated edition, the first such not to follow
or adapt, as had Orr or Gihon [39], the subjects of the Phiz illustrations.
Many of the Barnard illustrations are available in the Guiliano-Ford
edition (822). One point of interest is Barnard's emphasis on the sinister nature of Rosa Dartle and on the darkness of the fallen woman's
life as represented by Martha.
803. "Kyd" [pseud. Joseph Clayton Clarke]. "Mr. Peggotty," "Uriah
Heep," "Mr. Micawber."
In *The Characters of Charles Dickens Portrayed in a Series of Original
Water Colour Sketches.* London: Raphael Tuck and Sons [1889], 26
bound and unnumbered colored sketches, with brief passages from the
novels on separate pages.
Kyd's drawings anticipate many later illustrations which would break
from the Phiz originals by isolating the subject character, but in this
case the illustrations appeared separately from any edition of the novels. For each illustration, Kyd does quote a brief passage. For the
Peggotty picture, the textual link is with "I'm a-going to seek my
niece through the wuerld. I'm a-going to find my poor niece in her
shame and bring her back" (chapter 31); for the Heep picture, "I'm
well aware that I am the 'umblest person going, let the other be what

he may. My mother is likewise a very 'umble person. We live in a
humble abode, Master Copperfield, but have much to be thankful for''
(chapter 16); for the Micawber picture, ''. . . with a certain condescending roll in his voice, and a certain indescribable air of doing
something genteel'' (chapter 11).

804. *The Personal History of David Copperfield.* The Popular Edition of
the Complete Works of Charles Dickens. London. Chapman & Hall
Ltd., 1907.
A November 1910 reprint of this edition adds eleven photographs from
a stage version with ''Sir Herbert Tree As Dan'l Peggotty'' standing
before the first chapter. Photos are from *The Daily Mirror* studios and
one group shows Tree also as Micawber, Mr. Owen Nares as David
Copperfield, Miss Sydney Fairbrother as Mrs. Micawber, and Mr.
Deering Wells as Tommy Traddles.

805. *David Copperfield.* Collins' Clear-Type Press. London and Glasgow,
c. 1907.
The cover has an etching of the older Dickens at the center surrounded
by various characters from his work by Harry Furniss. There is a
frontispiece and a number of illustrations by W. H. C. Groome. This
was a volume in the Collins Illustrated Dickens. Groome (1881–1919)
was also a landscape painter.

806. *The Personal History of David Copperfield.* Ed. Edward C. Baldwin.
Chicago: Scott, Foresman, and Company, 1910; revised 1919.
A classroom edition with study materials; for Baldwin's introduction
see (1105).

807. *The Personal History of David Copperfield.* Illustrated in Colour by
Frank Reynolds, R. I. London: Hodder and Stoughton, 1911.
This deluxe edition highlighted the illustrations, for instead of a table
of contents listing chapter titles, it has a listing of the illustrations
along with quotations from the passages they illustrate. Reynolds
(1876–1953) was for many years the art editor of *Punch.*

808. Smith, Jessie W. ''David Copperfield and Mr. Peggotty by the Fire''
and ''Little Em'ly.'' In her *Dickens's Children: Ten Drawings.* New
York: Charles Scribners' Sons, 1912.
Color plates drawn from chapters 2 and 3. See also Kyd (803), and
Cameron (816).

809. *David Copperfield* Ed. William A. Nielson. Harvard Classics Edition,
2 vols. New York: P. F. Collier and Son, 1917.
Although not illustrated, this edition includes a biographical note, excerpts of criticism by Lang [381], Forster [730], Ward [522], Chesterton [253], Shore [479], and Gissing [321].

810. *The Personal History of David Copperfield* With Sixteen Coloured
     Illustrations by Gertrude D. Hammond. New York: Dodd, Mead and
     Company, 1921.
     The Hammond illustrations are of different subjects than those of the
     original illustrations.
811. *David Copperfield.* New York: Dodd, Mead and Company, 1935.
     Illustrated with 16 photos from the Metro-Goldwyn-Mayer film [see
     53, 122, 123, 127, 128, 131, 132] and including a list of the cast of
     characters from that film.
812. *David Copperfield.* Authorised Film Edition based on the Metro-Gold-
     wyn-Mayer Picture. London: The Literary Press Ltd., c. 1935.
     This is a twenty-one chapter abridgment and is introduced with "This
     is the Story": "Throughout the past century one great romance has
     lived to fascinate each new generation—David Copperfield, a name
     which spells magic to millions, a story that has cast a haze of enchant-
     ment on all who read it, an immortal among books. In these pages live
     some of the greatest characters in all literature; David and his child-
     wife Dora, the genial Mr. Micawber, the cringing Uriah Heap [*sic*],
     Peggotty, Aunt Betsey and Mr. Dick, all immortal creations of the
     magic pen of Charles Dickens, dipped deep in the well of human
     love and understanding. This great story has been filmed by Metro-
     Goldwyn-Mayer in a picture that has been justly hailed as a screen
     masterpiece, and the editing of the present edition has been based on
     the scenario of this wonderful picture." Hugh Walpole (856, 858,
     1101) wrote the script for the film [128].
813. *The Personal History of David Copperfield.* New York: Grosset and
     Dunlap, n. d. [1935?].
     From the Universal Library series, the dust jacket is illustrated with
     W. C. Fields and other cast members, and the book itself contains six
     line drawings from the 1935 movie [122]. Presumably this is an
     abridged version of the original, but no editor is listed.
814. *The Personal History of David Copperfield* by Charles Dickens. Illus-
     trated by John Austen. The Heritage Press. New York. 1937. [1935?].
     Austen's eight color plates and the Winterich introduction (799) were
     done for this edition.
815. "David Copperfield." Condensed by Mary L. Ashwell. Illustrated by
     Donald McKay.In *The Dickens Digest: Four Great Dickens Master-
     pieces Condensed for the Modern Reader.* New York: McGraw-Hill,
     1943, pp. 4–204.
     The "Editor's Note" acknowledges the difficulty of condensing Dick-
     ens but declares an intention to preserve "the essential narrative in

the words of its creator'' while eliminating circumlocution, ''padding,'' and some of the social satire that ''in tone and intention means little to the reader today.''

816. Cameron, William R. *David Copperfield in Copperplate.* Forty-six illustrations for the famous Dickens novel augmented by interpretative short passages taken from the original text. Berkeley, CA: Bern Porter, 1947.

This book of illustrations includes only brief passages from the novel, and its purpose is stated in a publisher's note: ''In offering this series of drawings by William Ross Cameron, the publisher is confident that their charm will be apparent to collectors & amateurs alike. Collectors of Dickensiana will find in them a fresh interpretation of *David Copperfield,* so often essayed by other artists, so seldom successfully. Through his painstaking researches into the life and manners of the period and through his piquant characterization—often just this side of caricature—that is Dickens, Will Cameron has added another bouquet to the great Victorian's wreath. Whether or not they have ever read the 800-odd pages of the novel amateurs from seven to seventy will find in these plates, with accompanying excerpts from the original text, a personally conducted tour of vivacity and sustained interest through the stirring scenes of David's fortunes & misfortunes. Children of seven will be led to read this truly remarkable novel, and those of seventy to reread and relive it!''

817. ''David Copperfield.'' Illustrated by Everett Shinn. Garden City, NY: The Literary Guild of America, Inc., 1948.

This abridged edition in 63 chapters contains numerous full-color illustrations plus quarter-page chapter-head drawings.

818. *David Copperfield.* 2 vols. Centennial Edition. General Introduction and Preface by J. B. Priestley. Illustrations by Phiz. Distributed by Heron Books. Geneva, c. 1950.

819. *David Copperfield.* Illustrated by Paul Degen. Franklin Center, Pennsylvania: The Franklin Library, 1980.

820. *David Copperfield.* Edited with an introduction and notes by Nina Burgis. The World's Classics Edition. Oxford: Oxford University Press, 1981.

This text is based on Burgis' Clarendon edition [72] but does not include that edition's many variant passages. See also Burgis (1108).

821. *The Personal History of David Copperfield.* Avon: The Folio Society, 1983.

Introduction by Christopher Hibbert (1092). Illustrated cloth cover, frontispiece, and 65 drawings by Charles Keeping. This is one of the most fully and originally conceived sets of illustrations among the many over the years. A few of the Charles Keeping illustrations are included in the Guiliano-Collins edition (822).

822. *David Copperfield*. In *The Annotated Dickens*. Ed. Edward Guiliano and Philip Collins. Vol. II. New York: Clarkson N. Potter, 1986.

This lavishly illustrated and annotated edition includes *David Copperfield* among seven of Dickens's major works. It claims to be the most thoroughly annotated version available, and provides much information about topographical and literary references, obsolete words and customs, slang and cant words and cultural allusions. It compares the public reading text with the episodes in the novel upon which the reading was based. The text includes all of the original illustrations, the many Fred Barnard illustrations from the Household Edition, selected illustrations by Harry Furniss, Frank Reynolds, William Rainey, and Charles Keeping as well as numerous photographs from stage and film versions. With the annotation, often comparative illustrations by various artists, and drawings and photos of contemporary reference, this edition provides a very visual reading of the novel, a sort of "hardcover hypertext," currently available only in its original two-volume boxed set.

Review: M. McGowan, *Dickensian*, 84 (1988), 52–54.

823. *David Copperfield*. Ed. Jerome H. Buckley. New York: W. W. Norton, 1990.

This paperback Norton Critical Edition includes text, backgrounds, and selected critical commentary. For more detail see (902, 1107).

824. *David Copperfield*. Ware, Herts.: Wordsworth Editions, Ltd., 1992.

Contains a brief introduction that offers no critical commentary, information on original publication, a biographical sketch, and a one-paragraph summary of critical reception by the first reviewers, and by G. K. Chesterton and Edgar Johnson.

825. *The Personal History and Experience of David Copperfield the Younger*. Everyman Edition. Edited by Malcolm Andrews. With illustrations by Hablot K. Browne (Phiz). London: J. M. Dent, 1993.

Andrews provides a critical introduction (885), notes, and an appended commentary on "Dickens and His Critics" in this paperback which will be helpful for teachers and students (1104). All the illustrations, a chronology of Dickens's life and times, notes on the text, author's preface to the Charles Dickens edition, 1867, are included as well. Identifies monthly parts.

826. *"David Copperfield."* Abridged for public reading by Charles Dickens. Illustrations by Alan Marks. Afterword by Anthea Bell. New York: North-South Books, 1995.

Because Marks's illustrations belong to the tradition of the illustrated novel text, this edition of Dickens's Public Reading text is listed among those of the novel. The text is based on Philip Collins [78], and Anthea Bell briefly discusses Dickens's reworking of the novel into readings, his careful preparation for his performances, and their impact on audiences. The many pen-and-ink and watercolor illustrations may appeal to readers of all ages, although this is presented as a children's book.

827. *David Copperfield.* Introduction and notes by Jeremy Tambling. London: Penguin, 1996.
This excellent edition replaces and considerably expands the illustrations and appended material of the earlier Penguin paperback [69]. See also (1065, 1131).

828. *David Copperfield.* Electronic text, created by Jo Churcher. Project Gutenberg, e-text #766.
Information about the nature and extent of Project Gutenberg texts is available at *http: //promo.net/pg/history.html* or through the Dickens home page (1120). The *David Copperfield* text includes the original and the Charles Dickens Edition prefaces, but there are no illustrations, notes, or other apparatus.

AUDIO ADAPTATIONS

829. "The Personal History of David Copperfield." Adapted by Betty Davies. BBC Radio, ten-part dramatization. 14 September–16 November 1991.
Particularly notable is Miriam Margolyes as Betsey Trotwood. Margolyes is also noted for her one woman show, "Wooman, Lovely Wooman," recorded in (862).

830. "Emma Micawber." Raymond FitzSimons. Dramatic monologue, BBC Radio, 17 September 1991.
We were unable to obtain either a copy of this broadcast or any further information about it.

831. "Uriah Heep from *David Copperfield.*" Victor Records, 1916.
William Sterling Battis presents a monologue in which Heep reveals his plans regarding Mr. Wickfield's business and his daughter, Agnes, and threatens any who might stand in his way.

832. *David Copperfield.* Read by Angela Cheyne. Books on Tape, 1977, 1996. 22 cassettes, 33 hours.
We were unable to obtain any further information about this production.

833. "*David Copperfield:* as excerpted and adapted by Dickens for his public readings." Read by Roger Rees. New York: Caedmon, 1982. 1 cassette, 58 *minutes.*

This recording also contains biographical and historical notes by Michael P. Hearn on the cassette container.

834. *"David Copperfield."* Abridged by Edward Phillips, produced by Richard Baldwyn, narrated by Anton Rogers. Listen for Pleasure Audiocassettes, 1988. 3 hours.

Reviewed by Mary Postgate in *Grammaphone* 66 (Dec. 88): 1070, who maintains that although it is abridged, many of the characters as well as the novelist's own manage to emerge. She finds it "as tempting an introduction to the complete work as one could find, and a pleasure in itself."

835. *"David Copperfield."* Abridged. Read by Ben Kingsley. Multilingua Inc., 1993. 2 cassettes, 3 hours.

Review: Michael Adams, *Library Journal,* 118 (Oct. 1 1993): 138. Adams finds that this retelling of the novel emphasizes the more somber episodes of David's life, and reduces such crucial characters as Mr. Micawber and Uriah Heep to "mere walk-ons."

836. *"The Real David Copperfield."* read by David Case. Books on Tape, 1993. 13 cassettes.

This is a recording of Robert Graves's 1933 retelling of Dickens's novel [167]. Feeling that "half the words in Charles Dickens's classic add nothing to the story," Graves rewrote the entire novel to make it "accessible to the modern reader."

837. *"David Copperfield."* Abridged by Neville Teller, produced by Stuart Owen, read by Nathaniel Parker. Penguin Audiobooks, 1996. 14 cassettes, 5 hours 45 minutes.

We were unable to obtain any further information about this broadcast.

COMMENTARY ON AUDIO ADAPTATIONS

838. Bolton, H. Philip. "David Copperfield" *Dickens Dramatized* (866).

The bulk of Bolton's 242 entries on *David Copperfield* are stage adaptations; see the entries in "Stage Adaptations," (854) and "Video Adaptations" (866) for further descriptions of his project. He does list seven radio broadcasts. Six are BBC productions, ranging from multipart broadcasts of the entire story to excerpts read or dramatized, such as "Mr. Micawber's Difficulties" on April 20, 1954, and "Betsey Trotwood" on March 29, 1962. The seventh is an American Armed Forces radio broadcast [134]. Bolton credits *David Copperfield* with the earliest Dickens broadcast ever on BBC, in a 1924 reading entitled

"Barkis is Willin'." Many of the later broadcasts were parts of educational series such as "Senior English II" or the popular series "Characters from Dickens" by Barry Campbell starting in 1970. See Bolton for complete listings, including rebroadcasts as well as original dates.

CHILDREN'S ADAPTATIONS

839. Benscoter, Grace A., and John Gehlmann. *"David Copperfield."* New York, Globe Book Co., 1945.
    This adaptation focuses on the central events of David's life, omitting or shortening the stories of marginal characters. The adaptors also, as they write in the introduction, took out what they considered "padding," or that portion of the installments that they believed included more to meet length requirements than for literary merit. In addition, the vocabulary is simplified, the spelling and punctuation modernized, and some incidents rearranged for clarification. The resulting 400 pages or so are aimed at juvenile readers who may be encountering this in a classroom. Also included are a map of "David Copperfield's Corner of England" on the frontispiece and several movie stills from the MGM 1935 film [122].

840. Campbell, Stuart. *The Boyhood of David Copperfield.* London: The Children's Press, 1935.
    We were unable to obtain a copy of this text to examine. According to the OCLC WorldCat record 37223420, it is only ninety-five pages long, suggesting that it is probably a retelling of the earlier parts of the story.

841. Darley, Felix O. C. [illustrator] *The Child-Wife: From the David Copperfield of Charles Dickens.* New York: Redfield, 1860.
    Part of the series "Dickens' Little Folks" which was "undertaken with a view of supplying the want of a class of books for children, of a vigorous, manly tone." Dickens was chosen especially for this project because of his excellent portrayal of children and their interests. The Preface indicates the more specific lesson to be learned from Dora's tale: "We must unite a child-like spirit with a high purpose in life, or we shall fall short of our desire to be useful, and to be best loved." In this abridgement, David's early years and childhood are condensed, focusing mostly on Clara Copperfield, however, for obvious reasons. Touching briefly on Miss Trotwood and the Wickfields, the text skips straight to the Spenlow household and Dora and Miss Mills. The greatest time is spent on David and Dora's courtship, marriage, and household difficulties, as well as his return after her death, his reunion with Agnes and their happy domestic scene at the end.

842. Dickens, Charles. *"David Copperfield."* Abridged for public reading by Charles Dickens. Illustrated by Alan Marks. Afterword by Anthea Bell. Also available in cassette. New York: North-South Books, 1995. See (826). This version of the story is particularly suitable for young readers interested in either book illustration or dramatic performance of Dickens's novels.

843. Dickens, Mary A., and Edric Vredenburg. *Little David Copperfield.* Illustrations by Frances Brundage and Harold Copping. Series: *Children's Stories from Dickens.* New York: London: R. Tuck, 1900.
This children's volume retells David's story from his infancy through his visits to the Peggotty houseboat, his mother's remarriage, his time at school, his mother's death, his subsequent experiences in London, and finally his adoption by his Aunt Betsey.

844. Severance, Annie D. *The Child's Dickens: David Copperfield and Oliver Twist.* New York: American Book Co., 1905.
Severance's project is "to simplify [the stories] by excluding from them the elements of unpleasantness and discursiveness which at times mar the original works," and thereby present them in a manner understandable and enjoyable for children. In her greatly abridged retelling of *David Copperfield,* she follows the main thread of the story, preserving the leading characters but leaving out such minor ones as Steerforth's family, Dora's friend Julia and her aunts, Traddles and Martha. Severance also includes several of Phiz's illustrations.

845. Sidlowski, Loretta. *Young David Copperfield; Abridged for Children 8–14 from Charles Dickens' Immortal Classic.* New York: Greenwich, 1957.
We were unable to obtain a copy of this text to examine; the information given comes from OCLC Worldcat record 18694047.

846. West, Clare. *"David Copperfield."* Oxford: Oxford University Press, 1994.
Part of the Oxford Bookworms Series, Stage 5. This ninety-two page retelling is aimed at developing readers, and includes a glossary at the end as well as several comprehension exercises.

847. Widdows, Richard. Adaptor. *David Copperfield.* New York: Gallery, 1985. Also an animated film by Burbank Films, 1985. Released by Children's Video of America, 1989.
The illustrations for this children's book are taken from the Burbank Films 1985 animated film (851). The book version also includes a brief biography of Dickens and a reproduction of R. W. Buss's painting *Dickens' Dream.* Widdows leaves out many minor characters and some plot lines, such as Rosa Dartle's relationship with Steerforth and the Strong's marriage, and condenses some episodes, but his use of samples of Dickens's own language in his adaptation makes for a reading

that feels true even in its brevity and should provide a fair introduction to the novel for children.

FILM AND VIDEO ADAPTATIONS

848. *David Copperfield: The Boy.* Film. MGM, 1935. 38 minutes.
   Excerpted from the 1935 MGM production [122, 128], this brief film focuses on the "formative years" of David, demonstrating the surroundings and people of Victorian England which influence his growth. Also see (849).
849. *David Copperfield: The Man.* Film. MGM, 1935. 38 minutes.
   Continuing *David Copperfield: The Boy* (848), this film, also excerpted from the 1935 MGM production [122, 128], picks up David's story as he is finishing school and setting out on his career.
850. *Tales from Dickens: David and Dora Marry.* Film. Cornet Instructional Films, 1962. 25 minutes.
   This film depicts the problems in David's marriage to Dora arising from her childishness and inexperience, as shown in the disastrous dinner for Traddles. Eventually David achieves some happiness in their final months together by accepting her limitations and not trying to make her more than she is.
851. *David Copperfield.* Animated video. Burbank Films, 1985. Released by Children's Video of America, 1989.
   Also listed under "Children's Adaptations" (851). Illustrations for Richard Widdow's adaptation were taken from this film.
852. *David Copperfield.* Video. Turner Entertainment/MGM, 1988.
   Videodisc release of MGM's 1935 production [128].
853. *Charles Dickens' David Copperfield.* Television. Don Arioli, 1993.
   Directed by Don Ariolo, this version of the story stars Julian Lennon as David, Sheena Easton as Agnes, Kelly LeBrock as Clara and Michael York as Murdstone. It is probably animated, and appears to be a Canadian production. What information we were able to find on this version comes from the Internet Movie Database.

COMMENTARY ON FILM AND VIDEO ADAPTATIONS

854. Bolton, H. Philip. "David Copperfield." *Dickens Dramatized* (866).
   The bulk of Bolton's 242 entries on *David Copperfield* are stage adaptations; see the entries in "Stage Adaptations" (866) and "Audio Adaptations" (838). He does list eight films and five television productions. He comments that stage productions of the novel had begun to

dwindle in the 1930s, after a period of popularity right after WWI, but the 1934 MGM film [128] took up the slack, creating such a memorable film that no other attempt was made to portray it on the silver screen until the 1970 Omnibus film [124]. Please see Bolton for complete listings, including rebroadcasts as well as original dates.

855. Gifford, Denis. *Books and Plays in Films, 1896–1915: Literary, Theatrical and Artistic Sources of the First Twenty Years of Motion Pictures.* London: McFarland, 1991.

This study of the first decades of film lists six very early movies made from Dickens's novel in whole or in parts: Edison's (USA) 1910 one-reel film *Love and the Law;* The 1911 Thanhouser (USA) films, each one reel, *The Early Life of David Copperfield, Little Emily and David Copperfield;* and *The Loves of David Copperfield;* Britannia's (Great Britain) 1911 one-reel *Little Emily;* and Hepworth's (Great Britain) 1913 eight-reel *David Copperfield* [123].

856. Hart-Davis, Rupert. *Hugh Walpole: A Biography.* New York: Macmillan, 1952, pp. 348–52.

Soon after receiving the commission to write the filmscript for the MGM production, Walpole purchased a house which he named Copperfield. Work in California on the film went more slowly than expected, and at six different points Walpole thought it finished. He had a small part in the film, playing the Vicar of Blunderstone.

857. Luhr, William. "Dickens's Narrative, Hollywood's Vignettes." In *The English Novel and the Movies.* Ed. Michael Klein and Gillian Parker. New York: Frederick Ungar, 1981, pp. 132–42.

In the novel, Luhr asserts, David's perceptions "emerge as a collection of simultaneous impressions, not necessarily consistent, and important not for what they build to, but for what they are." Selznick, the film's director, saw the novel primarily in terms of its distinctive characters and so structured his film, and David himself "is simply another character, and not a very interesting one." Generally the film is more optimistic than the novel, and, according to Luhr, it does not express, as does the novel, "a fear about the impossibility of establishing a unified family and happiness." Nonetheless, Luhr finds the 1935 film representing "the best of what the heyday of the Hollywood studio system" could do when dealing with Victorian fiction.

858. Ortman, Marguerite G. *Fiction and the Screen.* Boston: Marshall Jones, 1935.

In this broad analysis of adapting fiction to the still fairly new genre of film, Ortman searches for a "standard for a good picture" and discusses film in the context of theater history. Using the contemporary MGM film [128] as an example, Ortman concludes that Walpole was a "literary genius" who successfully reduced the "diffuse scattering" of the novel to order. Walpole's central problem, she maintains, was to dramatize what Dickens the novelist could describe. She commends him for only including what is dramatically involved in David's life, arguing that the elements Walpole leaves out are generally either duplication of events or themes already included elsewhere in the film or issues no longer relevant to modern society, such as the social injustice represented by Creakle's school. She provides a useful summary of the film, indicating what is omitted, changed, and condensed from the novel.

859. Parish, James Robert, Gregory W. Mank and Richard Picchiarini. "David Copperfield." In *The Best of MGM: The Golden Years (1928–59).* Westport, CT: Arlington House Publishers, 1981, pp. 52–53.

Synopsis and brief commentary, noting that one of the reasons Selznick so admired the novel was that his immigrant father had taught himself English by it and had used it to teach his children to read. Jackie Cooper was considered for the title role, but the authors indicate Cukor and Selznick preferred a British actor, Freddie Bartholomew. Charles Laughton, after clashes over interpretation with Cukor, withdrew from the role of Micawber, which then was played by W. C. Fields.

860. Petrie, Graham. "Dickens in Denmark: Four Danish Versions of His Novels." *Journal of European Studies,* 26 (1991), 185–193.

Petrie discusses the 1922 Nordisk film [122] of *David Copperfield* along with the 1921 *Great Expectations,* 1921 *Our Mutual Friend,* and 1924 *Little Dorrit,* also by Nordisk and directed by A. W. Sandberg (as was *Copperfield*). Placing the film in the context of broader film history, Petrie describes the narrative of the film as "episodic," presenting distinct scenes which rely on titles for explanation. By contrast, the one-reel 1911 Britannia film *Little Emily* (855) contains no titles at all, suggesting that it may have been accompanied by a lecturer. This shift in narrative technique, Petrie argues, arose from an increasing demand for more authentic portrayals of popular literary works. He praises the film for its "atmosphere, setting and acting" as well as for its fidelity to the novel, though it leaves out the Little Em'ly/Steerforth plot entirely. Petrie also notes several devices Sandberg uses to give his film respectability, such as dedicating it "in reverence to the memory of the world-loved author" and ending with a park scene of a bearded man with a woman and children, which the title tells us is the "famous author in the happiest time of his life. He calls himself . . . - David Copperfield . . . But his real name is CHARLES DICKENS."

861. Pointer, Michael. *Charles Dickens on the Screen: The Film, Television, and Video Adaptations.* London: The Scarecrow Press, 1996.

This book is both commentary and catalog (chronological, including parodies, pastiches, and spoofs). It is useful to learn that D. W. Griffiths's *True Heart Susie* included a partial reworking of *David Copperfield,* that an extract also appeared in 1910 as the one-reel Edison film, *Love and the Law.* In 1913 *David Copperfield* was the first eight-reel feature film. In the 1920s *David Copperfield* was one of four Danish produced feature films of Dickens (860). In addition to listing a number of the less well known adaptations, Pointer provides helpful commentary about the 1935 David Selznick production [128]. Because the Pointer and Bolton (854) listings are so complete, those seeking complete listings of stage, film and television adaptations should consult them because they supplement and complement the entries of the earlier volume of this annotated bibliography.

STAGE ADAPTATIONS

862. "Wooman, Lovely Wooman." Performed by Miriam Margolyes (829) and David Timson. Directed by Sonia Fraser. Devised by Miriam Margolyes and Sonia Fraser. Performed at the Edinburgh International Festival, 22–27 August 1989.

Review: M. Slater, *Dickensian* 85 (1989): 185. Slater describes the production as a "causerie," neither set readings nor lecture, with Margoyles performing a series of Dickens's female characters, ranging from "the girlish tones of Dora" to a "wonderfully leering Miss Mowcher." Her purpose is to show the influence of the women in Dickens's life on his characters, though Slater feels she underplays his mother and dismisses his wife Catherine a bit too easily. Slater's view of Dickens is that the sexism we find in his works is substantially counteracted by his ability to create haunting instances of female suffering.

863. *David Copperfield* Written by W. H. Skeen. London and New York: S. French, 1924, 1986.

Part of the series "French's Scenes from Dickens." Other notes describe this as "David's Guardians—An Eruption of Vesuvius." We were unable to examine a copy of this text; the information provided comes from OCLC Worldcat record 14959450.

864. Francis, Matthew, director. "Charles Dickens' *David Copperfield.*" Greenwich Theatre, December 1997–January, 1998.

Review: M. Andrews, *Dickensian,* (98) (1998), 62–63.

COMMENTARY ON STAGE ADAPTATIONS

865. Review of George Almar's *Born With a Caul; or, The Personal Adventures of David Copperfield.* [83] Strand Theatre, London. 29 Oct. 1850. *Athenaeum* No. 1200 (26 October 1850), 1123.

     The reviewer finds that "the most daring additions are hazarded to produce the required amount of stage-excitement" but that there are also "many striking situations well managed, and some good acting." In particular, he notes Mr. Atwood as Uriah Heep and Miss Mowcher, Mr. Turner as Mr. Micawber, and Miss Isabel Simpson as Martha Endell. Unfortunately for those not familiar with the story, "the plot is most mysteriously conducted; and the spectator has to make out the connexion of the incidents in the best way he can."

866. Bolton, H. Philip. "David Copperfield." *Dickens Dramatized.* London: Mansell, 1987, pp. 321–348.

     In this impressive project, Bolton lists some 3,000 dramatic productions of Dickens's works, ranging from contemporary stage adaptations to more recent film, television, and radio versions of his novels. He focuses on each novel in chronological turn, making for an intense study of the dramatic history of each work. It is, however, in his own words "not complete, not definitive, not exhaustive." It would be impossible to be so; but it is more extensive than anything else of its kind. In looking at the theater, Bolton focuses on New York and London and takes what he considers a representative sampling of provincial theaters of England and America. The annotations are the most substantial for those productions which occurred during Dickens's lifetime. Helpfully, he lists not only the first production or broadcast of a particular adaptation, but subsequent productions and broadcasts as well, indicating which versions have enjoyed more popularity. He does not, however, list recorded versions of the book. The substantial "Key to Abbreviation of Sources" is a handy bibliography of resources on nineteenth-century theater, film, collections, and related topics.

     Having examined so closely the history of Dickensian dramatic productions, Bolton is also in a position to provide some perspective on both the influence of dramatic media on Dickens's works and vice versa. He gives a good sense of the theatrical scene when Dickens was writing, discusses Dickens's own problems with various theaters and playwrights, and lists important playwrights, actors, and actresses who made their careers playing Dickens's characters. Each novel in turn is given its own introductory section before the lists. Bolton notes the appearance of parts of *David Copperfield* in no fewer than six theaters before it was even complete, and points out that it was the first Dickensian play to be performed in one of the "Patent" playhouses. However, it was not until the 1870s that the novel gained its highest theatrical popularity, with at least ninety productions in that decade alone. Many of these were not versions of the entire novel but popular sections of it, most notably the stories of Little Em'ly and the Micawbers. And, like *A Christmas Carol,* the popularity of *David Copperfield* only increased in the twentieth century with numerous radio, film, and television adaptations in addition to further stage versions. In all, Bolton lists 242 dramatizations of *David Copperfield,* including eight films, seven radio, and five television versions, in addition to the substantial list of stage adaptations. Note: because the Bolton and Pointer (861) catalogues are so complete, those seeking complete listings of stage, film, and television adaptations should consult them directly because they supplement and complement the listings of the earlier volume of this annotated bibliography.

MUSICAL ADAPTATIONS

867. Etherington, James W. "Peggotty, the Wanderer: Ballad, from David Copperfield Addressed to Emily." London and Richmond: Chappell; Cramer, Beale and Co.; R. Addison; J. Etherington, 1850.
     Set for voice and piano, this ballad begins with the line "Oh! Turn like some sing-wearied dove." The musical setting appears to be by William Martin, Esq. We were unable to obtain a copy of this ballad for examination; our information comes from OCLC WorldCat record 30939952.
868. Dickens, Charles. *Five Dickens Duets.* Program notes by Frank Pettingell. Produced and directed by Arthur L. Klein. Ocean, NJ: Musical Heritage Society, 1989.
     Contains duets from *David Copperfield* as well as *Oliver Twist, Martin Chuzzlewit, Great Expectations,* and *The Pickwick Papers.*

MISCELLANEOUS ADAPTATIONS

869. Caldwell, Roger. "Scene from *David Copperfield.*" *New Statesman and Society* 7 (9 December 1994), 41.
     In this brief poem, Caldwell describes the scene in which David and Mr. Peggotty discuss Mr. Peggotty's search for Little Em'ly while

Martha listens from behind the door, unnoticed by everyone but David. Caldwell makes it clear that David the narrator knows that everything will end happily for everyone involved in the scene, but skillfully keeps this knowledge out of the narrative. He then places himself and us as other patrons of the public house, existing in a sort of limbo, bereft of the kind of closure which we know even at this point in the novel will be reached by the central characters.

870. Dickens, Charles, and Sol Eytinge. *David Copperfield; and, Mr. Bob Sawyer's Party.* Boston: Ticknor and Fields, 1868.
We have been unable to locate a copy of this text. According to OCLC WorldCat, this is part of a series entitled "The Readings of Mr. Charles Dickens."

871. Martin, C. M. *"David Copperfield."* Stroud: Arthurs Press, 1935.
Number one in MGM's Souvenir Series. Martin retells and edits the novel, based on the Estabrook and Walpole screenplay, and he includes illustrations from the 1935 film [128]. This book should not be confused with those which actually abridge Dickens's original text; these are discussed in the "Editions" section.

872. Noyes, Alfred. "Epilogue." In *David Copperfield's Library.* By John B. Langstaff. London: Allen and Unwin, 1925, pp. 155–157.
In this poem, Noyes describes a boy, "his name—it might be Copperfield or Dickens," creeping up to an attic alone to read, finding in the works of such authors as Defoe and Cooper his escape from the world of daily toil and his path to the future.

873. Packer, Eleanor. *"David Copperfield."* Big Little Books, 1148. Racine, WI: Witman Publishing, c. 1934.
Retold in only 156 pages, this version contains 76 black and white photos from the MGM production [128]. This book should not be confused with those which actually abridge Dickens's original text; these are discussed in the "Editions" section.

874. Purdy, Robert J. *"David Copperfield."* Ed. Ann Price. Illustrations by Virginia Grilley. Chicago: Laidlaw, 1951.
Adapting the novel for junior and senior high school readers, Purdy and Price simplified vocabulary and sentence structure, cut back on many of the descriptive passages, and omitted many "non-essential elements" such as Steerforth's family, Miss. Mowcher, Littimer, Martha, the Strongs, and Jack Maldon. All in all, this adaptation comprises only 257 pages. However, there is a very helpful appendix, including a brief biography of Dickens as well as pictures of him and several of his residences.

875. Schilling, Bernard N. *The Comic World of Dickens.* Greenwich: Fawcett, 1961.

In his brief introduction, Schilling discusses Dickens's own sense of intimacy with his characters, which was so great that he even "disliked coming to the end of a beloved book, and he often grieved so much at the loss of a favorite character, that he might walk the streets for hours at night in sorrowing loneliness." Focusing on Dickens's comic works, he gives a brief history of his career, emphasizing his work up to and including *David Copperfield* as most thoroughly encapsulating his "comic world." The book then contains excerpts from *The Pickwick Papers, The Old Curiosity Shop, Martin Chuzzlewit,* and *David Copperfield* which highlight a specific character. In the case of *David Copperfield,* Mr. Micawber is shown in all his comic glory from David's first introduction to his household to their final parting. Schilling includes Mr. Micawber's confrontation with Uriah Heep, but unfortunately leaves out the newspaper editorial David receives from Australia, explaining the Micawber family successes.

876. Smith, Edith F. *"The Personal History and Experience of David Copperfield the Younger, by Charles Dickens."* Illustrations by Harriet S. Smith. New York: Macmillan, 1925.

In this adaptation, unlike others, Smith chooses to trim in small amounts along the way, rather than leaving out entire characters or plot lines. The resulting adaptation, still less than 500 pages, feels considerably close to the original, in that the component parts are there. The introduction includes a biographical sketch of Charles Dickens.

877. Uriah Heep, rock band, 1970s.

This band debuted in London in 1970 with their album *Very Heavy Very 'umble.* There appears to be no other connection to either the character or the rest of the novel in any songs or subsequent albums. One rock critic did write, at the time of their debut, "if this group makes it, I'll have to commit suicide."

Part II. Studies

RECEPTION BY DICKENS'S CONTEMPORARIES

878. Arnold, Matthew. "The Incompatibles." *Nineteenth Century,* 9 (June, 1881), 1026–43. Reprinted in *English Literature and Irish Politics.* Ed. R. H. Super. Ann Arbor: University of Michigan Press, 1973, pp. 273–85.

    Remarking that this is the first occasion he has taken in print to praise Dickens, Arnold calls *David Copperfield* sound and "rich in merit," and in this essay concerning the Irish Land Bill, he draws on the novel's portrayal of middle-schools. Arnold, himself an inspector of schools, cites Creakle's school as typical of the sort of training which "produces with fatal sureness the effect of lowering [the] standard of life," perpetuating "a defective type of religion, a narrow range of intellect and knowledge, a stunted sense of beauty, a low standard of manners." Arnold considers Mr. Murdstone a natural product of such schooling, and Murdstone (and his sister) as "just the type of the Englishman and his civilisation as he presents himself to the Irish mind by his serious side."

CRITICISM

879. Abbott, H. Porter. "Autobiography, Autography, Fiction: Groundwork for a Taxonomy of Textual Categories." *New Literary History,* 3 (1988), 597–615.

    There is but brief mention of *David Copperfield* in this essay which may assist readers in understanding the differing demands of fiction and autobiography. Abbott points out that "in autobiography the discourse is narrative action." In a fiction such as Dickens's novel, "innocence—in the sense of pure representation, disengaged from a life in progress" may be possible.

880. Ackroyd, Peter. *"David Copperfield."* In his *Introduction to Dickens.* London: Sinclair-Stevenson, 1991, pp. 114–21.

Appearing close to the publication of Ackroyd's biography of Dickens (1133), this briefer volume continues the biographical linking of Dickens with the "lineaments of the nineteenth century" itself. Noting the motivations for the novel's beginning and the comforts and discomforts Dickens experienced in the writing, Ackroyd suggests that "in the very act of inventing David Copperfield . . . Dickens for the first time confronted the shape and meaning of his own life." The result was a book Ackroyd thinks established Dickens uniquely as "the last of the great eighteenth-century novelists and the first of the great symbolic novelists, . . . the true heir of the Romantic poets."

881. Adrian, Arthur A. " 'The Heir of My Bringing-Up.' " In his *Dickens and the Parent-Child Relationship*. Athens: Ohio University Press, 1984, pp. 108–17.

Although he takes his title from *Martin Chuzzlewit,* Adrian also has much to say about the penetrating studies of harm done children by parents in *David Copperfield* and *Hard Times*. In the cases of Steerforth and Heep, "the end-product . . . is the same: each is concerned solely with himself, destroys the happiness of others, and ultimately suffers the consequences, whose impact also involves the mother." Parts of this chapter are reprinted in *Reading David Copperfield* (1127).

882. Anderson, Amanda. " 'The Taint the Very Tale Conveyed': Self-Reading, Suspicion, and Fallenness in Dickens." In her *Tainted Souls and Painted Faces: The Rhetoric of Fallenness in Victorian Culture*. Ithaca NY: Cornell University Press, 1993, pp. 66–107.

This chapter considers the portrayals of fallen women in *Dombey and Son* and *David Copperfield* along with Dickens's journalistic writings and coincident philanthropic work with Angela Burdett Coutts in the management of a refuge for fallen women. Commenting upon Emily, Martha Endell, and Annie Strong, Anderson deals with the question of what so many fallen (or near-fallen) women are doing in David's personal history. The novel is ambivalent, she believes, because it evokes sympathy for the women yet also has "instances of harshness, recoil, or scapegoating." Anderson is most interested in the complicated case of Annie Strong, for even though she is not fallen, through her we see "narrative strategies that have operated on the figure of the fallen woman generally." She concludes that these characterizations "suggest the contaminating and controlling powers of stories themselves, their capacity to communicate a fatal identity to their susceptible practitioners, auditors, and subjects." Although not endorsing his "Foucauldian frame," Anderson acknowledges a general debt to D. A. Miller (1014) as well as to Poovey (1029) for her discussion of interiority and character.

883. Andrade, Mary A. "Pollution of an Honest Home." *Dickens Quarterly,* 5 (1988), 65–74.

The intensely realized figures of Heep, Steerforth, and Murdstone test the domestic virtues the novel generally endorses, Andrade asserts. She finds a pattern of disruptive and irresponsible sexuality separating David from incestuous (mother and sister) love-objects. Significantly, the villains operate in isolation, never knowing one another, but linked solely through David.

884. Andrews, Malcolm. *Dickens and the Grown-Up Child.* London: Macmillan, 1994, pp. 135–71.

Two chapters, one centering on "Children and the Childlike" and one on "The Trials of Maturity," directly concern *David Copperfield,* which, for Andrews, dramatizes how far childhood may be regarded as a virtue or defect. The female characters with whom David is involved provide the most interesting studies of childhood or childlike qualities. Andrews finds the book lacking "any single coherent and stable idea of childhood," and he questions whether there can be a coherent idea of adulthood. Adding to the considerable critical commentary about the novel's "disciplined heart" theme, Andrews likens the growing control of head over heart to that in *Sense and Sensibility* or *Waverley,* and also as part of the cultural purging of the Byronic temper in the 1830s and 1840s. Nonetheless, a general discrepancy remains between David the narrator who links the man with the childhood self and the more stuffy, highly earnest adult David character. The great value of this study is its demonstrations of how the story of David's life vacillates "between progressive and retrogressive impulses," a pattern established in the projected views of childhood and childishness. Reviews: E. Eigner, *Dickensian,* 90 (1994), 200–202:A. Sadrin, *Dickens Quarterly* 12 (1995), 135–39; R. Newsom, *Nineteenth-Century Literature,* 50 (1995), 384–86; P. Marks, *South Atlantic Review,* 60 (1995), 166–67; R. DeGraaf, *Victorian Review,* 21 (1995), 199–201.

885. Andrews, Malcolm. "Introduction" and "Dickens and His Critics." In 1993 Dent Edition, pp. ix–xvi, 843–58 (825).

Andrews places the novel at transition point between the world which had produced *Pickwick* and a new Victorian world dominated by earnestness and purposefulness. He notes that we have no clear reasons for why Dickens regarded this as his favorite work, but it may have been because it was an exorcism of that past which had so haunted him. The appended survey of critical reaction to the novel provides a good overview both of the early and later criticism, noting in particular the serious interest the novel has received in recent years, and including lengthy quotation from Welsh's discussion (1073) of its anticipation of Freudian psychology and from Eigner's recognition of its basic pantomime structure (932).

886. Armstrong, Frances. *Dickens and the Concept of Home.* Ann Arbor: UMI Research Press, 1990.

Not treating the Dickens novels separately, this study provides a context both within Dickens's works and in Victorian culture for David's experiences of home and homelessness, for the novel's different representations of domestic life, and of the homes that Agnes keeps and represents.

887. Atteberry, Philip D. "The Fictions of David Copperfield." *Victorians Institute Journal,* 14 (1986), 67–76.

Atteberry approaches *Copperfield* as a "journey" novel, an extended expedition in search of life's meaning. Atteberry argues that David fictionalizes in order to counter the aimlessness and fragmentation he experiences. Like Mr. Dick, he reduces pain to metaphors, and he also exaggerates the influence of villains. According to Atteberry, Agnes is the ultimate fiction, the idealized goodness and part of the ending's small circle of family and friends seeming to share the benefits of divine justice.

888. Auerbach, Nina. "Performing Suffering: From Dickens to David." *Browning Institute Studies,* 18 (1990), 15–22.

Auerbach builds upon Welsh's reading (1073) of the blacking warehouse as more a product of Dickens's literary imagination than early trauma which directed that imagination. Auerbach finds Dickens withholding from David, as he did from other suffering fictional children, "his own genius for monumental self-creation." Therefore David, unlike Dickens, "the principal actor," searches vainly for an audience. The contrasted "shrinking creature" of the character and the expansive creativity of the author signals "the gulf between biography and novel as Dickens and his contemporaries understood these genres."

889. Auerbach, Nina. *Woman and the Demon: The Life of a Victorian Myth.* Cambridge: Harvard University Press, 1982, passim.

Although she does not discuss the novel separately, much of Auerbach's study is useful to readers interested in the women characters and ideals of womanhood projected in *David Copperfield.* She notes, in passing, the irony of Freud's having imposed Dora's name upon the recreant patient whose case became central to Freud's theories, and Auerbach discusses Agnes as a conventional angel who "is endowed with a virtually unlimited power of creation." Her chapter, "The Rise of the Fallen Women," provides from both literature and painting an excellent context for the attention Dickens gives the subject in *Copperfield.*

890. Ayres-Ricker, Brenda. "Dickens' Dissenting Women: Subversion of Domestic Ideology." *DAI,* 53 (1993), 3219A (Southern Mississippi, 1992).

In her study of women in Dickens's novels who "do not conform to the image of the angel in the house," Ayres-Ricker argues that though the narrative itself appropriately disciplines them, it nevertheless contains elements which undermine the domestic ideology otherwise professed. She takes on the typical interpretation of David's marriage to Dora as a mistake and suggests that there are fundamental conflicts "in the text's advocacy of domestic ideology." Ayres-Ricker also discusses *Oliver Twist, Barnaby Rudge,* and *Bleak House.* This work is forthcoming from Greenwood Press under the title *Dissenting Women in Dickens' Novels: The Subversion of Domestic Ideology.*

891. Barickman, Richard, Susan MacDonald, and Myra Stark. "Dickens." In their *Corrupt Relations: Dickens, Thackeray, Trollope, Collins and the Victorian Sexual System.* New York: Columbia University Press, 1982, pp. 58–110.

This chapter has no separate discussion of *David Copperfield* but cites its many views of women and families as instances of Dickens's perception that the patriarchal social system of the time was "thoroughly corrupt." The argument is that in every Dickens novel oppressive patriarchal effects on parent and child alike persist. The stereotypic mother is a weakling (Clara Copperfield), supplanted by masculinized surrogate mothers, to which Betsey Trotwood proves an exception because her mannerisms disguise true tenderness. The final union of Agnes and David "is a process of salvaging as well as a process of salvation," given the experience both have had with absent or ineffective parents.

892. Bauer, Matthias. "Orpheus and the Shades: The Myth of the Poet in *David Copperfield.*" *University of Toronto Quarterly,* 63 (1993), 308–27.

Although David the novelist has little to say about his profession, the character has some archetypal traits of the poet and engages in mythical role-playing. Incidents in his childhood resemble the classical journey in the underworld. The Orpheus parallel strikes Bauer, because David strives to recover several Eurydice figures (particularly Agnes) and because "Dickens attaches great importance to music in presenting David's mental and emotional development." Further, Bauer finds a Christian typology linking Christ, David, and Orpheus, which, involving the Biblical David, was a common configuration in the Middle Ages. As an approach to the poetic tone, the juxtapositions of present/past and life/death, this reading puts the novel in a context few readers would consider without Bauer's lead. At best, it alerts us to the seldom-noticed attention to music and to a fresh explanation of Dickens's phrase, "the shadowy world," in taking leave of his novel.

893. Baumgarten, Murray. "Writing and *David Copperfield.*" *Dickens Studies Annual,* 14 (1985), 30–59.

Through its many characters who in one way or another write, the novel explores some meanings of writing in its time. David, Micawber, and Mr. Dick are the principal writers, and Baumgarten sees David's writing as a version of the epistolary Micawber and the petitioning Mr. Dick. What counts for them most is more the act than the content of writing. Baumgarten's attention to the distinction between oral and written cultures defines class differences. Compared to David's written record, the oral narration of Dan Peggotty has a power greater than written memory; much of David's writing is an effort "to recover the lost innocence Peggotty embodies." Nonetheless, writing reinforces the class system, and, Baumgarten insists, David's writing about Steerforth shows how "writing's ideological function makes it possible to evade the natural blame we would heap on our cherished models and heroes were we dealing with them in a face to face culture." As self-proclaimed "written memory," Baumgarten notes, the novel is indebted to Wordsworth and Carlyle; like their writing, it is a "witnessing of the real existence of the past as well as of its contemporary power and meaning." See also Woodfield (1077), for expansion of many of Baumgarten's points.

894. Bell, John D. " 'Performing Funerals' and Dickens' Novels: Negotiating Culture in Victorian England." *DAI,* 53 (992), 179A (Tulane, 1992).

Bell compares Victorian funerals to Dickens's revival of the serial format for novels, claiming that both depict the "tension between the material impulse of commercialism and the spiritual desire for transcendence over the vicissitudes of industrialization and commercialization." He examines Dickens's use of funerals in three novels, including *David Copperfield,* to bring those tensions to light. These scenes, Bell argues, reflect not only a social anxiety about changing values but also Dickens's "own concerns and anxieties for both himself as an artist and for the serial novel as a form of art."

895. Berman, Ronald. "The Innocent Observer." *Children's Literature,* 9 (1981), 40–50.

Berman discusses *Copperfield* and *Jane Eyre* as examples of a fictional subgenre, the story of the child suffering the sins of the age vicariously. For Berman, education and religion are important subjects in both novels as institutional forms of public morality. David's views of the Murdstones are highly imaginative, weaving together "childish initiations of sexuality, hatred, and belief." For both writers, the child as social observer approximates the novelist, seeing "the social order both as it actually is and in metaphorical terms more useful than our ordinary perceptions.''

896. Blakey, Barbara F. ''Varieties of the Bildungsroman: Portraits of the Self in a Changing Society.'' *DAI,* 41 (1981), 292A (Arizona, 1980). Blakey examines the diversity of the Bildungsroman and in particular its ''increasing pessimism regarding the changes for self-fulfillment in an increasingly complex world'' during the Victorian period. Contrasting *David Copperfield* and *Great Expectations,* Blakey argues that the former represents an optimistic example of the genre, while the latter is more pessimistic. But the difference and similarities both here and with other Victorian Bildungsromane ''suggest both a consistent and identifiably British concept of self-fulfillment.''

897. Bloom, Harold, ed. *Charles Dickens's David Copperfield.* Modern Critical Interpretations Series. New York: Chelsea House, 1987. This volume reprints nine studies of *David Copperfield* which were published between 1970 and 1986. Bloom's short introduction links Dickens with Shakespeare and Freud, as one of ''the Great Originals.'' He terms *Copperfield* ''the first therapeutic novel, in part written to heal the author's self.'' The book's ''aesthetic puzzle . . . is why David has and conveys so overwhelming a sense of disordered suffering and early sorrow in his Murdstone phase.'' With little explanation, Bloom claims that ''Dickens's preternatural energy gets into David, and is at some considerable variance with the diffidence of David's apparent refusal to explore his own inwardness.'' Reprinted essays include: Barbara Hardy, ''The Moral Art of Dickens: *David Copperfield''* (956); Carl Bandelin, ''David Copperfield: A Third Interesting Penitent'' [215]; Barry Westburg, ''David Sees 'Himself' in the Mirror'' [527]; Robert E. Lougy, ''Remembrances of Death Past and Future: A Reading of *David Copperfield''* [391]; John P. McGowan, *''David Copperfield:* The Trial of Realism'' [397]; Philip M. Weinstein, ''Mr Peggotty and Little Em'ly: Misassessed Altruism?'' (1072); D. A. Miller, ''Secret Subjects, Open Secrets'' (1014); Ned Lukacher, ''Containing the Destructive Work of Remembrance'' (998).

898. Bloom, Harold, ed. *Major Literary Characters: David Copperfield.* New York: Chelsea House, 1992. Bloom includes the character David in this series of reprint collections because he finds him ''the great original of all the portraits of the artist as a young man,'' and because with this character we can see ''the genesis and the early development of a great novelist.'' In his four-page introduction, Bloom suggests that Dickens ''subtly conferred upon David a kind of blankness, . . . the sense of the novelist-in-waiting,'' and he says that ''what is most valuable in him never has to

mature at all.'' There are two sections of reprinted materials: ''Critical
Extracts'' and ''Critical Essays.'' Extracts are from Dickens's letters
[1], Chorley's 1850 review [176], the 1867 preface, Forster [307],
Matthew Arnold [185], William Samuel Lilly [''Dickens'' in *Four
English Humorists of the Nineteenth Century.* London: John Murray,
1895, p. 14], Chesterton [255], Woolf [538], Leacock [385], Shaw
[477], Orwell [443], Maugham [414], Hamilton [335], J. Hillis Miller
[419], Priestley [*Charles Dickens: A Pictorial Biography.* New York:
Viking, 1962, pp. 76–79], Beebe [223], Wilson [533], Gomme [326],
Ferris [298], Hawes [24]. Longer critical essays include Needham
[433], Kincaid [374], Hornback [344], Gilmour [320], Talbot [503],
Hennelly [340], McGowan [397], Crawford (918), Vanden Bossche
(1069), Eigner (932), Carmichael (912), Welsh (1073).

Review: Richard J. Dunn, *Dickens Quarterly,* 9 (1992), 89–91.

899. Bottum, Joseph. ''The Gentleman's True Name: *David Copperfield*
and the Philosophy of Naming.'' *Nineteenth-Century Literature.* 49
(1995), 435–55.

Bottum finds a fascination with names and the multiplicity of names
for individuals in *Copperfield* exceeding that in the other novels, for
here Dickens lets characters in on their naming and seems concerned
with the tension between meaning and reference. The philosophical
dimensions, for Bottum, are Dickens's use of a name to effect an
economy of power and desire as the character enacts a name. Bottum
further shows how a true name can push back on that economy with
the moral force of truth.'' Micawber is, for Bottum, both a text and an
exception to the expected, for he ''creates not himself but language''
through liberating circumlocution. David, often a victim of naming,
''must find in names a unity of concept and thing beyond the power
of the namer and the weakness of the named.'' This he does largely
by becoming a writer, and finally by reclaiming many of the names
that have pointed to his real distinction.

900. Brooke, Cheryl L. ''The Contributions of the Narrative Voice to the
Humor in Dickens' Novels.'' *DAI,* 42 (1982), 3162 (Case Western
Reserve, 1981).

Reclaiming Dickens as a humorist, Brooke compares the narrators in
Pickwick Papers, David Copperfield, and *Bleak House,* arguing that
the narrators' language is a significant part of Dickens's humor. For
her, David the narrator uses the double perspective of adult and child
to maintain throughout a ''continual, gently humorous tone'' and to
create an ironic distance which ''enables the reader to share his amuse-
ment at the characters whom he presents and at his youthful and
adult self.''

901. Brooks, Chris. " 'What the Waves Were Always Saying': Symbolic Realism in *Dombey and Son* and *David Copperfield.*" In Brooks's *Signs for the Times: Symbolic Realism in the Mid-Victorian World.* London: George Allen & Unwin, 1984, pp. 36–52.

Seldom cited by later commentators interested in the sea-imagery, such as Palmer (1027), or in more general considerations of the novel's narrative structure, Brooks's essay reconsiders *Copperfield* as a novel of education and as a work well demonstrating Dickens's particular blend of experience and imagination. Brooks discusses progressive stages of David's education as the means by which the hero registers a changing series of world-constructs, and Brooks notes, especially, the potency of the Edenic fallacy, "the need to believe in a lost world of innocent joy." Brooks persuasively shows Betsey Trotwood as "ethical counterweight to the Edenic fallacy," and finds her to be "the interpretative model" for David's understanding of his life. *David Copperfield,* more than any of the earlier novels, benefits from Dickens's conceiving of "symbolism, realism, ethic inquiry and conceptual patterning as parts of an imaginary whole."

902. Buckley, Jerome H. "The Identity of David Copperfield." In *Victorian Literature and Society: Essays Presented to Richard D. Altick.* Eds. James R. Kincaid and Albert J. Kuhn. Columbus: Ohio State University Press, 1984, pp. 225–39.

Buckley approaches the novel as David's rather than Dickens's autobiography, and he discusses David's character "in the autonomous context of the novel," a work which nonetheless "embodies many Victorian values and assumptions." Psychological criticism, taking a cue from Freud's admiration of *David Copperfield,* has made what Buckley terms "rather ominous clinical readings," and "attaching labels to [David's] affections and antipathies misrepresents rather than defines his identity." Comparable to *The Prelude* and *In Memoriam, David Copperfield* centers thematically on the power of memory as "the strongest sanction of identity."

903. Buckley, Jerome H. "Preface." *David Copperfield.* In 1990 Norton edition, pp. vii–xii (1107).

Buckley thinks that *David Copperfield* may be "the 'central' novel in quality, as it is in time, of the whole nineteenth-century English tradition" because of its amplitude, dramatic variety, well delineated characters, suspenseful plot, and "fertility of observation and invention and a master's command of an assured and eloquent style." Buckley finds the novel to be "a conspicuously successful example" of the Bildungsroman, and he likens its poetic reminiscence to that of Wordsworth's *Prelude* and Tennyson's *In Memoriam.* See Buckley [239, 240].

904. Buckton, Oliver S. " 'My Undisciplined Heart: ' Declassifying Homo-erotic Secrets in *David Copperfield.*" *ELH,* 64 (1997), 189–222.

Theoretically based on Philippe Lejeune's concept of autobiographical space, this essay finds the novel enacting a confusion between autobiography and fiction. Like D. A. Miller (1014), Buckton finds recurrent breakdown of "the disciplinary project" as he traces "David's trajectory from same-sex to heterosexual object-choices" and the resultant melancholy. Buckton extends Poovey's (1029) sense of the importance of gender, for he finds coexistent differing narratives of gender identification. Many of these involve the David-Steerforth-Heep relationship, about which Buckton concludes "David's heterosexual masculine narrative is achieved at the cost of a profound loss that eludes adequate representation or resolution." The sort of pact Dickens maintained with his future biographer, John Forster, "suggests an element of romance that anticipates the carefully-policed eroticism of David's scenes with Steerforth," but as with less familiar readers, Dickens also kept Forster "guessing as to the full extent of his confessional disclosures."

905. Budd, Dona. "When So, Not So: Voice and Gender in Dickens' Fiction." *DAI,* 55 (1995), 196A (Berkeley, 1993).

Budd argues that Dickens's "deep sympathies and identifications with the oppressed, the disempowered, the marginal" are inadequately represented by the primarily patriarchal voice which dominates his writing. In recompense, Dickens uses female voices which "compete with and challenge" the dominant voice and also "compensate for and repair its failures and brutalities." But even female voices which support the patriarchal voice, Budd argues, ultimately destablize its narrative authority, demonstrating an undercurrent of "feminine sympathies" which questions the novels' overall embracing of patriarchal values. Budd considers *David Copperfield, Bleak House,* and *Our Mutual Friend* in this light.

906. Burgan, Mary. "Bringing Up By Hand: Dickens and the Feeding of Children." *Mosaic,* 24 (1991), 69–88.

Burgan discusses instances involving Oliver Twist, David, and Pip concerning their nurture or lack of nurture. She combines Victorian social history with psychology in discussing Dickens's anger at the psychological as well as physical and social toll of malnutrition, and she suggests that his personal domestic problems lent "special urgency to his concern with the feeding of children."

907. Burgis, Nina. "Introduction." In 1981 World's Classics Edition, pp. vii–xv (1108).

Burgis, who also edited the full Clarendon edition [72], argues that the novel "is not fictionalized autobiography," but in this introduction she well links it with Dickens's thinking and writing over a number of years. She has an excellent discussion of the trial titles as signals of Dickens's fictional agenda, and she notes the importance of humor in enabling him to fictionalize painful memories. She points out that the novel's public events and social interests are those of 1850, not of the earlier period of David's life.

908. Busch, Frederick. "Suitors by Boz." *Gettysburg Review,* 6 (1993), 561–78.

Busch discusses how the narrators in *David Copperfield, Bleak House,* and *Our Mutual Friend* "knit the act of writing to the state of sorrow, to Dickens's state of sorrow." *Copperfield* "is about writing," and the urgent business of storytelling was for Dickens "a making of love and a challenge to death." Through David, "Dickens addresses his darkest, most secret, and most urgent needs 'to the reader whom I love,' his very self."

909. Byatt, A. S. "The Sins of Families and Nations." *New York Times Book Review,* 18 July 1993, pp. 3, 25–26.

This essay on envy includes some attention to Uriah Heep as Dickens's "masterpiece in the depiction of envy." Byatt terms Heep "a Victorian version of a medieval demon."

910. Carlton-Ford, Cynthia C. "Conversation, Gender, and Power: Dialogue in the Nineteenth-Century Novel." *DAI,* 48 (1988), 276A (Minnesota, 1987).

Arguing that dialogue has typically been neglected by critics, Carlton-Ford looks to it for depictions of power struggles between the genders. She finds that those in positions of power, usually males, have speech patterns "characterized most often by directness." For her, less powerful characters, usually females, have much more diverse speech patterns. Drawing on feminist language theory, linguistic anthropology and social psychology, Carlton-Ford examines dialogue in four Victorian novels to "ask how power is defined in that novel and who wields it." In *David Copperfield,* she finds that Dickens celebrates the submissive woman, "but represents a range of strategies that relatively powerless women use to cope with their places in the social structure."

911. Carabine, Keith. "Reading *David Copperfield.*" In *Reading the Victorian Novel: Detail into Form.* Ed. Ian Gregor. London: Vision Press, 1980, pp. 150–67.

Attending to the experience of the serial reader, Carabine registers "the different kinds of reading experiences the novel's shifting perspectives elicit," and finds the form "extraordinarily plural and unsettling" on the reader's mind. He sees in the first fourteen chapters "the paradigm for all the subsequent 'plots,' " and the remainder of the novel repeats "the curse of David's childhood." Carabine discusses the two threads of Heep's place in David's life and Dora's death. He finds David's final, alleged all-encompassing success embarrassing to the reader, who remains haunted by shadows removed in the closing moments of the narrative.

912. Carmichael, Virginia. "In Search of Beein': Non/Nom du Père in *David Copperfield.*" *ELH,* 54 (1987), 653–67.

Carmichael pairs Dickens's use of "beein'," a Yorkshire term for "home," with Lacan's pun to suggest "David's search for both social vocation and sexual bonding." She discusses interaction between the Lacanian Imaginary (pre-linguistic experience) and the Symbolic (primary Order, mediating and articulating the Imaginary and the Real) to suggest the extent to which both David and Dickens found language and writing problematic. The "pathologies of expression," reveal for Carmichael the difficulties various characters have when dealing with their past. David encounters different versions of triangulated desire as structural obstacles "to the recovery of the desired mother." Carmichael finds the ending undercutting David's asserted contentment with Agnes, because the imagery and narrative structuring betray the tone of resolution, showing him "still firmly imprisoned in the illusions of the Imaginary realm." She concludes that both David and Dickens "have produced a narrative text in which the Imaginary is radically bifurcated and transformed by the telling." This essay has been reprinted by Bloom (898) and by Peck (1124).

913. Carr, Jean F. "Dickens and Autobiography: A Wild Beast and His Keeper." *ELH,* 52 (1985), 447–69.

Taking her cue from language of Dickens's memoranda, Carr discusses Dickens's self-expression as "a secret, wild act, performed when the 'keeper' [himself] is not looking." Reluctant throughout his life to make public details about himself, Dickens nonetheless was susceptible to demands for portraits and life histories. The autobiographical fragment shows the inadequacy of the autobiographical form for recapturing Dickens's childhood feelings; his "regular habit was to transform whatever he saw or experienced into little dramas or fictions." Carr studies closely the influence Dickens exerted on the story of his own life by entrusting Forster with the autobiographical fragment. She notes, in particular, that the restlessness Dickens often mentioned in letters became a theme both in *Copperfield* and in John Forster's biography.

914. Carr, Jean F. "Dickens's Theatre of Self-Knowledge." In *Dramatic Dickens.* Ed. Carol H. MacKay. London: Macmillan, 1989, pp. 27–44.

Carr's essay centers on *Copperfield, Great Expectations,* and Dickens's production of *The Frozen Deep.* She finds Dickens struggling to articulate contradictions of his theatrical experience, as he used theater as scene and metaphor in his two most autobiographical novels. In *David Copperfield* this is most evident in the account of David's attending a production of *Julius Caesar* at the end of his school years, and in using a theatrical frame (momentarily "raising a curtain") for presenting David's childhood work experience. More generally, she asserts that "the metaphor of theatre also mitigates Dickens's ambivalence about the finality of self-expression," allowing quick changes of mood.

915. Chaston, Joel C. "Crusoe, Crocodiles, and the Cookery Books: *David Copperfield* and the Affective Power of Reading Fiction." *The University of Mississippi Studies in English,* 9 (1991), 141–53.

This essay argues that *David Copperfield* "is fundamentally concerned with the effects of reading fiction," can be read as a response to the charge that fiction is a dangerous waste of time, and is a sort of *Ars Poetica* for Dickens's ideas about the novel genre and relationship with his readers. The reading associated with various characters frequently signals their nature, and Chaston thinks that David finds reading both encouraging and confusing if not undertaken carefully. Like Dickens's, David's writing blends experience and imagination, Chaston concludes.

916. Colatosti, Camille. "Male versus Female Self-denial: The Subversive Potential of the Feminine Ideal in the Fiction of Charles Dickens." *Dickens Studies Annual,* 19 (1990), 1–24.

This article considers Dickens's depiction of "the complex desires that Victorian domestic—and, in fact, all patriarchal—ideologies have for women." For Colatosti, David Copperfield fails to consider the effect of Betsey's and Peggotty's maternal love, strengthens his image as a self-made man through appropriation of Agnes's letters, and discounts Mrs. Gummidge's grief as self-indulgent. For a contrasting reading of the impact of many women on David's life, see Eigner (932).

917. Craig, David M. "The Interplay of City and Self in *Oliver Twist, David Copperfield,* and *Great Expectations..*" *Dickens Studies Annual,* 16 (1987), 17–38.

Craig finds that in the imaginations of Oliver Twist, David, and Pip, Dickens's "terms of urban experience evolve as he becomes increasingly aware of the way in which reality is created by consciousness and consciousness is itself shaped by external reality." Craig notes that, like Oliver, David first finds the city confusing, presenting him with a problem of incommunicative isolation. Through his writing, David subsequently holds the stifling early urban experience at a rhetorical distance as "through the course of his narrative David literally

finds his way in the city." But Craig thinks that David does not metaphorically refigure the city to the extent Pip does in *Great Expectations.*

918. Crawford, Iain. "Sex and Seriousness in *David Copperfield.*" *Journal
of Narrative Technique,* 16 (1986), 41–54.
Crawford discusses the contrast between willed idea and insistent desire as presenting the truest image of David's self-development. Unresolved, the discrepancy between the two keeps the novel from
becoming a successful act of purgation. Crawford notes the novel's
terms of sexual attractiveness, its contrasts between dominated and
dominating characters, and Agnes as a variation on the Dickensian
earnest heroine. But on the whole, earnestness in *David Copperfield*
is a narrowing quality, lacking warmth and depth, and much of the
book's greatness, therefore, is in "characters and values quite inimical
to the orthodox beliefs its hero comes to voice." This essay has been
reprinted by Bloom (898).

919. Crick, Brian. " 'Mr. Peggotty's Dream Comes True': Fathers and Husbands; Wives and Daughters." *University of Toronto Quarterly,* 54
(1984), 38–55.
Acknowledging the Phiz illustration of Peggotty's reunion with Em'ly
and Q. D. Leavis's recognition, in *Dickens the Novelist* [386], of Peggotty's "horribly possessive love," Crick finds this uncle-niece relationship central to a "pattern of uncertainty and confusion" in the
novel's "ambiguous groups of fathers or surrogate fathers, 'lovers,'
and/or husbands and their loved ones." These include Annie and Dr.
Strong, Agnes and Mr. Wickfield, as each of these relationships, as
well as that of Dan Peggotty and Em'ly, is threatened by an unscrupulous young man. Generally the novel fails, claims Crick, in relating
the passionate love of adult men and women to the domestic ties of
brother and sister, parent and child.

920. Daldry, Graham. "The Novel as Narrative, I. *David Copperfield.*" In
his *Charles Dickens and the Form of the Novel: Fiction and Narrative
in Dickens' Work.* Totowa: Barnes and Noble Books, 1987, pp.
89–130.
Daldry finds the novel to be "not a narrative but an account of a
narrative, and a history of a narrative consciousness." David encounters people, like the Micawbers, who "half live a fictive existence,"
but perceive their world as "one of narrative." Aunt Betsey serves as
"the manager of the narrative, . . . providing [the generally melodra-
matic] literariness that transforms the literal details of David's life into
his story." But, notes Daldry, her own hidden history indicates that
there is no place in narrative for private feelings. Uriah Heep is "the

only other character in the book to share Betsey's knowledge of how narrative works.'' Daldry shows how Heep self-consciously exploits the parts of other players, as he "exists to torture the fictive imagination.'' David increasingly leaves behind the fictive world as his own narrative becomes literary, often "in an overwrought, artificial way.'' The consequence, argues Daldry, is that immediate reality disappears, "replaced by the consciousness that only the 'Narrative' is true.'' For David, but not for Betsey, "a life of narrative cannot risk an experience of the whole wide world.'' Daldry concludes that David's literary effort ultimately fails him, "as autobiography would have failed Dickens, for it has shut out the real life of imagination.''

921. Danon, Ruth. *Work in the English Novel: The Myth of Vocation.* London: Croom Helm, 1985, pp. 43–91, 98–99, 199–200.

Comparing *David Copperfield* to *Robinson Crusoe* which plays such a large part in David's imagination), Danon argues that the various homes in Dickens's novel are Crusoe's island domesticated, and are ultimately more important than the journeys undertaken to reach them. Although Danon finds the novel dominated by David's journeying, the happiness at the end is dependent upon the presence of work in all the characters' lives. This is not, she thinks, a Calvinist work ethic, which is dramatized in the figures of the Murdstones and Uriah Heep. Psychic wholeness is only to be found in the bringing together of vocation and home, such as in the Peggotty's houseboat. Work is also a source of pleasure, when it is connected with a home.

But it is in his marriage to Dora that the centrality of work to the novel comes to the surface, argues Danon. Dora is shown time and time again to be incapable of real, useful work, though even she eventually finds happiness in the appearance of usefulness, holding David's pens and copying out manuscripts for him. Danon finds readings of Agnes which focus only on her spiritual influence on David to be dismissive; "she is, at least, theoretically, an interesting and competent woman.'' Danon also cites Traddles as the model which David at first undervalues (in his infatuation with Steerforth) and grows ever closer to as he finds his true vocation.

922. Darby, Margaret F. "Dora and Doady." *Dickens Studies Annual,* 22 (1993), 155–69.

This, like a number of recent discussions of David's evasive fictionalizing (in particular 1031), asks that readers put aside David's interpretations "and the critical tradition that has taken David's word for truth.'' Even within the convention of the "ringletted heroine, Dora is an agent for subversion,'' and, unlike Flint (938), Darby argues that she has a space from which to speak; "the problem is that readers have colluded with David's refusal to listen.'' Darby points out that such a "gendered reading of Dora intensifies the bad light shed on David" through recent critical analyses of his "covert identification with Steerforth, with Traddles, with Uriah Heep, analyses which preclude acceptance of David's complacency and willful blindness.''

923. Davis, Philip. "Dickens and the Strong Art of the Autobiographical Novel.'' In his *Writing and Memory: From Wordsworth to Lawrence.* Liverpool: Liverpool University Press, 1983, pp. 196–225.

To the considerable body of commentary about memory, autobiography, and the relationships among David remembered and David remembering and Dickens himself, Davis takes the position that Dickens was showing a reduction in "the power and status of a presiding memory" from what "it had been to Wordsworth," although for David "memory was both himself *and* the witness of himself.'' But the relation between Dickens and David is "not so open to us as that between the writer of *The Prelude* and William Wordsworth.'' This, to some extent, is the nature of the autobiographical novel, which exists in "a middle distance between personal experience and consensus view of experience for the sake of their mutual criticism in an increasingly uncertain world.'' It was a form in which, for Davis, Dickens could exercise his strong "novelistic powers of deviousness, emotional cunning and manipulative artifice to defend and make strong immature experience.''

924. DeGraaff, Robert M. "Self-Articulating Characters in *David Copperfield.*" *Journal of Narrative Technique,* 14 (1984), 214–222.

Dickens, argues DeGraaff, should be taken on his own terms of creating characters as vividly realized individual personalities and not as either "flat" figures or "fragments, whose definition is determined by their place in a symbolic structure." Self-articulation is a principal technique for individualized characterization, and, for DeGraaff, almost every *David Copperfield* character at some point explains himself or herself. Betsey Trotwood's self-description gets beyond external eccentricities and establishes a sympathetic, conscious understanding.

925. Den Hartog, Dirk. *Dickens and Romantic Psychology: The Self in Time in Nineteenth-Century English Literature.* New York: St. Martin's Press, 1987, passim.

Like Raina (1031), Den Hartog is interested in the "aggressive dynamism of nineteenth-century bourgeois capitalism and the nostalgia for the sanctities this violated.'' He does not include a detailed reading of *David Copperfield* noting that he has little to add to Gilmour's discussion [320], and, like many more traditional readers, he finds this novel to be "an especially charmed interlude in an author's middle life.''

The introductory chapter on "Dickens, Romantic Psychology and 'the Experience of Modernity,' " provides a helpful context in an "emerging Wordsworthian-Romantic tradition." *Copperfield,* through its wistful witness of psychic continuity, "is Dickens's most successfully Wordsworthian novel."

Reviews: M. Steig, *Victorian Studies,* 32 (1989), 263–65; D. Sadoff, *Dickens Quarterly,* 5 (1988), 192–95.

926. Dennett, J. J. "Mighty Waters in the Work of Dickens and Turner." *Dickensian,* 90 (1994), 179–88.

This article points to parallels in the writer's and painter's uses of the storm at sea to represent "some omniscient force, usually God." Turner's *The Shipwreck* of 1805 and his *Slaves throwing overboard the dead and dying—Typhon [sic] coming on* of 1840 were well known to Dickens, and his writing of the tempest in *David Copperfield,* Dennett suggests, may allude to the earlier Turner work. Dennett, anticipating Palmer (1027), comments more broadly on Dickens's interest in shipwreck; see also Ruskin [197].

927. Dryden, Jonathan N. "Ixion's Wheel: Masculinity and the Figure of the Circle in the Novels of Charles Dickens." *DAI,* 58 (1997), 1291A (Arizona, 1997).

Dryden examines the connection between masculinity, authorial subjectivity and the figure of the circle in his Lacanian reading of *David Copperfield, The Pickwick Papers, A Tale of Two Cities,* and *Great Expectations.* The circle "functions both as a figure for an ideal narcissistic unity and as a sign of the individual's subjection to the metaphoric and metonymic movement of language within the symbolic order."

928. Dunn, Albert A. "Time and Design in *David Copperfield.*" *English Studies,* 59 (1978), 225–36.

Dunn, like John Lucas [394], argues that David is a representative character, a means by which Dickens examined such a Victorian social myth as that of innocent, romantic love. Paradoxically, David's spiritual adventure involves his differentiating himself from others, and this "process of individuation, like David's representative function, is an important aspect of *Copperfield's* complex use of time." Dunn finds David realizing both past and present in his union with Agnes, his authorial role permitting "him to achieve, despite his succession of new beginnings, the relation between past and present which gives his life continuity and the novel coherence."

929. Edwards, Simon. "*David Copperfield:* the Decomposing Self." *The Centennial Review,* 29 (1985), 328–352.

Edwards reads the novel in context of mid-nineteenth-century English literary culture, and makes comparisons with such other autobiographical fictions as *The Prelude, In Memoriam, Pendennis*—texts which "accompany and articulate a passage in historical time from crisis to triumph." They show particularly how the social construction of the age "was predicated upon the possibility of self-construction," usually an individualism "constrained by the appropriation of patriarchal authority and responsibility." Like Houston (968) and Crick (919), Edwards finds the novel embarrassing "in its unconscious snobberies and its repulsively coy treatment of sexuality and marriage." Noting the suggestive word "station" in the opening speculation about David's potential heroism, Edwards finds David's character developing from a set of "sibling" rivals—Traddles, Ham, Steerforth, and Uriah Heep, and the course of this development entails a number of class confusions. The relationships of David and Uriah provide the clearest illustration of the connections between class and sexuality. This essay has been reprinted by Peck (1124).

930. Eigner, Edwin M. "*David Copperfield* and the Benevolent Spirit." *Dickens Studies Annual,* 14 (1985), 1–15.

This article makes the case for Betsey as a character in the tradition of pantomime's magical, sometimes sexually ambivalent Benevolent Spirit, one who resorts readily to the pious fraud. For a fuller context of this connection of *Copperfield* with pantomime, see Eigner's *The Dickens Pantomime* (932).

931. Eigner, Edwin M. "Death and the Gentleman: *David Copperfield* as Elegiac Romance." *Dickens Studies Annual,* 16 (1987), 39–60.

Adding to the discussion of the gentleman by Gilmour (944), Eigner applies Kenneth A. Bruffee's definition, "elegiac romance," of the first-person retrospect concerning the death of a romantic figure who has captured the attention of a less heroic narrator. The question for Eigner is the extent to which the mourning survivor may free himself from the fallen hero and find a true identity. Eigner realizes that this question is complicated by the facts that in life Steerforth is a problematic representative of the idea of gentility, and in death he is one of several examples of loss David suppresses. As is often the case, a discussion of David and Steerforth also requires a discussion of David and Heep. This essay has been reprinted by Bloom (898).

932. Eigner, Edwin M. *The Dickens Pantomime.* Berkeley: University of California Press, 1989, passim.

Eigner centers his study on *David* Copperfield, because its various subplots present variations of basic pantomime structure, and it has a "constellation of pantomime characters—Harlequin, Columbine, Pantaloon, Dandy Lovers, Clown, and the benevolent Agent." Betsey

Trotwood is derived from the Benevolent Agent, the supernatural figure from pantomime, and she is the principal agent of change in David's life. Like Stone [496], Eigner also recognizes Betsey as a fairy-
tale character, but notes that both the real and fantastic natures of this
character are appropriate to this novel. In the chapter, "Pantaloon:
Some Dickensian Parents," Eigner comments upon the variety of
faulty parents, particularly those of the four major heroines—Mr. Spenlow, Mrs. Markleham, Mr. Wickfield, and Mr. Peggotty. To include
both Steerforth and Heep in a study of the dandy lover is to expand
the discussion of these characters who both cause and suffer from evil.
On the subject of "Columbine: A Pure Woman," Eigner provides
many insights about the novel's numerous sexually interesting women
and argues that David (himself an "androgynous Principal Boy" and
"both Harlequin and Columbine") must learn "to value feminine
qualities in himself and in other men." He and Agnes, with dual roles
in the pantomime according to Dickens, "are the most unattractively
complex figures." In the pantomime clown tradition, Martha appears
as an unfunny clown, Dora as the sacrificing clown, but Micawber "is
the ultimate Clown of *David Copperfield* and indeed of all Dickens'
novels." As Eigner says in his preface, Micawber is the principal
reason for his concentration on *David Copperfield,* and he regrets the
neglect of this character in the past generation of Dickens criticism.
Reviews: N. Auerbach, *Dickens Quarterly,* 6 (1989), 118–20; P.
Schlicke, *Nineteenth-Century Literature,* 44 (1989), 414–16; F.
Schwarzbach, *Times Literary Supplement,* 3 November 1989, 1214; R.
Tarr, *Journal of English and Germanic Philology,* 89 (1990), 426–28;
S. Monod, *Victorian Studies,* 33 (1990), 513–15; M. Sestito, *Modern
Language Review,* 86 (1991), 416; J. Pascoe, *Genre,* 23 (1990):
371–72; L. Woods, *NCTR,* 19 (1991), 130–38; G. Smith, *Dickensian,*
89 (1993), 141–43.

933. Eigner, Edwin M. "The Lunatic at the Window: Magic Casements in
David Copperfield." Dickens Quarterly, 2 (1985), 18–21.
Eigner notes the variety and frequency of the window motif in the
novel but is not ready to interpret it. He cites Michael Greenstein's
1974 York University (Canada) dissertation study of the window in
several of the arts in the nineteenth and twentieth century. See also
Greenstein (949).

934. Eigner, Edwin. "Shakespeare, Milton, Dickens and the Pious Fraud."
Dickens Studies Annual, 21 (1992), 1–25.
This article continues the attention Eigner gives in a chapter of his
earlier book (932). Pious frauds, where the deception benefits the character being deceived, were a dramatic device that was frequent and

unambiguous in Dickens's novels. They become incorporated in a serious way in *David Copperfield*, where most of them are perpetuated by Betsey Trotwood, though the most benevolent fraud that Eigner discusses is that in the Annie Strong story, which ultimately "sounds the keynote of the disciplined heart." Seeking in this novel to cure the disease of distrust of human nature, Dickens used this pious fraud to exploit his readers' presumed knowledge of a world where Annie arouses distrust.

935. Enemark, Richard D. "The Limits of David Copperfield's Retrospective Authority: The Many Voices of a 'Monologic' Fiction." *DAI,* 49 (1989), 218A (Columbia, 1986).

Enemark examines "apparently univocal works" for actual multivocality, citing two opposite impulses at work in such texts: on the one hand, the urge to create a central character who is also the "controlling creator, the maker of his or her own order," and on the other, the impulse to reflect in writing "the limits placed on any one structure that any one creative consciousness could provide." Focusing on *David Copperfield,* Enemark argues that the sentimentalism of the novel resists the seemingly dominant, univocal structuring principle, and ultimately sees this diversity of voices not as a flaw but as the very essence of Dickens's work.

936. Findlay, L. M. " 'Raly It's Give Me Such a Turn': Responding to the Reflexive in the Nineteenth-Century Novel." *English Studies in Canada,* 12 (1986), 192–209.

As part of a broader study of the reflexive, *Copperfield* is of interest as a Bildungsroman." Findlay finds "thought to propagate itself via fictional self-fashioning." In the few pages he devotes to this novel, Findlay describes "its enormously subtle and persistent self-reference." He finds the textual self subverting the narrative self's claims to "the truth" about himself, and he thinks the novel succeeds by admitting that the role of language is necessarily incomplete "in constituting both the story and the notion of humanity" Contrast McMaster (1001).

937. Fleishman, Avrom. "*David Copperfield:* Experiments in Autobiography." In his *Figures of Autobiography: The Language of Self-Writing in Victorian and Modern England.* Berkeley: University of California Press, 1983, pp. 201–18.

In its "narrative sophistication [variety of narrative modes to discover both an appropriate form and an interpretive principle for grasping experience], *David Copperfield* is surpassed only by [James Joyce's] *A Portrait of the Artist as a Young Man.*" Fleishman finds the novel constituting "the fullest version we have of the totality known as

Charles Dickens." He notes that the novel's world is inhabited by an inordinately large number of children, though for the first time Dickens begins to see childishness in adults as a defect. Although Fleishman acknowledges the interests of Freudean critics, especially Hutter [737] and Frank (940), he straightforwardly ranks it "as the paradigmatic autobiographical novel of the Victorian, perhaps of any, age." To complement and somewhat complicate this assessment, see Poovey (1029).

938. Fletcher, Luann M. "Gendered Fictions, Fictional Identities: Self-Narration in Dickens and Charlotte Brontë." *DAI,* 52 (1992), 1A (UCLA, 1991).

Fletcher compares male and female first-person narrators and finds that, regardless of the sex of the author, male narrators such as those in *David Copperfield* and *The Professor* attempt "to assume authority for the interpretation of his life" and are uncomfortable with threats to this authority, while female narrators such as those in *Bleak House* and *Villette* admit a number of possibilities for such interpretation. Thus the narrative of masculinity is that "of a stable, autonomous self" while that of femininity accentuates instead a "fluidity of identity." Fletcher draws considerably on the theories of Foucault, Bakhtin, and Benveniste. Also considered are *Great Expectations* and *Jane Eyre.*

939. Flint, Kate. *Dickens.* Brighton: Harvester Press, 1986, passim.

A volume in the Harvester New Readings series, this study speaks generally of Dickens to offer "what may be called new strategies of reading." Thus Flint's interest in *David Copperfield,* as well as in *Great Expectations,* is with narrative as dialogic. She does not think that the first-person method brings cohesion, and Flint discusses the doubleness of narrator and focaliser, a separation of present-time story teller and the earlier immediate experience. She finds David, "in command as both husband and narrator," asserting "his gender identity by assuming a protective, patronising paternalism."

940. Frank, Lawrence. "Introduction" and "The Autobiographical Imperative." In his *Charles Dickens and the Romantic Self.* Lincoln: University of Nebraska Press, 1984, pp. 3–30, 60–94.

Frank builds his study of Dickens's later novels on his readings of *Dombey and Son* and *David Copperfield,* and he uses the latter "to explain and to justify the relevance of psychoanalytic insights to an understanding of Dickens's world." Dickens wrote poised between Rousseau's confessional mode and Freud's psychoanalytic investigations (Frank notes that *The Copperfield Confessions* was one of Dickens's trial titles). Centering on the novel's narrative self-construct,

Frank discusses Mr. Dick, Mr. Micawber, and others who fail to complete their self-constructive narratives, and he is especially interested
in ways Steerforth, as tempting alter ego, presents "the most serious
challenge to the completion of David's personal history." Unlike many
commentators who see Steerforth (often with Heep) as David's double,
Frank finds him more autonomous. Ultimately the novel provides "a
coherent poetics of the self, . . . a poetics based upon a vision of man
as a narrative being." Although Frank finds a more complete and
complex David than have many other recent commentators, his understanding of the psychology of self-making and self-discovery and his
emphasis upon the narrative act provide means for reconsidering the
title character, the fictional autobiography, and the significance of the
novel in the Dickens canon. See also Welsh (1073), D. A. Miller
(1014), and Poovey (1029).

941. Gager, Valerie L. " 'The web I have spun': Shakespeareana in *Dombey
and Son* and *David Copperfield*." In her *Shakespeare and Dickens:
The Dynamics of Influence*. Cambridge: Cambridge University Press,
1996, pp. 223–44.
Part of a substantial study of the Shakespeare-Dickens dynamic, the
section begins with the argument that because many plays are alluded
to, and *Hamlet* in particular, "Shakespeare himself seems to preside
over *David Copperfield,* serving as the narrator's muse." The presence
is frequent in the text and in at least two illustrations. Many other
commentators mention Shakespeare in connection with Dickens's dramatic qualities; Gager argues for the strong influence of the play-
wright's narrative aspects. So considered, *Hamlet* can be seen as a
narrative frame for many layers of story, and the many references to
it in *Copperfield* make it a "unifying force both in representing memory and narrative thematically and structurally and as a key to David's
intellectual life."
Review John Glavin, *Nineteenth-Century Literature,* 52 (September
1997), 265–67.

942. Garnett, Robert R. "Why Not Sophy? Desire and Agnes in *David
Copperfield*." *Dickens Quarterly,* 14 (1997), 213–31.
Taking the view that Agnes's defects as a character are critically valuable to our understanding the nature of this novel, Garnett finds *David
Copperfield* to be "a spiritual aeneid [*sic*] that leads David to a beatific
detachment from all mundane involvements and ambitions." Various
experiences with Em'ly, Rosa, and Dora teach David "that sexual
desire is dangerously destablizing"; thus he projects spiritual impulses
onto Agnes and sensuality onto Uriah Heep. Traddles' wife, Sophy,

however seems a golden mean between Em'ly and Agnes, says Garnett, but even her liveliness might prove "too tempting and too perilous" for David. Many commentators recognize both Steerforth and Heep as projections of more aggressive energy; Garnett suggests that it is Mr. Peggotty who "embodies exactly the Dickensian qualities David most lacks."

943. Garson, Marjorie. "Inclusion and Exclusion: The Motif of the Copyist in *David Copperfield.*" *Etudes Anglaises,* 36 (1983), 401–13.

David, argues Garson, tends to include rather than exclude, an aspect both of his character and of his literary technique. He begins humbly as a copyist and is one of many copyists in the novel. Garson finds this recurrent motif suggesting a connection between this activity and self-surrender, helping Dickens to distinguish morally between good and bad kinds of mimetic behavior. Theoretically, the autobiographical novel combines the best aspects of copying and of acting on one's own, for it involves submission to and control over one's material.

944. Gay, Peter. "The 'Legless Angel' of *David Copperfield:* There's More to Her Than Victorian Piety." *New York Times Book Review,* 22 January 1995, p. 22.

This revaluation of the Agnes Wickfield character notes that she was an abused child, the victim of her "father's diseased attraction to her, masquerading as parental fondness." Gay argues that Dickens must have been aware that this character "is shot through with inhibitions," and he notes that a half century before Freud, "Dickens knew the innocent are never wholly innocent." He credits her with rightly holding to the role of sister "until David had lived enough to shed the belated manifestations of his Oedipus complex."

945. Gilmour, Robin. "Dickens and *Great Expectations.*" In his *The Idea of the Gentleman in the Victorian Novel.* London: George Allen & Unwin, 1981, pp. 112–18 and passim.

Gilmour makes comparative mention of *David Copperfield* in a discussion focused more on *Great Expectations.* He observes that in *Copperfield,* the myth of the orphan is less central than it had been in *Oliver Twist,* but, like Oliver, David is a gentleman whose "tenacious hold on an inner conviction of gentility . . . is rewarded."

946. Gilmour, Robin. "Dickens." In his *The Novel in the Victorian Age: A Modern Introduction.* London: Edward Arnold, 1986, pp.78–106.

Gilmour begins his chapter on Dickens with mention of *David Copperfield* in support of the point that "children and childhood are at the heart of Dickens's vision, both as a subject and as a way of seeing the world." His brief section on the novel notes that the book was both a popular early Victorian success-story and also a more poetic, humanly complex one. As in his earlier article [320] Gilmour stresses the function of memory, and he also comments upon Dickens's "exploitation of the analogical possibilities of serial form."

947. Golden, Morris. "*David Copperfield:* Memory and the Flow of Time." In his *Dickens Imagining Himself: Six Novel Encounters with a Changing World.* Lanham, Maryland: University Press of America, 1992, pp. 87–124.

This study of Dickens builds on three simple hypotheses: that Dickens's art reflects fantasies centering on himself; that it conceives others as self-projections; and that these actors operate in a metaphorical world satisfying readers' fantasies. The lengthy chapter on *Copperfield* discusses how, through David, Dickens traced his growth into the present, providing David at each stage with a young female symbolizing his ideal. His clearest alternative males are Heep, Steerforth, Traddles, and, more distantly, the older men like Micawber, Mr. Dick, Murdstone, and Mr. Peggotty. This reading of the novel may best serve as an introduction to its large cast of characters and as a summation of the traditional appreciative commentary, which found, as does Golden, David to be Everyman. Only at the chapter's end does Golden acknowledge the "irreconcilable intensities" within David, which have so interested recent commentary on the novel.

948. Golding, Robert. *Idiolects in Dickens: the Major Techniques and Chronological Development.* London: Macmillan, 1985, pp. 134–45.

Generally, this study recognizes ways Dickens stylized language "to such a degree that the idiolects of his characters come close to being language collages, to being wholly synthetic." Golding finds fictional speech in *Copperfield* maintaining a balance between Dickensian flamboyance and structural requirements, "unequalled in the author's canon." Golding senses a verbal ease in and with the language of "straight characters" such as Dora, Steerforth, and Traddles. Mr. Micawber, "one of Dickens' most complex comic images," belongs to the rhetorical tradition of Sam Weller, Dick Swiveller, Pecksniff and Sairey Gamp. Together with Mrs. Micawber, he represents for Golding "the idiolectal high spot of this novel, both in individual brilliance and structural significance." Golding urges that Miss Mowcher's different manners of speaking reflect the change of direction Dickens took with the characterization. Golding's notice that Dickens added non-standard deviations to Uriah Heep's speech should come as no surprise to close readers of *David Copperfield.*

949. Greenstein, Michael. "Between Curtain and Caul: *David Copperfield's* Shining Transparencies." *Dickens Quarterly,* 5 (1988), 75–81.

Suggests that the recurrent window imagery (see Eigner 933) may be a way of acknowledging the Freudean uncanny by looking in and out of "canny casements."

950. Grill, Neil. "Home and Homeless in *David Copperfield.*" *Dickens Studies Newsletter,* 11 (1980), 108–11.

Grill comments upon the "almost human vividness" with which houses and rooms mirror David's perceptions of their differing emotional textures. He notes also the association of particular characters such as Heep with buildings, and finds the words "house" and "home" are prominent in conveying authority in various households.

951. Grossmann, Maureen E. "Small Beginnings: The Recovery of Childhood and the Recovery from Childhood in the Victorian Novel." *DAI,* 50 (1989), 276A (Berkeley, 1988).

Comparing the experiences of childhood in *David Copperfield, Great Expectations, Jane Eyre,* and *The Mill on the Floss,* Grossmann identifies in each case "a particularly significant experience or psychological construct crucial to the subsequent development of the protagonist." These moments provide structures which the protagonists must either break free of, as in *Jane Eyre,* in order to emerge as an adult self, or which they must continue to reinforce "in order to reproduce a child self." Thus, for Grossmann, David's sense of balance depends on maintaining " 'everything just as it used to be,' " making the novel essentially regressive.

952. Guiliano, Edward, and Philip Collins. "Introduction." To the 1986 Annotated Dickens Edition, II, pp. 2–15 (822).

This introduction well situates the novel among Dickens's works, especially his writing of the 1840s, describes the relationship between the novel and the autobiographical fragment, and comments upon the "obvious artistic advantages, as well as prudential ones, in [the] distortion or refraction of biographical fact." The editors discuss the interest Henry James and Virginia Woolf had especially in the characterization of Mr. Micawber, who, in the opinion of Guiliano and Collins, was made even more memorable by "Phiz's graphic depiction."

953. Hager, Kelly. "Estranging David Copperfield: Reading the Novel of Divorce." *ELH,* 63 (1996), 989–1019.

Hager discusses the novel's many concerns with the miseries of marriage in the context of the novel's having appeared at the time a Royal Commission had been formed to study divorce law. Rather than finding marriage as the conventional solution for problems of identity, she sees it creating such problems, and this essay attempts to develop "a way of listening to the novel's silences . . . on subjects like adultery and divorce.'' Her focus is on women who want to leave husbands—Dora, Mrs. Micawber, Betsey Trotwood—and Hapke challenges the conventional view of Annie Strong (see [433]) as the model for the disciplined heart, for Annie's story distracts readers from the novel's truly failed marriages. Although it overtly endorses conventional views of marriage, Hager finds the book's ''cultural work'' implicitly ''feminist in that it offers a model for coping with the state of the law and for dealing with the inequities of the institution of marriage.'' This article stems from Hager's dissertation ''Plotting Marriage: Dickens, Divorce and the Failed-Marriage Plot'' (*DAI-A* 54/02 p. 532, UC Irvine, 1992) in which she discusses the way the failed-marriage plot complements the courtship plot of the domestic novel, highlighting both individual and social problems which lead to the dissolution of a marriage.

954. Hapke, Laura. ''He Stoops to Conquer: Redeeming the Fallen Woman in the Fiction of Dickens, Gaskell and Their Contemporaries.'' *Victorian Newsletter,* 69 (1986), 16–22.

Hapke discusses the role of women in the rescue of fallen women and questions whether female writers were more responsive than males to rehabilitation that stressed self-sufficiency over marriage. With Little Em'ly, Hapke points out that Dickens suggests her male rescuer must remain with her forever, and both Mrs. Steerforth and Rosa Dartle are hostile to her.

955. Hapke, Laura. ''Reflections on the Victorian Seduction Novel.'' *The Nassau Review* (Nassau Community College), 5 (1988), 35–43.

General discussion of how the Victorian seduction novel differed from Samuel Richardson's *Clarissa* because of Victorian class consciousness. For Hapke, Dickens's Em'ly, like victims in Gaskell and Eliot novels, is shattered by her failure to secure ''the love and financial security which in their minds is reparation for seduction.''

956. Hardy, Barbara. *''David Copperfield.''* In her *The Moral Art of Dickens.* New York: Oxford University Press, 1970, pp. 122–38.

Inadvertently missing from the 1981 *Annotated Bibliography,* this essay more anticipates studies of the future than represents the viewpoints of the 1960s and early 1970s because Hardy comments upon ways in which David ''reveals Victorian limitations which the author does not see but which the modern reader certainly does.'' She discusses Heep as a creature of his time. Acknowledging the presence of the disciplined heart theme, Hardy downplays it by finding the book ''not so much the moral and psychological study of the heart and its training, as the intense and local shafts which strike deep as human insights, honest revelations, and dramatic communications.'' She ranks this as a novel of education with George Eliot's *Middlemarch,* Henry James's *The Portrait of a Lady,* and D. H. Lawrence's *Sons and Lovers.* Especially in the presentations of the Micawbers and Betsey Trotwood, Hardy points out, Dickens's comedy creates surface effects and also trips readers "into feeling the depths beneath." Hardy abbreviates these comments in *Charles Dickens: The Writer and His Work.* (Windsor: Profile Books, 1983), pp. 63–69.

957. Hennelly, Mark M., Jr. "The 'Mysterious Portal': Liminal Play in *David Copperfield, Bleak House,* and *Great Expectations." Dickens Quarterly,* 15 (1998), 155–66.

Drawing upon anthropologist Victor Turner's theories about "ludic aspects . . . in liminal periods of protracted initiation," Hennelly takes this notion of "threshold" experience and discourse as his essay's general subject and finds Dickens "wonderfully well versed in the ritualistic nuances of initiatory phenomena." His cases in point in *Copperfield* are David's early visit to the Peggottys, his vacillations between structure and anti-structure in encounters with such contrastive "ritual elders" as Murdstone and Micawber, and his final status in "a shrinking communitas play group . . . whose camaraderie seems more and more tenuous."

958. Herst, Beth F. "*David Copperfield* and the Emergence of the Homeless Hero." In her *The Dickens Hero: Selfhood and Alienation in the Dickens World.* London: Weidenfeld and Nicolson, 1990, pp. 43–66.

Herst argues that David is a figure new to the Dickens world, one distinctively combining the qualities of the "natural hero" of the earlier books with the "time-haunted" sadness of the male protagonists in late Dickens novels. Herst discusses at some length the central motif of home and homelessness. The series of inadequate, unacceptable, or ruined homes David experiences or encounters from the first emphasize for Herst the novel's stress on the absent father. Even when the pattern is broken by Betsey Trotwood and the new start she provides David, he continues to be hindered by what Herst terms "the spectre of what has become for him a shameful and secret past." Steerforth, Heep, and Traddles are all fatherless, and in differing ways each functions as a reflection of David's self-image. Herst argues that both home and heroism are finally qualified by the ending's reliance upon "Agnes and the depleted domesticity she represents," for it and she "become a part of David's general chastening."

959. Hibbard, Christopher. "Introduction." To the 1983 Folio Society edition, pp. xiii–xviii (821).

Hibbard discusses the inception and composition of the novel, but errs in claiming that Dickens began his novel before attempting an autobiography. Hibbard, like a number of more recent readers, finds the novel sadder than he had first supposed, and he thinks it "far more skillfully constructed than its tumultuous energy, its apparently sprawling plots, and the method of its original presentation would seem to allow."

960. Hicks, Glenda L. "The Dream, the Romance, and the Real: The Synthetic Myths of Oliver, Pip, David, and Esther." *DAI,* 42 (1982), 240A (Oklahoma, 1981).

Choosing early, middle, and late novels, Hicks suggests an indebtedness on Dickens's part to the structure of romance as described by Northrop Frye. The protagonists embark on essentially inward journeys into "the nether world of the dream, undergo a trial and initiation in that world, and then return to synthesize the dream and the real worlds." Ultimately, reality is represented as the experience of one character "who creates and controls his own ways of being and the public and objective existence of every man."

961. Hirsch, Gordon D. "A Psychoanalytic Rereading of *David Copperfield.*" Victorian Newsletter, 58 (1980), 1–5.

Hirsch finds both the earlier interest in David's Oedipal neuroses—Manheim [401–06]; Pearlman [447], Spilka [486]—and also the more conventional intentionalist critics' attention to David's maturation "inadequate to describe the complexity and psychological verisimilitude of this book." More recent psychoanalytic theory, Hirsch points out, concerns "the sense in the individual of continuity, coherence, and integrity." Hirsch discusses the patterns of losses and separations in the novel, whose central question he finds to be one of how to overcome these blows. But one cannot read this "as simple sort of *Bildungsroman,*" for "what David achieves at the end is a rather fragile, tenuous, and probably reversible kind of mastery." See also Frank (940).

962. Hochman, Baruch, and Ilja Wachs. "Straw People, Hollow Men, and the Postmodernist Hall of Dissipating Mirrors: The Case of *David Copperfield.*" *Style,* 24 (1990), 392–407.

The first part of this essay discusses postmodernist dismantling of the sense of personhood or of identity, a discourse the authors find failing "to imitate other modes of self-organization" and deflecting "attention from the dramatic struggle, within texts and characters, for selfhood, or personhood, or identity." Like Fleishman (937), they regard *David Copperfield* as "the fullest nineteenth-century account of the development of a single individual," but find "David's shape is radically exclusionary and riddled by the contradictions of a prototypical . . . version of the Protestant Ethic and the premium it puts on productivity and accumulation.'' Through a ''panoply of doubles'' (with Micawber as the richest articulation), they assert, the novel embodies what must be displaced out of David, since these characters ''represent a variety of alternatives'' for dealing with identities and value systems.

963. Holland, Joy. ''Locations of Desire: Social Mobility and Ideal Space in Novels by Dickens, Charlotte Brontë, Stendhal and Sand, 1830–1860.'' *DAI,* 53 (1992), 320A (Brandeis, 1992).

Holland investigates the ways in which the narratives of Bildungsromane are shaped by characters' social mobility. She examines various methods and rationalizations given for upward mobility, looks at such narrative devices as ''orphanhood and refiliation,'' and identifies the ideal spaces towards which main characters move. She draws on Bakhtin and Bachelard to link those spaces to ideological positions.

964. Hollington, Michael. ''The Child's Perception of the Grotesque.'' In his *Dickens and the Grotesque.* Beckenham: Croom Helm Ltd., 1984, pp. 179–92.

Hollington is interested in the nature of childhood perception as Dickens renders it with precision that furthers the critical perspective for ''recognizing and laughing at the idealized picture.'' Hollington finds habits of language by various characters to be symptomatic of the ''cynical, manipulative, mystificatory deployments of thought and language'' that contrast young David's straightforward innocence. In the gallery of grotesque, Mr. Dick is, for Hollington, the principal ''innocent'' grotesque, Heep the ''demonic,'' and Miss Mowcher the most mixed grotesque as she operates like the fool in a Shakespearean play.

965. Hollington, Michael. ''*David Copperfield* and *Wilhelm Meister:* A Preliminary *Rapprochement.*'' *Q/W/E/R/T/Y: arts, literatures & civilisations du monde anglophone,* 6 (1996), 129–38.

Noting that in 1844 Dickens listed Carlyle's translation of *Wilhelm Meister* among his books, Hollington suggests that even though there is no evidence Dickens read this work, he was familiar with its leading characteristics and ideas. Through comparison of *Copperfield* with Goethe's work, Hollington argues that Dickens's novel retains a Germanic concept of Bildungsroman (contrasting Buckley's redefinition in Anglo-Saxon terms [240]).This has the advantage of downplaying the novel's personal and autobiographical dimensions and recognizing its concern for the public and social sphere. Jack Maldon, an often ignored character, is Hollington's example of the individual with an overt lack of concern for contemporary social issues. The Hegelian dialectic Dickens shared with Goethe provides grounds for Hollington to disagree with another important commentator, D. A. Miller (1014), who found David remaining "within the private sphere of the liberal subject." Hollington argues that both Dickens and Goethe subverted "the given bourgeois order through the creative imagination, which throws up grotesque, eccentric and oblique images of alternative worlds."

Review: A. Gavin, *Dickensian,* 93 (1997), 207–08.

966. Hornback, Bert G. *"The Hero of My Life": Essays on Dickens.* Athens: Ohio University Press, 1981, pp. 1–87, 100–104, 114–127, 145–155. Five of the nine chapters deal specifically with *David Copperfield,* the book Hornback thinks taught Dickens the most and which is "a novel about learning to love the world." Parts of this study appeared earlier as separate articles [343, 345]. Hornback considers implications of the novel's many trial titles, and by emphasizing the various elements in the full title of the novel finds that David Copperfield becomes *David Copperfield* "through the process Dickens outlines for us in the full title." Hornback differs from many critics by defending the significance of both David the narrator and David the character to the point that the novel's galaxy of characters represents "tests for David's imagination, . . . exemplary substances for him to imagine and comprehend." Like many other commentators, Hornback acknowledges the Wordsworthian quality of David's memory, but notes that the retrospect chapters resemble theatrical illusions. Hornback's third chapter's discusses *Copperfield* "insistently a novel whose theme is knowing and learning." Thus, when encountering evil in the persons of Jane Murdstone and Uriah Heep, David's comprehension proceeds "from description to metaphor to symbol and metaphysical identification." In the fourth chapter, discussing the serenity of the novel's conclusion, Hornback finds a sense of "kenosis," an unburdening. His fifth chapter surveys satisfaction and usefulness attained by various characters, and Hornback argues that David's heroism is "social rather than simply personal" as he works to improve the world.

Review: Roger Day, *Dickensian,* 78 (1982), 172–73.

967. Horton, Susan R. *The Reader in the Dickens World: Style and Response.* Pittsburgh: University of Pittsburgh Press, 1981, passim. Horton does not separately discuss particular novels, but her references to *Copperfield* are often illuminating. For example, she cites this as a book in which the reader often encounters "worlds beyond the Dickens world," because Dickens's "peripheral vision" includes such encounters as David's with strangers likely to lurch without warning out of the shadows. In discussing the dynamics of Dickens's descriptions, Horton mentions the stabilizing force of repetition as counterbalance to the uncertainty of the novelist's "peripheral worlds."

968. Houston, Gail T. *Consuming Fictions: Gender, Class, and Hunger in Dickens's Novels.* Carbondale: Southern Illinois University Press, 1994, pp. 99–122.

     In this examination of gendered codes of consumption, it is sexual and economic desire that is at issue in the familiar "disciplining of the heart" motif. Houston argues that David "only finds voracious hunger or maimed orality in the female economies that he expects will discipline his own appetite." Earliest childhood memories register, but do not directly state, "his desire for and fear of the maternal." Houston sees Steerforth and Heep as David's "two Cains," the former acting out David's "appetite to consume and discard," the latter's sexual and economic hunger for Agnes expressing David's own hidden motives. David's occupation as novelist "*is,* quite blatantly, the authorization of his own orality," Houston believes, but the problem with David's redeeming his appetites in his sister or other self, Agnes, is that hers, too, is a history "inextricably associated with the unrestrained male appetite" of her father. Houston cites and builds upon Mary Poovey's discussion of the novel (1029).

     Reviews: E. Westland, *Dickens Quarterly,* 13 (1996), 111–13; M. Bailin, *Dickensian,* 92 (1996), 133–35.

969. Houston, Gail T. "Gender Construction and the *Kunstlerroman: David Copperfield* and *Aurora Leigh.*" *Philological Quarterly,* 72 (1993), 213–36.

     This comparative study considers gendered construction of the artistic self within the constraints of a market system. Houston finds David "using the feminine to mask his materialistic motivations," and he has as foils "two feminized male writers"—Mr. Dick and Dr. Strong. Finally "co-opting the idealistic nature of the feminine Agnes," David conceals the material, elitist, masculinist nature of his profession."

970. Irwin, Michael. *Picturing: Description and Illusion in the Nineteenth-Century Novel.* London: George Allen & Unwin, 1979, passim.

     Copperfield serves as a frequent example through this study, beginning with Irwin's point that Dickens's method is one in which Dickens "imagines, he sees, and what he sees, he describes," with the three processes almost inseparable. Irwin notes that in the portrayal of human faces, Agnes remains abstract in contrast to the physically detailed portrait of Heep. Irwin's third chapter, "Gesture," has the most sustained commentary with attention to Mr. Omer, Heep, and Micawber as examples of contrasting styles of living and modes of energy. The concluding section of chapter 4, "Clothes and Accoutrements," argues that Dickens's attention to such details as Barkis's box or the interior of Dan Peggotty's house conveys "a sense of respect for human variety, oddity and unpredictability," and there is further commentary on these details in chapter 5, "Rooms and Houses."

971. Jackson, Arlene M. "Agnes Wickfield and the Church Leitmotif in *David Copperfield.*" *Dickens Studies Annual,* 9 (1981), 53–65.
This article begins with a good summary of critical readings of Agnes's importance, which, however, Jackson finds neglect the relationship of this character to the book's narrative perspective, image patterns, and iconography of the Phiz illustrations, even though Agnes as a character "is surely psychologically unrealized." She is closely associated with the image of the church, a presence of faith and stability, and Jackson makes a close reading of the illustration accompanying the domestic conclusion—"its iconography sums up the novel's themes and places the church and its associations as one of the novel's enduring images."

972. Jacobson, Karin K. "Unsettling Questions, Hysterical Answers: The Woman Detective in Victorian Fiction." *DAI,* 58 (1997), 1722A (Ohio State, 1997).
Analyzing female amateur detectives in Victorian novels such as Rosa Dartle in *David Copperfield,* Jacobson argues that these women unsettle the "male-gendering of power or knowledge," uncovering the hidden structure of the law and other social institutions. Through a position of open-ended questioning, she claims, these female detectives expose personal and institutional identity to "multiplicity and contradiction."

973. Jacobson, Wendy S. "Brothers and Sisters in *David Copperfield.*" *English Studies in Africa,* 25 (1982), 11–28.
This essay, by commentary on principal characters, expands Jacobson's observation that in each of the familial groups affecting David's imagination, failure or success is that of brotherhood and sisterhood. She approaches the novel as "a reconstruction of Dickens's own life," concluding that he was unable to live out his dreams, and only wrote about them.

974. Jaffe, Audrey "*David Copperfield* and *Bleak House:* On Dividing the Responsibility of Knowing." In her *Vanishing Points: Dickens, Narrative, and the Subject of Omniscience.* Berkeley: University of California Press, 1991, pp. 112–128.
This book considers omniscience as the fantasy of transcending individual consciousness and examines Dickens's various narrative strategies for producing an effect of omniscience. Jaffe finds that the self-effacing opening sentence of *David Copperfield* serves as the primary indication of the separations David the narrator establishes from his past. Jaffe argues that the narrator, in relation to his younger self,

remains unwilling and unable to articulate the implications of what he sees. The narrator therefore never attains the firmness of character that young David seems destined to develop, for the narrator lets the story meander and repeatedly "pictures" his earlier self as unknowing and innocent, keeping that characterization "free of the consequences of knowledge and action."

975. Johnson, Derek. "David Copperfield's Alpine Epiphany." In his *Pastoral in the Work of Charles Dickens.* New York: Peter Lang, 1992, pp. 21–31.

Johnson surveys previous commentary about this episode in chapter 58, noting that it "not only harvests critical abuse, but apparently also invites misreading." For all the echoes of Wordsworth, the passage for Johnson is not dependent upon Dickens's knowledge of *The Prelude,* for Dickens himself knew the Alps. He finds two "imperfectly imbricated myths" here—those of Nature as full presence and of woman as plentitude. Thus Dickens gave Agnes the last word in David's epiphany.

976. Jordan, John O. "The Social Sub-text of *David Copperfield.*" *Dickens Studies Annual,* 14 (1985), 61–92.

Making clear that it is David, rather than Dickens, who as narrator evades or distorts various social realities, this article examines textual effects that undermine David's narrative authority. Cases most in point are David's accounts of his relationships with Steerforth and the Peggottys and the projection of his social ambition and aggression onto Uriah Heep. Jordan finds the novel thus to be one in which "social themes and History are not absent but ... repressed," an argument later challenged by Palmer (1027). By treating Heep and Steerforth as "boundary figures in the class system," Jordan broadens the many readings of them as doubles for David's sexual desires. David's sentimental rendering of the Peggottys as hearty, simple people, and their internalizing of their social situation should alert us to his middle-class perspective which ignored the more complex facts of the working-class. Jordan calls attention to a growing class consciousness as Mr. Peggotty changes in the second half of the novel, where he seems less the hearty, good fellow and more the lonely, wandering modern man. So considered, especially when dealing with the concluding points about Heep in prison and the Peggottys and Micawber in Australia, David, Jordan argues, never becomes his novel's hero, for there is no single hero, only the collective heroism of the Peggottys.

977. Jordan, Mary E. "Absent Fathers and the Sons' Search for Identity in Four Victorian Prose Texts." *DAI,* 49 (1989), 269A (Minnesota, 1988).

Taking a psychoanalytic approach, Jordan analyzes four instances of the "negative Oedipus complex" in *David Copperfield,* Thomas Hardy's *Return of the Native,* Cardinal Newman's *Apologia Pro Vita Sua,* and George Eliot's *Daniel Deronda.* The physical lack of fathers in these novels causes the sons to focus on the fantasy, Jordan shows, of the internal, all-powerful figure, to the detriment of the sons' feelings towards their mothers. The sons show varying levels of awareness of this fantasy; David shows "no consciousness of . . . being in thrall to the oedipal father," whereas others attempt to get behind this identification to an examination of their own natures.

978. Kearns, Michael S. "Associationism, the Heart, and the Life of the Mind in Dickens' Novels." *Dickens Studies Annual,* 15 (1986), 111–44.

Although attention has been given to Dickens's interests in abnormal psychology, mesmerism, and hypnotism, Kearns argues that "Dickens' psychology incorporated his era's most generally accepted explanation of the life of the mind, associationism." For Kearns, Dickens particularly stresses the reforming of the mind through the agency of the heart, the inner force counteracting the external world's power over the individual. David Copperfield is one of Kearns's several cases in point of this psychological reformation. Associationist principles help explain David's feelings of guilt that were stimulated in childhood by Murdstone, his early schooling, and his demeaning work at Murdstone and Grinby. Other early associations, ones linked to his heart, prompted his decision to flee to Betsey. A similar subconscious process accounts for David's later sudden realization that he loved Agnes, and the images and diction of the moment of this discovery show how the Alpine scene was creating associational complexes for David. Even so, as Kearns carefully explains, David finally may be seen "as a middle-aged adolescent unable to accept all of the mental laws of his world."

979. Kellogg, David. " 'My Most Unwilling Hand': The Mixed Motivations of *David Copperfield.*" *Dickens Studies Annual,* 20 (1991), 57–73.

Observing that it is easy to understand how this text has become vulnerable to "perhaps overly speculative psychological readings," Kellogg finds recent critical response taking a decisive turn toward social concerns. Kellogg examines the "collisions of self and society," particularly those involved in David's acts of writing. The novel's principal collision of motives is between happiness (implying a psychological state independent of others) and utility (depending on the value others assign). David's writing is both "an act of personal recovery and an affirmation of privileged social standing," with the economic motive undercutting and subverting the personal recovery motive. The overall product is "two strikingly different *David Copperfields:* the autobiography, which the author 'never meant to be Published on any Account,' and the public fiction by one Charles Dickens."

980. Keyte, J. M., and M. L. Robinson. "Mr. Dick the Schizophrenic," *Dickensian,* 76 (1980), 36–37.

This note suggests that because Mr. Dick attributes his own thoughts to others he manifests various thought disorders, and catatonia. The authors note that Dickens, unlike such contemporaries as Charlotte Brontë, when dealing with lunacy did not lapse into vague, lay terms.

981. Kim, Soong Hee. "A Resistance to Growing-Up: A Comparative Study of *The Prelude* and *David Copperfield.*" *DAI,* 52 (1992), 148A (North Texas, 1991).

Kim traces what he calls the "retrogressive rather than progressive aspect" of these two explorations of maturation. Each hero survives by "keeping his child-self alive in the imaginative world he creates." This unchangeability in the heroes undermines the very structure of the works, which inherently focuses on the concept of change, Kim believes. For Kim, both heroes ultimately express a deep affection and concern for the world around them, but neither engages that world of other people directly, in David's case turning to writing and observing the world from a "fit-distance." All in all, Kim argues, these texts do not offer any solution to individuals attempting to face reality instead of evading it.

982. Kim, Tag-Jung. "Ghosts of the Past in Dickens' Later Novels: Transformations of Memory in Author and Characters." *DAI,* 58 (1997), 884A (Texas Tech, 1997).

In this biographical reading of Dickens's later novels, Kim argues that it is his failed marriage which affects the author more lastingly than any other event. This surfaces in the prevalence of the symbol of the past in both plot and characters; the trauma suffered as the result of this failed marriage emerges, for example, as David's ambivalence towards his past memories in *David Copperfield.*

983. Kincaid, James R. "Desiring David Copperfield." In his *Child-Loving: The Erotic Child and Victorian Culture.* New York: Routledge, 1992, pp. 306–09.

This brief commentary is part of Kincaid's explanation of what it means "to read with longing, to try to maintain the currents of desire through our seeing." To the Lacanian explanation of decentering discourse, Kincaid suggests that playful deconstructive reading may be playfully disinterested in the power of possessing textuality. The opening thirteen chapters of *David Copperfield* are a case in point for him.

The comforts of childhood experienced are in "the land of cuddles, one where the connections between mother, child, and nurse are so fibrous and tactile that there are hardly any clear demarcations among the bodies." Thus "for the voyeur-reader, it is like having front-row seats at Eden." Even the adult narrator's "pedophile reflections confirm and enable our own, . . . framing them outside of time." As David encounters such intruders as Murdstone and abusers as Creakle, Kincaid asserts, we share with David in a "constricted game of resentment."

984. Kincaid, James R. "Performance, Roles, and the Nature of the Self in Dickens." In. *Dramatic Dickens.* Ed. Carol H. MacKay. London: Macmillan, 1989, pp. 11–26.

Kincaid discusses the contradictory suggestions of character performance in Dickens, those earnestly completing tasks and the more irresponsible acting or playing at tasks. Kincaid points out that David Copperfield himself has a difficult time locating his real self behind the roles that he plays, and he doggedly tries to define other characters as solid, self-contained, determinate. But, in Kincaid's view, such characters as the Micawbers are "endlessly versatile role-players" improvising their lives.

985. Kincaid, James R. "Viewing and Blurring in Dickens: The Misrepresentation of Representation." *Dickens Studies Annual,* 16 (1987), 95–111.

Kincaid questions what it means "when we say we are reading Dickens—or watching him." Perspective is multiple and uncertain, and Kincaid notes that "a film-maker must construct, not represent or reflect, a Dickens novel." Kincaid cites David Copperfield's first departure from home on Barkis's cart as an example of how even conventional set pieces are disrupted by "an inexplicable shift of visual fields that disallows any attempt we might make to naturalize the description, bring it into coherent focus." This novel also presents the problem of how a film can handle the privileged view of the narrator, how close can the camera come to David's eyes and troubled heart? Most films of the novel have focused on the monsters (Murdstone) David sees surrounding him. But, Kincaid insists, the challenge for the film-maker, as for the reader, is in how David sees his own life, the extent to which he is or is not the product of what he encounters. "The perception, however, that he is trapped trying to tell a progressive narrative with materials that refuse, finally, to budge from a stasis, an idealized infancy and young childhood, haunts the novel." Kincaid stresses the contrast of David, an individualized self, and the Micawbers who "embody a notion of being that is without clear boundaries."

986. Kinkead-Weekes, Mark. "The Voicing of Fictions." In *Reading the Victorian Novel: Detail into Form.* Ed. Ian Gregor. London: Vision Press, 1980, pp. 150–67.

This essay notes that the actual experience of reading a Victorian novel "is of a fluctuating human relationship in time," and in *David Copperfield* "the changing voice requires different kinds of listening." Kinkead-Weekes traces four major phases of reading with differing relations of "author and hero, of inner and outer, and of author and reader." This essay separately discusses Charlotte Brontë's *Villette* and Thackeray's *Vanity Fair.*

987. Knoepflmacher, U. C. "From Outrage to Rage: Dickens's Bruised Femininity." In *Dickens and Other Victorians: Essays in Honour of Philip Collins.* Ed. Joanne Shattock. London: Macmillan, 1988, pp.75–96.

Taking issue with Slater's reading (1056) that Dickens's women characters are mimetic replications, this essay uses *David Copperfield* and *Great Expectations* "to say that Dickens's most powerful responses to the feminine are far more likely to be dramatised through the action of male self-personfications." In both works Dickens attempted to feminize a male psyche, Knoepflmacher argues, shielding it more in *Copperfield* "from sadistic expressions of anger" (even though there is obvious anger originating from the intrusion of Murdstone into his and his mother's lives). Although Dickens fends off "resentment of Steerforth's seduction of a child-angel because he manages to convert her into a lower-class woman," Knoepflmacher believes, he does strike Heep in outrage over the "lower-class Uriah's presumption." For Poovey (1029) Agnes is the victim of David's power; for Knoepflmacher, "she epitomizes a type of femininity he has both coveted and himself displayed by adopting the role of a victim incapable of anger." Where David encounters female anger such as Rosa exhibits toward the fallen Em'ly, he passively watches, as she acts out his rage, and because Rosa shares his allegiance to Steerforth, David here through inaction sides with "the humiliator of women rather than with Steerforth's victims."

988. Korte, Barbara. *Body Language in Literature.* Toronto: University of Toronto Press, 1997, pp. 133–34.

Korte includes Uriah Heep as an example of a character whose body language constantly contradicts his verbally asserted humility. She finds the narrator's explicit comments about the body language evoking the reader's hostility toward the character.

989. Kucich, John. "Charles Dickens." In his *Repression in Victorian Fiction: Charlotte Brontë, George Eliot, and Charles Dickens.* Berkeley: University of California Press, 1987, pp. 201–83.

David Copperfield is a frequent point of discussion in this chapter, which focuses on it and the Dickens novels which followed, for in these works Kucich finds Dickens emphasizing "the dominant role of repression in his protagonists' lives, and the inevitability of an inward struggle between passion and repression." David's love for Agnes, about which Kucich provides one of the most intelligent readings, involves both passion and restraint, a complex doubleness that gives complexity to the character. It is finally a "balanced paradox of intense self-abandon and personal circumspection, in which both passion and repression sustain this tension in each other." Like D. A. Miller (1014), Kucich notes the novel's "tenuous cycle of secrecy and disclosure," in both David's life and the lives around him. Excerpts from this study are reprinted in Peck (1124).

990. Kucich, John. *Excess and Restraint in the Novels of Charles Dickens.* Athens: University of Georgia Press, 1981, passim.

Although there is no extensive separate discussion of *David Copperfield,* Kucich's is one of the most important critical reconsiderations of Dickens to appear in the past twenty years. The chapter titles themselves point to matters of content and style that will interest readers of *Copperfield*—"Storytelling," "Melodrama and Sentimentality," "Villains," "Heroes," "Endings," "Mechanical Style." In his discussion of endings, Kucich sees in *Copperfield* "the deliberate evocation of loss that also contains loss within the safety of a reassured, shared, narrative present," and in mention of the novel's "retrospects" as examples of Dickensian excess, he points out that here, as elsewhere, the novelist counterbalances his effusions.

991. Kurtz, Emily. "The Vision Splendid: The Victorian Novel's Wordsworthian Muse." *DAI,* 57 (1997), 1A (NYU, 1996).

Kurtz examines the way certain Victorian novelists whom she calls "Victorian Romantics" adopt and adapt elements of Wordsworth's poetics, including language, ideology, and motifs such as an intensely personal narrator, use of the "Pathetic Fallacy," relationships, and the "privileging of the sense of vision." One of the primary deviations from a "pure" Wordsworthian poetics, Kurtz points out, involves the loss of immediate connection between the physical sense of vision and the inner, emotional sense of "I." For Victorian Romantics, factors of urban life and social change present new problems for the narrator's vision. Considered along with *David Copperfield* are Charlotte Brontë's *Jane Eyre* and *Villette,* Emily Brontë's *Wuthering* Heights, and George Eliot's *Adam Bede* and *The Mill on the Floss.*

992. LaRocque, Carolyn B. "The Initiation of David Copperfield the Younger: A Ritual Passage in Three Acts." In *Dramatic Dickens.* Ed. Carol H. MacKay. London: Macmillan, 1989, pp. 52–67.

Drawing upon anthropological study of ritual drama, LaRocque closely examines the first four numbers of the novel, in which David undergoes rites of passage marking the end of childhood. She points out that Dickens's infusion of Victorian stage business animates these rites.

993. Leavis, L. R. "*David Copperfield* and *Jane Eyre.*" *English Studies: A Journal of English Language and Literature,* 67 (1986), 167–73.

Based on Q. D. Leavis's sense [386] that Brontë's novel strongly influenced *David Copperfield,* this commentator discusses similarities and some differences between the novels. Certainly the two novels provide mutually illuminating views of Victorian childhood, and L. R. Leavis traces direct and indirect influences from *Jane Eyre* in an effort to confirm the fairly obvious differences between the two writers. Even though he concludes that "Dickens clearly found a mass of suggestive material in *Jane Eyre,*" Leavis has no evidence that Dickens had even read the Brontë book.

994. Lee, Hsaio-Hung. "*Possibilities of Hidden Things*": Narrative Transgression in Victorian Fictional Autobiographies. *Studies in Nineteenth-Century British Literature* Vol. 5. New York: Peter Lang, 1996.

Starting with Foucault's ideas of narrative transgression and Derrida's notion of erasure, Lee argues that the narrative continuity of the novel is always challenged by other stories and voices which "dwell on the shifting and unstable representations of identity of the 'self.' " This subversive "shadow" narrative attempts to decenter the "causal and realistic narrative" of David's telling. Lee sees this decentering, right from the start, in the narrator's wondering whether he will be the hero of his own novel; this is carried further as the young David links the everyday world with his fictional readings, and further yet when Steerforth periodically takes over as the hero of young David's life. In other ways, Lee indicates, the dominant narrative is haunted by several figures: David's affinity with his deceased father; his sister who never was; Betsey Trotwood; and Steerforth's death, which he sees before him " 'growing larger and larger' " as he approaches it in the narrative. Even the nature of David's relationship with Dora is otherworldly, and is disrupted by his longings for something more from her. Ultimately, Lee argues, the historical events of David's narrative "have melted into the world of the imagination, and fantasy takes over reality." The imaginative narrative, Lee concludes, is what allows the narrator to make the historical absence present, and in the process deconstructs the apparently stable ordering system of that historical narrative. Lee originally wrote this as his dissertation for Drew University in 1990.

995. Leger, J. Michael. "Triangulation and Homoeroticism in *David Copperfield.*" *Victorian Literature and Culture,* 23 (1995), 301–25.

If David's is the story of heart-disciplining, his attachment to Steerforth is not condemned and is, in fact, "celebrated by its centrality to and superiority in the text," Leger postulates. This essay considers three triangular relationships involving David and Steerforth. In the first, the feminine article is the fictive "evocation of feminine psychic material in both men"; in the second Rosa and Dora "mirror one another in the feminine corner"; in the third, David must choose between Steerforth and Em'ly. Finally entrusted with Steerforth's story, David "provides himself safe and eternal emotional access" to the most enduring of the triangles, his original relationship with Steerforth, complicated first and last by his love for Em'ly. Thus his love for Steerforth "is narratively productive," contrasting the more literal "heterosexual-romantic ending of this novel," and even though David remains within "paradigms his patriarchal society prescribes," this love "transcends his culture's constraints." See also D. A. Miller (1014) and Weinstein (1072), whose somewhat parallel works Leger acknowledges.

996. Leitch, Thomas M. "Closure and Teleology in Dickens." *Studies in the Novel,* 18 (1986), 143–56.

Leitch shows that the endings of Dickens's later novels become more teleological than did the more contrived earlier endings. See Dunn [288]. David is the first of Dickens's heroes whose problematic personal identity is presented explicitly in teleological terms. But even with the attention on disciplining the heart and with different versions of David represented through other characters' names for him, Leitch finds that the novel fails to "be as insistently end-oriented as the three novels which follow." He also discusses the endings of *Bleak House, Hard Times,* and *Little Dorrit.*

997. Levenson, Michael H. "The Private Life of a Public Form: Freud, Fantasy, and the Novel." In *Critical Reconstructions: The Relationship of Fiction and Life.* Ed. Robert M. Polhemus and Roger B. Henkle. Stanford: Stanford University Press, 1994, pp. 52–70.

Levenson's case in point is a Freudian study of fantasy/fancy in *David Copperfield.* Levenson argues that fantasy "stands as a third term between experience and art, that it is indeed a mediating term between the actual and the aesthetic." The "great thematic labor" of Dickens's novel "is the overcoming of fantasy," and by the end the word "fancy" loses its sense of idle romantic imaginings and "appears as the name for creative vision." As David's story expands through the stories of those around him, Levinson indicates, autobiographical fiction becomes a form of fictional sociology, an expansiveness of fantasy paralleled in Freud's patients. Levenson concludes that *Copperfield* finally demonstrates the capacity of fantasy to enlarge its domain and bring "the social world within the realm of greatest personal intimacy," and, more generally, that the novel form "has taught us how to dream the real and to hallucinate the moral."

998. Lukacher, Ned. "Dialectical Images: Benjamin/Dickens/Freud." In his *Primal Scenes: Literature, Philosophy, Psychoanalysis.* Ithaca: Cornell University Press, 1986, pp. 314–22.

After Lukacher discusses Dickens's previous efforts "to master the memory of what he calls 'the slow agony' of his youth" and after describing the novelist's experiences of the streets as "inseparable from the political confusion and mystification that intensified throughout his career," Lukacher reads *Copperfield* as a novel in which Dickens's sense of "no thoroughfare" structures "historical experience in the modern world." David's encounters with Martha, Micawber, Rosa, and Murdstone are cases in point. Against debilitating experience, Lukacher finds that Dickens writes "as a way of managing or containing the destructive work of remembrance." Reprinted in Bloom (897).

999. Lund, Michael. "Clocking the Reader in the Long Victorian Novel." *Victorian Newsletter,* 59 (1981), 22–25.

Lund considers how serial readers found themselves moved through the worlds of their novels, and over time seemed involved in expanded certain textual elements, and in a sense contributed to the development of fictional characters. The monthly clock of installment publication, argues Lund, kept both novelist and readers aware of changing events in their own lives, a process that enhanced the sense of a developing central character. With parallel fictional lives such as that of Pendennis in process, *Copperfield* readers could measure the comparative growth of Thackeray and Dickens protagonists.

1000. Lund, Michael. "Novels, Writers, and Readers in 1850." *Victorian Periodicals Review,* 17 (1984), 15–28.

Lund discusses both *Copperfield* and *Pendennis* in the context of 1850 views of the writing profession and suggests that Dickens may have decided to make David a novelist in response to the debate about writing waged by Thackeray, *The Morning Chronicle,* and John Forster. He points out that Dickens's first readers would have less reason than do modern readers to complain about how little David mentions his profession.

1001. McMaster, Juliet. "Dickens and David Copperfield on the Act of Reading." *English Studies in Canada,* 15 (1989), 288–304.

McMaster notes Dickens's frequent attention to various branches of reading, with the last half of the essay discussing David as someone

"often defined for other characters by his role as reader." The novel,
like *Tristram Shandy*, "emerges as a treatise on the relation of language to experience." Although some of the characters "are arrested
and stymied by colliding with the clamourous alphabet," McMaster
concludes, the novel as a whole expresses optimism about language
as the medium for learning.

1002. McMullen, Buck. "Allergies of Reading: Some Ambiguities of Literacy in Nineteenth-Century British Fiction." *DAI*, 53 (1993), 1A (Colorado at Boulder, 1992).

Examining the novels of such authors as Dickens, Charlotte Brontë,
Gaskell, Gissing, and Mary Shelley, and using the methodologies of
Jacques Derrida and Paul de Man, McMullen concludes that nothing
whatsoever can be concluded about instances of reading, not reading,
literacy, and illiteracy in such novels. "[L]iteracy, as these texts may
or may not show, is a deeply clouded issue, of which little of historical,
cultural, psychological, or literary importance can be reliably concluded."

1003. McSweeney, Kerry. "*David Copperfield* and the Music of Memory."
Dickens Studies Annual, 23 (1994), 93–119.

Among numerous discussions of memory in *David Copperfield*, this
essay stresses the relationship of memory and imagination in narrative
reconstruction of a life, compares Dickens with Wordsworth and
Proust, and considers the operation of memory in *Oliver Twist* and in
The Haunted Man. McSweeney finds the first-person retrospection
less seamless than it at first appears, and he discusses the value such
characters as Betsey, Micawber, Julia Mills, and Mr. Dick ascribe to
memory. For David the writer, "recollection is one of the tools of the
trade," for David the explorer of his past, "memory is less conscious
recollection than a felt contact between past and present and a vital
part of the life experience" (comparable to Proust's distinction between habitual and spontaneous memory). The deepest current of David's life, McSweeney holds, is in the memories of Agnes and
Canterbury, filled with "quotidian particular" through which David
recovers his life.

1004. MacKay, Carol H. "Surrealization and the Redoubled Self: Fantasy
in *David Copperfield* and *Pendennis*." *Dickens Studies Annual*, 14
(1985), 241–65.

MacKay's central distinction between these fictionalized lives is that
in the Dickens novel readers are inside, "caught up and even trapped"
by David's fantasies, but in *Pendennis* readers are invited to share the
omniscient narrator's larger insights and perspective. To some extent,
the adult David recognizes the shaping role fantasy had in his life, but,

MacKay asserts, seeking solace, he is likely to be caught up in it again. For her, surrealized characterization suppresses such personal provocation as the blacking warehouse experience, and the clash of stereotypes and personal experiences leads to Dickens's problematic characterizations of women. In both novels, the doubling of characters seems to confirm the point that heroism is problematic and no self is whole.

1005. MacLeod, Norman. "The Discussion of Prose Style: An Example from *David Copperfield." Edinburgh Studies in the English Language,* 1 (1988), 156–67.

MacLeod analyzes the last three paragraphs of chapter 7 "to demonstrate the central necessity to the passage of the linguistic form it takes." The significance of this passage is that it models the novel's larger "progressive coalescing of the temporal poles of narration and experience."

1006. MacLeod, Norman. "Lexicogrammar and the Reader: Three Examples from Dickens." In *Language, Text, and Context: Essays in Stylistics.* Ed. Michael Toolan. London: Routledge, 1992, pp. 138–57.

The opening paragraph of *David Copperfield* is one of MacLeod's examples of the Dickens reader's unsettling experience of having to become self-conscious while processing subtle lexicogrammatical arrangements. The novel's beginning disconcerts the reader, he indicates, until it becomes evident that David is himself approaching his story from a reader's perspective. See also Kinkead-Weekes (986). MacLeod also considers *Hard Times* and *Great Expectations.*

1007. Magee, Mary M. "Postscript: Theatricality and Dickens's End Strategies." In *Dramatic Dickens.* Ed. Carol H. MacKay. London: Macmillan, 1989, pp. 184–93.

Complementing the accompanying Carr (914) and Kincaid (984) essays in this volume, Magee also finds "the structure and very nature of David's autobiographical narration . . . richly susceptible to theatrical interpretation." She centers on the concluding chapter, but also considers the previous retrospect chapters and also the beginning. She argues the need to be "alert to the many-voiced qualities of David's ostensible univocality," if readers are to understand Dickens's characterization of David. The control David ultimately attains is through a dramatic persona as director, allowing him "to channel and even determine both his own plot and those of the other characters, while denying (and controlling) subversive energies."

1008. Malone, Cynthia N. "Fictions of Identity in Dickens' First-person Narratives." *DAI,* 48 (1988), 195A (Boston U., 1987).

Malone studies the "fiction of a unified 'self' as the center" of Dickens's fictional autobiographies. This self, i.e., the narrative voice, seems to be positioned at the center of the narratives, and the plots trace the development of those selves from youth to maturity, but Malone argues that these "centering strategies" are disrupted by unstable representations of identity, making "otherness" always a part of self-representation. In her chapter on *David Copperfield* she focuses on the erasure of self and other early in the novel, when David's mother and his infant brother die.

1009. Manigault, Shirley F. "Time in Charles Dickens' First-Person Retrospective Narratives." *DAI*, 43 (1983), 164A (Chapel Hill, 1982).

Focusing on *David Copperfield, Bleak House,* and *Great Expectations,* Manigault traces Dickens's changing views of people's experience of time and the "nature and quality of human existence" over the course of a decade. Ultimately, these changes culminate in the darker tone and mood in Dickens's later writings, she believes. For her, the various narrators' experiences of time are central to the various problems posed by first person, retrospective narrations. In examining *David Copperfield,* Manigault concentrates on David's "romantic quest" to "reunify his divided self" and eventually be integrated into society.

1010. Manning, Sylvia. "David Copperfield and Scheherazada: The Necessity of Narrative." *Studies in the Novel,* 14 (1982), 327–36.

Manning finds the powers of language providing "the defense against memory that the dreamer lacks," and she finds in *Copperfield* Dickens dealing with memory's mixed blessings. She cites such examples as Barkis or Annie and Dr. Strong to show that silence is not an alternative to language's power. She finds the novel presenting "the familiar Dickensian battle against the tendencies of language to reify and falsify." Manning takes issue with Gilmour [320], whom she thinks disproportionately glorifies the power of memory, and like Lankford [383] she is interested in memory's more treacherous potential. In this novel memory is mainly visual and non-chronological, she believes; narrative, however, controls it by fixing it in time and thus stabilizing the past.

1011. Marlow, James E. *Charles Dickens: The Uses of Time.* Selinsgrove, PA: Susquehanna University Press, 1994, passim.

There is not a separate discussion of *Copperfield,* but in a section on "The Dead Hand of the Past," Marlow argues that, following Betsey Trotwood's advice, David works to come to peace with his past so it may "render benefits to the present." In Betsey's and Mr. Dick's experience, as in that of Mr. Spenlow, and differently in the person of Uriah Heep, there is an "insidious power of the past to interrupt the present," Marlow asserts. Through their conservative deference to the past, the privileged such as the Steerforths are the first of many later Dickens portrayals of recklessness and passionless upper class. In another section, "Trust in the Present," Marlow notes that beginning with *Copperfield,* the situation of the central character threatened with annihilation goes beyond melodrama to envision a "complex relationship . . . between an individual and society founded upon the premise of hunger." See also Houston (968).

1012. Matus, Jill. "Proxy and Proximity: Metonymic Signing." *University of Toronto Quarterly,* 58 (1988), 305–26.

This is a study of ways metonymy has been construed and the difference a sensitivity to it makes to the way we approach texts. Her chief case in point is George Eliot's *The Mill on the Floss,* but Matus briefly mentions David Copperfield's association of Dora with the scent of geraniums.

1013. Meisel, Martin. *Realizations: Narrative, Pictorial, and Theatrical Arts in Nineteenth-Century England.* Princeton: Princeton University Press, 1983, pp.80–82 and passim.

In his discussion of *David Copperfield,* Meisel contrasts conventional dramatic effects with what he calls "theatricalism," in which the dramatic acts and words of a character come naturally from the characters themselves. An example of the conventional is the scene of David's learning of Dora's death; an examples of "theatricalism" are the self-dramatizings of Micawber and Heep. Meisel finds Agnes's gesturing out of character, seemingly staged for an audience external to the novel, though she herself is unconscious of performing. Mr. Micawber and Uriah Heep, Meisel explains, perform for an internal audience and are very conscious of themselves as performers. In another instance of this theatricalism, David and Steerforth burst in on Mr. Peggotty's household, and David the narrator describes the scene as exactly that, a scene that he imagines to have been staged just for his and Steerforth's benefit.

1014. Miller, D. A. "Secret Subjects, Open Secrets." In his *The Novel and the Police.* Berkeley: University of California Press, 1988, pp. 192–220. Previously appeared in *Dickens Studies Annual,* 14 (1985), 17–38.

For the reader tantalized by the narcissistic lure of autobiographical representation as well as for Dickens and David, Miller finds secrecy "to be a mode whose ultimate meaning lies in the subject's formal insistence that he is radically inaccessible to the culture that would otherwise entirely determine him." Using this definition, Miller reconsiders the book's patterns of disclosure and secrecy that resonate from the promises of the title, self-confessions of the preface, and David's narrative. Paradox abounds; in writing the self, "the self is most itself

at the moment when its defining inwardness is most secret, most with-
held from writing.'' More broadly, Miller argues, secrecy is ''the subjective practice in which the oppositions of private/public, inside/
outside, subject/object, are established, and the sanctity of their first
term kept inviolate.'' Appropriately, there is much coupling of characters with boxes and other containers. Some box themselves in; sometimes boxes open in dramatic explosions of secrets. The novel's
essential drama, for Miller ''stems from David's desperate attempt not
to be boxed in, or confounded with a box, like the other characters.''
But, notes Miller, David with his resolute discipline fails to transcend
the boxed-in state. ''*David Copperfield* everywhere imitates a dreary
pattern in which the subject constitutes himself against discipline by
assuming that discipline in his own name.'' Miller's is one of the key
new readings of *David Copperfield*. He finds the novel ''particularly
relevant to the problematics of modern subjectivity,'' posing ''a sharp
contrast in the extreme difference and distance between the character,
who is so thoroughly extroverted that his inner life seems exiguous,
and the narrator, who is so completely defaced.''
Reviews: P. Garrett, *Journal of English and Germanic Philology,* 88
(1989), 541–44; S. Cohan, *Novel,* 22 (1989), 650–53; D. Riede, *Studies
in English Literature,* 28 (1988), 728–31; R. Hull, *Studies in the Novel,*
21 (1989), 108–11; W. Day, *Victorian Studies,* 32 (1989), 577–79.

1015. Morgan, Nicholas H. *Secret Journeys: Theory and Practice in Reading
Dickens.* London: Associated University Presses, 1992, passim.
Discussing *David Copperfield* alongside *The Old Curiosity Shop, Little
Dorrit,* and *Great Expectations,* Morgan emphasizes the practical experience of reading the works rather than finding some essential meaning
behind them. For him, *David Copperfield* demonstrates the tensions
native to first-person narration; David attempts to illuminate the buried
mysteries of his inner being, but also creates a teleology from those
discoveries, writing his own personal mythology out of the events
which are the most important to him. In a reading drawing heavily on
Freud's theories of childhood and development, Morgan sees David
in ''a dialectical battle with himself,'' pitting ''David the dreamer
against David the self-disciplined worker.'' At times, David seems
torn between his dreams and a more structured reality; between his
mother and Peggotty on the one hand, and the Murdstones on the
other; between Mr. Dick, Mr. Wickfield and the Strongs, and Uriah
Heep. Viewing David's marriage to Dora, in this light, Morgan argues
that it represents a step backwards into the more dreamlike realm of
David's childhood. Throughout these struggles, Agnes and Aunt Betsey remain as the important new element in David's life, providing

both love and firmness, the structure he needs. Morgan suggests that we assume David's psyche, provisionally, as we read, for we are seduced into believing that "our own efforts to find meaning and control will also triumph in the end," just as David's do. But, notes Morgan, the spectre-like recurrence of such characters as the Murdstones and Uriah Heep at the fringes of the novel warns us about the dangers of such self-deception. Thus the reader too must undergo his or her own dialectical investigation before taking a side in the struggle between dream and restraint.

1016. Morris, Pam. "*David Copperfield:* Alienated Writer." In her *Dickens's Class Consciousness: A Marginal View.* New York: St. Martin's Press, 1991, pp. 63–80.

Like Welsh (1073), Morris finds the ideological issues of *David Copperfield* as a continuation of those of *Martin Chuzzlewit,* but finds the novel to be politically innocent. In psychological terms, "the primary unity of the Imaginary phase, before the imposition of the Reality Principle in the form of the Father's Law, is only maintained by projecting threats of disintegration to the margin." Childhood and the childlike and powerless, thus, are cast to the side as David, through the narrative making of an English gentleman, represses "all that is other to this genteel identity." Moral progress so defined "seems inimical to a convincing construction of the hero as a creative writer," and Morris suggests that the text may articulate "an anxiety Dickens himself felt about feminine aspects of his own creative energy." See also Shires (1054), Hirsch (961), and Houston (9689.

1017. Mugglestone, Lynda. "Fictions of Speech: Literature and the Literate Speaker in the Nineteenth-Century Novel." *The Yearbook of English Studies,* 25 (1995), 114–27.

Mugglestone finds that David's speech is an example of fiction's literal applications of prescriptive ideals of literate language, and the novel "is marked by Dickens's habitual acuity" in texturing discourse to demarcate various strata of society. But as Mugglestone points out in respect to the Peggottys, Dickens values speech forms less than deeds as marks of character. Thus Dickens exposed, rather than endorsed, stigmatizing speech forms.

1018. Mundhenk, Rosemary. "*David Copperfield* and 'The Oppression of Remembrance.'" *Texas Studies in Literature and Language,* 29 (1987), 323–41.

Like Gilmour [320] and Shelston (1053), Mundhenk approaches *Copperfield* as "a particularly complex novel about remembering." The return to the past to find or clarify the present is an embedded structure in most of Dickens's novels; here the focus is directly "on the complexities and paradoxes of the act of remembering." This is evident

not only in David's own story but, as Mundhenk points out, also in
the stories of Mr. Wickfield and Betsey Trotwood, and numerous other
characters troubled by memory. Most of David's direct statements
about memory come in connection with painful recollections, a sign
"of the nearness and intensity of the past," Mundhenk believes. When
David deliberately screens memories to filter out regrets, "the effect
is incomplete and temporary."

1019. Murray, Brian. *Charles Dickens.* New York: The Continuum Publishing Company, 1994, pp. 122–36.
One of the "Literature and Life: British Writers" series, Murray's
book provides a general introduction to Dickens with attention to the
major works. He finds Dickens's narrative voice more subdued in
Copperfield, a relaxed and conversational first-person. Murray follows
the traditional critical opinion that the adult David is of little interest,
and that the moral is the straightforward one articulated by Betsey
Trotwood. With both Micawber and Betsey, Murray indicates, Dickens
provides more than the caricatured eccentric, for these characters well
represent the contradictory complexities of human personality. Also
Murray discusses the significance of Steerforth, Little Em'ly, and Uriah Heep.

1020. Musselwhite, David E. "Dickens: The Commodification of the Novelist." In his *Partings Welded Together: Politics and Desire in the Nineteenth-Century English Novel.* London: Methuen, 1987, pp. 143–226.
This is one of few commentaries to question the standard readings
of Dickens's autobiographical fragment, for Musselwhite finds it "a
brilliantly fictive achievement, . . . the retrospective construction of an
eminently marketable identity." He calls *Copperfield* a sad book, continuing "a split that was so traumatic in *Dombey*" between patterns
of desire. He discusses the basic structure of "sets of relationships
which exist in forlornly separate cells," a panopticon with the observant David at the center.

1021. Myers, Margaret. "The Lost Self: Gender in *David Copperfield.*" In
Gender Studies: New Directions in Feminist Criticism. Ed. Judith
Spector. Bowling Green OH: Bowling Green University Popular Press,
1986, pp. 120–32.
Like Poovey (1029), Myers addresses gender questions in David's
search for a self, arguing that as an adult he must integrate "those
aspects of his male selfhood culturally designated as feminine." Although the final chapter attempts to project a larger social optimism
based on David's self-integrative effort, "the masculine-identified
world . . . cannot finally admit the feminine-identified into the prevailing social and economic structures." This essay was reprinted by
Peck (1124).

1022. Nelson, B. R. *The Basis of Morality and Its Relation to Dramatic Form in a Study of David Copperfield.* (Studies in Comparative Literature, Vol. 3.) Lewiston NY: Edwin Mellen, 1998.

In a detailed first section, drawing on Hume, Freud, and Kant, Nelson forms a theory of morality based on the premise that although morality is not a direct expression of one's self-interest, it is nevertheless "in certain fundamental cases, necessarily determined by the concern of a moral being about its own worth." He then argues, in a second section on *David Copperfield,* that dramatic form (as opposed to discursive) can "achieve a true representation" by showing a person "in the actual circumstances of his or her psychological development." The narrator's mode of telling the events of his life as they occurred to him at the time, without analysis or extensive reflection, reveals to us the frequent irony and mistaken impressions David is prey to, such as in his assessments of his mother and Steerforth. In reference to these relationships, Nelson indicates, his moral attitudes are determined by his perception of his own moral worth, which he demonstrates dramatically rather than discursively. In turn, these moral attitudes also depend upon David's various relationships with others which inform that sense of personal worth. Thus, for example, David is unwilling to condemn Steerforth, Nelson finds, but must retain his memories of what was best in him, because to abandon his idol so completely would be a blow to David as well. The supportive nature of his relationship with Agnes, confirming his belief in stability, makes bearable his hectic, married life with Dora. Nelson examines David's other relationships as well, giving an exhaustive close reading of the novel and the formation of David's moral character.

1023. Newcomb, Mildred. *The Imagined World of Charles Dickens.* Columbus: Ohio State University Press, 1989, passim.

This study deals with the "non-discursive" nature of Dickens's imagination, "materials that show rather than tell, that paint a picture without explaining its significance." There is frequent mention but no sustained discussion of *David Copperfield.* Newcomb finds the Dickensian view of childhood differing from that of Wordsworth because of "its radically different conclusion—rather than intimations of immortality, Dickens found in recollected childhood intimations of an earthly paradise that would make of him a humanist and a humanitarian." So regarded, *Copperfield,* along with *Martin Chuzzlewit, Bleak House, Little Dorrit,* and *Great Expectations,* extensively explores the transitional period between child and adult.

1024. Nicholls, Maria C. "A Beloved Mother and a Resented Mother: The Maternal Influence on the Portrayal of Women in Stendhal and Dickens." *DAI,* 52 (1991), 239A (SUNY Binghamton, 1991).

Comparing Dickens's resentment of his mother (over what he saw as
her neglect in making him work at a factory) to Stendhal's "passionate
and erotic love" for his mother, Nicholls traces the results of this
difference in the novelists' portrayals of female characters and, in
particular, mothers.

1025. Olson, Ted. "His Changing Nature: Comparing Dickens's Two 'Autobiographical' Novels." *Publications of the Mississippi Philological
Association,* 1992, 119–24.

Accepting without question Phyllis Rose's assertion (1139) that Dickens's mid-life crisis came between the writing of *David Copperfield*
and *Great Expectations,* thus greatly complicating and intensifying his
art in the later work, Olson argues that Dickens's Edenic view of
the natural world became more sophisticated, and his animal imagery
(occurring "gratuitously and inconsistently" in *Copperfield*) was precise in *Great Expectations.* Simplistic in analysis and conclusions, this
essay is not informed by the principal discussions of Dickens's thought
and art.

1026. Oxenford, Rosemary A. "Narrative Structure and the Pursuit of Identity in *Nicholas Nickleby, David Copperfield, Our Mutual Friend* and
The Mystery of Edwin Drood." DAI, 52 (1992), 140A (Harvard, 1991).

Claiming that in order to "mean" a Dickensian character must have
"a place (meaning both home and occupation), a name and a story,"
Oxenford argues that David makes these claims primarily through
asserting his story, making a visible text of his life and establishing
himself as hero. This attempt at creating meaning is paralleled, Oxenford asserts, by the narrative's attempt at closure i. e., the typical
"happy ending," she believes, with its resolution of all plots and
proper meting out of punishment and reward. This drive for closure
and meaning, however, is undermined by "disruptive desires, drives,
and realities" which can never be entirely purged from the text, reaffirming "the perpetual dialectic between order and disorder."

1027. Palmer, William J. *Dickens and New Historicism.* New York: St. Martin's Press, 1998.

The principal discussion of *David Copperfield* is in chapter 3, "Dickens and Shipwreck," of which an earlier version appeared in *Dickens
Studies Annual,* 18 (1989), 39–92. As Palmer claims, to enter his novel
by sea, "in terms of one of its most prominent and controlling metaphors," is to make a "sociohistorical reading in which psychological
struggles become secondary to a historical commentary on the loss of
faith and heroism in the face of the 'Condition of England' in the
1840s." This places *Copperfield* in the contexts of an age experiencing
"the very real and personal effects that . . . shipwrecks had" and of a

considerable body of shipwreck journalism and fiction. For a different focus on the drowning motif's stylistic character, see Stewart (1061). There is more brief and speculative consideration of *David Copperfield* in Palmer's discussion (chapter 4) of the persistence of the George Barnwell motif in Dickens. Although every novel up to this point in Dickens's career had directly mentioned the story of the murderous apprentice, it, "in a much more sinister and subtle psychological way drive[s] both the novel's characters and theme," in the fictionalizing of the blacking factory experience and in the characterization of Uriah Heep.

Review: Richard J. Dunn, *Dickens Quarterly,* 15 (1998), 232–36.

1028. Pettersson, Torsten. "The Maturity of Dickens." *English Studies: A Journal of English Language and Literature,* 70 (1989), 63–74.

Noting the principal differing views of David's self-development, Pettersson, like Hirsch (961) but without the psychoanalytic perspective, finds the character reaching neither full resolution nor "irresolvable and damning conflict." Although he never directly states it, David is aware of ambivalence toward his mother, Steerforth, and Dora. David's willing recreation of past emotions "is both less contradictory and less subversive," because his moral emphasis on self-control is not totally controlling. Pettersson agrees with Buckley's [240] argument that David is Dickens's counterpart rather than double.

1029. Poovey, Mary. "The Man-of-Letters Hero: *David Copperfield* and the Professional Writer." In her *Uneven Developments: The Ideological Work of Gender in Mid-Victorian England.* Chicago: University of Chicago Press, 1988, pp. 89–125.

Poovey's study has had significant impact on subsequent discussions of class and gender in *David Copperfield*. One facet of nineteenth-century literature's ideological work, she notes, was the psychological narrative of individual development, a process explicitly "part of the legitimation and depoliticization of capitalist market and class relations." Identity in *Copperfield* "takes the form of a physical and emotional development in which the male subject tempers his sexual and emotional desires by the possibilities of the social world." Poovey finds Clara Copperfield's contradictory roles critical, and Dora is but another version of her. David's relationship with Em'ly, complicated by class consciousness, provides an example of the Victorian tendency to make women bear the burden of sexuality. Poovey explores the implications of Heep's relationship to David and Agnes, noting that in differing ways, both he and the hero tend to manipulate others for self-serving ends. She finds that just as young David and the narrator are simultaneously similar and different, so are Copperfield and Heep;

thus the hero's identity "is never fully individuated because the main character is split and distributed among so many other characters and parts." As literary man, David ultimately "derives the source of his ideological work from the idealized vision of domestic labor epitomized in Agnes." Poovey's work is reprinted by Peck (1124).
Review:.E. K. Helsinger, *Nineteenth-Century Literature,* 45 (1990), 94–97.

1030. Puttock, Kay. " 'The Fault . . . of Which I Confusedly Felt Guilty Yet Innocent': Charles Dickens's Evolving Championship of the Child." *Children's Literature Association Quarterly,* 17 (19929, 19–22.

This discussion mainly surveys Dickens's presentations of childhood guilt and shame, straightforwardly claiming that in *David Copperfield* and *Great Expectations* Dickens worked through his childhood trauma to a mature acceptance of his and his parents' failings. However, depending on Dickens criticism and biography, Puttock asserts that at the time of writing *David Copperfield* the novelist could not yet "distinguish fully between rational guilt and the 'agony' of irrational shame."

1031. Raina, Badri. "*David Copperfield:* The Price of Success." In Raina's *Dickens and the Dialectic of Growth.* Madison: University of Wisconsin Press, 1986, pp. 77–101.

This book argues that the forms of Dickens's novels are "closely implicated in the scope of his social thinking." Countering the extensive critical influence of Needham's "benign reading of David's career" [433], Raina, like Edmund Wilson [536], Manheim [401–06], and Spilka [486], considers the novel's less innocent aspects. This chapter reconsiders the David-Steerforth relationship, noting that here as elsewhere in the novel, Tommy Traddles "functions as a reliable comment [generally by contrast] on David." David chooses not to see many of Steerforth's faults, for, although Dickens may see Steerforth's rottenness, he uncritically gives David a tone of "endless accommodation" toward Steerforth. Contrasted to Traddles' responsiveness toward the Micawbers, David seems never "to admit the *reality* of their condition, or the reality of his bonds with them." These failures of the self-absorbed imagination are most emphatically clear in intermeshing details of the David-Heep story, which Raina neatly summarizes by noting that Uriah's "is what the story of David's life might have been had there been no Betsey Trotwood." *Copperfield,* even with some protective nostalgia, dramatizes "the debasement attendant upon a pursuit of the goal that capitalism has set for the ambitious individual." Thus the characterization of Heep "acquired the status of a new thesis," one given fuller reign in *Bleak House, Hard Times,* and *Little Dorrit.*

Reviews: P. Rogers, *Comparative Literature,* 42 (1990), 271–72; W. Burgan, *Victorian Studies,* 31 (1988), 298–99; S. Monod, *Etudes Anglaises,* 40 (1987), 474–75.

1032. Ramchandani, Dilip. "The Hypomanic Personality of Wilkins Micawber." *Psychiatric Quarterly,* 63 (1992), 245–49.
This article begins by acknowledging the risks of literary descriptions in justification of clinical entities, but claims that "art can sometimes capture the essence of a universally shared cultural conflict or phenomenon." Micawber, "a picture of overconfidence, robustness, and dramatic flair," exemplifies the "cognitive style of a hypomanic individual."

1033. Ranson, Nicholas. "Dickens and Disability: *David Copperfield.*" *The Kaleidoscope,* Summer-Fall 1986, pp. 11–15.
This article considers Dickens's attitudes and feelings toward both physical and psychological disability. Dickens turned Mr. Dick's disability to powerful social use, Ranson claims, and after a lapse of judgment with his first plans for the character of Miss Mowcher he reconstructed her to caution readers against associating physical disability with moral worth. Mr. Dick, portrayed as the wise child, Ranson considers "a most notable achievement."

1034. Rearick, Anderson M., III. "Loss and Reclamation in *David Copperfield.*" *DAI,* 53 (1993), 448A (Rhode Island, 1992).
Rearick examines *David Copperfield* through the lens of the Christian cycle of loss and reclamation, seeing it not as an allegory of simple theological concepts but instead as David's personal "process of creating order out of his chaotic and painful past." This spiritual message is clear not only in David's own life, but in such other lives as those of Little Em'ly, Martha Endell, Mr. Wickfield, Mrs. Strong, Mr. Micawber, and Mrs. Gummidge. In David's life, Rearick traces five "moments of crisis in which his sense of self is in real peril" and out of which he is pulled by another character.

1035. Reed, John R. "*David Copperfield.*" In his *Dickens and Thackeray: Punishment and Forgiveness.* Athens: Ohio University Press, 1995, pp. 187–206.
More traditionally than many of the commentators of the 1980s and 1990s, Reed continues to regard *Copperfield* as having a narrative tenor reflective of the hero's moral education, well-learned lessons in humility and sympathy. In the treatment of evildoers, it is more gentle than most of Dickens's novels. The most threatening forces "are those who are positioned to alter David's perception of himself by insinuating some aspects of their own nature into his—namely, Murdstone, Steerforth, and Heep." Reed also comments upon female transgressors, those who either violate or appear to violate the rules of sexual

morality—Martha, Em'ly, and Annie Strong. The novel's concluding chapters "provide an interesting example of the nature of forgiveness and punishment as Dickens understood them." Reed finds the general structure of melodrama inadequate for David, who at the end cannot accept melodrama's absolute separation of good and evil, but Dickens, the implied author, metes rewards and punishments to provide "the ordering of the world's moral economy."

1036. Reed, John R. "Charles Dickens." In his *Victorian Will*. Athens: Ohio University Press, 1989, pp. 245–74.

In brief commentary on *David Copperfield*, Reed treats Steerforth's errors as failings of will, and points out that heart and will cannot be separated in Dickens's values. As narrator, David transforms "the flat plain that Steerforth used as a metaphor for purposeless human existence into a landscape to set in relief the monumental event that organizes that waste space."

1037. Riebetanz, J. M. "Villain, Victim and Hero in *David Copperfield*." *Dalhousie Review*, 59 (1979), 321–37.

This essay considers the question of heroism as a structural tool for organizing and developing the novel's many plots. Reibetanz lists seven plots and subplots, "arranged in three basic roles, victim, villain, and hero." Extending the Needham focus [433] on the disciplined heart, Reibetanz notes that Dickens's own conception of discipline was less pejorative than that of our age; his ideal of a new and integrated selfhood "has been argued by Bruno Bettelheim in strikingly similar terms." Although David never intervenes in the resolutions of the various plot complications, "he reflects all three roles on which the novel's plots are structured," and finally reaches some "knowledge and mastery of suffering"—this novel's definition of heroism.

1038. Reifel, Karen F. "The Work of Believing: Labor as Self-Definition in Carlyle, Dickens, and Brontë." *DAI*, 51 (1990), 211A (Texas-Austin, 1990).

Reifel examines the authors' depiction of "self-definition" as a continuous labor of reconciling "private desire and public form." The spiritual concerns involved in such labor thus necessarily become intertwined with material concerns as well. In *David Copperfield*, Reifel points out, David rereads his life in order to bring together his public and private lives in his work in print. The product of this work, the novel, traces David's emergent self-definition through a framework of profit and loss.

1039. Reynolds, Kimberley, and Nicola Humble. "Victorian Men and Feminine Autobiography." In their *Victorian Heroines: Representations of Femininity in Nineteenth-Century Literature and Art,* London: Harvester Wheatsheaf, 1993, pp. 156–64.

The authors construe feminine autobiography as "constructing the self in collective rather than individual ways, acknowledging the fragmented and protean nature of experience." For them, *David Copperfield* is in this mode, and they outline ways this novel resembles fictionalized autobiographies by women. Early in their study (pp. 18–19), they comment on Em'ly as the innocent changed into dangerous woman.

1040. Rodolff, Rebecca. "What David Copperfield Remembers of Dora's Death." *Dickensian,* 77 (1981), 32–40.

This essay examines the key elements of chapter 53, suggesting an analogy between the weeks of Dora's dying and the years of David's remembered progress toward his own end. Rodolff finds Dora finally shedding her earlier self to the point where "it appears that her centre is Agnes," and Agnes serves the plot by serving as the device whereby David acquires maturity. Rodolff's is thus a late reiteration of the "disciplined-heart" readings of the novel.

1041. Roston, Murray. "The Fallen Woman." In his *Victorian Contexts: Literature and the Visual Arts.* New York: New York University Press, 1996, pp. 41–67.

Roston includes Em'ly and Martha in his discussion of a number of representations of fallen women, noting that in the painting, drama, and literature of the early 1850s there was a striking convergence of interest in the subject of the fallen woman. Roston discusses it as a counter-image to the Angel in the House and regards it as a growing perception that the morality of the Victorian era was itself sullied.

1042. Rubinson, Jill L. "Stages of Maturity: Transitions of Life in the Victorian Novel." *DAI,* 44 (1984), 186A (Harvard, 1983).

In this study, Rubinson focuses on certain Victorian novels which she claims extend the tradition of the Bildungsroman by reflecting "a developmental view of adult experience," focusing "not on the process of fashioning one's dreams but on the complicated business of living them out." *David Copperfield,* which she compares with *Villette,* deals with the period of early adulthood and the changes which follow childhood. These novels, she believes, emphasize periods of isolated self-assessment which form bridges between stages of maturity, require a review of the past and an exploration of the self, make possible more advanced relationships, and provide space for the accommodation of loss.

1043. Sadoff, Dianne F. "The Dead Father: *Barnaby Rudge, David Copperfield,* and *Great Expectations.*" *Papers on Language and Literature,* 18 (1982), 36–57.

To the psychological study of fathers and sons in Dickens, Sadoff brings Jacques Lacan's point about the figurative murder of the father

enabling the son's individual growth, amounting to the transformation
of "the imaginary Murdered father into the symbolic Dead father."
She does not discuss the individual novels in detail, but points out the
significance of the apparently dead father seeming to return to David
in the figure of Murdstone, and she sees David the writer taking revenge against fathers.

1044. Sadoff, Dianne F. "Language Engenders." In her *Monsters of Affection: Dickens, Eliot & Brontë on Fatherhood.* Baltimore: The Johns
Hopkins University Press, 1982, pp. 39–51.

This section of Sadoff's study discusses *David Copperfield, Great
Expectations,* and Dickens's autobiographical fragment as retroactive
structural searches through which the writing son becomes a figurative
father. Thus "the narrative project serves to originate and engender
the son himself." Sadoff notes that David questions the theory of
language as a vehicle for worldly success, especially through his portrayals of Mr. Dick, Dr. Strong, and Micawber. Reprinted in Bloom
(897).

1045. Sadrin, Anny. "Davy Who?" *Etudes Anglaises,* 49 (1996), 413–24.

This article is in French, but provides the following English summary:
"This essay bears on the full title of *David Copperfield the Younger*
and on what Michael Ragussis calls 'acts of naming.' The idea is to
analyze Dickens's attitude to the concept of naming, examined in the
light of Plato's *Cratylus.* The stress is put on the eponymous hero's
name and on the relationships between son and father. But in any final
analysis, it appears that David's question is not so much 'Who am I?'
as 'What am I?' Conversely many other characters ask themselves the
question, 'Who is he?' and each gives his or her answer."

1046. Sadrin, Anny. *Parentage and Inheritance in the Novels of Charles
Dickens.* Cambridge: Cambridge University Press, 1994.

The first chapter has a brief but incisive commentary about Betsey
Trotwood's ambivalent nature and power as a name-transmitter.

1047. Schacht, Paul. "Dickens and the Uses of Nature." *Victorian Studies,*
34 (1990), 77–102.

Schacht discusses the image of the infant at the mother's breast as
both a symbol of naturalness in human relations and as a synecdoche
for "nurture" as a preparation for socialization. He includes Mrs.
Micawber among his examples.

1048. Schad, S. J. "The I and You of Time: Rhetoric and History in Dickens." *ELH,* 56 (1989), 423–38.

Schad considers broadly the understanding of time and history in Dickens's novels as a rhetorical sensibility. In *Copperfield* "the communi-
cative you is most notably made into the image of the future"

concerning Agnes, "the narrative's virtual addressee." As such, she is by David's words ("My narrative proceeds to Agnes") transformed into his subject, a speech-act Schad finds to be a "highjacking" of future time. Although there is little direct commentary about *Copperfield,* this deconstruction argues that Dickens's "rhetoric disorders the articulation and indeed meaning of time-past."

1049. Schaumberger, Nancy E. "Partners in Pathology: David, Dora, and Steerforth." *Dickensian,* 84 (1988), 154–59.
Noting that the Copperfields, Spenlows, and Steerforths are the principal single parent-only child families, Schaumberger finds David an exception in his growth beyond what was imposed upon him in formative years.

1050. Schroeder, Natalie E., and Ronald A. Schroeder. "Betsey Trotwood and Jane Murdstone: Dickensian Doubles." *Studies in the Novel,* 21 (1989), 268–78.
Seeming opposites, Betsey and Jane are in some ways "chillingly similar," and David's experiences with them "are disturbingly repetitious," the Schroeders argue. But as the psychological double of the harsh and unyielding Jane Murdstone, Betsey Trotwood struggles "to accept her responsibility and to repudiate the unloving side of her own character." Many of the parallels the Schroeders discuss help to explain the complexity of this doubling, but their final attention to differing connotations of these characters' names seems over-simplistic.

1051. Sell, Roger D. "Projection Characters in *David Copperfield.*" *Studia Neophilogica,* 55 (1983), 19–29.
Particularly well informed by the major critical arguments concerning the David-Dickens, David-and various double characters, and David-development questions, Sell provides a comprehensive reading of *Copperfield* and argues that the book's vitality and complexity emerge from David's ways of seeing the people around him. Against readings that tend toward one-to-one relationships between the hero and this or that other character, Sell notes recurrences and shifts in values associated with characters. The question of how intuitively or deliberately Dickens projected revelations about David through other characters cannot be resolved, Sell points out, but much of Dickens's creative power stems from "his inability to substantiate his conscious design." What results is a "tension between David's respectability and inadvertent honesty, ... flowing in and out of consciousness, in and out of art."

1052. Shaw, George B. "From Dickens to Ibsen." In *Shaw on Dickens.* Eds. Dan H. Laurence and Martin Quinn. New York: Frederick Ungar Publishing Co., 1985, pp.17–21.

Shaw labels *David Copperfield* as principally "a romantic autobiography," but he finds it to be "a book of pain, doubt, anxiety, and unfulfillment." This previously unpublished fragment has only brief comments about *David Copperfield.* Shaw did credit Dickens for dealing seriously with the failure and disillusion of his marriage and for "a remarkable combination of tenderness and ruthlessness in the picture of Dora." Laurence and Quinn also reprint Shaw's preface to *Great Expectations,* which includes some attention to *Copperfield;* see [477].

1053. Shelston, Alan. "Past and Present in *David Copperfield.*" *Critical Quarterly,* 27 (1985), 17–33.

Shelston, differing from many who have found David's growth resulting from his coming to terms with his past, argues that "in a particularly honest, if disturbing way," *Copperfield* deals with the Victorian question of how the isolated individual consciously uses memory in confronting realities of the present. More private than either Wordsworth or George Eliot, Dickens, in his novel, "asserts the difficulty of relating past to present," Shelston maintains. The narrator has less than absolute capacity to re-order the experience of his past, and even the observant child David has minimal capacity to make sense of his present. The Steerforth story gives impetus to the novel's Carlylean concern with the question of how a noble life is to be led. Shelston finds Steerforth allowing "the past to control the present in what amounts to a denial of the human will," but David, conscious of his past, ultimately accepts and surmounts its conditioning influence. Even so, the novel shows that "for Dickens in mid-career, past memories and present experience were alike traumatic."

1054. Shires, Linda M. "Literary Careers, Death, and the Body Politics of *David Copperfield.*" In *Dickens Refigured: Bodies, Desires, and Other Histories.* Ed. John Schad. Manchester: Manchester University Press, 1996, pp. 117–35.

Like Welsh (1073) in stressing the importance of his American experience to Dickens's writing from *Chuzzlewit* through *Copperfield,* and like Poovey (1029) in recognizing the class and gender implications of David's history, Shires makes particularly striking parallels among three writers—Charlotte Brontë, Tennyson, and Dickens—who attempted to reconcile public with private selves when confronted with death. She argues that the first two gained "authorial strength through confronting the dead bodies of others," but "*David Copperfield* foregrounds the struggle and cost of gaining authority through discarding and decorporealising bodies." As did Morris (1016), Shires finds that to succeed with his middle-class agenda David must excise passions.

1055. Simon, Irene. *"David Copperfield:* A Kunstlerroman?" *Review of English Studies,* 43 (1992), 40–56.
To raise the question of the extent to which the novel is a portrait of the artist is to raise questions of the extent to which David resembles Dickens and of the book's thematic coherence. Simon, disagreeing with those who have found David saying too little about himself as a writer and also with those like Shelston (1053) who find David more protective than exploitative of his earlier experience, insists that "David is at once like his creator and a persona." First and foremost, she asserts, David as narrator orders experience according to the viewpoint of "a man fully integrated in his society, yet critical of it." See also John Jordan (996) and Shires (1054).
1056. Slater, Michael. "The Women of his Novels" and "The Womanly Ideal." Parts I and II of his *Dickens and Women.* Stanford: Stanford University Press, 1983, pp. 243–54.
The first part of Slater's book provides considerable biographical background for various women in Dickens's life. Critically, in the second and third parts of this study, he centers on the portrayals of Dora, whom he finds more complex than have most readers, for at times she "has a deeper insight into the truth about life and love than David does." He finds her to be a dramatization of Dickens's traditional belief that women are instinctively wiser and more sensitive than men about human relations, and he finds her uttering "some implicit social criticism of a feminist kind." The true heroine, however, for Slater, is the poorly characterized Agnes, Dickens's most complete conception of the feminine ideal. Slater finds several convincing reasons why the characterization fails to give this ideal sufficient life. Other women receive briefer treatment in Slater's extensive study of women characters and various idealizations of women.
1057. Spilka, Mark. "On the Enrichment of Poor Monkeys by Myth and Dream; or, How Dickens Rosseauisticized and Pre-Freudianized Victorian Views of Childhood." In *Sexuality and Victorian Literature.* Ed. Don R. Cox. Volume 27 of *Tennessee Studies in Literature.* Knoxville: University of Tennessee Press, 1984, pp. 161–79.
Noting that the Victorian novelists transposed Romantic ideas of childhood, Spilka credits Dickens with making the child the emotional center of fiction, a touchstone for human worth. In *Copperfield,* Dickens exercises "a projective artistry," giving a psychological dimension to David. Spilka cites two basic motives for nineteenth-century fiction's preoccupation with childhood—"the desire to come to grips with the terms of childhood conflict" and the nostalgic "desire to return to a period of conscious innocence."

1058. Spurgin, Timothy A. "Presenting Charles Dickens: The Author and His Public Image in *Nicholas Nickleby, David Copperfield* and *Great Expectations.*" *DAI,* 52 (1991), 225A (Virginia, 1990).
Tackling the issue of Dickens's "true identity" and personality, Spurgin argues not for one coherent authorial self but rather many different possibilities carefully managed by Dickens "in order to manage his career and maintain his enormous popularity." Spurgin does not attempt to privilege one possibility but analyzes the construction and the relationship of authorial selves established between Dickens and his audience. In *David Copperfield,* Dickens is particularly concerned with "his personal reputation and his status as a conspicuous public figure."

1059. Sroka, Kenneth M. "Dickens' Metafiction: Readers and Writers in *Oliver Twist, David Copperfield,* and *Our Mutual Friend.*" *Dickens Studies Annual,* 22 (1993), 35–65.
Although throughout Dickens's work there is much attention to imagining, reading, and writing, Sroka indicates, these three novels illustrate the importance of literacy and reflect the author's "sense of the progressive devaluation of Fancy." In *David Copperfield,* Sroka believes "literacy becomes a . . . key to experience and self-knowledge." The novel's "real action" is David's writing of the story, and the reader looks over his shoulder as writing becomes the means for self-discovery. As does Palmer (1027) more recently, Sroka stresses the metaphor of sea-journey both in the composing process and in the story itself. He also notes that in contrast to David as the major "author," other characters—Julia Mills, Mr. Dick, Dr. Strong, and Mr. Micawber—lack his courage and write only to escape the present.

1060. Steig, Michael. "*David Copperfield's* Plots Against the Reader." In his *Stories of Reading: Subjectivity and Literary Understanding.* Baltimore: Johns Hopkins University Press, 1989, pp. 127–43.
An expansion of Steig's earlier discussion of reader-response-based teaching of the novel; see (1111). This chapter considers reasons for Steig's sense that this is one of the most violent of Dickens's works, with David as narrator and Dickens as author perpetrating "violence within the story-line, and thus against me as reader." Student responses to David's views toward his mother, Dora, and particularly Agnes lead Steig to understand these views as manipulative, self-serving mirrorings of David's fantasies.

1061. Stewart, Garrett. *Death Sentences: Styles of Dying in British Fiction.* Cambridge: Harvard University Press, 1984, pp. 72–83.
In part of a chapter discussing Dickens's handling of "the envisaged and traversed instant of death," *David Copperfield* is a key text because of its "symbolic proliferation of the scene of drowning"; see

also Palmer (1027). Stewart describes "the prevalence of both narrated and analogized drowning," and argues that unlike the memorialists Mr. Dick and Dr. Strong, David finds the literary means to "get beyond death." Thus, "this autobiographic chronicle makes the process of narration taken whole an enterprise profoundly comparable to the *topos* of drowning as a recovery of the past." Also, as does no other Dickens novel, *Copperfield* explores "not just the complexly plotted intervals of deathbed rhetoric, but also the psychology of narrating and receiving such scenes."

1062. Stone, Harry. *The Night Side of Dickens: Cannibalism, Passion, Necessity.* Columbus: Ohio State University Press, 1994, passim.

This richly referential discussion of the related fascinations of Dickens and his age with cannibalism, passion, and necessity, has frequent mention of *David Copperfield.* In regard to cannibalism, Stone discusses scenes he finds central, although they "seem at first to have no overt cannibalistic elements." They are David's return from school to find his mother nursing his half brother and subsequently his learning of the deaths of both mother and child. Stone suggests, that among a number of other influences, Dickens's "profoundly disturbing and deeply ambivalent feelings toward his mother," revealed in these scenes, are a source of his obsession with cannibalism. Thus Stone gives particular attention to David's encounter with the used-clothing dealer who threatens to eat him alive. Likewise, he notes that in David's young adulthood, he seems to feed upon his beloved Dora, even as he reacts negatively to the aggressive hungers of Uriah Heep, who desires to devour Agnes.

Reviews: S. Connor, *Dickensian,* 91 (1995), 127–30; J. Cunningham, *Dickens Quarterly,* 12 (1995), 75–79; S. Monod, *Etudes Anglaises,* 48 (1995), 236–37; R. Newsom, *Journal of English and Germanic Philology* 94 (1995), 576–79; R. Dunn, *Nineteenth-Century Literature,* 50 (1995), 113–17; M. Smith, *Victorian Review* 21 (1995), 90–94; A. Sadrin, Victorian Studies, 38 (1995), 498–99.

1063. Stone, Harry. "What's in a Name: Fantasy and Calculation in Dickens." *Dickens Studies Annual,* 14 (1985), 191–204.

In four novels, Stone traces Dickens's formulation of related character names that "incorporate the potent fusion of fantasy and calculation, concealment and revelation." The name Murdstone, evolved in manuscript from "Mr. Harden" and "Murden," gains its importance through connection with David's fears and fantasies, he points out, and at its most elemental level "is for Dickens a personal conflation of horror, revulsion, coldness, and mortality."

1064. Tambling, Jeremy. "Doing the Police in Different Voices." In his *Confession: Sexuality, Sin, the Subject.* Manchester: Manchester University Press, 1990, pp. 136–40.

This chapter includes a brief but incisive discussion of the relationship between autobiography and fiction in *David Copperfield,* noting that the events of the blacking factory complete in the novel "a previous fictionalising . . . either by Dickens or by Forster." David, Tambling finds, has few secrets to reveal; "the confessional material adheres to the figures constructed round the neutral figure of the hero, and the confessional relates back to Dickens." Thus, argues Tambling, the text safeguards Dickens's confessional note from appearing too strongly. Many of the important voices in the novel are those of women, and "Rosa Dartle has the most interesting revelations of self to offer," because, in Tambling's reading, she is "the image of the repressed in the text, the object of male authorial and narrator surveillance."

1065. Tambling, Jeremy. "Introduction." To the 1996 Penguin Edition, pp. vii-xxii (1131).

This superb introduction so well balances nineteenth-century context with twentieth-century criticism and theory that it introduces readers to the novel and also invites their multiple readings of it. Recognizing the extraordinary number of major works that were published in England at mid-century by Carlyle, Tennyson, and Wordsworth, Tambling describes *David Copperfield* as a book about "the making (and unmaking) of identity." "Identity" is complex and problematic, for as Foucault has argued, it is a product "of an active and directive discourse or ideology." Tambling discusses the functions of memory, the mode of autobiography, gender and sexuality, socially constructed discipline, heroism (especially as it resonates in the doubling of David and Uriah Heep), and the ambiguity of the father-figure represented in Micawber.

1066. Thurin, Susan S. "The Relationship between Dora and Agnes." *Dickens Studies Newsletter,* 12 (1981), 103–08.

Beginning with notice of how this novel divides characteristics of the conventional heroine between Dora and Agnes, this brief commentary makes a conventional reading of how "the relationship between Dora and Agnes hinges upon their [complementary] functions as agents in David's education." For a more extensive and different conclusion, see Garnett (941).

1067. Tick, Stanley. "Dickens, Dickens, Micawber . . . and Bakhtin." *Victorian Newsletter,* 79 (1991), 34–37.

Tick discusses the "refictionalizing" in the novel of Dickens's previously private autobiographical fragment as an example of what Paul

Ricoeur calls "the redescriptive power of narrative fiction. The autobiographical piece, argues Tick, was monologic, but with the presence of Mr. Micawber in the novel, David engages in dialogic narrative. Thus, as Bakhtin said of the dialogic form, the isolated memory of autobiography was transformed into the knowledge of the novel.

1068. Tracy, Robert. "Stranger than Truth: Fictional Autobiography and Autobiographical Fiction." *Dickens Studies Annual,* 15 (1986), 275–89.

This comparison of Dickens's autobiographical fragment, *David Copperfield,* and Anthony Trollope's *Autobiography,* shows how both forms of writing "employ the same literary strategies to transform experience into art." Tracy points out that to impose a theme on his life, the autobiographer uses imagination rather than absolute historical veracity, and thus autobiography is "fictional in form and to some extent perhaps in content." Autobiographical fiction, when autobiography proves too refractory, frees the author from depending entirely upon the facts of his own experience. So considered, Tracy notes that autobiographies explain the "why and how" of the protagonist's life, but the fictions more dramatically tell the story. In the Dickens versions or autobiography and fiction, young Charles and David are rescued by unexpected benevolence, a theme recurrent in Dickens's novels. Tracy argues that David, whose passivity troubles many readers, here differs from Dickens, who rather than running away from the blacking warehouse, tamely stuck with his work until rescued. Tracy concludes that a novel more often satisfies than does autobiography, because it purports to tell us everything about its characters, but with autobiography there is truncation (as in the unfinished Dickens effort) or much deliberate omission (as evident in Trollope).

1069. Vanden Bossche, Chris R. "Cookery, not Rookery: Family and Class in *David Copperfield.*" *Dickens Studies Annual,* 15 (1986), 87–109.

The catchy title, taken from an observation by Betsey Trotwood, describes the changing parameters of David's search for family and identity. This is one of several recent studies—see Jordan (976)—to define alternative types of families, correspondent to his three loves (Em'ly, Dora, and Agnes), in "a complex structure of class relations in which no single one could exist without the other." Thus Vanden Bossche finds the Peggottys' Yarmouth home to be "full-blown pastoral," appearing "timeless, classless, and innocent." There David for the first time becomes conscious of his social position; see also Raina (1031). For Vanden Bossche, the Steerforth family (and the Micawbers as its parodic mirror) provides David with the genteel family ideal he wishes to establish with Dora Spenlow. The Dover and Canterbury families—Betsey, the Strongs, the Wickfields—represent the virtues of middle-class life. The comic conflict between David and Dora is set up by the middle-class domestic economy rejecting the wasteful, genteel style of living. Vanden Bossche provides useful commentary about the books of household management that Dora receives, noting that "domestic economy becomes socially significant . . . because one's commitment to it signifies one's values and class loyalty." The final part of this new historicist essay points out contradictions and discontinuities in the novel's divisions between the private home and the public world, and it connects divisions between the novel's "domestic fiction of wedded bliss and its excluded domestic fictions" with discontinuities between David Copperfield and Charles Dickens. Retitled, "Family and Class in *David Copperfield*," this essay has been reprinted by Bloom (898) and under its original title by Peck (1124).

1070. Vargish, Thomas. *The Providential Aesthetic in Victorian Fiction.* Charlottesville: University Press of Virginia, 1985, pp. 127–30.
Vargish devotes a chapter to Dickens but gives only slight attention to *David Copperfield.* He cites two good male characters, Mr. Peggotty and Dr. Strong, as positive models for David's moral self-disciplining. Also he notes that, as in Charlotte Brontë's *Jane Eyre,* the natural world operates to awaken the protagonist to love. Vargish considers this the last of Dickens's novels to attempt "straightforward providential fiction, one which ends with poetic justice for almost everybody."

1071. Walder, Dennis. "The Social Gospel: *David Copperfield* and *Bleak House*." In his *Dickens and Religion.* London: George Allen & Unwin, 1981, pp. 140–53.
"Social gospel" to Dickens, Walder asserts, was "a continuing deep conviction of our collective responsibility for the poor and dispossessed," and Walder finds Dickens expressing this long before it became respectable in orthodox religious circles. Agnes fulfills "the role of woman as semi-divine mediator of wisdom," and also through memory and sensitivity to nature, David seems aware of the existence of another world. Counter to the bullying hypocrisy of the Murdstones' fierce religion, Walder believes, the movement of the novel is "towards compassion and service to others, as exemplified by Mr. Peggotty."

1072. Weinstein, Philip M. "The Nocturnal Dickens: A Palimpsest of Motives in *David Copperfield.*" In his *The Semantics of Desire: Changing Models of Identity from Dickens to Joyce.* Princeton: Princeton University Press, 1984, pp. 21–47.
This discussion, one of several explicitly opposing Needham's insistence upon the disciplining of the heart [433], explores "an unresolved tension between Dickens's involuntary imaginary vision and his moral assessment of that vision." Weinstein finds the book overflowing "the

limits of its conceptual framework,'' creatively disturbing ''insofar as it surreptitiously reveals the wayward heart overpowering'' discipline and altruism. Given a Nietzschean reading, Mr. Dick and Dr. Strong anticipate a ''slave morality,'' reflexively identifying ''good'' as their own incapacity Weinstein thinks a Nietzschean self-deception characterizes David's ultimate relationship with Agnes as through her he ''insists upon what he would like to be: a discarnate figure of sublime selflessness.'' Like Poovey (1029), Weinstein parallels Dora with David's mother, and he finds in her relationship with David ''a shadowy repetition of the denouement of Clara Murdstone's marriage.'' There is a resonating pattern of ''older men [David's father, Wickfield, Strong, Mr. Peggotty] uneasily doubling as fathers and husbands'' shadowed by ''potential betrayers [Murdstone, Heep, Maldon, and Steerforth].'' These and such other relationships as Annie and Strong, David and Agnes, David and Dora, Peggotty and Em'ly ''bristle with unintended meanings'' to disturb ''the authorized script of sublime motives'' by a ''covert semantics of desire.''

1073. Welsh, Alexander. *From Copyright to Copperfield: The Identity of Dickens.* Cambridge, MA: Harvard University Press, 1987, passim.
Challenging the idea that childhood trauma is the best ground for biographical criticism, Welsh closely studies the period ''in early middle life when Dickens *recalled* his traumatic experience,'' a time when Dickens was reaffirming his vocation and was involved in the controversy over international copyright. This book deals with *Martin Chuzzlewit, Dombey and Son,* and devotes the final five chapters to *David Copperfield.* For all the problematics of the novel's famous first sentence, Welsh demonstrates that Dickens the novelist came to this book with considerable professional confidence and satisfaction. The chapter, ''Women Passing By,'' discusses Agnes in particular as an image of a discontinuous self, a complicated analogue to David himself. Another chapter, ''Perfection of English Mirth,'' challenges readings of the humor as innocent by finding it incorporating ''the combined passive and aggressive longings that Dickens so successfully imitated from fairy tales and employed for his own fictionalized confession of progress.'' In the ''Young Man Copperfield'' chapter, which is reprinted by Bloom, (898), Welsh views Dickens's contrastive use of the fairy tale and the Oedipal references as ways of responding to the cultural ''need to justify a rise in the world, so desired by the sons of the nineteenth century.'' Welsh, in the larger context of his study, finds Dickens in *Copperfield* codifying ''the very assumptions about early life that bring psychoanalysis into being. . . . The rise of the hero is prepared but also justified by a fall and recovery in childhood.''

Reviews: D. Sadoff, *Dickens Quarterly,* 5 (1988), 192–95; J. Sutherland, *London Review of Books,* 10 Nov 1988, 22–23; R. Dunn in *Nineteenth-Century Literature* 43 (1988), 268–72; R. Ashton *Times Literary Supplement,* 27 May 1988, 576; N. Auerbach, *Victorian Studies* 32 (1988), 116–17; M. Baumgarten, *Style,* 23 (1989), 165–67; A. Fleishman, *Journal of English and Germanic Philology* 88 (1989), 119–21; S. Monod, *Etudes Anglaises* 42 (1989), 219–20; David G. Riede, *Studies in English Literature,* 28 (1988), 736; G. Smith, *Year's Work in English Studies* 20 (1990), 303–04; K. Rosador, *Archivist,* 227 (1990), 380–382; D. Parker, *Modern Language Quarterly,* 50 (1991), 58–63.

1074. Wiley, Margaret C. "The Fallen Woman in the Victorian Novel: Dickens, Gaskell, and Eliot." *DAI,* 58 (1998), 3544A (Massachusetts, 1997).

Wiley draws on Foucault's ideas about power and discourse as well as new historicism, feminism, and autobiographical criticism in her argument that the Victorian idea about the figure of the "fallen woman" was closely tied to the ideas about both the "Angel in the House" and the "gentleman." Dickens's involvement with Urania Cottage, a house for former prostitutes, affected his attitude towards such women, she holds, from portraying them as victims in *Oliver Twist* to seeing them more cynically as sexually transgressive in *David Copperfield* and *Dombey and Son.* Also considered are Gaskell's *Mary Barton* and Eliot's *Adam Bede, The Mill on the Floss,* and *Daniel Deronda.*

1075. Wilkes, David M. "Dickens's *David Copperfield.*" *Explicator,* 51 (1993), 157–59.

Brief commentary upon the pejorative labels associated with snake, bandit, beast, monster, and spider—especially in regard to David's character in relationship with Dora.

1076. Winnifrith, Tom. "Dickens." In his *Fallen Women in the Nineteenth-Century Novel.* London: St. Martin's Press, 1994, pp. 93–112.

Winnifrith notes that Dickens takes more conventional views of fallen women in his fiction than in his philanthropic work concerning Urania Cottage, a home for them. Winnifrith briefly discusses the Annie Strong story as "a muddled account of a marriage which does come right in the end," and in connection with the novel's fallen women—Martha and Em'ly—he finds Dickens raising more questions than he answers about their guilt and fate.

1077. Woodfield, Malcolm J. "The Endless Memorial: Dickens and Memory/Writing/History." *Dickens Studies Annual,* 20 (1991), 75–102.

Comprehensive in its recognition of much critical attention to Mr. Dick (Woodfield's responses to it provide a running bibliographic essay), this substantial essay argues that he "characterizes the metaphorical madness of modern culture." Dickens makes use of him "to dramatize or simulate matters of which he can neither speak directly nor write without dissimulation," matters of general epistemological crisis and of "the success or failure of narrative stories or histories to resolve that crisis." Woodfield considers Mr. Dick's efforts in the context of the self-questioning of John Stuart Mill's *Autobiography,* and he contrasts Mr. Dick (who finds the seventeenth century "a site of fracture and loss") with Carlyle's picturing of Cromwell. For Mr. Dick and for Dickens, "histories are means of both memorializing and displacing. David is Dickens' Charles I, constantly interrupting the narrative, forcing a new beginning which questions the role of the past in the present."

APPRECIATIONS

1078. Anon. "Theodore Roosevelt on Dickens." *Dickensian,* 82 (1986), 118–20.
In letters to his children, T. R. made several references to Dickens, noting in connection with *David Copperfield* that he had known "plenty of women of the Dora type," whom he "felt were a good deal better than the men they married." He particularly appreciated the characterization of Sophy Traddles.

TOPOGRAPHY

1079. Davies, James. A. "Dickens and the Region in *David Copperfield.* In *Writing, Region and Nation: Proceedings of the Fourth International Conference on the Literature of Region and Nation.* Swansea: University of Wales, 1994, pp. 187–96.
Davies regards *David Copperfield* as one of the great London novels and in this essay shows that as the book proceeds David finds London changing "from a place of threat and horror to a setting for that very Victorian combination of marital bliss, material success and sustaining religiosity." Many of the negative qualities originate in various suburbs. Highgate, Norwood, Blackheath, and Putney are all settings for trauma or crisis. Davies also examines the characters and experiences

associated with locales more remote from London—Yarmouth, Canterbury, and Dover—and concludes that "Dickens's treatment of region raises questions about what might be called 'regional orthodoxy.' "

1080. Johnson, Derek. "Dickens's Two Boyhoods." In his *Pastoral in the Work of Charles Dickens*. New York: Peter Lang, 1992, pp. 69–90.

In discussing Dickens as both country boy and urban drudge, Johnson notes the impact of Dickens's degrading childhood labor upon his portrayal of Camden Town and London. Also he compares Dickens's and Wordsworth's renderings of the contrast between country and city. Unlike Wordsworth, he asserts, Dickens was drawn imaginatively to the teeming city life. Johnson argues that Dickens "moved in a psychologically retrograde fashion from one version of pastoral to another" (toward "a metropolitan pastoral myth").

1081. Langstaff, John B. *David Copperfield's Library*. London: Allen and Unwin, 1925.

Langstaff describes the process of identifying the Micawbers' house in Windsor Terrace, City Road, where David stays while working at the factory, as Number 13 Johnson Street, where Dickens himself lived as a child during the similar period in his life. The house now serves as a children's library. As an epilogue, Langstaff includes a poem by Alfred Noyes (872). Originally listed in the "Appreciations" section of the first edition of this bibliography [565].

1082. Murphy, Colonel. N. T. P. "Around Charing Cross with David Copperfield." *Punch,* 9 December 1988, 24.

Murphy points out that it is yet possible to walk many of the dark alleys and lanes young Dickens knew in the 1820s, and that in the Charing Cross area, Rules Restaurant, The Adelphi Arches, the Red Lion pub, and Buckingham Street survive from Dickens's time.

LITERARY INFLUENCES AND PARALLELS

1083. Anon. "Who Was the Imitator—Dickens or Thackeray?" *Atlantic Monthly,* 78 (1896), 139–51.

This note from a contributor points out a number of parallels between *David Copperfield* and *Pendennis,* particularly those of the Steerforth/ Emily and Pendennis/Fanny Bolton relationships. The answer this writer finds to the title question is that Thackeray was the imitator, even though "there was borne into the English mind at that period a strong tidal movement toward better views of life."

1084. Allen, Brooke. "The Man Who Didn't Like Dickens: Evelyn Waugh and Boz." *Dickens Quarterly,* 8 (1991), 155–61.

Notes that in *Decline and Fall* Waugh reworked David Copperfield's visit to the model prison.

1085. Arnds, Peter O. *Wilhelm Raabe's Der Hungerpastor and Charles Dickens's David Copperfield: Intertextuality of Two Bildungsromane.* New York: Peter Lang, 1997.

Arnds begins with a chapter presenting Raabe (1831–1910) as the German Dickens, even though the authors differ considerably in style and manner of characterization. He argues that Raabe was influenced by the immense popularity of *David Copperfield* in Germany; see [37]. Principally, Raabe found an exemplary model for a Bildungsroman in Dickens's novel. Major chapters discuss Raabe's knowledge of Dickens's works, a comparison of the two plots, similarities between the protagonists who undergo phases of development, similarities between antagonists (including Steerforth and Heep), and a consideration of angels (Agnes Wickfield) and fallen women (Emily).

1086. Cain, Tom. "Tolstoy's Use of *David Copperfield.*" In *Tolstoy in Britain.* Ed. W. Gareth Jones. Oxford: Berg, 1995, pp. 67–77.

This reprint from *Forum for Modern Language Studies,* 4 (1968), 45–52, notes the excellent timing of Dickens's work for Russian writers and readers and observes that Tolstoy praised most what many modern Dickens readers chiefly mistrust—"the 'Christian' imagination that too readily creates an Agnes Wickfield."

1087. Cronin, Mark. "The Rake, The Writer, and *The Stranger:* Textual Relations between *Pendennis* and *David Copperfield.*" *Dickens Studies Annual,* 24 (1996), 215–40.

Contemporaneous monthly publication of the Dickens and Thackeray novels kept the writers' rivalry active, and Cronin finds Thackeray's work having a significant influence on *Copperfield.* He discusses three major points of textual connection—similarities between Arthur Pendennis and James Steerforth as "gentleman-rake" characters, competing depictions of the artist as hero, the title characters' shared theatrical experience with Kotzebue's *The Stranger.* The Steerforth-Mrs. Steerforth-Rosa Dartle triangle has its *Pendennis* parallel, although "ultimately diverging paths of Pendennis and Steerforth [are] scripted early in each book." As part of the Victorian revaluation of the status of the writer, Cronin further indicates, Dickens views the writer as hero, Thackeray portrays him as a prose laborer, and by saying little about David the writer, Dickens may have been countering Thackeray's unflattering presentation of the writing life. Cronin adds to Welsh's commentary (1073) on the Kotzebue parallel by finding the play serving "as a subtle omen to David and Pendennis, who must learn to navigate the perilous course of romantic entanglement" and to "examine the pattern of transgression and reconciliation."

1088. Curry, William M., Jr. "Appreciating the Unappreciated: Washington Irving's Influence on Charles Dickens" *DAI,* 57 (1996), 186A (Southwestern Louisiana, 1996).

Curry extends previous examinations of Irving's influence on Dickens, adding to Ernest Boll's evidence and refuting Christof Wegelin's dismissal of that evidence. Curry finds parallels between certain Irving and Dickens characters, such as Irving's Arabian philosopher and Uriah Heep and Irving's Dolph Heylinger and Mr. Micawber, suggesting that Dickens drew on Irving's work for sources.

1089. Dennett, J. J. "Mighty Waters in the Work of Dickens and Turner." *Dickensian,* 90 (1994), 179–88.

See (926) for critical commentary Dennett makes about common interest Dickens and Turner had in the sea and in shipwreck. Noting that Turner's 1805 "The Shipwreck" features red clothing on sailors, Dennett points to David Copperfield's eye being drawn to the drowning Steerforth's red cap in the novel's Tempest chapter.

1090. Fleissner, Robert F. "Caulfield and Copperfield." *Word Ways: The Journal of Recreational Linguistics,* 27 (1994), 249–50.

Fleissner contests several suggested sources for Holden Caulfield's name and points out a number of parallels between Salinger's and Dickens's novels—the first person narration, focus on school experiences, attractions of David and Holden to Steerforth and Stradlater, and similarity between Em'ly and Phoebe. See also Martin (1096).

1091. Hawes, Donald. *Who's Who in Dickens.* London: Routledge, 1998.

See (1116); Hawes provides some information about the prototypes for *David Copperfield* characters.

1092. Hibbert, Christopher. "Introduction." To the 1983 Folio Society Edition, pp. xiii–xviii (821).

Hibbert cites Dickens's recent reading of Thomas Holcraft's autobiography and of *Tom Jones* as inspirations for *Copperfield.* He briefly discusses the serial writing, autobiographical aspects of the novel, and notes that although it can be read as a joyous book, it also has more somber qualities. Hibbert mentions the numerous orphan characters in a novel "to a large extent preoccupied with the relationship of children to their parents."

1093. Irving, John. *The Cider House Rules.* New York: William Morrow, 1985.

With *Great Expectations* and Charlotte Brontë's *Jane Eyre, David Copperfield* is the repeated text for nightly reading aloud at the unusual orphanage run by Dr. Wilbur Larch.

1094. Lucas, John. "Dickens and Shaw: Women and Marriage in *David Copperfield* and *Candida.*" *The Shaw Review,* 22 (1979), 13–22.
Lucas notes that Shaw thought Dickens's novel failed as autobiography, with the grown-up David not telling the truth and even the child David being "more remarkable for the reserves than for the revelations." Lucas thinks that Shaw's principal concern was that the novel did not reveal more about Dickens's own marriage, especially in a fictional autobiography "crucially concerned with the nature of relationships between men and women." Despite some parallels between David's coming to understand Dora and a similar situation in *Candida,* Shaw and Dickens differ, Lucas insists, totally on their notions of marriage as the opportunity both for private contentment and for promoting artistic success.

1095. Marsden, Malcolm M. "Dickens' Mr. Micawber and Mark Twain's Colonel Sellers: The Genesis of an American Comic." *Dickens Studies Annual,* 21 (1992), 63–77.
Traces a number of personal parallels in the lives and thoughts of Dickens and Twain, and notes their common comic aptitude to affirm human goodness and attack those who endanger it. Despite many similarities between the characters in *Copperfield* and *The Gilded Age,* Marsden notes important differences in the characters' social standing and moral sensitivities.

1096. Martin, John S. "Copperfield and Caulfield." *Notes on Modern American Literature,* 4 (1980), Item 29.
Martin cites several earlier notices in Salinger commentary of incidental parallels between *The Catcher in the Rye* and *David Copperfield.* His own point is that the parallels establish a thematic relationship between the phoniness Holden rejects and the very concrete Victorian world evident in Dickens. See also Fleissner (1090).

1097. Nies, Frederick, and John Kimmey. "*David Copperfield* and *The Princess Casamassima.*" *Henry James Review,* 10 (1989), 179–84.
Noting James's various expressions of regard for Dickens's work, the authors find that James's very personal involvement with Dickens is most evident in *The Princess Casamassima,* especially in specific borrowings of a description of the Thames and of Betsey Trotwood's advice to young David. Further, James, despite his complaint about Dickens's methods of characterization, seemed to model characters after Steerforth, Em'ly, and Martha. The nature and extent of parallels between the novels suggest to Nies and Kimmey that Dickens's fiction taught James "how to take possession of" London both as home and setting for most of his fiction.

1098. Priestley, J. B. "Charles Dickens" and "Introduction." To c. 1950 Centennial Edition, pp. vii–xviii (818).

The biographical note to this centennial edition is interpretative, providing the picture of Dickens becoming increasingly "divided and at war with himself." Like the critics and biographers of the 1940s and 1950s—Edmund Wilson [536], Humphry House [346], Edgar Johnson [738]—Priestley recognizes Dickens's increasing concern with social issues, "an ever-increasing depth, weight,and significance" in the novels after *Copperfield,* which he does not find concerned with society, a judgment much challenged recently—see, for example, Palmer (1027). Priestley argues that Dickens considered this his favorite novel, not because it was autobiographical but rather because through an adopted first-person point of view a novelist seems "to come closer to that story and that character" than when unfolding a novel "in terms of a group of characters." Priestly speaks from the experience of his own first-person novel, *Bright Day.* "From a strictly literary point of view," the chapters dealing with David's childhood are Dickens's best work, "a marvel of the novelist's art."

1099. Rogers, Philip. "A Tolstoyan Reading of *David Copperfield.*" *Comparative Literature,* 42 (1990), 1–28.

Rogers, noting that there are few specific reasons for Tolstoy's appreciation of *Copperfield,* argues that it is necessary to read back to Dickens from Tolstoy's works, particularly from his early trilogy, *Childhood, Adolescence,* and *Youth.* Noting a number of resemblances in an essay that focuses increasingly on *Copperfield,* Rogers provides an illuminating discussion of Heep (who warrants Tolstoy's "boldly imaginative interpretation") and his qualifying perspective of David's world. Tolstoy seems to have anticipated many of the more recent readers, Rogers believes, by understanding that David's surrogates call his narrative authority into question to the extent that "his complacent self-appraisal is not the final word."

1100. Salinger, J. D. *The Catcher in the Rye.* New York: Little, Brown, 1951.

From the familiar opening line denouncing "all that David Copperfield kind of crap," Salinger's novel resonates with echoes from *Copperfield;* see Fleissner (1090) and Martin (1096) The narrator-hero's surname, "Caulfield," recalls both David's name and a feature of his birth. Also there are similarities in the hero's relationship to his young sister (an Em'ly type of character) and to his schoolmate Stradlater (a modern Steerforth).

1101. Steele, Elizabeth. "The Question of Imitation." In *Hugh Walpole.* New York: Twayne, 1972, pp. 51–54.

Steele notes that "Walpole clearly intended" *Fortitude,* his novel about a writer, "to be the modern *David Copperfield.*" The central character even calls a school friend "my Steerforth." The parallel is interesting particularly because Walpole wrote the script for the MGM film version of *Copperfield* (856).

1102. Sullivan, Patricia R. "A Student Response to the Genuine Fear and Pain in *Mort à Credit* and *David Copperfield.*" *Recovering Literature: A Journal of Contextualist Criticism,* 7 (1979), 42–55.

Compares David's childhood experience with Mr. Murdstone to the experience with a harsh parent figure portrayed in Celine's novel.

1103. Tillotson, Kathleen. "Steerforth's Old Nursery Tale." *Dickensian,* 79 (1983), 167–69.

In chapter 22, Tillotson points out, Steerforth alludes to a boy who became food for lions. Tillotson traces this, through a reference by Dickens in 1837 to the instructive story of Tommy and Harry in Daniel Fenning's *Universal Spelling Book,* which was published in 1756. She summarizes the story and notes its pertinence to Steerforth's faults of character.

TEACHING AND STUDY MATERIALS

1104. Andrews, Malcolm, ed. *David Copperfield.* In 1993 Everyman edition (825).

Andrews provides much useful material for teachers and students. The table of contents indicates monthly number division; there is a chronology of Dickens's life and times, Andrews's critical introduction (885), explanatory notes, and an appended commentary on Dickens and his critics that focuses on the critical reception of this novel over the years. The text includes all of the original illustrations.

1105. Baldwin, Edward C. "Introduction and Notes." *The Personal History of David Copperfield.* To the 1910, revised 1919, Scott, Foresman edition (806).

This edition contains a short general preface, a thirty-page introduction, a bibliography, and a chronological list of Dickens's works. An appendix has helps to study, questions about the life of Dickens and about *David Copperfield* in general, details of the story, theme subjects, selections for class reading, and suggestions for dramatization. Comparison of this with subsequent classroom editions (1107, 1108, 1131) shows the scope and development of instructional approaches and interests both in America and England over the years.

1106. Bland, Joellen. "The Fall of Uriah Heep: From *David Copperfield.*" In *Stage Plays from the Classics.* Boston: Plays, Inc., 1987.

A half-hour dramatization of the scene in which Mr. Micawber presents his evidence against Uriah Heep. Bland makes good use of much of Dickens's own dialogue to give students an introduction to the work as a whole. She also includes some stage direction for assembling a mid-nineteenth century set.

1107. Buckley, Jerome H., ed. *David Copperfield.* 1990 Norton Critical Edition (823).

This critical edition includes a note on the illustrations, the number plans, the 1850 and 1869 prefaces, Dickens's Autobiographical Fragment, selections from Dickens's letters relating to the novel, and (in regard to the Maria Beadnell-Dora Spenlow connection), an excerpt from Chapter III of *Little Dorrit.* Buckley also includes critical excerpts from John Forster [730], Matthew Arnold [185], E. K. Brown [234], Gwendolyn B. Needham [433], Monroe Engel [294], J. Hillis Miller [419], Mark Spilka [486], Harry Stone [498], Bert Hornback [344], Garrett Stewart [495], Robert L. Patten [444], and Alexander Welsh (1073). Also there is a chronology of Dickens's life and works and selected bibliography.

Reviews: Joel J. Brattin, *Dickens Quarterly,* 8 (1991), 179–87; J. A. Davies, *Notes & Queries,* 38 (1991), 244.

1108. Burgis, Nina, ed. 1981. *David Copperfield.* World's Classic Edition (820).

Like recent paperback texts edited by Andrews (1104), Buckley (1107), and Tambling (1131), this one provides much useful material for students and teachers of the novel. It has all the original illustrations and also facsimiles of the monthly parts cover and 1850 title page. Original serial part numbers are clear, and appendices include Dickens's 1867 preface, his trial titles, and number plans. Explanatory notes concisely deal with literary and cultural allusions.

1109. Burton, H. M. *Dickens and His Works.* London: Methuen Educational Ltd., 1968.

A brief, general introduction to Dickens, which lists *David Copperfield* among the five most recommended Dickens novels. Noting the changes Dickens made to his own life story, Burton finds parallels between fact and fiction in the early parts of the novel close and poignant. "It is unnecessary to relate the story of David Copperfield, partly because everybody has read the book, partly because there is no real plot, only the adventures and the development of David himself and of his family and friends," concludes Burton.

1110. "*David Copperfield* (1849–50). In "Works and E-texts" section of *The Dickens Page. Http://lang.nagoya-u.ac.jp/~matsuoka/Dickens.html* October, 1998.

The listed academic resources of this page include a Project Gutenberg E-text of the novel (828), George Landow's commentary on the blacking factory and Dickens's imaginative world, excerpts from Chesterton

[253] and Forster [308], and Joseph Bottum's article on naming (899). The larger Dickens Page includes a concordance to the novel (798), access to homepages of The Dickens Fellowship, The Dickens Society, The Dickens Project, and links also with the Victorian Web. See also (1120).

1111. Dunn, Richard J., ed. *Approaches to Teaching David Copperfield.* New York: The Modern Language Association, 1984.

. There are two parts to this book: Materials and Approaches. The first discusses the relative merits of available editions, recommends background readings, lists some aids to teaching, and also includes a brief bibliographic essay, "The Instructor's Library" now superseded particularly by the "Teaching and Study Materials" section of *David Copperfield: Supplement I-1981-1998.* The second part includes sixteen brief essays describing ways instructors use *David Copperfield* in courses of varied subject emphasis, size, and student experience. These include Daniel Sheridan, "*David Copperfield:* Different Readers, Different Approaches," pp. 23–32; Susan J. Hanna, "*Copperfield* on Trial: Meeting the Opposition," pp. 33–39; Thomas M. Leitch, "Dickens' Problem Child," pp. 40–48; Beverly Lyon Clark, "*David Copperfield* in a Children's Literature Course," pp. 49–53; Margaret Scanlan, "An Introduction to Fiction: *David Copperfield* in the Genre Course," pp. 54–60; Willis Konick, "The Chords of Memory: Teaching *David Copperfield* in the Context of World Literature," pp. 61–70; Gerhard Joseph, "Fathers and Sons: *David Copperfield* in a Course on Victorian Autobiographical Prose," pp. 71–80; Stanley Friedman, "*David Copperfield:* An Introduction to Dickens Course," pp. 81–87; Jean Ferguson Carr, "*David Copperfield's* 'Written Memory,' " pp. 88–94; Melissa Sue Kort, " 'I have taken with fear and trembling to authorship': *David Copperfield* in the Composition Classroom," pp. 95–101; J. Gill Holland, "*David Copperfield:* Parallel Reading for Undergraduates," pp. 102–6; George J. Worth, "Multum in Parvo: The Ninth Chapter of *David Copperfield,*" pp. 107–13; Michael Lund, "Testing by Installments the 'Undisciplined Heart' of *David Copperfield,*" pp. 114–21; Dianne F. Sadoff, "Teaching *David Copperfield:* Language, Psychoanalysis, and Feminism," pp. 122–30; Susan R. Horton, "Making Sense of *David Copperfield,*" pp. 131–40; and Michael Steig, "*David Copperfield* and Shared Reader Response," pp. 141–50.

1112. Dunn, Richard J. " 'Whether . . . these pages . . . must show': Teaching *David Copperfield* Again." In *Reading David Copperfield* (1127), pp. 190–94.

This lecture deals with the question of how to teach this novel with the recognition that it is a work about learning and also one that is self-conscious about its performances and performers. Dunn demonstrates how the first sentence's concern over what the novel's pages must show provokes significant questions about its entire design and success.

1113. Garrigus, Fred. "David Copperfield." In *You're On the Air*. Ed. Fred Garrigus and Theodore Johnson. Boston: Baker's Plays, 1946, passim. This collection of short radio dramas is intended "to serve as an introduction to the field of radio dramatics" in classrooms. Only a brief scene from *David Copperfield* is used, in which Barkis takes Peggotty and David to Yarmouth, where he meets Little Em'ly, Ham, Mr. Peggotty and Mrs. Gummidge. Garrigus remains quite faithful to Dickens's own dialogue throughout the adaptations, and includes many helpful hints regarding sound effects and music for the benefit of students.

1114. Grant, Allan. *A Preface to Dickens*. London: Longman, 1984. There are three parts to this book: "The Writer and His Setting," "Critical Commentary," and "Reference Section." Reference materials include information about Dickens's various illustrators and his circle of friendships. In discussing *David Copperfield,* Grant focuses on its Wordsworthian "incidents and situations from common life," and he warns against too direct association of David with Dickens. The function of memory and imagination, he argues, is to locate beginnings of moral life in fantasy and early experience.

1115. Hardy, Barbara. *Charles Dickens: The Writer and His Work.* Windsor: Profile Books, 1983, pp. 63–69. Hardy includes a biographical sketch and brief critical commentaries on each of the works. The *Copperfield* section, pp. 63–69, reiterates key points of Hardy's earlier study (956).

1116. Hawes, Donald. *Who's Who in Dickens*. London: Routledge, 1998. Superseding various earlier handbooks of Dickens characters, Hawes's aim is "to give fuller accounts of the major characters than are found in many reference books, noting some of Dickens's possible sources and referring, in a limited way, to critical opinion, especially when questions of influence and interpretation have arisen [Miss Mowcher is a case in point]." The introduction is an informative discussion of Dickensian characterization; there are many illustrations showing "how characters were understood by contemporaries and near contemporaries of Dickens." Listings are alphabetical, but there is a helpful prefatory list of characters by work, including over 50 from *David Copperfield.*

1117. Hollington, Michael. *Charles Dickens: David Copperfield.* Capes/ Agregation d'anglais coedition Didier-Erudition, 1996, pp. 170.

Our information about this work comes entirely from the 1998 review which appeared as this bibliography was going to the publisher. Hollington's book is designed for those studying to enter the teaching profession in France. His reading incorporates his critical study (965) of the novel as Bildungsroman, particularly in relation to Goethe and Carlyle. Review: Robin Gilmour, *Dickens Quarterly,* 15 (1998), 236–40.

1118. Lipscomb, George, adaptor. *"David Copperfield."* Art by Henry Kiefer and Gene Ha. New York: Acclaim, 1997.

Part of the Classics Illustrated Study Guides series. In the forty-three pages of this graphic novel, probably most suitable for middle-school or early high-school students, Lipscomb manages to provide a fairly comprehensive adaptation of Dickens's novel, frequently encapsulating entire scenes or chapters into a single panel with some commentary and key dialogue, so that although he loses Dickens's subtleties, he at least shows the scope of the original. The admirable essay at the end by Emily Woudenberg provides an impressive amount of helpful information for readers who are probably unfamiliar with Dickens and the Victorian period; she includes a biography of Dickens and many asides on such topics as money, the notion of separate spheres, social ranking, debtors' prisons and the legal system. Woudenberg also gives thorough character descriptions and a healthy plot summary to round out the graphic novel, and suggests several ways to view the novel, as an autobiography and through such themes as the vulnerable child and the quest for home. Most importantly, she does not oversimplify the novel but gives several different interpretations of David's life, acknowledging the problematic sides to his character as well as the admirable ones.

1119. Lund, Michael. "Teaching Long Victorian Novels in Parts." *Victorian Newsletter,* 58 (1980), 29–32.

Lund offered students the independent study opportunity to read *Copperfield* in parts, and he cites papers they wrote as evidence of the value of studying the book in parts. For a more complete discussion see Lund's chapter in Dunn (1111).

1120. Matsouka, Mitsuharu. "The Dickens Page." *http://lang.nagoya-u.ac.jp/~matsouka/Dickens.html* (December, 1998).

Links from this homepage include the Dickens Fellowship, the Japan Branch of the Dickens Fellowship, the Dickens Society, the Dickens Project, various other Dickens homepages, works and E-texts (see 828) and the *David Copperfield* concordance (see 798). Rather than list further the many currently available resources at this site, students and teachers may find it to be the single best source for supplementing this annotated bibliography, but as with any largely public website, the accuracy and completeness of information may not be certain.

1121. Nelson, Harland S. *Charles Dickens.* Boston: Twayne Publishers, 1981.

Except for some passing references and a plot summary this general introduction to Dickens does not discuss *David Copperfield.* Nelson focuses on imagination, energy, and will as the characteristics which "helped make Dickens what he was, as he himself knew." Readers new to Dickens should benefit from Nelson's chapters on the author's relationships to his audience and on his forms of serial publication.

1122. Newlin, George. *Every Thing in Dickens: Ideas and Subjects Discussed by Charles Dickens in His Complete Works, A Topicon.* Westport, CT: Greenwood Press, 1996.

This is the fourth volume of Newlin's *Windows into Dickens,* with the first three bearing the title, *Everyone in Dickens.* As Fred Kaplan says in his foreword, this is a reference work that "can be read for pleasure, for casual browsing in the distinctiveness of Victorian things and thoughts; but it can also be mined for selective gold by the social historian, the political historian, and by those who simply need or want to know something specific about Dickens himself or about Victorian manners, morals, thoughts and things."

1123. Page, Norman. *"David Copperfield."* In his *A Dickens Companion.* New York: Schocken Books, 1984, pp. 157–68.

Page provides basic information about composition, serialization, publication, and reception. His commentary notes Dickens's fondness for the book, his struggles in finding a title, the focus on memory, and the uncovering of buried experiences. There is a listing of some sixty characters, with brief paragraphs identifying their roles. Page was unable to anticipate the revival of critical interest in this novel in the 1980s, as he deemed its "limited topicality, and its lack of the comprehensive vision of society" as reasons for having not much interested contemporary criticism. For a summary of the newer directions of *Copperfield* criticism, see John Peck (1124).

Reviews: A. Maio, *Choice,* 26 (Dec. 1988), 622; R. Mason, *Notes & Queries,* 36 (1989), 525–27; G. Storey, *Times Literary Supplement,* 17 Feb 1989, p. 173; A. Watts, *Dickensian,* 85 (1989), 55–56; D. Paroissien, *Dickens Quarterly* 7 (1990), 343–48; S. Monod, *Victorian Studies* 33 (1990), 513–15.

1124. Peck, John, ed. *David Copperfield and Hard Times.* New York: St. Martin's Press, 1995, pp. 1–154.

This is a New Casebooks volume, reprinting and excerpting from Vanden Bossch (1069), Edwards (929), Poovey (1029), Myers (1021), Carmichael (912), and Kucich (990). Peck's introductory essay surveys surging new historicist, feminist, and psychoanalytic critical interest in *David Copperfield* in the 1980s. Broadly surveying the move from traditional to more recent criticism, Peck finds the latter regarding the novel's "text as a site where the ideological contradictions of a period are exposed, and to some extent examined, but not necessarily contained and judged." Peck's introductory commentary about his selections not only relates them to each other but also explains their connections with deconstruction, new historicism, feminism, and psychoanalytic criticism.

1125. Pocock, Guy N., ed. *David Copperfield as a Boy.* London: Dent, 1935.
In his brief introduction, Pocock describes the early chapters of *David Copperfield* as "the best part of one of the world's best books. In the later part of the book the hero grows less and less substantial. . . . But in this first part David Copperfield is a boy, and he is Dickens; and the whole thing is alive, and stupendous, and beyond all criticism." Pocock follows David through his days at Dr. Strong's school, and then includes some later passages such as David's visit to the Barkis household and Mr. Barkis's death, and the great storm in which Ham and Steerforth are killed. Following the text are a series of "Questions and Suggestions" ranging from basic reading comprehension questions to simple analysis. The focus of this text on David's childhood and the tone of the introduction and questions seem to indicate that it is intended for older children, perhaps in late grade school or middle school.

1126. Pool, Daniel. *What Jane Austen Ate and Charles Dickens Knew: From Fox Hunting to Whist—the Facts of Daily Life in Nineteenth-Century England.* New York: Simon and Schuster, 1993.
Pool frequently mentions *David Copperfield* in this book's highly readable brief discussions of nineteenth-century popular culture and in its useful glossary of terms that annotate this and other Victorian novels. His bibliography is very dated, with very few citations to works after 1980.
Reviews: *Times Literary Supplement,* 3 July 1998, 28; Schickle, *Dickens Quarterly,* 11 (1994), 90–92.

1127. *Reading David Copperfield: Resource Handbook for Teaching and Study.* The Dickens Project. Santa Cruz: University of California, 1990.
John O. Jordan, Director of the Dickens Project, describes this handbook as neither a teacher's guide nor a step-by-step curriculum, but as a resource "designed to clarify, develop, and enrich the teaching and reading of this remarkable novel." It includes a video tape of a dramatization of parts of the novel and also an audio tape of the same sections; a slide talk on Dickens's legal London; illustrations from

the novel; numerous background reading materials; suggested writing assignments and classroom activities. There are reprints from various interpretations: Stone on Dickens's working notes (780); Gilmour on the novel's place in the Dickens canon (944) and on memory in the novel [320]; Kincaid on laughter and the Micawbers [373]; Manning on David and Scheherazade (1010); George Bernard Shaw on Dickens (1052); Jordan on the novel's social sub-text (11439; Eigner on elements of pantomime (932); Matthew Arnold's appreciative remark (878); Adrian on parents and children (881). First published in this volume are lectures by Dunn (1112) and Schor (1128), as well as Regul's essay on the novel's use of illustrations (796). The Dickens Project at The University of California, Santa Cruz, may have a limited number of printed copies of this handbook, and according to information on the Project's homepage, the handbook will become part of the Dickens Project's electronic archive (1120).

1128. Schor, Hilary M. "The Heroine of His Own Life: Charles Dickens, *David Copperfield*, Feminism, and the Classroom." In *Reading David Copperfield* (1127), pp. 195–197.

As the abstract for this lecture notes, Schor is interested in "How heroic is David really?" She notes his passivity, lack of narrative authority, and the numerous characters who compete with him for prominence. If the novel ultimately has no hero, perhaps it provides a heroine instead, and thus she asks, "What would happen . . . if we listened more carefully to the suppressed story of Agnes Wickfield?"

1129. Selman, James E. *Readings and Scenes from David Copperfield.* New York: Edgar S. Werner, 1898.

This stage adaptation is an "outgrowth of a deeply-felt need, that the public exercises of our schools should combine the elements of true literary and popular taste." *David Copperfield* meeting both these needs, Selman presents a broad but selective set of readings from the novel interspersed with scenes for schoolchildren to act out. "[A]rranged to be presented by girls alone," the abridgement excludes such plot lines as Steerforth's seduction of Little Em'ly and Uriah Heep's interest in Agnes.

1130. Storey, Graham. *David Copperfield: Interweaving Truth and Fiction.* Boston: Twayne Publishers, 1991.

Part of Twayne's masterwork series, this volume includes discussions of the novel's historical background, influence and critical reception, and a critical reading of the novel. Because the volume best serves as an introduction to Dickens and *David Copperfield,* it is listed here, rather than in the "Critical Studies" section of this bibliography. In his reading of the novel, Storey provides brief discussions of the "The

Child's-Eye Vision," the thematic and narrative structure, the distinctive voices of the many characters, the attention the novel gives to marriage and to parents and children and orphans. There is a brief separate discussion of Rosa Dartle, and a brief chapter on social criticism (although Storey finds the social criticism less in the foreground than in most Dickens works). He comments also, following Stone [496], on the importance of fairy tale to *David Copperfield,* and concludes with a note on the pathetic fallacy. His bibliography is very dated, with few citations to works after 1980.

Reviews: L. Peters, *Dickensian,* 88 (1992); 49–52; B. Rosenberg, *Dickens Quarterly,* 10 (993); 115–17; S. Smith, *Review of English Studies,* 45 (1994), 121.

1131. Tambling, Jeremy, ed. *David Copperfield.* 1996 Penguin Edition (827). This is the first Penguin edition to provide all the original illustrations, but it does not retain the facsimile of the monthly parts cover that was in the previous Penguin edition; see [69]. The introduction (1065) is excellent, and Tambling appends the descriptive headlines Dickens added in 1867 and also his number plans for the novel. Notes comment on points of interpretation, indicate important material Dickens deleted before the novel was published, and provide glosses to difficult passages. Tambling acknowledges the assistance of the Clarendon edition [79] in his determinations about numerous textual variants. See also Andrews (1104), Buckley (1107), and Burgis (1108) for comparable paperback editions for students and teachers.

1132. Watts, Alan S. *"David Copperfield."* In his *The Life and Times of Charles Dickens.* New York: Crescent Books, 1991, pp.88–93. Watts's book introduces Dickens to the general reader, particularly the younger reader. Well illustrated, it includes various plates from the novels, photographs from major films, and related Dickensiana.

BIOGRAPHICAL STUDIES

1133. Ackroyd, Peter. *Dickens.* New York: Harper Collins, 1990. Also an abridged edition, London: Mandarin, 1994. Like Kaplan (1137), Ackroyd (himself also a novelist) benefits from much information and scholarship not available to biographers before the publication of the Clarendon edition of *David Copperfield* [72] or of the volumes of the Pilgrim edition of Dickens's letters (729) most germane to the inception, composition, and reception of this novel. For the reader seeking understanding of the relationship between Dickens's fragment of autobiography, the subsequent biographies, and *David*

Copperfield as fictional autobiography, it may seem that this novel is everywhere yet nowhere in biographies that try to come to terms with both the life Dickens had and the ones he imagined. The biographer particularly recognizes in this novel "that strange concatenation . . . of time past" when talking about David's musings upon the death of his mother (comparing it with the death of the author's sister, Fanny). So, too, can the biographer appreciate the novel's contrapuntal movement as memory is "triumph and restoration" and also "loss and grief." On the Dickens-David question, Ackroyd has Dickens "seeing his own face everywhere," noting, for example that he even signed one of his letters "Wilkins Micawber." But though the life and the fiction are greatly entangled, "it would be death itself" to work it all out.

1134. Allen, Michael. *Charles Dickens' Childhood.* New York: St. Martin's Press, 1988.

Allen's purpose is to "correct and supersede past biographers" with information about the homes of the Dickenses (all but two are located precisely). The restlessness of experiencing fourteen homes in as many years, Allen believes, is reflected in the lives of many of Dickens's characters, including David Copperfield. Allen provides considerable information about John Dickens's imprisonment for debt and young Charles's period of work at the blacking factory (arguing that this lasted somewhat longer than had been previously thought).

1135. Dunn, Richard J. "Charles Dickens." In *St. James Guide to Biography.* Ed. Paul E. Schellinger. Chicago and London: St. James Press, 1991, pp. 211–12.

This brief essay surveys Dickens biography from Forster [730] through Kaplan (1137).

1136. Gitter, Elizabeth G. "The Rhetoric of Reticence in John Forster's *Life of Charles Dickens.*" *Dickens Studies Annual,* 25 (1996), 127–39.

Gitter contends that because Forster structured his narrative around the parallels between Dickens and David, the principal difference of Dickens's surviving wife "created an awkward situation" for Forster, who had to conceal or obscure "information that might damage his subject's dignity." But by virtually eliminating Catherine Dickens from the biography, Forster, in effect, collaborates with Dickens, suggests Gitter, in noting how Dickens's adult experiences "unavoidably reawaken the 'shrinking sensitiveness' of his Copperfieldian childhood . . . that is as much an apologia as it is a Rousseauian psychical analysis."

1137. Fred Kaplan. *Dickens: A Biography.* New York: William Morrow, 1988.

This is the most complete biography since Edgar Johnson's [738]. Kaplan had access to many yet unpublished letters, focused more on the life than on the fiction, but is adept at chronicling the multiple personal and professional pressures Dickens had as he wrote *David Copperfield.* The Dickens that Kaplan sees behind David was beginning to find fatherhood and marriage troublesome, was haunted by memories, and was engaged in various projects. Kaplan notes that at the time he wrote *David Copperfield,* Dickens "had a future whose patterns promised to be similar to those he already knew, his opportunities for adventure limited by his personal and professional obligations, by the restraints of success, and by the pressure to keep earning at a high point."

1138. Page, Norman. *"David Copperfield."* In his *A Dickens Chronology.* London: Macmillan, 1988, pp. 62–72.

Page's preface well indicates the usefulness of this chronology: "the student of, say, *David Copperfield* is likely to find it fascinating as well as useful to know just when Dickens was at work on each part of that novel, what other literary enterprises he was engaged in at the same time, whom he was meeting, what places he was visiting, and what were the relevant circumstances of his personal and professional life. Such a chronology is not, of course, a substitute for a biography; but its arrangement, in combination with its index . . . may be acceptable as a form of 'alternative' biography."

1139. Rose, Phyllis. "Catherine Hogarth and Charles Dickens." In her *Parallel Lives: Five Victorian Marriages.* New York: Alfred A. Knopf, pp. 141–91.

Rose finds, as had many earlier commentators, *David Copperfield* marking the end of the earlier, more humorous Dickens. Her commentary on Dickens's growing discontent with Catherine, and his interest in and various relations with other women include a discussion of his reunion with Maria Beadnell, an inspiration for Dora. Rose's work complements the newer Dickens biographies and the increasing number of studies of his relationships with and portrayals of women. Biographically innovative and at times provocative, Rose nonetheless reads *Copperfield* more in the context of the comic and sentimental early works rather than as a precursor of the darker novels which followed.

1140. Slater, Michael. "Experience into Art." Part I of his *Dickens and Women.* Stanford: Stanford University Press, 1983, pp. 1–217.

In the first half of his biographical and critical study, Slater devotes separate chapters to the relationships Dickens had with his mother, sister, early loves, wife, two sisters-in-law, daughters, and mistress. He argues that Dickens's mother furnished a partial prototype for Clara Copperfield and Jane Murdstone—"the light and dark of Dickens's childhood memories of his mother.'' Emma Micawber, for Slater, represents a more objective view of Elizabeth Dickens. Em'ly and Dora, as many others have suggested, emanate from childhood sweetheart Lucy Stroughill and subsequent infatuation with Maria Beadnell. In Agnes Wickfield, Slater finds an enshrined composite of Dickens's early loves.

Author and Subject Index

Author and Subject Index

Wilkes, David M., 1075
Williams, William A., Jr., 798
Winnifrith, Tom, 1076
Winterich, John T., 799
Woodfield, Malcolm J., 1077
Woolf, Virginia, 952

Wordsworth, William, 893, 903, 923,
   925, 966, 975, 991, 1003, 1023,
   1053, 1080, 1114. *See also The
   Prelude*
Worth, George, 1111
Wuthering Heights, 991

INDEX

(The *David Copperfield* bibliographical supplement has its own Author and Subject Index beginning on page 459.)